Interpreting Objects and Collections

Leicester Readers in Museum Studies
Series editor: Professor Susan M. Pearce

Care of Collections
Simon Knell

Collections Management
Anne Fahy

The Educational Role of the Museum
Eilean Hooper-Greenhill

Interpreting Objects and Collections
Susan M. Pearce

Museum Management
Kevin Moore

Museum Provision and Professionalism
Gaynor Kavanagh

Interpreting Objects and Collections

Edited by Susan M. Pearce

ROUTLEDGE

London and New York

First published 1994
by Routledge
11 New Fetter Lane, London EC4P 4EE

Simultaneously published in the USA and Canada
by Routledge
29 West 35th Street, New York, NY 10001

Typeset in Sabon by Florencetype Ltd, Stoodleigh, Devon

Printed and bound in Great Britain by T J Press Ltd, Padstow, Cornwall

British Library Cataloguing in Publication Data
A catalogue record for this book is available from the British Library

Library of Congress Cataloging in Publication Data
A catalog record for this book has been requested

ISBN 0–415–11288–5 (hbk)
ISBN 0–415–11289–3 (pbk)

Contents

List of figures   viii
List of tables   ix
Series preface   x
Acknowledgements   xi

Introduction   1
Susan M. Pearce

Part I Interpreting objects

 1 Museum objects   9
    Susan M. Pearce

 2 The contextual analysis of symbolic meanings   12
    Ian Hodder

 3 Things ain't what they used to be   13
    Daniel Miller

 4 Objects as meaning; or narrating the past   19
    Susan M. Pearce

 5 Death's head, cherub, urn and willow   30
    J. Deetz and E. S. Dethlefsen

 6 Behavioural interaction with objects   38
    Susan M. Pearce

 7 A view of functionalism   41
    Edmund Leach

 8 Culture as a system with subsystems   44
    David Clarke

 9 Theoretical archaeology: a reactionary view   48
    Ian Hodder

10 A view from the bridge   53
    Edmund Leach

11 Ivory for the sea woman: the symbolic attributes
of a prehistoric technology   59
Robert McGhee

12 Interpreting material culture   67
Christopher Tilley

13 Commodities and the politics of value   76
Arjun Appadurai

14 Why fakes?   92
Mark Jones

15 Cannibal tours, glass boxes and the politics of interpretation 98
Michael Ames

16 Craft   107
M. Shanks

17 Towards a material history methodology   109
R. Elliot et al.

18 Thinking about things   125
Susan M. Pearce

19 Mind in matter: an introduction to material culture theory
and method   133
Jules Prown

20 Not looking at kettles   139
Ray Batchelor

21 Home interview questionnaire, with coding categories and definitions 144
M. Csikszentmihalyi and E. Halton

Part II Interpreting collections

22 The urge to collect   157
Susan M. Pearce

23 The collection: between the visible and the invisible   160
Krzysztof Pomian

24 Notes on the history of collecting and of museums   175
Eva Schulz

25 Another past, another context: exhibiting Indian art abroad   188
B. N. Goswamy

26 Collecting reconsidered   193
Susan M. Pearce

27 Psychological aspects of art collecting   205
Frederick Baekeland

28 No two alike: play and aesthetics in collecting   220
    Brenda Danet and Tamar Katriel

29 Of mice and men: gender identity in collecting   240
    Russell W. Belk and Melanie Wallendorf

30 Objects of desire   254
    Susan Stewart

31 Collecting ourselves   258
    J. Clifford

32 The filth in the way   269
    M. Thompson

33 Art museums and the ritual of citizenship   279
    Carol Duncan

34 'The People's Show'   287
    Cathy Mullen

35 Leicester Contemporary Collecting Project's questionnaire   291
    Susan M. Pearce

36 Beyond the Odyssey: interpretations of ethnographic
    writing in consumer behaviour   296
    Annamma Joy

37 Collectors and collecting   317
    Russell W. Belk

38 Why they collect: collectors reveal their motivations   327
    Ruth Formanek

    Further reading   336
    Index   338

Figures

0.1   Semiotic analysis of objects and collections   3

4.1   Analysis of communication in material culture terms,
     using Saussure's system   22

6.1   Behavioural action: young woman and clothes   39

8.1   A static model representing the dynamic equilibrium
     between the subsystem networks of a sociocultural
     system and its environment   45

8.2   A schematic model suggesting the oscillating subsystem
     states and values in the networks of a sociocultural system
     in dynamic equilibrium with the oscillating states of its
     coupled environment   46

8.3   A static and schematic model of the dynamic equilibrium
     between the subsystem networks of a single sociocultural
     system and its total environment system   47

18.1   Model for artefact studies   127

18.2   Proposed model for artefact studies   129

31.1   The art–culture system: a machine for making authenticity   263

32.1   'Transient' and 'durable' objects   270

32.2   The covert 'rubbish' category   272

32.3   Dynamic system of cognitive categories   272

32.4   The rubbish triangle   276

32.5   Model representing one of the historic conditions of distribution
     and exchange   276

32.6   Chicken-and-egg image representing various possible
     and impossible transfers   277

Tables

11.1 Proportions of selected artefact classes made from ivory,
      bone and antler   61
17.1 Graphic representation of model   113
17.2 New model configuration, rotating grid of original   114
17.3 The analysis method   116
28.1 Strategies to pursue closure/completion/perfection   231
29.1 Mouse Cottage is to Fire Museum as . . .   245
29.2 Feminine images and characters   247
29.3 Masculine images and characters   249

Series preface

Museums are established institutions, but they exist in a changing world. The modern notion of a museum and its collections runs back into the sixteenth or even fifteenth centuries, and the origins of the earliest surviving museums belong to the period soon after. Museums have subsequently been and continue to be founded along these well-understood lines. But the end of the second millennium AD and the advent of the third point up the new needs and preoccupations of contemporary society. These are many, but some can be picked out as particularly significant here. Access is crucially important: access to information, the decision-making process and resources like gallery space, and access by children, ethnic minorities, women and the disadvantaged and underprivileged. Similarly, the nature of museum work itself needs to be examined, so that we can come to a clearer idea of the nature of the institution and its material, of what museum professionalism means, and how the issues of management and collection management affect outcomes. Running across all these debates is the recurrent theme of the relationship between theory and practice in what is, in the final analysis, an important area of work.

New needs require fresh efforts at information-gathering and understanding, and the best possible access to important literature for teaching and study. It is this need which the Leicester Sources in Museum Studies series addresses. The series as a whole breaks new ground by bringing together, for the first time, an important body of published work, much of it very recent, much of it taken from journals which few libraries carry, and all of it representing fresh approaches to the study of the museum operation.

The series has been divided into six volumes each of which covers a significant aspect of museum studies. These six topics bear a generic relationship to the modular arrangement of the Leicester Department of Museum Studies postgraduate course in Museum Studies, but, more fundamentally, they reflect current thinking about museums and their study. Within each volume, each editor has been responsible for his or her choice of papers. Each volume reflects the approach of its own editor, and the different feel of the various traditions and discourses upon which it draws. The range of individual emphases and the diversity of points of view is as important as the overarching theme in which each volume finds its place.

It is our intention to produce a new edition of the volumes in the series every three years, so that the selection of papers for inclusion is a continuing process and the contemporary stance of the series is maintained. All the editors of the series are happy to receive suggestions for inclusions (or exclusions), and details of newly published material.

Acknowledgements

The publishers and editors would like to thank the following people and organizations for permission to reproduce copyright material:

Susan M. Pearce, 'Museum objects' reprinted from Susan M. Pearce, *Objects of Knowledge* (1990) The Athlone Press; © 1990 The Athlone Press. Ian Hodder, 'The contextual analysis of symbolic meanings', in Ian Hodder, *The Archaeology of Contextual Meanings* (1987) reprinted by permission of the author and Cambridge University Press. Daniel Miller, 'Things ain't what they used to be', in *Royal Anthropological Institute Newsletter* 59 (1983), pp. 5–7, reprinted by permission of the Royal Anthropological Institute. Susan M. Pearce, 'Objects as meaning; or narrating the past', reproduced from *Objects of Knowledge* © 1990 The Athlone Press. J. Deetz and E. S. Dethlefsen, 'Death's head, cherub, urn and willow', reproduced with permission from *Natural History* (March 1967); copyright the American Museum of Natural History. Extracts from *Museums, Objects and Collections* by Susan M. Pearce, 1992, by permission of Leicester University Press (a division of Pinter Publishers Ltd., London). Edmund Leach, 'A view of functionalism' in Edmund Leach, *Social Anthropology* (1982) Fontana, reprinted by permission of Harper Collins Publishers Ltd. David Clarke, 'Culture as a system with sub-systems', reproduced from *Analytical Archeology* (1968) London: Routledge. Ian Hodder, 'Theoretical archaeology: a reactionary view' in Ian Hodder (ed.), *Symbolic and Structural Archaeology* (1982) reprinted by permission of the editor and Cambridge University Press. Edmund Leach, 'A view from the bridge' in M. Spriggs (ed.), *Archaeology and Anthropology*, British Archaeological Reports Supplementary Series 19 (1977), pp. 170–3. Robert McGhee, 'Ivory for the sea woman: the symbolic attributes of a prehistoric technology' in *Canadian Journal of Archaeology* 1 (1977), pp. 141–9. Christopher Tilley, 'Interpreting material culture' in I. Hodder (ed.) (1991) *The Meaning of Things*, London: Routledge, pp. 185–94. Arjun Appadurai, 'Commodities and the politics of value', in A. Appadurai (ed.), *The Social Life of Things* (1986) reprinted by permission of the author and Cambridge University Press. Mark Jones, 'Why fakes?' in Mark Jones, *Fake? The Art of Deception and Collections* (1990) reprinted by permission of British Museum Press. Michael Ames, 'Cannibal tours, glass boxes and the politics of interpretation': this excerpt is reprinted with permission of the publisher from *Cannibal Tours and Glass Boxes: The Anthropology of Museums* by Michael Ames (Vancouver: UBC Press 1992), pp. 139–50; copyright University of British Columbia Press; all rights reserved. M. Shanks, 'Craft' in M. Shanks (1992) *Experiencing the Past*, London: Routledge, pp. 167–70, reprinted by permission of the publishers. R. Elliot *et al.*, 'Towards a material history methodology', *Material History Bulletin* 22 (1982), pp. 31–40. Susan M. Pearce, 'Thinking about things', reproduced from *Museums Journal* 85(4) (1986), pp. 198–201 by permission of the Museums

Association. Jules Prown, 'Mind in matter: an introduction to material culture theory and method', in *Winterthur Portfolio* 17 (1982), pp. 1–19, reprinted by permission of the University of Chicago Press. R. Batchelor, 'Not looking at kettles' reproduced from *Museum Professionals Group News* 23 (1986), pp. 1–3. M. Csikszentmihalyi and E. Halton, 'Appendix B: Home Interview Questionnaire', 'Appendix C: Coding Categories and Definitions', pp. 256–77, in *The Meaning of Things* edited by M. Csikszentmihalyi (1981) reprinted by permission of Cambridge University Press. K. Pomian, 'The collection: between the visible and the invisible', in K. Pomian, *Collectors and Curiosities* (1990) Polity Press, reprinted by permission of Blackwell Publishers. Eva Schulz, 'Notes on the history of collecting and of museums', *Journal of the History of Collections* 2(2), 1990, pp. 205–18, by permission of Oxford University Press. B. N. Goswamy, 'Another past, another context: exhibiting Indian art abroad', in I. Karp and S. Lavine (eds), *Exhibiting Cultures: the Poetics and Politics of Museums Displays*, the Smithsonian Institution (1991), pp. 68–73; by permission of the Smithsonian Institution. Susan M. Pearce, 'Collecting reconsidered', reproduced from G. Kavanagh (ed.) (1991) *Museum Languages*, by permission of Leicester University Press (a division of Pinter Publishers Ltd), London. All rights reserved. Frederick Baekeland, 'Psychological aspects of art collecting' in *Psychiatry* 44 (1981), pp. 45–59, reprinted by permission of Guildford Publications. B. Danet and T. Katriel, 'No two alike: play and aesthetics in collecting' in *Play & Culture* 2(3), pp. 255–71. Copyright 1989 by Human Kinetics Publishers; reprinted by permission; all rights reserved. Russell W. Belk and Melanie Wallendorf, 'Of mice and men: gender identity in collecting': this article will appear in Kenneth L. Ames (ed.) *Gender and Material Culture* (Winterthur, Delaware: Henry Francis du Pont Winterthur Museum, forthcoming 1994). Reprinted by permission. Susan Stewart, 'Objects of desire' reprinted from *On Longing: Narratives of the Miniature, the Gigantic, the Souvenir, the Collection* (Duke University Press 1984), by permission of the author and Duke University Press. James Clifford, 'Collecting ourselves', in *The Predicament of Culture* by James Clifford, Cambridge, Mass.: Harvard University Press, copyright © 1988 by the President and Fellows of Harvard College. Excerpts from Michael Thompson, *Rubbish Theory: the Creation and Destruction of Value*, © Michael Thompson (1979) by permission of Oxford University Press. Carol Duncan, 'Art museums and the ritual of citizenship', reproduced from I. Karp and S. Lavine (eds) (1991) *Exhibiting Cultures: the Poetics and Politics of Museums Displays*, pp. 88–103, by permission of the Smithsonian Insititution Press, Washington, DC. Cathy Mullen, 'The People's Show' in *Visual Sociological Review* 6(1) (1991), pp. 47–9 reprinted by permission of the author. Susan M. Pearce, 'Leicester Contemporary Collecting Project's questionnaire' (1993), Department of Museum Studies, University of Leicester. Annamma Joy, 'Beyond the Odyssey: interpretations of ethnographic writing in consumer behaviour' reproduced from R. Belk (1991) *Highways and Buyways*, Association for Consumer Research (1991), pp. 216–33, © 1991 the Association for Consumer Research. Russell W. Belk, 'Collectors and collecting' reproduced from *Advances in Consumer Research*, Vol. 15 (1988), pp. 548–53, © 1988 the Association for Consumer Research. Ruth Formanek, 'Why they collect: collectors reveal their motivations' in W. F. Rudmin (ed.), *To Have Possessions: Handbook on Ownership and Property, Journal of Social Behaviour and Personality* 6(6), pp. 275–86. Reprinted by permission.

Every attempt has been made to obtain permission to reproduce copyright material. If any proper acknowledgement has not been made, we would invite copyright holders to inform us of the oversight.

Introduction

The starting point for this volume of collected papers (as for all other similar work undertaken by the editor) is the belief that museums exist to hold particular objects and specimens which have come to us from the past (i.e. the period up to midnight yesterday), that museums therefore constitute a specific social phenomenon with a unique and explicit role in the western scheme of things, and that material arrives in museums as a result of practice (or practices) which can be described as collecting. It is, therefore, incumbent upon the investigator to try to find ways in which, first, the social meanings of individual objects can be unravelled; second, the significance of the museum as a cultural institution can be understood; and third the processes through which objects become component parts of collections, and collections themselves acquire collective significance, can be appreciated.

These are enormous topics, because material objects are as much a part of the weave of our lives as our bodies are; indeed these two aspects of our lives have the fundamental characteristic of physicality not possessed by most other facets of our existence. The papers collected here are primarily intended to illuminate the first of these topics and the last, the meaning of objects and the nature of collecting, and therefore have a relevance which extends beyond material formally received by a museum, into the world of objects in normal social use, and that of private collections. But because all existing museum material was once, one way or another, a part of these twin processes, an understanding of them is fundamental to museum practice.

This volume also stems from the conviction that both objects and collections can and should be studied in their own right, as part of the broader pattern of cultural studies. The reader will not, therefore, find here papers which are written from the perspectives of the traditional disciplines of art history, archaeology and so on, although, of course, many themes overlap, and cultural analysis, in any case, draws from the same wells of philosophy, psychology and historiography that water discipline studies. One particular point needs to be made. I would contend that specimens from the natural world work within human society in exactly the same ways as human artefactual material, whatever they may do in nature and under only the eye of God. They are a part of the human construction of the world both as single pieces and (but rather more obviously) as collections. However, it must be admitted that the great majority of the texts here are written in terms of artefactual rather than natural material (that great distinction at the heart of early museology), and acknowledgement of natural science specimens is only, as it were, by the way. This is a great pity, and it is to be hoped that we shall soon have a body of writing which helps us to understand natural history as culture.

The structure of this volume reflects the distinction between studying objects as such, and studying those groups of objects which we usually think of as 'collections', however

1

difficult this notion may be to define. The amount of study which has been devoted to these topics is very uneven. The meanings of objects has been the subject of a body of research, usually called material culture theory, which reaches back immediately to the 1960s and beyond that to the pioneers of archaeology (largely) in the mid- and later nineteenth century. Collection studies is a new field, which has found a place in the broader scope of cultural studies only in the course of the last decade or so, although of course individual collections and collectors have been the subjects of a huge range of publications, mostly directed either at discipline or at biographical perspectives. Nevertheless, the two groups of papers presented here are deliberately of more or less the same length, in order to reflect the work which has been done and to represent the equal weight accorded to the two aspects of objects.

The relationship of the two aspects needs to be made clear. It is, of course, obvious, that all collected objects begin life outside a collection, and it is possible to build up individual biographies for particular objects which cover first their lives in general circulation, then their entry into a collection, and then perhaps the entry of that collection into an established museum, with its concurrent professional repertoire of documentation, display, photography and publication. The life story of an object may not run as smoothly as this; for the great majority of objects, as of people, it does not. There may be episodes in which the object comes and goes within various collected relationships, as collections are assembled and then broken up. There may be phases in which the object is lost to sight, literally in the case of excavated material, figuratively perhaps when objects find their ways into attics and cellars. Objects can be subject to great fluctuations in value, when despised rubbish becomes first collectable and finally major acquisition; in fact, the capacity of objects to stimulate social changes of this kind is one of their most fascinating characteristics, and one in which the process of collecting plays a major part. Nevertheless, all individual vicissitudes notwithstanding, there seems to be a qualitative difference between objects in circulation and objects in collection, and this distinction is most easily approached through the use of a simple semiotic scheme which employs the basic Saussurian notions.

Fig. 0.1 shows how this analysis works. Each society – let us say that of late twentieth-century Britain – operates within social parameters which are, broadly, the legacy of the historical past, up to and including the immediate past. As a result of this we have available to us in the social structure the *langue*, a body of objects, material culture, with which to produce our social lives. In order to create social sense, these are structured according to generally understood categories, and give rise to the *parole*, the actual objects in daily circulation doing their social jobs. Because objects (like everything else) are only meaningful in relation to each other, these social objects work in groups or sets, and are so shown in the diagram. So, for example, because we have become a highly literate, bureaucratic culture as a result of our history, our ideas about appropriate objects include writing materials, structured into categories which both reflect and reinforce social norms. These give rise to the actual object sets in use, the different sets of pens, pencils, paper blocks, blotting-pads, desk toys, tables and chairs, and so on, as are thought appropriate to children, teenage girls, elderly ladies and business executives.

These objects in circulation are the subject of material culture study, which aims to show how and why they have meaning as they come and go in use. But we and objects together are capable of entering into a qualitatively different kind of relationship, the relationship here described as collecting. Obviously, the same broad social parameters come into play, as the linking time arrow shows, although more or less change may have taken place, depending upon the extent of the time lapse. The earlier *parole*, i.e. the writing materials in circulation, becomes part of the *langue*, the material to be

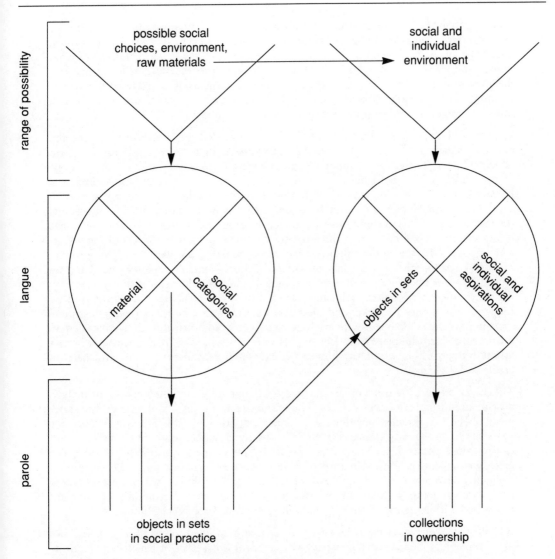

range of possibility

langue

parole

possible social
choices, environment,
raw materials

social and
individual
environment

material

social
categories

objects in sets

social and
individual
aspirations

objects in sets
in social practice

collections
in ownership

Fig. 0.1 Semiotic analysis of objects and collections

worked upon, in the second action. These are structured a second time against the cross-references of the individual collector, his (or her) history, psychological quirks and imaginative notions of value. In the *parole* of actual life arise the collections which result from these choices. These might be collections of pre-war fountain-pens of the great makes, Swan, Waterman's, Conway Stewart, complete with their gold nibs; they might be pens used by famous people on famous occasions; they might be biros collected by the owner on trips abroad. People normally make the very clear distinction between the two kinds of accumulation which the diagram reflects.

A moment's thought shows that a range of collecting processes is brought within the embrace of this scheme. Collections may be the result of large sums spent in the sale-rooms, or carefully calculated excavation campaigns, or well-designed fieldwork across the social sciences. They may equally be the results of forays into car-boot sales or genteel gift-shops. A second thought shows up a range of issues which it would be inappropriate for me to discuss in detail in an Introduction to the writings of others. Social class has a bearing on the collection process, and so does gender. Notions of what creates value are very complex and so are the related processes of social change and the relationship of the material world to these movements. Our relationship to the accumulation of objects is as profound and as significant as our relationships to each other, to language, and to time and space, and as complex.

In each of the two Parts, the same principles have guided the choice of material, and the arrangement of the pieces follows the same pattern. First comes a general statement which offers a perspective of the material under discussion; both extracts quote some of the widely discussed definitions of, respectively, material culture and collections. In Part I: 'Interpreting objects' this is followed by the very brief but extremely signifi-cant piece from Hodder in which he distinguishes between the historical, functional (or technomic or sociotechnic) and symbolic, or structuralist, aspects of the meanings of objects. Part I continues with three papers representing various aspects of the histor-ical approach to the understanding of objects. Miller gives us an insight into the historical development of the study of material culture. Pearce's paper on the Waterloo jacket discusses the accretion of historical meaning in semiotic terms, and suggests how our engagement with objects helps to create a diversity of meanings. The study of New England gravestones by Deetz and Dethlefsen shows how objects can carry historical meaning which is unique to themselves, and which complements that contained in documents. The brief piece from Pearce puts our relationship to objects within a behav-ioural framework in order to show how individual responses develop and help to create social change.

These are followed by three pieces devoted to illuminating the functionalist (or materi-alist or utilitarian) aspect of objects. The extract from Leach's book is a classic state-ment of the functionalist position, and Clarke's discussion, although now twenty-five years old, is an equally classic dissection of the functionalist working of material cul-ture in social patterning. Hodder presents a critique of the functionalist position. The next two papers pursue the nature of objects in their symbolic guise. Leach gives a brilliantly imaginative and impressionistic account of how structuralist thinking can work, and this is followed by McGhee's analysis of the symbolic relationships embedded within Central Inuit material culture and other aspects of Inuit life.

As Tilley's paper makes clear, however, all meaning, of whatever kind, is a matter not of objective fact, but of social construction, the ideological basis of which can be unrav-elled, or 'deconstructed'. An important part of this ideology is the way in which objects, commodities, or objects in their marketable aspect interweave with the political ways in which value is ascribed to individual pieces: Appadurai's contribution gives us an important insight into this web of relationships. The nature of fakes, analysed by Jones, is one aspect of this, and an important one for museum material. The acquisition and interpretation of material from the 'Other', that is from those parts of the world whose traditions are now western but which the western world has appropriated, has its own world of politics, as Ames shows. In a not dissimilar way, we all appropriate the 'other' which comes to us as material from the past, or as pastiches of it: 'craftwork' has its own political dimension, as Shanks shows us.

Part I concludes with a group of papers concerned with the methodology of study. Those by Elliot, Pearce, Prown and Batchelor describe particular approaches to the organization of the study of individual objects, and offer research procedures, or models for object studies. All of these spring from the perspectives of particular disciplines, and those of Elliot, Pearce and Prown, in particular, arose from work carried out in relation to post-graduate seminars in museum studies. Each of these models, in its different way, starts by framing particular steps in which data about each object can be gathered by the normal procedure of description, historical research, scientific dating and characterization, analysis of technological and manufacturing techniques, and so on. Similarly, each places within its procedures the need to compare the piece under examination with others of its kind. Each provides scope, usually towards the end of the process, for discussion based upon the appreciation of the object from the historical, behavioural functionalist, symbolic-structuralist and political perspectives already discussed. Each should be regarded as a guide, not a set of rules. The piece from Csikszentmihalyi and Halton is taken from their pioneering study of the ways in which people regard their own material possessions, and shows how a questionnaire and related definitions can be devised as the core of a research enquiry. All five of these pieces should be regarded as describing the application of material culture theory to actual objects, within both a museum and a broader social context.

After its introductory piece on definitions Part II: 'Interpreting collections', is given a similar tripartite structure, the elements of which consider the historical process of collecting, its relation to individual psychology, and collecting as part of the politics of value. The historical practice of collecting in the western, or European, tradition is represented by the extract from Pomian's book and the paper by Schultz. This is an area where material has had to be kept to a minimum, and much fascinating and important material relating to early European practices, and Renaissance and modern collecting, has had, perforce, to be omitted. Pomian takes a broad view of the social practices which relate to collecting, and Schultz analyses the key moment in the history of collecting when modernist practices gather momentum. This is followed by Goswamy's paper, which serves to remind us that cultures outside the West also have their own traditions of connoisseurship and collecting.

The next group of papers, by Pearce, Baekeland, Danet and Katriel, and Belk and Wallendorf consider the ways in which collecting is used to structure individual identity in relation to a sense of temporal and spatial ordering, to relationships with others, and to the construction of genders. The pieces from Stewart's significant book link up with these internal parameters but carry the investigation over into the world of ideology and social action. The same political motifs appear in the arguments mounted by Clifford in the essay 'Collecting ourselves'. The same note is struck in Thompson's investigation into ideas of 'rubbish' and 'value'. In similar vein, but for a broadly Marxist standpoint, Duncan discusses the relationship of collected material in museums, particular art material, to notions of 'good citizenship' and the modern state. A very different view of the relationship between collecting and museum display is offered by the People's Show Project, started by Peter Jenkinson at Walsall Museum, England, in 1991. This encouraged local collectors to display their own material in the museum and Mullen presents an account of the enterprise.

Finally, as in Part I, there is a group of papers concerned with the methodology of collection study. The Leicester Contemporary Collecting Project questionnaire was used in 1993–4 in the investigation into contemporary collecting in Britain carried out by Pearce and Wheeler. Joy describes some of the implications of the Odyssey Project (University of Utah), and Belk's paper presents some of the associated fieldwork and its significance. Finally, Formanek's paper describes a research project carried out in New York on contemporary collecting practice. Taken together, these papers point the way towards further investigations in the area.

The choice of papers has been extremely difficult, and much interesting material has had to be omitted. I have tried to include pieces not only representative of all the main trains of thought, but also of all the main practitioners of material culture study, but nevertheless there are some exclusions which I regret. Some pieces are deliberately included in their entirety while others have been cut to the bare bones of their arguments, and this is, of course, particularly true of excerpts from single-author books. Similarly, decisions have had to be taken about the inclusion of endnotes and references or bibliographies: here a variety of solutions have been adopted as seems fit in each case. The papers gathered here offer, I hope and believe, a coherent account of the contemporary state of play in a relatively new but rapidly developing field of study. It is now time to let them speak for themselves.

Part I
Interpreting objects

1

Museum objects

Susan M. Pearce

Setting the parameters of material culture studies has always been difficult because the term is capable of a range of definitions, some of them very broad. In this introductory piece, Pearce discusses some of the terms in use and their differing connotations, and suggests that in Museum Studies it is most useful to concentrate upon those relatively small, movable pieces for which 'object' or 'thing' is our term in ordinary speech. 'Artefact' can also be used in the same way, and these three words are best employed without any particular distinctions being made between them, their potential distinctiveness in formal philosophical discourse notwithstanding. 'Material culture' is then the phrase used as a collective noun.

It will be helpful to clear some paths through the undergrowth by picking out some of the key words relating to museum material, and taking a closer look at them. One group comprises those words which are used to describe an individual piece, or in general terms a number of pieces, and this group includes 'object', 'thing', 'specimen', 'artefact', 'good' usually used in the plural as 'goods', and the term 'material culture' used as a collective noun. All of these terms share common ground in that they all refer to selected lumps of the physical world to which cultural value has been ascribed, a deceptively simple definition which much of this book will be devoted to discussing, but each carries a slightly different shade of meaning because each comes from a distinguishably different tradition of study.

One problem common to them all, and one which throws up the characteristic cleft between philosophical speculation and the everyday meanings attached to words, revolves around the scope to be attributed to them. Strictly speaking, the lumps of the physical world to which cultural value is ascribed include not merely those discrete lumps capable of being moved from one place to another, which is what we commonly mean when we say 'thing' or 'artefact', but also the larger physical world of landscape with all the social structure that it carries, the animal and plant species which have been affected by humankind (and most have), the prepared meals which the animals and plants become, and even the manipulation of flesh and air which produces song and speech. As James Deetz has put it in a famous sentence: 'Material culture is that segment of man's physical environment which is purposely shaped by him according to a culturally dictated plan' (Deetz 1977: 7).

This is to say, in effect, that the whole of cultural expression, one way or another, falls within the realm of material culture, and if analytical definition is pushed to its logical conclusion, that is probably true. It is also true that the material culture held today by many museums falls within this broader frame, like the areas of industrial landscape which Ironbridge exhibits. However, for the purposes of study, limits must be set, and this book will concentrate upon those movable pieces, those 'discrete lumps' which have always formed, and still form, the bulk of museum holdings and which museums were, and still are, intended to hold.

This brings us to a point of crucial significance. What distinguishes the 'discrete lumps' from the rest – what makes a 'movable piece' in our sense of the term – is the cultural value it is given, and not primarily the technology which has been used to give it form or content, although this is an important mode of value creation. The crucial idea is that of selection, and it is the act of selection which turns a part of the natural world into an object and a museum piece. This is clearly demonstrated by the sample of moon rock which went on display in the Milestones of Flight hall at the National Air and Space Museum, Washington, D.C.:

> The moon rock is an actual piece of the moon retrieved by the Apollo 17 mission. There is nothing particularly appealing about the rock; it is a rather standard piece of volcanic basalt some 4 million years old. Yet, unlike many other old rocks, this one comes displayed in an altar-like structure, set in glass, and is complete with full-time guard and an ultrasensitive monitoring device (or so the guards are wont to say). There is a sign above it which reads, 'You may touch it with care.' *Every-one touches it.*
>
> (Meltzer 1981: 121)

The moon rock has been turned into material culture because, through its selection and display, it has become a part of the world of human values, a part which, evidently, every visitor wants to bring within his own personal value system.

What is true of the moon rock is equally true of the stones which the Book of Joshua tells us Joshua commanded the twelve tribes of Israel to collect from the bed of the River Jordan and set up as a permanent memorial of the crossing of the river, and of all other natural objects deliberately placed within human contexts. It is also equally true of the millions of natural history pieces inside museum collections for which 'specimen', meaning an example selected from a group, is our customary term. It is clear that the acquisition of a natural history specimen involves selection according to contemporary principles, detachment from the natural context, and organization into some kind of relationship (many are possible) with other, or different, material. This process turns a 'natural object' into a humanly defined piece, and means that natural history objects and collections, although like all other collections they have their own proper modes and histories of study, can also be treated as material culture and discussed in these terms. The development of contemporary epistemology suggests that no fact can be read transparently. All apparently 'natural' facts are actually discursive facts, since 'nature' is not something already there but is itself the result of historical and social construction. To call something a natural object, as Laclau and Mouffe say (1987: 84), is a way of conceiving it that depends upon a classificatory system: if there were no human beings on earth, stones would still be there, but they would not be 'stones' because there would be neither mineralogy nor language with which to distinguish and classify them. Natural history specimens are therefore as much social constructs as spears or typewriters, and as susceptible to social analysis.

'Thing' is our most ordinary word for all these pieces, and it is also used in everyday speech for the whole range of non-material matters (a similarly elusive word) which have a bearing on our daily lives. 'Object' shares the same slipperiness both in ordinary speech and in intellectual discourse, where it is generally the term used. The ways in which we use these terms, and the implications of this usage for the ways in which our collective psyche views the material world are very significant. The term 'artefact' means 'made by art or skill' and so takes a narrow view of what constitutes material objects, concentrating upon that part of their nature which involves the application of human technology to the natural world, a process which plays a part in the creation of many, but by no means all, material pieces. Because it is linked with practical skills, and so with words like 'artisan', 'artefact' is a socially low-value term, and one which is correspondingly applied to material deemed to be humble, like ordinary tables and chairs, rather than paintings and sculptures.

'Goods' comes to us from the world of economics and production theory and relates to that aspect of material pieces which embraces the market-place value which is set upon them, and their exchange rate in relation to other similar or different goods and services. This is the treatment of material culture as commodity, and the work of social anthropologists, particularly Douglas and Isherwood (1979), has shown how shallow the purely economic discussion of material is until social or cultural dimensions of value are added to it.

This paper first appeared in S. Pearce (ed.) (1992) Museums, Objects and Collections, *Leicester: Leicester University Press, pp. 4–6.*

REFERENCES

Deetz, J. (1977) *In Small Things Forgotten*, Garden City, N.Y.: Doubleday Natural History Press.
Douglas, M. and Isherwood, B. (1979) *The World of Goods: Towards an Anthropology of Consumption*, London: Allen Lane.
Laclau, E. and Mouffe, C. (1987) 'Post-Marxism without apologies', *New Left Review* 166: 79–106.
Meltzer, D. J. (1981) 'Ideology and material culture' in R. A. Gould and M. B. Schiffer (eds) *Modern Material Culture: The Archaeology of Us*, New York: Academic Press, 113–25.

2

The contextual analysis of symbolic meanings

Ian Hodder

Ian Hodder is one of the leading proponents of what might be called the Cambridge School of material culture theorists, archaeologists who, in the 1970s and 1980s, started to interpret ancient material culture in terms of contemporary theories in social anthropology. This brief but very important piece sums up Hodder's view that meaning in objects is threefold. Objects have use value through their effect on the world: this is the significance which they hold for a functionalist, materialistic or utilitarian perspective (these words are often used to convey similar ideas). Objects have structural or coded meanings, which they can communicate: this is their symbolic meaning. Finally, objects have meaningful interest through their past associations: this is their historical meaning. All objects are, always, working in all three of their ways. Hodder's analysis has stood the test of time, and is a useful way of structuring object analysis.

All objects can be given meaning, and of varied types. Beyond the meanings of an object as matter, to be studied by physicists, chemists and biologists for example, it can be argued that cultural objects have three broad types of meaning. First, there is the object as involved in exchanges of matter, energy and information. We can talk of how the object is used, and how it conveys information about social characteristics, personal feelings and religious beliefs. This is to talk of the technomic, sociotechnic and ideotechnic functions of the object. The object's meaning is the effects it has on the world. Second, we can say that the object has meaning because it is part of a code, set or structure. In fact its particular meaning depends on its place within the code. Third, there is the content of meaning. The first and second types of meaning are little concerned with the non-arbitrariness of cultural objects. In the first, the object is assessed in terms of its ability to do a job (cut down a tree or convey information), and there is no way of choosing between equivalently efficient tools. Particularly in the realm of information exchange, any object will do as long as it conveys the correct information. In the second type of meaning any object will do as long as it has found a place within the code – the sign is arbitrary. So the third type of meaning is the historical content of the changing ideas and associations of the object itself, which makes its use non-arbitrary.

This paper first appeared in I. Hodder (ed.) (1987), The Archaeology of Contextual Meanings, *Cambridge: Cambridge University Press, p.1.*

3

Things ain't what they used to be

Daniel Miller

Material culture as a study has had its ups and downs, and in part at least, these match both the popularity of different approaches to anthropological studies as these have developed over the last century and a half, and the prestige which has been accorded to museums and their collections over the same period (particularly collections in the broad field of human history). Here Miller analyses the development of approaches to the study of things. Careful reading of his paper will show how the movements he discusses relate to the perspectives of object meanings given by Hodder in the previous piece.

It has been the policy of the Royal Anthropological Institute to promote those kinds of studies which act in an integrative fashion in relation to the subject as a whole. One area of such studies has been material culture. By the study of material culture, I mean simply the study of human social and environmental relationships through the evidence of people's construction of their material world. The term applies equally to aspects of ethnography that analyse the production, consumption and symbolism of contemporary artefacts as well as to the archaeologist uncovering the material evidence of past societies, and it has often been viewed, in particular, as a meeting point of these two branches of anthropology. By taking a historical framework we can see how far, at different periods, material culture has played an integrative or merely a peripheral role within anthropology. The point of this survey is, however, assertive, because it leads to reasons why an expansion of studies in material culture appears both worth while and probable at the present time.

This brief history of material culture studies will be focused mainly on Britain, where such studies appear, from an early period, to have acted as an integrative and also a core field within anthropology. Its centrality in nineteenth-century British anthropology is clear from reading the works of influential figures such as Tylor, Haddon, Lubbock, Balfour and Pitt Rivers (e.g. Haddon 1895; Tylor 1881). Its importance is also reflected in the role played by the establishment of museums as a means by which anthropology became better known to the public. If material culture studies played a core role in the emergence of anthropology, this was not for any one reason, but because of a constellation of mutually reinforcing factors.

The first role of the object was to symbolize the people who created it. For the travellers, explorers and missionaries, before the emergence of mass photography, the object provided the major means of representing the exotic places and people visited. The original anthropology was largely practised in the drawing-room, where objects were a convenient symbol for actual peoples whose presence was neither required nor desired. The selection of objects is significant: the insignia of power, emblems of status, fetishes of supernatural power taken from colonial realms. Pieces were used to objectify the notion of the romantic innocent or the barbaric savage depending upon the argument being engaged upon.

In a recent book by an architect Phil Steadman called *The Evolution of Designs* (1979), it becomes clear how the need to provide order in assemblages of such objects was a key factor in the emergence of the first dominant models in anthropological theory. The sequence into which such weapons and ornaments were placed was itself, as the analogue for the systematization of species and cultures, one of the means of intrusion of nineteenth-century evolutionist theory into anthropology. Placed in an array from simplicity to complexity the material stood for the proposed developmental sequences, as evidence affirming the primitive nature of the Australian Aborigines and hunter-gatherer modes of subsistence in general. This creation of order in the presentation of such objects, to the public, in the museums, may be taken as the stem from which two ways of thinking about time and place developed. Put most crudely, from an emphasis on the vertical in such displays flourished evolutionist theory, while an emphasis on the horizontal emerged as diffusionism.

This development was not only convenient for the ethnographer. It was the perfect model for the archaeologist, who is supposed to have developed the model of Stone–Bronze–Iron Ages as much through the museum display as through excavation. Indeed at this stage it is archaeology that is in the vanguard as Lowie stated 'prehistory proved evolution by the rigorous technique of geologic stratigraphy at a time when ethnographers were still groping for the proper methods of investigating living aboriginies' (1937: 22). The peoples who use ground stone tools could be equated with the Swiss Neolithic, the Australian Aborigines using flake tools equated with the Mousterian. It is curious how archaeologists in their histories (e.g. Daniel 1962) place the emphasis on geological methods, but the contemporary writers such as Lubbock and Pitt-Rivers seem to be working as undifferentiated anthropologists using archaeology and information on contemporary populations equally within the model of social evolution.

From its inception, then, material culture studies played a highly integrative role, in that objects stood for societies in a number of related planes. They could stand for distance in terms of time and space, simplicity as against complexity, they could stand for the dominant theoretical models, and they could stand for the entire discipline as presented in the museums to the public at large.

It was the very success of these interwoven connotations based around the evolutionary model that led to the subsequent shift in the position of material culture studies. A new anthropology arose, that in part defined itself precisely by its opposition to all aspects of the evolutionary and diffusionist perspectives. The relationship to the informant was to be direct, not mediated through objects, and in particular, it was to be through language. Faced in the mid-twentieth century with a participatory, relativistic and synchronic consensus, objects retained the implications of the theories they had been used to support, and that had in turn given them meaning. Photography and other methods of recording visual information made objects less important. In Britain, unlike some other areas, museums retained their older pre-functionalist traditions and did not become the base for the long-term fieldwork now expected in the discipline. Material culture studies continued as ethnographic and especially museum collections, but their relationship with the concept of anthropology itself was fundamentally altered. The objects, the museum studies, the older theories were now a peripheral pursuit, secondary, in some senses dated, and unlikely to contribute to the development of modern 'advanced' theories and perspectives, but better used as a secondary and simplified level of signification to the general public. This was especially the case in Britain, but after a lag, material culture studies have also declined in continental Europe.

Archaeology, in a sense, went in the opposite direction. There was a shift to a more autonomous role for artefacts as objects of scientific analysis rather than as symbols of societies. Stone tools and ceramic sequences were increasingly studied in themselves. This resulted in a kind of fetishism that archaeology is always prone to. Objects start by standing for prehistoric peoples, who are the intended subject of study, but the symbolic process is easily inverted, and peoples under terms such as 'cultures' become viewed principally as labels for groups of artefacts, which are the immediate subjects of analysis. The focus is then on the relationships between the objects themselves, which in the 1960s became the centre of interest (e.g. Clarke 1968). In recent decades, these divisions have grown, with the emphasis on different external disciplines. Social anthropology has seen a steady growth in the dominance of models derived from linguistics. Despite the claim of semiotics to an interest in non-linguistic modes of communication, the emphasis in structuralism and post-structuralism is on 'word', 'text' and 'discourse'. In archaeology, by contrast, the goal was represented by the physical sciences. Although the 'New Archaeology' of the 1960s and 1970s proclaimed an interest in anthropology as a whole, the practice, and a strident epistemology, was increasingly geared towards the emulation of the natural sciences.

By this stage material culture studies is clearly no longer playing an integrative role in relation to anthropology. From the earlier studies and as found in volumes such as *Notes and Queries in Anthropology*, a triad of concerns developed that came to constitute 'material culture studies'. These are (a) the study of technology, which breaks down into two parts, first that of technology as a process of manufacture, such as firemaking and pottery production, and second technology as the means of coping with the environment in the manner of Forde's *Habitat, Economy and Society* (1934); (b) the study of 'primitive' art; (c) the study of archaeology.

If, as has been argued, what material culture studies have come to represent depends upon the dominant concept of anthropology as a whole, then a return of these studies to a more central and integrative role can only occur because a new set of mutually reinforcing factors has begun to emerge. What changes are apparent in anthropology that make such a shift seem plausible? There are factors that relate to developments both within the discipline and outside it. A good place to start is with what is now the most pronounced cleavage, that between social anthropology and archaeology.

One recent trend suggestive of integration is the rise of 'ethno-archaeology', but this may prove illusory. Ethnoarchaeology has developed as a series of studies in which an archaeologist undertakes some contemporary ethnography in order to investigate phenomena helpful in the interpretation of prehistory: for example, the processes by which archaeological sites are formed. This 'as if they were dead' approach is disingenuous, tending to impose the categories archaeology has developed in isolation onto contemporary materials, rather than allow itself to be challenged by the changed context. It does so in a parasitic manner that fails to impinge upon social anthropology and thereby reproduces the asymmetrical relationship that has grown up between them.

Quite different from this has been the return to some older traditions including evolutionary and materialist perspectives. These (e.g. Friedman and Rowlands 1977) have used both ethnographic and archaeologically derived material to tackle questions about the nature of social development that neither subject was able to approach in isolation, and thereby have enriched both approaches and dissolved their differences. Similarly in the recent work of Hodder and colleagues (Hodder 1982) there has been an attempt to build on studies of material culture, in both past and present contexts, to create models of the nature of material artefacts, to which both archaeology and ethnography contribute and from which both prehistorians and social anthropologists can derive ideas about the interpretation of the object world. Both of these projects lead towards a form of material culture studies that integrates, precisely by demonstrating what is achieved when boundaries are transcended.

The other 'residual' elements of material culture studies can also be reintegrated within the more general concerns of anthropology. Materialist studies that include technology, for example blacksmithy work or the carving of wooden tables, from the point of view of the social organization of productive relations may have this effect. The study of art has been analysed from sociology (e.g. Bordieu 1979; Wolff 1981) and also expanded into the more general question as to the nature of form as objectification.

There is a second shift that might at first seem contrary, but the coincidence of whose development is not fortuitous. As anthropology starts to struggle towards a more critical role, assumptions that were once current in critical studies about the primary nature of technology as a means of coping with the environment, and then productive organization as dominant in the structure of social relations in general, have come increasingly into question. The object then becomes studied equally for what it represents in the field of consumption and in the construction of images. The potential for expansion within such fields has been pointed out in recent years in *The World of Goods* by Douglas and Isherwood (1979), and by the French social theorist Baudrillard (1981). Both, though in quite different ways, see this as the rise of another form of critical study, and both relate this to a shift, mediated through anthropology, in what had been seen as the arena of the political economy. We might expect within economic anthropology to see more attention given not just to worldwide systems of production but to how commodities work towards the 'homogenization' of the 'styles' of living, and the implications for society in the ways these are resisted and transformed in different social contexts, studies of motor vehicles, clothes, packaged foods, modernist style constructions and so forth.

Both of these shifts sprang originally from the rise of structuralist studies which left no part of anthropology unaffected. The influence that arose through structural-Marxism in one direction, and through studies of the symbolism of the artefact is still pronounced. In material culture studies, in particular, symbolic analysis has become the constant complement to the social. It may be that current work in social theory with its emphasis on the recontextualization and interpretation of 'texts' by the consumer, as opposed to merely the 'authors' of images, might provide insights for the development of these studies of consumption in different societies.

Similar changes may result from shifts in disciplines outside anthropology. In history and in particular archaeology, the study of the material object has always provided a representation of the common person, to oppose the 'high' history of the academics. There is, for example, the recent growth of the folk museum, which works alongside the continued popular base for prehistory. Recently the study of 'everyday life', through the history of furnishing and fashions, has been extolled and exemplified by the influential work of Braudel in France and in studies in Britain of the changing pattern of consumption in the eighteenth century prior to the changes in production discussed under the title of the 'industrial revolution'.

A major source of interest arises from studies that have traditionally looked to the material works for examples: studies of buildings, or of fashion, have in recent years developed an increasing interest in fields such as semiotics. This may be part of a more general movement in the study of material culture outside anthropology, which stems from a certain disillusionment with the formalism of modernist studies, and from caution and concern about the implications of dominant scientific and technological models for the development of new forms. Anthropology is looked to in order to provide methods for the study of the nature of buildings and other artefacts in their social context. The vernacular and localized traditions have become more prominent, and again there is a concern with the consumer reception and inception of design.

I have detailed here a series of recently developed interests that seem to suggest a reference point in theories about the nature of the material world. They help to engender, from a narrow and peripheral category, the possibility of a positive contribution to a wide range of questions in contemporary anthropology. Material culture may offer a particular contribution because of the nature of its subject. Barthes (1973), Bourdieu (1977) and others have emphasized the 'naturalizing' effect of the material world, new forms can quickly become established as the everyday environment, the taken-for-granted context for living. Even in anthropology, which prides itself on the subtlety of its enquiry, the basic construction of self and social relations as they are mediated by images in clothes, household furnishings and so on, may be relatively neglected because they are quite coarsely articulated in language. An example arises in recent studies inspired by feminism, in which the critique of structures of dominance can be supplemented by the analysis of the subtle reproduction of asymmetry in the covert nature of the everyday world.

This may form part of the more general problem of 'culture' as posed by Simmel at the turn of the century. Our modern world's increasing range and complexity of form and commodity become ever more difficult to 'capture'. Yet given the comparative absence of 'critical' literature on this subject between, or example, Veblen writing at the same period as Simmel, and Baudrillard or Douglas and Isherwood today, it is almost as though the theoretical writings that take as their subject the social manipulation of the material world have declined as this subject has become central to the art of living in society and to the construction of social identity. It may be, however, that studies developed during this period, for example, the German work on *Ideologiekritik* and objectification, or the current attempts to free the image from its connotations as mere product (for the study of its positive recontextualization), provide a theoretical foundation for further studies today. It is clear that there is a strong base in Britain for the development of a range of research in this area.

Archaeology has, for its own logistical reasons, retained a sensitivity to the material world. Studies of subjects such as category variability and prestige goods are central features of its analysis. The ideas suggested here have direct implications for a subject whose interpretation is dependent upon a core relationship between objects and people. From this perspective, material culture studies may help to break down the boundaries between the study of, for example, small-scale peasant villages, industrial Britain and the Bronze Age, taking from and contributing to historical, archaeological and ethnographic forms of enquiry. As such, it may, in a modest way, once again act as an integrative element within the overall structure of contemporary anthropology.

This paper first appeared in Royal Anthropological Institute News (RAIN), *No. 59 (December 1983), pp. 5–7.*

REFERENCES

Barthes, R. (1973), *Mythologies*, London: Paladin.
Baudrillard, J. (1981) *For a Critique of the Political Economy of the Sign*, St Louis: Telos Press.
Bourdieu, P. (1977) *Outline of a Theory of Practice*, Cambridge: Cambridge University Press.
—— (1979) *La Distinction*, Paris: Editions de Minuit.
Clarke, D. (1968) *Analytical Archaeology*, London: Methuen.
Daniel, G. (1962) *The Idea of Prehistory*, Harmondsworth: Penguin Books.
Douglas, M. and Isherwood, B. (1979) *The World of Goods*, London: Allen Lane.
Forde, C. D. (1934) *Habitat, Economy and Society*, London: Methuen.
Friedman, J. and Rowlands, M. (eds) (1977) *The Evolution of Social Systems*, London: Duckworth.
Haddon, A. (1895) *Evolution in Art*, Newcastle-on-Tyne: Walter Scott Press.
Hodder, I. (ed.) (1982) *Symbolic and Structural Archaeology*, Cambridge: Cambridge University Press.
Lowie, R. (1937) *The History of Ethnological Theory*, New York: Rinehart.
Steadman, P. (1979) *The Evolution of Designs*, Cambridge: Cambridge University Press.
Tylor, E. (1881) *Anthropology*, New York: Macmillan & Co.
Wolff, J. (1981) *The Social Production of Art*, Cambridge: Cambridge University Press.

4

Objects as meaning; or narrating the past

Susan M. Pearce

This paper pursues the theme of the content of meaning which historical associations give to objects. It employs a particular semiotic approach, broadly that of Saussure, to analyse the way in which individual objects accumulate meanings as time passes. It also discusses the ideas of Wolfgang Iser, a literary critic whose thoughts (like those of many contemporary analysts of literature) are very pertinent to our understanding of objects. These help us to understand how objects are both active and passive (not just passive, as older views held), and how meaning develops as an interactive process between thing and viewer. The semiotic analysis set out in diagram form here can be compared with the similar one given in the Introduction: the framework is the same, and it is a very useful simple way of approaching an understanding of how objects work.

In the collections of the National Army Museum, London, there is an infantry officer's red jacket, of the type known as a coatee, which was worn by Lieutenant Henry Anderson at the battle of Waterloo, in what is now Belgium, on Sunday 18 June 1815.[1] The coatee is on exhibition in the National Army Museum, where it forms a part of the permanent displays. The jacket has been lovingly preserved from that June day to the present, and so we must suppose that it carries a genuine significance for the generations who have lived and died since the battle, up to and including our own. It is the nature and the implications of this significance which this paper sets out to explore.

As a first step, it is necessary to establish the specific context of the jacket in time and space, and to describe the historical moment of which it was a part. Anderson served in the Waterloo campaign as a lieutenant in the light company, 2nd battalion, 69th Regiment of Foot. On 16 June 1815, his regiment had fought at Quatre Bras, the action between the British Army and its allies and the French, which preceded the decisive encounter at Waterloo two days later. Due to a confusion of orders, the 69th were caught in extended line by the charge of Kellermann's brigade of cavalry. They were badly cut up, suffering some hundred and fifty casualties, and their colours were captured by the enemy. At Waterloo, the 2/69th took its place in the line of infantry regiments which held the ridge at Mont St Jean, and in the final phase of the battle, about seven o'clock in the evening, formed square with the 33rd Regiment as the British and Allied line prepared to receive the assault of the Imperial Guard (Whitehorne 1932).

The precise events of this, the most celebrated passage of arms in the entire Napoleonic Wars, has been a matter of dispute ever since. The square next to that of the 33rd and 69th seems to have been driven back in confusion, and that in which Anderson and the 69th stood began to give way until their commanding officer, General Halkett, himself took the 33rd's standard and encouraged them to stand their ground. At this moment, in the crisis of the battle, Anderson fell, wounded severely 'by a musket ball which broke his left shoulder, passed through the lungs, and made its exit at the back, breaking the scapula' (Army List, 1860). The coatee shows the tears and stains which would have resulted from such a wound. Anderson remained unconscious while the Imperial Guard was halted and turned, first by the attack of the 52nd Regiment and the 1st Foot Guards, and then by the mass of the Allied line: the battle was won and the French formations destroyed (Naylor 1968: 78–80, 159–65; Howarth 1968: 203–7).

Anderson's own, very brief, account of these final events survives in a letter which he contributed to Capt. Siborne's collection as a result of Siborne's requests for information from officers who had served in the battle; the collected letters were ultimately edited and published by his son in 1891 (Siborne 1891: 338). Anderson's slow promotion after 1815, and the considerable time he spent in 'desk jobs', suggest that his injuries at Waterloo left him something of an invalid for the rest of his life.

A number of points about this should be noticed, because they are of importance in the discussion which follows. The historical circumstances of time, place and action in which Anderson wore the surviving coatee, and in which he was wounded and the jacket damaged, are 'facts' as 'real' as any we shall ever have. The defeat of the Imperial Guard was recognized as decisive militarily and politically, and as glorious emotionally, within a few moments of its happening and, in at least some quarters, has been so seen ever since. The part played by the 69th, however, throughout the two battles, was much less prestigious and does not, therefore, form part of the extensive public mythology of the campaign. Anderson himself had his health affected, and we can only guess at the, probably complicated, mixture of feelings which led him to preserve his damaged jacket.

The jacket shows characteristics common to a great many pieces in museum collections, especially those within the broad fields of social history, applied art, and ethnography. Its connotations and historical context are extremely personal, giving it the value and emotional tone of a souvenir: nostalgic, backward-looking and bitter-sweet. It is intensely romantic, in that, for its owner in later life, who was the first person to cherish it, it probably represented a time when life seemed more exciting and more meaningful than the dull present of middle age. It serves, also, to sum up, or make coherent in personal and small-scale terms, an important event which seemed confused, spasmodic and incoherent to most of the individuals who took part in it. Finally, it acts as the validation of a personal narrative: when the original owner told his story of the great battle, he referred to his souvenirs to bear out the truth of what he was saying, and to help him make his personal selection of the moments which he wished to recall (Stewart 1984).

These intensely individual experiences are often of very limited interest to anybody else, and it is this which makes so much of this kind of museum material very intractable to deal with, either in terms of research or for the purposes of a display (or at any rate, of a modern display which aspires to make the past meaningful), because both research and display strive to operate within a broad and generalizing intellectual tradition, to which our jacket, of itself, seems to bear little relationship. But we know that many people *do* find the jacket worth looking at, because it has a quality which moves and excites us. In museums we are accustomed to call this the 'power of the real thing' and to regard it as the greatest strength which a collection-holding institution commands.

There is a problem here, upon which the concepts of semiotics may enable us to shed some light. We shall hope to show how the jacket works as a message-bearing entity, acting in relationship to Waterloo both as an intrinsic sign and as a metaphorical symbol, which is capable of a very large range of interpretations; and to explore how this relates to the way in which the present is created from the past. The nature of interpretation is then examined in terms of viewer-response, and this leads to a discussion of the relationship between individual responses and the social consensus of meaning, and so of the role of the curator. Finally, objects are seen as one of several ways of narrating the past.

We may start by viewing the jacket in terms of the fundamental insights achieved by Ferdinand de Saussure, adapting what he offers for an understanding of language to the analysis of other communication systems, in this case material culture (1973). Fig. 4.1, Section A, shows the three conceptual elements and their relationships. Each society 'chooses' from the large (but not infinite) range of possibilities what its individual nature is going to be. This 'choice' is not forever fixed, but will alter as circumstances change, a point to which we shall return. The choice gives each society at any particular moment a large range of communication possibilities, including a body of material culture within which, in the Britain of 1815, was our jacket. To be of social use, this range must be structured according to socially understood rules which command a sufficiently broadly based range of social support. This support is part of the local system of domination and subservience and therefore forms part of the local ideology. The rules, which can be called categories and which are the material equivalent to the grammar of language, and the range of possibilities equivalent to the vocabulary, together make up the deep structure of the society under analysis, and Saussure calls this structured whole the *langue*.

Later writers, like Barthes (1977), identify the *langue*, broadly, as the *signified*, that is to say, the body of social understanding which must operate through a social action of some kind. From the *langue* of society issues *parole*, that is the actual action, spoken sentence or performed deed, by means of which each society creates itself and continues its daily life. For Barthes, these concrete performances or embodiments, which he calls *signifiers*, have no necessary connection with the signified meaning which they carry (although this is debatable). Together, the union of signified and signifier gives us a *signe*, that is the social construct which members of the group can recognize and understand (Fig. 4.1, Section A).

The position of the jacket in all this seems quite clear. The *langue* of western European society in 1815 held a mass of material and human 'vocabulary', which included the production of coloured cloths and brass fittings, gunpowder, horse wagons and so on. Its categories included a desire to define armies, and within these armies different ranks and different regiments. The jacket, with its special cut, its red colour, its regimental insignia and its elements indicating rank, shows material structuring at work in classic form. There was, however, no obvious reason why this particular choice should have been made, for there are other ways in which the same social categories could have been expressed. The jacket is then a *signe* in Barthes's sense, uniting the message (the signified) and the physical embodiment (the signifier).

Saussure shows that the structuring process means that *parole* works not in discrete pieces but in sets, in which meaning depends upon relationships, and categories are created by the distinction which divides one set from another. The rank which the jacket expresses would be meaningless if there were not other, higher and lower, ranks with which it forms a set. Equally, the category 'army' acquires clearer meaning in relationship to the different category 'navy', where everyone wears blue jackets, and both are distinguished from the category 'civilian'. So, to the lower part of Fig. 4.1, Section A, we can add some of the sets which this society's *langue* produces as *parole*.

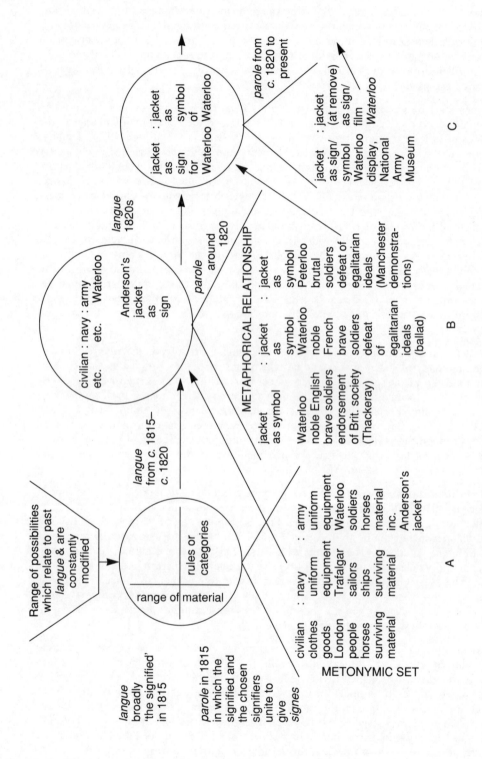

Fig. 4.1 Analysis of communication in material culture terms, using Saussure's system

We may take the discussion an important stage further by employing the analysis of communication devised by Leach (1976: 12). The message-bearing entity (jacket as signifier) stands for the message (the signified categories) as a result of human choice. At this point, Leach makes a crucial distinction between his sign and his symbol, which is very helpful in enabling us to understand better how the jacket works (confusingly, Leach and Barthes use the same word to describe different things; here the French spelling will be used when Barthes's meaning is intended, and the English when Leach's is). Objects (and other messages) operate as a *sign* when they stand for the whole of which they are an intrinsic part, as the jacket does for the actual events of Waterloo; and in this case the relationship between the different parts of the whole is said to be metonymic. They operate as a *symbol* when they are brought into an arbitrary association with elements to which they bear no intrinsic relationship, and in this case the association is said to be metaphoric. This association is a human device which bears no logical investigation, but apparently we instinctively behave as if it were true, particularly when objects or actions are connected with our deepest hopes and fears. We are inclined, for example, to invest considerable spiritual capital in religious ritual, which works precisely in this symbolic way, even though both rational thought and accumulated empirical experience suggest that this is misplaced.

This analysis of distinctions gives us a framework for expressing how Waterloo, both in immediate retrospect and ever since, has been experienced and interpreted in a large number of ways, or, to put it in post-structuralist terms, a number of discourses or narratives have been constructed around the event. Some of the broadly contemporary interpretations can be distinguished very readily. The socially approved norm, ideologically endorsed, saw the battle as embodying bravery, loyalty, worthy self-sacrifice and national pride, so that its events became proverbial and all contact with it, like Anderson's jacket, was lovingly cherished. In *Vanity Fair*, published in 1847, but dealing chiefly with events around 1815, Thackeray, after a paragraph musing on the brave folly of war, described the battle in one of the most famous passages in English letters (chapter 32):

> All our friends took their share and fought like men in the great field. All day long, whilst the women were praying ten miles away, the lines of the dauntless English infantry were receiving and repelling the furious charges of the French horsemen. Guns which were heard at Brussels were ploughing up their ranks, and comrades falling, and the resolute survivors closing in. Towards evening, the attack of the French, repeated and resisted so bravely, slackened in its fury. They had other foes beside the British to engage, or were preparing for a final onset. It came at last: the columns of the Imperial Guard marched up the hill of Saint Jean, at length and at once to sweep the English from the height which they had maintained all day, and spite of all: unscared by the thunder of the artillery, which hurled death from the English line – the dark rolling column pressed on and up the hill. It seemed almost to crest the eminence, when it began to wave and falter. Then it stopped, still facing the shot. Then at last the English troops rushed from the post from which no enemy had been able to dislodge them, and the Guard turned and fled.
>
> No more firing was heard at Brussels – the pursuit rolled miles away. Darkness came down on the field and city; and Amelia was praying for George, who was lying on his face, dead, with a bullet through his heart.

The view of the contemporary British labouring poor was rather different. A ballad in the BBC Sound Archive, recorded from the singing of Robert Cinnamond in Belfast, which seems to have originated soon after 1815, and which shows a detailed knowledge of Waterloo, gives one expression of the widespread sympathy which the underclass felt for the ideals of the French Revolution and for Napoleon as their glorious embodiment (*Folk Songs of Great Britain*, vol. 8, 'A soldier's life for me', Topic Records, 1961):

> 1 Attention pay, both young and old,
> To these few lines that I unfold.
> It is the deeds of great Napoleon
> I'm going to relate.
> He was a gallant Corsican,
> As ever stood on Europe's land,
> I'm inclined to sing his praises,
> So noble was his heart,
> For in every battle manfully
> He strove to gain that victorie,
> And to the world a terror
> Was Napoleon Bonyparte.
>
> 2 On that fatal June at Waterloo
> It caused Napoleon for to rue,
> When he saw the tricks of Grouchy.[2]
> It struck terror to his heart,
> For there upon that fatal day;
> He was forced to yield or run away,
> Like a bullock sold in Smithfield
> Was Napoleon Bonyparte.

Egalitarian ideals and a hatred of the British soldiers at the command of the class oppressors are explicitly linked in the period of abortive revolutionary action following 1815. The men who attempted revolution in the Derbyshire Peak in the early days of June 1819, sang:

> Every man his skill must try,
> He must turn out and not deny;
> No bloody soldier must he dread,
> He must turn out and fight for bread.
> The time is come you plainly see
> The government opposed must be.

> (Thompson 1968: 723–5)

As the marching men approached Nottingham, they were faced by a small force of Hussars, and their attempt collapsed: three men were ultimately executed and fourteen were transported.

The Derbyshire failure emphasized the dangers of armed conspiracy and, in Thompson's words (1968: 736–7), Peterloo, on 16 August 1819, followed directly as 'the outcome of an extraordinarily powerful and determined "consitutionalist" agitation, largely working class in character, within a potentially revolutionary context'. On that day about 60,000 peaceful demonstrators in St Peter's Fields, Manchester, were deliberately ridden down by the Manchester Yeomanry (local men serving part-time) and the regular 15th Hussars, on the orders of the local magistrates. The number of killed and wounded is uncertain, but there seems to have been about eleven dead and over 500 injured. To quote Thompson again, 'The epithet itself – Peter-Loo – with its savagely sardonic confidence, indicates better than any other evidence, the tone of feeling' (1968: 755). We can still hear the contempt for the soldiery and the disparagement of military glory which brought the name to birth, and perhaps, too, echoes of wistful sympathy for the ideals, if not the realities, of the French armies which we hear in the ballad already quoted, and many others of its kind. To the survivors of Peterloo, Anderson's coatee would have been experienced in a way quite different from that felt by Thackeray and most of his readers. These examples show the range of interpretations in which the battle and its elements were directly involved. A finer mesh would ultimately bring us down to the feelings of each single individual who was alive at the time with his or her perceptions of loss, gain or indifference; and all these perceptions share an equal validity.

It is clear that, in the terms which we have already described, each of these perceptions forms its own metonymic 'Waterloo set', and that these sets have a metaphorical relationship to that of Waterloo itself, and to each other (Fig. 4.1, Section B). The jacket as part of the set to which it has an intrinsic relationship – Waterloo – exists as a sign, but when it is part of the other sets it is acting as a symbol, although, as has been said, it is its metonymic sign nature which enables it to do this. The range of possible metaphorically related sets is very large, because each contemporary was capable of seeing the battle in a very large number of ways. The jacket is correspondingly rich in symbolic possibilities. It is capable of acting as a signifier for much signification, with each one of which the meaning of the *signe* changes; or, to put it another way, it is polysemantic.

All these shifting perceptions of the battle and the jacket went in to the imaginations (*langue*) of those who continued to live after the battle was over, forming part of an ever-shifting flux of experience which was passed on as an inheritance to their successors (Fig. 4.1, Section C). The perceptions which matched the aspirations of the class in power naturally tended to suppress or dislodge those which were officially regarded as more subversive, and it is these perceptions which ultimately brought the jacket into its museum collection. In semiotic terms, what happens is that those objects which were once signifiers become themselves the signified, as they become a chosen part of the society's *langue*, in which they play a role in modifying both the existing categories and the rules of their use. Put in historical terms, the experience of Waterloo, in all its guises and including its physical souvenirs, becomes part of the collective consciousness, in which it will play its role in bringing about social change. It may be added here that society is an agglomeration of individuals, and although in some senses the whole may be greater than the sum of its parts, it is also true that each individual's experience follows much the same patterning as has been discussed throughout this paper in social terms.

The jacket and the battle, now part of the signified held in the *langue*, give rise to a fresh range of signifiers which will find their own appropriate *signes*, among which, again, may well be the jacket itself. The crucial aspect of the jacket, which differentiates it from most other kinds of message-bearers (or elements in *parole*), is that while it survives physically it retains its metonymic relationship to the battle itself; of Waterloo, whatever meaning may be attached to it, the jacket remains *not* in Leach's terms a 'symbol' (however much it may be so described in ordinary speech) but, in his terms, a 'sign', an intrinsic part. So we have a sign available for constant symbolic reuse in the strict sense, in the creation of fresh sets of signifiers. The cycle of signified – signifier – *signe* (= sign: symbol) is constantly repeating itself throughout the span of an individual's consciousness, and in the course of social action, and it is the sum of these perpetually shifting meanings which makes up our perception of social change. In the example chosen here, the sign which carries meaning is able to do so because, unlike we ourselves who must die, it bears an 'eternal' relationship to the receding past, and it is this that we experience as the power of 'the actual object'.

This analysis helps us to understand the working of the emotional potency which undoubtedly resides in many supposedly 'dead' objects in our collections. It gives a framework for understanding better how our relationship with the material culture of the past operates, and shows that this is part of the way in which we construct our ever-passing present. This rests on the assumption that our reaction to the coatee is as important as the object itself, and the nature of this interaction bears further investigation. We have, as it were, the text created by the coat and its contexts, both originally and as a result of the signification chains already described; and we have the act of realization accomplished by the reader or viewer, the process which Roman Ingarden called *Konkretisation* (Iser 1974: 274). The meaning of the object lies not wholly in the piece itself, nor wholly in its realization, but somewhere between the two. The object only takes on life or significance when the viewer carries out his realization, and this is dependent partly upon his disposition and experience, and partly upon the content of the object which works upon him. It is this interplay which creates meaning; however, the precise convergence can never be exactly pinpointed but 'must always remain virtual, as it is not to be identified either with the reality of the text or with the individual disposition of the reader' (Iser 1974: 274).

It is this 'virtuality', to use Wolfgang Iser's word, which gives rise to the dynamic nature of objects, as it does of texts. As the viewer stands in front of the showcase, he makes use of the various perspectives which the object offers him, some of which have already been suggested: his creative urges are set in motion, his imagination is engaged, and the dynamic process of interpretation and reinterpretation begins, which extends far beyond the mere perception of what the object is. The object activates our own faculties, and the product of this creative activity is the virtual dimension of the object, which endows it with present reality. The message or meaning which the object offers is always incomplete and each viewer fills in the gaps in his own way, thereby excluding other possibilities: as he looks he makes his own decisions about how the story is to be told of, for example, Lieutenant Anderson's feelings on that day.

In this act, the dynamics of viewing are revealed. The object is inexhaustible, but it is this inexhaustibility which forces the viewer to his decisions. The viewing process is selective, and the potential object is richer than any of its realizations. When the same person sees the same coat ten years later, it may appear in a new light, which seems to him more 'correct', richer and more perceptive, so that artefact is transformed into experience. In one sense, it is reflecting the developing personality of the viewer and so acting as a kind of mirror; but at the same time the effect of the object is to modify or change the viewer, so that he is a slightly different person from the one he was before. So we have the apparently paradoxical situation in which the viewer is forced to reveal aspects of himself in order to experience a reality which is different from his own, because it is only by leaving behind the familiar world of his own experience that he can take part in the excitement which objects offer; and many of us would feel that this lies at the heart of the museum experience.

The viewer's process may be taken a stage further. He will endeavour to bring all his imaginative impressions together into the kind of consistency for which we are always searching, since, it seems, that the creation of satisfactorily complete sets, which have a parallel or metaphorical relationship to other perceived sets, is the way in which our minds work to provide distinctions and explanations. This brings us to the final problem to be considered here. The object as it survives has a fixed form and a definite factual history, without which it could not exist and we could not begin to understand it; but if viewing and interpreting it were to consist only of uninhibited speculation, uninterrupted by any 'realistic' constraints, the result would be a series of purely individual sequences with little relationship to each other, and meaningful only in terms of the individual personality, no matter how bizarre, idiosyncratic or simply ill-informed this may be.

If the viewer cannot conjure up the kind of consistency just mentioned, which may be described as an act of interpretation, with all the claims to validity which this implies, he will lose interest in the object. But if his interpretation departs too far from contemporary norms, his community will lose interest in him, at least as far as this subject is concerned. This can certainly happen, but more usually it does not and the reason seems to rest in the relationship between object and viewer. The object provokes certain reactions and expectations which we project back on to it in such a way that the polysemantic possibilities are greatly reduced in order to be in keeping with the expectations that have been aroused. To paraphrase Iser, the polysemantic nature of the object and the interpretation-making of the viewer are opposed factors. If the interpretation-making were limited, the polysemantic nature would vanish, but if the polysemantic nature were all-powerful, the interpretation would be destroyed (Iser 1974). Much the same point may be made by saying that the object only exists if it is 'made meaningful' through somebody reacting with it; but, at the same time, that somebody only exists, as a social being, as he is in the process of interaction (as, of course, he is most of the time). The balance is held by the object itself, with its tangible and factual content. About the nature of these, there is a consensus within each individual's community, and so the act of interpretation will bear a relationship to this consensus. Herein lies the dialectical structure of viewing. The need to decipher gives us the chance to bring out both what is in the object and what is in ourselves; it is a dynamic, complex movement which unfolds as time passes, and in the act of interpretative imagination we give form to ourselves.

The nature of this consensus is complex. Among other things, it embraces the body of traditional knowledge and expertise which we may call scholarship or curatorship, and the ability to apply this to a particular object or collection in order to extend the boundary of understanding. But the curator faces both ways. He possesses traditional knowledge, which in the case of the Waterloo jacket means the ability to appreciate its specific nature and history, precisely the qualities which give it its unique value. However, he is also part of the dialectical process, so that each presentation of an object is a selective narrative, and the curator is engaging in a rhetorical act of persuasion, which has an uncertain outcome. The whole process assists each of us to make some kind of sense of our relationship to our past and so to our present, the perpetual re-creation in which meaning is always just through the next door.

Two further points remain to be made. The constant use, in this paper and others like it, of words like 'cypher', 'code', and, above all, 'text', gives us a broad clue to the first: objects and our relationship to them are analysed as if they were written narratives, and this approach needs a little more elaboration. The material to which we react, combining as it does both external events like the coatee and internal events like our own imaginative response, always lies in the past, although this past may be as distant as Waterloo or as recent as a moment ago. The past survives in three ways: as objects or material culture; as physical landscape (the difference between which and artefacts is conventional rather than essential); and as narratives (which may, of course, take the form of film or tape as well as of written text). To these should be added a further dimension, that of individual memory, but it seems likely that this memory forms itself as images of objects and places, linked with physical remembrances like heat and cold and with remembered emotions, to construct narratives similar to those which have external form.

27

The distinction between narrative as 'historical' writing, which claims to 'tell the truth about the past', and narrative which is 'fiction', like a novel or a poem, becomes increasingly flimsy the harder it is looked at. Both will have to bear a relationship to 'external' fact and to a generally received view of the human condition which they illumine, if they are to hold our interest and stimulate our imaginations (and they are generally held to be the greater, the more they achieve this), and both are equally 'true' in the sense that they set out a view of the human social past as conceived by the writer in his day. Both require their present meaning to be constructed in the ways already described, and both, therefore, are subject to Barthes's famous 'death of the author' (1977). But narratives of these various kinds all require a degree of explication to help in the creation of most of their meaning, which is another way of saying that the cultivation of curatorship and scholarship, in the traditional sense, is fundamental to our enhanced understanding of them, in spite of the fact that, as we have seen, scholarship is itself a dialectical process. Precisely the same applies to the objects and the landscapes which survive from the past. These also tell their story, like a verbal or pictorial narrative, and they do this more meaningfully the more they have been studied. Hence the fact that both technical history (the events of Waterloo and Peterloo), and technical fiction (*Vanity Fair*), together with that shifting, moody, quicksilver construction which is each individual, have all been drawn into this attempt to unravel the nature of our relationship with the coatee on display; and hence, also, the title of this paper.

Second, it is important to remember that we ourselves – I who write this paper and you who find yourself reading it – are actors in the story. It is our better understanding, as we live our lives, of the processes of making meaning which enables us to analyse the nature of our relation to the objects which come from the past, and to perceive how they affect us, both individually in the dialectical creation of meaning and self, and socially in the ideological creation of unequal relationships. Better understanding in both these modes brings discontent, since it is seldom comfortable to know more either about one's self or about one's position in the world, but equally, understanding is a liberating project, even though forever bound in self-related subjectivity. So tension is generated, and it is precisely for these reasons that authors write narratives, museums collect objects and display them, people visit galleries, and we all construct our explaining stories from what we see, read and remember; and all these meanings, as we have seen, are the continuous re-creation of significance through the perpetual play of metaphor and metonymy, of signification and signifier. So the jacket which was once part of Lieutenant Anderson's past and present now becomes part of our own, carrying the objective reality of its red cloth and its bullet hole along the chain of meanings.

This paper first appeared in S. Pearce (1990) New Research in Museum Studies: Objects of Knowledge, London: Athlone, pp. 125–40.

NOTES

1   I am very grateful to Michael Ball and Simon Davies, both of the National Army Museum, London, who supplied me with details about Lt. Henry Anderson and his coatee.

2   On 15 June Napoleon divided his army into three groups, and command of the right wing was given to Marshal Grouchy. On the 17th Grouchy was ordered to pursue the Prussian army, presumed (wrongly) to be in disarray after the action at Ligny on the 16th, and prevent a junction between the Prussians and Wellington. Grouchy's force spent the crucial hours of the 18th partly in delay and partly in useless pursuit of part of the Prussian Army. If Grouchy had interpreted his orders differently, or ignored them, or received more sensible orders much earlier, he might have turned towards Waterloo sooner and pre-vented the arrival of the Prussians on the field and so, perhaps, the French defeat. This muddle was used in some quarters to make Grouchy the scapegoat for Napoleon's failure, in many ways unfairly because the responsibility for the orders which Grouchy was given rests with Napoleon himself. The pro-Bonapartist ballad quoted here takes an extreme view of Grouchy's actions, and even hints that Napoleon was 'betrayed'.

REFERENCES

Army List (1860).

Barthes, R. (1977) *Image–Music–Text*, trans. S. Heath, London: Fontana.

Howarth, D. (1968) *Waterloo*, London: Fontana.

Iser, W. (1974) (trans. C. Macksey and R. Macksey) *The Implied Reader: Patterns of Communication in Prose Fiction from Bunyan to Beckett*, Baltimore: Johns Hopkins University Press.

Leach, E. (1976) *Culture and Communication*, Cambridge: Cambridge University Press.

Naylor, John (1968) *Waterloo*, London: Pan Books, British Battles Series.

Saussure, F. de (1973) *Course in General Linguistics*, trans. Baskin Wade, London: Fontana.

Siborne, H. T. (1891) *Waterloo Letters*, London: Macmillan.

Stewart, S. (1984) *On Longing: Narratives of the Miniature, the Gigantic, the Souvenir, the Collection*, Baltimore: Johns Hopkins University Press.

Thompson, E. P. (1968) *The Making of the English Working Class*, Harmondsworth: Penguin Books.

Whitehorne, A. C. (1932) *The History of the Welch Regiment*, Cardiff: The Welch Regiment.

5

Death's head, cherub, urn and willow

J. Deetz and E. S. Dethlefsen

This paper similarly analyses historical meaning in objects, through the discussion of a group of seventeenth- and eighteenth-century New England gravestones and their motifs. It has come to be a classic statement of the fundamental techniques – dating, seriation, diffusion, typology and style classification – that the working material culturalist uses every day. It combines this methodological ease with an interpretative analysis which aims to sharpen our understanding of cultural process and cultural change. The authors ask, 'Where does innovation in a society's material culture first begin? How is cultural change diffused?' They show how the answers to these questions can be approached through an appreciation of their historical contexts.

Enter almost any cemetery in eastern Massachusetts that was in use during the seventeenth and eighteenth centuries. Inspect the stones and the designs carved at their tops, and you will discover that three motifs are present. These motifs have distinctive periods of popularity, each replacing the other in a sequence that is repeated time and time again in all cemeteries between Worcester and the Atlantic, and from New Hampshire to Cape Cod.

The earliest of the three is a winged death's head, with blank eyes and a grinning visage. Earlier versions are quite ornate, but as time passes, they become less elaborate. Sometime during the eighteenth century – the time varied according to location – the grim death's head designs were replaced, more or less quickly, by winged cherubs. This design also went through a gradual simplification of form with time. By the late 1700s or early 1800s, again depending on where you are observing, the cherubs were replaced by stones decorated with a willow tree overhanging a pedestalled urn. If the cemetery you are visiting is in a rural area, the chances are quite good that you will also find other designs, which may even completely replace one or more of the three primary designs at certain periods. If you were to search cemeteries in the same area, you would find that these other designs have a much more local distribution. In and around Boston, however, only the three primary designs would be present.

If you were to prepare a graph showing how the designs changed in popularity through time, the finished product might look something like three battleships viewed from above, the lower one with the bow showing, the centre one in full view, and the third visible only in the stern. This shape, frequently called a 'battleship-shaped' curve, is thought by archaeologists to typify the popularity career of any cultural trait across time. Such curves can be prepared from controlled data taken from the Stoneham cemetery, north of Boston, where the style sequence is typical of the area around this eighteenth-century urban centre of eastern Massachusetts.

It is appropriate here to interrupt and pose the question: Why would an archaeologist study gravestones from a historic period?

Whether archaeology can be considered a science in the strict sense of the word is much debated. One of the hallmarks of scientific method is the use of controls in experimentation that enable the investigator to calibrate his results. Since archaeology deals largely with the unrecorded past, the problem of rigorous control is a difficult one. Much of modern archaeological method and theory has been developed in contexts that lack the necessary controls for precise checking of accuracy and predictive value. For this reason, any set of archaeological data in which such controls are available is potentially of great importance to the development and testing of explanatory models, which can then be used in uncontrolled contexts.

For a number of reasons, colonial New England grave markers may be unique in providing the archaeologist with a laboratory situation in which to measure cultural change in time and space and relate such measurements to the main body of archaeological method. All archaeological data – artefacts, structures and sites – can be said to possess three inherent dimensions. A clay pot, for example, has a location in space. Its date of manufacture and use is fixed in time, and it has certain physical attributes of form. In a sense, much of archaeological method is concerned with the nature and causes of variation along these dimensions, as shown by excavated remains of past cultures.

The spatial aspect of gravestones is constant. We know from historical sources that nearly all of the stones in New England cemeteries of this period were produced locally, probably no more than 15 or 20 miles away from their resting places; an insignificant number of them came from long distances. This pattern is so reliable that it is possible to detect those few stones in every cemetery that were made at a more remote town. Once placed over the dead, the stones were unlikely to have been moved, except perhaps within the cemetery limits.

Needless to say, the dimension of time is neatly and tightly controlled. Every stone bears the date of death of the individual whose grave it marks, and most stones were erected shortly after death. Like the spatial regularity, this temporal precision makes it possible to single out most of the stones that were erected at some later date.

Control over the formal dimension of gravestone data derives from our knowledge of the carvers, who, in many instances, are known by name and period of production, and who, even if anonymous, can be identified by their product with the help of spatial and temporal control. Thus, in most cases stones of similar type can be seen to be the product of a single person, and they reflect his ideas regarding their proper form.

Furthermore, it is known that the carvers of the stones were not full-time specialists, but rather they were workers at other trades who made stones for the immediate population as they were needed. We are dealing, then, with 'folk' products, as is often the case in prehistoric archaeology.

Other cultural dimensions can also be controlled in the gravestone data with equal precision, and with the addition of these, the full power of these artefacts as controls becomes apparent: probate research often tells the price of individual stones, and status indication occurs frequently on the stones, as well as the age of each individual. Since death is related to religion, formal variations in the written material can be analysed to see how they reflect religious variations. Epitaphs provide a unique literary and psychological dimension. Spatial distributions can be measured against political divisions. In short, the full historical background of the seventeenth, eighteenth and nineteenth

31

centuries permits both primary and secondary control of the material, and with the resulting precision, explanations become quite reliable.

With such controls available to the archaeologist, the pattern of change in colonial gravestone design and style can be used with great effect to sharpen our understanding of cultural process in general.

To return to the battleship-shaped curves, what does this mean in terms of cultural change? Why should death's heads be popular at all, and what cultural factors were responsible for their disappearance and the subsequent rise of the cherub design? The most obvious answer is found in the ecclesiastical history of New England. The period of decline of death's heads coincided with the decline of orthodox Puritanism. In the late seventeenth century, Puritanism was universal in the area, and so were death's head gravestones. The early part of the eighteenth century saw the beginnings of change in orthodoxy, culminating in the great awakenings of the mid-century. In his recent, excellent book on the symbolism of New England gravestones, *Graven Images*, Allan Ludwig points out that the 'iconophobic' Puritans found the carving of gravestones a compromise. While the use of cherubs might have verged on heresy, since they were heavenly beings whose portrayal might have led to idolatry, the use of a more mortal and neutral symbol – a death's head – would have served as a graphic reminder of death and resurrection.

Given the more liberal views concerning symbolism and personal involvement preached by Jonathan Edwards and others later in the eighteenth century, the idolatrous and heretical aspects of cherubs would have been more fitting to express the sentiment of the period.

It is at this point that available literary controls become valuable. The epitaph on each stone begins by describing the state of the deceased: 'Here lies' or 'Here lies buried' being typical early examples. Slowly these were replaced by 'Here lies (buried) the body (corruptible, what was mortal) of'. This slightly, but significantly, different statement might well reflect a more explicit tendency to stress that only a part of the deceased remains, while the soul, the incorruptible or immortal portion, has gone to its eternal reward. Cherubs reflect a stress on resurrection, while death's heads emphasize the mortality of man. The epitaphs that appear on the bottoms of many stones also add credence to this explanation of change in form over time. Early epitaphs, with death's head designs, stress either decay and life's brevity:

> My Youthful mates both small and great
> Come here and you may see
> An awful sight, which is a type
> Of which you soon must be.

Or there may be a Calvinistic emphasis on hard work and exemplary behaviour on the part of the predestined: 'He was a useful man in his generation, a lover of learning, a faithful servant of Harvard College above forty years.' On the other hand, epitaphs with cherub stones tend to stress resurrection and later heavenly reward:

> Here cease thy tears, suppress thy fruitless mourn.
> His soul – the immortal part – has upward flown.
> On wings he soars his rapid way
> To yon bright regions of eternal day.

The final change seen in gravestone style is the radical shift to the urn-and-willow design. It is usually accompanied by a change in stone shape; while earlier stones have a round-shouldered outline, the later stones have square shoulders. 'Here lies the body of' is replaced by 'In memory of' or 'Sacred to the memory of', quite different from all earlier forms. The earlier stones are markers, designating the location of the deceased or at least a portion of him. In contrast, 'In memory of' is simply a memorial statement, and stones of this later type could logically be erected elsewhere and still make sense. In fact, many of the late urn-and-willow stones are cenotaphs, erected to commemorate those actually buried elsewhere, as far away as Africa, Batavia, and in one case – in the Kingston, Massachusetts, cemetery – 'drowned at sea, lat. 39 degrees N., long. 70 degrees W'. The cultural changes that accompanied the shift to urn-and-willow designs are seen in the rise of less emotional, more intellectual religions, such as Unitarianism and Methodism. Epitaphs changed with design and in the early nineteenth century tended more to sentiment combined with eulogy.

This sequence of change did not occur in a vacuum, unrelated to any cultural change elsewhere; indeed, the sequence of three major types also took place in England, the cultural parent of the Massachusetts colony, but about a half-century earlier. Thus cherubs became modal by the beginning of the Georgian period (1715), and urns and willows made their appearance, as a part of the neo-classical tradition, in the 1760s. In fact, the entire urn-and-willow pattern was a part of the larger Greek revival, which might explain the squared shoulders on the stones – a severer classical outline.

Thus far we have been discussing formal change through time and some of the fundamental causes. We have seen that New England was changing in harmony with England, with an expectable time interval separating the sequences. But we have not identified the relationship of all of this to archaeological method.

The battleship-shaped curve assumption is basic to many considerations of cultural process in general and to such dating methods as seriation. Seriation is a method whereby archaeological sites are arranged in relative chronological order based on the popularity of the different types of artefacts found in them. The approach assumes that any cultural item, be it a style of pottery or a way of making an arrowhead, had a particular popularity period, and as it grew and waned in popularity, its prevalence as time passed can be represented graphically by a single peaked curve. Small beginnings grew to a high frequency of occurrence, followed in turn by a gradual disappearance. If such an assumption is true, it follows that a series of sites can be arranged so that all artefact types within them form single peaked curves of popularity over time. Such an arrangement is chronological and tells the archaeologist how his sites relate to one another in time.

By plotting style sequences in this manner in a number of cemeteries we find that the assumption, not previously measured with such a degree of precision, is a sound one: styles do form single peaked popularity curves through time. By adding the control of the spatial to the form–time pattern explained above, we gain a number of understandings regarding diffusion – the spread of ideas through time and space and how this, in turn, affected internal change in style. In looking now at the three dimensions, we will see that all of the secondary cultural controls become even more important.

The style sequence of death's head, cherub, and urn-and-willow design is to be found in almost every cemetery in eastern Massachusetts. However, when we inspect the time at which each change took place and the degree of overlap between styles from cemetery to cemetery, it becomes apparent that this sequence was occurring at a widely varying rate from place to place. The earliest occurrence of cherubs was in the Boston Cambridge area, where they began to appear as early as the end of the seventeenth century. Occasional early cherubs might be found in more distant rural cemeteries, but in every case we find them to have been carved in the Boston area and to be rare imports from there. The further we move away from the Boston centre, the later locally manufactured cherubs make their appearance in numbers. The rate at which the cherub style spread outward has even been approximately measured and shown to be about a mile per year. It is not common in archaeology to make such precise measurements of diffusion rate – the usual measurements are cruder, such as hundreds of miles in millennia.

We can view Boston and, more significantly, nearby Cambridge as the focus of emphasis of Puritan religion with its accompanying values and enquire what factors might have contributed to the initial appearance of cherubs and the change in religious values in this central area. We have noted that the change had already been accomplished in England by the early eighteenth century, so that when the first cherubs began to appear in numbers in Cambridge, they were already the standard modal style in England. While cherubs occurred in Boston, they never made a major impression, and as many death's heads as cherubs were replaced by the urn-and-willow influx.

On the other hand, in Cambridge cherubs made an early start and attained a respectable frequency by the late eighteenth century. Although they never attained a full 100 per cent level there, as they did in most rural areas, they did at least enjoy a simple majority. When the cherub stones in Cambridge are inspected more closely, we find that roughly 70 per cent of them mark the graves of high-status individuals: college presidents, graduates of Harvard, governors and their families, high church officials, and in one case, even a 'Gentleman from London'. From what we know of innovation in culture, it is often the more cosmopolitan, urban stratum of society that brings in new ideas, to be followed later by the folk stratum. If this is true, then the differences between Boston and Cambridge indicate a more liberal element within the population of Cambridge, reflected in the greater frequency of cherub stones there. This is probably the case, with the influence of the Harvard intellectual community being reflected in the cemetery. It would appear that even in the early eighteenth century, the university was a place for innovation and liberal thinking. Cambridge intellectuals were more likely to be responsive to English styles, feelings and tastes, and this could well be what we are seeing in the high number of cherub stones marking high-status graves.

Introduced into Cambridge and Boston by a distinct social class, the cherub design slowly began its diffusion into the surrounding countryside. Carvers in towns further removed from Cambridge and Boston – as far as 14 miles west in Concord – began to change their gravestone styles away from the popular death's head as early as the 1730s, but 50 miles to the south, in Plymouth, styles did not change until the 1750s and 1760s and then in a somewhat different cultural context. We find, however, that the further the cemetery was from Boston, and the later the cherubs began to be locally manufactured, the more rapidly they reached a high level of popularity. The pattern is one of a long period of co-existence between cherubs and death's heads in the Boston centre, and an increasingly more rapid eclipsing of death's heads by cherubs in direct proportion to distance, with a much shorter period of overlap. One explanation is that in towns further removed from the diffusion centre, enforcement of Puritan ethics and values was lessened, and resistance to change was not so strong. Furthermore, revivalism and the modification of orthodox Puritanism was widespread from the late 1730s through the 1760s in rural New England, although this movement never penetrated Boston. Such activity certainly must have conditioned the rural populace for a change to new designs.

We have, then, a picture of the introduction of a change in the highly specific aspect of mortuary art, an aspect reflecting much of the culture producing it. We see the subsequent spread of this idea, through space and time, as a function of social class and religious values. Now we are in a position to examine internal change in form through time, while maintaining relatively tight control on the spatial dimension.

One significant result of the use of gravestone data, with its accompanying controls, is the insight it provides in matters of stylistic evolution. The product of a single carver can be studied over a long period of time, and the change in his patterns considered as they reflect both ongoing culture change and his particular manner of handling design elements. The spatial axis extending outward from Boston shows not only systematic change in major style replacement rates but also a striking pattern of difference in style change. We find that in many cases the further removed we become from Boston, the more rapid and radical is change within a given single design. This has been observed in at least five separate cases involving a number of the styles of more local distribution; we can inspect one of these cases closely and attempt to determine some of the processes and causes of stylistic evolution.

The design in question is found in Plymouth County, centring on the town of Plympton. Its development spans a period of some seventy years, and the changes effected from beginning to end are truly profound. Death's heads occurred in rural Plymouth County, as they did elsewhere in the late seventeenth century. However, in the opening decade of the eighteenth century, the carver(s) in Plympton made certain basic changes in the general death's head motif. The first step in this modification involved the reduction of the lower portion of the face, and the addition of a heart-shaped element between nose and teeth. The resulting pattern was one with a heartlike mouth, with the teeth shrunken to a simple band along the bottom. The teeth soon disappear entirely, leaving the heart as the sole mouth element. This change was rapidly followed by a curious change in the feathering of the wings.

While early examples show all feather ends as regular scallops crossing the lines separating individual feathers, shortly after the first changes in the face were made, every other row of feather ends had their direction of curvature reversed. The resulting design produces the effect of undulating lines radiating from the head, almost suggesting hair, at right angles to curved lines that still mark the feather separation. These two changes, in face and wing form, occupy a period of thirty-five years from 1710 to 1745. During the later 1740s this development, which had so far been a single sequence, split into two branches, each the result of further modification of wings. In the first case, the arcs marking feather separations were omitted, leaving only the undulating radial lines. Rapid change then took place leading to a face surmounted by wavy and, later, quite curly hair. The heart mouth was omitted. We have dubbed this style 'Medusa'. In the second case, the separating lines were retained, and the undulating lines removed; the result in this case was a face with multiple haloes. At times, space between these haloes was filled with spiral elements, giving the appearance of hair, or the haloes were omitted entirely. The heart-shaped mouth was retained in this case and modified into a T-shaped element.

Both of these styles enjoyed great popularity in the 1750s and 1760s, and had slightly different spatial distributions, suggesting that they might have been the work of two carvers, both modifying the earlier heart-mouthed design in different ways. Yet a third related design also appeared in the 1740s, this time with tightly curled hair, conventional wings, and a face similar to the other two. Although this third design seems to be a more direct derivative of the earlier death's head motif, it is clearly inspired in part by the Medusa and multiple-halo designs. This tight-haired style has a markedly different spatial distribution, occurring to the west of the other two, but overlapping them in a part of its range. Of the three, only the Medusa lasted into the 1770s, and in doing so presents us with something of an enigma. The final form, clearly evolved from the earlier types, is quite simple. It has a specific association with small children and has never been found marking the grave of an adult and rarely of a child over age five.

The carver of the fully developed Medusa was probably Ebenezer Soule of Plympton; a definitive sample of his style is found in the Plympton cemetery. Normal Medusas, except for the late, simple ones marking children's graves, disappeared abruptly in the late 1760s. In 1769, and lasting until the 1780s, stones identical to Soule's Medusas, including the simple, late ones, appeared in granite around Hinsdale, New Hampshire. Fortunately, a local history has identified the carver of some of these stones as 'Ebenezer Soule, late of Plympton'. This alone is of great interest, but if Soule did move to Hinsdale in 1769, who carved the later children's stones in Plymouth County? As yet, no answer is known.

This development raises two interesting considerations. First, we see that a style, the Medusa, which had been used for the general populace, ended its existence restricted to small children. This pattern has been observed elsewhere, with children's burials being marked by designs that were somewhat more popular earlier in time. In other words, children are a stylistically conservative element in the population of a cemetery. While no clear answer can be given to this problem, it may well be that small children, not having developed a strong, personal impact on the society, would not be thought of in quite the same way as adults and would have their graves marked with more conservative, less explicitly descriptive stones.

The second problem raised by the Medusas is their reappearance in Hinsdale. If, as archaeologists, we were confronted with the degree of style similarity seen between Hinsdale and Plympton in mortuary art, might we not infer a much greater influence than a single individual arriving in the community? After all, mortuary art would be about the only distinctively variable element in material culture over eighteenth-century New England, and such a close parallel could well be said to represent a migration from Plympton to Hinsdale. One man did move.

Placing this striking case of stylistic evolution in the broader context of culture change and style change in eastern Massachusetts, we find that it is paralleled by other internal modifications of death's head designs in other remote rural areas. The closer we move towards Boston, the less change takes place within the death's head design, and in Boston proper, death's heads from 1810 are not that different from those from 1710. Yet 1710 death's heads in Plympton and elsewhere had changed so radically by 1750 that it is doubtful that we could supply the derivation of one from the other in the absence of such an excellently dated set of intermediate forms. This difference in rate of change can be explained by referring back to the long, parallel courses of development of both death's head and cherub in the diffusion area's Boston centre. However, culture change in the area of religion, marked by a shift of emphasis from mortality to immortality, probably generated a desire for less realistic and less grim designs on stones. Given this basic change in religious attitudes, what were the alternatives facing carvers in Boston as opposed to the Ebenezer Soules of rural New England? In Boston it was simply a matter of carving more cherub stones and fewer death's head stones; neither had to be altered to suit the new tastes. The choice between cherub and death's head in Boston has been interpreted as ultimately a social one, and if there was a folk culture component within Boston, there was nothing but folk culture in the more democratic, less stratified rural areas. With no one to introduce cherubs and to call for them with regularity in the country, carvers set to work modifying the only thing they had – the death's head. The more remote the community, the later the local cherubs appeared, diffusing from Boston, and the more likely the tendency to rework the common folk symbol of skull and wings. Thus we get Medusas and haloed T-mouthed faces populating the cemeteries of Plymouth County until cherubs finally appeared. Even then, the waning popularity of the death's head in this area might be more the result of Soule's exit than their unsatisfactory appearance compared to the new cherubs.

Only a few applications of gravestone design analysis have been detailed here. There is a large and important demographic dimension to these data; since precise date of death is given, as well as age at death, patterns of mortality and life expectancy through time and space can be detailed. The results of this work, in turn, will add a biological dimension of style to the cultural one described above. Studies of diffusion rate and its relationship to dating by seriation will be continued. Relationships between political units – countries, townships and colonies – and style spheres will be investigated to determine how such units affect the distribution of a carver's products. Finally, a happy by-product will be the preservation on film of over 25,000 gravestones, a vital consideration in view of the slow but steady deterioration these informative artefacts are undergoing.

Aside from the value of this work to archaeology and anthropology in general, one final comment must be made. Compared to the usual fieldwork experienced by the archaeologist, with all of its dust and heavy shovelling under a hot sun, this type of archaeology certainly is most attractive. All the artefacts are on top of the ground, the sites are close to civilization, and almost all cemeteries have lovely, shady trees.

This paper first appeared in Natural History 76 (March 1967), pp. 29–37.

REFERENCE

Ludwig, A. (1966) *Graven Images: New England Stone Carving and its Symbols 1650–1815*, Cambridge, Mass.: Harvard University Press.

6

Behavioural interaction with objects

Susan M. Pearce

This short piece from Pearce picks up on the two preceding pieces, and offers a behavioural perspective which helps to show how objects and people interact. This process of interaction has already been described in a slightly different way through the use of Iser's terms in relation to the Waterloo jacket. The way in which the New Englanders related to the gravestones described in the previous piece could also be put in these terms. Together, the papers give perspectives on how objects acquire historical meaning, and how this is part of the process of social change.

Let us try to demonstrate the process of this interaction in more explicit and concrete terms, using a deliberately simple scheme to represent the behavioural framework within which social action takes place. Within this we shall set a fashion-conscious woman in her late teens as the acting individual, and the clothes of the late 1980s as the acting objects (Fig. 6.1). The framework sets out the main parameters within which action happens, giving us the environment both physical and social, the individual, and the psychological or cognitive processes of perception and learning which form a continuous cycle and link the whole together. The physical environment is straightforward enough, and for our example will be southern urban England with the normal English climate. The social environment is broken down into three groups, all fairly standard in social science: primary groups like family, peer groups comprising people of the same age and background who may or may not be friends, and reference groups who for our woman are likely to be members of the youth culture scene. The individual, the woman herself, is presumed to have a personality, sets of attitudes, beliefs and values, and motives, all of which derive from her nature and nurture.

The Punk style of dressing (and incidentally, it is interesting that it had to look back to the subculture diction of seventeenth-century England where 'punk' meant 'ruffian' or even 'goblin', to find itself a name) had caught the attention of the public by 1976. It has been described as

> a classic case of avant-garde shock tactics. An assault on all received notions of taste, it is significant in being almost the only one of the post-war youth/culture/music movements fully to have integrated women. The style alluded to sado-masochism, porn, sleaze and tawdry glamour and inscribed itself by means of shaven or partially shaven heads and a sort of anti-make-up (reddened eyes, black lips, make-up painted in streaks across the face or in a pattern) on the surface of the body. Punks created an alienated space between self and appearance by means of these attacks on their own bodies; this was truly fit wear for the urban dispossessed, constructed out of the refuse of the material world; rusty razor blades, tin cans, safety pins, dustbin bags and even used tampons.
>
> (Wilson and Taylor 1989: 196)

The style was, not surprisingly, actually worn only by a few, but by the late 1980s it had modified the mainstream of young fashion. Bright lipstick and heavy black eye make-up, 'ugly' short hair, shaved necks, sometimes spiky hair stiffened with gel, together with black leather, short black skirts and black tights became the normal metropolitan uniform for young women in the late 1980s. These fashions and the life style, for both men and women, that went with them were encouraged by the new style magazines of the 1980s, like *The Face*, *i-D* and *Blitz*. As Wilson and Taylor say,

> The newly glamorous, male style setter of the eighties became as familiar in magazines and advertisements as his female counterpart, with his hair, short at the back, long at the front, sleekly gelled, his looks mean and tough, yet simultaneously blankly narcissistic. This new man is the empty object of anyone's desire, his sexuality ambiguous. It is unclear whether this beauty is destined for men or for women.
>
> (1989: 204)

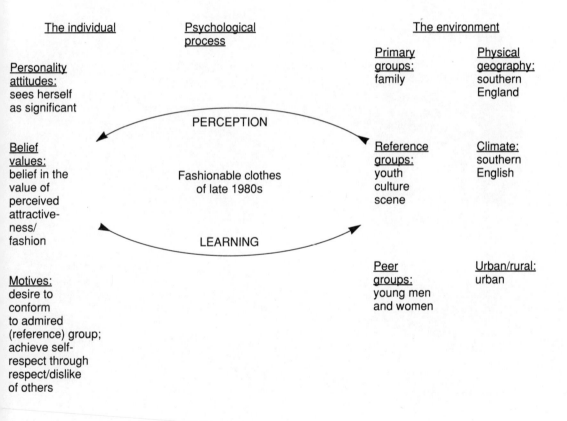

Fig. 6.1 Behavioural action: young woman and clothes

We can see what is happening in terms of the behavioural model. There is a large range of clothes available for wear, but our teenage woman learns in relation to her own personality and motives, that the pressure of her peer group, and of the reference groups which they admire, will lead her to buy and wear the fashionable black clothes and the look that goes with it, in opposition probably to some primary groups and rejected reference groups (e.g. parents). Once she has done this, however, she is herself perceived differently by all the groups to which she relates. This perception may for some take the form of greater acceptance and admiration, but it may suggest to others that the black clothes are now old hat, and that the time has come to turn into, say, a Laura Ashley milkmaid. So the cycle of learning and perception is matched by a cycle of old and new clothes, and the two interact at the level of actual individuals to produce the particular kind of social change which we call fashion, and all that this implies.

This paper first appeared in S. Pearce (1992) Museums, Objects and Collections, *Leicester: Leicester University Press, pp. 214–17.*

REFERENCE

Wilson, E. and Taylor, L. (1989) *Through the Looking Glass*, London: BBC Books.

7

A *view of functionalism*
Edmund Leach

Edmund Leach is one of the foremost social anthropologists of the post-war period. Here he describes the genesis and character of the view of the world generally lumped under the term 'functionalist', the second of Hodder's parameters of meaning. Functionalism as a social theory is now something of a fossil in the history of ideas, but as an analytical approach it retains its importance in the understanding of objects. A functionalist stance stands behind most museum displays in the human history areas, often linked to a pre-sentation of historical depth, and with 'special' pieces highlighted as 'artworks'.

The functionalist anthropologists were not all of one breed. Although outsiders tended to apply the label quite indiscriminately to the disciples of both Malinowski and Radcliffe-Brown and although some of the earlier writings of these two gurus had much in common, they and their followers later became sharply opposed. This is not surprising for they had entirely different personalities and, from the start, each had adopted his own definition of what the term 'function' was supposed to mean.

For Malinowski the central issue of anthropology was the problem which faces every fieldworker: How should one interpret the bizarre quality which pervades so much of the behaviour which is encountered in the exotic settings which anthropologists usually choose as the arena for their research? The essence of his answer was that as soon as the social context is fully understood the bizarre quality disappears. In context, the various aspects of human social behaviour – domestic, economic, legal, political, magico-religious, technological – fit together and 'make sense'.

'Making sense' for Malinowski here meant 'common sense', practical utility as the anthropological observer perceives it, even this might sometimes mean giving a very peculiar twist to the notion of utility.

Up to a point this line of argument is acceptable and important even if it can some-times seem naive. It is always highly desirable that the fieldworker should rid himself of the notion that there is something altogether extraordinary about the situation he is observing.

'Magic' is not a strange mystery which can only be encountered in travellers' tales and medieval romances. Everyone who shows above average competence at producing a cup of coffee or growing tomatoes achieves his results by 'magic' (or, as we usually say, 'art') rather than by strict adherence to scientific principle. In other words, it is crucial for the fieldworker to recognize that what the observer finds strange and mysterious the actor may regard as entirely obvious.

But for Malinowski this was not enough. He felt he needed a casual explanation for the behaviours he observed and he believed that such an explanation was provided by the dogma that every social institution must, in one way or another, serve the immediate practical needs of the human individual.

On this issue Malinowski was quite un-Durkheimian. He was still assuming that the object of anthropological enquiry was to understand the nature of man rather than the nature of human society. He believed that if the research worker can come to understand the fitting together of institutions in a really comprehensive way, even in just one social context, he will have learnt something of fundamental importance about human nature everywhere. Malinowski viewed the integration of society from the inside rather than the outside; as the consequence of individual self-interest rather than of social necessity.

This approach to the observable facts can often prove very illuminating but the trouble is that, in Malinowski's presentation, the argument is banal. It is self-evidently true but trivial. In the last analysis the basic needs of the individual are biological; the need to survive and to procreate. But the functionalist dogma then becomes a kind of just-so story. For after all, if social institutions did not make it possible for individuals to survive and procreate, there would be no social institutions anyway!

In the outcome Malinowski's explanations for the oddities of ethnographic data were often very similar to those which are currently being advanced by the sociobiologist followers of E. O. Wilson. Wilson's dogma is that all custom is the outcome of a process of Darwinian adaptation to the environment which serves, in some sense or other, to maximize the chance that an individual's genetic endowment will be perpetuated in the gene pool of the collective society. It should not be difficult to see that this is again a just-so story borrowed from Dr Pangloss. Everything is for the best in the best of all possible worlds. But as a form of 'explanation' this king of thing rates rather low.

Radcliffe-Brown's functionalism was very different. His performances as a fieldworker in the Andaman Islands, Africa and Australia had been notably undistinguished and, unlike Malinowski, he does not seem to have had much interest in the complex problems of translation and interpretation that fieldwork necessarily entails. His famous account of the Andamanese value system is an exercise in Durkheimian exegesis rather than a felt experience. He was essentially a stay-at-home theorist. He claimed that social anthropology was 'a generalizing science', 'a comparative sociology' which was expected to arrive at universally valid 'laws' concerning human society by means of the systematic comparison of the structure of total social systems.

Although Radcliffe-Brown had begun his study of anthropology at Cambridge, where in 1904 he was a pupil of Rivers, his subsequent academic career until 1937 was peripatetic and always outside Britain. He thus had little face-to-face interaction with Malinowski. His functionalism was in the tradition established by Durkheim's *De la division du travail social* (1893) and most of his ideas can be seen to derive from a wide, if somewhat insensitive reading of contributions to Durkheim's journal *Année Sociologique*. Following in this convention Radcliffe-Brown wrote of society as a thing in itself, a self-sustaining organism or system which already exists when the individual is born into it and which constrains the freedom of the individual through a complex structure of jural rules and sanctions which are implicit (rather than explicit) in the traditional mythology and ceremonial of the people concerned. He saw Malinowski's 'commonsense' functionalist explanations as an example of the 'danger that the ethnologist may interpret the beliefs of a native people not by reference to *their* mental life but by reference to his own'. This may be fair criticism but it could equally well be levelled against Radcliffe-Brown's own comments on the beliefs of the Andamanese!

Like Malinowski, Radcliffe-Brown was concerned with the nature of social integration. Why do human beings co-operate together within a social matrix? Malinowski looked at the problem from the inside and came up with a dogma of individual self-interest; Radcliffe-Brown looked at it from the outside and laid emphasis on what he saw as a diversity of types of integration each of which finds expression in a distinctive, yet coherent, system of belief and ceremonial practice.

As a derivation from this model Radcliffe-Brown held that the first task or a scientific and sociological anthropology should be to establish a taxonomy of types of society classified according to their internal structural organization. The imagery was zoological and anatomical. Societies with segmentary unilincal descent groups were to be distinguished as species from societies stratified by social class much as mammals are distinguished from fish.

In this version of the social anthropological style which subsequently came to be described as 'structural-functionalism' (in order to distinguish it from the plain functionalism of the Malinowskians), the central issue was that of social continuity. The anthropologist's task was not to discover how customs serve the (biological) needs of the individual but to understand how social structures persist through time.

Social structure was here taken to mean the articulation of a set of clearly definable and directly observable social institutions which were considered to constitute the basic framework of the society concerned. The *function* of such an institution was formally defined as the part that it played in the maintenance of the system as a whole, on the analogy that, in a mammalian body, the function of the heart is to pump blood through the circulating network of arteries and veins.

This paper first appeared in E. Leach (1982) Social Anthropology, *London: Fontana, pp. 28–32.*

8

Culture as a system with subsystems

David Clarke

A functionalist approach can have a good deal in common with a system analysis approach to understanding material culture. David Clarke was the founding father of the Cambridge Material Culture study school, and his book of 1968, Analytical Archaeology, was a major force for change. Clarke's systems analysis of social action is given here because it remains one of the clearest, as well as one of the most influential, presentations of its kind. Here all kinds of artefactual meaning – historical and symbolic as well as 'utilitarian' – are treated as if they are geared to the goal of social continuity; there is clearly a functionalist side to both the historical legacy and symbolic value. This brings us close to a Marxist view of society and of material culture in which all individual elements are bound together in an ideology which gives authority to patterns of dominance.

The internal setting of subsystems within the general system constitutes 'cultural morphology', as opposed to the external setting of the system in its environment, comprising 'cultural ecology'. Both of these fields are sufficient to fill several books with discussion and elaboration but the intention here is merely to sketch in two successive sections the implications of the developing general model for these specialist fields. If the model is well constructed it should be possible to say succinctly and in general what should prove to be the case in particular instances. Since the subsystems within culture are the subject of highly specialized studies, we are here only interested in seeing them in a particular light in preparation for their use as a setting for archaeological data.

It is, of course, quite as arbitrary and dangerous to describe a sociocultural system as having component subsystems as to describe any unitary and highly complex system in terms of a number of its component circuits, for the self-same reasons. Not only are the subsystems really different aspects of the same system but even could we define them adequately in terms of content and boundaries one would still not have defined the system containing them. Such complex systems cannot be treated as an interlaced set of more or less independent subsystems since, as we have seen, the 'behaviour' of such a unit is more complex than simply the expression of the sum of its components' 'behaviours'. Nevertheless, as long as we continue to realize the arbitrary nature of this kind of component description it will perhaps serve to partially describe an otherwise extremely complex reality. In the full realization that where we arbitrarily describe, say, five component subsystems the system generators may have conceptualized only one, or possibly three, or perhaps sixty – but as long as we are consistent this arbitrariness will temporarily serve our purpose.

In the arbitrary setting devised here it is intended to distinguish five subsystems within which we will imagine the information in sociocultural systems to be more richly interconnected than externally networked within the system as a whole:

1 *Social subsystem.* The hierarchical network of inferred personal relationships, including kinship and rank status.
2 *Religious subsystem.* The structure of mutually adjusted beliefs relating to the supernatural, as expressed in a body of doctrine and a sequence of rituals, which together interpret the environment to the society in terms of its own percepta.
3 *Psychological subsystem.* The integrated system of supra-personal subconscious beliefs induced upon the individuals in a society by their culture, their environment and their language; essentially the subconscious system of comparative values.
4 *Economic subsystem.* The integrated strategy of component subsistence methods and extraction processes which feed and equip the society.
5 *Material culture subsystem.* The patterned constellations of artefacts which outline the behaviour patterns of the system as a whole and embody that system's technology.

These five subsystem headings are transparently based on the prejudices of current opinion, underlining their arbitrary nature. Even by the standards of this biased basis, many will find them unsatisfactory and will wish to reorganize them accordingly – for example, language might well rank as a full subsystem. However, we will arbitrarily conceptualize cultural systems as integrating these five main information subsystems as a coherent ensemble in dynamic equilibrium at the three levels:

(i) within each subsystem,
(ii) between the subsystem outputs,
(iii) between the whole system and its environment (Fig. 8.1)

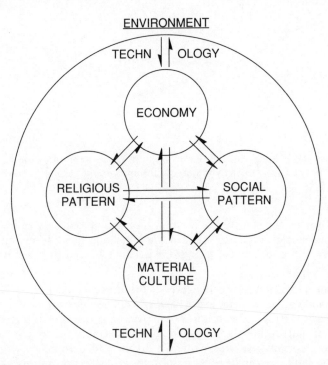

Fig 8.1 A static model representing the dynamic equilibrium between the subsystem networks of a sociocultural system and its environment. The, psychological subsystem may be envisaged as centrally encased by the other subsystems – a genetic inheritance modified by an induced field; see Fig. 8.3

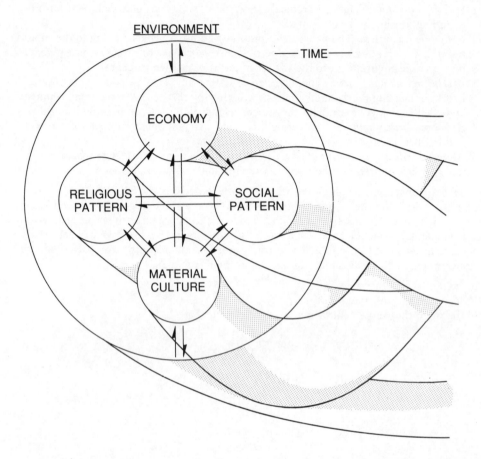

Fig. 8.2 A schematic model suggesting the oscillating subsystem states and values in the networks of a sociocultural system in dynamic equilibrium with the oscillating states of its coupled environment

Equilibrium being defined in terms of the information concepts earlier discussed – minimizing immediate system dislocation. These relationships can be crudely summed up in a diagram, first in a static background (Fig. 8.1), and then against a changing background (Fig. 8.2).

The environment of a culture system expresses the attributes external to that system and their varying and successive states in time and space. These environmental attributes may be partly perceived by the enclosed culture and partly not; from the culture's point of view some environmental attributes are inessential, some essential, and some are key attributes for that culture system. Conventionally, we organize the external environment under many headings but these can be roughly subsumed under – other sociocultural systems, fauna, flora, climate and geology; taking these terms in their broadest sense so that geography and topography are mere manifestations of geology, for example. These five subsystems are taken as interconnected networks of attributes forming complex wholes and themselves an ensemble within the environmental system.

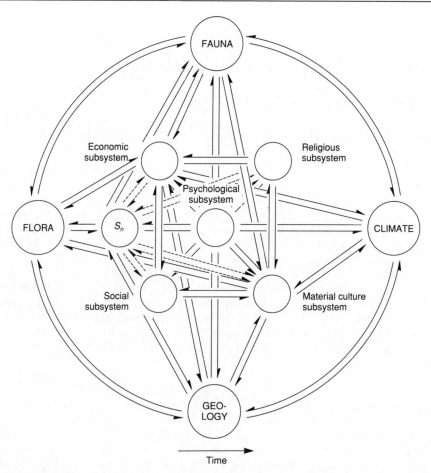

Time

Fig. 8.3 A static and schematic model of the dynamic equilibrium between the subsystem networks of a single sociocultural system and its total environment system. S_n represents the summation of the effects of alien sociocultural systems connected to S by cultural 'coactions' (dashed lines) and to the environment by 'interactions' (solid lines). To set the model in motion all the components must oscillate randomly along intercorrelated trending trajectories

We have artificially conceptualized sociocultural systems as five component subsystems coupled in a moving equilibrium with a five-component environmental system (Fig. 8.3):

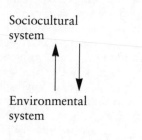

Sociocultural system

Environmental system

(1) Social subsystem
(2) Religious subsystem
(3) Psychological subsystem
(4) Economic subsystem
(5) Material culture subsystem

(1) Other sociocultural systems
(2) Fauna subsystem
(3) Flora subsystem
(4) Climate subsystem
(5) Geology subsystem

This paper first appeared in D. Clarke (1968) Analytical Archaeology, *London: Methuen, pp. 101–4, 124–6.*

9

Theoretical archaeology: a reactionary view

Ian Hodder

In this piece Hodder offers a critique of functionalist theory, and in doing so supplies information about its significant practitioners and its history as an idea. The bibliography given with this paper will be found very useful by those who wish to pursue this theme. Several of Hodder's criticisms of functionalism look back to ideas about the active nature of objects, and the active natures of individuals, which have already figured in the previous pieces by Pearce and by Deetz and Dethlefsen. Underlying much of what Hodder says is the notion that, while it is possible to carry out functionalist needs in a variety of ways, actual societies and individuals choose to do so in very particular ways – the key words here are 'choice' and 'particular' – which relate to actual social arrangements ('cultures') and to individual characters.

Functionalism is defined as the use of an organic analogy in the explanation of societies, with particular reference to system, equilibrium and adaptation. A critique of functionalism is put forward, centring on the dichotomies between culture and function, individual and society, statics and dynamics, and on the links to positivism. Criticisms of an alternative approach, structuralism, include the lack of a theory of practice, the dichotomies between individual and society, statics and dynamics, and the paucity of rigour in the methods employed. A contextual or cultural archaeology is described which is based on the notion of 'structuration', and which attempts to resolve many of the difficulties associated with functionalism and 'high' structuralism. The main concern is with the role of material culture in the reflexive relationship between the structure of ideas and social strategies.

In defining functionalism, a simplified version of Radcliffe-Brown's (1952) account will be used since his approach can be shown to be close to that followed by many New Archaeologists (those who in the 1960s and 1970s were concerned with explanations and approaches of the types outlined by Binford and his associates). Functionalism introduces an analogy between social and organic life. Emile Durkheim (*Règles de la méthode sociologique* 1895) defined the 'function' of a social institution as the correspondence between it and the needs of the social organism. In the same way that the stomach provides a function for the body as a whole and allows it to survive, so any aspect of a past society can be assessed in terms of its contribution to the working of the whole society. A society is made up of interrelated parts and we can explain one component by showing how it works in relation to other components. But these are all very general statements, and there is room for a great variety of views within these general propositions. Indeed, Radcliffe-Brown (1952: 188) stated bluntly that the 'Functional School does not really exist; it is a myth'. Functionalism often appears to be little more than a 'dirty word' used by the opponents of anthropologists such as Malinowski, Boas and Radcliffe-Brown himself, and it may convey little meaning. So if it is to be used of the New Archaeology, a more specific definition needs to be provided.

The concept of function is closely linked to the notion of system. In the middle of the eighteenth century Montesquieu used a conception of society in which all aspects of social life could be linked into a coherent whole. What Comte called 'the first law of social statics' held that there are relations of interconnection and interdependence, or relations of solidarity, between the various aspects of society. It is possible analytically to isolate certain groups of particularly close interrelationships as systems.

According to the functionalist viewpoint as stated in systems theory, societies reach a healthy organic equilibrium, called homeostasis. Plato, in the Fourth Book of his *Republic*, saw the health of a society as resulting from the harmonious working together of its parts. The Greeks distinguished good order, social health (*eunomia*), from disorder, social illness (*dysnomia*), while the notion of malfunction and social pathology was a central concern of Durkheim. (In recent systems archaeology, pathologies have been listed and their effects examined by Flannery (1972).)

Pathologies occur during periods when the organic unity and equilibrium are upset as a result of maladaptation. A society can only continue to exist if it is well-adjusted internally and externally. Three types of adaptation can be distinguished. The first concerns the adjustment to the physical environment, the ecological adaptation. The second is the internal arrangement and adjustment of components of the society in relation to each other. Finally, there is the process by which an individual finds a place within the society in which he lives. It is through these three types of adaptation that societies survive and evolve. Many anthropologists and archaeologists, however, have discussed change largely in terms of ecological adaptation, the meeting of external constraints. It is an ecological functionalism which prevails today in archaeology.

I do not intend to examine the problems of applying systems theory in archaeology (Doran 1970), nor whether systems theory has really aided archaeologists in their functionalist aims (Salmon 1978). Rather, I want to consider the criticisms of functionalism itself.

Many of the problems and limitations of the organic analogy as applied to social systems have long been recognized. Radcliffe-Brown (1952: 181) noted that, while an animal organism does not, in the course of its life, change its form, a society can, in the course of its history, undergo major organizational change. Other problems are not inherent to the approach but result from the particular emphasis that is given by archaeologists, perhaps as a result of the limitations of their data. For example, a systems approach which assumes that homeostatic equilibrium is the natural state of things results in the notion that all change ultimately has to derive from outside the system. Negative feedback occurs in reaction to outside stimuli, and positive feedback and deviation amplifying processes need initial external kicks. According to Hill (1977: 76), 'no system can change itself; change can only be instigated by outside sources. If a system is in equilibrium, it will remain so unless inputs (or lack of outputs) from outside the system disturb the equilibrium.' The result of this view has been to place great emphasis on the impact of supposed 'independent' variables from outside the sociocultural system under study. The favourite external variables have been environmental factors, long-distance trade and population increase, although it is not often clear why the latter is assumed to be an independent variable. Little advance has been made in the study of factors within societies that affect the nature of change. But Flannery (1972) has shown how the systems approach can be extended to include internal forces of change and those forms of internal adaptation within the organic whole which have been described above.

A more fundamental limitation of the functionalist viewpoint centres on the inadequacy of function and utility in explaining social and cultural systems, and on the separation made between functional utility and culture. All aspects of culture have utilitarian purposes in terms of which they can be explained. All activities, whether dropping refuse, developing social hierarchies, or performing rituals, are the results of adaptive expedience. But explanation is sought only in terms of adaptation and function. The problem with such a viewpoint is not so much the emphasis on function, since it is important to know how material items, institutions, symbols and ritual operate, and the contribution of the New Archaeology to such studies is impressive. It is rather the dichotomy which was set up between culture and adaptive utility which restricted the development of the approach.

In archaeology the split between culture and function took the form of an attack on what was termed the 'normative' approach. In Binford's (1965) rebuttal of the 'normative school', he referred to American archaeologists such as Taylor, Willey and Phillips, Ford, Rouse and Gifford who were concerned with identifying cultural 'wholes' in which there was an ideational basis for the varying ways of human life within each cultural unit. Such archaeologists aimed at identifying the normative concepts in the minds of men now dead. Binford more specifically criticized the normative studies which tried to describe the diffusion and transmission of cultural traits. It is not my concern here to identify whether the normative paradigm, as characterized by Binford, ever existed. Certainly, as will be shown below, European archaeologists such as Childe were already able to integrate a concern with cultural norms and a notion of behavioural adaptability. But in Binford's view, the normative approach emphasizing homogeneous cultural wholes contrasted with the study of functional variability within and between cultural units. The normative school was seen as historical and descriptive, not allowing explanation in terms of functional process. So he moved to an opposite extreme where culture, norms, form and design had only functional value in, for example, integrating and articulating individuals and social units into broader corporate entities. In fact Binford suggested that the different components of culture may function independently of each other. Functional relationships could thus be studied without reference to cultural context, and regular, stable and predictable relationships could be sought between variables within social systems. As a result, an absolute gulf was created between normative and processual studies. 'An approach is offered in which culture is not reduced to normative ideas about the proper ways of doing things but is viewed as the system of the total extrasomatic means of adaptation' (Binford 1972: 205).

The dichotomy set up between culture and function limits the development of archaeological theory because 'functional value is always relative to the given cultural scheme' (Sahlins 1976: 206). All actions take place within cultural frameworks and their functional value is assessed in terms of the concepts and orientations which surround them. That an item or institution is 'good for' achieving some end is partly a cultural choice, as is the end itself. At the beginning of this chapter Durkheim's definition of the function of a social institution as the correspondence between it and the needs of the social organism was described. But the needs of the society are preferred choices within a cultural matrix. It follows that function and adaptation are not absolute measures. All daily activities, from eating to the removal of refuse, are not the results of some absolute adaptive expedience. These various functions take place within a cultural framework, a set of ideas or norms, and we cannot adequately understand the various activities by denying any role to culture. An identical point is made by Deetz (1977) in his comparison of cultural traditions in two historical periods in North America.

The above discussion is particularly relevant to the functionalist view of material items. As already noted, Binford assumes that culture is man's extrasomatic means of adaptation.

According to David Clarke (1968: 85), 'culture is an information system, wherein the messages are accumulated survival information'. In this way material culture is seen as simply functioning at the interface between the human organism and the social and physical environment in order to allow adaptation. It has a utilitarian function (Sahlins 1976). The result of this view is that cultural remains are seen as *reflecting*, in a fairly straightforward way, what people *do*. Even work on deposition and postdepositional processes, while adding complexity to the situation, still assumes that material culture is simply a direct, indirect or distorted reflection of man's activities. This is a continuation of earlier views of material culture as 'fossilized action'. As Fletcher (1977: 51–2) has pointed out, material culture is seen simply as a passive object of functional use, a mere epiphenomenon of 'real' life. But there is more to culture than functions and activities. Behind functioning and doing there is a structure and content which has partly to be understood in its own terms, with its own logic and coherence. This applies as much to refuse distributions and 'the economy' as it does to burial, pot decoration and art.

Linked to the separation of function and culture has been the decreased emphasis on archaeology as a historical discipline. If material items and social institutions can be explained in terms of their adaptive efficiency, there is little concern to situate them within a historical framework. The evolutionary perspective has emphasized adaptive relationships at different levels of complexity, but it has not encouraged an examination of the particular historical context. However, it is suggested here that the cultural framework within which we act, and which we reproduce in our actions, is historically derived and that each culture is a particular historical product. The uniqueness of cultures and historical sequences must be recognized. The resolution of the culture/function dichotomy which is sought here will also reintroduce historical explanation as a legitimate topic of concern in archaeology.

Another limitation of the functionalist perspective of the New Archaeology is the relationship between the individual and society. The functional view gives little emphasis to individual creativity and intentionality. Individual human beings become little more than the means to achieve the needs of society. The social system is organized into subsystems and roles which people fill. The roles and social categories function in relation to each other to allow the efficient equilibrium of the whole system. In fact, however, individuals are not simply instruments in some orchestrated game and it is difficult to see how subsystems and roles can have 'goals' of their own. Adequate explanations of social systems and social change must involve the individual's assessments and aims. Some New Archaeologists have recognized the importance of this. 'While the behaviour of the group, of many individual units, may often effectively be described in statistical terms without reference to the single unit, it cannot so easily be *explained* in this way. This is a problem which prehistoric archaeology has yet to resolve' (Renfrew 1972: 496). The lack of resolution is inherent in the functionalist emphasis in archaeology.

Further criticism of functionalist archaeology concerns the emphasis on cross-cultural generalizations. Because of the preferred hypothetico-deductive nature of explanation, it became important to identify rules of behaviour and artefact deposition which were used regardless of cultural context. As already noted, such an approach was feasible because the particular historical and cultural dimensions of activity were denied. Different subsystems were identified, such as subsistence, exchange, settlement, refuse disposal and burial, and cross-cultural regularities were sought. Since the role of cultural and historical factors was not examined, it was necessarily the case that the resulting generalizations either were limited to mechanical or physical aspects of life or were simplistic and with little content. Some aspects of human activity are constrained by deterministic variables. Smaller artefacts are more difficult for humans to hold and find than large artefacts and so the patterns of loss may differ. Cross-cultural predictive laws or generalizations can be developed for these mechanical constraints on human behaviour, and ethnoarchaeology has been most successful in these spheres, but attempts to extend this approach to social and cultural behaviour have been severely criticized and the result has been the frustration implied by Flannery's (1973) characterization of Mickey Mouse laws. As soon as any human choice is involved, behavioural and functional laws appear simplistic and inadequate because human behaviour is rarely entirely mechanistic.

This paper first appeared in I. Hodder (1982) Symbolic and Structural Archaeology, *Cambridge: Cambridge University Press, pp. 1–5.*

REFERENCES

Binford, L. R. (1965) 'Archaeological systematics and the study of cultural process', *American Antiquity* 31: 203–10.
—— (1972) *An Archaeological Perspective*, New York: Seminar Press.
Clarke, D. L. (1968) *Analytical Archaeology*, London: Methuen.
Deetz, J. (1977) *In Small Things Forgotten*, New York: Anchor Books.
Doran, J. (1970) 'System theory, computer simulations and archaeology', *World Archaeology* 1: 289–98.
Flannery, K. V. (1972) 'The cultural evolution of civilisations', *Annual Review of Ecology and Systematics* 3: 399–426.
—— (1973) 'Archaeology with a capital S', in C. Redman (ed.) *Research and Theory in Current Archaeology*, New York: Wiley.
Fletcher, R. (1977) 'Alternatives and differences', in M. Spriggs (ed.) *Archaeology and Anthropology*, Oxford: B.A.R. Supplementary Series 19.
Hill, J. N. (ed.) (1977) *The Explanation of Prehistoric Change*, Albuquerque: University of New Mexico Press.
Radcliffe-Brown, A. R. (1952) *Structure and Function in Primitive Society*, London: Cohen & West.
Renfrew, C. (1972) *The Emergence of Civilisation*, London: Methuen.
Sahlins, M. (1976) *Culture and Practical Reason*, Chicago: University of Chicago Press.
Salmon, M. H. (1978) 'What can systems theory do for archaeology?', *American Antiquity* 43: 174–83.

10

A view from the bridge
Edmund Leach

Structuralist theory is an enormous field in its own right, with its own array of schools, orthodoxies and heresies. Leach's piece is given here because it offers an imaginative and impressionistic account of how this kind of thinking can work and what sort or poetic insights it has to offer. Leach himself draws upon, or relates to, the work of Claude Lévi-Strauss, Victor Turner and Mary Douglas. In essence, their ideas revolve around a recognition that social patterning sometimes (or often, or always, depending upon the point of view) shows organization around opposed, or binary, pairs and that the 'betwixt and between' which separates these pairs is the area of the ambiguous, the sacred, the dangerous and the exciting. It is therefore the focus of much anxiety and ritual activity. Reading Leach's piece with objects in mind helps to show how things can have poetic or symbolic (or religious) meanings.

So let me light my Catherine wheels. No doubt most potential readers will soon give up in total exasperation; this method of discourse is altogether too unfamiliar. But let me explain. I am not trying to make statements of a straight forward linear kind like 'the cat sat on the mat'. I am trying to generate free associations of a symbolic, metaphorical kind.

1 BASIC PREMISSES

1.1 First basic premiss: All human beings think in the same way. The mammoth hunters of 50,000 BC, the men of Lascaux, the men of the Neolithic Revolution, the architects of Athens, Rome, medieval London and contemporary Birmingham are/were all 'people like us'.

1.2 Second basic premiss: All human beings are interested in their own bodies. They are interested in what distinguishes the inside from the outside. They are interested especially in the orifices through which the inside connects with the outside – mouth, anus, urethra, penis, vagina, nipples, eyes, nose, ears. In all religions known to history, to ethnography and to archaeology such orifices have major symbolic significance even though we are not always certain just what they are symbolic of.

1.3 Third basic premiss: 'In the beginning Man created God in his own (mirror) image.'

2 A FANTASY OF MAMMOTH HUNTERS

2.1

I (We)	//	Other (They)
Live Man		Live Mammoth
(Culture)		(Nature)

2.2 *Transform*

Man	uses a *weapon* to kill	Mammoth
Live Man	//	Dead Mammoth

2.3 *Transform*

Man	dissects	Mammoth
Man	*cooks and eats* leaving residue of bones	Mammoth meat

Inside the camp (Tame)	Well fed live man	//	FIRE cooking hearth / BONES // eating place		Outside the camp (Wild)

2.4 *Transform* (alternative to 2.3)

Man	dissects	Mammoth
Man	*freezes and preserves* in ice pit	Mammoth meat

Inside the camp (Tame)	Hungry live man	// ICE ice pit shrine Dead/Live Mammoth (God)	//	Outside the camp (Wild)

2.5 *Inference*

FIRE : ICE :: Food : Hunger :: Life : Death (for man)

:: Death : Life (for god)

Therefore: Life above ground for men = Life below ground for God

Implication: Bury dead men so that they become like living gods.

Alternatively: Fire converts dead gods into food for living men.

Implication: Burn dead men and they will be reincarnated in some other form. (You could of course eat the body instead.)

(NB At least two-thirds of the world's population still act as if they believed in one or other of these 'implications'.)

2.6   By condensation of 2.1–2.4 we may infer that in the triad:

CULTURE [This World]	/	Betwixt & Between	/	NATURE [The Other World]

The following classes of material object may appropriately symbolize the boundary category 'betwixt and between':

(i) anything which moves across the boundary in the course of the proceedings: excretions of the human body (faeces, urine, semen, head hair, saliva, vomit, tears, blood), 'things ingested by the human body – (food, drink)', 'things which express exchange relationships with others, the others being either natural or supernatural ('offerings, women in marriage, ceremonial valuable, animals which are killed' ('sacrificed', i.e. 'made sacred'), 'actors' (they are in this world as human beings but as fictional characters they are 'other'), 'priests', 'shamans' (i.e. men who communicate with gods).

(ii) anything which acts as an agent for converting things in this world into things in the other world or vice versa – 'weapons', 'fire', 'cooking as a process', 'washing as a process', 'birth as a process', 'death as a process'

(iii) residues of the conversion process – ash, bones, corpses, relics of all kinds

(iv) self-contradictory images – a dead god, a virgin mother

Surely this is moving rather fast? I am not so sure. Some mammoth hunters seem to have collected the bones of slaughtered mammoths and formed them into boundary walls.

3 BURIAL PRACTICES

3.1 What then shall we do with a corpse ?

The answer is plain enough: Eat it, burn it, bury it.

But where shall we bury it?

But that too is plain: In the 'betwixt and between' at the boundary of the Other World.

But where is this Other World?

Have you not understood? The Other World is the inaccessible Other, the *not* Here. It is (a) below the ground, (b) above the sky, (c) beyond the city walls, (d) the holy of holies in the temple shrine.

3.2 So where shall we put our corpse ?

Beneath the floor of the dwelling house, beneath the dancing floor where the living approach the other world through the path of ecstasy, in a cemetery adjacent to the church, in a tomb house high among the trees, in a tomb which itself becomes a temple. . . .

So corpses can be put anywhere?

Not really. The land of the dead is always 'other than' the land of the living. If you can understand the logic of where men place their dead you will begin to understand something about how they perceive themselves .

'This world' and 'the other world' form a binary opposition, the two halves of which are bound together into a unity by 'that which lies between'. The dead lie between. In classical Athens, the Akropolis and the Agora were above and below, with tombs in between as well as outside both. And so it is too in my Lancashire home town of Rochdale. In medieval times they built the Parish Church on a 150-foot high crag and the cemetery grew up around it. Then the market-place grew up at the foot of the crag. And finally in the nineteenth century they built the Town Hall immediately below the Parish Church. There is a pattern to these things which expresses the feelings that men have about themselves and their relations with the Other.

4 CITIES AND EMPIRES

| We Civilized Men Citizens | // | The boundary limits of 'our' territory
 (City Walls)
 (Territorial Frontiers) | // | Barbarians and Savages |

4.1 The great classical empires were not content just to mark it out on a map. The boundary must be marked with a fosse, even a major wall. . . . Hadrian's Wall, the Great Wall of China. But the significance of such structures is symbolic as well as military.

During the closing years of the British regime in Burma, when you might have supposed that there were many other matters of more pressing importance, a number of senior British Administrative Officers were engaged full time on demarcating the precise boundary between 'administered' and 'unadministered' territory. It was an exercise entirely devoid of practical significance though I do not doubt that many of the boundary markers, appropriately decorated with phallic symbols, are still in place waiting to provide some baffling puzzles for future generations of Asian archaeologists.

4.2 But cities engage in trade, in political and marital alliances, and in war, therefore:

| Civilized men in our city | // | *Our* city walls | / | Wilderness area inhabited by vagabonds and bandits but also by wandering hermits prophets, saints | / | *Their* city walls | // | Civilized men in other cities (possible friends, foes) |

Notice that, in this case, the 'Other World' is in the middle rather than on the outside.

5 BUILDINGS AND GROUPS OF BUILDINGS

5.1 The orifices of my dwelling-house are like the orifices of my body. If a building has more than one entrance, as is commonly the case, these entrances will be of very different moral status, as mouth is to anus or penis to vagina. Generally the more ostentatious the entrance to a building the less frequently it will be used. The grandeur is symbolic rather than utilitarian. This is true also of the city as a whole. It is the impressiveness of gateways that matters rather than their efficiency; they are sacred precincts.

5.2 Buildings differ among themselves not only in their prestige status – royal palace, commoner's hovel – but on the spectrum sacred/profane – cathedral/town hall. The organs of the human body are comparably discriminated. By introspection I come to feel that the mysterious entity the conscious 'I' is 'inside' my body, yet I also feel that it is somehow 'other than' my body. This illusion provides the basis for the Protean doctrine of the 'soul', and the 'seat of the soul' within the body is, like the orifices on the boundary of the body, a sacred precinct.

The heart, the liver, the spleen, the spine, the head and so on are credited with ritual value in accordance with locally prevalent notions of the spiritual anatomy.

The same is true of the relative status of buildings within cities; there are parts of the other world which lie at the centre of things and other parts which lie on the outside. This radically affects the way the inhabitants of a city perceive the urban environment in which they live.

Quite apart from the possibility of status-loaded symmetries and asymmetries, north/south, east/west, cities tend to have a concentric structure. A shrine at the centre is surrounded by an area of ambiguity which is surrounded by an area of secular activity, which is surrounded by the city wall (again sacred), which is surrounded by the outer wilderness.

6 RIVERS

A river constitutes a natural boundary but also, like the alimentary canal of the body, it may provide economic sustenance to the city. The resulting ambiguities are manifested in various forms.

The sacred Ganges is a boundary to the sacred city of Benares to which the dead and dying are brought so that they may achieve instant oblivion (*moksha*) when their ashes are cast into the Ganges waters. Of Benares itself it is said, not wholly without justice, that there are more temples than there are dwelling-houses. There has been no urban development on the 'other' side of the river which is secular and evil. However, there *is one* solitary and impressive structure on the other side: it is the Rajah's Palace!

London grew up in rather similar fashion. The city was all on the North Bank. South-wark was simply a bulwark to guard the southern entrance to London Bridge. It was not a fort but a church! In Shakespeare's day there was only a single line of buildings close to the water's edge along the South Bank but also there were low-status secular places of amusement – brothels, the Bear Pit and the Globe Theatre. The discrimination in status still survives.

Rome likewise. In early Imperial Rome the inhabited city was all on the east bank of the Tiber, the cemeteries were outside the city walls to the south and also across the river to the west. Christianity in part inverted these values. The Mausoleum of Hadrian on the west bank became the Castel S. Angelo; the cemetery further west was developed as the Cathedral of St Peter and the Palace of the Popes. The present-day situation, with the secular offices of the Italian state on the east bank and the Vatican City on the west bank, derives, in an immediate historical sense, from the circumstances of Italian politics since 1871. But to the local inhabitants Rome has 'seemed' to be divided in this way for centuries. A German woodcut view of Rome dated 1493, when the whole city was part of the Pope's domain, shows, on the east bank, only buildings surviving from *Imperial Rome*: the Colosseum, Pantheon, Trajan's Column and so on; the west bank is entirely filled by the papal palace and other buildings with specifically *Christian* associations.

Our own day-to-day experience shows us quite clearly that human beings do *not* perceive their physical environment to be as it actually is; they mould their experience to fit the expectations which emerge from the categories of their thought.

What I have suggested in this paper is that it is not necessarily a wholly fatuous enterprise to try to discover the categories of thought which dominated the builders of ancient cities and the users of ancient burial grounds. If the mammoth hunters were really, as I believe, people like us, then so also was everyone else.

This paper first appeared in M. Spriggs (ed.) (1977) Archaeology and Anthropology, *British Archaeological Reports Supplementary Series 19, Oxford, pp. 170–3.*

11

Ivory for the sea woman: the symbolic attributes of a prehistoric technology

Robert McGhee

McGhee's paper is a classic account of structuralist analysis of social life, and material culture is shown to be an integral element it its patterning. McGhee analyses a prehistoric way of life, that of the Central Inuit, and in so doing also gives a useful account of many of the foregoing arguments. His paper draws together the physical environment of the culture, its material culture and its myths into a unified account, which is shown to have a symbolic structure.

A few years ago Edmund Leach (1973), in commenting on a symposium devoted to the 'newer' approaches to archaeology, pointed out that changes in the paradigms of archaeological interpretation appeared to follow those of ethnology, but with a time-lag of several decades. Having recently rejected the naive historicism and evolutionism which characterized nineteenth-century ethnology, the new archaeological paradigm is closely related to the naive functionalism characteristic of ethnology during the first half of the twentieth-century. In this paradigm, cultures are seen as primarily economic systems interacting in various predictable ways with their environments. The structuralist paradigm favoured by Leach, in which cultures are seen as primarily communications systems and which has produced much of the more interesting ethnological work of the past twenty years, has yet to make an impact on archaeology. In large part, this is a result of the simple fact that functional attributes of archaeological artefacts are more easily recognized than are symbolic attributes. However, it may also be due, in part, to the blindness to other interpretive modes which Thomas Kuhn has attributed to the users of any scientific paradigm. That the functionalist bias of archaeological thinking may indeed be obscuring the existence of certain symbolic attributes of prehistoric technologies is suggested by a chance observation on the archaeological remains of the Thule culture of arctic Canada.

The Thule culture, a concept formulated by Mathiassen (1927), and one which has changed remarkably little over the half-century since its original definition, comprises a distinctive set of archaeological materials found in northern Alaska, and across the arctic mainland and islands of Canada to Greenland and Labrador. The Thule people are thought to have originated in northern Alaska, where they or their ancestors had developed an extremely efficient maritime-oriented adaptation. About AD 1000 they began to spread eastward across the North American Arctic, expanding to become the primary population of the area north of the tree-line. Although Thule groups adapted their ways of life to local environments, most retained an orientation to the coast and an economy based on the hunting of sea mammals including the large baleen whales. After approximately AD 1600 the uniform cast of the Thule culture becomes less apparent, as adaptations changed and diverged in apparent response to regional variations in a general climatic deterioration and environmental change. The Thule way of life continued virtually unchanged to the Historic period in Labrador and southwestern Greenland, while elsewhere it was transformed to the patterns characteristic of the historic Inuit. The Thule people are considered to have been Eskimos, almost certainly speaking dialects of the Inupik Eskimo language, and to have been directly ancestral to the present Inuit populations of arctic Canada and Greenland.

The observation which led to this essay is very simple, yet the possible significance of this observation appears to have escaped those of us who have studied the remains of the Thule culture: certain classes of Thule artefacts tend to be made from ivory, other classes from antler, and yet others from sea-mammal bone. Ivory, antler and bone are materials basic to Thule technology, substitutes for the hardwoods used in most preindustrial technologies. Archaeologists have generally assumed that attributes such as shape, toughness, brittleness and local availability of each material were the criteria used in deciding whether to make a particular artefact from ivory, antler or bone. These criteria must have been important, as certain materials are more suited in shape, more easily worked, and are more readily available than others. But were these the only criteria used by the Thule craftsman in selecting one material over another? Is it possible that these various materials were characterized by symbolic, as well as by what we would call empirically functional, attributes? And if so, can we determine the nature of these symbolic attributes by examining the association of each material with the various functional classes of artefacts?

The possible existence of symbolic attributes was first suggested by an examination of artefacts from the Debliquy site (QiLe–1), a Thule winter village located on Bathurst Island in the Canadian High Arctic. All six of the harpoon heads from this site are made from either ivory or sea-mammal bone, while all eight of the arrowheads are made from caribou antler. In this small assemblage, the exclusive use of sea-mammal bone and ivory to fashion weapons for hunting sea mammals, and of caribou antler for weapons used in hunting caribou, suggests something other than purely functional considerations in the selection of materials. Unfortunately for ease of interpretation, such a clear picture does not emerge from the examination of other Thule collections.

Table 11.1 lists the proportions of harpoon or lance heads, and of arrowheads, made from the various materials for five of the larger Thule assemblages for which such information is available. These assemblages were selected on the basis of size, in order to illustrate the range in material use over the temporal and geographical range of the Thule tradition. The Walakpa assemblage from the North Alaskan coast (Stanford 1976) is derived from a series of occupations spanning the Birnirk (ancestral Thule) and Thule periods. The Lady Franklin Point collections, from southwestern Victoria Island, are from two sites which appear to represent a western-oriented middle Thule occupation in which the economy emphasized the hunting of caribou and ringed seals rather than larger sea mammals. The Nunguvik assemblage is from an early to middle Thule occupation of northern Baffin Island in the eastern High Arctic. Silumiut represents an early to middle Thule adaptation to the west coast of Hudson Bay, and the Cumberland Sound collections are from a number of middle to late Thule sites on the Davis Strait coast of southeastern Baffin Island (Schledermann 1975).

In each of these five collections, all of the barbless or single-barbed arrowheads, of types used by the historic Inuit to hunt caribou, are made from antler. On the other hand, aside from the Lady Franklin Point collection in which almost all harpoon heads are made from antler, the proportion of harpoon and lance heads made from ivory or sea-mammal bone ranges from 42% in the Alaskan Walakpa collection (57% if only harpoon heads from the

Table 11.1 Proportions of selected artefact classes made ivory, bone and antler. N: number in assemblage; I: % made from ivory or sea-mammal tooth; B: % made from sea-mammal bone; A: % made from antler. The Lady Franklin Point, Nunguvik and Silumiut assemblages were examined in the collections of the Archaeological Survey of Canada. The Walakpa and Cumberland Sound proportions were calculated from lists of artefacts identified by material in Stanford (1976) and Schledermann (1975)

Artefact class	Walakpa				Lady Franklin Point				Nunguvik				Cumberland Sound				Silumiut			
	N	I	B	A	N	I	B	A	N	I	B	A	N	I	B	A	N	I	B	A
caribou arrowhead	400	0	0	100	87	0	0	100	29	0	0	100	2	0	0	100	10	0	0	100
harpoon and lance heads	52	40	2	58	35	0	10	90	21	5	52	43	51	26	41	33	64	33	39	28
Harpoon equipment:																				
foreshaft	10	100	0	0	3	0	0	100	4	25	75	0	12	0	100	0	2	100	0	0
foreshaft socket	5	0	100	0	3	0	0	100	5	40	40	20	3	0	100	0	5	20	60	20
ice pick	25	68	0	32	0	0	0	0	7	72	14	14	4	50	25	25	5	20	60	20
finger rest	0	0	0	0	0	0	0	0	2	50	0	50	4	50	25	25	3	100	0	0
tension piece	0	0	0	0	0	0	0	0	0	0	0	0	0	100	0	0	0	0	0	0
line stopper	0	0	0	0	0	0	0	0	0	0	0	0	0	0	0	0	1	100	0	0
float mouthpiece & nozzle	3	100	0	0	2	0	0	100	0	0	0	0	5	40	60	0	7	100	0	0
wound pin	5	80	20	0	18	0	0	100	2	100	0	0	0	0	0	0	1	100	0	0
Bird-hunting weapons:																				
multibarbed arrowhead	?	0	0	100	2	0	0	100	2	0	50	50	6	17	66	17	5	20	0	80
bird dart sideprong	4	100	0	0	4	0	0	100	2	50	0	50	2	0	50	50	1	100	0	0
bolas ball	46	59	41	0	0	0	0	0	4	0	100	0	1	0	100	0	9	11	89	0
Winter equipment:																				
sled shoe	1	0	100	0	2	0	50	50	8	0	100	0	50	4	96	0	8	0	100	0
trace buckle & swivel	1	100	0	0	1	0	100	0	9	45	45	10	22	5	95	0	1	100	0	0
snow knife blade	1	0	0	100	0	0	0	0	5	20	80	0	7	29	71	0	9	33	56	11
snow probe & furrule	0	0	0	0	0	0	0	0	2	50	50	0	0	0	0	0	2	50	50	0
Women's equipment:																				
needle case	0	0	0	0	1	100	0	0	1	100	0	0	1	100	0	0	0	0	0	0
thimble holder	1	100	0	0	0	0	0	0	0	0	0	0	0	0	0	0	1	100	0	0
comb	0	0	0	0	1	100	0	0	3	100	0	0	2	100	0	0	2	100	0	0
pendant	0	0	0	0	0	0	0	0	2	100	0	0	8	100	0	0	3	100	0	0
bird-woman figures	1	100	0	0	0	0	0	0	4	100	0	0	0	0	0	0	12	100	0	0

Thule period levels are counted) to 72% in the Silumiut collection. The anomalous proportions in the Lady Franklin Point collection can probably be attributed largely to the unavailability of ivory or the bones of large sea mammals, the remains of which account for only 0.3% of refuse bone identified at the site (Taylor 1972: 40). The antler harpoon heads in this collection are made in the same range of forms as ivory or bone heads from other sites, and from an empirical viewpoint they probably worked as well in capturing sea mammals. Antler is more easily carved than ivory or bone, is less brittle, and widely available to almost all Thule people. Why, then, was it used less frequently than ivory or bone in the manufacture of harpoon and lance heads by most Thule people? One might suggest that the proportions of ivory, bone and antler harpoon heads in each collection merely reflect the relative availability of these materials to the people who lived at each site. But if this were so, one must ask why barbless and single-barbed arrowheads are made exclusively from antler. From a purely functional viewpoint, such arrowheads could have been made from other materials; the endbladed and multiple-barbed arrowheads which we interpret as having been used for hunting bears and birds are frequently made from ivory or bone, as are the prongs for bird-darts which are similar in shape and function.

From this brief examination of five collections which probably illustrate the general range of variability in Thule technology, we may suggest that the observation made on the Debliquy assemblage – that ivory and sea-mammal bone are associated with harpoon heads but not with arrowheads – may be extended to Thule culture in general. Before attempting to explain this association, we may gain a few hints regarding the nature of the phenomenon by examining the materials from which other classes of Thule artefacts were manufactured.

Because of their qualities of toughness, workability and availability, bone and antler were the material from which the majority of Thule artefacts were manufactured. Ivory, being more difficult to work and usually available in smaller quantities, was used for a more limited and apparently somewhat selective range of artefacts. Table 11.1 lists the proportions of various materials in the five Thule assemblages described above, for artefact classes with which ivory is often associated. As can be seen from this list, many component parts of the harpoon and associated gear were often made from ivory in areas where the material was available. Items more vaguely associated with sea-mammal hunting, such as snow goggles, kayak mountings, and dog trace buckles, were frequently fashioned from ivory. Ivory, and secondarily sea-mammal bone, also seems to be associated with equipment used for bird hunting: arrows, dart prongs and bolas balls. Snow knives and the ferrules for snow probes, tools used in building snow houses, were often made from ivory.

Although items of equipment such as drill bows, fish spear barbs, or men's knife handles, are occasionally of ivory rather than bone or antler, most of the remaining artefact classes with which ivory is closely correlated may be categorized as tools associated with women. This includes, perhaps most importantly, sewing tools: needle cases, thimble holders, and occasionally handles for ulus. Women's combs, and plaques which were probably worn as browbands or hair ornaments similar to those of the Historic period, were generally made from ivory and ornamented with incised designs using motifs worn as tattoos by historic Inuit women. Ivory drop pendants and chains closely resemble those which decorated the parkas of nineteenth-century Baffin Island women (Boas 1888: fig. 509). An artefact class for which ivory, or other sea-mammal tooth, seems to be the exclusive material, is that of small bird or bird-woman figures. These very characteristic Thule artefacts, some representing swimming birds and others birds with women's heads, are similar to those used in a hand-game (*tingmiujaq*) by the historic Eastern Inuit (Boas 1888: 567); their significance in prehistoric Thule culture is not known, and may have been somewhat esoteric.

To summarize the above, we may suggest that in Thule technology, ivory is associated with a limited number of artefact categories: weapons for hunting sea mammals; weapons for hunting birds; tools associated with winter life on the sea ice; women's sewing tools; women's ornaments; and bird-woman figures. Ivory, and sea-mammal bone as well, is negatively associated with the arrowheads used in hunting caribou. These associations must be suggested solely on the basis of subjective judgements, since most classes of ivory artefacts are so small in number that statistical testing is not useful.

If the suggested associations of ivory and antler with specific artefact categories are judged to be valid, and since there are no obvious functional explanations for such associations, we might suggest that an explanation may be found in the symbolic attributes of these materials in the minds of the Thule people. We might postulate that ivory was linked symbolically by the Thule craftsman with a set of mutually associated concepts: sea mammals, women, birds, and winter life on the sea ice. Antler, the most useful alternative to ivory in Thule technology, may have been linked with a set of concepts opposed to these: land mammals, particularly the caribou, men and summer life on the land. From the archaeological evidence alone, such a hypothesis must be judged to be extremely tenuous. The hypothesis does gain support however, from a consideration of the culture of the historic Inuit. Assuming that the historic Inuit are the direct cultural descendants of the Thule people, we may usefully search for such a set of associations in Inuit culture as described by ethnographers. If such associations are found to exist, we may legitimately suggest that they derived from a Thule prototype which may then be related to our archaeological observations.

Ethnographic evidence pertaining to the reasons why particular artefact classes are manufactured from particular materials are practically non-existent. Few ethnographers of Inuit cultures have bothered to elicit statements on the use of materials, and these seem to have assumed that such decisions were based solely on empirically functional criteria. For example, Murdoch (1892: 205–25) states that the nineteenth-century Point Barrow Inuit made caribou arrowheads from antler, bird arrowheads from ivory, sealing harpoon heads from sea-mammal bone, and walrus harpoon heads from ivory, but suggests no reasons for these choices of materials. Balikci (1970: 43, 69), working in the memory culture of the central arctic Netsilingmiut, states only that lances and arrowheads used for hunting caribou were made from antler, and that sealing harpoon heads were made from the bones of bear. Lacking direct ethnographic statements on the nature of the associations postulated above, we must attempt to derive information from more indirect sources, those pertaining to the customs, rituals, mythology and seasonal changes in the organization of historic Inuit life.

Most ethnographers have reported that the historic Inuit concept of their environment was centred around one major dichotomy: that between the land and the sea. This dichotomy, the implications of which were analysed most thoroughly in Mauss's (1906) classic discussion, expressed itself most obviously in a set of practical rules maintaining the separation of land and sea animals. The meat of caribou and sea mammals could not be cooked in the same pot, and in some areas could not be eaten on the same day (Birket-Smith 1959: 168). Caribou skins could not be sewn on the sea ice, or while seal or walrus hunting was taking place. Among the Iglulingmiut of the central Arctic, walrus skins or clothing made from walrus skin could not be taken into the interior during the summer caribou hunt (Rasmussen 1929: 193). The Caribou Eskimos of the Barren Grounds considered it dangerous to work walrus skins or ivory in the vicinity of caribou hunting stations (Rasmussen 1930: 48).

It would seem likely that these separation taboos might be extended to weapons, on the assumption that caribou would be repelled by an ivory arrowhead, or sea mammals by an antler harpoon head. The only specific reference to such a practice, however, is Jenness's (1922: 183) statement that the Copper Eskimo used caribou blood, and never seal blood, as glue on arrows used for hunting caribou. From the archaeological association of antler with arrowheads, and to a lesser extent of ivory and sea-mammal bone with harpoon heads, we might suspect, however, that the separation taboos did extend to weapons at one time in the past, or at least that these materials had implicit associations with certain types of activities in the minds of prehistoric Inuit craftmen and hunters.

Since our archaeological observations noted an apparent selective use of ivory in technological categories other than weapons, it may be useful to examine other aspects of the land–sea dichotomy. The separation taboos of the historic Inuit were not restricted to animals, but were also applied to other products of the land and sea. The Copper Eskimos could not work soapstone, a land product, while living on the ice during the winter (Jenness 1922: 184). The Iglulingmiut substituted powdered ivory for the more usual moss as a wick for winter lamps burning walrus oil, and if a whale had been captured, summer fires had to be built of bones and blubber rather than wood (Rasmussen 1929: 186–8). The Point Barrow Inuit could not work wood during the whaling season (Murdoch 1892: 274), nor could the Mackenzie Eskimos dig in the ground while whales were being hunted (Stefansson 1919: 128). From these and other customary practices, we might suggest that the opposition between land and sea mammals was extended to the fields of technology and the raw materials for technology: on the one hand, materials collected during summer life on the land, including caribou antler, stone, wood and moss; on the other, material collected from the sea during the winter, primarily ivory and sea-mammal bone. The association of ivory with equipment used during winter life on the sea suggests that such an extension of the land–sea dichotomy may have been relevant to the selection of materials by Thule craftsmen.

In order to construct a comprehensive explanation for the selective use of ivory in Thule technology, however, we must look to the realm of historic Inuit mythology, a sort of charter from which were derived the practical rules of life noted above. And in mythology, we do find a set of associations similar to those postulated on the basis of our study of ivory artefacts. For example, the association of women with birds is suggested not only by the bird-woman *tingmiujaq* figures of Thule and Historic technology, but by the widespread swan-maiden myth, a bird–woman transformation story (Kleivan 1962).

An apparent association between women and sea mammals can also be found in historic Inuit mythology. According to the most widespread myth, the ringed seals, bearded seals and whales were created from the finger joints of the girl who married the fulmar and who now lives at the bottom of the sea, from where she controls the availability of these animals and is the most important deity of the Inuit pantheon (Nungak and Arima 1969: 116). In another widespread myth, the narwhal was transformed from a woman, the mother or grandmother of the blind boy whose sight was restored by the loon (Savard 1966: 126). The symbolic linking of women and sea mammals in the hunting rituals of many Inuit groups may be related to such myths. From Alaska to Greenland, the hunter's wife must remain quietly at home and refrain from movement while her husband hunts whale, lest the whale be active and escape; in north Alaska the whaler's wife overtly symbolizes the whale, and is symbolically harpooned as a prelude to the hunt (Soby 1970: 47, 53).

On the other hand, summer life on the land has a mythological association with men. The moon, a deity second in importance to the sea woman, is a man. He lives in the sky, which is seen as a vast plain with herds of caribou (Rasmussen 1931: 316). One of the Iglulingmiut afterworlds is in the sky, where souls live with the moon spirit and hunt animals; this is contrasted with a second afterworld beneath the sea, where souls live with the sea woman and hunt sea mammals (Rasmussen 1929: 94). The land itself has a mythological association with masculinity, judging from the widespread myth of the fox-wife who deceives her husband with a giant penis emerging from an interior pond or, in the Mackenzie Delta version, from the earth (Savard 1966: 187–202).

The opposition of woman–sea–ivory to man–land–antler is nicely summed up in the myth of the origin of the walrus and the caribou. According to this myth, the walrus and caribou were created at some time after the original creation of sea mammals, by an old woman who is sometimes explicitly identified with the sea woman. During a famine she took two pieces of fat; one she threw into the water and it became a walrus which swam quietly away. The other she cast on the land, where it became a caribou and attacked her, so she knocked out its teeth and has disliked caribou ever since. A more complex version of the myth from Baffin Island (Boas 1888: 588) states that the caribou originally created by the sea woman had ivory tusks, while the walrus had antlers. These were dangerous to hunters, who were stabbed by the tusked caribou and had their kayaks overturned by the antlered walrus. An old man changed the tusks and antlers around, and created the animals in their present forms which are not as dangerous to his fellow male hunters.

The arguments presented above should not be considered as anything like a thorough structural analysis of Inuit mythology or custom, and the interpretations differ considerably from those of the more thorough analysis presented by Savard (1966). Nevertheless, I feel that from the ethnographic evidence it is reasonable to postulate the existence, in historic Inuit thought, of a set of implicit associations and oppositions which might be presented as follows:

land:sea :: summer:winter :: man:woman, and perhaps :: antler:ivory
(where : can be read 'is to', :: can be read 'as')

If the latter opposition is a valid member of the set, we may be able to use the archaeological products of this opposition as a means of tracing the entire structured set into the prehistoric past. The apparent association of ivory in Thule technology with weapons for hunting sea mammals, women's tools, and tools associated with winter life suggests that a similar set of oppositions existed in the Thule mind, and was expressed in Thule technology to a greater extent than in the technology of their historic descendants. If the associations between specific materials and artefact categories listed in Table 11.1 represent something other than choices based simply on the empirical attributes of each material and the relative availability of each material. I feel that they can best be explained in terms of a symbolic framework similar to that outlined above.

In conclusion, it seems highly unlikely that archaeology will be 'overwhelmed by structuralist fashion', as predicted by Leach (1973). Archaeologists might usefully recognize, however, that prehistoric man was not altogether a functional animal, and that prehistoric cultures were not purely functional adaptive systems. We should give consideration to Schwimmer's (1974: 233) argument that to preindustrial peoples, objects are often 'multivalent phenomena'. Our functional interpretations of the past may be usefully complemented by a search for the symbolic associations of the artefacts which we excavate, and for the relationships of these symbolic associations to the more perishable aspects of past cultures.

This paper first appeared in Canadian Journal of Archaeology *1 (1977), pp. 141–9.*

REFERENCES

Balikci, Asen (1970) *The Netsilik Eskimo*, Garden City, N.Y.: Natural History Press.
Birket-Smith, Kaj (1959) *The Eskimos*, London: Methuen.
Boas, Franz (1888) *The Central Eskimo*, Washington: Bureau of Ethnology, Smithsonian Institution, Sixth Annual Report.
Jenness, Diamond (1922) *The Life of the Copper Eskimos*, Ottawa: Report of the Canadian Arctic Expedition, 1913–18, 12 Pt B.
Kleivan, Inge (1962) 'The swan maiden myth among the Eskimos', *Acta Arctica* 13.
Leach, Edmund (1973) 'Concluding address', in Colin Renfrew (ed.) *The Explanation of Culture Change*, Pittsburgh: University of Pittsburgh Press, 761–71.
McCartney, Allen P. (1970) 'Thule Eskimo prehistory along northwestern Hudson Bay', unpublished PhD dissertation, University of Wisconsin, Madison.
Mathiassen, Therkel (1927) *Archaeology of the Central Eskimos*, Copenhagen: Report of the Fifth Thule Expedition, 1921–24, 4 (1 & 2).
Mauss, M. (1906) 'Essai sur les variations saisonnières des sociétés eskimos', *L'Année Sociologique* 9: 39–130.
Murdoch, John (1892) *Ethnological Results of the Point Barrow Expedition*, Washington: Bureau of Ethnology, Smithsonian Institution, Ninth Annual Report.
Nungah, Z. and Arima, E. (1969) *Inuit Stories*, Chicago: University of Chicago Press.
Rasmussen, Knud (1929) *Intellectual Culture of the Hudson Bay Eskimos*, Copenhagen: Report of the Fifth Thule Expedition, 1921–24, 7 (1).
—— (1930) *Intellectual Culture of the Caribou Eskimos*, Copenhagen: Report of the Fifth Thule Expedition, 1921–24, 7 (2).
—— (1931) *The Netsilik Eskimos, Social Life and Spiritual Culture*, Copenhagen: Report of the Fifth Thule Expedition, 1921–24, 8 (1 & 2).
Savard, Rémi (1966) *Mythologie esquimaude, analyse de textes nord-groenlandais*, Quebec: Centre d'Etudes Nodiques, Travaux Diverses, 14.
Schledermann, Peter (1975) *Thule Eskimo Prehistory of Cumberland Sound, Baffin Island, Canada*, Ottawa: Archaeological Survey of Canada, Mercury Series 38.
Schwimmer, Erik G. (1974) 'Objects of mediation: myth and praxis', in Ino Rossi (ed.) *The Unconscious in Culture*, New York: Dutton, 109–37.
Soby, Regitze Margrethe (1970) 'The Eskimo animal cult', *Folk* 11/12: 43–78.
Stanford, Dennis (1976) *The Walakpa Site, Alaska*, Washington: Smithsonian Contributions to Anthropology, 20.
Stefansson, Vihalmar (1919) *The Stefansson–Anderson Arctic Expedition: Preliminary Ethnological Report*, New York: Anthropological Papers of the American Museum of Natural History, 14.
Taylor, William E. (1972) *An Archaeological Survey between Cape Parry and Cambridge Bay, N.W.T., Canada*, Ottawa: Archaeological Survey of Canada, Mercury Series 1.

12

Interpreting material culture
Christopher Tilley

As Tilley himself says, this paper looks back at some of the assumptions involved in the structuralist encounter and then charts a course which leads from structuralism to the post-structuralism of Derrida, Barthes and Foucault, three of the leading contenders in what is recognized as the French school of post-structuralist (or, in some versions post-modernist or deconstructionist) thinkers. Tilley's paper is an exceptionally clear and reader-friendly account of a difficult, but very important, interrelated set of ideas. We arrive at the position that the interpretation of the objects which comes to us from the past (as they all must and do) has little to do with a 'real' or 'direct' interpretation of that past, and much to do with projects in the present and future. However, the reader may care to bear in mind that, although this is undoubtedly true, it is also true that objects do genuinely come from their own past time, a point Pearce makes in Chapter 4 about the Waterloo jacket (pp. 19–29).

If one wishes to talk about paradigms in archaeology, where the term 'paradigm shift' means a fundamental change in the way in which archaeologists actually see the world of material culture, the decisive break occurs not in 1962 with the substitution of one form of empiricism for another (Binford 1962), but in 1982 with the appearance of *Symbolic and Structural Archaeology* (Hodder 1982a). This break involves, primarily, the conception of material culture as a signifying system in which the external physical attributes of artefacts and their relationships are not regarded as exhausting their meaning. This chapter briefly looks back at some of the assumptions involved in the 'structuralist' encounter in archaeology, then charts a course leading from structuralism to the post-structuralism of Derrida, Barthes and Foucault.[1] The change now occurring in archaeology is a move away from attempts to establish what basically amounted to the search for a methodology for assigning meaning to artefact patterning to a more fully self-reflexive position involving consideration of what is involved in the act of *writing the past*.

SAUSSURE AND THE DIACRITICAL SIGN

Saussure, the father of contemporary linguistics, drew a fundamental distinction between *langue* and *parole*. *Langue* constitutes the system of codes, rules and norms structuring any particular language, whereas *parole* refers to the situated act of utilization of this system by an individual speaker (Saussure 1960). The object of linguistics was, according to Saussure, the *synchronic* analysis of *langue* as opposed to the diachronic analysis of specific changes in elements of languages through time. The essential building-block of *langue* on which linguistic analysis was to work was the diacritical linguistic sign consisting of a union of two facets or components, the 'signifier' and the 'signified'. The signifier is an audible utterance or a sound 'image' referring to a particular concept, the signified:

SIGN: signifier   :   signified
          (acoustic image)   (concept)

A number of points may be noted about this conception of the linguistic sign. It exists in no direct relationship with reality, because the relationship between the signifier and the signified is entirely arbitrary, a matter of convention. The arbitrariness involved here is directly analogous to that existing between words and things. In English we use the utterance 'dog' to refer to a class of creatures with four legs, whereas in other languages an equally arbitrary sound image (e.g. *chien*, *Hund*) may be used. The sign only gains meaning diacritically because the meaning is derived from the system in which it is constituted as different from other signs. In other words, 'dog' is only meaningful because it is *not* cat, rope or axe, and vice versa. Meaning therefore resides in a system of *relationships between signs* and not in the signs themselves. A sign considered in isolation would be meaningless. Furthermore, the meaning of a sign is not predetermined, but is a matter of cultural and historical convention. Consequently, it does not matter how a signifier appears, so long as it preserves its difference from other signifiers.

Saussure was not interested in actual speech or the social utilization of signs in encounters between individuals or groups, or both, but with the objective structures making such *parole* possible. This position had a number of consequences:

(a) the study of linguistics moves from concrete manifestations of speech to unconscious rules and grammars;
(b) an emphasis on relations between signs rather than the signs themselves;
(c) a conception of signs forming part of an overarching system; and
(d) an aim of determining principles underlying different linguistic systems.

FROM LANGUAGE TO CULTURE

Saussure regarded the study of linguistic systems as eventually forming part of a general science of signs – semiology. Language might then be regarded as one sign system among many which would have relative degrees of autonomy from each other. By the 1960s semiology or semiotics had, indeed, developed as a major intellectual field. It is difficult, and perhaps undesirable, to draw any clear distinction between structuralism and semiology, other than to say that the former constitutes a general method of enquiry, whereas the latter forms a field of study of particular sign systems, e.g. advertising, fashion and facial gestures. What they have in common is to use, modify or build on aspects of the linguistic theory outlined above in order to study areas of human culture other than language.

Language becomes the paradigm for understanding all other aspects of social life. If language is an exchange of messages constituted in their difference, governed by an underlying system of codes and grammatical rules, then the move made by Lévi-Strauss is quite understandable. Marriage practices are analysed in terms of systems of underlying rules, such systems being variant realizations of a limited number of structural oppositions defined in their relational difference. Totemism is explained as a way of structuring the relationship between social groups (Lévi-Strauss 1969). If clan A traces descent from the iguana and clan B from the kangaroo, then this is merely a way of stating that the relation of clan A to clan B is analogous to that between the two species. So iguana and kangaroo are logical operators, concrete signs. Hence, one can deduce the canonical formula, archetypal of any structural analysis:

iguana : kangaroo   ::   clan A : clan B

To understand the meaning of 'iguana' and 'kangaroo' they must be situated within an overall structured system of signs. Lévi-Strauss' most ambitious project is the study of myth (1970, 1973), in which he aims to show that the seeming arbitrariness of myths is in fact only tenable in terms of a superficial surface reading of the narratives. Instead myths can be understood in terms of fundamental principles or laws operating at a deeper level. The consequence is that if the human mind can be shown to be determined even in its creation of myths, then *a fortiori* it will also be determined in other spheres. He isolates a number of fundamental oppositions such as male–female, culture–nature, day–night, raw–cooked, and others of a less obvious nature. In doing so Lévi-Strauss is analysing codes and the manner in which categories drawn from one area of experience can be related to those in other areas and used as logical tools for expressing relations. He does not ask so much what the codes are that account for the meaning that myths have in a particular culture, since he is interested in constructing a transcultural logic of myth. This means that myths are always, and primarily, signs of the logic of myth itself. Myths can be broken down into 'mythemes' which, like phonemes (the basic sound units of language), acquire meaning only when combined in particular ways. The rules governing the combinations constitute the true meaning of myth residing beneath the surface narrative, and ultimately to be related to universal mental operations. People do not so much make up myths, but rather myths think themselves through people.

MATERIAL CULTURE AND STRUCTURE

Barthes, in *Mythologies* (1973), is not concerned with general structures, but with particular cultural practices. All such practices are endowed with signification, and this is a fundamental feature running throughout the entire gamut of social life from a wrestling match to eating steak and chips to hairstyles – the list is endless. There is no 'innocent' or transparent fact or event. All facts and events 'speak' to their culturally conditioned observers and participants. Culture is a kind of speech embodying messages coded in various forms and requiring decoding. Furthermore, the meaning of signification may be analogous for those who 'produce' and those who 'consume' the signs. At other times signs act asymmetrically, becoming ideological, linked to the maintenance of power.

Given the intellectual force and power of the general perspectives outlined above, it seems, in retrospect, almost inevitable that archaeologists would come to reframe an understanding of their basic data – material culture – as constituting a meaningful significative system, the analysis of which should go far beyond a reductionist conception of it as merely constituting an extrasomatic means of adaptation, or as vaguely functioning in utilitarian or social terms. Such frameworks have no way of coping with variability or specific form. All that a functional argument can ever be expected to do is to rule on conditions of existence or non-existence. For example, ritual may exist because it performs the function of asserting social solidarity – but why any particular ritual? Such a question remains unanswered. Similarly, a consideration of economic practices must go far beyond simplistic accounts of how food resources might be obtained efficiently or inefficiently. The economy has a style, is part of a cultural and symbolic scheme. Of course, people eat to survive, but eating is a cultural practice. It involves a way of thinking and provides a medium for thought. This symbolic dimension is part of that which is to be explained. It might be said that the primary significance of material culture is not its pragmatic use-value, but its significative exchange value.

In archaeology the particular use of a structuralist or semiological perspective has not been concerned to analyse material culture in terms of the transcultural perspective of Lévi-Strauss. Rather, there has been a concern with historical and social specificity and context: particular rather than universal structures. Much of this work has been indelibly linked with Marxism, involving consideration, in particular, of ideology and power and dynamic processes of structuration or structural change. Here it is not the intention either to review or to analyse the strengths or shortcomings of this work, but rather to focus in a more abstract manner on archaeology as being a pursuit of sign systems.

If archaeology is anything, it is the study of material culture as a manifestation of structured symbolic practices meaningfully constituted and situated in relation to the social. This relationship is active, and not one of simple reflection. Material culture does not provide a mirror to society or a window through which we can see it. Rather, there are multiple transformations and relationships between different aspects of material culture and between material culture and society of, for example, parallelism, opposition, inversion, linearity and equivalence. In order to understand material culture we have to think in terms that go entirely beyond it, to go beneath the surface appearances to an underlying reality. This means that we are thinking in terms of relationships between things, rather than simply in terms of the things themselves. The meaning of the archaeological record is always irreducible to the elements which go to make up and compose that record, conceived as a system of points or units. Such a study involves a search for the structures, and the principles composing those structures, underlying the visible and the tangible. The principles governing the form, nature and content of material culture patterning are to be found at both the level of microrelations (e.g. a set of designs on a pot) and macrorelations (e.g. relations between settlement space and burial space). Such relations may be held to be irreducibly linked, each forming a part of the other. So each individual act of material culture production and use has to be regarded as a contextualized social act involving the relocation of signs along axes defining the relationship between signs and other signs which reach out beyond themselves and towards others becoming amplified or subdued in specific contexts.

Such an analysis is undeniably difficult, but it does at least have the merit of trying to capture the sheer complexity of what we are trying to understand. Several points require emphasis.

(a) Material culture is a framing and communicative medium involved in social practice. It can be used for transforming, storing or preserving social information. It also forms a symbolic medium for social practice, acting dialectically in relation to that practice. It can be regarded as a kind of text, a silent form of writing and discourse; quite literally, a channel of reified and objectified expression.

(b) Although material culture may be produced by individuals, it is always a social production. This is because it does not seem to be at all fruitful to pursue a view of the human subject as endowed with unique capacities and attributes, as the source of social relations, font of meaning, knowledge and action. As Foucault (1974) pointed out, this 'liberal' humanist view of humanity is largely an eighteenth-century creation. In regarding material culture as socially produced, an emphasis is being placed on the constructedness of human meaning as a product of shared systems of signification. The individual does not so much construct material culture or language, but is rather constructed through them.

STRUCTURE AND ARCHAEOLOGICAL ANALYSIS

An underlying assumption of much structuralist work in archaeology has been that such studies either have discovered the real structures generating the observed variability in the archaeological record, or at the very least, are working painfully towards this end. The questions become: What are the signs at work? How can we recognize them? How do they differ? How did they operate in a past life-world? This involves a search for recurrent associated elements in relation to their contextual patterning. The meaning of the past is something that the archaeologist does not have but wants to work towards by means of an analysis going 'beneath' the materials to reveal the underlying principles at work, principles which may be held to be not only structuring the observed archaeological materials, but also implicated in the overall structuration of the social order.

The problem has always been the precise assignation of meaning. For example, a formal analysis of pottery decoration (e.g. Hodder 1982b; Tilley 1984) is not concerned with the actual perceived designs, whether a triangle or a zig-zag line, but with the differences between these designs, which may then be recoded in various ways – for example, in terms of horizontal and vertical distinctions, or alphabetically. How far does such an analysis take us? The structure so arrived at remains a simulacrum (almost Platonic!) of the design sequence, something previously invisible. A paradox is involved here. On the one hand, analysis becomes a form of repetition. We are not told anything about the pot design which is not already there in it. On the other hand, the implication of the analysis is that something new has indeed been produced. The archaeologist has discovered the inner essence residing in the object, in this case the pot design, but what is the meaning of this 'recovery'?

Several strategies may be utilized. Meaning may be established by linking the pot design structure to other structures in the overall material culture patterning, e.g. refuse disposal and burial practices, such that these different structural aspects of the material culture can be regarded as being transformations of each other. The same basic structure may then be held to 'generate' how people are buried, how they design their pots, organize their disposal of refuse and the use of space in settlements. Ultimately, general overarching structuring principles (principles which structure structures) may be recognized. In the case of Hodder's (1982c) study of the Nuba these are:

pure–impure: cattle–pig: male–female: clean–dirty: life–death

So pure is to impure as cattle is to pig, and so on – all very neat.

Another way of assigning meaning, this time in a 'purely' archaeological study, involves a more abstract double-edged conceptual strategy. First, again, different types of material culture are analysed in terms of structural oppositions (usually entirely abstract), e.g. left–right and bounded–unbounded, in different contexts such as settlement and burial. So pot designs may be analysed in terms of boundedness and the treatment of human body parts (Tilley 1984). Second, a conceptual link is then drawn between boundedness in body parts and boundedness in pot designs and, through time, the archaeological record can be examined to see whether such an 'expression' of boundedness intensifies or decreases. The abstracted reconceptualized 'data' may then have its assigned meaning further mobilized by the introduction of social concepts such as contradiction, power and ideology.

In both these and other studies, a notion of 'context' and 'wholeness' is invoked, into which the material culture fitted as meaningful code. This whole may, or may not, be conceived as a fissured or contradictory totality. The archaeologist stands outside this whole, his or her gaze directed towards its internal structuring. A commentary is then produced, bringing order to the superficial chaos of the external appearances and forms of the artefacts. What is happening is the enclosure of the enigmatic (interpreted) object within the interpretative theory's pre-existent system, which then further comments on it.

THE METACRITICAL SIGN AND POLYSEMY

More comments on these commentaries are now required. First, is the notion of the diacritical sign one which can be sustained? If the meaning of a sign is just a matter of difference from other signs, then this conception can be pressed further until it breaches Saussure's notion of language forming a closed and stable synchronic system. This is because if a sign is what it is by virtue of its differences from all other signs, then each sign must be made up of a vast and never-ending network of differences from other signs. The outcome of such a line of reasoning is that there can be no clear symmetrical unity between one signifier and one signified. Meaning is then to be related to a potentially endless play of signifiers, and signifiers keep on changing into signifieds, and vice versa. So the signifier and the signified become conceptually split (Derrida 1976, 1978). We arrive at what might be termed the metacritical sign. The meaning of the metacritical sign is never transparently present in it, but is a matter of what the sign is not. So meaning is both present and absent – to state this more simply, meaning is dispersed along chains of signifiers. Another piece of willed and deliberate obfuscation? Perhaps, but no more so than to mention a minimax satisficer strategy, ringing a dulcet tone of clarity in the attuned economistic archaeological ear. The corollary to the position just taken is quite simple – the meaning of material culture can never be objectified or exactly pinned down. Its meaning always, to some extent, evades the analyst.

Considering the concept of polysemy may clarify this further. An object, any object, has no ultimate or unitary meaning that can be held to exhaust it. Rather, any object has multiple and sometimes contradictory meanings. The meanings depend on a whole host of factors. One appropriate example is the safety-pin in contemporary Britain (Hodder 1985: 14), which, according to who wears it – an infant, a grandmother or a 'punk' – changes its meaning. However, this is only part of the story. The meaning also changes according to the context in which the interpretation takes place (a kitchen or an underground station); who is carrying out the interpretation (to various people the safety-pin may mean aggression, pity, children or bondage); and why they are bothering to interpret it in the first place. This last point is an appropriate cue to draw the archaeologist into the text.

FROM READING THE PAST TO WRITING THE PAST

The previous section left the intrepid archaeologist grappling with the notion of meaning not being so much present in the artefact but absent, and being faced with a situation in which the notion of any unitary meaning residing in the past to which our analyses might strive to reach – whether by producing a structural simulacrum or by any other means – as a dangerous chimera. Meaning therefore becomes indeterminate and problematic. What is to be done, if anything? On one point we can at least be certain, the archaeological pursuit of signs is no easy business.

One possible escape route might be to renounce linguistic imperialism and develop a theory of the meaning of material culture not based on linguistic analogies. We might strongly assert that what material culture communicates is totally different from language. For example, it would require a vast number of material objects to 'say', in a material form, even the simplest sentence. If someone makes a statement and you do not understand what they mean, there is the possibility that a Socratic dialogue may bring illumination. Such dialogue is not possible with a pot! On the other hand, a stress can be made on the fact that material culture acts in multidimensional channels as a non-verbal mode of communication. In this respect its meanings could be held to be more complicated than those conveyed in speech. We could say that material culture is a material language with its own meaning product tied to production and consumption. Endless permutations of such arguments could be produced, but none of them can escape language. Thinking about material culture inevitably involves its transformation into linguistic concepts. However much we might try to escape from language, we are trapped in its prison house. So, although it might appear a laudable aim to escape a linguistic frame, this is an impossibility. There can be no meaningfully constituted non-linguistic semiological system.

The detour of attempting to embrace a radically non-linguistic analogy for the interpretation of material culture has apparently failed, leading us back once more to the archaeologist. Undecidability then, ambivalence: a free play of meaning? The 'structuralist', 'contextualist' or 'dialectical-structuralist' encounter as it has appeared in archaeology seems to be too important to be abandoned. In favour of what? The fact that such an enterprise leads inexorably towards its own critique and extension may be a sign of its vitality. A notion of metacritical and polysemous signs leads us to the margins of such an approach and our better understanding of it as an active interpretative exercise creating a past in a present which must renounce either finality or the notion that in the future we will be producing better, truer or more-precise accommodations to the truth of the past – whatever that might be

The interpretation of the meaning and significance of material culture is a contemporary activity. The meaning of the past does not reside in the past, but belongs in the present. Similarly, the primary event of archaeology is the event of excavation or writing, not the event of the past. Consequently, the archaeologist is not so much reading the signs of the past as writing these signs into the present: constructing discourses which should be both meaningful to the present and playing an active role in shaping the present's future. Here an irony crops up. Archaeologists write, but many do not feel they should be writing! At best such textual production may be regarded as a transparent resource, a mere medium for expression. However, writing always transforms. The process of writing the past in the present needs to become part of that which is to be understood in archaeology. The ultimate aim of much contemporary archaeological discourse is to put an end to writing, to get the story right. Empiricism inexorably encourages such a futile goal. To the contrary, there will be no correct stories of the past that are not themselves a product of a politics of truth. There can only be better or worse re-presentations of history: his [*sic*] story.

What is important is the development of a truly self-reflexive archaeological discourse, aware of itself as discourse and systematically refusing the usual imperative of producing yet another methodology for grasping the past's meaning. Archaeological discourses are, by and large, framed in specific institutional settings and transmitted and disseminated through definite forms of media in which archaeological knowledge is located. Such disclosures have their bases in forms of pedagogy imposing 'a will to truth'. As yet there is no true alternative discourse in archaeology. A crucial act in creating one will be the disruption of the discursive authority of the texts we have to hand at present. This will involve an awareness of the politics of discourse and the power structures in which it is embedded. This requires consideration of what kind of past we want in the present and why we produce the past in one manner rather than another.[2]

The general position being taken in this chapter suggests that material culture can be regarded as providing a multidimensional 'text' from which the archaeologist can construct his or her texts: not, therefore, an entirely free process. The text that the archaeologist writes will consist, in part, of a tissue of 'quotations' drawn from the material record and meaningfully activated in fresh constellations in relation to a particular argumentative frame of reference. The assignation of the meaning of the quotations drawn from the archaeological record requires a self-reflexive problematic.

We might set up a chain of signifiers to help us to understand the process of writing the past. First we might put interest. We are interested in interpreting some aspect of the archaeological record, making it meaningful for ourselves and others. However, this interest is at the outset dependent on our values (why we are carrying out this activity in the first place). These values are, in turn, dependent on our politics and our morality, which relate more generally to the sociopolitical context in which we find ourselves situated and positioned as agents. The chain we actually end up with is: positioned subject – politics, morality – values – interests – meanings – text.

The meaning of the past has to be inserted into the present through the medium of the text. So there is no meaning outside the text (conceived broadly to include film, etc.). This *meaning* has to be argued for and against. The act of writing always presupposes a politics of the present, and such writing is a form of power. It cannot escape power. Any kind of writing about the past is inevitably simultaneously a domestication of the difference of the past, an imposition of order. Writing the past is not an innocent and disinterested reading of an autonomous past produced as image. Writing the past is drawing it into the present, re-inscribing it into the face of the present.

This text is a pastiche or montage, a material production built on other texts, an extended footnote which, if anything interesting has been said, may become incorporated into another text. A formal conclusion is out of keeping with the spirit in which it is written. It will suffice to mention that in ending this contribution I wonder whether I should be saying what I have said. I would like to be looking over your shoulder and saying 'No, no – I didn't exactly mean it to be interpreted like *that*!'

This paper first appeared in I. Hodder (ed.) (1991) The Meaning of Things, London: Routledge, pp. 185–94.

NOTES

1   These authors are names for problems rather than formalized doctrines, and this is precisely their interest. Both Foucault and Barthes, in their early work, have been labelled structuralists. Both have renounced the structuralist enterprise. Post-structuralism is characteristically a term not amenable to any rigid definition. It is simply a term applied to work without any unitary core that is temporally removed from a structuralist position. Those interested might look at Barthes (1974, 1977), Foucault (1972, 1984), Derrida (1976, 1981) and Sturrock (1979).

2   Aspects of post structuralism, discourse, textuality, power, ideology and politics in relation to archaeology are discussed in detail in *Re-Constructing Archaeology* and *Social Theory and Archaeology* (Shanks and Tilley 1987a, 1987b).

REFERENCES

Barthes, R. (1973) *Mythologies*, London: Paladin.
—— (1974) *S/Z*, New York: Hill & Wang.
—— (1977) *Image, Music, Text*, New York: Hill & Wang.
Binford, L. (1962) 'Archaeology as anthropology', *American Antiquity* 28(2): 1–37.
Derrida, J. (1976) *Of Grammatology*, Baltimore: Johns Hopkins University Press.
—— (1978) *Writing and Difference*, London: Routledge & Kegan Paul.
—— (1981) *Dissemination*, London: Athlone Press.
Foucault, M. (1972) *The Archaeology of Knowledge*, London: Tavistock.
—— (1974) *The Order of Things*, London: Tavistock.
—— (1984) *The Foucault Reader*, ed. P. Rabinow, Harmondsworth: Penguin Books.
Hodder, I. (ed.) (1982a) *Symbolic and Structural Archaeology*, Cambridge: Cambridge University Press.
—— (1982b) 'Sequence of structural change in the Dutch Neolithic', in I. Hodder (ed.) *Symbolic and Structural Archaeology*, Cambridge: Cambridge University Press, 162–78.
—— (1982c) *Symbols in Action*, Cambridge: Cambridge University Press.
—— (1985) 'Postprocessual archaeology', in M. Schiffer (ed.) *Advances in Archaeological Theory and Method* vol. 8, New York: Academic Press.
Lévi-Strauss, C. (1969) *Totemism*, Harmondsworth: Penguin Books.
—— (1970) *The Raw and the Cooked*, London: Cape.
—— (1973) *From Honey to Ashes*, London: Cape.
Saussure, F. de (1960) *Course in General Linguistics*, London: Peter Owen.
Shanks, M. and Tilley, C. (1987a) *Re-Constructing Archaeology*, Cambridge: Cambridge University Press.
—— (1987b) *Social Theory and Archaeology*, Cambridge: Polity Press.
Sturrock, J. (ed.) (1979) *Structuralism and Since*, Oxford: Oxford University Press.
Tilley, C. (1984) 'Ideology and the legitimation of power in the middle Neolithic of southern Sweden', in D. Miller and C. Tilley (eds) *Ideology, Power and Prehistory*, Cambridge: Cambridge University Press.

13

Commodities and the politics of value

Arjun Appadurai

Tilley's contention that objects are interpreted for the present and future is one insight into their political nature. Another facet of their political lives is their capacity to act as goods to be exchanged and hence to carry values; the link, as Appadurai says, between exchange and value is politics, and in order to start an analysis of this he draws upon the work of Georg Simmel, an economist whose work was first published in 1907, but who is now attracting considerable attention among students of material culture theory. Appadurai analyses some Marxist ideas, and also those surrounding the notion of 'gift' and adds this broad argument to the proposition that objects have social lives of their own.

This essay is intended to propose a new perspective on the circulation of commodities in social life. The gist of this perspective can be put in the following way. Economic exchange creates value. Value is embodied in commodities that are exchanged. Focusing on the things that are exchanged, rather than simply on the forms or functions of exchange, makes it possible to argue that what creates the link between exchange and value is *politics*, construed broadly. This argument, which is elaborated in the text of this essay, justifies the conceit that commodities, like persons, have social lives.

Commodities can provisionally be defined as objects of economic value. As to what we ought to mean by economic value, the most useful (though not quite standard) guide is Georg Simmel. In the first chapter of *The Philosophy of Money* (1907; English translation 1978), Simmel provides a systematic account of how economic value is best defined. Value, for Simmel, is never an inherent property of objects, but is a judgement made about them by subjects. Yet the key to the comprehension of value, according to Simmel, lies in a region where 'that subjectivity is only provisional and actually not very essential' (Simmel 1978: 73).

In exploring this difficult realm, which is neither wholly subjective nor quite objective, in which value emerges and functions, Simmel suggests that objects are not difficult to acquire because they are valuable, 'but we call those objects valuable that resist our desire to possess them' (p. 67). What Simmel calls economic objects, in particular, exist in the space between pure desire and immediate enjoyment, with some distance between them and the person who desires them, which is a distance that can be overcome. This distance is overcome in and through economic exchange, in which the value of objects is determined reciprocally. That is, one's desire for an object is fulfilled by the sacrifice of some other object, which is the focus of the desire of another. Such exchange of sacrifices is what economic life is all about and the economy as a particular social form 'consists not only in exchanging *values* but in the *exchange* of values' (p. 80). Economic value, for Simmel, is generated by this sort of exchange of sacrifices.

Several arguments follow this analysis of economic value in Simmel's discussion. The first is that economic value is not just value in general, but a definite sum of value, which results from the commensuration of two intensities of demand. The form this commensuration takes is the exchange of sacrifice and gain. Thus, the economic object does not have an absolute value as a result of the demand for it, but the demand, as the basis of a real or imagined exchange, endows the object with value. It is exchange that sets the parameters of utility and scarcity, rather than the other way round, and exchange that is the source of value: 'The difficulty of acquisition, the sacrifice offered in exchange, is the unique constitutive element of value, of which scarcity is only the external manifestation, its objectification in the form of quantity' (p. 100). In a word, exchange is not a by-product of the mutual valuation of objects, but its source.

These terse and brilliant observations set the stage for Simmel's analysis of what he regarded as the most complex instrument for the conduct of economic exchange – money – and its place in modern life. But Simmel's observations can be taken in quite another direction. This alternative direction, which is exemplified by the remainder of this essay, entails exploring the conditions under which economic objects circulate in different *regimes of value* in space and time.

Contemporary western common sense, building on various historical traditions in philosophy, law and natural science, has a strong tendency to oppose 'words' and 'things'. Though this was not always the case even in the West, as Marcel Mauss noted in his famous work *The Gift*, the powerful contemporary tendency is to regard the world of things as inert and mute, set in motion and animated, indeed knowable, only by persons and their words (see also Dumont 1980: 229–30). Yet, in many historical societies, things have not been so divorced from the capacity of persons to act and the power of words to communicate. That such a view of things had not disappeared even under the conditions of occidental industrial capitalism is one of the intuitions that underlay Marx's famous discussion, in *Capital*, of the 'fetishism of commodities'.

Even if our own approach to things is conditioned necessarily by the view that things have no meanings apart from those that human transactions, attributions and motivations endow them with, the anthropological problem is that this formal truth does not illuminate the concrete, historical circulation of things. For that we have to follow the things themselves, for their meanings are inscribed in their forms, their uses, their trajectories. It is only through the analysis of these trajectories that we can interpret the human transactions and calculations that enliven things. Thus, even though from a *theoretical* point of view human actors encode things with significance, from a *methological* point of view it is the things-in-motion that illuminate their human and social context. No social analysis of things (whether the analyst is an economist, an art historian, or an anthropologist) can avoid a minimum level of what might be called methodological fetishism. This methodological fetishism, returning our attention to the things themselves, is in part a corrective to the tendency to excessively sociologize transactions in things, a tendency we owe to Mauss, as Firth has recently noted (1983: 89).

Commodities, and things in general, are of independent interest to several kinds of anthropology. They constitute the first principles and the last resort of archeologists. They are the stuff of 'material culture', which unites archeologists with several kinds of cultural anthropologists. As valuables, they are at the heart of economic anthropology and, not least, as the medium of gifting, they are at the heart of exchange theory and social anthropology generally. The commodity perspective on things represents a valuable point of entry to the revived, semiotically oriented interest in material culture, recently remarked and exemplified in a special section of *RAIN* (Miller 1983). But commodities are not of fundamental interest only to anthropologists. They also constitute a topic of lively interest to social and economic historians, to art historians and, lest we forget, to economists, though each discipline might constitute the problem differently. Commodities thus represent a subject on which anthropology may have something to offer to its neighbouring disciplines, as well as one about which it has a good deal to learn from them.

THE SPIRIT OF THE COMMODITY

Few will deny that a commodity is a thoroughly socialized thing. The definitional question is: in what does its sociality consist? The purist answer, routinely attributed to Marx, is that a commodity is a product intended principally for exchange, and that such products emerge, by definition, in the institutional, psychological and economic conditions of capitalism. Less purist definitions regard commodities as goods intended for exchange, regardless of the form of the exchange. The purist definition forecloses the question prematurely. The looser definitions threaten to equate commodity with gift and many other kinds of thing. In this section, through a critique of the Marxian understanding of the commodity, I shall suggest that commodities are things with a particular type of social potential that they are distinguishable from 'products', 'objects', 'goods', 'artefacts' and other sorts of things – but only in certain respects and from a certain point of view. If my argument holds water, it will follow that it is definitionally useful to regard commodities as existing in a very wide variety of societies (though with a special intensity and salience in modern, capitalist societies), and that there is an unexpected convergence between Marx and Simmel on the topic of commodities.

The most elaborate and thought-provoking discussion of the idea of the commodity appears in Volume I, Part I, of Marx's *Capital*, though the idea was widespread in nineteenth-century discussions of political economy. Marx's own reanalysis of the concept of commodity was a central part of his critique of bourgeois political economy and a fulcrum for the transition from his own earlier thought (see especially Marx 1973) on capitalism to the full-fledged analysis of *Capital*. Today, the conceptual centrality of the idea of commodity has given way to the neo-classical, marginalist conception of 'goods', and the word 'commodity' is used in neo-classical economics only to refer to a special subclass of primary goods and no longer plays a central analytic role. This is, of course, not the case with Marxian approaches in economics and sociology, or with neo-Ricardian approaches (such as those of Piero Sraffa), where the analysis of the 'commodity' still plays a central theoretical role (Sraffa 1961; Seddon 1978).

But in most modern analyses of economy (outside anthropology), the meaning of the term 'commodity' has narrowed to reflect only one part of the heritage of Marx and the early political economists. That is, in most contemporary uses, commodities are special kinds of manufactured goods (or services), which are associated only with capitalist modes of production and are thus to be found only where capitalism has penetrated. Thus even in current debates about proto-industrialization (see, for example, Perlin 1983), the issue is not whether commodities are associated with capitalism, but whether certain organizational and technical forms associated with capitalism are solely of European origin. Commodities are generally seen as typical material representations of the capitalist mode of production, even if they are classified as petty and their capitalist context as incipient.

Yet it is clear that this is to draw on only one strand in Marx's own understanding of the nature of the commodity. The treatment of the commodity in the first hundred or so pages of *Capital* is arguably one of the most difficult, contradictory and ambiguous parts of Marx's corpus. It begins with an extremely broad definition of commodity ('A commodity is, in the first place, an object outside us, a thing that by its properties satisfies human wants of some sort or another'). It then moves dialectically through a series of more parsimonious definitions, which permit the gradual elaboration of the basic Marxian approach to use value and exchange value, the problem of equivalence, the circulation and exchange of products, and the significance of money. It is the elaboration of this understanding of the relationship between the commodity form and the money form that allows Marx to make his famous distinction between two forms of circulation of commodities (Commodities–Money–Commodities and Money–Commodities–Money), the latter representing the general formula for capital. In the course of this analytic movement, commodities become intricately tied to *money*, an impersonal market, and exchange value. Even in the simple form of circulation (tied to use value), commodities are related through the commensuration capabilities of money. Today, in general, the link of commodities to postindustrial social, financial, and exchange forms is taken for granted, even by those who in other regards do not take Marx seriously.

Yet in Marx's own writings, there is the basis for a much broader, more cross-culturally and historically useful approach to commodities, whose spirit is attenuated as soon as he becomes embroiled in the details of his analysis of nineteenth-century industrial capitalism. By this earlier formulation, in order to produce not mere products but commodities, a man must produce use values for others, social use values (Marx 1971: 48). This idea was glossed by Engels in a parenthesis he inserted into Marx's text in the following interesting way: 'To become a commodity a product must be transferred to another, whom it will serve as a use-value, by means of an exchange' (Marx 1971: 48). Though Engels was content with this elucidation, Marx proceeds to make a very complex (and ambiguous) series of distinctions between products and commodities, but for anthropological purposes, the key passage deserves quotation in full:

> Every product of labour is, in all states of society, a use-value; but it is only at a definite historical epoch in a society's development that such a product becomes a commodity, viz. at the epoch when the labour spent on the production of a useful article becomes expressed as one of the objective qualities of that article, i.e., as its value. It therefore follows that the elementary value-form is also the primitive form under which a product of labour appears historically as a commodity, and that the gradual transformation of such products into commodities, proceeds *pari passu* with the development of the value-form.
>
> (Marx 1971: 67)

The difficulty of distinguishing the logical aspect of this argument from its historical aspect has been noted by Anne Chapman (1980), whose argument I will return to shortly. In the above passage from *Capital*, the shift from product to commodity is discussed historically. But the resolution is still highly schematic, and it is difficult to specify or test it in any clear way.

The point is that Marx was still imprisoned in two aspects of the mid-nineteenth-century episteme: one could see the economy only in reference to the problematics of production (Baudrillard 1975); the other regarded the movement to commodity production as evolutionary, unidirectional, and historical. As a result commodities either exist or do not exist, and they are *products* of a particular sort. Each of these assumptions requires modification.

Despite these epistemic limitations, in his famous discussion of the fetishism of commodities, Marx does note, as he does elsewhere in *Capital*, that the commodity does not emerge whole-cloth from the product under bourgeois production, but makes its appearance 'at an early date in history, though not in the same predominating and characteristic manner as nowadays' (Marx 1971: 86). Though it is outside the scope of this essay to explore the difficulties of Marx's own thought on precapitalist, non-state, non-monetary economies, we might note that Marx left the door open for the existence of commodities, at least in a primitive form, in many sorts of society.

The definitional strategy I propose is a return to a version of Engels's emendation of Marx's broad definition involving the production of use-value *for others*, which converges with Simmel's emphasis on exchange as the source of economic value. Let us start with the idea that a commodity is *any thing intended for exchange*. This gets us away from the exclusive preoccupation with the 'product', 'production', and the original or dominant intention of the 'producer' and permits us to focus on the dynamics of exchange. For comparative purposes, then, the question becomes *not* 'What is a commodity?' but rather 'What sort of an exchange is commodity exchange?' Here, and as part of the effort to define commodities better, we need to deal with two kinds of exchange that are conventionally contrasted with commodity exchange. The first is barter (sometimes referred to as direct exchange), and the other is the exchange of gifts. Let us start with barter.

Barter as a form of exchange has recently been analysed by Chapman (1980) in an essay that, among other things, takes issue with Marx's own analysis of the relationship between direct exchange and commodity exchange. Combining aspects of several current definitions of barter (including Chapman's), I would suggest that barter is the exchange of objects for one another *without* reference to money and *with* maximum feasible reduction of social, cultural, political, or personal transaction costs. The former criterion distinguishes barter from commodity exchange in the strict Marxist sense, and the latter from gift exchange by virtually any definition.

Chapman is right that, in so far as Marx's theory of value is taken seriously, his treatment of barter poses insoluble theoretical and conceptual problems (Chapman 1980: 68–70), for Marx postulated that barter took the form of direct exchange of the product (x use-value $A = y$ use-value B), as well as direct exchange of the commodity (x commodity $A = y$ commodity B). But this Marxist view of barter, whatever problem it may pose for a Marxist theory of the origin of exchange value, has the virtue of fitting well with Chapman's most persuasive claim – that barter, as either a dominant or a subordinate form of exchange, exists in an extremely wide range of societies. Chapman criticizes Marx for inserting the commodity into barter and wishes to keep them quite separate, on the grounds that commodities assume the use of money objects (and thus congealed labour value), and not just money as a unit of account or measure of equivalence. Commodity exchange, for Chapman, occurs only when a money object intervenes in exchange. Since barter, in her model, excludes such intervention, commodity exchange and barter are formally completely distinct, though they may coexist in some societies (Chapman 1980: 67–8).

In her critique of Marx, it seems to me, Chapman takes an unduly constricted view of the role of money in the circulation of commodities. Though Marx ran into difficulties in his own analysis of the relationship between barter and commodity exchange, he was right to see, as did Polanyi, that there was a *commonality of spirit* between barter and capitalist commodity exchange, a commonality tied (in this view) to the object-centred, relatively impersonal, asocial nature of each. In the various simple forms of barter, we see an effort to exchange things without the constraints of sociality on the one hand, and the complications of money on the other. Barter in the contemporary world is on the increase: one estimate has it that an estimated $12 billion a year in goods and services is bartered in the United States alone. International barter (Pepsico syrup for Russian vodka; Coca-Cola for Korean toothpicks and Bulgarian forklifts are examples) is also developing into a complex alternative economy. In these latter situations, barter is a response to the growing number of barriers to international trade and finance, and has a specific role to play in the larger economy. Barter, as a form of trade, thus links the exchange of commodities in widely different social, technological and institutional circumstances. Barter may thus be regarded as a special form of commodity exchange, one in which, for any variety of reasons, money plays either no role or a very indirect role (as a mere unit of account). By this definition of barter, it would be difficult to locate any human society in which commodity exchange is completely irrelevant. Barter appears to be the form of commodity exchange in which the circulation of things is most divorced from social, political, or cultural norms. Yet wherever evidence is available, the determination of what may be bartered, where, when, and by whom, as well as of what drives the demand for the goods of the 'other', is a social affair. There is a deep tendency to regard this social regulation as a largely negative matter, so that barter in small-scale societies and in earlier periods is frequently regarded as having been restricted to the relation *between* communities rather than *within* communities. Barter is, in this model, held to be in inverse proportion to sociality, and foreign trade, by extension, is seen to have 'preceded' internal trade (Sahlins 1972). But there are good empirical and methodological reasons to question this view.

The notion that trade in non-monetized, pre-industrial economies is generally regarded as antisocial from the point of view of face-to-face communities and thus was frequently restricted to dealings with strangers has as its close counterpart the view that the spirit of the gift and that of the commodity are deeply opposed. In this view, gift exchange and commodity exchange are fundamentally contrastive and mutually exclusive. Though there have been some important recent attempts to mute the exaggerated contrast between Marx and Mauss (Hart 1982; Tambiah 1984), the tendency to see these two modalities of exchange as fundamentally opposed remains a marked feature of anthropological discourse (Dumont 1980; Hyde 1979; Gregory 1982; Sahlins 1972; Taussig 1980).

The exaggeration and reification of the contrast between gift and commodity in anthropological writing has many sources. Among them are the tendency to romanticize small-scale societies; to conflate use-value (in Marx's sense) with *Gemeinschaft* (in Toennies's sense); the tendency to forget that capitalist societies, too, operate according to cultural designs; the proclivity to marginalize and underplay the calculative, impersonal and self-aggrandizing features of non-capitalist societies. These tendencies, in turn, are a product of an oversimplified view of the opposition between Mauss and Marx, which, as Keith Hart (1982) has suggested, misses important aspects of the commonalities between them.

Gifts, and the spirit of reciprocity, sociability and spontaneity in which they are typically exchanged, usually are starkly opposed to the profit-oriented, self-centred and calculated spirit that fires the circulation of commodities. Further, where gifts link things to persons and embed the flow of things in the flow of social relations, commodities are held to represent the drive – largely free of moral or cultural constraints – of goods for one another, a drive mediated by money and not by sociality. I aim to show that this is a simplified and overdrawn series of contrasts. For the present, though, let me propose one important quality that gift exchange and the circulation of commodities share.

My view of the spirit of gift exchange owes a good deal to Bourdieu (1977), who has extended a hitherto underplayed aspect of Mauss's analysis of the gift (Mauss 1976:

70–3), which stresses certain strategic parallels between gift exchange and more ostensibly 'economic' practices. Bourdieu's argument, which stresses the temporal dynamics of gifting, makes a shrewd analysis of the common spirit that underlies both gift and commodity circulation:

> If it is true that the lapse of time interposed is what enables the gift or counter-gift to be seen and experienced as an inaugural act of generosity, without any past or future, i.e., without *calculation*, then it is clear that in reducing the polythetic to the monothetic, objectivism destroys the specificity of all practices which, like gift exchange, tend or pretend to put the law of self-interest into abeyance. A rational contract would telescope into an instant a transaction which gift exchange disguises, by stretching it out in time; and because of this, gift exchange is, if not the only mode of commodity circulation practised, at least the only mode to be fully recognized, in societies which, because they deny 'the true soil of their life', as Lukács puts it, have an economy in itself and not for itself.
>
> (Bourdieu 1977: 171)

This treatment of gift exchange as a particular form of the circulation of commodities comes out of Bourdieu's critique not only of 'objectivist' treatments of social action but of the sort of ethnocentrism, itself a historical product of capitalism, that assumes a very restricted definition of economic interest. Bourdieu suggests that 'practice never ceases to conform to economic calculation even when it gives every appearance of disinterestedness by departing from the logic of interested calculation (in the narrow sense) and playing for stakes that are non-material and not easily quantified' (ibid. 177).

I take this suggestion to converge, though from a slightly different angle, with the proposals of Tambiah (1984), Baudrillard (1968, 1975, 1981), Sahlins (1976) and Douglas and Isherwood (1981), all of which represent efforts to restore the cultural dimension to societies that are too often represented simply as economies writ large, and to restore the calculative dimension to societies that are too often simply portrayed as solidarity writ small. Part of the difficulty with a cross-cultural analysis of commodities is that, as with other matters in social life, anthropology is excessively dualistic: 'us and them'; 'materialist and religious'; 'objectification of persons' versus 'personification of things'; 'market exchange' versus 'reciprocity'; and so forth. These oppositions parody both poles and reduce human diversities artificially. One symptom of this problem has been an excessively positivist conception of the commodity, as being a certain *kind* of thing, thus restricting the debate to the matter of deciding *what kind* of thing it is. But, in trying to understand what is distinctive about commodity exchange, it does not make sense to distinguish it sharply either from barter on the one hand or from the exchange of gifts on the other. As Simmel (1978: 97–8), suggests, it is important to see the calculative dimension in all these forms of exchange, even if they vary in the form and intensity of sociality associated with them. It remains now to characterize commodity exchange in a comparative and processual manner.

Let us approach commodities as things in a certain situation, a situation that can characterize many different kinds of thing, at different points in their social lives. This means looking at the commodity potential of all things rather than searching fruitlessly for the magic distinction between commodities and other sorts of things. It also means breaking significantly with the production-dominated Marxian view of the commodity and focusing on its *total* trajectory from production, through exchange/distribution, to consumption.

But how are we to define the commodity situation? I propose that *the commodity situation in the social life of any 'thing' be defined as the situation in which its exchangeability (past, present or future) for some other thing is its socially relevant feature*. Further, the commodity situation, defined this way, can be disaggregated into: (1) the commodity phase of the social life of any thing; (2) the commodity candidacy of any thing; and (3) the commodity context in which any thing may be placed. Each of these aspects of 'commodityhood' needs some explication.

The idea of the commodity phase in the social life of a thing is a summary way to capture the central insight in Igor Kopytoff's important essay (1986), where certain things are seen as moving in and out of the commodity state. I shall have more to say on this biographical approach to things in the next section, but let us note for the moment that things can move in *and* out of the commodity state, that such movements can be slow or fast, reversible or terminal, normative or deviant. Though the biographical aspect of some things (such as heirlooms, postage stamps and antiques) may be more noticeable than that of some others (such as steel bars, salt or sugar), this component is never completely irrelevant.

The commodity *candidacy* of things is less a temporal than a conceptual feature, and it refers to the standards and criteria (symbolic, classificatory and moral) that define the exchangeability of things in any particular social and historical context. At first glance, this feature would appear best glossed as the *cultural* framework within which things are classified, and it is a central preoccupation of Kopytoff's paper (Kopytoff 1986). Yet this gloss conceals a variety of complexities. It is true that in most stable societies it would be possible to discover a taxonomic structure that defines the world of things, lumping some things together, discriminating between others, attaching meanings and values to these groupings, and providing a basis for rules and practices governing the circulation of these objects. In regard to the economy (that is, to exchange), Paul Bohannan's (1955) account of spheres of exchange among the Tiv is an obvious example of this type of framework for exchange. But there are two kinds of situations where the standards and criteria that govern exchange are so attenuated as to seem virtually absent. The first is the case of transactions across cultural boundaries, where all that is agreed upon is price (whether monetary or not) and a minimum set of conventions regarding the transaction itself. The other is the case of those intracultural exchanges where, despite a vast universe of shared understandings, a specific exchange is based on deeply divergent perceptions of the value of the objects being exchanged. The best examples of such intracultural value divergence are to be found in situations of extreme hardship (such as famine or warfare), when exchanges are made whose logic has little to do with the commensuration of sacrifices. Thus a Bengali male who abandons his wife to prostitution in exchange for a meal, or a Turkana woman who sells critical pieces of her personal jewellery for a week's food, are engaging in transactions that may be seen as legitimate in extreme circumstances, but could hardly be regarded as operating under a rich shared framework of valuation between buyer and seller. Another way to characterize such situations is to say that in such contexts, value and price have come almost completely unyoked

Also, as Simmel has pointed out, from the point of view of the individual and his subjectivity, all exchanges might contain this type of discrepancy between the sacrifices of buyer and seller, discrepancies normally brushed aside because of the host of conventions about exchange that *are* complied with by both parties (Simmel 1978: 80). We may speak, thus, of the cultural framework that defines the commodity candidacy of things, but we must bear in mind that some exchange situations, both inter- and intracultural, are characterized by a shallower set of shared standards of value than others. I therefore prefer to use the term *regimes of value*, which does *not* imply that every act of commodity exchange presupposes a complete cultural sharing of assumptions, but rather that the degree of value coherence may be highly variable from situation to situation and from commodity to commodity. A regime of value, in this sense, is consistent with both very high and very low sharing of standards by the parties to a particular commodity exchange. Such regimes of value account for the constant transcendence of cultural boundaries by the flow of commodities, where culture is understood as a bounded and localized system of meanings.

Finally, the commodity *context* refers to the variety of *social* arenas, within or between *cultural* units, that help link the commodity candidacy of a thing to the commodity phase of its career. Thus in many societies, marriage transactions might constitute the context in which women are most intensely, and most appropriately, regarded as exchange values. Dealings with strangers might provide contexts for the commoditization of things that are otherwise protected from commoditization. Auctions accentuate the commodity dimension of objects (such as paintings) in a manner that might well be regarded as deeply inappropriate in other contexts. Bazaar settings are likely to encourage commodity flows as domestic settings may not. The variety of such contexts, within and across societies, provides the link between the social environment of the commodity and its temporal symbolic state. As I have already suggested, the commodity context, as a social matter, may bring together actors from quite different cultural systems who share only the most minimal understandings (from the conceptual point of view) about the objects in question and agree *only* about the terms of trade. The so-called silent trade phenomenon is the most obvious example of the minimal fit between the cultural and social dimensions of commodity exchange (Price 1980).

Thus, commoditization lies at the complex intersection of temporal, cultural and social factors. To the degree that some things in a society are frequently to be found in the commodity phase, to fit the requirements of commodity candidacy, and to appear in a commodity context, they are its quintessential commodities. To the degree that many or most things in a society sometimes meet these criteria, the society may be said to be highly commoditized. In modern capitalist societies, it can safely be said that more things are likely to experience a commodity phase in their own careers, more contexts to become legitimate commodity contexts, and the standards of commodity candidacy to embrace a large part of the world of things than in non-capitalist societies. Though Marx was therefore right in seeing modern industrial capitalism as entailing the most intensely commoditized type of society, the comparison of societies in regard to the degree of 'commoditization' would be a most complex affair given the definitional approach to commodities taken here. By this definition, the term 'commodity' is used in the rest of this essay to refer to things that, at a certain *phase* in their careers and in a particular *context*, meet the requirements of commodity candidacy. Keith Hart's (1982) analysis of the importance of the growing hegemony of the commodity in the world would fit with the approach suggested here, except that commoditization is here regarded as a differentiated process (affecting matters of phase, context and categorization, differentially) and the capitalist mode of commoditization is seen as interacting with myriad other indigenous social forms of commoditization.

Three additional sets of distinctions between commodities are worth making here (others appear later in this essay) The first, which is a modified application of a distinction originally made by Jacques Maquet in 1971 in regard to aesthetic productions, divides commodities into the following four types: (1) commodities by *destination*, that is, objects intended by their producers principally for exchange; (2) commodities by *metamorphosis*, things intended for other uses that are placed into the commodity state; (3) a special, sharp case of commodities by metamorphosis are commodities by *diversion*, objects placed into a commodity state though originally specifically protected from it; (4) *ex-commodities* things retrieved, either temporarily or permanently, from the commodity state and placed in some other state. It also seems worth while to distinguish 'singular' from 'homo-geneous' commodities in order to discriminate between commodities whose candidacy for the commodity state is precisely a matter of their class characteristics (a perfectly standardized steel bar, indistinguishable in practical terms from any other steel bar) and those whose candidacy is precisely their uniqueness *within* some class (a Manet rather than a Picasso; one Manet rather than another). Closely related, though not identical, is the distinction between primary and secondary commodities; necessities and luxuries; and what I call mobile versus enclaved commodities. Nevertheless, all efforts at defining commodities are doomed to sterility unless they illuminate commodities in motion. This is the principal aim of the section that follows.

PATHS AND DIVERSIONS

Commodities are frequently represented as mechanical products of production regimes governed by the laws of supply and demand, I hope to show in this section that the flow of commodities in any given situation is a shifting compromise between socially regu-lated paths and competitively inspired diversions.

Commodities, as Igor Kopytoff points out, can usefully be regarded as having life his-tories. In this processual view, the commodity phase of the life history of an object does not exhaust its biography; it is culturally regulated; and its interpretation is open to indi-vidual manipulation to some degree. Further, as Kopytoff also points out, the question of what sorts of object may have what sorts of biography is more deeply a matter for social contest and individual taste in modern societies than in smaller-scale, non-monetized, preindustrial ones. There is, in Kopytoff's model, a perennial and universal tug-of-war between the tendency of all economies to expand the jurisdiction of com-moditization and of all cultures to restrict it. Individuals, in this view, can go with either tendency as it suits their interests or matches their sense of moral appropriateness, though in premodern societies the room for manoeuvre is usually not great. Of the many virtues of Kopytoff's model the most important, in my view, is that it proposes a gen-eral processual model of commoditization, in which objects may by moved both into and out of the commodity state. I am less comfortable with the opposition between sin-gularization and commoditization, since some of the most interesting cases (in what Kopytoff agrees are in the middle zone of his ideal–typical contrast) involve the more or less permanent commoditizing of singularities.

Two questions can be raised about this aspect of Kopytoff's argument. One would be that the very definition of what constitutes singularities as opposed to classes is a cultural question, just as there can be unique examples of homogeneous classes (the perfect steel bar) and classes of culturally valued singularities (such as works of art and designer-label clothing). On the other hand, a Marxist critique of this contrast would suggest that it is commoditization as a worldwide historical process that determines in very important ways the shifting relationship between singular and homogeneous things at any given moment in the life of a society. But the important point is that the commodity is not one kind of thing rather than another, but one phase in the life of some things. Here, Kopytoff and I are in full agreement.

This view of commodities and commoditization has several important implications, some of which are touched upon in the course of Kopytoff's argument. But my imme-diate concern is with one important aspect of this temporal perspective on the com-moditization of things, which concerns what I have called paths and diversions. I owe both these terms, and some measure of my understanding of the relationship between them, to Nancy Munn's contribution (Munn 1983) in an important collection of papers on a phenomenon that is of great importance to this topic, the celebrated kula system of the western Pacific (Leach and Leach 1983).

The exchange path taken by the necklaces and armrings of the kula system is both reflective and constitutive of social partnerships and struggles for pre-eminence. But a number of other things are worth noting about the circulation of these valuables. The first is that their exchange is not easily categorized as simple reciprocal exchange, far from the spirit of trade and commerce. Though monetary valuations are absent, both the nature of the objects and a variety of sources of flexibility in the system make it possible to have the sort of calculated exchange that I maintain is at the heart of the exchange of commodities. These complex non-monetary modes of valuation allow partners to negotiate what Firth (following Cassady 1974) calls 'exchange by private treaty', a situation in which something like price is arrived at by some negotiated process other than the impersonal forces of supply and demand (Firth 1983: 91). Thus, despite the presence of broad conventional exchange rates, a complex qualitative calculus exists (Campbell 1983: 245–6) which permits the competitive negotiation of personal estimates of value in the light of both short-and long-term individual interest (Firth 1983: 101). What Firth here calls 'indebtedness engineering' is a variety of the sort of calculated exchange that, by my definition, blurs the line between commodity exchange and other, more sentimental, varieties. The most important difference between the exchange of these commodities and the exchange of commodities in modern industrial economies is that the increment being sought in kula-type systems is in reputation, name or fame, with the critical form of capital for producing this profit being people rather than other factors of production (Strathern 1983: 80; Damon 1983: 339–40). Pricelessness is a luxury few commodities can afford.

Perhaps even more important than the calculative aspect of kula exchanges is the fact that these recent studies make it very difficult to regard the exchange of kula valuables as occurring only at the boundaries between communities, with more giftlike exchanges occurring within these communities (Damon 1983: 339). The concept of *kitoum* provides the conceptual and technical link between the large paths that the valuables take and the more intimate, regular and problematic intra-island exchanges (Weiner 1983; Damon 1983; Campbell 1983; Munn 1983). Though the term *kitoum* is complex and in certain respects ambiguous, it seems clear that it represents the articulation between the kula and other exchange modalities in which men and women transact in their own communities. *Kitoums* are valuables that one can place into the kula system or legitimately withdraw from it in order to effect 'conversions' (in Paul Bohannan's sense) between disparate levels of 'conveyance' (Bohannan 1955). In the use of *kitoum* we see the critical conceptual and instrumental links between the smaller and bigger paths that constitute the total world of exchange in Massim. As Annette Weiner has shown, it is a mistake to isolate the grander interisland system of exchange from the more intimate, but (for men) more suffocating local transfers of objects that occur because of debt, death and affinity (Weiner 1983: 164–5).

The kula system gives a dynamic and processual quality to Mauss's ideas regarding the mingling or exchange of qualities between men and things, as Munn (1983: 283) has noted with regard to kula exchange in Gawa: 'Although men appear to be the agents in defining shell value, in fact, without shells, men cannot define their own value; in this respect, shells and men are reciprocally agents of each other's value definition.' But, as Munn has observed, in the reciprocal construction of value, it is not only paths that play an important role, but diversions as well. The relations between paths and diversions is critical to the politics of value in the kula system, and proper orchestration of these relations is at the strategic heart of the system:

Actually, diversion is implicated in the path system, since it is one of the means of making new paths. Possession of more than one path also points to the probability of further diversions from one established path to another, as men become subject to the interests and persuasiveness of more than one set of partners. . . . In fact, men of substance in kula have to develop some capacity to balance operations: diversions from one path must later be replaced in order to assuage cheated partners and keep the path from disappearing, or to keep themselves from being dropped from the path.

(Munn 1983: 301)

These large-scale exchanges represent psychological efforts to transcend more humble flows of things, but in the politics of reputation, gains in the larger arena have implications for the smaller ones, and the idea of the *kitoum* assures that both conveyances and conversions have to be carefully managed for the greatest gains overall (Damon 1983: 317–23). The kula may be regarded as the paradigm of what I propose to call *tournaments of value*.

Tournaments of value are complex periodic events that are removed in some culturally well-defined way from the routines of economic life. Participation in them is likely to be both a privilege of those in power and an instrument of status contests between them. The currency of such tournaments is also likely to be set apart through well-understood cultural diacritics. Finally, what is at issue in such tournaments is not just status, rank, fame or reputation of actors, but he disposition of the central tokens of value in the society in question. Finally, though such tournaments of value occur in special times and places, their forms and outcomes are always consequential for the more mundane realities of power and value in ordinary life. As for the kula, so in such tournaments of value generally, strategic skill is culturally measured by the success with which actors attempt diversions or subversions of culturally conventionalized paths for the flow of things.

The idea of tournaments of value is an attempt to create a general category, following up a recent observation by Edmund Leach (1983: 535) comparing the kula system to the art world in the modern West. Baudrillard's analysis of the art auction in the contemporary West allows one to widen and sharpen this analogy. Baudrillard notes that the art auction, with its ludic, ritual and reciprocal aspects, stands apart from the ethos of conventional economic exchange, and that it 'goes well beyond economic calculation and concerns all the processes of the transmutation of values, from one logic to another logic of value which may be noted in determinate places and institutions' (Baudrillard 1981: 121). The following analysis by Baudrillard of the ethos of the art auction deserves quotation in full since it could so easily be an apt characterization of other examples of the tournament of value:

Contrary to commercial operations, which institute a relation of economic *rivalry* between individuals on the footing of form *equality*, with each one guiding his own calculation of individual appropriation, the auction, like the fête or the game, institutes a concrete community of exchange among peers. Whoever the vanquisher in the challenge, the essential function of the auction is the institution of a community of the privileged who define themselves as such by agonistic speculation upon a restricted corpus of signs. Competition of the aristocratic sort seals their *parity* (which has nothing to do with the formal equality of economic competition), and thus their collective caste privilege with respect to all others, from whom they are no longer separated merely by their purchasing power, but by the sumptuary and collective act of the production and exchange of sign values.

(1981: 117)

In making a comparative analysis of such tournaments of value, it may be advisable not to follow Baudrillard's tendency to isolate them analytically from more mundane economic exchange, though the articulation of such value arenas with other economic arenas is likely to be highly variable. I shall have no more to say on tournaments of value in the discussion of the relationship between knowledge and commodities late in this essay.

Though commodities, by virtue of their exchange destinies and mutual commensurability, tend to dissolve the links between persons and things, such a tendency is always balanced by a counter-tendency, in all societies, to restrict, control and channel exchange. In many primitive economies, primitive valuable display these socially restricted qualities. We owe to Mary Douglas (1967) the insight that many such valuables resemble coupons and licences in modern industrial economies. That is, although they resemble money, they are not generalized media of exchange but have the following characteristics: (1) the powers of acquisition that they represent are highly specific; (2) their distribution is controlled in various ways; (3) the conditions that govern their issue create a set of patron–client relationships; (4) their main function is to provide the necessary condition for entry to high-status positions, for maintaining rank, or for combining attacks on status; and (5) the social systems in which such coupons or licences function is geared to eliminating or reducing competition in the interests of a fixed pattern of status (Douglas 1967: 69). Raffia cloth in central Africa, wampum among the Indians of the eastern United States, shell money among the Yurok and the shell currency of Rossell Island and other parts of Oceania are examples of such 'commodity coupons' (in Douglas's phrase), whose restricted flow is at the service of the reproduction of social and political systems. Things, in such contexts, remain devices for reproducing relations between persons (see also Dumont 1980: 231). Such commodity coupons represent a transformational midpoint between 'pure' gifts and 'pure' commerce. With the gift, they share a certain insensitivity to supply and demand, a high coding in terms of etiquette and appropriateness and a tendency to follow socially set paths. With pure barter, their exchange shares the spirit of calculation, an openness to self-interest, and a preference for transactions with relative strangers.

In such restricted systems of commodity flow, where valuables play the role of coupons or licences designed to protect status systems, we see the functional equivalent but the technical inversion of 'fashion' in more complex societies. Where in the one case status systems are protected and reproduced by restricting equivalences and exchange in a *stable* universe of commodities, in a fashion system what is restricted and controlled is *taste* in an *ever-changing* universe of commodities, with the illusion of complete interchangeability and unrestricted access. Sumptuary laws constitute an intermediate consumption-regulating device, suited to societies devoted to stable status displays in exploding commodity contexts, such as India, China and Europe in the premodern period.

Such forms of restriction and the enclaved commodities they create sometimes provide the context and targets of strategies of diversions. Diversion, that is, may sometimes involve the calculated and 'interested' removal of things from an enclaved zone to one where exchange is less confined and more profitable, in some short-term sense. Where enclaving is usually in the interests of groups, especially the politically and economically powerful groups in any society, diversion is frequently the recourse of the entrepreneurial individual. But whether it is groups or individuals who are involved in either kind of activity, the central contrast is that, whereas enclaving seeks to protect certain things from commoditization, diversion frequently is aimed at drawing protected things into the zone of commoditization. Diversion, however, can also take the form of strategic shifts in path within a zone of commoditization.

Of course, the best examples of the diversion of commodities from their original nexus is to be found in the domain of fashion, domestic display, and collecting in the modern West. In the high-tech look inspired by the Bauhaus, the functionality of factories, warehouses and workplaces is diverted to household aesthetics. The uniforms of various occupations are turned into the vocabulary of costume. In the logic of found art, the everyday commodity is framed and aestheticized. These are all examples of what we might call commoditization by diversion, where value, in the art or fashion market, is accelerated or enhanced by placing objects and things in unlikely contexts. It is the aesthetics of decontextualization (itself driven by the quest for novelty) that is at the heart of the display, in highbrow western homes, of the tools and artefacts of the 'other': the Turkmen saddlebag, Masai spear, Dinka basket. In these objects, we see not only the equation of the authentic with the exotic everyday object but also the aesthetics of diversion. Such diversion is not only an instrument of decommoditization of the object but also of the (potential) intensification of commoditization by the enhancement of value attendant upon its diversion. This enhancement of value through the diversion of commodities from their customary circuits underlies the plunder of enemy valuables in warfare, the purchase and display of 'primitive' utilitarian objects, the framing of 'found' objects, the making of collections of any sort. In all these examples, diversions of things combine the aesthetic impulse, the entrepreneurial link and the touch of the morally shocking.

Nevertheless, diversions are meaningful only in relation to the paths from which they stray. Indeed, in looking at the social life of commodities in any given society or period, part of the anthropological challenge is to define the relevant and customary paths, so that the logic of diversions can properly, and relationally, be understood. The relationship between paths and diversions is itself historical and dialectical, as Michael Thompson (1979) has skilfully shown in regard to art objects in the modern West. Diversions that become predictable are on their way to becoming new paths, paths that will in turn inspire new diversions or returns to old paths. These historical relationships are rapid and easy to see in our own society, but less visible in societies where such shifts are more gradual.

CONCLUSION: POLITICS AND VALUE

Apart from learning some moderately unusual facts, and regarding them from a mildly unconventional point of view, is there any general benefit in looking at the social life of commodities in the manner proposed in this essay? What does this perspective tell us about value and exchange in social life that we did not know already, or that we could not have discovered in a less cumbersome way? Is there any point in taking the heuristic position that commodities exist everywhere and that the spirit of commodity exchange is not wholly divorced from the spirit of other forms of exchange?

In answering these questions, I shall not conduct a tedious review of the main observations made in the course of this essay, but shall go directly to the substance of my proposal. This essay took as its starting point Simmel's view that exchange is the source of value and not vice versa

Politics (in the broad sense of relations, assumptions and contests pertaining to power) is what links value and exchange in the social life of commodities. In the mundane, day-to-day, small-scale exchanges of things in ordinary life, this fact is not visible, for exchange has the routine and conventionalized look of all customary behaviour. But these many ordinary dealings would not be possible were it not for a broad set of agreements concerning what is desirable, what a reasonable 'exchange of sacrifices' comprises, and who is permitted to exercise what kind of effective demand in what circumstances. What is political about this process is not just the fact that it signifies and constitutes relations of privilege and social control. What is political about it is the constant tension between the existing frameworks (of price, bargaining and so forth) and the tendency of commodities to breach these frameworks. This tension itself has its source in the fact that not all parties share the same *interests* in any specific regime of value, nor are the interests of any two parties in a given exchange identical.

At the top of many societies, we have the politics of tournaments of value, and of calculated diversions that might lead to new paths of commodity flow. As expressions of the interests of elites in relation to commoners we have the politics of fashion, of sumptuary law and of taboo, all of which regulate demand. Yet since commodities constantly spill beyond the boundaries of specific cultures (and thus of specific regimes of value), such political control of demand is always threatened with disturbance. In a surprisingly wide range of societies, it is possible to witness the following common paradox. It is in the interests of those in power to freeze completely the flow of commodities, by creating a closed universe of commodities and a rigid set of regulations about how they are to move. Yet the very nature of contests between those in power (or those who aspire to greater power) tends to invite a loosening of these rules and an expansion of the pool of commodities. This aspect of elite politics is generally the Trojan horse of value shifts. So far as commodities are concerned, the source of politics is the tension between these two tendencies.

We have seen that such politics can take many forms: the politics of diversion and of display; the politics of authenticity and of authentication; the politics of knowledge and of ignorance; the politics of expertise and of sumptuary control; the politics of connoisseurship and of deliberately mobilized demand. The ups and downs of the relations within and between these various dimensions of politics account for the vagaries of demand. It is in this sense that politics is the link between regimes of value and specific flows of commodities. Ever since Marx and the early political economists, there has not been much mystery about the relationship between politics and production. We are now in a better position to demystify the demand side of economic life.

This paper first appeared in A. Appadurai (ed.) (1986) The Social Life of Things, *Cambridge: Cambridge University Press, pp. 3–30.*

REFERENCES

Alsop, J. (1981) *The Rare Art Traditions: A History of Art Collecting and its Linked Phenomena*, Princeton, N.J.: Princeton University Press.
Baudrillard, J. (1968) *Le Système des objets*, Paris: Gallimard.
—— (1975) *The Mirror of Production*, St Louis, Mo.: Telos Press.
—— (1981) *For a Critique of the Political Economy of the Sign*, St Louis, Mo.: Telos Press.
Bohannan, P. (1955) 'Some principles of exchange and investment among the Tiv', *American Anthropologist* 57: 60–70.
Bourdieu, P. (1977) *Outline of a Theory of Practice*, Cambridge: Cambridge University Press.
Campbell, S. F. (1983) 'Kula in Vakuta: the mechanics of Keda', in J. W. Leach and E. Leach (eds) *The Kula: New Perspectives on Massim Exchange*, Cambridge: Cambridge University Press, 201–27.
Cassady, R. Jr, (1974) *Exchange by Private Treaty*, Austin: University of Texas Bureau of Business Research.
Chapman, A. (1980) 'Barter as a universal mode of exchange', *L'Homme* 20(3): 33–83.
Damon, F. H. (1983) 'What moves the kula: opening and closing gifts on Woodlark Island', in J. W. Leach and E. Leach (eds) *The Kula: New Perspectives on Massim Exchange*, Cambridge: Cambridge University Press, 309–42.

Douglas, M. (1967) 'Primitive rationing: a study in controlled exchange', in R. Firth (ed.) *Themes in Economic Anthropology*, London: Tavistock, 119–47.

Douglas, M. and Baron Isherwood (1981) *The World of Goods*, New York: Basic Books.

Dumont, I. (1980) 'On value' (Radcliffe-Brown Lecture), *Proceedings of the British Academy* 66: 207–41.

Firth, R. (1983) 'Magnitudes and values in kula exchange', in J. W. Leach and E. Leach (eds) *The Kula: New Perspectives on Massim Exchange*, Cambridge: Cambridge University Press, 89–102.

Gregory, C. A. (1982) *Gifts and Commodities*, London: Academic Press.

Hart, K. (1982) 'On commoditization', in Esther Goody (ed.) *From Craft to Industry: The Ethnography of Proto-industrial Cloth Production*, Cambridge: Cambridge University Press, 37–54.

Hyde, L. (1979) *The Gift: Imagination and the Erotic Life of Property*, New York: Random House.

Kopytoff, I. (1986) 'The cultural biography of things', in A. Appadurai (ed.) *The Social Life of Things*, Cambridge: Cambridge University Press, 64–91.

Leach, E. (1983) 'The kula: an alternative view', in J. W. Leach and E. Leach (eds) *The Kula: New Perspective on Massim Exchange*, Cambridge: Cambridge University Press, 529–38.

Leach, J. W. and Leach, E. (eds) (1983) *The Kula: New Perspective on Massim Exchange*, Cambridge: Cambridge University Press.

Marx, K. (1971) *Capital* vol. 1, *A Critical Analysis of Capitalist Production*, Moscow: Progress Publishers. (Original publication 1887)

—— (1973) *Grundrisse: Foundations of the Critique of Political Economy*, New York: Vintage Books.

Mauss, M. (1976) *The Gift*, New York: Norton.

Miller, D. (ed.) (1983) 'Things ain't what they used to be', Special section of *RAIN* (*Royal Anthropological Institute News*), 59: 5–7.

Munn, Nancy D. (1983) 'Gawan kula: spatiotemporal control and the symbolism of influence', in J. W. Leach and E. Leach (eds) *The Kula: New Perspectives on Massim Exchange*, Cambridge: Cambridge University Press, 277–308.

Perlin, F. (1983) 'Proto-industrialization and pre-colonial South Asia', *Past and Present* 98: 30–94.

Price, J. A. (1980) 'The silent trade', in G. Dalton (ed.) *Research in Economic Anthropology*, Greenwich, Conn.: JAI Press, vol. 3: 75–96.

Sahlins, M. (1972) *Stone Age Economics*, New York: Aldine.

—— (1976) *Culture and Practical Reason*, Chicago: University of Chicago Press.

Seddon, D. (ed.) (1978) *Relations of Production: Marxist Approaches to Economic Anthropology*, London: Frank Cass.

Simmel, G. (1978) *The Philosophy of Money*, London: Routledge & Kegan Paul.

Sraffa, P. (1961) *Production of Commodities by Means of Commodities*, Cambridge: Cambridge University Press.

Strathern, A. J. (1983) 'The kula in comparative perspective', in J. W. Leach and E. Leach (eds) *The Kula: New Perspectives on Massim Exchange*, Cambridge: Cambridge University Press, 73–88.

Tambiah, S. J. (1984) *The Buddhist Saints of the Forest and the Cult of Amulets*, Cambridge: Cambridge University Press.

Taussig, M. T. (1980) *The Devil and Commodity Fetishism in South America*, Chapel Hill: University of North Carolina Press.

Thompson, M. (1979) *Rubbish Theory*, Oxford: Oxford University Press.

Weiner, A. B. (1983) 'A world of made is not a world of born: doing kula on Kiriwana', in J. W. Leach and E. Leach (eds) *The Kula: New Perspectives on Massim Exchange*, Cambridge: Cambridge University Press, 147–70.

14

Why fakes?

Mark Jones

Fakes are a way of subverting the established order of object value through the arts of deception. From another point of view they are, as Jones points out, legitimate histori- cal documents which tell as much (and sometimes more) about the time in which they were made, and the history of collecting and taste, as any other piece. They capture two important aspects of objects: they relate directly to notions of object value, usually in a straightforward saleroom price sense, and they are deeply implicated in the often mali- cious personalities of the fakers and the weaknesses of the collectors. Fakes are, of course, a particular focus of hazard and interest in the museum world: this piece is tak- en from the catalogue which accompanied the exhibition Fake? *put on at the British Museum in 1990.*

Fake? is an exhibition about deception, or rather the material evidence of the myriad deceptions practised by men upon their fellows over three millennia. It is a record of human frailty, of the deceit of those who made fakes and of the gullibility of those who were taken in by them – a curious subject at first sight for exhibition in the British Museum. Yet it can be argued that fakes, scorned or passed over in embarrassed silence by scholar, dealer and collector alike, are unjustly neglected; that they provide unri- valled evidence of the values and perceptions of those who made them, and of those for whom they were made.

Fakes can teach us many things, most obviously perhaps the fallibility of experts. Not a single object has been included here merely because it deceived an untutored layman. Most have been validated thrice over, on initial purchase by an experienced collector, on publication by a leading scholar and on acquisition by a great museum. What is being asserted is not that the less well-informed may sometimes make mistakes, though that is evidently true, but that even the most academically and intuitively gifted of individuals, even the most rigorously organized of institutions, can and will occasionally be wrong. And this is not, or not simply, because knowledge and experience can never be complete, but because perception itself is determined by the structure of expectations that under- pins it. Present Piltdown Man to a palaeontologist out of the blue and it will be rejected out of hand. Present it to a palaeontologist whose predictions about the 'missing link' have been awaiting just such evidence and it will seem entirely credible. Bring an excep- tionally rare Athenian coin to a classical numismatist and he will examine it with careful scepticism. Allow one of the greatest of all classical numismatists, Sir George Hill, a Director of the British Museum, to find such a coin *for himself*, mounted as a jewel around a lady's neck, and he will take its authenticity for granted.

This omnipresent fallibility is of wider significance than might be suggested by a misidentified coin or even a misapprehension about the whole course of human evolution. It can affect our conception of reality itself. One whole section of *Fake?* is devoted to the changing boundaries of belief, boundaries that were often marked and sometimes determined by fakes. The fabricators of the Vegetable Lambs of Tartary that grazed on the surrounding grass while joined to mother earth by an umbilical cord, of the 'Sea Bishop' that visited the King of Poland in 1531, or of the numerous mermen that reached Europe from Japan, altered, for a while at least, the mental universe inhabited by those who saw them. And this is not just a question of medieval credulity. Elsie and Frances Wright's fabricated photographs convinced Conan Doyle, creator of that paradigm of sceptical intelligence Sherlock Holmes, and millions of others, that there really were fairies at the bottom of the garden.

Even those resistant to such beliefs may be vitally affected by fakes. Though the disseminator of the 'Zinoviev letter' may have exaggerated when he claimed that it had lost the British Labour Party the 1924 general election and fundamentally altered the balance of power between the main political parties, there is no denying that smear campaigns based on forgeries, most notoriously the *Protocols of the Elders of Zion*, have influenced public opinion – and not only public opinion. A rather earlier forgery, the Donation of Constantine, was the legal basis of the medieval Papacy's claim to temporal power in the West and so, among other things, as Nicolas Barker points out, of Pope Adrian IV's grant of Ireland to Henry VI of England.

Such forgeries were far from being exceptional aberrations. It has recently been estimated that the great monastic houses of England were so busy forging writs in the century after the Norman Conquest that over half the surviving charters of Edward the Confessor may be spurious. No one can be sure, because their forgeries are so clever that it can still be difficult to detect them today. This illustrates the unrivalled potential of fakes as evidence of the sense of history possessed by their creators. In the fakers' work we can see exactly what it was that they believed to characterize the antiquity of the object faked; exactly what was necessary to meet expectations about such objects and so secure their acceptance.

The sense of history revealed by fakes is sometimes remarkable. As John Taylor notes, the ancient Egyptian forgers of the Shabaka Stone, which located the creation of the world in their home town of Memphis, not only claimed that they were copying an ancient, worm-eaten document, but also actually reproduced the layout of just such a document, and introduced archaic spelling and grammatical forms to give it credibility. There could be no better demonstration of the existence of a sophisticated sense of anachronism among the educated elite of Pharaonic Egypt.

Equally surprising is the almost total lack of any such sense demonstrated by some of the fakes surviving from Renaissance Europe. Neither the Constantine and Heraclius medals, nor the severed head of Pompey in the Cabinet des Médailles, Paris, nor the coin portraits of ancient worthies by Valerio Belli look remotely classical to the modern eye. There has therefore been a general tendency among art historians to assume that they could not have been intended to deceive. Andrew Burnett, however, has shown that they were. The earliest books on numismatics were in fact motivated in part by the existence of such fakes and by a desire to help the collector to avoid them.

Just as the fake itself is evidence of the historical sense of its maker and recipients, so its critical history is a gauge of the development, or decline, of such a sense thereafter. The denunciation of the Constantine and Heraclius medals in the early seventeenth century reflects the emergence of a perception of the stylistic norms of late classical and early

Byzantine art, and the realization that such pieces lay outside them. In much the same way the gradual exposure of the *Corpus hermeticum*, a highly influential collection of religious texts purporting to prefigure many of the central tenets of Christianity, began with the simple observation, in the late sixteenth century, that a letter from Hermes to Aesculapius could hardly be genuine if it included a reference to the sculptor Phidias (since it would have antedated his birth). It continued with Isaac Casaubon's much more sophisticated demonstration, in the early seventeenth century, that the whole collection was written in the Greek of the first century, not that of Herodotus or Hippocrates, let alone that of the much earlier period to which its composition was ascribed.

The development of a critical tradition has thus been intimately connected, in every field, with the exposure and even the production of fakes. As Christopher Ligota demonstrates, it was in a work purporting to establish the central position of the Etruscans in world history that Annius of Viterbo attacked the unreliability of certain ancient Greek historians and proposed new and highly influential rules for the assessment of historical evidence. This is a world in which poachers act simultaneously as gamekeepers, alerted to others' frauds by their own

Fakes are, however, only secondarily a source of evidence for the outlook of those who made and uncovered them. They are, before all else, a response to demand, an ever-changing portrait of human desires. Each society, each generation, fakes the thing it covets most. For the priests of ancient Memphis this was, as we have seen, the promotion of their cult and of their city. For a nineteenth-century nationalist, like Václav Hanka, it was a medieval tradition of epic poetry that would fire the heart of the Czech nation and lead it to statehood. For medieval monks it was the relics of saints and martyrs that would perform miracles, attract the faithful and ensure the endowment of their foundation. For Renaissance humanists it was relics of a different kind, of that source of all beauty and enlightenment, the ancient world. Succeeding generations added demand for the work of famous artists, for things associated with famous people and, by the late nineteenth century, for almost anything that spoke to them of the calm certainties of the vanished past.

It may be significant then that the great growth area for faking today is not the creation of religious relics, national epics, or works of art, nor even some specifically modern area like the production of spurious scientific data (though that is on the increase), but the massive counterfeiting of brand-named goods. Wherever there is a market for the perfume of Chanel or Dior, the watches of Rolex or Cartier, shirts by Giorgio Armani, luggage by Louis Vuitton or footware by Adidas, the counterfeiter is at work. Most of the purchasers of their work know that at the price they are paying they cannot be buying the real thing. They are buying an illusion – the illusion of status, of belonging, of success, conferred by the fraudulent reproduction of a famous name.

If fakes provide a unique portrait of the changing focuses of human desires, they also delineate the evolution of taste with unrivalled precision. Where there are fakes it is clear that there was a booming market in the things thus imitated: fakers are above all creatures of the market. Unencumbered by the individualism of a great artist or thinker, they move quickly to take advantage of the high prices produced by a new fashion before the development of expertise makes their task more difficult or, worse still, their activities undermine the market altogether (as was the case with the market for classical gems in the mid-nineteenth century). If the market concerned is in antiques, however broadly defined, the fakes produced for it will reflect its demands more accurately than the genuine works traded in it. The former mirror the perceived desires of collectors; the latter may pass unchanged through their hands.

Not all genuine objects remain untouched by their owners, however. Some are rendered more acceptable by restoration, a process that provides the same kind of evidence for the history of taste as fakes themselves. The history of restoration is indeed inextricably linked with that of fakes, as the section of *Fake?* devoted to the collection of classical antiquities in the late eighteenth century demonstrates. At this period the restoration of sculpture was not in itself controversial: no classical figure, however beautiful, was considered worthy of display unless complete. Since classical antiquities were almost always found damaged, restorers were much in demand and their skill lay in the creation of an illusion of completeness, in modifying the old and adding the new in such a way as to create a single unified whole. Faking only came into it when, as was commonly the case, the purchaser was deceived as to the extent of the restoration carried out. In the case of the famous Venus, now at Newby Hall in Yorkshire, the dealer Jenkins created one of the most expensive pieces of classical sculpture ever sold by joining an alien and recut head to a headless body, and selling the result as a complete figure. This is a paradigmatic example of a fake.

Restoration, however, also raises questions of a more complicated kind about the search for authenticity. In the early nineteenth century the crucial decision was taken not to restore the Elgin Marbles. To subsequent generations, reared on the notion that the peak of beauty was to be found in these fragmentary examples of ancient sculpture, previous attitudes to restoration seemed wrong. What had once been seen as returning works of art to their original state, so that they could be seen and appreciated in as near as possible the form that they had had in classical times, was now regarded as deception. So, for example, it was asserted that the restoration of the Aegina marbles by the famous Danish neo-classical sculptor Thorwaldsen amounted to forgery, and in the 1960s his additions were removed by the Munich Glyptothek, so that the original fragments could once again be seen as they really were. Now a new concept of authenticity is emerging which encourages us to accept that objects have a continuing history, that they are damaged and repaired, cleaned and restored, and that their present state records not only the moment of creation but also a whole subsequent sequence of events. Whether, in the light of this, the pursuit of authenticity requires the restoration of the Thorwaldsen restorations, or whether their removal should be accepted as another significant event in the continuing history of the Aegina marbles, is not yet clear. What is certain is that this controversy has a direct bearing on the treatment of fakes. These have too often been ruthlessly dismantled, victims of a puritanical zeal that would strip away the lie and reveal the truth behind it, even if the truth is a heap of uninteresting fragments and the fake was a construct of historical and aesthetic value.

If *Fake?* poses questions about authenticity, and the problems posed by the application of different concepts of authenticity by different groups of people to different types of object, it also, and most painfully, challenges the authenticity of our responses to them. Why, if what we value from a work of art is the aesthetic pleasure to be gained from it, is a successfully deceptive fake inferior to the real thing? Conscious of this problem, some have attempted to deny the importance, to them, of authorship. The great collector and scholar Richard Payne Knight, when attempting to ascertain the truth about the Flora cameo, which he had purchased as antique but which the contemporary gem-engraver Benedetto Pistrucci claimed to have made himself, told the dealer who had sold it to him that it did not matter whether it was old or new since its beauty was unaffected by its age. Similarly, the purchasers of the supposedly Renaissance bust of Lucrezia Donati expressed their pleasure, on discovering that it was a fake, that an artist of such talent was still alive. But it would be unwise to rely on museums, dealers or private collectors taking that attitude today.

What most of us suspect, that aesthetic appreciation is not the only motor of the art market, becomes evident when a work of art is revealed as a fake. When a 'Monet' turns out not to be, it may not change its appearance but it loses its value as a relic. It no longer provides a direct link with the hand of a painter of genius, and it ceases to promise either spiritual refreshment to its viewer or status to its owner. And even though the work in question remains physically unaltered, our aesthetic response to it is profoundly changed. The great art historian Abraham Bredius wrote of Van Meegeren's 'Vermeer' forgery *Christ at Emmaus*:

> It is a wonderful moment in the life of a lover of art when he finds himself suddenly confronted with a hitherto unknown painting by a great master, untouched, on the original canvas, and without any restoration, just as it left the painter's studio! And what a picture! Neither the beautiful signature . . . nor the pointillé on the bread which Christ is blessing, is necessary to convince us that what we have here is a – I am inclined to say – *the* masterpiece of Johannes Vermeer of Delft.
>
> (*Burlington Magazine*, November 1937)

After Van Meegeren's exposure, however, it became apparent that his forgeries were grotesquely ugly and unpleasant paintings, altogether dissimilar to Vermeer's. His success is, retrospectively, literally incredible . M. Kirby Talley Jr concludes his piece on Van Meegeren with the observation 'had Van Meegeren been a better artist . . . he might just have succeeded in producing "Vermeers" which would have fooled more people longer than the ones he created'. Yet as he himself tells us, Van Meegeren was exposed not because he ceased to fool people but because he fooled one art lover too many, Hermann Goering, and was forced to prove himself a forger in order to clear himself of the more serious charge of having sold a national treasure to the enemy.

Van Meegeren's success seems incredible. But what is really extraordinary about it is that the pattern revealed by his case is in fact commonplace. The reaction of Bredius and his numerous distinguished colleagues, far from being exceptionally foolish, was normal; fakes are very often greeted with rapture by *cognoscenti* and general public alike. It is generally true that fakers are known to us only because they have revealed themselves, overcoming considerable public and scholarly scepticism to prove the works in question theirs only to find that what was so admired as the work of another is now seen as trite and even maladroit.

From this it is clear that both private and public collections must still contain many works by fakers less boastful, quarrelsome or unlucky than Bastianini, Dossena or Van Meegeren. And they will continue to do so. Some will be exposed by advances in scientific techniques; but many objects cannot be scientifically dated, and even where analysis is appropriate its conclusions must be based on a control group of 'genuine' objects which may itself be contaminated. Others, anchored in their own time, may become 'dated' and expose themselves – as Lord Lee's Botticelli was betrayed by her resemblance to 1920s film stars. But while sensitivity to stylistic anachronism is a powerful tool, it is far from an infallible one. When a group of fakes is accepted into the canon of genuine work all subsequent judgements about the artist or period in question are based on perceptions built in part upon the fakes themselves. Had Bastianini not become enraged by the profits being made from his work we, like Kenneth Clark's art master, might have a conception of Renaissance art formed around his work.

This, finally, is our complaint against fakes. It is not that they cheat their purchasers of money, reprehensible though that is, but that they loosen our hold on reality, deform and falsify our understanding of the past. What makes them dangerous, however, also makes them valuable. The feelings of anger and shame that they arouse among those who have been deceived are understandable, but the consequent tendency to dispose of or destroy fakes, once identified, is misguided. Even if the errors of the past only provided lessons for the future, they would be worthy of retention and study. But fakes do far more than that. As keys to understanding the changing nature of our vision of the past, as motors for the development of scholarly and scientific techniques of analysis, as subverters of aesthetic certainties, they deserve our closer attention, while as the most entertaining of monuments to the wayward talents of generations of gifted rogues they claim our reluctant admiration.

This paper first appeared in M. Jones (1990) Fake? The Art of Deception, *London: British Museum Publications Ltd, pp. 11–16.*

15

Cannibal tours, glass boxes and the politics of interpretation

Michael Ames

An important aspect of the western view of the material world is how it has treated the material culture of those outside the western tradition. These traditions are often described as 'the Other', either implicitly or, increasingly, explicitly as writers explore how 'us' and 'the other' are constituted, and how the other, including the material other, has been appropriated to serve western interests. Since much of the non-western material in the West is held in museum collections, these issues are of particular importance to museum staff and visitors, and the surrounding issues are particular sharp when, as in the situation Ames discusses, the land has its own indigenous and non-western cultures.

The film *Cannibal Tours* (O'Rourke 1987), a sardonic portrayal of a group of European tourists travelling through Papua New Guinea villages, also parodies anthropology. It opens with the statement: 'The strangest thing in a strange land is the stranger who visits it.' There too lies the irony of anthropology and the anthropologist as professional tourist, for when we attempt to make others less strange to us, we make those others strangers to themselves.

The problems involved in representing others to ourselves, as Virginia Dominguez (1988) notes in her paper 'On creating a material heritage', are common to the entire discipline of anthropology and beyond, not just to the museum branch. The following remarks therefore should be taken in that broader, discipline-wide sense, even though the examples are specific to museums. If there is a need to reconstruct anthropology – and a good case can certainly be made for that (as for other disciplines) – then there is an opportunity here for museum anthropologists to play leading roles because of the ways museums are embedded in the social, economic and political complexities of contemporary society. Because public criticisms frequently have immediate implications for museums, museum anthropologists are frequently more inclined than their academic colleagues to seek immediate, practical solutions. Thus critiques of museum anthropology usually also provide assessments of the broader discipline of which it is a part and suggest directions for general reconstruction. Considering Parezo's (1988) observation that vastly more people learn about anthropology from museums than from universities, what museums do will drastically affect the rest of anthropology. The future of anthropology in museums, therefore, may very well be central to the future of the discipline as a whole.

Most of the criticisms of museums flow from the simple fact that they are the self-appointed keepers of other people's material and self-appointed interpreters of others' histories. They circle around the question of who controls the rights to manage and interpret history and culture. Parezo, for example, indicates that many of the methods of museum collecting, especially during the nineteenth and early parts of the twentieth centuries, would be questionable by today's moral standards. And museum exhibition techniques continue to impose academic classifications – our 'glass boxes' of interpretation upon diverse cultures. The sizes and shapes of these boxes have changed with the theoretical fashions within anthropology – ranging from progressive technology exhibits, comparative, cultural displays of family and work groups, and dioramas or stage sets to demonstrations and performances. They always remain anthropological boxes, however, 'freezing' others into academic categories and to that mythical anthropological notion of time called the 'ethnographic present'.

Those boxed in, especially the indigenous peoples who have served as the primary subjects of anthropological study, were never terribly happy about their museumification and often objected. What is significant is that by the 1980s, after one hundred years and more of boxing others, museums (and their academic counterparts) are only now beginning to hear what the objects of classification, especially those same indigenous groups, have been saying all along: they want to be out of the boxes, they want their materials back, and they want control over their own history and its interpretation, whether the vehicles of expression be museum exhibits, classroom discourses or scholarly papers, textbooks and monographs. Since those who control history are the ones who benefit from it, people should have the right to the facts of their own lives. This is surely a cornerstone of postmodernist ideology and one of the central political implications of interpretation.

The criticisms are encouraging museum professionals and those interested in museums to reconsider and re-evaluate the very foundations upon which museum work is based. Witness the five papers presented in the 'Objects of Culture' symposium at the 1988 annual meeting of American anthropologists: the three by curatorial specialists (Parezo, Jacknis and Welsh) and two by interested non-museum, academic anthropologists (Dominguez and Errington) are all, in one way or another, critical of anthropology. How then do we proceed? Criticizing our past is the first step; reconstructing for the future is perhaps the next. Criticism also needs to be placed in perspective, and with some limits placed upon it, for museums alone cannot shoulder all the burdens of the past. Although there is much that museums have done wrong, or did not do at all, they also do some things right. Thus, when mounting criticisms it helps to recognize not only the bad and the ugly but also the good and the useful, to give credit where credit is due, and to build upon the good examples.

These papers suggest some ways in which we might break the glass to liberate indigenous peoples from the hegemony of our systems of classification and in turn liberate ourselves from an unwelcomed over-dependence on other people's material. Jacknis points to the importance of considering 'the historical contextualization of the collecting process', recording what might be called the 'social patina' that accrues over time as an object moves from maker to user to collector to preserver to exhibitor. Tom McFeat (1967), when he was chief ethnologist at the National Museum of Canada, proposed the formula: 'Objects + data = specimen'. Jacknis would have us look at these data as embodying an evolutionary development of meanings which have been superimposed one upon the next as objects are continually recontextualized throughout their careers. 'The character . . . of an ethnological phenomenon,' Jacknis quotes Franz Boas (1887:66) as saying, 'is not expressed by its appearance, by the state in which it is, but by its whole history.'

The object as palimpsest? Milton Singer quotes the late Jawaharlal Nehru's metaphor to describe the civilizations of India, a task which may appear rather different from the one considered here, but which shares some epistemological problems. Nehru wrote in *The Discovery of India* (1946: 47, quoted in Singer 1988: 13) that Indian civilization is 'like some ancient palimpsest',

> on which layer upon layer of thought and revery had been inscribed, and yet no suc-
> ceeding layer had completely hidden or erased what had been written previously.
> All of these existed together in our conscious or subconscious selves, though
> we might not be aware of them. And they had gone to build up the complex and
> mysterious personality of India.

Is a museum also a palimpsest, Singer asks (telephone conversation, Dec. 1987)? If we follow Dominguez, yes it is, just like the object. (And why not, to make a fair trade, use 'living museum' as a metaphor for the civilization of India?)

Jacknis's reference to process combined with the palimpsest metaphor suggest at least two levels of analysis: (1) the social history of the object from origin to current destination, including the changing meanings as the object is continually redefined along the way; and (2) the museum itself as layered object and machine for recontextualization or, to borrow Dominguez's term, 'objectification'. The Heard Museum's 1988–9 exhibition, 'Exotic Illusions', described in Peter Welsh's paper, which dealt with how we interpret objects from other cultures – as art, exotic curios, commercial souvenirs (our perceptions chang-ing according to the context of representation) – illustrates these levels. The first level con-cerns the way objects are recontextualized when they are collected; the second, with how museums actively assist that redefinition, sometimes directing it and other times confirm-ing it, through their acquisition and interpretation programmes.

Jacknis and Dominguez suggest that anthropologists need not limit themselves to study-ing the first or original meaning of the objects (that is, to the makers and initial users) or to spending all their energies on attempts to reconstruct that early meaning – the archaeology of objects, as it were. They can also explore the evolution of meaning over object careers and the history of the institutional mechanisms that produce and repro-duce those meanings. Anthropology, the late Harvard anthropologist Clyde Kluckhohn liked to say to his students, was the study of others in order to understand ourselves. Tracking the semantic career, the acquiring of social patina, of objects and museums – the 'anthropology of museums' – illustrates how people over time reveal themselves through the ways they interpret or recontextualize others.

Another illustration of a museum 'doing it right', by presenting both sides of the inter-pretive equation (one's own and the other), is the Native-operated Woodland Indian Cul-tural Education Centre (Brantford, Ontario), whose 1988 exhibition, 'Fluffs and Feathers', drew a connection between white stereotypes of Natives expressed in history books, literature, art and the media – 'the Myth of the Savage' – and their own self-images. 'Every culture creates images of how it sees itself and the rest of the world,' cura-tor Deborah Doxtator (1988a: 13–14; see also 1988b) wrote in the exhibition Resource Guide. 'Incidental to these images of self-definition are definitions of the "Other".' Stereotypes, the exhibition suggests, institutionalize forms of privilege, empowering those who are exalted and disempowering those portrayed as the 'Other'. 'What then happens to a culture whose symbols are chosen by outsiders, by those who do not under-stand its deepest beliefs, structures and ways of life?' Joanna Bedard (1988), executive director of the Woodland Centre, asks in her Foreword to the Resource Guide. Stereo-types of the Indian, Doxtator notes (ibid.: 14), 'often operate as a form of social control, [justifying] why it is all 'right to deny other racial groups access to power and financial rewards'. Every society creates its own images about itself and other people connected to it, Doxtator (ibid.: 67–8) continues:

The non-Indian use of Indian symbols operates within a hierarchical society that is based on the principle of economic and social inequality. From the day children start school, they are ranked and judged according to their academic performance, their athletic abilities, their creative talents. It is not surprising, then, that non-Indian images of Indians are either at one extreme of the 'ranking' spectrum or the other – either Indians are depicted as 'savages' below Euro-Canadian 'civilization' or as 'noble savages' who are more moral, faster, stronger, kinder than any Euro-Canadian. Rarely have Indians been treated by Canadian society as equals.

This one fact alone is probably the key factor in understanding the destructive effects of the images created by non-Indians. It is not right that anyone should define someone else, tell them who they are and where they 'fit in.' You cannot do this to someone if you think of them as your equal.

The introductory panel in the 'Fluffs and Feathers' exhibition asks visitors to think about their own images of Indians. What it is really asking, Doxtator continues (ibid.: 68), is, 'How do you see yourself?'

The Heard's 'Exotic Illusions' and the Woodland's 'Fluffs and Feathers' expose those who collect and classify the works of others. To reiterate Virginia Dominguez's point (1988), museums provide fruitful information about people's continual struggles to control their worlds (including alien worlds) through their objectifications or classifications. 'Our own processes of objectification provide us not just with the objects but also with the categories by which we may see some things and not others as objects,' she continues. Museums are not only machines for recontextualization; they also document the process itself, through their histories and the collections they appropriate over time. Through our objectifications we study the objectifications of others. Dominguez says cultural institutions are 'continuous sources of data about their varying constituencies' objectifications of the world and their struggles for control'. They are 'objects of culture, objects of heritage, objects of power made possible by particular combinations of social, ideological, cognitive, economic, and political conditions'. They recall for Dominguez Foucault's thesis on the emergence of 'Man' in the nineteenth century,

> when, he argued, the idea of human beings as actors or doers (subjects) converged with the idea of human beings as objects of knowledge and study. The awkward duality of being both subject and object generated enormous creative tension then, giving birth to most of the 'human sciences' – both 'natural' and 'social.'

This view brings the study of museums in line with other theoretical interests. Objects, like people, have social lives, Appadurai (1988: 5) tells us in his discussion of commodities (objects with economic value), and this life history (Nehru's palimpsest process) needs study:

> We have to follow the things themselves, for their meanings are inscribed in their forms, their uses, their trajectories. It is only through the analysis of these trajectories that we can interpret the human transactions and calculations that enliven things. Thus, even though from a *theoretical* point of view human actors encode things with significance, from a *methodological* point of view it is the things-in-motion that illuminate their human and social context [emphasis in the original].

The object as commodity, as artefact, as specimen, as art, as someone else's heirloom, treasured cultural heritage, or sacred emblem: these are different ways of seeing the same thing. They are all properties or values of the object, all phases in its life. Values may be imposed by those wishing to possess or appropriate the object, and others asserted by those claiming moral jurisdiction. These transformations of meaning and use during the objects' careers could be better represented in museum interpretations. The longer the career of an object, however, the more segmented its history becomes, and the more knowledge about it becomes fragmented, contradictory differentiated, and fodder for commodification (Appadurai 1988: 56) and dispute.

Dominguez and Appadurai remind us that objects are, along with everything else, expressions of power relationships. Reconstruction involves repowering the object, investing it with the authority and privilege of those currently possessing it, who then impose upon it (and upon those whom it represents) their own histories. The process of reconstruction thus entails a shift in power and status of the object and of those formerly and presently associated with it. Once an object has been acquired by a museum, Balfe (1987: 4) says in reference to 'art' objects, that context attracts the power plays of status seekers who appropriate art to their own ends:

> Not surprisingly, like individual patrons, both corporations and governments seek the reflected glory, the gilt by association, with artworks supposedly beyond price and above politics. At the same time, such sponsors seek to re-embed the decontextualized art in wider systems of meaning which they (more or less) control. The less aesthetically aware the audience, the more likely the recontextualizing is to occur according to the sponsors' agenda.

Here are a number of issues to resolve: an object's checkered, commodified, disputatious, palimpsest-like career; competition for power and status; appropriation of others; the tensions between viewing and being viewed; the mixed and contradictory messages; and the presence of different audiences not all equally aware of what is going on nor all seeing the same thing. In both his paper and the 'Exotic Illusions' exhibition he curated, Peter Welsh (1988) provides an example of the competing objectifications, the realities or illusions – which, given the layered nature of objects, may amount to the same thing – museums construct for different constituencies. He calls these the 'visiting audience' (those who come to view) and 'the constituents' (those whose cultures are being viewed). Shelly Errington (1988) describes the 'magic realism' or 'hyper-realism' that has become a prominent, almost standard form of museum objectification ('mystification' would be more compatible with her perspective, though that probably amounts to the same thing): the artificial construction of a real-world diorama or stage set. Like the emperor and his new clothes, when the hyper-realistic dioramas are identified as the imaginary fabrications they are, rather than the realistic portrayals they are meant to be, will museums continue to create them? Probably. And will visitors care if they are told that the exhibits are artificially made to depict an arbitrary realism? Probably not. Welsh's classification of audience types, each expecting something different, each entering with a different knowledge, suggests a way of understanding such conundrums.

The question of audience leads to other issues. Museums serve multiple audiences, including the visitors and constituents Welsh identified, each of whom can be subdivided into very different groups. Many are anything but indifferent to museums and some are hardly benign. Museum visitors expect, and will frequently demand, to be educated and entertained, whereas those whose cultures are being exhibited (Welsh's (1988) constituents who are our 'originating populations') express concern over how they are being used for others' entertainment: 'What, or whom, exhibits represent, and to whom it, or they, may be represented,' Welsh notes, 'is the question that concerns us here.'

At 'Preserving our Heritage', a 1988 conference of indigenous people and museum workers held in Ottawa, Tommy Owlijoot, who was director of the Eskimo Point Cultural Centre in northern Canada, said that whites have benefited from the display of Inuit culture for a hundred years or more, and it was time to redress the balance. As Parezo observed, anthropology provided a past for a new, expanding country by appropriating the past of the recently subjugated Native Americans. Once seemingly reasonable, it is no longer acceptable appropriation. Owlijoot and many other Native Americans are calling upon museums to start repaying their 'debt' by balancing the scales. At the same conference, Christopher McCormick (Watts 1988: 16; Assembly of First Nations 1989: 11), spokesperson for the Native Council of Canada, said:

> Today, Native people are talking about reconquering our homeland. . . . We are not talking about a violent reconquest, a war of peoples. We are talking about taking control over our own lives, our cultures, and most importantly, the interpretation of our cultures past and present. . . .

> The pattern in Canada, as in the United States, has been to assume our imminent demise, take our sacred objects and lock them up in mausoleums for dead birds and dinosaurs. . . . It is not surprising then that the cultural professionals – anthropologists, archaeologists, museum directors – have often been the handmaidens of colonialism and assimilation.

The politics of representation – who can represent whom, how, where, and with what, Dominguez's 'questions of authenticity, authority, appropriation, and canonization of knowledge and meaning' – have become central for museums and for all students of culture. Who controls history, who has the moral right to control it, and who benefits? The traditional museum privilege is being challenged. 'The new project is the reconquest,' McCormick continued (Watts 1988: 17):

> We *were*, we *are* and *will be* the First People. We will refuse to allow people to appropriate or interpret our Cultures for their own ends. It will be our elders, our specialists, our historians and our anthropologists, our scientists who from now on will be the interpreters of our Culture. That is what self-determination means and we will have no less.

'We are well aware that many people have dedicated their time, careers, and their lives to showing what they believe is the accurate picture of indigenous peoples', Georges Erasmus, national chief of the Assembly of First Nations, co-sponsors of 'Preserving Our Heritage', said in his opening remarks (Assembly of First Nations 1989: 2). 'We thank you for that,' he continued, 'but we want to turn the page.'

If representations of others – our 'magic realisms' – are inventions, Dominguez (1988) asks, how should we judge the inventors? 'Should they be viewed as unethical, manipulative, opportunistic, normal, creative, unaware?' Are museum curators the cultural imperialists and missionaries of the postmodern age? The controversy surrounding the Glenbow Museum's 1988 exhibition, 'The Spirit Sings: Artistic Traditions of Canada's First Peoples', mounted in association with the Calgary Winter Olympics, demonstrated how cultural interpretation and political interest can become inextricably entwined in the minds of the public, professional and Native communities, and how those involved on *all* sides of the controversy, both Native and non-Native, viewed the others and were viewed, interchangeably, as *both* unethical and creative, *both* manipulative and normal, *both* victim and aggressor. The Lubicon Lake Indian Band in northern Alberta called for a boycott of the Calgary Olympics and of 'The Spirit Sings' to call attention to its long-standing land claims. Many individuals and organizations supported the boycott. In the process public debate shifted from land claims to questions about the propriety of a museum mounting an exhibition of Native artefacts in the face of Native political protests and while the major corporate sponsor of the exhibition was drilling on lands claimed by the Lubicon. The exhibition went ahead and so did the boycott. The Lubicon land claim was still unresolved when representatives of museums and Native organizations met in Ottawa in September 1988 and later in November to discuss the political implications of heritage management and interpretation highlighted by the exhibit and its boycott; it remained unresolved when the exhibition closed in November 1988 (and remains unresolved as of December 1991). A joint First Peoples–Canadian Museums Association Task Force was established following the November 1988 meeting. After meeting over several years it produced recommendations on how to improve relations between First Nations and museums (Nicks and Hill 1991).

Additional examples of disputed interpretations were cited at both national Canadian conferences and at a third in October associated with the 'Fluffs and Feathers' exhibition (Doxtator 1988a). Native delegates on all three occasions made it clear that museums were expected to repatriate artefacts and histories and to allow Natives to represent themselves or at least to share control. Minorities and indigenous peoples everywhere are making similar demands, of course. To give one example, Maori scholar Sidney Moko Mead stated (quoted in McManus 1988: 12): 'Maori people are taking charge of their heritage. No longer will they tolerate other people speaking for them and about their *taonga* [treasured cultural possessions].'

There is a natural move everywhere towards self-determination, for the benefits of democracy are self-evident. Interesting, for museums at least, is a growing public sentiment, both among anthropology audiences and within the profession, favouring this move among indigenous peoples, at least towards self-interpretation if not towards full economic and political self-determination. This call is made to art museums and galleries as well as to anthropology and history museums. It should be noted, however, that the 'art' problem is in some ways the reverse of the 'artefact' problem. Anthropology and history museums control indigenous histories by *including* in their collections and exhibitions heritage materials they classify as 'artefacts' or 'specimens'; art museums and galleries control more by *excluding*, by not collecting or exhibiting indigenous 'arts' except for those that fall within the hegemonic domain of the western theory of aesthetics, Appadurai's (1988: 28) 'aesthetics of decontextualization'. Indigenous artists (in Canada many are represented by the Society for Canadian Artists of Native Ancestry) call for acceptance of their work by the art establishment, while Native elders, religious groups, and politicians challenge the traditional recognition provided by museums. This is no contradiction, simply the quest for some control in two different cultural arenas – to be included in one and emancipated from the other.

Let the art establishment take its lumps at another time. Museums and anthropology are responding to these initiatives, though how effectively remains to be seen. 'As representatives of a kind of institution whose short history can be traced directly to colonial expansion and domination,' says Welsh, echoing Dominguez's consideration of appropriation and domination and McCormick's castigation of the professional handmaidens of colonialism, 'some of us are, understandably I think, concerned with the shape of museums in the future.' And with actively shaping that future, we might add.

If museums empower people to speak for themselves, will they consequently lose their own institutional or professional voices? Welsh contends they need not. He rejects the relativist thesis that museums should only allow constituents to speak; self-representation is not the only appropriate representation. Museums and anthropologists can continue to speak about others, though of course no longer *for* them (a right they once may have assumed but never really had). They can speak jointly with those whose materials they keep or study. They can continue to speak about cultural encounters, the careers of objects and institutions, and the complicated objectifications that occur during them. Anthropologists can continue to explore with others the 'symbolic mediation of cultural diversity' (Phillips 1988: 60) in an increasingly complex world. They can speak more frequently about the cultures of their audiences, as 'Exotic Illusions' does so well. Important roles for museums remain. In this world of 'mixed-up differences', Clifford Geertz concluded in his recent analysis of anthropology literature (1988: 60), there is a persistent need to facilitate conversation across the ubiquitous divisions of ethnicity, class, gender, language and race. The task for anthropology, he continues, is 'to enlarge the possibility of intelligible discourse between people quite different from one another in interest, outlook, wealth, and power, and yet contained in a world where, tumbled as they are into endless connection, it is increasingly difficult to get out of each other's way'.

In this tumbled world remains the museum's problem of having multiple responsibilities to diverse audiences. What, Welsh asks (1988), happens to the educational and scientific missions when a museum honours the constituents' demand for privacy ahead of the visitors' desire for information? 'What do visitors need to know?' he continues, 'and how do we let visitors in on the fact there are things we do not feel it appropriate to tell them?' Can we serve the needs and meet the standards of colleagues and scholars if we withhold information from exhibitions and publications? The rights to privacy always need to be balanced with the rights to know. The challenge for museums is not to present the 'facts' about cultures, Welsh (1988) concludes, but rather 'to find ways to educate visitors about the very nature of facts. About the fact that information is not only power, but also a responsibility and is deserving of respect.'

We might conclude with Welsh and Dominguez, using the latter's words, that museums are 'prime participants in the much broader sociopolitical arena which conceptualizes and reconceptualizes OBJECTS'. Having these meaningful things around, she says, 'reminds us vividly of the power and the limitations of representation – that when all is said and done, we human beings will still (and probably always) have to grapple with ways to relate to, signify, employ, and dispose of things we see, touch, smell, and feel that play some role in our lives'. Turning the page and empowering people to speak for themselves, however worthy a project, will not dissolve this inventive quality of objectification. Indigenous peoples are equally prone to 'inventing culture', of course, and they should have equal rights to do so. One task for anthropology is to make that process – 'the very nature of facts' – more visible, comprehensible and accessible to all the audiences. Our purpose is not just to identify the careers of objects and institutions, like collecting and arranging so many butterflies, but also to use this information to liberate dominated peoples from the hegemonic interpretations of others so that they can speak for themselves. It is part of the struggle for control over the production of commonsense understandings of our world, a task to which a critical theory of museums can contribute.

What we can learn from 'The Objects of Culture' (a comfortable academic symposium) and 'Preserving Our Heritage' (a nervous meeting between indigenous peoples and museum professionals) is that the interconnected circumstances of a tumbled world in which museums, anthropologists and their audiences work are changing in complex, tangled ways and will continue to do so. Museums, therefore, need to chart their futures with care and sensitivity since they are very much an integral part of the larger picture and play some part in its production and reproduction. As Georges Erasmus (Assembly of First Nations) told delegates in Ottawa at the November 1988 conference, 'We are embarking on the beginning of a different kind of relationship.' The time has come to break a few old glass boxes to make room for new ones, and never mind the cannibals.

This paper first appeared in M. Ames (ed.) (1991) Cannibal Tours and Glass Boxes: the Anthropology of Museums, *Canada: University of British Columbia Press, pp. 139–50.*

REFERENCES

Appadurai, Arjun (1988) 'Introduction: commodities and the politics of value', in Arjun Appadurai (ed) *The Social Life of Things: Commodities in Cultural Perspective*, Cambridge: Cambridge University Press, 3–63.

Assembly of First Nations (1989) Minutes of 'Preserving Our Heritage' Conference, Ottawa, 3–5 November 1988. (Dated 18 January 1989)

Balfe, Judith H. (1987) 'Affinities of art and politics: gilt by association', *Controversies in Art and Culture* 1(1): 1–17.

Bedard, Joanna (1988) 'Foreword', in D. Doxtator (ed.) *Fluffs and Feathers: An Exhibition on the Symbols of Indianness. A Resource Guide*, Brantford, Ontario: Woodland Indian Cultural Education Centre, 5.

Boas, Franz (1887) 'Museums of ethnology and their classification', *Science* 9: 587–9.

Dominguez, Virginia R. (1988) 'On creating a material heritage', paper presented to the symposium 'The Objects of Culture', annual meeting of the American Anthropological Association, Phoenix, Ariz., 19 November.

Doxtator, Deborah (1988a) *Fluffs and Feathers: An Exhibition on the Symbols of Indianness. A Resource Guide*, Brantford, Ontario: Woodland Indian Cultural Education Centre.

—— (1988b) 'The home of Indian culture and other stories in the museum: erasing the stereotypes', *Muse* 6(3): 26–31.

Errington, Shelly E. (1988) 'Objects of power', paper presented to the special symposium, 'The Objects of Culture', annual meeting of the American Anthropological Association, Phoenix, Ariz., 19 November.

Geertz, Clifford (1988) *Works and Lives: The Anthropologist as Author*, Stanford: Stanford University Press.

McFeat, Tom F. S. (1967) 'The object of research in museums', *Contributions to Ethnology 5*. Bulletin 204, Ottawa, National Museums of Canada, 91–9.

McManus, Greg (1988) 'The question of significance and the interpretation of Maori culture in New Zealand museums', *AGMANZ Journal* 19(4): 8–12.

Nehru, Jawaharlal (1946) *The Discovery of India*, New York: John Day.

Nicks, Trudy and Hill, Tom (1991) *Turning the Page: Forging New Partnerships between Museums and First Peoples*, Ottawa: Canadian Museums Association.

O'Rourke, Dennis (director) (1987) *Cannibal Tours* [film], Los Angeles: Direct Cinema.

Parezo, Nancy J. (1988) 'A glass box for everyone: displaying other cultures', paper presented to the special symposium, 'The Objects of Culture', annual meeting of the American Anthropological Association, Phoenix, Ariz., 19 November.

Phillips, Ruth (1988) 'Indian art: where do you put it?' *Muse* 6(3): 64–71.

Singer, Milton (1988) 'A changing American image of India: the palimpsest of a civilization', foreword to Carla M. Borden (ed.) *Contemporary Indian Tradition: Voices on Culture, Nature and the Challenge of Change*, Washington: Smithsonian Institution, 1–17.

Watts, Dolly (1988) 'Cultural empowerment within museums and anthropology', unpublished paper, Vancouver, University of British Columbia Museum of Anthropology.

Welsh, Peter H. (1988) 'Exotic illusions: museum exhibits and cultural interpretation', paper presented to the special symposium 'Objects of Culture', annual meeting of the American Anthropological Association, Phoenix, Ariz., 19 November.

16

Craft
M. Shanks

The past is another kind of Other, and its material is equally open to political appro-
priation in the present. This can be done in a number of ways, all of them deeply sig-
nificant, which include the construction of heroes and monuments at a national or
regional level, and the offering of comforting nostalgia at a personal level. In this piece
Shanks looks at the ways in which the idea of 'craftwork' can be used and abused.

At the craft fair. Market stalls laid with 'hand-made' goods: pottery, especially wheel-
thrown bowls and jugs, the more idiosyncratic or up-market called 'studio' pottery;
colourful 'designer' knitwear; silver wire jewellery; basketry (hanging baskets for house
plants); furniture perhaps, often made with hardwoods; leather bags and belts; a cake-
stall in the corner sells home-made lemonade and sticky buns. The term 'craft' invites
caricature: comfortable middle-class people in fishermen's smocks expressing themselves
in activities which were once the livelihood of the working class when they were known
as trades. Arty pretence, complacent, conservative, safe. A honey-glazed milk jug sitting
on a stripped-pine Welsh dresser. It has undertones of regressive ruralism – getting back
to the securities of preindustrial village life and community, preserving 'traditional'
ways and natural materials. Overtones of utopian nostalgia.

The potters sitting at their wheel look absorbed in the work. The concentration requires
no effort; the work draws the potter in. It looks care-free, far from the pressures of
car assembly line. The potter is envied. It looks relaxing. People may take up crafts as
hobbies or pastimes for these reasons; physical activities with clear untaxing guidelines
in which they can lose themselves and escape.

It is for these reasons also that crafts may not be taken seriously. Traditional and safe,
homely and affirmative craftwork is not challenging and critical, subversive avant-garde
art appearing in public gallery and discussed in the media. The gallery art piece, product of creative inspiration, seems to invite contemplation and close scrutiny. Handling
the pot invites consideration of skill and technique, price and decorative appeal. Art is
intellectual and singular; craft is practical and everyday. Craft is also associated with
provincial folk art and tourist crafts, articles (often considered spurious) produced by
locals as souvenirs for a tourist market. This is not the appeal of high-culture art.

Craftwork has moved to the gallery. This began in the nineteenth century with museums
of style and taste such as the Victoria and Albert in London. It continued with the studio
pottery of Bernard Leach and others. Since the 1970s, craft criteria of truth to material
and suitability for purpose have been questioned, traditional and accepted qualities scru-
tinized in experimental works in textiles, clay and all the main craft materials.

An attempt has been made to question also the boundary between art and craft. This has been particularly evident in the United States. Here are new experiences in woven materials: ceramic sculptural teapots which do not look like fired clay and do not pour tea in the way you might expect.

Especially since the nineteenth century the crafts have been for many an aesthetic in opposition. The arts and crafts movement, defined in the writings of John Ruskin and expressed in the political works of William Morris, was a reaction against the products of the industrial revolution. In his business company Morris championed hand craft, workshop-based authentic labour, as opposed to machine-based alienated labour of capitalist industry. This was an attempt to restore a dignity and respectability to labour, to oppose the separation of art and politics, morality and religion. Craft was to be art in society.

This paper first appeared in M. Shanks (1992) Experiencing the Past, *London: Routledge, pp. 167–70.*

17

Towards a material history methodology

R. Elliot *et al.*

Elliot's paper is the first of four which endeavour to draw the threads of the analysis of objects into an organized procedure which can be used as a model for object study. As has already been stressed in the Introduction, these are to be regarded as guides and aides-mémoire rather than as sets of rules. Most of these models, including that of Elliot and his colleagues, arose from work in postgraduate Museum Studies or material history classes. Elliot's model arises from an essentially historical perspective. His paper describes the process of developing a methodology, the research model itself, and the application of it to a sample artefact, a nineteenth-century caulking mallet.

INTRODUCTION

During the academic year 1983–4, a graduate history seminar at the University of New Brunswick in Fredericton attempted to construct a methodology for the analysis of artefacts.[1] This was the first seminar in what would become the Diploma Programme in Material History offered in conjunction with the MA Programme in History at the university.[2] The course was taught by Dr Stuart Smith of the Department of History whose creative leadership provided the climate for group discovery which has resulted in this report.

The article has been divided into three sections: a description of the class process in developing a methodology and research model; the research model described; and a test case application of the methodology using a sample artefact. No attempt has been made to integrate this line of enquiry within the broader questions posed by the discipline of history. Rather, it is presented as an end in itself and, as such, will hopefully serve as a useful catalyst for discussion and a departure point for those interested in material history and the analysis of artefacts.

THE CLASS PROCESS

The search for a workable methodology began with a general, surface investigation of several past cultures and attitudes held towards the object in those cultures. This process was repeated, more or less, when a number of social science disciplines were examined and their relationship with material evidence measured. Of this group, archaeology appeared the closest methodological link to the class objective in view of its basic procedure of commencing investigation with the object, a direction no doubt born of necessity because of the paucity of other forms of evidence available in the course of the archaeologists' work. In spite of or perhaps because of this factor, the seminar adopted archaeology's initial stage of scientific description of material evidence as a core philosophy.

Equipped with this outlook the class then began to digest and qualify a number of methodological proposals contained in pertinent literature that attempted to formulate a line of enquiry for the analysis of artefacts. Two of the more promising models appeared in recent issues of the *Winterthur Portfolio* – E. McClung Fleming's 'Artifact study: a proposed model' and Jules Prown's 'Mind in matter: an introduction to material culture theory and method'.[3] Aspects of Fleming's methodological framework were in fact altered and adapted in a generalized sense for use in a preliminary class model emphasizing several basic properties of the object. Fleming's basic artefact properties included History, Material, Construction, Design and Function. To each of these he applied four analytical operations: Identification (factual description), Evaluation (judgements), Cultural Analysis (relationship of the artefact to its culture) and Interpretation (significance).

Upon reflection, the class decided to reduce the perceived complexity of this framework by abandoning the four analytical operations and creating a cleaner, basic model with aspects of Fleming's methodology intact. History, for example, was omitted as the initial artefact property and replaced by Material, a move that seemed consistent with the archaeologist's method of beginning analysis with the artefact. Next, as in Fleming's model, Construction (including physical description) would be considered, followed by Provenance (History). Design was eliminated in the belief it would be incorporated by Construction and other elements of the model and therefore did not warrant separate classification. Function was viewed as essential to determine the artefact's use and what implications, if any, were intended or unintended through that use. Finally, a property termed Value was added to the basic framework. This was seen as the most interpretive portion of the model despite its shallow monetary connotation. Aside from the price an object might bring in a contemporary auction setting or the consideration of its purely aesthetic value, this property represented a more complex level of analysis and was related, in large part, to the object's cultural associations with, and perceived value to, the society in which it was produced. At the same time, it was recognized that an artefact's value could be interpreted differently by a range of observers from its point of creation to the present day.

Material, Construction, Provenance, Function and Value thus formed the seminar's core model. These properties would be considered as listed, an order that anticipated the examination of an artefact as the starting point of analysis before the consultation of supplementary source material. The arrangement of the properties also reflected a gradual shift from the more empirical observations gained in Material and Construction to the largely interpretive property of Value.

The seminar viewed the basic model structure as a necessary retreat from Fleming's more complex proposal, which it felt attempted to synthesize too much information from several sources too early in the investigation procedure. Class members did note that their model might itself develop further through discussion and testing but anticipated a slower, more controlled evolution to the interpretive aspects of artefact analysis.

A more central question confronting the seminar at this point, however, was the model's adaptability. Could a broad range of artefacts be approached using this line of enquiry or was it necessary to develop separate methodologies for different categories of artefacts? Indeed, was it even necessary to categorize artefacts for analytical purposes? Jules Prown, in his article, felt that artefact categories were useful because of the broad range of material produced or modified by man. He based his classification system on function and listed several categories which progressed from the decorative to the utilitarian (i.e. Art, Diversions, Adornment, Modifications of the Landscape, Applied Arts and Devices).[4] Proceeding from this arrangement, he proposed a methodology in which direct contact with the artefact would be established using the analytical stages of Description, Deduction and Speculation followed by a programme of research designed to validate these stages by considering external forms of evidence. That evidence would be gathered through a variety of methodologies and techniques developed by established disciplines (i.e. social history, cultural geography, social anthropology, etc.).[5]

Prown emphasized that these methodologies should not be applied until the artefact itself was thoroughly analysed, a direction supported by the seminar. At the same time, however, it was noted that Prown's model could be tightened considerably, particularly the Speculation stage, which involved the formulation of theories and hypotheses based primarily on physical evidence. The seminar viewed these processes as having application near the end of the investigation and felt that Prown proposed their introduction too early with less effect. If anything, Prown relied too much on physical evidence, posing questions it could not answer. In addition, his system of artefact classification appeared, without testing, to be redundant and potentially harmful to the investigation process. Once a group of artefacts were categorized, for instance, they might receive questions not asked of artefacts in other categories and vice versa. This perceived diversity was thought dangerous to the seminar's desire for a flexible research model. It was instead decided to test the class approach on a sample artefact chosen by each student for analysis, an exercise that would hopefully serve to indicate whether the model required any alterations.

The initial test produced some interesting results, as well as several problems, and ultimately, the need for an expanded model format. The examination of the assigned properties of each artefact produced a number of instances in which the hands-on approach applied in Material and Construction yielded observations contradicting held assumptions. For example, a bowler hat's material composition, component parts and their assembly revealed moulded cardboard as a base material with a circle of wire beneath the brim to help maintain the hat's shape. The seminar member who examined the hat had always assumed that bowlers were made primarily of felt, but these new findings contributed directly to subsequent observations regarding the hat's perceived value to the society in which it was produced.

Next, during consideration of Provenance as an artefact property, a British army sword was presented and the question posed as to whether it had ever been used in a major historical event such as the war of 1812. In discussing this matter it was eventually agreed that the sword's individual history and connoisseurship were less important than its more general connections to the era in which it was produced. If swords like the example presented were used during the war of 1812, then study of that artefact would likely reveal certain conclusions about the general nature of warfare at that time. The sword's property of Function, beyond its implied basic use, would consider the weight of the weapon and its place in a soldier's pack. Did it in fact retard movement? Was it awkward to swing in use, etc.?

The properties of Function and Value were confirmed as being more productive in an interpretive sense than expected. Value, in effect, was seen as the collection point for the build-up of information through the preceding stages. Hence, for example, elements of the bowler hat's construction technique contributed to observations regarding the values of the society that produced and used this form of head wear (uniformity, durability, formality, etc.).

While seminar members felt that the model performed reasonably well during this run-through, a number of problem areas were discovered. The gradual build-up of information through the artefact properties, although seen as essential, also created uncertainty in some cases as to where one property ended and the other commenced. Function seemed to flow into Value and elements of Provenance became confused with Function. In addition, the exact time and place for the introduction of supplementary data remained unclear. This included comparative data derived from objects similar to the artefact under consideration as well as documentary and other evidence in support of (or contrary to) information revealed to the observer through the hands-on approach encouraged during Material and Construction. In the course of the presentations, seminar members usually began introducing supplementary data during Construction after having made initial observations derived from a direct examination of the artefact. A mixture of observable and supplementary evidence then continued through the remainder of the properties from Provenance to Value.

Finally, an area of major concern developed regarding the perception that some artefacts yielded more information than others when treated by the model. A number of seminar members subsequently proposed that time could thus be spent more profitably analysing artefacts of higher information value. Others, however, felt this point of view seemed reminiscent, in some respects, of Prown's artefact categories and their progression from the decorative (aesthetic) to the primarily utilitarian: To Prown, ultimately, the decorative/aesthetic dimension of objects as embodied primarily in fine art, architecture and the applied arts resulted in greater communication value between the observer and the original producing culture than the more utilitarian artefacts, which he referred to as devices.[6] It was felt, perhaps unfairly, that, as an art historian, Prown had advanced his opinion because of his professional background. Yet the core of his argument confirmed the seminar's observation that the analysis of some artefacts was more profitable than others, whether this conformed to Prown's aesthetic–utilitarian construct or not. After much discussion, it was ultimately decided to abandon a scale of artefact information value since questions raised through the application of the mode were seen as equally valid whether applied to a mid-nineteenth-century hammer or a late eighteenth-century landscape painting. The landscape might yield more information about the culture that produced it, but if the hammer was not questioned at all, potentially useful information might be lost. In addition, any rest of the model's flexibility would be skewed in one direction.

Although this issue was resolved, earlier concerns regarding the lack of a clear division among the model's artefact properties and the place of introduction of supplementary data seemed to indicate a need for structural change. A partial answer to these difficulties came during one of the final class presentations in which a nineteenth-century firearm was analysed by applying a series of three general question categories to each artefact property in turn, from Material to Value. These categories each contained very general standardized questions in view of the broad range of artefacts the model would conceivably seek to analyse. For the sake of convenience, these were labelled A, B and C, where questions marked A involved those that could be answered through direct observation of the artefact, B those that could be answered through comparisons with similar artefacts, and C when supplementary evidence such as printed or written sources were consulted. In addition, a final non-question category, labelled D, was created for the formulation of conclusions derived from the preceding questions.

This standardized format appeared to give each artefact property more definition through the application of an ordered series of question categories. Introduced in turn to Material, Construction, Provenance, Function and Value, the A, B and C questions also served as a guide for the timing and use of observable, comparative and supplementary data. Given the fact that most seminar presentations to that point had attempted to answer unordered questions of no particular type, the most recent approach was seen as a promising direction.

As the autumn term ended, further development occurred when it was proposed that the model might achieve greater clarity if represented in graphic format. A grid system was suggested containing the five artefact properties along its vertical dimension and the three question categories and conclusions along the horizontal dimension (see Table 17.1).

Table 17.1 Graphic representation of model

	Observable data	Comparative data	Supplementary data	Conclusions
Material				
Construction				
Provenance				
Function				
Value				

When the next term commenced, the seminar continued its examination of the proposed model. After considerable reflection and discussion it was eventually realized that the methodology, though heading in the right direction, exhibited problems and required additional modification. The existing procedure of examining an artefact through each of its properties in succession meant, for instance, that material composition was subjected to three groups of question categories and a set of conclusions derived therefrom before the property of construction was considered, and so on. In effect, the model did allow for the accumulation of knowledge about an artefact but did so at a tedious rate in a repetitive, rigid manner.

A solution, suddenly proposed, was simply the rotation of the grid system to one side. Rather than gathering all available data (observable, comparative and supplementary) for a single property before proceeding to the next, it was now suggested that observable data be recorded for all properties before moving on to the comparative process. After comparative data were acquired, the researcher could proceed to an examination of supplementary sources. It was further proposed during discussion that the conclusion categories be amalgamated to form one unit at the base of the model configuration in the interests of efficiency. Finally, the order of two artefact properties, Provenance and Function, was reversed so that Function would henceforth be considered before Provenance in each of the three question categories. This was proposed because Function entailed a greater reliance on observable data than Provenance and thus conformed to the general procedure of considering this form of evidence as early as possible within the model construct (see Table 17.2).

The new orientation appeared more logical and less rigid than its predecessor but required testing to determine if it contained inconsistencies. To that end, seminar members were once again instructed to select an artefact for analysis and to ensure, if possible, that a variety of man-made objects were represented in that selection. If the model was able to accommodate these disparate items successfully, it would demonstrate a universal and flexible application in terms of artefact research. Selections included a tea-caddy, caulking mallet, lithographic prints, a pressed-glass goblet, a piece of lace, a Pembroke table, architectural drawings and a Bricklin automobile.

This exercise involved more research and preparation time than the first round of enquiries in the autumn and resulted in some fairly detailed papers. As these were presented, however, it became clear that the class was not in complete accord regarding the methodology. What had inspired agreement and seemed a logical structure and progression in theory did not always find adherence in practice. Some members had not followed the proposed methodology and several felt that the model remained too rigid, unduly complicating the researcher's progress by preventing freedom of movement within its structure. Others disagreed, believing that the method as developed forced the examiner to adopt an orderly approach to artefact analysis. This would permit other researchers easy access to recheck the data and conclusions and thus form a retraceable system.

While the concept of a retraceable analysis procedure did find agreement, debate continued over the methodology's perceived rigidity. This was manifested primarily in the fact that some had introduced documentary sources into their research before a complete examination of the artefact had been attempted. A number of seminar members felt this missed the point of the model and its indicated progression. It was their opinion that examination of the artefact by itself was essential before consultation of other sources if preconceived notions regarding objects were to be avoided and inconsistencies discovered.

Table 17.2 New model configuration, rotating grid of original

	Material	*Construction*	*Function*	*Provenance*	*Value*
Step 1 Observable data					
Step 2 Comparative data					
Step 3 Supplementary data					
Step 4	Conclusions				

The seminar presentation analysing a Bricklin automobile was advanced as a case in point. It was noted that available documentation, including a Bricklin Vehicle Corporation press kit, advertised the safety aspects of the automobile.[7] Yet, upon initial examination of a Bricklin, it was discovered that no handles existed on the outside of its doors to release the latches. This might present a serious problem during an emergency if the occupant were incapacitated and a potential rescuer were forced to lose valuable seconds gaining entry by other means. The seminar member who gave the presentation felt that this example appeared to justify the adoption of the analysis procedure as developed.

While a consensus on this issue was not established during class presentation, other aspects of the methodology were refined. A general checklist of questions in their appro-priate categories continued to be developed over the course of the spring term and these were applicable to a wide range of objects. The checklist was expected to be a guide only, and it was recognized that some of the questions could not elicit a response at any particu-lar step in the analysis procedure. Thus, while the answers to some questions were com-monly found during one particular level of investigation (i.e., during comparative analysis), the data to answer others might be discovered in any one of the information-gathering steps. This depended entirely on the nature of the object under examination. It also remained true, as established earlier, that the amount of information that artefacts might convey to the researcher could vary widely and that some questions presented in the checklist might remain unanswered.

Many of the questions encouraged the researcher to look for evidence of cultural expres-sion in the object since this fusion had been well established early in the seminar's inves-tigations. It was also advanced that the researcher should re-examine the artefact after the initial hands-on stage, especially if new information became available through comparative data or documentary evidence that would help the analysis of the object's properties more fully. Indeed, though insistence remained that the artefact must be examined by itself during the opening steps of the analysis process, it was agreed that any single source of information could prove misleading and all available evidence should be consulted. Some felt that the methodology represented or reinforced a state of mind consistent with artefact research. Rather than succumbing to the temptation to consult printed or written works when confronted with an unknown object, it was stressed that the material historian must develop a grammar in order to read the arte-fact. Use of the model would hopefully encourage this development and thus alleviate the charge of rigidity in its application.

As the spring term neared its conclusion, the seminar appeared satisfied that the analy-sis model was capable of handling a broad sample of artefacts ranging from the com-plexity of a Bricklin automobile to the relative simplicity of a caulking mallet. (Note: an analysis of a caulking mallet appears later in this paper.) In addition, the model formed a retraceable line of enquiry combined with an accessible overview of the entire analysis procedure. Thus, while disagreement on individual aspects of procedure remained, a general mental construct had been fashioned which, at least, could serve to reduce the researcher's preconceptions of an artefact's meaning. Its ultimate value, of course, would only be determined by continued testing.

THE MODEL DESCRIBED

The proposed analysis method encourages the historian to discard, as much as possi-ble, preconceived notions about the artefact under study and to begin by studying the artefact itself. The investigative procedure suggests that the researcher perform a derailed examination (which may be either a written or a mental exercise) of the artefact before proceeding to other sources of information. After all observable data have been gathered, the examiner is directed to compare the artefact with objects similar to the one being analysed. Other sources of information (documents, etc.) are introduced as supplementary data only after a complete examination has been made of the artefact and similar objects. At any stage during the process, the historian is able to re-examine the artefact, especially if new information becomes available that would help to analyse the object's properties more fully. The final step in the analysis procedure is to draw conclusions based upon all observable, comparative and supplementary data. At this point, contradictory evidence might be recognized and hypotheses formulated to explain these contradictions.

Table 17.3 The analysis method

	Question Categories				
Analysis procedure	*Material*	*Construction*	*Function*	*Provenance*	*Value*
Step 1 Observable date (examination of the single artefact)					
Step 2 Comparative data (comparisons made with similar artefacts)					
Step 3 Supplementary data (other sources of information introduced)					
Step 4	Conclusions				

During each phase of the information-gathering process, the historian is seeking data from specific sources. The types of data are refined:

Step 1: Observable data
Data that can be determined through sensory engagement with the artefact beginning with material composition, then construction, function, provenance and value.

Step 2: Comparative data
Information acquired by comparing the artefact with similar (or identical) objects produced by the same maker or by other manufacturers during the same time period. Comparisons made with similar artefacts produced by the same manufacturer or different manufacturers over a period of time either before or after the artefact in question was produced. Comparisons with contemporary objects similar in function (if not design). Such comparisons move from material composition through to value.

Step 3: Supplementary data
Generally written or printed sources of information that are seen as useful in supplying additional data concerning the properties of the artefact. Any other form of evidence (i.e., oral history, photographs of artefacts) consulted outside the artefact itself and others like it (or dissimilar to it).

A checklist of questions

Each of the steps outlined in the analysis method is subdivided into five categories or broad areas of enquiry (material, construction, function, provenance and value). General questions, which apply to a wide range of very different objects, have been developed for these categories or artefact properties. Since the material historian is primarily interested in what an artefact can reveal about the culture that produced it, many of the questions encourage the researcher to look for evidence of cultural expression in the object. The generalized questions are meant to be used as a guide or checklist for the examiner throughout the entire research process, while gathering all observable evidence from the individual artefact, through the comparative analysis phase, to the use of available supplementary data. The questions on the following pages do not represent an attempt to produce a definitive list. They are only offered as a guide for the researcher during the examination process.

During the examination of a variety of entirely different artefacts, it becomes obvious that many of the questions are not always answerable at any particular step in the analysis process. While the answers for some questions are commonly found during one particular level of investigation (for example, during comparative analysis), the data to answers might be discovered in any one of the information-gathering steps. It depends entirely on the nature of the object under examination. It is also true that the amount of information artefacts are capable of conveying to the researcher varies widely, and therefore some of the questions presented in the checklist may remain unanswered.

Material

The natural, organic and/or man-made materials composing the artefact and completing its appearance. Also the investigator's sensory response to the use or occurrence of those materials in the artefact.

1 What materials were used to produce the artefact and complete its appearance? (Quality of materials used?)
2 Did the materials used influence the object's final form?
3 Are these materials used in similar artefacts?
4 Where did the unworked materials originate?
5 Do the materials employed suggest trade patterns/practices?

Construction

The methods employed to produce the artefact (or, if completely natural and/or organic, the methods used to arrange such materials physically for the physical or mental benefit of man). A physical description of the artefact's appearance to the observer and the qualitative intuitive judgement of the piece as viewed by itself, and later, in comparison with others like itself.

1 How was the artefact fabricated and finished? (A detailed examination including texture, size, etc.)
2 What construction methods (and tools) would be required to produce this artefact? (Handmade/ machine-made? Quality and complexity of construction?)
3 How was the object's appearance affected or influenced by the construction techniques employed?
4 Is any form of ornamentation/decoration present? If so, what type?
5 How does this ornamentation/decoration affect the artefacts appearance?
6 Are there any markings or inscriptions present?
7 Are there any signs of wear or repair?
8 Does the construction of this artefact differ greatly from similar objects? (Objects by the same maker and others?)
9 Is its design comparable to like objects? (Is the overall design a set style?)
10 What stage of development or evolution does this artefact represent when compared with both older and more recent objects of a similar type? (Does the design aid in dating?)
11 What degree of sophistication is represented by the artefact? (Style, method of construction, etc.)
12 Is the artefact a reproduction?

Function

The reason(s) for the artefact's production and the use that was made of it. Its effectiveness for the role intended, including attendant social function whether intended or not .

1 Why was the artefact produced?
2 What function did this artefact perform?
3 How well did the artefact perform its intended function?
4 Was the object's functional performance affected by its design, materials used, construction methods employed or the ornamentation applied? (Do any of these hinder or reduce the artefact's effectiveness?)
5 Does the artefact's function reveal anything about its maker/owner?
6 What is its function today and has its function changed?

Provenance

The artefact's geographic place and time of origin, its maker or arranger (if naturally occurring such as a walkway made of flagstone), its owner if different from the maker and its history, including alterations or evolution from its point of origin to the present. The design of the artefact, including that represented through the artefact's content as articulated through observable data, comparisons with other artefacts, both similar and dissimilar, and the use of supplementary data.

1 Where and when was the object produced?
2 Who was the maker?
3 Where and how was the artefact used?
4 Who was the original owner of the object?
5 When and where did the original owner live and what was his social status, trade, etc.?
6 Who were the subsequent owners and where? Plus any other information on the object's history, owners and maker(s), etc.

Value

The artefact's value to its original producer and/or owner. Its value (if any) to its contemporary society in terms of the cultural values it depicts through observable evidence, comparisons with others like it and supplementary data. Its value as determined by subsequent owners, caretakers, etc.

1 What was the artefact's value to its original owner?
2 Did ownership of this type of artefact reflect the social or economic status of the original owner?
3 What value was placed on the object by society.
4 What cultural values does it reveal?
5 What value does the object have to the society in which it was produced? (extrinsic/monetary)

THE METHOD APPLIED

Even though, for this example, the analysis procedure has been written, the proposed analysis method may be performed as either a mental or a written exercise. It is an approach for artefact analysis. The procedure is meant to encourage the researcher to examine the artefact more closely for observable data before relying on documentary sources. Naturally, the amount of information that may be extracted from an artefact depends heavily on that object (plus the examiner's observation skills and background knowledge).

The secret to gaining as much information as possible from an artefact rests in the interdisciplinary nature of material history studies and the observational powers of the examiner. A wide variety of relevant sources may be drawn upon to analyse and understand the artefact fully. For example, specialists from other disciplines may be able to answer questions concerning the artefact's structure or composition that few historians could answer.

Although an artefact of relatively simple construction (a nineteenth-century caulking mallet) is examined on the following pages, the analysis procedure has been tested on a wide selection of different objects; several were very complex. For the sake of brevity, this particular test case has been abbreviated and footnotes and a bibliography have been omitted.

Step 1: Observable data

Material

The artefact is composed principally of hardwood with iron as a secondary material. Both the handle and the head of the implement appear to be made from the same type of wood, probably live oak (*Quercus virginiana*), although the handle may be of locust wood, possibly honey locust (*Gleditsia triacanthos*). (A hardness test was used to determine that the head of the object is live oak. More detailed analysis would prove whether the handle is locust wood or another hardwood species.)

Two other materials are present: a short length of rope and a small quantity of light cardboard.

Construction

The artefact weighs about 1.5 kg (3 lb). It consists of a head or striking portion of live oak, 30.5 cm long with a circumference ranging from 15 cm to 18 cm in the middle area where the handle joins the head. The joining of the handle to the head gives the object a T-shaped appearance. The ends of the head, as previously mentioned, are smaller in circumference than the middle section, measuring 15 cm for a distance of 10 cm from one end and 9.5 cm from the other. A thicker area in the middle of the head, for a length of 10 cm, is 18 cm in circumference. A tapered hole, around 2.5 cm in diameter, of oblong shape nearly bisects the head. The handle measures 37 cm long and is consistently 10 cm in circumference with the exception of a slight tapering that begins 10 cm from the end inserted into the head of the implement. A 1-cm hole has been drilled 2. 5 cm from the end of the handle to admit a short length of rope (about 30 cm long) which has been spliced to form a loop.

Thin iron bands have been driven over the centre portion of the head to either side of the handle. These metal rings measure 1.2 cm wide and 0.3 cm thick. Tapering iron bands are located at either end of the head, having been driven to the full width of the metal to the point of being flush with the wood at each extremity.

Narrow slots about 8 cm long and 0.3 cm wide have been cut entirely through the head in a longitudinal fashion in the area of the head to either side of the handle. One slot runs very nearly to the metal ring on one end of the head, while the other actually extends under the tapering iron at the other end. A 0.6-cm hole has been drilled through each slot and centred 2.5 cm from each narrow iron ring near the handle. Between each iron ring and the wood of the head is a light cardboard substance, apparently to help lodge the rings in place. A small quantity of packing is visible where the handle has been spread somewhat to prevent the head from slipping off.

One iron ring (at the end of the head) is misshapen from use and the fact that one end of the head is slightly shorter than the other indicates uneven use. Numerous gouges, scratches and paint spots are visible on both metal and wood surfaces. The striking surfaces on either end of the head exhibit relatively little wear and the tool is still in fairly good condition.

The skills of two main craftsmen were required to produce this artefact. The iron rings were made in an iron foundry, while the wooden handle and head were produced by a woodworker who also might have assembled the implement. Since the artefact is of relatively simple construction, implements of this type could possibly be mass-produced very easily.

Function

The wear marks on either end of the head clearly indicate that the object is a tool used for striking. (Unless the examiner was familiar with caulking mallets and the operations required to caulk a wooden ship, the artefact's actual role would not be apparent.) Being constructed of hardwood and iron, the implement has considerable heft, weighing about 1.5 kg. The head, being slightly loose, detracts somewhat from the feel of confidence one would otherwise have in swinging the tool. One can easily adjust the force of the blow due to the implement's balance, which is sufficiently heavy to enable the person employing the tool to use its heft to advantage or, on the other hand, check its force of impact with relative ease.

One might also assume, because the tool does not have any applied ornamentation, that the artefact was originally produced for a purely functional purpose. The wear marks and general condition of the tool are consistent with this conclusion.

The size and shape of the tool show that it can be used by only one individual at a time.

Provenance

The provenance of this particular artefact cannot be determined from the object. Maker's marks and other data that would allow the examiner to formulate general conclusions concerning the tool's place and date of origin are not present. However, the use of iron rather than steel for its metal hardware probably indicates that the tool was produced prior to the twentieth century if it is of a North American origin.

Value

Although we may assume that the tool was relatively inexpensive to purchase or produce because it is of simple construction, this cannot be determined with absolute certainty.

The functional nature of the tool seems to indicate that the individual using it would only value the implement for the task(s) which it could perform.

Step 2: Comparative data

Material

When comparisons were made between similar implements, it was found that many had heads composed of live oak, while others were made from lignum vitae (*Guaiacum officinale*). A significant number of the artefacts examined had locust wood handles, but other species of hardwood were also used to produce the heads and handles for this type of tool. A number of early twentieth-century examples in museum collections had steel hardware, while earlier specimens employed iron bands.

Construction

The artefact is very similar to many tools in public and private collections in North America, Europe and Britain. However common the materials and general structural appearance compared with other tools of this type, there are facets of construction that lend a unique character to each artefact. The length of the slots in the head (described previously) are peculiar to each tool. The number of holes drilled to enlarge the slots also varies. Apparently, the slots and holes were made by the tool's user or were at least modifications to suit his individual tastes or requirements.

Tools of this type, despite the fact that their slots differ, appear to have changed very little over the last several hundred years. Since the tool being examined is of similar construction when compared with other examples and exhibits similar wear marks, it is very likely an authentic artefact and not a reproduction.

Function

Although the size and weight of the specimens varied, all were constructed along similar lines and therefore must have been employed for a task that was essentially the same.

The existence of many other tools of this type seems to suggest that they were mass-produced for sale.

Provenance

After comparing the artefact with others, nothing more could be determined regarding the object's provenance.

Value

The number of these artefacts in widely scattered collections indicates that they were relatively common tools at one time.

Step 3: Supplementary data

Note: Since the purpose of this exercise has been to show the type of information that may be acquired directly from artefacts (using a systematic analysis procedure) without the aid of documentary sources, only selected pieces of supplementary evidence are included in the third step. To gain as much knowledge as possible about the artefact under examination, a wide variety of supplementary data sources may be consulted. These include the use of both primary and secondary sources, oral history and the assistance of specialists from various fields.

Material

According to Niels Jannasch of the Maritime Museum of the Atlantic in Halifax, those caulking mallets having heads composed of live oak were fabricated in the United States, whereas the head made of lignum vitae would likely have been manufactured in Britain. In a hardness test, it was determined that the head of this tool is of live oak, which helps locate its origin to a degree, but the determination of a more precise location is difficult.

Function

This mallet and others like it were used to caulk the seams of ships and boats of wood-plank construction to make them watertight. Caulking irons were struck by the mallet to force oakum into the seams. Obviously, the artefact performed a very necessary function, then, in both new construction and in ship repair. A caulker was considered to be a skilled worker and inefficient or careless use of this tool and caulking material could result in sprung seams and consequent damage to the hull. It is, perhaps, a tribute to their status that a caulker was more highly paid than an unskilled labourer and by 1864 a Caulker's Association of the City and Company of Saint John was set up.

In *Tools of the Maritime Trade*, Horsely claims the slot was the cause of a musical note created with each impact on the iron and that the pitch of the note could be varied by the size, number and location of the drilled holes. It was said that a good foreman could determine which caulker in his crew was applying his trade without having to actually witness his endeavours. The slots and holes also reduced the noise level of hardwood striking iron, and were necessary to prevent hearing loss. Fred G. Heans, the mallet's present owner, testified that the slot provides resonance and reduces the rebound effect and vibration in the handle. This may be speculation on his part as it was difficult to test this theory to our satisfaction. It is apparent at least that the slots and holes did serve a practical function.

Provenance

Information acquired from the mallet's present owner, Fred G. Heans:

> This caulking mallet is known to have been used by William Heans (1831–1912) personally in the construction of the yacht *Canada*, built in 1898, and in ship repair and construction prior to this date. The *Canada* was constructed in the Hilyard boat yard (Saint John, New Brunswick) in a specially constructed shed at the foot of Main Street, on the edge of the Joseph A. Likely Co. millpond. The son of William Heans, Fred S. Heans (1868–1943) was also an experienced caulker and used this mallet in repairs to the *Canada* and in the construction of other yachts. In later years before the sale of the *Canada* in 1967, Fred G. Heans and his son Howard employed this particular mallet in preparing the yacht for the annual spring launchings from the yard of the Royal Kennebecasis Yacht Club of Saint John.

Value

When new, the mallet would have been a relatively inexpensive piece of hardware, available locally in Saint John through a ship's chandler. However, mallets of this type are relatively rare today and therefore its value has increased. Today, the Heans family, although not willing to put a dollar value on this family treasure, would not be easily enticed to part with it. The tool is in fairly good condition, as a worn mallet would have a much shorter head, perhaps to the width of the iron rings on each end of the striking portions. Since the caulking iron must be struck with the wood portion of the head, not the metal ring, the relatively unworn condition of the head renders it still quite capable of employment in the purpose for which it was designed, adding to its value.

Step 4: Conclusions

Note: Only the major conclusions have been summarized. Most of the data gathered during the first three steps do not require further explanation.

After examining all observable, comparative and supplementary data, the following facts become clear. The caulking mallet was probably purchased by William Heans (1831–1912) directly from a ship's chandler in Saint John, New Brunswick, and according to family tradition, it was used to caulk the seams of numerous vessels prior to the construction of the yacht *Canada* in 1898. This particular caulking mallet is an example of a mass-produced tool of the nineteenth century, and the wood (live oak) used to construct the tool's head seems to indicate that it was manufactured in the United States and shipped to Saint John for sale.

When used by Fred G. Heans in later years, the mallet was employed exclusively to repair the seams of the yacht, *Canada*. Earlier in its history it saw more heavy-duty use in caulking the seams of larger vessels in a section of the Hilyard yard rented by William and later Fred S. Heans. Since most modern pleasure craft are constructed of materials other than wood, it is not apt to function in the future as it was originally intended. However, the continued use of caulking mallets of this design over several centuries indicates that the tool was well suited for its intended function.

There are signs of misuse, as indicated by the flattening of one of the wide metal rings. In normal use these rings were driven to the centre of the head as the wood wore down to prevent metal from striking metal. It may be that Howard, the son of Fred G. Heans, has put the mallet to uses other than for which it was intended and in doing so damaged the ring.

The original purpose of the mallet, however, is clear. It represents an integral part of the shipbuilding process in Saint John and other marine locations when wood was the primary material of construction. As witness to the transition years in ship construction, this caulking mallet is evocative of a period of maritime history very recent, yet remote.

This paper first appeared in Material History Bulletin 22 *(Fall 1982), pp. 31–40.*

NOTES

1 The class consisted of Darrel Butler, Elizabeth Earl, Robert Elliot. Gregg Finley, Kim Godwin, Gary Hughes, Milford Lewis and Gerald Thomas.
2 For more information on the Diploma Programme in Material History see *Material History Bulletin* 19 (Spring 1984): 57.
3 E. McClung Fleming (1973) 'Artifact study: a proposed model', *Winterthur Portfolio* 9: 153–73. Jules Prown (1982) 'Mind in matter: an introduction to material culture theory and method', *Winterthur Portfolio* 17(1): 1–19.
4 Prown, op. cit. 2–3.
5 Prown, op. cit. 7.
6 Prown, op. cit. 14.
7 Robert S. Elliot 'A case study in New Brunswick material history: testing a method for artifact analysis', term paper, History 6700, pp. 17, 32.

18

Thinking about things
Susan M. Pearce

This paper presents another approach to the development of a model for artefact studies, one which draws heavily on an archaeological perspective. The paper also includes an account of McClung Fleming's model, which was developed by Fleming in the context of the study at Winterthur, Delaware, of early American applied arts. Fleming's model has influenced most subsequent work in this model-building area.

In the view of most curators – the present writer among them – collections are at the heart of a museum. In a fundamental sense, the possession of collections, of actual objects and specimens, is what distinguishes a museum from other kinds of institution. These collections are the basis from which spring most forms of museum service. For those of us on the human history side of museums – fine and applied arts scholars, ethnographers, social historians, science and technology historians, military historians and archaeologists – our collections are composed of artefacts, which may be defined as objects made by man through the application of technological processes. In practice, the term 'artefact' is usually reserved for movable pieces rather than structures, and is concerned with inorganic or dead materials; refined arguments over the artefact status of hybrid tea roses or miniature dachshunds need not detain us here.

The curating of artefacts is, therefore, a central concern; but over the years very much less effort has been put into developing the discipline of material culture study than into the other aspects of collection care. This is not surprising; many of us took over collections whose glaring needs were for documentation and storage rather than for artefact study and, in any case, material culture itself was given a low rating by the academic world at large. But four decades of post-war hard-working, professional curatorship have made their mark on our store rooms, while the study of objects is now receiving serious attention, especially among the 'new' anthropologists and archaeologists. Museum material culture studies need to be put upon a fuller and more secure theoretical basis by a willingness to grasp at the large issues, however difficult or elusive some of these may be, or however great a gulf there may seem between the theoretical stance and the poorly documented material, or collections in some of the smaller museums, or the availability of special expertise for study. An awareness of this is reflected in the number of object-orientated articles which have appeared recently (e.g., Porter and Martin 1985).

Objects embody unique information about the nature of man in society: the elucidation of approaches through which this can be unlocked is our task, the unique contribution which museum collections can make to our understanding of ourselves. The potential insights are fascinating enough in their own right, but they can have many spin-offs for the ways in which we approach exhibitions and museum teaching. Charges of arid intellectualism or elitism are quite beside the mark, for no profession can afford to neglect its theoretical roots.

THE NATURE OF ARTEFACTS

As the linguistic philosophers would tell us, artefacts, man-made objects, are objective in relationship to man, the subject. They have an external reality and so it should be possible to view the whole diversity of artefact types and to distinguish properties possessed by every artefact which are accessible to the appropriate modes of analysis and interpretation, and which together offer us a perception of the role of the artefact in social organization. To put it another way, it should be possible to ask the questions *how*, *what*, *when*, *where*, *by whom* and *why* about every artefact, and to achieve interesting answers.

Bearing these questions in mind, a useful way of organizing the properties of an object for the purposes of artefact study is to divide these into four main areas: *material*, which includes raw material, design, construction and technology; *history*, which includes a descriptive account of its function and use; *environment*, involving all its spatial relationships; and *significance*, which embraces its emotional or psychological messages. The sum of our understanding of these properties may be described as the interpretation.

MODELS FOR ARTEFACT STUDIES

Most of the work aimed at putting artefact studies on a systematic and coherent footing has been based upon this kind of approach to the properties of objects, and much of it has been carried out in North America. One of the pioneer papers was that by Montgomery (1961) in which he distinguished a series of fourteen 'steps or exercises' through which the connoisseur might achieve his goal of determining 'the date and place of manufacture; the author if possible; and where within the range of its fellows the object stands in terms of its condition, excellence of execution and success as a work of art.'

The steps cover artefact attributes like form, materials analysis, techniques employed, function, history and evaluation, all of which in one guise or another will always form part of any formal artefact study; but the emphasis on connoisseurship and the assumption that the trained eye can judge an artefact's 'success as a work of art' confines its application to the field of European/North American applied art, for which, indeed, Montgomery developed it. For the material culture field as a whole, words like 'success' and 'failure' are an irrelevance, although the quality of the object compared with others of its kind in the eyes of both its maker and user and of its students, will be important in our overall understanding of the piece, and we should aspire not simply to evaluation but to ways of understanding why an object's values have a particular character and why these are important.

Like Montgomery, E. McClung Fleming developed his approaches in connection with the Winterthur Museum – University of Delaware study programme in Early American Culture, and in 1974 he published a proposed model for artefact studies. This model, as Fleming says, uses two conceptual tools – a five-fold classification of the properties of an artefact, its history, material, construction, design and function, and a set of four operations to be performed on these properties in association with supplementary information

(Fig. 18.1). Each operation may involve each of the five properties; identification is the foundation for everything that follows and interpretation is the crown.

Fleming's model is applicable across the range of material culture, and we have cause to be grateful for its systematic presentation. In scheme, it adopts a cross-referencing approach in which a series of properties and analyses are applied to each other, and this can be cumbersome when an individual artefact is being studied. More fundamentally, the properties distinguished are open to criticism. The construction and design of an artefact are too closely related to stand separately and may be regarded as aspects of its material body. The practical function is concerned with how the piece has been used and is therefore better regarded as a part of its history. The spatial relationships of the artefact are omitted as an integral attribute, to emerge only during the process of cultural analysis. The significance property of the object is obscured by the word 'function' used in the paper to cover both uses and roles, described as including delight and communication as 'unintended

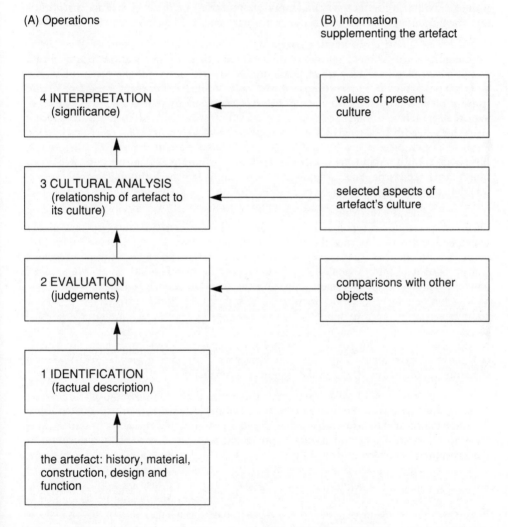

Fig. 18.1   Model for artefact studies (after E. McClung Fleming 1974)

functions', an adjective which begs a great many questions. The cultural analysis operation will indicate how objects convey status, ideas and so on, as Fleming rightly says, and he suggests some ways in which this may carry artefact study beyond description towards explanation, but this endeavour is capable of considerable expansion and difficult although it undoubtedly is, it must be our prime concern.

The model for artefact studies proposed here (Fig. 18.2) is framed around the properties which were distinguished in the earlier section. The column of boxes on the left develops the theme of artefact properties, while that on the right suggests the studies and analyses appropriate to each property. The obvious starting point is the object's physical body, the components from which it has been constructed, and any ornament which may have been added to them, and so an artefact study will begin with a physical description of the piece. This will include a full written description of the construction and ornamentation cast in the appropriate technical language, together with relevant measurements, drawings, photographs and X-ray photographs, or in other words, the normal documentation which, circumstances permitting, a curator would hope to include as part of basic accessioning.

The identification of these physical attributes and their rationalization into a cluster of significant characteristics which make up the overall design of the piece (in a non-aesthetic sense) enable it to be compared with other artefacts of its own broad type so that its position on its typological band can be established, at any rate to a degree. The typological approach to artefact study has come in for a good deal of criticism over recent years. It can readily be argued that the rationalization of significant characteristics referred to above is so subjective a process that types are born not among the objects themselves, but in the curator's mind, from whence they issue to impose categories into which the objects are forced to fit, if necessary by special pleading. However, this will not do. Objects do relate to each other in an objective sense, they do fall into groups with shared characteristics and it is our business to use our minds so that these groupings may emerge.

Once the principle of typological grouping has been conceded, there are techniques which endeavour to minimize the subjective element. Most of these involve the recording of a wide range of measurements and the processing of these by a computer, which can be used to establish object groups in which the members all fall within limited bands. In the writer's experience, gained in the study of Bronze Age metalwork, these approaches take us little further forward. The same object groups are thrown up by the computer as are yielded by hand-and-eye sorting, and in both cases the same awkward pieces are left over to linger in grey areas of uncertainty. Be that as it may, the comparison of a newly acquired silver spoon, for example, with other spoons, or of a newly discovered portrait with the line and brushwork of other portraits, will remain a fundamental technique to aid in dating and provenancing.

The third pair of boxes in Fig. 18.2 cover the material characterization of the artefact – that is, the analysis of the materials of which the object is made, in order to establish the provenance of the metal, stone, clay, wood and so on, and the ways in which these have been treated before and during the manufacture of the piece. The application of the appropriate petrological, metallurgical and other scientific techniques have been for some years commonplace in the study of strictly archaeological objects and also of fine art pieces, but they are beginning to be employed with social history, applied art material and ethnography, and it is clear that if analysis programmes could be developed in these fields on the kind of scale to which they have been applied, say, to prehistoric pottery, then the yield in knowledge could be very considerable and long vistas across patterns of exchange and industrial techniques would be opened up.

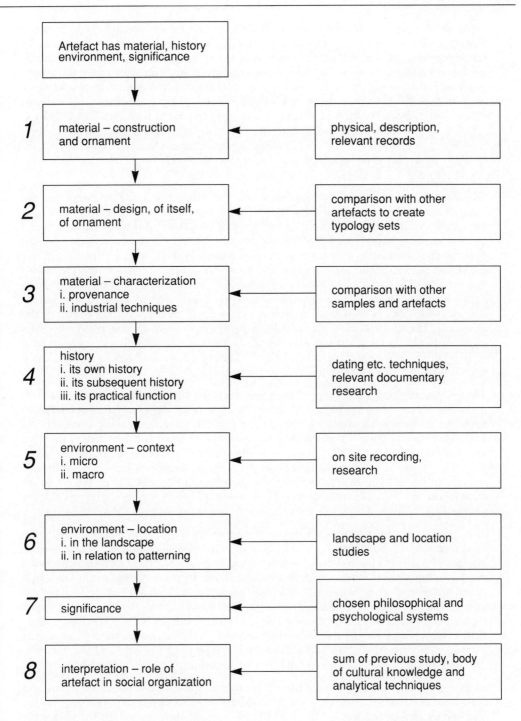

Fig. 18.2 Proposed model for artefact studies

From the material characteristics of an artefact, we may turn to its history. This conveniently divides into two: its 'own' history, that is the details (in so far as these may be recovered) of its maker and manufacture, and its use in its own time and place; and its subsequent history of collection, publication and exhibition. This will involve the appropriate scientific dating techniques and historical research into contemporary and other relevant documents in order to establish details of the maker's career and associations, and as many facts about the object as possible. Closely linked with this is investigation which aims to establish the function of the object in its own time and perhaps subsequently: wooden shuttles which once formed a part of the mechanized looms in the Lancashire mills are now converted to hold thermometers and decorate domestic sitting-rooms.

Objects exist in a locational relationship to other artefacts and to the landscape and the study of these relationships can be very fruitful for our understanding of the role of the artefact. Inevitably, material in old collections will lack much of the necessary recorded detail and the insights which this might have conveyed are irretrievably lost, but the opportunities are there for material now being accessioned. In order to understand this dimension of the artefact it is necessary to establish its context, divisible into the micro-context, covering, say, the cubic metre of the object's immediate environment and giving details of surrounding related objects, containers, debris and so on; and the macro-context, which can be as wide as seems helpful, and will certainly involve details of the workshop, church or bedroom from which the artefact came, and the building, settlement or parish in which these were situated. To take an obvious example, it adds considerably to our appreciation of a Friendly Society's brass staff head if we can know what it was normally stored with, and where it was kept.

The plotting of distribution maps of typological sets of objects in the landscape has been a standard archaeological technique since the pioneering days, and it is intended to show the patterning of artefact classes in the context of natural geology, upland and lowland, river systems, travel routes and resources of food and raw materials. This approach is used to a much lesser extent in the other material culture disciplines, probably, one suspects, because much of the detailed work upon which it depends still remains to be undertaken; for example, the distribution of particular classes of goods from recent small, local manufacturing centres in both urban and rural districts has not yet been much studied, but when it has, it will need to be analysed along these lines.

The application of the techniques of the human geographers, particularly those of the location analysis school like Lösch and Christaller (usefully summarized and discussed in Haggett 1956) are in the same case. The work of these men and their increasingly sophisticated followers and critics suggests that social life forms patterns in the landscape which are repetitive and which reflect in their character the character of the society concerned. The application of their approaches also depends upon the creation of object types through detailed local work, but it would be interesting to build up bodies of information about material in our collections which would enable us to plot locational patterns of blacksmiths' shops, village general stores or potteries large and small in relation to the areas which they served and to other social territories like parishes.

Finally, we are bound to consider the significance of the artefact, for its own time and place and for ourselves, since these are often different: a nineteenth-century Yoruba mask had one set of significances for the Yoruba and a rather different set for the twentieth-century collector. Here we face the question of the psychological role of the artefact, and in some ways this, together with material characterization, touches most closely the heart of artefact studies, since it is objects – tangible, external, enduring objects – which can embody a freight of emotional significance, collective and individual, and so it is in the development of insights here that material culture scholars may be able to make their most important particular contribution to our understanding of men in society.

Objects are important to people because they demonstrate prestige and social position; in social terms, most of the pieces which survive in our fine and applied art and costume collections do so for this reason. Objects, especially those in the religious or ceremonial spheres or those made from highly valued materials like precious metal, amber or ivory, symbolize states of mind and social relationships between men and men, and men and their gods, in a unique way. Ceremonial objects take their form from a combination of socially appropriate craftwork and impulses deriving from a profound level in the human psyche: Victoria Crosses are cast in bronze because metal-casting was pre-eminent among the mid-nineteenth-century industrial techniques, but their cross shape follows Christian ideas of passion and sacrifice deeply embedded in the western tradition.

Is it possible to analyse these roles in a more systematic way, to produce a theoretical basis which will render them intelligible in a more universal and less specific fashion? A follower of Jung might argue that we invest with symbolic significance those objects which form bridges between the conscious and unconscious or shadow elements in our personalities, helping us to come to terms with socially undesirable characteristics. It is arguable that what we mean when we talk of beauty in an object is superb hand-and-eye craftmanship linked with a subject and a perceptive treatment of that subject which corresponds most closely to our needs for inner reconciliation and reassurance. The choice of subject and the expression of the insights with which it is clothed will differ from one society to another; beauty is in the eye of the beholder. A structuralist, following Lévi-Strauss and his disciples, might seek to establish opposed pairs of material types, or object types, and to link these into the binary structure of human society and the human mind; McGhee (1977) has suggested that among the Eskimo caribou antler and walrus ivory occupy the material culture sphere in a set of opposed pairs which, together with the other pairs in the set, land/sea, summer/winter and man/woman, structure Eskimo life. Objects would then take their place alongside other creations of man-in-society, like kinship systems or settlement plans, all manifesting universal patterns underlying immense superficial variety.

The last pair of boxes in Fig. 18.2 represent the final phase in an artefact study, the interpretation. This will bring together the yield of information and insight already gathered, and will deploy the fullest possible suite of social analyses – knowledge of the local kinship patterns, authority, structures, economy forms and so on – in order to form a view of the meaning of the object in its society, in the way, for example, that Nigel Barley has discussed the significance of textiles among the Dowagos of North Cameroon (1983).

SOME CONCLUSIONS

Several conclusions seem to arise from this discussion. It must be repeated that not all the material now in our collections is capable of responding to these approaches, nor can we expect to study all our material in equal depth; but one of the aims of this paper has been to set out an approach to artefact study which can potentially be applied across the range of material culture, although obviously artefacts will differ in the degree to which they will respond to the various techniques. It is no accident that some of the approaches discussed here are likely to be more familiar to archaeologists and anthropologists than they are to students in the other material culture fields and one of my hopes in writing this paper is to encourage discussion here.

Some of the topics broached here, particularly the symbolic and structuralist interpretations, together with the other interpretive techniques, are very important subjects, which I hope to pursue in further articles. Meanwhile this paper and this model for artefact studies is offered as a contribution to the debate.

This paper first appeared in Museums Journal *85(4) (1986), pp. 198–201.*

ACKNOWLEDGEMENTS

I am very grateful to Jim Roberts who prepared the two figures.

REFERENCES

Barley, N. (1983) 'The warp and woof of culture', *Royal Anthropological Institute News* 59: 7–8.
Fleming McClung, E. (1974) 'Artefact study: a proposed model', *Winterthur Portfolio* 9: 153–61.
Haggett, R. (1956) *Locational Analysis in Human Geography*, London: Arnold.
McGhee, R. (1977) 'Ivory for the sea woman: the symbolic attributes of a prehistoric technology', *Canadian Journal of Archaeology* 1: 141–9.
Montgomery, C. (1961) 'Some remarks on the practice and science of connoisseurship', *American Walpole Society Notebook* 720.
Porter, J. and Martin, W. (1985) 'Learning from objects', *Museums Journal* 85: 35–7.

19

Mind in matter: an introduction to material culture theory and method

Jules Prown

Jules Prown also works from a background in the applied arts, although he is very aware of theoretical developments in the fields of social studies and linguistics. Prown's approach, which is not tabulated into diagrammatic form, offers three stages of analysis: description, deduction and speculation, and possesses the great advantage of admitting the subjective nature of much analysis, and of bringing the interpreter's understanding and response into the interpretative frame.

METHODOLOGY

How does one extract information about culture, about mind, from mute objects? We have been taught to retrieve information in abstract form, words, and numbers, but most of us are functionally illiterate when it comes to interpreting information encoded in objects. Several academic disciplines, notably art history and archaeology, routinely work with artefacts as evidence and over the years have built up a considerable amount of theoretical and methodological expertise. Work done in these fields is often directed inward, towards the accumulation and explication of information required by the discipline itself. In the history of art this takes the form of resolving questions of stylistic and iconographic influence, of dating and authorship, of quality and authenticity. In archaeology it is the basic task of assembling, sorting, dating and quantifying the assembled data. But art history and archaeology also have fundamental concerns with the cultures that produced the objects, and the methodologies of these two fields, to the extent that they provide means for the interpretation of culture, are essential to material culture. At present they are the two disciplines most directly relevant to the actual work of investigating material culture. But, as they are usually defined, they are not adequate to the total task. The exploration of patterns of belief and behaviour, in an intellectual borderland where the interests of humanities and social sciences merge, requires an openness to other methodologies, including those of cultural and social history, cultural and social anthropology, psychohistory, sociology, cultural geography, folklore and folk life, and linguistics. But the approach to material culture set forth below dictates that these broader concerns and methodologies *not* be brought into play until the evidence of the artefact itself has been plumbed as objectively as possible. Therefore the first steps are most closely related to the basic descriptive techniques of art history and archaeology, and in this there is more overlap with the natural than with the social sciences. The initial descriptive steps in the approach to objects resembles fieldwork in a science such as geology, and description can also involve the use of scientific equipment.

The method of object analysis proposed below progresses through three stages. To keep the distorting biases of the investigator's cultural perspective in check, these stages must be undertaken in sequence and kept as discrete as possible. The analysis proceeds from *description*, recording the internal evidence of the object itself; to *deduction*, interpreting the interaction between the object and the perceiver; to *speculation*, framing hypotheses and questions which lead out from the object to external evidence for testing and resolution.[1]

Description

Description is restricted to what can be observed in the object itself, that is, to internal evidence. In practice, it is desirable to begin with the largest, most comprehensive observations and progress systematically to more particular details. The terminology should be as accurate as possible; technical terms are fine as long as they can be understood. The analyst must, however, continually guard against the intrusion of either subjective assumptions or conclusions derived from other experience.

This is a synchronic exercise; the physical object is read at a particular moment in time. The object is almost certainly not identical to what it was when it was fabricated; time, weather, usage will all have taken their toll. At this stage no consideration is given to condition or to other diachronic technological, iconographic or stylistic influences.

Substantial analysis

Description begins with substantial analysis, an account of the physical dimensions, material and articulation of the object. To determine physical dimensions, the object is measured and perhaps weighed. The degree of precision depends on the interests of the investigator. If he will be considering a series of objects, a certain amount of precision is desirable, given the possible subsequent significance of and need for quantification. However, it is not desirable to carry decimals to the point of losing an immediate sense of dimension in a welter of numbers; real significance may lie in general measure, as with Glassie's discovery of the modal importance of spans and cubits in the vernacular architecture of Virginia.[2] Next comes a description of the materials – what they are, how extensively they are used, and the pattern of their distribution throughout the object. Finally, the ways in which the materials are put together in the fabrication of the object, the articulation, should be noted. For example, with fabrics one would look at the weave; with metals, the welding, soldering, riveting; with wood, the dovetails, dowels, mitre joints, mortise-and-tenon joints, glue.

Substantial analysis is a descriptive physical inventory of the object. It is achieved with the assistance of whatever technical apparatus is appropriate and available. Simple tape measures and scales, ultraviolet lamps and infrared photographs, or complex electron microscopes and X-ray diffraction machines are all basically enhancements of one's ability to perceive and take the measure of the physical properties and dimensions of the object.[3]

Content

The next step in description is analysis of content. The investigator is concerned simply with subject matter. This is usually a factor only with works of art or other decorated objects. The procedure is iconography in its simplest sense, a reading of overt representations. In the case of a painting, this may simply be what is represented, as if the work were a window on the world (or on some kind of world). Content may include decorative designs or motifs, inscriptions, coats of arms, or diagrams, engraved or embossed on metal, carved or painted on wood or stone, woven in textiles, moulded or etched in glass.

Formal analysis

Finally, and very important, is analysis of the object's form or configuration, its visual character. It is useful to begin by describing the two-dimensional organization – lines and areas – either on the surface of a flat object or in elevations or sections through a solid object.[4] Next comes the three-dimensional organization of forms in space, whether actual in a three-dimensional object or represented in a pictorial object. Subsequently, other formal elements such as colour, light and texture should be analysed with, as in the case of the initial description of materials, an account of their nature, extent and pattern of distribution (rhythm) in each case. Determination of the degree of detail must be left to the discretion of the investigator; too much can be almost as bad as too little: the forest can be lost for the trees.

Deduction

The second stage of analysis moves from the object itself to the relationship between the object and the perceiver. It involves the empathetic linking of the material (actual) or represented world of the object with the perceiver's world of existence and experience. To put it another way, the analyst contemplates what it would be like to use or interact with the object, or, in the case of a representational object, to be transported empathetically into the depicted world. If conditions permit, he handles, lifts, uses, walks through, or experiments physically with the object. The paramount criterion for deductions drawn from this interaction is that they must meet the test of reasonableness and common sense; that is, most people, on the basis of their knowledge of the physical world and the evidence of their own life experience, should find the deductions to be unstrained interpretations of the evidence elicited by the description. If these deductions are not readily acceptable as reasonable, they must be considered hypothetical and deferred to the next stage.

Although the analyst in the deductive stage moves away from a concern solely with the internal evidence of the object and injects himself into the investigation, the process remains synchronic. Just as the object is only what it is at the moment of investigation, and as such may be more or less different from what it was when it was made, so too the analyst is what he is at the moment of investigation. Ten years hence he might respond differently to the object because of different interests and a different mix of life experiences near the surface of conscious awareness. The particular encounter between an object with its history and an individual with his history shapes the deductions. Neither is what they were nor what they may become. Yet the event does not occur within a vacuum. The object is at least in some ways what it was or bears some recognizable relationship to what it was; the same, although less germane, is true of the investigator. The object may not testify with complete accuracy about its culture, but it can divulge something. It is the analyst's task to find out what it can tell and, perhaps, deduce what it can no longer tell.

Sensory engagement

The first step in deduction is sensory experience of the object. If possible, one touches it to feel its texture and lifts it to know its heft. Where appropriate, consideration should be given to the physical adjustments a user would have to make to its size, weight, configuration and texture. The experience of architecture or a townscape would involve sensory perceptions while moving through it. If the object is not accessible, then these things must be done imaginatively and empathetically. In the case of a picture, the engagement is necessarily empathetic; the analyst projects himself into the represented world (or, in Alois Riegl's sense, considers that the pictorial space continues into the viewer's world of existence) and records what he would see, hear, smell, taste and feel.[5]

Intellectual engagement

The second step is intellectual apprehension of the object. With a tool or implement this is a consideration of what it does and how it does it, and in such cases may need to precede or accompany the sensory engagement. The degree of understanding at this stage (prior to the admission of external evidence) depends on the complexity of the object and the analyst's prior knowledge and experience. It is unnecessary to ignore what one knows and feign innocence for the appearance of objectivity, but it is desirable to test one's external knowledge to see if it can be deduced from the object itself and, if it cannot, to set that knowledge aside until the next stage.

In the case of a pictorial object, there are a number of questions that may be addressed to and answered by the object itself, especially if it is representational. What is the time of day? What is the season of the year? What is the effect on what is depicted of natural forces such as heat and cold or the pull of gravity? In the relation between the depicted world and our world, where are we positioned, what might we be doing, and what role, if any, might we play? How would we enter pictorial space? What transpired prior to the depicted moment? What may happen next?

Emotional response

Finally, there is the matter of the viewer's emotional response to the object. Reactions vary in kind, intensity and specificity, but it is not uncommon to discover that what one considered a subjective response is in fact widely shared. A particular object may trigger joy, fright, awe, perturbation, revulsion, indifference, curiosity or other responses that can be quite subtly distinguished. These subjective reactions, difficult but by no means impossible to articulate, tend to be significant to the extent that they are generally shared. They point the way to specific insights when the analyst identifies the elements noted in the descriptive stage that have precipitated them.

I have stressed the importance of attempting to maintain rigorous discreteness and sequence in the stages of object analysis. In fact, this is difficult if not impossible to achieve. Deductions almost invariably creep into the initial description. These slips, usually unnoted by the investigator, are undesirable since they undercut objectivity. But in practice, while striving to achieve objectivity and to maintain the scientific method as an ideal, the investigator should not be so rigorous and doctrinaire in the application of methodological rigour as to inhibit the process. Vigilance, not martial law, is the appropriate attitude. Often an individual's subjective assumptions are not recognized as such until considerably later. In fact, it is instructive in regard to understanding one's own cultural biases, one's own cultural perspective, to mark those assumptions that remain undetected the longest in the descriptive stage. These are often the most deeply rooted cultural assumptions.

Speculation

Having progressed from the object itself in description to the interaction between object and perceiver in deduction, the analysis now moves completely to the mind of the perceiver, to *speculation*. There are few rules or proscriptions at this stage. What is desired is as much creative imagining as possible, the free association of ideas and perceptions tempered only, and then not too quickly, by the analyst's common sense and judgement as to what is even vaguely plausible.

Theories and hypotheses

The first step in speculation is to review the information developed in the descriptive and deductive stages and to formulate hypotheses. This is the time of summing up what has been learned from the internal evidence of the object itself, turning those data over in one's mind, developing theories that might explain the various effects observed and felt. Speculation takes place in the mind of the investigator, and his cultural stance now becomes a major factor. However, since the objective and deductive evidence is already in hand, this cultural bias has little distorting effect. Indeed, it is an asset rather than a liability; it fuels the creative work that now must take place. Because of cultural perspective, it is impossible to respond to and interpret the object in exactly the same way as did the fabricating society, or any other society that may have been exposed to and reacted to the object during its history and peregrinations. Where there is a common response, it provides an affective insight into the cultural values of another society. Where there is divergence, the distinctive cultural perspective of our society can illuminate unseen and even unconscious aspects of the other culture. There was gravity before Newton; there was economic determinism before Marx; there was sex before Freud. We are free to use the insights afforded by our cultural and historical perspective, as long as we do not make the mistake of assigning intentionality or even awareness to the fabricating culture. Our cultural distance from the culture of the object precludes affective experience of those beliefs that are at variance with our own belief systems, but the process now begun can lead to the recovery of some of those beliefs. That is a goal of the exercise.

Programme of research

The second step in the speculative stage is developing a programme for validation, that is, a plan for scholarly investigation of questions posed by the material evidence. This shifts the enquiry from analysis of internal evidence to the search for and investigation of external evidence. Now the methodologies and techniques of various disciplines can be brought into play according to the nature of the questions raised and the skills and inclinations of the scholar.

The object is not abandoned after the preliminary analysis – description, deduction, speculation – is complete and the investigation has moved to external evidence. There should be continual shunting back and forth between the outside evidence and the artefact as research suggests to the investigator the need for more descriptive information or indicates other hypotheses that need to be tested affectively.

This paper first appeared in Winterthur Portfolio *17 (1982), pp. 1–19.*

NOTES

1   The issue of sequence undoubtedly needs further study. I am aware that the insistence upon strict adherence to a particular series of steps seems rigid and arbitrary, an uncalled-for fettering of the investigator. Yet, I have come to appreciate the virtues of sequence empirically on the basis of considerable classroom experience with artefact analysis. It simply works better. The closer the sequence suggested below is followed, especially in regard to the major stages, and the greater the care taken with each analytical step before proceeding, the more penetrating, complex and satisfying the final interpretation. Obviously, the procedure is time-consuming, and there is a natural impatience to move along.

My experience has been, however, that this should be resisted until the analysis is exhausted and the obvious next question requires advancing to the next step.

2 Henry Glassie (1975) *Folk Housing in Middle Virginia: A Structural Analysis of Historic Artifacts*, Knoxville: University of Tennessee Press.

3 The procedures outlined here for collecting internal evidence have other significant applications. Physical analysis, including the use of scientific apparatus, can provide crucial information in regard to authenticity. Other procedures noted below, notably formal analysis, can also be exceedingly useful in determining authenticity. These applications of the methodology can take place at any time, but it is preferable for the issue of authenticity to be resolved before the analysis proceeds beyond *description*. If a material culture investigator is to arrive at cultural conclusions on the basis of material evidence, the specimen being studied *must* be an authentic product of the culture in question. The investigator must determine what aspects of the objects, if any, are not authentic products of the presumed culture. A fake may be a useful artefact in relation to the culture that produced the fake, but it is deceptive in relation to the feigned culture.

4 The procedures of formal analysis summarized briefly here will be familiar to any art historian. They are not, however, arcane, and investigators need not be specially trained. Formal analysis is a matter of articulating and recording what one sees, preferably in a systematic sequence as suggested here.

5 See Sheldon Nodelman (1970) 'Structural analysis in art and anthropology', in Jacques Ehrmann (ed.) *Structuralism*, Garden City, N.Y.: Anchor Books/Doubleday, 87. This splendid article sets forth succinctly the basis for contemporary structural analysis in the early art historical work of the German school of *Strukturforschung*, especially as initiated by Riegl and developed by Guido von Kaschnitz-Weinberg, and the *anthropologie structurale* of Claude Lévi-Strauss.

20

Not looking at kettles

Ray Batchelor

Batchelor's model stemmed from his work at the Science Museum, London, and was intended to highlight the point that objects are capable of multifaceted interpretation through the analysis of a deliberately mundane, mass-produced object, a twentieth-century kettle. Like Prown, Batchelor eschewed the creation of a model diagram, but his analysis was through the clearly demarcated areas of idea or invention, material, manufacture, marketing, history of design and use.

Writing just before the Second World War, E. M. Forster in his essay 'Not Looking at Pictures' remarked 'Ours is an aural rather than a visual age'. I'm not sure he was right, even then. Certainly, since then, the growth of television has ensured that today's public has grown used to sophisticated visual imagery, and this in turn has influenced museum display techniques. In the Lower Wellcome Gallery in the Science Museum, for example, some of the most successful reconstructions were designed and built with the help of a TV set designer. No museum, however modest its scope, seems complete these days without its Victorian shop or parlour or kitchen. The approach has much to recommend it. Many visitors, especially children, who may not linger over detailed labels, however scholarly, can see at once the significance of a variety of objects. But there are pitfalls, of which we are all becoming increasingly aware. Accuracy is one. A 'Victorian parlour' may well have been a rare commodity in Victorian England when one reflects on the mixture of furnishings found in one's own or one's parents' home. The public is constantly bombarded with 'historical' or 'nostalgic' drama. They have seen it on Telly; they *know* what it was really like. Do we have the sense to strive after genuine authenticity, and after that, the courage to disabuse or enlighten? We must not ignore the various and distinct significances an object can present, by giving trivial prominence to just one. None of these difficulties is insuperable, and I am sure that the reconstruction as a means of passing on information has a long way to go yet. But, conscious of these dangers, I would like to put in a plea for a more scrupulous and methodical analysis of some of the apparently obvious objects in our care. Before we allow our desire to please the public to influence the decisions we take about how objects should be interpreted, we should at the very least assemble all the information at our disposal relating to it. Only then can we decide which of the departure points the object presents are worth pursuing on our public's behalf.

Unless I give it away, which is quite unlikely, my kettle belongs not to the public, but to me. I bought it at Brick Lane Market, in the East End of London about four years ago, because it was cheap and I liked its shape. As it turned out, it worked as well. The method of examining objects I would like to outline gives plenty of scope for the imaginative application of specialist knowledge. But more than anything else, it hinges on doing the one thing we probably already think we do: *looking at it*. For the purposes of this explanation I would like you to join me in imagining my kettle is a museum object, and less plausibly perhaps, that we are its curators. We are going to analyse its design, examining each of the forces which have made it the way it is. In 'real life' these are interdependent and altered by one another. None the less, in our museum laboratory we should attempt to separate and label them.

FIRST: THE IDEA OR THE INVENTION

Behind most domestic appliances is an evolution of ideas, a discovery or an invention. Kettles in different forms have been with us for thousands of years. The first patent for electrically heated food was taken out in 1879. Electrical elements were eventually incorporated into other appliances including frying-pans and food warmers. The first electrical kettle appeared in Chicago in 1894, and in this country in 1902. The potentially hazardous mixture of electricity and water meant that early electric kettles had their elements mounted directly *under* the base of the kettle. Only later, some time prior to 1922, did the manufacturers, Bulpitts, incorporate an element which was – safely – immersed in the water itself, a much more efficient arrangement. Armed with this knowledge it becomes apparent that this kettle is of the earlier sort, with the element mounted separately in the base. However, closer examination of the inside reveals that the designer had some appreciation of the inefficiency of this arrangement. The inner base of the kettle is not flat but a shallow dome, giving greater surface area of metal for the heater to act on. Heat radiating from the sides of the element which might otherwise have been lost is used instead to heat the water.

SECOND: THE MATERIAL FROM WHICH IT IS MADE

Setting aside for the moment the form the materials may take, cheap materials such as cast iron, enamelware or block tin tend to indicate a cheap utilitarian article. Precious metals – or, more unusually in the case of domestic appliances, some form of plating – whatever their practical advantages for the device, suggest at least a gesture towards show. Most of the metal parts of this kettle are sheets of brass plated with nickel. Of course there are also sound utilitarian reasons for the selection of materials. Brass is a good conductor of heat; but nickel is easier to keep clean than brass. The black knob on the lid is wooden – a poor conductor of heat. For similar reasons, the hinged metal handle is sheathed in woven cane. Apart from fulfilling some of the aesthetic and practical demands put on the object in use, the choice of materials will in some part be governed by the ease with which they can be worked.

THIRD: MAKING, OR MANUFACTURE

The choice of manufacturing methods is in turn governed by the choice of materials. Then there is the state of the manufacturing arts at any time, in any one place. The methods must satisfy the practical and aesthetic demands of the design, yet at the same time their cost must be justified relative to the wholesale price the maker or manufacturer can expect to realize. This kettle was made in Germany in about 1910. The principal sheets of brass from which it has been constructed would have started life flat, and then been cut into – mostly circular – shapes. These would have been mounted in a lathe and spun to the requisite profiles over carefully measured patterns. At the same time the decorative grooves and imitation planishing effect could easily have been added. The individual metal parts would then have been electrically nickel-plated, and afterwards soldered together. The electric element and remaining components would then have been incorporated, and the electric kettle have been complete. In all likelihood the hand-work put into the cane covering for the handle would have been performed by women – a perennial way of keeping manufacturing costs to a minimum. All the other steps in the manufacturing process would have been straightforward by the standards of the day. None the less, it is very well made.

Most of this information can be assembled just by looking at this kettle very closely indeed. It is a skill anyone working with such material – be their background so-called 'arts', or so-called 'technical' – ought to possess.

FOURTH: MARKETING

Marketing is an area where, in our interpretation of this object, it is worth while drawing back a little, and considering trade activities in a wider context than simply as an influence on design. Certainly it is an aspect of the 'natural life' of many modern objects – domestic appliances are no exception – which is often neglected by museums. If one is fortunate, a retail price is sometimes given on a museum label. Better still, it is occasionally expressed relative to the incomes of different levels of society. Seldom is an analysis of the price attempted from the other side of the counter, yet this can often be very worth while. A retail price, as I have said, is influenced by the cost of raw materials, and of working them into the finished product; added to these basics is the cost of transport, including import and export tariffs where appropriate; usually there is also a wholesaler's cut, tax, everyone's overheads and, perhaps most significantly, what the market will bear. Recently, in the case of Cabbage Patch dolls, this seems to have been the overriding factor. But it is more common for a retail price to reflect more evenly all these influences. This kettle was made in Germany in 1910. Its high-quality finish is a reflection of Germany's increasingly sophisticated industrialization and rapid economic growth. This growth was financed to a large extent by a vigorous exploitation of old and new export markets.

If this kettle, as seems most probable, was bought new in Britain in about 1910, it provides a graphic illustration of one of the most fiercely fought political issues of the early twentieth century – 'Tariff Reform'. In the General Election of 1906, Joseph Chamberlain exhorted the electorate to support the Tory proposals for tariff barriers against imported goods, to protect those produced at home. They lost, and a landslide victory went to the Liberals. It would have been under the conditions of free trade which they espoused that this kettle was imported

It may well have been competitively priced against other electric kettles. Yet it would inevitably have been more expensive than kettles heated in the more conventional way. Not only that, it holds only very little water – about two pints – and takes about twenty minutes to boil: the simplest gas burner took only ten. To understand why these apparent handicaps did not prevent it from enjoying a fair measure of success, we must now return to the examination of its design, but this time looking at it from an aesthetic point of view. This should provide conclusive proof of how this kettle, in its early life at least, would probably have been used.

FIFTH: ART

The prettiness of this kettle is no accident of its utilitarian function. It is a careful, sophisticated composition. Its overall form, and in particular the little heart shape of the hinges, are derived from 'lugendstil' – still very much an active influence on design in 1910. The cane handle is perhaps a gesture towards Japan, the East, and cane-handled teapots; and this, together with the planished effect – even if it was achieved on a machine – subtly plants the erroneous idea that this kettle was not mass-produced at all, but hand-made by craftsmen. Japan and the 'Crafts' were other fashionable influences on design. At about the same time in 1906 when Chamberlain was trying to protect British goods from, amongst others, a barrage of German imports, the Allgemeine Elektrizitäts-Gesellschaft was busy adding a further piece of artillery to its commercial force. By engaging the services of Peter Behrens, AEG had secured for themselves the proven talents of a daring and capable designer and, more recently, architect. Soon all AEG electrical goods were manufactured to his designs; the shapes became simpler more sophisticated and – most importantly for them – found favour with the buying public. Peter Behrens designed this kettle.

SIXTH (AND FINALLY): USE

This good, attractive design was not just a way of competing in the marketplace with uglier, more efficient rivals. The key to understanding why this kettle is the shape that it is lies in its use. It is highly probable that it was never intended primarily for boiling water in the *kitchen* at all, but more an article of *drawing-room* equipment for the preparation of tea or coffee. That is why AEG lavished such attention on its design, why its comparative inefficiency was not crucial, and why its high purchase price did not prevent its commercial success. One simply would not have a gas ring in the drawing-room. The traditional arrangement of a silver kettle, previously filled with boiling water in the kitchen and then kept at simmering point over a spirit lamp, was not without its disadvantages. For one thing, it did not provide *freshly boiled* water for making tea. Spirit lamps could be uncertain in their action, and required a degree of skill in their management. This electric kettle was, in 1910, a modern alternative. It held just enough water to make a pot of tea for two or three guests, it was elegant, respectable and required absolutely no skill whatsoever.

Design is a tricky word. Like 'technology', which always suggests to me endless acres of graph paper, or like 'Art', it sets off all sorts of alarm bells in different people. My analysis of the design of this kettle has been necessarily superficial. Nowhere, for example, apart from the women who worked the cane handles, Peter Behrens the designer, and those who drank the tea, have I mentioned the thousands of people's lives that this kettle would have affected: the miners in the nickel mines, the sheet-metal dealer, the workers at AEG, the wholesalers, shopkeepers – the scope is absolutely enormous. Many of those occupations continue today. We are in the business of explaining to people of the present the meaning of objects in the past. The implications are obvious.

When I bought this kettle I was not a museum curator but a postman. I bought it because, four years ago, I just liked its shape. In the sense that I have just indicated I was 'not looking' at it. As museum curators we really cannot afford to do just that. Objects *are our primary archives*. We must understand their various meanings as widely as we can. That said, I doubt that the public wants to know everything about everything. It may well be that the most effective way of explaining the function of this kettle would be to furnish a corner of our museum as a 1910 drawing-room, people it with a trio of appropriately dressed glass-fibre women ordered from Gems; put teacups and coloured plaster cakes on a little table, and let the kettle – as its makers would have wanted – blend discreetly into the background. But before we settle on this charming and attractive scene, we must first examine all the information the object presents or illustrates, and actively decide that within the function of our museum, *its use* is more important than:

- the inventions it incorporates,
- the manufacturing methods it illustrates,
- its place in commercial or political history,
- the principles on which it operates,
- the aspects of applied art which it embodies.

Of course, it may be desirable and possible to incorporate some of these points in our display. We have a duty to entertain the postman, but more than that, we have an obligation to stop him from 'not looking' at his kettle, for just a little while at least. After all, once started, we do not know what he might see, or what he might do as a consequence.

'Not looking at kettles' was originally delivered as a paper to a Museum Professionals Group Annual Study Weekend in Liverpool in 1984. Ray Batchelor was then a curator at the Science Museum. The paper was first published in *Museum Professionals Group News* 23 (1986), pp. 1–3.

21

Home interview questionnaire, with coding categories and definitions

M. Csikszentmihalyi and E. Halton

In 1977–8 the authors undertook a major study into a socioeconomically stratified sample of three-generation families from Evanston and Rogers Park, Chicago, and the ways in which they viewed material objects, principally those objects which formed part of their domestic surroundings. The study explored the relationship between individuals, families and material culture, and showed how these three elements interact. The basis of the study was the interviews conducted with participants. This extract gives the text of the Home Interview questionnaire, and the categories and definitions against which the replies were coded in order to allow analysis.

The paper first appeared in M. Csikszentmihalyi and E. Halton (eds) (1981) The Meaning of Things, Cambridge: Cambridge University Press, pp. 256–77.

HOME INTERVIEW

1 Could you describe your home to me, as if I were someone who had never seen it? (Interviewer – if respondent describes social atmosphere, feeling or mood but not physical description, then probe for physical description. If physical description given, then vice versa.)

2 What are the rooms in your home?

3 Where in your home do you feel most 'at home'? Why there?

4   Are you trying to have a certain style or atmosphere in your living-room? Describe.

5A What are the things in your home which are special for you? Could you name the rooms these things are in and tell us why they are special? (Interviewer – remember that parts B, C and D of this question will be asked sequentially. Also, use additional sheets for any section if necessary.)

ROOM   OBJECT   WHY SPECIAL

_____

_____

_____

_____

_____

5B What would it mean to you not to have this thing? (Interviewer – list the objects the person has already named in 5A.)

OBJECT   WITHOUT OBJECT

_____

_____

_____

_____

_____

5C When did you acquire these things? D. How did you acquire each of these things? (Interviewer – D is only for objects for which the circumstances of acquisition have not already been described.)

OBJECT   WHEN ACQUIRED   HOW ACQUIRED

_____   _____

_____   _____

_____   _____

_____   _____

_____   _____

6   If you had a fire in your home, what objects would you save?

145

7   Are there any objects that have been special in your life, but which you no longer possess?

8   What do you think are your parents' most special objects? Your spouse's most special objects? Your children's most special objects?

PARENTS   SPOUSE   CHILDREN

9   What objects are special for you to give to your children? Why? (Interviewer – if respondent has no children ask '. . . would be special *if* you had children?')

10   What are your most private or personal objects – either ones that you've already mentioned or others?

11   What do all of your special objects, taken together as a whole, mean to you?

CODING CATEGORIES AND DEFINITIONS

Object categories

The first step in analysing the data consisted in grouping the household artefacts that people mentioned as special into a limited number of categories. The 41 categories that are subsequently listed seemed adequate to account for all the 1,694 objects mentioned by the 315 respondents. Some of the 1,694 'objects' are groupings of objects, for example if a respondent ['R'] said 'my plants' or 'my art' and did not choose to differentiate separate objects, it would be scored as one object. In formulating the main kinds of objects, the attempt was inductively to draw the categories from the objects named by respondents. Some of the categories are grosser than others, e.g. furniture may be broken down into separate categories of dining-room sets, chairs, and so on. But the intention was to draw out categories that would characterize different general kinds of objects and the resulting categories did seem accurate, because interrater reliability was 95 per cent.

1 *Furniture*. Refers to objects on or in which to place things or sit, e.g. tables, chairs, dressers, desks, etc. Beds, lamps, carpets and other appliances will be scored separately.

2 *Bed*. R explicitly names a bed, not a couch.

3 *Visual art*. Refers to the full range of two-dimensional representations other than photographs, commonly hung on a wall (e.g., an original Picasso as well as a *Last Supper* reproduction from a 5¢ & 10¢ store would be included in this category. Paintings by children or other family members are included in this category.)

4 *Sculpture*. Refers to all plastic art, or the range of three-dimensional representations and crafted objects, excluding weavings and furniture, which are usually displayed for generalized 'aesthetic' reason. Like the Visual art category, it includes the range from 'high art' (e.g., a maquette by Chicago artist Richard Hunt) to mass-produced items (such as a Don Quixote statue), and objects made by friends or relatives (e.g., a burnt match crucifix made by one woman's son).

5 *Collections*. Refers to objects that people collect, *which do not fall into any of the other object categories*, e.g., an art collection named as an object would be coded under Visual art, not under Collections. The kinds of objects that would be coded under Collections would include rock or butterfly collections, comic books, letters.

6 *Musical instruments*. Includes the mention of all musical instruments, e.g., piano, guitar, etc.

7 *TV*.

8 *Stereo, Tape players*.

9 *Radio*.

10 *Books*. Includes books in general, as well as particular books, e.g. Bible, Proust.

11 *Photos*. All mention of photos under this category. If R mentions 'pictures', check to see if this refers to Photos or Visual art.

12 *Plants*.

13 *Plates*. This category includes the mention of 'dishes', china, 'cups', 'mugs', pewter dishes.

14 *Silverware*.

15 *Glass*.

16 *Pets*. Make sure the animal is alive and not a stuffed toy.

17 *Aquariums*.

18 *Appliances*. Includes the mention of washers, dryers, toasters, microwave, etc.

19 *Refrigerator*.

20 *Lamps, Chandeliers, Sconces*.

21 *Clocks*. Includes all wall clocks, alarm clocks, grandfather clocks, etc.

22 *Tools*. Includes lathes, hammers, 'tools' in general, and electric *tools*.

23 *Sports equipment*. Includes golf clubs, basketballs, jogging shoes, etc. Does not include athletic *clothes*, which will be coded under Clothes.

24 *Trophies*. Includes all trophies, awards, medals, ribbons, badges, citations or merit of achievement, and animals caught or shot and stuffed, e.g., dolphin, moose.

25 *Camera*. Refers to all photographic *equipment*, not the photographs, which will be coded under Photos. Includes cameras, tripods, dark rooms and other photographic equipment.

26 *Toys*. All mention of toys, excluding objects that are explicitly athletic equipment and the subcategory of stuffed animals.

27 *Stuffed animals*. Includes all mention of toy stuffed animals. Be careful to check that the named animal is stuffed and not alive, especially when a name is used, e.g., 'Arfie'. A formerly live animal that has been stuffed by a taxidermist should be coded under Trophy, e.g. dolphin, moose.

28 *Clothes.* Includes all mention of attire, excluding athletic footwear.
29 *Jewellery.* Includes all mention of jewellery, wedding rings, high-school rings, watches.
30 *Quilts, Textiles.* Includes all forms of weaving, excluding carpets.
31 *Carpets.*
32 *Fireplace.*
33 *Bath.*
34 *Room.* Kitchen, breakfast nook, bedroom, recreation room, etc.
35 *Miscellaneous.* Refers to the idiosyncratic objects that do not fit any of the other categories. *Make a separate list* of any object that falls into this category, e.g. clubhouse.
36 *All.* 'Everything' includes mention of the whole house or all objects.
37 *Scrapbook.* Family trees, papers, poetry, diaries.
38 *Vehicles.* Cars, trucks, bicycles.
39 *Telephone.* C.B. radio, two-way communication devices.
40 *Yard.* Garden, backyard, etc.
41 *Candlesticks.*

For some operations the object categories were grouped into two broad classes: action objects and contemplation objects. Those objects whose use involves some physical handling, interaction or movement were coded in the action category; those whose use is mainly through reflection or contemplation were coded in the contemplation category.

Action objects

2 Bed	22 Tools
6 Musical instrument	23 Sports equipment
7 Television	25 Camera
8 Stereo	26 Toys, games
9 Radio	27 Stuffed animals
12 Plants	28 Clothes
16 Pets	32 Fireplace
17 Aquariums	33 Bathroom
18 Appliances	38 Vehicles
19 Refrigerator	39 Telephones, etc.

Contemplation objects

3 Visual art
4 Sculpture
5 Collections
10 Books
11 Photos
13 Plates
14 Silverware
15 Glass
30 Quilts, textiles
41 Candleholders

Meaning classes and categories

The next step was to develop 'meanings' categories (such as the object is valued as a 'souvenir', or because it was a 'gift', or for the 'experiences' it provides) in an attempt to classify and statistically compare the meanings embodied in the various kinds of objects by respondents. Like the object categories, the meanings categories were drawn out of what seemed to be the most common descriptions given by respondents, and were proved to be statistically reliable by comparing the results of two independent coders (approximately 85 per cent for all generations). The two coders spent considerable time and effort to define the rules for coding, because this portion of the coding was so context-bound. A total of 7,875 'significations' were recorded for the 1,694 objects, and these were coded into the following 35 categories of meaning. These 35 categories of meaning were also grouped into 11 broader meanings *classes* for comparisons that did not need as much detail. The broad class of Memories, for example, includes the categories of meanings referring to Mementos, Recollections, Heirlooms, Souvenirs, and 'Had it for a long time'.

Non-persons coding classes and categories

I Past

  A Memories

    1 *Memento*. Memories in general, not associated with particular occasion. Includes description of sentimental associations.

    'It gives me memories of my aunt in California'

    'It connects me with the past'

    'Reminds me of family dinners we used to have'

    'I guess it's just a lot of sentiment'

    'Because I love them'

    'We've had it for so many years' is *not* coded for memento but will be coded under 'Had it for so long' category.

    2 *Recollection*. Memories of *specific* occasion(s) in respondent's lifetime.

    'Reminds me of last Christmas'

    'I got it as a wedding present'

    'I got it for my birthday'

    'We signed the bottom of this'

    3 *Heirloom*. Object handed down in family.

    'It belonged to my grandfather'

    'These pewter mugs have been in my family since the 1700s'

    4 *Souvenir*. Memory of a place. The object was purchased at the place either by the respondent or by someone known to the respondent who gave it to the respondent, e.g., 'We got these in Tunisia.' Don't forget that this is a memory of a place, so a description of a memory of some place would be coded here instead of under 'memento'.

    5 *'Had it for a long time.'* The respondent describes the object as special because he has had it for such a long time, either in R's own possession or in the environment that the person has lived in (e.g., 'this clock has been here since before I was even born, and so it's special just because I'm used to it always being here').

    The reference must be to the length of time the object has been around. E.g., simply stating, 'I've had it since the kids were born' would not be sufficient to be scored for this category, because the reference might be to the birth of children. This would include examples indicating an actual time period the object was in the respondent's possession, e.g., 'We've had it for 15 years.' Any time reference of *10* years or longer will fall under this category.

  B Associations

  6 & 7 *Ethnic, Religious*. Some reference is given to R's *own* ethnic or religious group (or own religious belief).

    'This porkskin plate comes from Mexico and reminds me of my country'

    Check R's ethnic identity before coding this one.

    8 *Collections*. Object or set of objects are explicitly valued as a collection.

    'My comics'

    But 'We have a lot of art' would *not* be a collection because there is no mention of the art as a *collection* as being special.

    9 *Gift*. Object is special because it was given as a gift. 'I would never want to part with that *egg cup* because it was given to me by a very dear friend.'

II Present–Future

A Experience

10 *Enjoyment*. Refers to positive feelings associated with the object and somehow explicitly described by the respondent.
'It makes me happy'
'I like to work with these tools'
'Entertaining'
'I dig it'
'Unhappy without object' does not get coded as enjoyment.

11 *Ongoing occasions*. Object used for events or everyday activities that regularly occur. Includes descriptions of regular use of object.
'We sit in front of this fireplace each Christmas'
'We sit in front of this fireplace on weekends'
'I enjoy the piano and I learn a lot from my lessons *each week*'
'My bed is very special because it's warm and because I sleep in it *every night*'
'Kitchen – *I cook all the meals* here and like the room'
'Silverware – we use this for our Sunday dinner'

NOT: 'I like to cook gourmet meals', no indication of frequency.

12 *Release*. The feeling of release that some of the respondents said the object enabled them to achieve – escape, venting frustration.
'My piano is a release for me'
'Venting frustration'

B Intrinsic qualities of object

13 *Craft*. Made by hand either by respondent, kin, friend, or someone or someone known by respondent. Tools used to make other things are not Craft but Accomplishment.
'My daughter made this potholder for me'

14 *Uniqueness*. The object is described as being one of a kind, unique. The object is either physically unique or explicitly described as unique because of personal associations *connected with that object* for the respondent. The object is unique, not the personal association.
'I could never replace this'
'I made this at a certain point in my life and could never do the same thing again'
'It's one of a kind'

NOT unique: 'These are very rare'

'There were only 100 of these ever made'
Original oil painting. Even though this is a unique object, it must be explicitly described as such by the respondent.
'It's all I have from my father's family. I wouldn't have it to pass on'

15 *Physical description*. Respondent gives a physical description of the object. Usual descriptions include references to size, texture or colour, and employ such characteristic words as: large, wood, brass, copper, mahogany, chipped, naugahyde, etc. For painting and sculpture, a description of the representation itself will be coded as a physical description (even though this will sometimes be coded as style also), e.g. 'Painting. It is a fiesta scene'
'I like his work, especially the way he depicted the cloud formation'

'Sculpture. It's all brass. It's fourth-century Sumerian [*sic*] sculpture'
The preceding example would be coded for physical description *as well as* for style.
'Painting. This is a painting of someone in my wife's family'
Descriptions of people represented in family photos, etc., are to be taken as physical descriptions.
This also includes references to the *contents* of an object – e.g. enumerating different kinds of pictures in a photo album.
Examples of Style not Physical description:
'Living-room. That's a very warm room. It has a comfortable atmosphere'
'Chair. It's a good piece of furniture'
'Painting. It's got a sense of antiquity'

C Style
  16 *Style*. Some decorative, fashion or design aspect is mentioned.
     Also includes descriptions of ambiance, atmosphere.
     'The colours match the rest of the room'
     'My new Jaguar says something – it is distinctive'

D Utilitarian
  17 *Utilitarian*. The object is valued for convenience, saving time, money, energy.
     Also includes a description of the value of the object as an investment.
     'My washer allows me to have more time'
     'And someday I'll be able to sell these paintings at a tremendous profit'
     Be careful that descriptions of appliances, etc. actually include a functional referent: 'my new sewing machine was a Christmas gift' would *not* be scored as utilitarian.

E Personal values
  18 *Embodiment of an ideal*. The object is described as embodying personal values, aspirations, goals, achievement, *that are desired or sought after*. The object embodies the sought goal, not just something already achieved, which will fall under the Accomplishment category. If the object embodies the sought goal *and* the achieved goal, it will he coded for both. But there must be some explicit description of the object as embodying an ideal for the respondent.
     'I've been taught to live by the Bible as close as I can'
     'Books. Cause you can learn a lot and grow from them'
     'Plants. Because my plants are a symbol of life for me'
     'Reminds me of what a good friend he was, of our relationship and the friendship.' Here the value of friendship is embodied.

  19 *Accomplishment*. The object is described as manifesting the creativity or accomplishment or some achievement of the respondent. It refers to something *already achieved*. The object indicates that the respondent is competent in some endeavour or in life in general. This category refers to the accomplishment of the actual respondent. It refers to the respondent's immediate family only when it is clear that the respondent is a part of the activity or signification.
     'It makes me feel like I can do something'
     'It makes me feel like I'm accomplishing something'
     'These pots show that even though I'm handicapped, I can still create something beautiful'
     'Our whole family pitches in on decorating these Christmas eggs. It shows our talent'

20 *Personification*. The object is described as having the qualities of a person, either an actual person or a metaphoric person. The object represents some known person or the respondent himself or has a quality *of personhood* itself. The object should have the quality of a whole person, not just a partial quality.
'Dog He's a part of the family'
'I feel almost like I was missing a person with it'
'It's me'
'Poochie is like one of the family'
NOT Personification: 'It reminds me of my grandmother'
'It reflects her warmth'

Person codes

A Self
  1 *Self*. Code for Self any time the respondent is an explicit reference of the object. The respondent singles out something about himself or herself in relation to the object, e.g.
  'Tools. Because I like to work with tools'
  'TV. Because I like to watch TV'
  'Air conditioner. You really need it in the summer. It keeps you cool'
  'This is special because I can make something'
  'Game. I love to play it'

  BUT: 'I love to play pool with my family' would *not* be scored as Self; it would be scored as Family, and all family references implicitly include the respondent.

  HOWEVER: 'TV. I love watching it by myself, or with the whole family' would be scored for both Self *and* Family, because R singles himself or herself out.

  'Books. I learn from my books. You can get lost in them'
  'Guns. Shooting is my hobby'

B Immediate family
  2 *Spouse*.
  3 *We*. We or us use when description is vague – any mention of other person *not* specified.
  4 *Children*.
  5 *Parents*. Mother/Father.
  6 *Siblings*.
  7 *Grandparents*.
  8 *Grandchildren*.
  9 *Whole family (nuclear)*. Respondent refers to the whole family, e.g., 'I enjoy watching it with *my whole family*', or names all the members of the nuclear family, e.g., '*The children and my wife and I* all get around the table for breakfast on Sundays'
  Code 2 through 9 when one of these family members is mentioned, BUT if the entire nuclear family is mentioned individually, code under Whole family (nuclear) only, not for each individual.

C Kin
  10 *Relatives*. (Outside immediate family. e.g., the three generations)
  'It used to belong to my *uncle*, who I thought a lot of'
  'Photo. It was taken when we were visiting my *cousins* . . .'

11 *Ancestors.* (Outside respondent's own grandparents)
'Family tree. You can trace our family all the way to 1600'
'Photo. This is an old family photo from the last century'

12 *In-Laws*

D Non-family
13 *Friends.* Person is described as a friend, e.g.
'We got this from *friends*'

14 *Associates.* Respondent names someone from an associational context. Relation of the respondent to the person named is primarily through the association, e.g.
'I got that from a *friend at work*' (person named in work context)
'Cadillac. *My clients* may resent it, but I think I deserve it'

15 *Role models, Heroes, Admired people.* Object is valued in reference to some public figure or role model, e.g. teacher.
'Books. I admire all of Robbie-Grillet's books. They have so much personality'
'TV. I love to watch *The Hulk*'

Acquisition categories

The following are the categories used in coding how special objects were originally acquired (interrater reliability for all generations 86 per cent). For a discussion of how acquisition affects the meaning of special objects see Rochberg-Halton 1979b, Chapter 6.

1 *Purchased.* The object was acquired as a purchase regardless of who bought it.

2 *Gift.* The object was given as a present to the respondent.

3 *Inherited.* The respondent must mention the fact that the object was *owned* and not recently purchased by the previous generation, or the respondent lived with the object as a child and it was out of his possession for a number of years (e.g., in parents' possession) or the object was part of an inheritance (e.g., 'When my grandfather died my sister got the statue and I got this plinth').

4 *Crafted.* The respondent either made the object, designed it, grew it, created the idea, or somehow performed the operations that yielded the object (e.g., took the photos, grew the plants, etc.). Or someone else made the object in one of these ways but has *not* given the object to the respondent (e.g., 'I like the wall hanging my sister made').
The object must be accessible to the respondent and is usually found in his home. If someone else made it and then gave it to the respondent, code it as Gift.

5 *Found.* The respondent found the object.

6 *Award.* The object was acquired as an award or trophy (e.g., a diploma. bowling trophies, etc.).

7 *Hand-me-downs.* An older sibling or relative has outgrown the object (e.g, clothes, toys) and these now belong to the respondent.

8 *Traded.* The respondent traded or bartered something for the object.

9 *Moved into house.* The object was acquired when the respondent moved into the house.

10 *Other.*

Gift: subcodes

Occasions	Persons
1 Birthday	1 Spouse/Lover
2 Christmas	2 Parents or Parents-in-law
3 Wedding	3 Grandparents
4 Anniversary	4 Grandchildren
5 Religious occasion	5 Children
6 Multiple occasions	6 Relatives or 'Family gave it to me'
	7 Non-relatives
	8 Sibling(s)
	9 Multiple persons

Attitudes towards the home

By using the following coding system below, two raters scored blindly all protocols with a 90.8 per cent agreement.

Coding of home interview question no. 1

Three codes to be used: 1 Positive
2 Neutral
3 Negative

1 *Positive*

  a Any description of the home that uses adjectives connoting a positive emotional tone; e.g., 'warm; happy; fun; affirmative; cheery; cosy; special ambience; friendly; free'
  Do Not code 'comfortable' here, nor positive descriptions of physical characteristics, i.e., 'large; beautiful; warm' (when referring to temperature)

  b Or any statement of positive affect towards the home, e.g., 'I really like it; There are a lot of things in it I like; I love my home'

2 *Neutral*

  a Any description of the home that *does not* use adjectives connoting positive emotional tone.
  i.e., 'It is pretty; it is a good home; it's medium-sized; it's OK; it's nice; it's relaxing; it's comfortable; it's spacious'

  b Qualified descriptions, i.e., 'we work to make it feel somewhat homey, sometimes we succeed'; 'cluttered, disorganized, but comfortable'; 'I wouldn't say it's serene . . . I wouldn't say it's chaotic': 'it's warm . . . messy mostly'
  When such statements are accompanied by unqualified positive feelings, Score 1 (Positive).

3 *Negative*

  a Any description of the home that uses adjectives connoting negative emotional tone.
  e.g.: 'It's kind of dead; it makes me feel scared; frustration; oppression; no family spirit; it's cold; disorganized'

Part II
Interpreting collections

22

The urge to collect

Susan M. Pearce

Forming a worthwhile definition of what makes a collection, and distinguishing it from other kinds of accumulation, is difficult, not least because all such definitions tend to be self-serving and circular, and so leave out much interesting material for reasons which do not bear much investigation (for example, many accumulations created by women fall outside the traditional view of what constitutes a collection). Nevertheless, definitions have been attempted, and some of the most important are given here. Some useful characteristics (rather than a new definition) of collecting arise in the course of discussion.

In a world of objects, different people will take different things into their hearts and minds, and so objects cross the threshold from the outside to the inwardness of collection. A number of definitions of what makes a collection have been attempted, and although definition-making is an arid affair at best, with each definition inevitably open to a variety of niggling objections based on specific examples, definitions are a useful way of gaining a perspective on the subject, both of itself and of the way in which it has been regarded. In 1932 Durost, one of the earliest students of collecting, offered:

> A collection is basically determined by the nature of the *value* assigned to the objects, or ideas possessed. If the *predominant* value of an object or idea for the person possessing it is intrinsic, i.e., if it is valued primarily for use, or purpose, or aesthetically pleasing quality, or other value inherent in the object or accruing to it by whatever circumstances of custom, training, or habit, it is not a collection. If the predominant value is representative or representational, i.e., if said object or idea is valued chiefly for the relation it bears to some other object or idea, or objects, or ideas, such as being one of a series, part of a whole, a specimen of a class, then it is the subject of a collection.
>
> (Durost 1932: 10)

This holds the valuable distinction between objects held for use, with a helpfully wide idea of what constitutes 'use', and objects held as part of a sequence: it is the idea of series or class which creates the notion of the collection. Probably Durost had in mind collections, like those of butterflies or cigarette cards, in which the notion of series is particularly clear, but in an extended form in which sequence is a largely subjective creation of the collector, the idea has a potentially wide application.

Alsop has offered a refreshingly simple approach. He says: 'To collect is to gather objects belonging to a particular category the collector happens to fancy . . . and a collection is what has been gathered' (Alsop 1982: 70). The stress here is laid on the mentality of the collector, for essentially a collection is what he believes it is, provided there are at least some physical objects gathered together. This expresses the essentially subjective element in collecting very well. The late 1980s have produced two further efforts at definition. Aristides offers: 'collection . . . [is] "an obsession organized." One of the distinctions between possessing and collecting is that the latter implies order, system, perhaps completion. The pure collector's interest is not bounded by the intrinsic worth of the objects of his desire; whatever they cost, he must have them' (Aristides 1988: 330). This recognizes the subjective element in its use of the word 'obsession', and suggests that the crucial difference between 'possessing' and 'collecting' is the order and possibility of completion which collecting possesses. This is open to a number of objections: a group of working tools, for example, will have order and may be complete, but they do not hold the place in the imagination which a collection would occupy.

Belk and his colleagues have arrived at the following: 'We take collecting to be the selective, active, and longitudinal acquisition, possession and disposition of an interrelated set of differentiated objects (material things, ideas, beings, or experiences) that contribute to and derive extraordinary meaning from the entity (the collection) that this set is perceived to constitute' (Belk *et al.* 1990: 8). This definition takes on board the idea of the interrelated set, Durost's series or class, and adds to it the notion that the collection as an entity is greater than the sum of its parts, an important contribution to the discussion. It brings in the actively selecting collector, with his personal or subjective slant on what he is doing, and it recognizes that collecting is a prolonged activity, extending through time. We might take issue with the unglossed use of the word 'active'. The study of collectors makes clear that collections can creep up on people unawares until the moment of realization: it suddenly dawns on a woman that the old clothes at the back of the wardrobe constitute an important group of Mary Quant or Carnaby Street dresses, which then in her mind becomes a collection to which she may actively add. Even more difficult to bring into Belk's and the other definitions are the collections of personalia or memorabilia: the little group of German helmet, bayonette, piece of shrapnel and shell case cigarette-lighter which represent somebody's memories of the Somme, or the lifetime's accumulation of an important figure like Thomas Hardy. Perhaps the real point is that a collection is not a collection until someone thinks of it in those terms.

A good deal of ink has been spilt in the effort to pin down the difference between 'collecting' and 'accumulating' or 'hoarding'. Baudrillard suggests:

> Le strade inférieur est celui de l'accumulation de matières: entassement de vieux papiers, stockage de nourriture – à mi-chemin entre l'introjection orale et la retention anale – puis l'accumulation sérielle d'objets identiques. La collection, elle, émerge vers la culture . . . sans cesser de renvoyer les uns aux autres, ils incluent dans ce jeu une extériorité sociale, des relations humaines.
>
> (Baudrillard 1968: 147–8)

Perhaps notions of anal retention should be taken with a dose of salts, but 'accumulating' is usually seen as the simple magpie act, the heaping-up of material without any kind of internal classification, often covered by some pretence at a utilitarian purpose. Belk quotes the case of a man in his seventies who had accumulated three garages full of miscellaneous possessions and was facing pressure from his family to begin to discard these things so that they were not faced with the burden of doing so after his death (Belk 1988: 13). Nevertheless, the line between collecting and accumulating is a very fine one, which individual groups of material can cross in each direction, depending upon the view taken by their owner at different points in his life. Motive is all-important, and motives change. Hoarding is more difficult. In everyday use it means the gathering of material like Baudrillard's old papers or tins of food, sometimes carried to miserly excess, which comes within the accumulation mode just discussed. However, to archaeologists it means the deliberate gathering of selected materials for clearly social purposes, even if we do not know for certain what these purposes were: this kind of hoarding in ancient Europe is best regarded as an ancestor of modern collecting. The term is therefore liable to confusion and, except in relation to the ancient past, it will be avoided here.

From this discussion we glean that ideas like non-utilitarian gathering, an internal or intrinsic relationship between the things gathered – whether objectively 'classified' or not – and the subjective view of the owner are all significant attributes of a collection, together with the notion that a collection is more than the sum of its parts. At some point in the process the objects have to be deliberately viewed by their owner or potential owner as a collection, and this implies intentional selection, acquisition and disposal. It also means that some kind of specific value is set upon the group by its possessor, and with the recognition of value comes the giving of a part of self-identity. But collecting is too complex and too human an activity to be dealt with summarily by way of definitions.

This paper first appeared in S. Pearce (ed.) (1992) Museums, Objects and Collections, *Leicester: Leicester University Press, pp. 48–50.*

REFERENCES

Alsop, J. (1982) *The Rare Art Traditions: A History of Collecting and Its Linked Phenomena*, New York: Harper & Row.

Aristides, N. (1988) 'Calm and uncollected', *American Scholar* 57(3): 327–36.

Baudrillard, J. (1968) *Le Système des objets*, Paris: Gallimard.

Belk, R. (1988) 'Possessions and the extended self', *Journal of Consumer Research* 15: 139–68.

Belk, R. Wallendorf, M., Sherry, J. Holbrook, M. (1990) 'Collecting in a consumer culture', *Highways and Buyways*: 3–95, Provo, Utah: Association for Consumer Research.

Belk, R., Wallendorf, M., Sherry, J., Holbrook, M. and Roberts, S. (1988) 'Collectors and collecting', *Advances in Consumer Research* 15: 548–53.

Durost, W. (1932) *Children's Collecting Activity Related to Social Factors*, New York: Bureau of Publications, Teachers' College, Columbia University.

23

The collection: between the visible and the invisible

Krzysztof Pomian

Krzysztof Pomian is a scholar of international reputation whose interest in the history and nature of European collecting has done much to define the development of the study. This short piece is intended, in part, to give a taster as an introduction to Pomian's wider work. It is also intended to show how wide is the range of social activities to which the notion of 'collecting' can be applied, and how these form, and historically have formed, very significant aspects of social life. Pomian takes a very helpful deep historical perspective on collecting practice.

It would take more than one large tome to list the contents of every museum and private collection, even if these contents were only referred to once, and by category. In Paris alone, there are apparently 150 museums, not only the world-famous art galleries, but also museums devoted exclusively to the army, to nature and hunting, the cinema, counterfeiting, Freemasonry, the history of France, natural history, the history of man, old-fashioned spyglasses and telescopes, the navy, musical instruments, gramophones, speech and gesture, locksmithing, the table, techniques and technology and so on and so on. For their part, private collections often contain the most unexpected objects, whose banality is such as to make one wonder who on earth could possibly be interested in them. One lady in Poland even picks up orange, lemon and grapefruit wrappings. Which all goes to prove that every natural object known to man and every artefact, however strange, will show up somewhere in the world as part of a museum or private collection. This begs the question of how this universe, which comprises so many and such sundry elements, can ever be given an overall definition without the danger of succumbing to simple list-making. Our task is therefore one of finding out what, if anything, they all have in common.

The trucks and locomotives lined up in the railway museum carry neither freight not passengers. Nobody is slain by the swords, cannons and guns on display in the military museum, and not one single worker or peasant uses the utensils, tools, and costumes assembled in folklore collections or museums. The same is true of everything which ends up in this strange world where the word 'usefulness' seems never to have been heard of, for to say that the objects which now await only the gaze of the curious were still of some use would be a gross distortion of the English language: the locks and keys no longer secure any door, the machines produce nothing and the clocks and watches are certainly not expected to give the precise time of day. Although they may well have served a definite purpose in their former existence, museum and collection pieces no longer serve any at all, and as such acquire the same quality as works of art, which are never produced with any definite use in mind, but simply to adorn people, palaces, temples, apartments, gardens, streets, squares and cemeteries. Even so, it cannot really be said that museum and collection pieces serve a decorative purpose: decoration is the art of using pictures and sculptures to break the monotony of blank walls which are already there and in need of enhancement, whereas walls are built or specially adapted in museums and in some of the larger collections, for the specific purpose of displaying works. Collectors with more modest means have showcases built, boxes and albums made or else clear a space somewhere for objects to be placed, the aim every time seemingly being the same, namely that of bringing objects together in order to show them to others.

Museum and collection pieces may be neither useful not decorative, yet enormous care is nonetheless lavished on them. The risk of corrosion caused by physical and chemical factors is reduced to a minimum by careful monitoring of variables such as light, humidity, temperature and levels of atmospheric pollution. Damaged objects are always restored to their former glory whenever possible, and every effort is made to ensure that the public's only contact with them is visual. The existence of a market where these objects circulate at sometimes astronomical prices emphasizes their great value; indeed when a self-portrait of Rembrandt was sold on 29 November 1974, at the Palais Galliera in Paris for the sum of 1,100,570 francs, one of the expert journalists found this figure completely derisory. A black market, fed with stolen goods from private collections and museums, operates alongside the official one, and in 1974 alone, 4,785 old masters went missing. Besides these, thieves also go for objects which, although less spectacular, are nonetheless valuable in the eyes of the collectors, which means that, along with museum curators, they too are constantly faced with a major security problem. The presence of a police station within the precincts of the Grand Palais in Paris, where the most prestigious works are exhibited, exemplifies the extent of the surveillance system which has been set up. Put in simple terms, collectors and curators alike are forced to act as if they were guarding treasure.

Given that this is the case, it might seem surprising that treasures like these should still be on show to the public, unlike those which languish in bank safes and strongrooms. Even more surprising is the fact that as often as not their owners do not profit from them financially. True, some collections are built up with a purely speculative end in mind, and most private collections are dispersed upon the death of their owners, to the benefit of their heirs. Yet this is by no means always the case, and one could cite dozens of examples of collections which have been turned into museums. In Paris, the Cognacq-Jay, Jacquemart-André and Nissim de Camondo Museums all started life this way, as did Geneva's Ariana Museum, the Làzaro Galdiano in Madrid, the Federico Marés in Barcelona, the Peggy Guggenheim Foundation in Venice, Boston's Gardner House and New York's Frick Collection. The creation of a private collection cannot, therefore, be reduced to outright and unambiguous hoarding, and the same is, of course, even more true for museums. The objects these latter possess are inalienable, and no move is ever made to sell them off, even when a museum is afflicted by the very worst financial crisis imaginable. The only known exception to this, since the beginning of the twentieth century, has been the sale of pictures from the Hermitage Museum in Leningrad by the Soviet government from 1929 to 1937. Even museums which reserve the right to sell certain pieces in their possession, such as the New York Museum of Modern Art, only do so in order to acquire other works which will widen the range of styles and movements the museum covers. Unlike private collectors, museums do not seek to keep works out of circulation for a limited period of time, but for always.

The world of private collections and museums seems to be one of endless diversity, and yet the few remarks which have just been made, albeit provisionally, reveal a certain unity, certain points in common shared by every single one of those extremely hetero-geneous objects which are amassed in such great quantities in private homes and pub-lic buildings alike. These remarks enable one to gain a clearer definition of the particular institution which concerns this volume, namely the collection, an institution which must satisfy the following criteria: a set of natural or artificial objects, kept temporarily or permanently out of the economic circuit, afforded special protection in enclosed places adapted specifically for that purpose and put on display. This definition is obviously rigorously descriptive, and one which immediately bars all exhibitions from the cate-gory of collection, since they only represent the very briefest of moments in the process of circulation or production of material goods. Excluded too are the piles of objects which chance alone has thrown together, as well as all hidden treasures, regardless of their other characteristics. On the other hand, the same definition does include most libraries and archives in the category of collection, alongside museums and private collections, though this does require a distinction to be made straightaway between archives and mere repositories of documents which remain part of the administrative and economic circuits of activity. The Polish dictionary of archives does, in fact, furnish a view coinciding with our own definition: 'an institution called upon to guard, collect, sort, preserve, keep and render accessible documents which, although they are no longer useful on a daily basis as before, and are therefore considered superfluous in offices and stores, nonetheless merit being preserved'. Libraries pose a slightly more compli-cated problem. Books are, it is true, sometimes regarded as objects, collected for their beautiful bindings or illustrations, for instance, and in this case the issue is simple, just as it is when a library acts as an archive or contains books intended solely for enter-tainment. Certain libraries, however, house only works of reference needed for the pursuit of some form of economic activity, and these cannot come under the heading of collection.

This topic will be discussed later on, as will that of the coexistence in our societies of two types of collections, the private collection and the museum. The descriptive stage, which had enabled the collection to be defined, appears otherwise to be something of a cul-de-sac, though it does harbour an implicit paradox which now needs to be discussed, for it is an undoubted paradox that objects which are kept temporarily or permanently out of the circuit of economic activity should even so be afforded the kind of special protection normally reserved for precious objects. The fact is that they are precious objects, yet they paradoxically have an exchange value and no practical or usage value. Indeed they could have no practical value as they are bought not to be used but to be displayed. This could in itself be seen as a very particular use, but at that point the term 'use' might end up devoid of all meaning altogether. Any and every object can be used in many different ways of course, but it seems important to maintain the difference between these uses, however strange, and the very special behaviour reserved for certain objects, when they are simply looked at and admired. This is the fate of every item purchased for a collection, and even when it is carefully preserved or repaired, the sole aim is to render it more presentable. It must be remembered that when a work of art enters a museum or a collection, it loses its usage value, if one is of the opinion that its ability to decorate constitutes such a value, for it no longer serves that purpose in such an environment. It can now be taken as read that objects which become collec-tion pieces have an exchange value but no practical value, yet the origin of this exchange value still needs to be elucidated, and our next task is to establish exactly what it is that makes these objects so precious in our eyes.

Answers to this puzzle are frequently based on a sort of primitive psychology which can conjure up any postulation it needs, such as the existence of a property instinct or a tendency to hoard inherent in certain individuals and probably all civilized beings, if not in the whole of mankind. More seriously, it is claimed that certain collection pieces are sources of aesthetic pleasure, and that others, or indeed the very same ones, constitute the key to greater historical or scientific knowledge. Lastly, it is observed that their possession confers a certain prestige on their owners, since they serve as proofs of their good taste, of their considerable intellectual curiosity, or even of their wealth and generosity, if not all these qualities at the same time. It is hardly surprising, or so the argument continues, that there are a number of people who seek to own such pieces and are willing to sacrifice some of their fortune in the process, while other similar individuals, this time without sufficient means, seek at the very least the right to view them. This in turn creates demand, which attributes value to potential collection pieces the purchase of which gives rise to a new market. It also leads to pressure being exerted on the state for it to provide visual access to these objects for those who have not the wherewithal to purchase for themselves the aesthetic pleasure, the historical and scientific knowledge or even the prestige they afford.

This explanation has its merits, but remains unsatisfactory. Aesthetic pleasure is left undefined, the reason behind the urge to acquire historical and scientific knowledge is not explored and we never learn precisely how the possession of certain objects confers prestige. Even if all these answers were given, an explanation would still need to be found for the presence of collections in societies different from our own. The existence of a collection in contexts differing slightly from those of private collections and museums would immediately render the above explanation inapplicable, even if we were fully to understand and accept it. In this case, it would, at the very best, apply only to a local modification of a more general phenomenon; at worst, it would be entirely irrelevant, and would turn out to be a very secondary explanation of the behavioural trait which consists in considering collection pieces as precious, and whose true motives remain a total mystery to us. Accordingly, the real truth can only be ascertained if we leave the confines of our society and embark on the quest for collections elsewhere.

A COLLECTION OF COLLECTIONS

The quest is not an arduous one. Piled up in tombs and temples are sets of natural and artificial objects, kept temporarily or permanently out of the economic circuit, afforded special protection and placed on display, and it is time to take a closer look.

Funeral objects

Though not universal, the custom of burying the dead along with their possessions is extremely widespread, and the existence of funeral objects, sometimes precious, sometimes less so, has been proved as far back as Neolithic times. In the most ancient city to be discovered so far, Çatal Hüyük in Anatolia, which flourished between 6500 and 5700 BC, the contents of the tombs already differed widely according to the gender and social status of the person buried there. These differences were reinforced later on in many civilizations, where tombs were filled with various different examples of tools, weapons, articles of toiletry, jewellery and ornaments, tapestries, musical instruments, works of art and so on. Accounts of digs and exhibition catalogues provide countless descriptions of the decoration and contents of tombs. An example from China, and a particularly spectacular one at that, the description of the tomb of Princess Tong-T'Ai dating from AD 706, will suffice to give a good idea of this.

The tumulus measuring some twelve metres high, rose up from the tomb which was in turn some twelve metres below ground. A slope measuring sixty metres in length, and decorated on each side by four recesses three metres deep gave on to a corridor which opened on to an antechamber ten metres further on, and this antechamber was linked by a passage more than six metres long to the funeral chamber. A stone sarcophagus had been placed within this chamber. Overall, the tomb measured some fifteen metres long by five metres wide. It was excavated from August 1960 to April 1962. It was noticed, as is often the case, alas, with the large tombs, that it had been visited by thieves. . . . In spite of the pillage, it still contained over a thousand objects: eight hundred and seventy-eight funeral statuettes, a great many vestimentary ornaments, ceramics, eight objects made from gold in the passage, which the thieves must have dropped as they left, around one hundred bronzes, one hundred and five door embellishments, roughly thirty iron objects, including pieces of harness, as well as a dozen jade pieces, also found in the passage. Seven hundred and seventy-seven statuettes were made of painted terracotta; sixty had 'Three Colour' glazing, while thirty more were made from wood. . . . No less exceptional were the murals decorating the walls of the tomb and corridor.

('Trésors d'art chinois' 1973)

Two further facts need to be underlined. First of all, a whole series of measures was taken to protect the tombs from pillage, that is the reuse in this life of what is intended to remain with the dead for ever in the life beyond. Attempts were made to disguise the location of the tomb or to make intruders lose their way, by building mazes or digging false graves. Divine assistance was sought in the form of curses invoking heavenly wrath upon the heads of possible robbers or profaners. Inspection and monitoring systems were set up. Second, and very importantly, the objects were placed in the tombs to be seen by those living in the next world. It is hard to believe that the Chinese or the Scythians really expected their sacrificed slaves to perform the usual tasks for their masters and their slaughtered horses to carry horsemen. Moreover, it is a fact that human and animal sacrifices were replaced almost everywhere by statuettes, and objects in actual use by models. This phenomenon is explained by invoking economic considerations: the tendency to hold on to what could still be of use. However, this is a specious argument, as the replacement models were often more difficult to execute than the original objects, and the materials used often far rarer and therefore more precious. The advent of replacement models would seem thus to have been dictated not by economic motives but rather by the belief that funeral objects were not to be used but perpetually gazed upon and admired.

Offerings

Our museums owe their name to the ancient temples of the Muses, though the most famous of these, the Museum of Alexandria, did not owe its fame to any collection of objects, but rather to its library and the team of scholars who formed a community within its walls. There is, nevertheless, more than one similarity between the Greek and Roman temples and our own museums, for it was in these temples that offerings were amassed and displayed. 'The object, which had been given to the god and received by him in accordance with the rites, becomes ἱερόν or *sacrum*, and shares in the majesty and inviolability of the gods. Stealing or moving it, preventing it from fulfilling its function or even simply touching it constitute acts of sacrilege.' To talk of use in this context is in fact impossible. Once the object crossed the threshold of the sacred enclosure, it entered into a domain which was strictly opposed to utilitarian activities. Within this enclosure, 'one can neither extract stone, take earth, chop wood, build, cultivate nor live'. Accordingly, objects could play only one single role, and were placed on display either in the sacred buildings which they then adorned, or else in buildings erected specially to house offerings, when these became so numerous that they threatened to clutter up the places of worship. As well as coming to pray, the pilgrims, who were also tourists, visited the temples in order to admire the objects they contained. Indeed, a whole body of literature, the most well-known being the work by Pausanias, was written with the aim of describing the examples which were the most remarkable because of their material, their size, the difficulty of their execution, the extraordinary circumstances surrounding their placing in the temple or because of yet other features which set them apart from the rest.

In theory, once an object had been offered to the gods it had to remain forever in the temple in which it had been deposited. Every object was listed in an inventory and protected from theft. Even when they deteriorated they were not disposed of in any old way.

> If they were made of silver or gold, the following course of action was taken: a decree of the people resulting from a proposal from the priest or holy treasurer, in accordance with advice from the council, ordered that the offerings which were in a poor state be melted down into ingots or amalgamated to form one single offering; the same procedure was followed when dealing with all scraps of precious metal. If they proved to be an encumbrance or were broken, less valuable objects were taken from the temple and buried. Their dedication had consecrated them for eternity, and they were in no circumstances to be put back into circulation, so in order to shield them better from all secular use, they were often broken on purpose, if they were not already broken. This accounts for the piles of terracotta or bronze objects to be found in the vicinity of certain sanctuaries, for example at Tegea, Cnidus and Olympia.
>
> (Pliny the Elder, XXXVII, 12–14)

Treasures amassed in temples as offerings did sometimes, however, return to the economic circuit, converted, in other words, into money. In spite of the belief that temples should not be touched even in times of war, armies did not always resist the temptation of pillaging the riches of their enemies, even when the enemies in question were Greek. Thus, when the Phocaeans gained control of the sanctuary of Delphi, they sold off the gold and silver offerings they found there in order to pay their mercenary army. This action was looked upon as sacrilege, and when the Phocaeans were in their turn conquered in 346 BC, they were forced to reimburse the temples for all that they had stolen from them. There did exist a legal procedure for lifting restrictions on sacred treasures. This required the vote of the people to whom the temple belonged, and was resorted to when the country was in danger, as was the case when the Athenians borrowed money from their gods during the Peloponnesian War. This was in fact a loan granted by the gods to the city and which had to be reimbursed with interest, and in 422 BC the Athenians had run up a debt of 4,750 talents to Athena Polias, 30 talents to Athena Nike and 800 talents to the other gods, meaning that, taking the interest into account, they owed a total sum of around 7,000 talents.

Gifts and booty

Objects kept out of the economic circuit accumulated not only in temples but also in the seats of power. Tributes and booty flowed in, while ambassadors would come armed with gifts, which would always be shown to the courtiers and sometimes also to the crowds which gathered to witness their official visits. These objects were stored under strict guard in treasure-houses, and were rarely accessible, being exhibited solely during festivals or ceremonies. Funeral cortèges and coronation processions proved good opportunities to display the splendour the country possessed, and the dazzled public was given the chance to feast its eyes on all the precious stones, fabrics, jewels, *objets d'art* made of precious metals and so on, which had been amassed. This was so not only in oriental monarchies but also in European countries during the Middle Ages, and we will come back to this later.

We must now turn our attention to Rome, in which a general returning there from a victorious campaign would be granted the privilege of displaying the men he had subjugated and the treasures he had seized. Thus,

> on the occasion of his third victory over the pirates, Asia, Pontus and the nations and kings listed in the seventh book of this work . . . Pompey paraded a chess-board, along with its pieces made from precious stones, which measured three feet wide and four feet long . . . three dining-room couches, dishes of gold and gemstones, sufficient for nine credence tables, three gold statues of Minerva, Mars and Apollo, thirty-three pearl crowns, a square mountain of gold with stags, lions and fruit of every kind, surrounded by a gold vine, a pearl grotto topped with a sundial. . . .

After being carried round in triumphant display, some of the objects seized from the enemy were offered to temples, where they were put on view; Pompey, for example, dedicated wine cups and murrhine cups to Jupiter's temple on the Capitoline. Others remained in the possession of the victorious general.

Booty seems to have formed the basis of private collections in Rome. This, at any rate, was the opinion of Pliny the Elder:

> It was the victory of Pompey over Mithridates that made fashion veer to pearls and gemstones. The victories of Lucius Scipio and of Cnaeus Manlius had done the same for chased silver, garments of cloth of gold and dining couches inlaid with bronze; and that of Mummius for Corinthian bronzes and fine paintings.

It is patently obvious that the objects which the great Roman collectors (as well as either generals or proconsuls), Sulla, Julius Caesar and Verres, amassed and put on display in their residences or else in the temples where they had been placed as offerings, were booty, and the story of Verres is a good case in point. Only during the Empire did collecting gain such popularity that when Vitruvius designed a house he would reserve a special place for housing pictures and sculptures.

Two features characterizing the Roman collectors still need to be outlined. The first of these was their supreme disdain for the usefulness of the objects they amassed, the second their constant efforts to outbid each other, risking in so doing not only their fortunes but also their personal dignity. The best illustration of this comes in a passage from Pliny the Elder, which is worth quoting despite its length.

> An ex-consul drank from a murrhine cup for which he had given 70,000 sesterces, although it held just three pints. He was so fond of it that he would gnaw its rim; and yet the damage he thus caused only enhanced its value, and there is no other piece of murrhine ware even today that has a higher price set upon it. The amount of money squandered by this same man upon the other articles of this material in his possession can be gauged from their number, which was so great that, when Nero took them away from the man's children and displayed them, they filled a private theatre. . . . When the ex-consul Titus Petronius was facing death, he broke, to spite Nero, a murrhine dipper that had cost him 300,000 sesterces, thereby depriving the emperor's dining-room table of this legacy. Nero, however, as was

proper for an emperor, outdid everyone by paying 1,000,000 sesterces for a single bowl. That one who was acclaimed as a victorious general and as Father of his Country should have paid so much in order to drink is a detail that we must formally record.

(Pliny the Elder, xxxvii, 18–20)

This seems to bear a curious resemblance to the potlatch of the North American Indians, but whereas in Rome dignity was associated with the ability to spend money in exchange for utterly useless objects, dignity for the Kwakiutl people, for example, is linked to the ability to give blankets, chests, canoes or food to others without asking for anything in return. This observation in turn raises two further questions. The first concerns the presence of collections in societies which historians of this institution are not accustomed to studying; the second, and more important, concerns the relationship between the collection and competitive behaviour. This will be discussed in more detail further on.

Relics and sacred objects

Relics, or objects supposed to have been in contact with a god or hero or to constitute the remains of some great event in the mythical or far-distant past, were equally well known in Greece and Rome. Pausanias describes a great many of them, including the clay Prometheus used to fashion the first man and woman, the rock Cronos devoured instead of his son, the egg from which Castor and Pollux hatched, the remains of the tree at the foot of which the Greeks made their sacrifices before setting off for the Trojan War, and many others besides. Pliny also mentions them from time to time, one example being the sardonyx put on display in the temple of Concord in Rome, and which was said to have belonged to Polycrates of Samos, the hero of a famous tale. It was Christianity with its cult of the saints which was responsible for the cult of relics reaching its apogee. It would be impossible to trace the history of this cult here, and for the purposes of our study we need only repeat that a relic was any object said to have been in contact with a character from sacred history, and whenever possible was an actual part of his body. However minute it was, and whatever its nature, this object retained all the grace with which the saint had been invested during his lifetime, which explains how a relic was able to sanctify the place where it was situated just as effectively as the saint himself would have done. Some put a halt to the spread of disease and restored sufferers to health; others protected towns and kingdoms from their enemies. All guaranteed assistance from the saints along with prosperity, and all were, not surprisingly, regarded as the most precious of treasures. When Queen Matilda returned to England in 1125, after the death of her husband, the Emperor Henry V, she brought with her a relic of St James, and the events were described in the following way by a chronicler: 'Queen Matilda travelled to her father in England taking the hand of St James with her and by this she did irreparable damage to the *regnum Francorum*.' This was by no means an isolated opinion: Frederick Barbarossa embarked on diplomatic negotiations in an attempt to recover the relic, but the English refused to relinquish it.

Gifts of land were not sufficient in themselves to found a religious establishment; relics were also needed. Once they entered a church or abbey, they would only ever leave it as the result of a theft or, most exceptionally, because they had been given to some powerful figure or other. In this way they became extremely numerous, and required catalogues to be drawn up. The relics were contained in reliquaries, shown to the faithful during religious ceremonies and carried in processions. As contact rendered the miraculous powers of the relics even more effective, the faithful did not content themselves with merely looking on, but touched the reliquaries and kissed every inch of them.

In northern France, between 1050 and 1550 it was relics that the monks exhibited when collecting donations towards the building of churches and abbeys. Finally, relics were much coveted, often obtained through theft, and this meant that the most famous of them had to be guarded by soldiers. Trading based on relics also took place, and the Roman cemeteries functioned, dare one say it, as quarries from which great quantities of saintly relics were extracted for sale in the rest of Europe.

As well as relics, churches also kept and put on show other objects, including natural curiosities and above all offerings: altars, chalices, ciboria, chasubles, candelabras and tapestries sometimes retain even today the names of their donors, while certain pictures even include the faces of them and their families. Funeral monuments, stained-glass windows, jubes and historiated capitals should all be added to the list, and doubtless other items too. Thus, besides being places of worship, each church also constituted a permanent exhibition of dozens of objects. This, however, is so familiar a subject that it needs no further elaboration.

Royal treasures

The objects gradually accumulating in the residences of those in power have already been alluded to in our discussion on gifts and booty. Gifts and booty were, however, not the only things to be found there. The Attalids of Pergamum, to quote a well-known example, prized sculptures and pictures, and they were not alone in doing so. However, we have chosen a number of inventories from the Middle Ages in order to highlight the contents of the homes of princes and kings in ancient times, as they give a fairly accurate picture. The first striking feature of these inventories is that most of the objects they list had some kind of use. In the case of regalia, rings and belts, the use was a ceremonial one; in the case of crosses, crucifixes, images, reliquaries, altars, chalices, crooks, mitres and copes a religious one, while dishes, knives, seat covers and so on were all part of secular life. From time to time, natural curiosities and various odd instruments, such as astrolabes and globes, find their way into these collections, and it becomes obvious that we are not dealing here with objects kept out of use and out of the economic circuit. Two features should, nevertheless, prevent any rapid assumptions being made. The first is the sheer number of objects: the inventory of King Charles V of France, lists 3,906 items, and such a huge quantity could not possibly have been used all at the same time, however extended the court may have been, and must therefore not have served any function at all. The second is that, in general, the objects were made from the precious metals gold and silver, and decorated with precious stones such as sapphires, rubies, onyx, amethysts, emeralds, diamonds and pearls. This would appear to be a further reason for supposing that most of these objects would never be used in everyday life.

Involvement in the economic circuit does not necessarily mean an object has to serve some practical purpose, since it can also stem from the accumulation of objects where the aim is to build up capital. It cannot be denied that in times of need princes dipped into their stores of treasure: when Charles V had part of his collection of dishes taken to the Mint he was neither the first nor the last to make use of this expedient. The inventories themselves contain references to sales made in order to finance royal expenditure elsewhere. The authors of the inventory of the jewels of King Charles VI of France wrote the following caption concerning a certain small gold crown with thirteen flowerets: '117 pearls were extracted from this crown and given to a silversmith by the name of Charles Poupart, in payment for a number of doublets and jewels he had made for the king for his journey to St Omer where the King of England himself was to be present.'

And several other events of this kind could be cited. Philippe de Valois sent a famous piece known as Le Grand Camée from the Sainte Chapelle to Pope Clement VI as security for a loan, and in 1253 the Hohenstaufen family jewels were given as security, or possibly sold, to a company of merchants and bankers for the sum of 2,522 Genoese pounds, the equivalent of two years' wages for a *podestà* in Genoa, one year's wages for 500 craftsmen, the price of the largest ship to be built at that time, complete with crew and enough supplies to last for four months, 630 cows or 400 ordinary horses.

All these various equivalents, which indicate a treasure much less valuable than that of Charles V, for example, help to illustrate just how much wealth was stored up in the royal palaces. Yet it is impossible to reduce the amassing of precious objects by royalty to the simple accumulation of capital. Indeed, distinctions were apparently made at the time between 'joyaux' and 'épargne' just as a distinction was made between 'joyaux' and 'vaisselle'. In view of this, our task is to determine whether and in what circumstances the jewels were displayed, and in fact the inventories make it clear that they were normally shut away in chests or cupboards, these being placed in their turn in well-guarded chambers. They were taken out mostly for various different ceremonies and festivals: at the death of the king, the regalia were paraded during the funeral procession, while they were also displayed on solemn visits to the different towns of the realm, along with ceremonial arms and armour, decorated harness and richly embroidered cloths covered in gems. Here is King Charles VII of France, entering Paris on 12 November 1437.

> Le roy estoit armé de toutes piesses, sur ung biau coursier; et avoit ung cheval couvert de velloux d'azur en coullour, semé de fleurs de lis d'orfaverie. Et devant luy, son premier escuier d'escurie monté sur ung coursier couvert de fin blanchet couvert d'orfaverie semee de serfs [*sic*] vollans. Et estoient quatre coursiers tous pareulx, dont il y avoit trois chevalliers avec l'escuier, leurs coursiers pareillement couverts que l'escuier, et eulx en armes de tous harnois; et portoit ledit escuier, sur ung baston, le harnois de teste du roy; et sur ledit harnois, une couronne d'or; et au milieu, sur la houppe, une grosse fleur de lis doublée de fin or moult riche, et son roy d'armes devant luy portant sa cotte d'armes moult riche de veloux azuré à trois fleurs de lis de fin or de brodeure (et estoient les fleurs de lis brodees de grosses perles;) et ung autre escuier d'escuerie monté sur ung genest, qui portoit une grande espee toure semee de fleurs de lis de fin or d'orfaverie.
>
> (Berry 1968: 73)

The scene which has just been described is in no way exceptional, and it is clear, even without constant reference to source material, not only that the jewels were put on show, but also that this was their chief function.

Our case rests here, even if it does seem to rest on a mere assortment of bric-à-brac. The so-called collections which have been described so far differ in almost every aspect from ones which exist today, as well as from each other. Established in widely differing locations, and of different natures and origins, even the behaviour of their visitors or viewing public differs. True, in each case there is a set of objects which, subject to certain reservations, satisfy the conditions stipulated in our definition of a collection, yet by assimilating such heterogeneous sets we perhaps risk resembling the madman, created by the novelist Julio Cortàzar, who firmly believed he was surrounded by collections. For him, an office was nothing but a collection of clerks, a school a collection of pupils, a barracks a collection of soldiers and a prison one of prisoners. The moral of this anecdote is that no comparison of institutions can be valid unless it is based not on external appearances but on functional similarity.

COLLECTIONS: THE INVISIBLE AND THE VISIBLE

The objects which are shut up in tombs are, to the living, sacrificed. As gifts to the dead, they should remain in their possession for ever. No matter how this sort of proceeding is justified – and it has been variously justified by successive societies and in successive periods – the relationship between the living and the dead has always and everywhere been perceived as an exchange: the living give up not only the use but even the sight of certain objects, in return for the benevolent neutrality, if not actual protection, of the dead. Pursuing this idea to its extremes, the ancient Chinese invented special offertory currencies, which 'constituted from the very outset exchange values for use with the world beyond. As early as Neolithic times, there existed imitations of stone and bone cowries, and tombs dating from the third century BC contain considerable quantities of clay slabs symbolizing gold'; paper money appeared later on. Obviously, this exchange presupposed the division of human beings into two groups, those in this world and the others in the next.

The same can be said of offerings, although in this case the dividing line ran not between the living and the dead but between man and god. This difference did, however, become blurred as the gods were actually deified men while ancestors benefited from almost divine status. Whatever the case, the important thing to remember is that offerings placed in the temple became the property of the gods. The gods stipulated that these objects should not leave the sacred enclosure once they had entered it, except in the very special circumstances discussed earlier on. It was therefore possible to bury them in the *favissae*, the pits where the objects cluttering up the temple were deposited, as in this way they continued to be the property of the gods. Moreover, instead of being sent to the temple, objects could be ritually destroyed, and if this was deliberately done to dedicate them to the gods, they remained true offerings. Herodotus recounts how Croesus 'burnt on a great pyre couches covered with gold and silver, golden goblets, and purple cloaks and tunics; by these means he hoped the better to win the aid of the god of Delphi', to whom he also sent rich gifts. Offerings also formed part of the exchange process, therefore, and along with prayers and sacrifices guaranteed the favour of the divinity for whom they were intended.

When objects were intended for gods or for the dead, they did not necessarily have to be put on display. Funeral objects were not, nor were offerings, except in certain societies, and this, of course, poses a problem, as we have defined the collection as a set of objects . . . put on display. But for whom? We had implied that they were intended for the eyes of the living, yet the inhabitants of the world beyond also had visual access to them, at times when it was barred to the former. One possibility would be to disregard the non-human gaze and to limit discussion to sets of objects displayed to human eyes. This seems unnecessary, even though it does complicate the picture somewhat, since objects remained visible to the gods and even to the dead after having been physically destroyed, crushed and burned. However, funeral objects and offerings should, in our view, be considered as collections, as the important factor is not that they were intended for gods or for the dead, but the acknowledgement of the existence of a potential audience, in another temporal or spatial sphere, implicit in the very act of placing the objects in a tomb or temple. This is the belief, which could be expressed in actions alone, but which words have often been used to describe, that another kind of observer can or does exist, who should be allowed to rest his eyes on objects belonging to us.

We should now look more closely at what happens when the objects intended for the gods, namely the offerings, are placed on public show. As well as serving as intermediaries between mortals and immortals, they also came to represent to visitors the fame of the gods, since they were proof that this fame reached all four corners of the world: after all, even the Hyperboreans sent offerings to Delphi. . . . In the same way, they represented peoples who lived in far and remote if not fabulous lands. For present-day visitors they were a reminder of past benefactors, along with the circumstances surrounding the sending of offerings, and even of groups and individuals who had been involved in bygone events. Some of the offerings were testaments to the ability of certain craftsmen, sculptors or painters to produce extraordinary works the likes of which are no longer seen today. The weirdest, strangest, most spectacular offerings stood out from the ranks of more commonplace articles, exciting the curiosity and imagination of the visitors by challenging them to go beyond the simply visual and to listen to or read more on the subject. Thus it was that stories or anecdotes, some of which have come down to us through the works of Herodotus, Pausanias, Pliny the Elder and several other authors, revolved around offerings of this kind. These offerings could continue to function as intermediaries for this world and the next, the sacred and the secular, while at the same time constituting, at the very heart of the secular world, symbols of the distant, the hidden, the absent. In other words, they acted as go-betweens between those who gazed upon them and the invisible from whence they came.

Objects found in places of worship, especially painted or sculpted images of gods or saints, also played this role, by representing normally invisible personages, living on the other side of the boundary separating the sacred from the secular. These images were representative in that they were supposed to be flat or three-dimensional replicas of features, giving the onlooker an opportunity to associate a name or perhaps even a life history with a face. In fact, the link between a model and its image can be considered as being much stronger than that which consists merely of resemblance, and images were therefore arttibuted a certain power, which gave them a direct role in all that was sacred, and the capability to represent not only the features of a person but also the active force that was his. Phenomena of this sort are not hard to find: one only has to think of all the miracle-performing Madonnas populating European churches and all those images and statues from which miracles are still awaited. It is also an accepted fact that objects did not need to resemble a sacred personage in any way in order to represent him. This was particularly true of relics, which owed their significance to having either been in contact with a saint or constituted part of his body. However, relics represented not only the sacred but also the past, or more exactly they represented the sacred because they were supposed to have come from a personage belonging to sacred history. This explains why they were always accompanied by authenticating documents, either sealed certificates attesting their origin or small strips of parchment bearing brief explanations. While those who saw these images followed up this experience in the composition of a new theology or hagiography, those who had studied relics went on to write history and, from the twelfth century, when Guibert de Nogent wrote his *De pignoribus sanctorum*, critical history. In short, images and relics too were intermediaries between those who looked at and touched them and the invisible.

We arrive at the same conclusion when we analyse the objects hotly fought over by wealthy Romans. There is no point in embarking on yet another discussion of statues and paintings, of images that is, since it is obvious that they represent the invisible. Indeed, the same can be said of precious stones and pearls, of Corinthian vases, crystal ladles and dishes, engraved silverware and so on. Gemstones in particular simultaneously represented several different aspects or domains of what has been termed *en bloc* the invisible. They encapsulated the whole of nature; 'Hence very many people find that a single gemstone alone is enough to provide them with a supreme and perfect aesthetic experience of the wonders of Nature.' As well as being at the heart of many a legend associating them with mythical heroes or events, they also came from far-distant places, not only from the Orient as in the case of murrhine and crystal, but also from India and Arabia in the case of pearls. They possessed health-giving powers: '"Adamas" prevails also over poisons and renders them powerless, dispels attacks of wild distraction and drives groundless fears from the mind.' For their part, the Corinthian bronzes were a reminder of a casting method forgotten by the Romans and of a historical event: the fire which followed the taking of Corinth by Roman troops. All these objects were, once again, intermediaries between the onlooker and the invisible, with statues representing gods and ancestors, pictures scenes from the lives of the immortals or historical events, precious stones the power and beauty of nature and so on.

It now only remains to be said that various different traditions surrounding stones thrived during the Middle Ages in western societies, and that these stones were also believed to have certain powers. The inventory of Charles V's jewels spoke, for instance, of a 'stone which cures gout', while gold and silver were considered to be extraordinary substances, the very purest and, as such, the most representative products of the earth. They were noble and extraordinary substances used to produce or decorate images, reliquaries and more generally everything the king used, including his dishes, clothes, furniture, weapons, armour and regalia, in short, everything which represented either the realm as an undivided whole or else the power and wealth of its sovereign. Put another way, the contents of the treasure-houses belonging to kings and princes represented the invisible first because of the materials from which they were made, second because of the forms they were given, such as the crown, as these were the legacy of an entire tradition, and last because they had been acquired from a particular individual and thus constituted a reminder of past events, or else were either very old or came from exotic places. Yet again, we find ourselves dealing with objects mediating between their admirers and the invisible.

It now seems clear that the collections which have just been discussed have not been compared uniquely on the basis of external likenesses. In spite of their apparent disparity, all these collections consisted of objects which were in certain respects homogeneous. This homogeneity sprang from their involvement in the exchange process which took place between the visible and invisible worlds. While funeral objects and sacrificial offerings moved from the first to the second of these worlds, other objects moved in the opposite direction, sometimes directly, sometimes by depicting elements of the invisible world in sculpted or painted images. It will be shown later on that it was the role forced upon them, the role of guaranteeing communication between the two worlds into which the universe is cleft, which kept these objects out of the economic circuit. Yet it will also be seen that it was this very same role which caused them to be attributed such a high value and meant that there was always a considerable temptation to reintroduce them into the circuit, in return for usage values and goods, which is why they had to be afforded special protection. Needless to say, they could not guarantee communication between the two worlds unless they were displayed to the inhabitants of both: only when this condition was met could they become the intermediaries between their admirers and the world they represented.

To avoid any misunderstanding, it must be emphasized straightaway that the opposition between the visible and the invisible can take many and diverse forms. The invisible is spatially distant, not only beyond the horizon but also very high or very low. It is also temporally distant, either in the past or in the future. In addition, it is beyond all physical space and every expanse or else in a space structured totally differently. It is situated in a time of its own, or outside any passing of time, in eternity itself. It can sometimes have a corporeity or materiality other than that of the elements of the visible world, and sometimes be a sort of pure antimateriality. At times it will be an autonomy *vis-à-vis* certain or even all the restrictions placed on the visible world, at others it will be an obeying of laws different from our own. Even so, these are, of course, merely empty compartments capable of containing the most diverse of beings, from ancestors and gods to the dead and to people different from ourselves, as well as events and circumstances. The objects going from one exchange partner to another between the visible and the invisible vary greatly according to the identity of these partners. Just as the ways of transmitting messages to the invisible can take varying forms, such as human and animal sacrifices, offerings, libations and prayers, so the phenomena representing the invisible can greatly vary, including heavenly apparitions, meteors, animals and plants (sacred cows in India, and the Romans' sacred forests), striking changes in the relief, such as mountains, and rivers.

Collections, or at any rate those which have been examined here, represent only one of a number of measures adopted in order to guarantee communication between the two worlds and the unity of the universe. This enables us to understand more clearly why there is such diversity in the objects making them up, in the places in which they are located and in the behaviour of their visitors, as it reflects the diversity in the ways the visible can be contrasted with the invisible. This diversity by no means rules out an equivalence of functions, but rather is a symptom of it. All the collections which have been discussed fulfilled one identical function, that of allowing the objects they contained to play the role of intermediaries between their onlookers, whoever they might be, and the inhabitants of the world to which the former did not belong: the visible world, if the onlookers were invisible and vice versa. However, this function diversified into a multitude of equivalent functions, and for those reasons which have just been outlined.

The term 'collection' immediately implies the grouping together of a certain number of objects. In this very work, the *genus proximum* is given as 'a set of objects'. Yet how many objects are needed to form a collection? In an abstract sense, it is clear that a question of this kind cannot possibly have an answer, and with the exception of one or two special cases, which need not be discussed here, such quantitive considerations do not need to be bothered with. This is because the number of objects going to make up a collection depends on several different factors, including the place where they are amassed, the type of the particular society, the state of its technology and its way of life, its production capacity and ability to stock the surplus, and the importance it attaches to the use of objects to establish communication between the visible and invisible. This means that the number necessarily varies considerably in time and space and can only be used in very exceptional circumstances to distinguish a collection from a mere heap of objects. It is its function which is the really important factor, and the one which is expressed through observable characteristics which were listed in the definition of the collection. Given this fact, we are forced to accept that collections are also present in so-called primitive societies, and to extend our discussion to cover the *churinga* of the Australian Aborigines and the *vaygu'a* of the Trobriand Islanders, which Malinowski rightly compares to the crown jewels in Europe, as well as examples of tools which are apparently conserved in Bambara villages and shown to adolescents during initiation ceremonies and, of course, the statuettes, masks, blankets and large items of copperware belonging to the peoples of the north-west coast of America. All these objects are kept temporarily or permanently out of the economic circuit, afforded special protection in enclosed spaces adapted specifically for that purpose and put on display. All, without exception, act as intermediaries between those who can see them and an invisible world mentioned in myths, stories and accounts. Even without a large number of examples, we can therefore show that the collection is a universally widespread institution, though this should come as no surprise, given that the opposition between the visible and the invisible is a universal phenomenon.

This paper first appeared in K. Pomian (1990) Collectors and Curiosities, *Oxford: Polity, pp. 6–25.*

REFERENCES

Berry, Le Heraut (1968) *Chronîque du roi Charles VII*, Bibl. nat., MS fr. 5052, in Bernard Guenée and Françoise Lehoux, *Les Entrées royales françaises de 1328 à 1515*, Paris.

Pliny the Elder (1963) *Natural History*, trans, W. H. S. Jones, Loeb Classical Library, London: Heinemann and Cambridge, Mass.: Harvard University Press.

'Trésors d'art chinois, récantes découvertes archéologiques de la République populaire de Chine' (1973) exhibition catalogue, Petit Palais, Paris.

24

Notes on the history of collecting and of museums

Eva Schulz

Schulz's paper reflects on the early development of collections and on the history of collecting, with particular reference to the sixteenth to eighteenth centuries, the period in which modernist approaches to knowledge and understanding crystallized and in which appropriate institutions developed, the modern museum among them. Four key texts – by Quiccheberg, Major, Valentini and Neikelius – dating from this time are chosen to shed light on the purpose of, and approach to, collecting as it was perceived during the period. The implications of this historic collecting practice shape many collections and museums in the modern world.

Since the sixteenth century, collections have been amassed with the aim of transmitting information by means of a systematic arrangement of objects.[1] The wish to perpetuate and to disseminate this information gave rise to a particular kind of publication. These museological tracts provide insights into the preoccupations of collectors from the sixteenth to eighteenth century, although they tend to contain only rather vague statements concerning the appearance and the function of the collections themselves.[2]

On the other hand, our knowledge of the materials which feature in such collections towards the end of the fifteenth century and more especially from the beginning of the sixteenth century is steadily becoming more concrete. Changing perceptions at this time had the consequence that the scholar emerged as a third leading power in society alongside the 'sacerdotium' and the 'regnum'. The scholar, who was not bound to any particular social class, needed a place in which he could pursue, without interruption, his intellectual occupation. His researches provided him with higher knowledge and wisdom, so that he was no longer a passive element in the godly plan, 'sondern Baumeister seiner Welt'. [3]

Having established the necessity of such a place, the question of its furnishing was considered. In this connection Pliny's *Historia naturalis* emerged, as it were, as a connecting thread. This song of praise for 'the mother of all objects' is an encyclopaedia of nature comprising thirty-six volumes and developed out of the author's wish to transmit his 'scientific strivings' to the reader. For reasons which will be discussed, it gains in importance for the history of collections during the succeeding centuries.

After the description of the world, of its movements and those of the planets, Pliny describes the place of man and nature in the macrocosm and their relationships with God's purposes. According to Pliny the aim of all human research is self-knowledge of human triviality in the face of the infinite power of nature which he represents by the word 'God'.[4] Man can never fully understand nature, although, as a godly creation, it has been conceived solely for the benefit of man. This unique position, designated for man in creation, can be deduced from his role within the macrocosm even though he is prone to frailties and mistakes (vii, i). Not only was nature created for man, but its recording, analysis and investigation represented the highest goal of all human activities. In order that its constituents could be examined, they had to be collected in one place, and the scholar also found in Pliny instructions concerning what was to be collected. His detailed description of the three realms of nature (viii ff.) embraces everything from elephants to insects, from the cultivation of plants to the influence of the heavenly bodies upon the times of sowing; the arts of healing and magic are elucidated in as much detail as minerals, precious stones and the rudiments of sculpture.

The history of collections is clearly bound up with this concept of the scholar as it emerged during the Renaissance. Science was first directed to the service of realizing the causality of all existence as conditioned by God, which man began to question. As a result, the desirability emerged of conducting these studies in one place in which all such materials – Pliny lists them – were assembled. Collectors south and north of the Alps were soon no longer content with the mere creation of a collection as comprehensive as possible, but they themselves compiled encyclopaedias which in effect praised the ordered universe of godly creation, which none the less remained beyond the grasp of the human intellect. Furthermore, they served to transmit this knowledge to visitors, describing the qualities of the objects in the collections and explaining their organizing principles. Already at the end of the sixteenth century, works of art and artistically arranged *naturalia* were introduced into collections, especially in Italy. Encyclopaedic writing and the history of collections in Italy since the sixteenth century have been analysed elsewhere, so that we will here deal with comparable writings north of the Alps.[5]

The treatise of the physician Samuel Quiccheberg (1529–67)[6] is one such encyclopaedia, arranged as a set of instructions for compiling an ideal collection. Quiccheberg's supposed position as personal physician to Albrecht V of Bavaria (1528–79) or as an occasional counsellor at court, cannot be firmly established. Evidently of Flemish origin, he lived in Antwerp and Ghent only until the tenth year of his life and then spent some time in Nuremberg. He can be further traced through the universities of Basle and Freiburg up to 1548 and to the 'Reichstag' of Augsburg, where he may first have come into contact with the Fugger family. After a period in Padua, he seems to have returned to take up an administrative position with Johann Jakob Fugger, as successor to his teacher Hieronymus Wolf, with responsibility for the library and the collection of the Fuggers. During this time he seems also to have served at the court of Albrecht V. To judge from the numerous journeys he undertook at this time, he evidently enjoyed a large measure of freedom.

In 1565 his first printed work, today's oldest known museological tract, appeared in quarto. It was printed in the 'Adam Bergschen Offizin' in Munich with the Emperor Maximilian II's approval and has the title *Inscriptiones vel tituli theatri amplissimi . . .*

Quiccheberg divides the contents of his 'Theatrum', covering sixty-two pages, into four chapters. In the first chapter he identifies the five main fields of collection ('classes') of the whole of the universe. In these principal fields the infinity of real objects is arranged according to relationships of sense, and within the classes they are again ordered into ten or eleven subclasses ('inscriptiones'). In the second chapter, he comments on the importance of a library within a collection: in the selection of relevant literature a hierarchy of individual faculties is to be observed, with theological writings occupying the first place, followed by jurisprudence, mathematics, medicine and literature on museums. In the third chapter advice is given on what is to be arranged in the individual classes – or rather 'inscriptiones' – using the collection of Albrecht V of Bavaria as an example. In the fourth and last chapter are listed all the collections of princes and scholars in the German Reich and in Italy with which the reader and collector should familiarize himself. The last five pages contain, in the form of an appendix, quotations from the Bible, verses praising the author and a justification of the publication. According to Quiccheberg, sacred objects, paintings and artistic works are to be arranged first amongst the 'inscriptio prima' of the 'classis prima'. Following the sacred objects, a genealogy of the founder of the 'Theatrum' is to be given in the 'inscriptio secunda' in the form of a series of portraits. These portraits are intended not only to demonstrate the origins of the collector and the importance of his family, but are also to assure the collector of a respected place in the genealogy of all well-known founders of collections, which is to be presented in the 'inscriptio tertia, again by way of portraits The 'inscriptiones quarta ad decima' list maps, topographical views and illustrations of well-known monuments as further fields of collection.

In the second 'classis' Quiccheberg lists all manner of works of art and items which can be produced by man from the *naturalia*. Here are goldsmith's products alongside works of art made of stone, wood and glass, side by side with exotic vessels of metal and marble; it includes also weights and measures, contemporary and antique coins, and portrait medallions of famous personalities in plaster and wax, while diverse ornamental pieces are to be found in the consecutive subclasses.

This 'classis', mainly of inorganic materials, is followed by the third 'classis' of predominantly organic materials. The three realms of nature are to be represented – earth, water and air. Man is categorized amongst the earth-dwellers and his skeleton appears grouped with those of apes and frogs. Plants, fruits and roots are also to be arranged in this 'classis'. Unaltered nature in the 'classis tertia' is opposed to 'modelled nature' in the form of manufactured materials of the 'classis secunda' In the 'quarta classis', this representation of nature is contrasted with man and his activities: here, man is shown researching, cultivating and artistically reproducing nature, by means of his natural aptitudes and the tools he has developed; consequently, all necessary instruments such as rulers, dividers and the tools of artists are to be found here, alongside medicinal and hydraulic machines etc. Yet, man is also marked by his desire to amuse himself quite unproductively, as evidenced by the inclusion of a collection of European and other games and clothing.

The 'quinta classis' might be called a collection of 'two-dimensional products', originating from distinguished artists. However, according to Quiccheberg, all graphic techniques belong to this class as well. For the second time in the collection, therefore, portraits of famous men, together with a genealogical family tree of the collector, are to be found here. This glorification of the collector and his genealogical links with other scholars finds its conclusion in a collection of emblems and arms.

Quiccheberg entitled this instruction in collecting and systematization 'Rich theatre of objects of the whole universe, unique materials and extraordinary representations . . .' While the names 'Theatri rerum universitatis' or 'universo theatro' seem adequate to Quiccheberg as characterizations of collecting and writing, yet in the heading to the second chapter he gives the terms 'Musea' (museums), 'Officinae' (workshops) and 'Reconditoria' (repositories) as synonyms. Quiccheberg defines a 'museum' as a place (or a text?) in which spectacular and extraordinary things are arranged in all their abundance and diversity as in a chamber. Furthermore, these objects are to be accessible for purposes of study, by which they are ennobled.[7] The elevated claims that are attributed to a universal collection by these tasks have to be expressed in its naming. For

Quiccheberg, the term 'Theatrum' is not enough – according to him one has to speak of an 'amphitheatrum': 'unde et accommodari aliquo modo amphitheatri nomen ipsi posset . . .'[8] Thus, the model for sixteenth-century collections north of the Alps was not quite that of the Greek *museion* or temple: the amphitheatre or *theatrum* in its original etymological sense had the meaning of 'to look at, to examine', and hence to name. This 'universo theatro' evolved into a model of the universe, in the sense both of a collection of real objects and of an encyclopaedic text. In either case, the purpose was to study and to admire the collection.

Besides the 'Theatrum, vel museum' which was to house objects of all sorts, Quiccheberg saw a need for special collections which were to concentrate on the exhaustive representation of a specific field of collection. These specialized collections were given special names, which once again were Greek in origin. Thus, terms such as 'Bibliotheca', 'Tornatilis', 'Pharmacotheca' and 'Myrothecium', or for collections of paintings 'Promptuarium Imaginum', are to be found according to the nature of the contents. But here Quiccheberg emphasizes that these collections can exist only as part of the 'Theatrum' or 'museum' (used synonymously in this case).

Surprisingly enough, Quiccheberg already gives a definition of 'Kunst- und Wunderkammern'. He remarks on the usual name for special collections north of the Alps as follows: 'Cuius equidem promptuarium vulgo Germanorum non iam Kunstkammer (quod est artificiosarum rerum conclave) sed solum Wunderkammer (id est miraculosarum rerum promptuarium).'[9] Here we may ponder whether Quiccheberg was precocious in this matter or whether the term had been in circulation for some time. 'Kunstkammer' as a chamber for artistic objects and 'Wunderkammer' in the sense of a repository for extraordinary objects, were terms commonly used in the eighteenth century, yet it is surprising that no reference is made by later authors to Quiccheberg as the originator or first authority for the name. Quiccheberg expounds on the advantages of total specialization in a single field. In this way, he suggests, are to be uncovered the explanations for the individual objects and phenomena which shape the universe.

With his 'Theatrum' Quiccheberg takes up the idea of an encyclopaedic text as encountered in Pliny's *Historia naturalis*. Pliny was particularly preoccupied with the need for a written catalogue – as complete as possible – of all the things that form the universe. Quiccheberg wanted in addition to provide a book of instructions for the arrangement of a collection, of a 'museum' in which tangible objects are presented. Such a 'theatrum' was not only to serve for the glorification of the creative God, but was also to be a place of study. Here Quiccheberg postulates and ideal 'Wunderkammer on paper' as a model, the realization of which he leaves not only to prices and scholars, but to everyone: 'museums and workshops and repositories for the treasure of wisdom and famous works of art are located in the royal palace, sometimes separately, sometimes together . . . (Musea et officinae, ac reconditoria, qualia ad sapientae et iucundi artificii suppellectilem quandoque peculiaria in regis extruuntur, quandoque vero coniunctim habentur . . .)'.[10]

Not only does the format correspond to his aim of producing a 'handbook for all collectors of materials of the universe', but so too does his use of Latin, 'the language of the scholar'. It would be inappropriate to draw any conclusion concerning the public function of museums at that time from what has been said, but in this museological text demands for the purposefulness of collections were stated which were to become a cardinal feature of museums in the following centuries. Therefore, Quiccheberg's proposals for a catalogue must not remain unmentioned: 'sed solum catalogus theatri cultorum succinctus debeat appellari',[11] by which he meant the enumeration, description and categorization of all objects collected. The objects were not only to exist for inspection and glorification, but the catalogue – as indeed the collection itself – was to be a reflection of the collector's sublime spirit. Here, Quiccheberg takes up the contemporary Italian conception of the *studiolo*, which had become a metaphor for intellectual activity.[12] From here the idea had developed, that the scholar – as an intellectual ruler – should occupy a special position in society on account of his pursuits. For Quiccheberg, however, this was not in itself sufficient reason for establishing a collection. According to him, the first collections were already described in the Old Testament, the desirability being thereby established that true Christians should also form such collections. According to Quiccheberg, these exemplary collections are the collection of King Hezeki'ah (2 Kings 20: 12–21) and the Temple of Solomon (1 Kings 5 and 6). In 2 Kings 20, 13 the revised standard version reads as follows:

> And Hezeki'ah welcomed them, and he showed them all his treasure house, the silver, the gold, the spices, the precious oil, his armoury, all that was found in his storehouses: there was nothing in his house or in all his realm that Hezeki'ah did not show them.

Quiccheberg concludes his quotation from the Bible with verse 19 (after the prophet Isaiah has predicted the dispersal of all that Hezeki'ah has stored up), in which Hezeki'ah hopes instead for times of peace that will last for the rest of his days.

Hiram was, likewise, able to build 'a house for the name of the LORD my God' (1 Kings 5: 5), because of peace between him and King Solomon. This most sagacious ruler built the temple that is described in 1 Kings 6: 1–83 and 1 Kings 7: 1–51 with full details of its costly decoration, its provision with an abundance of ornaments and rich textiles. God speaks to Solomon: 'Concerning this house which you are building, if you will walk in my statutes . . . then . . . I will dwell among the children of Israel' (1 Kings 6: 12–13). The Temple of Solomon becomes a symbol for the Church, God's habitation on earth, in which man praises him. God's omnipotence can be represented and praised not only in church, but also in a collection. In Quiccheberg's eyes, the Temple of Solomon forms a prototype for the 'Kunst- und Wunderkammer'. This 'Theatrum mundi' assembled by man formed, in fact, a mirror of the universe. Yet, only a limited lifespan was assigned to it because it had been assembled by the hand of man (see 2 Kings). In spite of the praise of scholars, a reference was embedded here to the transitoriness of everything that is wrought by man in the face of the infinity and order of God's omnipotence.

Quiccheberg praises the collection of Albrecht V of Bavaria as especially exemplary, although he did not live to see its establishment (in 1578) in the Munich *Residenz*. This collection, as well as that of Ferdinand II of Tirol at Schloss Ambras, allows certain conclusions to be drawn on the influence of Quiccheberg's writing.[13] Contrary to the situation in the Italian *studioli*, the task of assembling the products of the godly creation predominated in the 'theatrum' north of the Alps towards the end of the sixteenth century. The *raison d'être* of such a collection was deduced from the Bible. Thus, the *naturalia* were considered more important at first, but later on the *artificialia* became the stuff of collections. In spite of the importance of the treatise as an ideal plan for a collection, as has been outlined here, references to Quiccheberg are not to be found in other works of the seventeenth and eighteenth centuries. The present writer has been unable to discover exactly how far, Quiccheberg's work was distributed nor how well-known it was. Today it occupies pride of place at the beginning of the series of museological discourses, the number and scope of which increased considerably in the course of the seventeenth century.

As a second exemplar we may consider the work of the collector Johann Daniel Major (1636–93),[14] a physician and a native of Kiel. In October 1674 his publication appeared in Kiel under the pseudonym 'D.B.M.D.', with the title: *Unvorgreiffliches Bedencken von Kunst- und Naturalien-Kammern insgemein*. Major's text, which is rare in the original, was reprinted in its entirety in the first volume of Michael Bernhard Valentini's encyclopaedic *Museum museorum*, published in Frankfurt in 1704. In contrast to Quiccheberg's work, Major's treatise is a folio, of twenty-eight sheets without illustrations. After studying in Wittenberg and Leipzig and following the completion of his medical studies in Padua, Major worked as a general practitioner in Hamburg from 1664. He compiled his treatise while holding the position of medical professor and inspector of the botanical gardens of the academy in Kiel, to which he was appointed in 1665. In doing so, he had two intentions: the first was private, for it was to be dedicated to an old colleague and was to be a wedding-gift for him; the second intention was more important for the history of the development of museums in general. for Major wanted to present an 'Inventarium der meisten Natural-Sachen'. To his knowledge, no such work existed up to that time, although such a piece would undoubtedly be useful for the 'Beförderung guter Künste'.[15] In the course of eight chapters, Major introduces the reader to the ways in which a collection might be arranged and ordered, and additionally he lists the most important collections known to him. First of all, he deals with the basic question of why man collects. In the fourth and fifth chapters he gathers some forty different names for collections of all kinds, the differences between which he defines as in a reference-book. Chapters six to eight give practical instructions on the ordering and care of the contents of a collection. Major, who believed himself to be the first to compose such a tract on 'das Sammeln', makes no reference anywhere to Quiccheberg, although he must have known his works, as shown below. Surpassing Quiccheberg's museological writings, Major's treatise gives instructions on how to arrange and how to work with the objects.

In 'I Capitel §1', Major points to the fact that collecting is an inborn human urge which is to be found in young and old alike, in believers and non-believers, in the 'mittleren und niedrigerm Stande. . . . Unter allen weltlichen Wissenschaften ist keine so lieblich, keine den Mensch so vergnügend, und die Begierde dazu ihm gleichsam angeboren, als die Wissenschaft von den Dingen der Natur.' The scholar achieves his fame by collecting alone, not by birth. For Major, this urge to collect everything from heaven and earth is explained by the human consciousness: 'es müsse dieses Alles von einer weit höheren und göttlichen Kraft seinen Anfang von einer verborgenen übernatürlichen Ursach sein Wesen und Ursprung haben'.[16] Man, though, had almost completely lost his preeminent position in God's creation by virtue of the Fall, but has been restored to a state of grace by Christ's intercession with the 'richtenden Vater'.[17] In Major's view, the true character of man is expressed in his striving for good and, furthermore, in his being prepared 'von der Natur gern etwas Neues [zu] wissen'.[18] Major likens man's insatiable desire for knowledge to a clockwork automaton, the body of which is formed like a vessel: the highest task of this automaton is to give expression to the wonderful acts of God and its mechanism to refill the vessel that has been emptied by the Fall of man. This can be effected in two ways: on the one hand by studying the 'göttliche Wort' of the Bible and, on the other hand. by the 'inextinguishable perfection' of man 'die auf Erfahrung gegründete gesunde Vernunft'.[19]

In broad terms, this inference is reminiscent of Quiccheberg. After it has been demonstrated that the accumulation of a collection is a natural human urge, with the ultimate aim of recognizing the sublime, Major turns to the enumeration and interpretation of different commonly used expressions for collections. *Artificialia* are simply to be counted among the *naturalia* in order to explain the latter more exactly, or they are to be deposited in totally separate *Kunstkammern*.[20] Such artistic objects are of little value in Major's eyes and are, according to him, much less significant than the *naturalia*. The following expression is most appropriate for a completely furnished collection: 'Naturalien Gemälde-Schrank und Kammer'.[21] This is the conclusion he draws at the end of his enumeration of names for collections. This enumeration stretches from the Greek word *museion*, which he derives from the temple of the nine Muses on Mount Olympus, to *studio*, a term which would be used in Italy. Major names Pliny (XIV, 14) and Vitruvius (VI, 3) as sources in addition to his own enumerations. Before finally listing the owners and the contents of the most famous collections in an appendix, he describes how the 'Natural-Sachen und Raritäten recht zu disponieren [seien]'. For this purpose he suggests an arrangement of real objects according to their materials in different 'classes' (Cap. 8 §11) and 'nach Orgel-Pfeiffen-Manier' (Cap. 8 §6) as the only practicable organizing principle. Here, the similarities to Quiccheberg's ideas are so striking that Major's knowledge of the work seems indisputable. Or was this arrangement of collections already a generally practised reality? Furthermore, Major demands the marking of boxes (Cap 5/3 §7) with the identity of their contents. This, however, can be realized only if a scholar and not a 'Handwerker' is in charge of the collection (Cap. 8 §3): only such a person can undertake the grouping of objects according to their natural 'classe', i.e. according to collective terms rather than by alphabetical order.

According to Major, the whole arrangement of the collection has to do justice to the diversity and singularity of the universe. A complete collection should, in addition to the cabinet of *naturalia*, be provided with four corresponding but spatially separated individual collections within the same building. Although in Major's opinion the 'Naturalien-Kammer' has the most prominent role among all these collections, he refers to the installation of a reading room (with reference to Pliny, XXXV, 2) as an asset of almost equal importance. In this 'Antiquarium' books, sculptures, coins, urns, etc. are to be deposited. The three other collections identified are: 'ein Cabinet von vielerley Mathematischen Instrumenten', 'eine Rüstkammer (Armamentarium)' and a 'Technicarcheum oder Technicotheca, von gewissen Kunst-Sachen geringerer Nothwendigkeit' (Cap. 8 §7). According to Major, this concept can be realized only if it is well devised and committed to writing in the form of 'Universal-Catalogi' (Cap. 8 §4) before the real objects are actually collected. This 'catalogue' is to be a 'Raritäten-Buch', in which all known real objects are assembled. Even objects which are not themselves represented in the particular collection, are to be described and illustrated. Furthermore, the reader is to be able to deduce the qualities, advantages and disadvantages etc. of the objects from the catalogue. Here, Major extends considerably Quiccheberg's requirements for a catalogue in that it no longer serves exclusively to establish the organizing principle of a collection. Such a 'Catalogus' makes possible for the collector a completeness which is hardly possible in reality. Thus, he is able to compile an encyclopaedia of all real objects in the macrocosm.

The only collections whose arrangements are complete, according to Major, were those of King Solomon and King Hezeki'ah, as described in the Bible. To them he devotes a detailed description of contents, from precious stones to an artificial pond, in the appendix of his work. Major recommends these as models for all other collections[22] as they are, according to him, the most complete that can be created by the hand of man. Then he enumerates the most exemplary collections – in his opinion – of princes and scholars and describes them in full. He devotes a whole chapter to the collection of natural objects of Ferrante Imperato in Naples[23] as well as to those of Augustus, Cicero, the Mogul of India and King Montezuma – for the latter no mention is made of the source of his knowledge. He also mentions the collection of the Medici in Florence. All these collections, though, pale into insignificance alongside God's natural chamber of art. His organizing principle and structure are best realized in the 'weltberuffenen Kunst- und Raritäten-Kammer Ihrer Chur-sächsischen Durchl. zu Dresden' (Cap. 8 §2). These collections and their associated inventories have been discussed elsewhere.[24] Thus, only the 'Catalogus' of 1671 and that of 1755 need be mentioned here as examples of Major's theories. In this description of the collection of 1671 with the title *Cedretum oder Churfürstlicher sächsischer stets grünender hoher Cedernwald, auf dem grünen Rautengrunde*, the author, Tobias Beutel, mentions that the third of seven chambers contained 'Schatzkästlichein und Kunstgemählde'. Here, he observes, 'alte und neue künstliche Gemählde' were assembled, and he quotes the names of Dürer, Lucas van Leyden, Cranach, Tintoretto, Titian, Rubens 'und andern künstlichen Mahleren'.[25] The intrinsic value of a work of art was clearly already taken into account in Dresden, and the value of the work was judged according to the name of the artist. At the urgent request of Augustus the Strong, the two-volume catalogue of the picture gallery was already compiled in 1753/7, preceded in 1755 by the bilingual (German–French) catalogue of the 'königlichen Naturalienkammer zu Dresden'. According to the wish of the author, who is not named, this catalogue was meant for interested visitors, who in 'Zukunft die hiesigen Cabinetter besuchen möchten sich auf das sie sehen wollen, desto nutzbarer gefaßt machen, und durch diese Beyhülfe, sich desto leichter wieder erinnern'. In this collection of natural products of God's creation, visitors were also able to admire a model of Solomon's Temple, which was earlier in the possession of a merchant from Hamburg. This model, which could be opened up and entered in order to be properly examined, was evidently so well known that an account of it had already been compiled by 1752: 'The Temple of Solomon, with all its Porches, Walls, Gates, Halls, Chambers, etc.'. There it is described as the product of seventeen years' work, containing 6,737 columns with capitals and other details, such as the Ark of the Covenant, the altar etc., in silver and gold.[26] It was set up in the cabinet of *naturalia*, in which the works of God's creation were assembled, yet it represented one of only two exemplary human collections mentioned by Major.

His work, composed in German in 1664, is important in several respects. It was the first source to supply a large circle of readers with such a clearly structured enumeration of the diverse definitions of collections. The detachment of the 'Kunstkammer' from the collections of *naturalia* and the revalidization of works of art as man's own creation developed at a varying pace in the collections of the time. The 'Raritäten-Buch' which Major demanded was already customary at the beginning of the eighteenth century. A catalogue no longer merely listed the objects within collections, but extended to form a reference-book with explanations of the importance, origin, cosmological significance and miraculous power of the individual natural products. In these encyclopaedias, the glorification of God's work progressively diminishes and the task of conveying writings and realities to the scholar grows in importance. But at first it was not learning and research in the encyclopaedic sense, of education of the mind in the power of observation and critical ability, that gave the name 'Museum' to the collections: rather, it became the title of this literary genre. By and large, these 'catalogues' are similar in their mode of presentation and in their contents. They are compilations of all objects that were regarded as being unalterably components of a collection that could justly bear the name 'museum'.

Michael Bernhard Valentini's manual which appeared in two volumes in 1704–14, illustrated with copperplate etchings, is a 'museum in words' in this sense. The princely Hessian physician, who was also an experimental scientist and professor of medicine at Giessen University, entitled his work as follows: *Schaubühne oder Natur- und Materialienkammer. Auch Ost-Indisches Sendschreiben und Rapporten. Museum Museorum oder vollständige Schaubühne aller Materialien und Specereyen nebst deren Natürlichen Beschreibungen / Election / Nutzen und Gebrauch ... Zum Vorschub der studierenden Jugend / Materialisten / Apotheker und deren Visitoren / wie auch anderer Künstler*

Jubelierer/ Mahler / Färber usw. also verfasst und mit etlichen hundert sauberen Kupfer-stücken unter Augen gelegt. . . . He adds Major's complete text to his 'Vorbilder- und Studiensammlung' for the benefit of collectors and as an explanation for the organizing prin-ciple. In his introduction, Valentini emphasizes that the formation of a collection of natural products is the wisest way for man to recognize 'Gottes Allmacht'. Not only, he remarks, do the collections of King Hezeki'ah and King Solomon prove this, but God's Creation is one sin-gle immeasurable collection. He doubts that there is a complete collection in the world, but each collection surely has something that appeals to the 'curios Gemüth'.

Valentini believed that pure collections of *naturalia*, as he (erroneously) supposed the 'Anatomie Theater' in Leyden and the collection of the Anatomy School of Oxford University to be, were especially important. According to him, the electoral collection in Dresden, which offered something for everyone, also lived up to the measure of a good collection. In Italy, however, there were only 'wenig dergleichen vollständige Musae Publica'. Only Aldrovandi's collection in Bologna and Settala's in Milan were thought worthy of mention. Valentini excludes from his list collections dedicated exclusively to the fine arts. As far as the aim of his tract is concerned, he points out that all other publications on this topic are so incomplete that he wants to make up for this in his own publication. For this purpose, he includes all 'Musea oder sogenannten Kunst-Kammern / curiose Zeit- und Tag-Register / Reis-Beschreibungen und anderer Bücher der Naturkundiger', which he lists in his bibliography in alphabetical order. Here Kunckel's *Ars vitraria experimen-talis*, Major's work and the Italian authors Aldrovandi and Settala are to be found, as well as the writing of Paracelsus. He has also studied Pliny's *Naturalis historia*, Vitruvius's *De architectura* and Virgil's *Aeneid*. He makes no reference, however, to Quiccheberg. Valentini adds a detailed enumeration, description and elucidation of natural products, each illustrated with an etching. He embraces the concept of the three realms of nature from Pliny (or Quiccheberg?), beginning with a description of insects, birds, fish and mammals and extending to trees, the essences and magical powers of which are noted. Then he turns to describing gold, silver, precious stones, pigments, varnishes and other materials of painting. He separately lists exotics in the 'Ost-Indisches Send-Schreiben'.

In Part II, published in 1714, Valentini presents individual collections, including his own, in the form of a tabulated list of contents. At the end of the double volume is an index of key-words. It is this index and the bibliography which give rise to the claim of this 'Museum' as being a universal reference-book, a guide for the collector. Scientific studies in the eighteenth century were no longer limited to collecting and arranging elements of the universe according to a concept: now collectors wanted to make their knowledge, acquired by way of their own researches, available to a wider circle. In order to be able to relay information on individual objects and on their significance within the wider uni-verse, usable, intelligible and generally accepted encyclopaedic manuals were a necessity.

At the same time a development in collecting procedure is to be observed through the rise of special collections and the revalidization of the artistic creations of man's own hand. This is to be observed in the work of the son of a Hamburg merchant named Jenckel, who composed his writing under the pseudonym 'C. F. Neikelius'. *Museo-graphia oder Anleitung zum rechten Begriff und nützlicher Anlegung der Museorum oder Raritäten Kammern* was edited in 1727 by Dr Johann Kanold, a member of the Kaiserlich Leopoldinischen-Carolinischen Akademie of Vienna, who added a preface in which he briefly introduces the author in the manner described above.[27] As Neikelius emphasizes in his foreword, he sees his work – also in quarto format with one copper-plate etching – as a reference-book. As he aimed to assemble everything 'in beliebter Kürze', he asks the reader to excuse a certain incompleteness, for he has no intention of filling a folio on the topic. This work is also marked by a clear and convenient structure, including a bibliography and an index. His bibliography cites Major's as well as Valentini's works, and includes also the catalogues of Aldrovandi and Imperato and of the Tradescant Collection in London. Again, there is no reference to Quiccheberg.

Neikelius views his writing as an 'Opferung an Gott' and devotes it to 'Gott dem Vater, Sohn und Heiligem Geist, also von dem alle Weisheit und Wissenschaft ihren Ursprung haben'. As in the work of Major, very complex reasoning is to be found in Neikelius on the question of man's insatiable desire for knowledge of the universe, in spite of the Fall. Neikelius realizes, as well, that this desire applies not only to 'Hochgelehrte und Kluge' and consequently he also directs his work to the 'Ungelehrte und Einfältige'. Nevertheless, God has properly equipped all human beings – Neikelius compares man with a tablet on which all knowledge is noted down, the blank surface being 'beschrieben' from youth onwards. Man can, however, acquire knowledge of physical things only by way of libraries and curiosity collections: only if there are libraries can man conduct the scientific studies which are indispensable for the maintenance of a cabinet of curiosities.[28] For, according to Neikelius, the real function of the cabinet is to serve 'zur Beförderung der Ehre Gottes absonderlich, und dann zum gemeinen Besten'.[29] By and large, Neikelius takes over from Major the whole list of names and definitions of expressions for collections, but he includes a new definition for 'Museum'. He divides the creation of nature into three realms 'Regno animali / regno vegetabili / regno minerali', while he defines art a little less precisely: 'Ars est multiple, die Kunst ist mancherley.' In his opinion, however, art adds the 'Vollkommenheit einer Raritätenkammer'. Neikelius also redefines the term 'Rarität', which he derives from Latin *raritas* and translates it as 'selten, dünn' in German. A 'Rarität' is marked by having been 'ausgearbeitet und verfertigt' by the hand of a 'künstlerischen Menschen'.[30] He understands 'Kunstsachen' as 'köstliche Gemählde von den berühmtesten Mahlern, als Michel Angelo, Raphael, Titian, Rubens, Dürer &c.'. Here, he demands the presentation of 'geistliche und weltliche Gemählde' in a large collection. Neikelius holds to the opinion that it is very important to observe that they are: '(1) Originalia und keine Copien und (2) von den berühmtesten Meistern, wie bereits gedacht worden'.[31] The selection is to be made according to the taste of the owner. He also gives here some guidelines for the storage of paintings: the conditions must not be too damp, and the light must be prevented from falling directly on to the surface, since it might damage the painting.

In contrast to the preceding works – excepting the catalogue of the Dresden collection – the difference between original works of art and imitations is emphasized and collectors are encouraged to collect only high-quality originals. This estimation of art presupposes that it is regarded as an original product of the human mind. Created by man, it can also be evaluated and judged by man. Man has this ability since he studies and educates himself. In this way, Neikelius found a new definition for 'Museum' in which 'allerley natürliche[r] Wunder im Original' as well as 'unterschiedlichen künstlich ausgearbeiteten Naturalien' were collected, 'die zwar gleicher Gestalt ihren Ursprung aus der Natur hätten', but 'durch die von Gott in den Menschen gelegte Kunst aber unseren Augen desto angenehmer vorkommen. Ein solcher Ort wird insgemein ein Museum genannt.' He continues that this name is derived from the nine Muses and goes on, 'Museum bedeutet also ein solches Gemach oder Kammer, worinnen man findet (1) ein Cabinet entweder mit Naturalibus oder Artificiosis natürlichen und künstlichen Dingen . . . ; (2) einen Schrancken und Repositorium mit Büchern, und vornehmlich solchen, deren Material von dem Inhalt des dabey befindlichen Cabinets handelt',[32] as otherwise the collection is of limited use.

In the first half of the eighteenth century the theories of preceding centuries were consolidated, bringing about a re-evaluation of the objects which were to be collected. The possibilities afforded for research, as outlined in preceding works, led to a realization of the intrinsic value of *naturalia* and *artificialia*, which were then assembled in separate collections. In addition to self-contained collections of natural products, the museum was also to encompass an art collection of its own – God's creations to be shown beside man's creations.

On the need for a well-structured order for a collection, Neikelius goes further. The location of the collection within a building has its own significance.[33] Study of the ten books of Vitruvius' *De architectura* led Neikelius to suggest the desirability of a favourable circulation of air and a south-easterly orientation for the room containing the collection. He also takes over Vitruvius's recommendation of painting the room in a light colour. Vitruvius remarks in the third chapter of Book IV on the arrangement of a room for the display of paintings, that it should be twice as long as it is broad. Neikelius further elaborates this recommendation by suggesting a central entrance and the placing of a large table directly on the longitudinal axis of the room. Bookshelves are to be installed on one side and shelves for the natural products on the other side of the room – each separated by a window. These shelves are to be orderly; thus, the large objects have to be on the lower shelves, the smaller ones on the higher shelves. At the end of the room, facing the entrance, the 'curioso Artificialia . . . antique und moderne' are to be presented in cabinets for detailed study. For purposes of deterrence two 'fürchterliche Löwen, Bären und Tieger' are to sit at the entrance in order to symbolize the silence that is necessary for study. Three further points have to be observed in order to uphold the necessary order of such a museum. According to Neikelius, a register of new acquisitions, the mode of access and all further information in the form of an 'Inventarium' is indispensable. Furthermore, a 'General-Catalogum'[34] must be on hand, by which the use of the 'Museum' for scientific purposes is to be facilitated. From this fact Neikelius's third demand follows logically: the need to observe a 'Besucherordnung'.[35] In order to visit the collection repeatedly, the visitor must always appear with clean hands and neatly dressed. On no account must the order of the collection be interfered with. Neikelius recommends the purchase of the catalogue for further study of the objects at home.

But it was not only the definition of a 'Museum' or the introduction of organizational guidelines that made this work a reference-book for the museum of the eighteenth century. It contains in addition an alphabetically ordered list of all famous collections known to the author. These collections are described in considerable detail, the naming of the specific works of art taking up a large amount of space. He describes with some precision Italian art collections such as the Tribuna of the Uffizi, enumerating the works of Titian, Raphael, Leonardo da Vinci, etc., which are to be seen there. For the depiction of the Belvedere Court in the Vatican, which is very detailed, he quotes Michelangelo, who called it 'sein Studium'. Here, the *Apollo* and the *Torso* of the Belvedere caught his attention; the *Laocoön* group fascinated him especially, and it is striking that he takes over the description and co-ordination of the group almost exactly from Pliny.[36] On the basis of this detailed depiction of Italian art collections, which is noteworthy in Neikelius's work as it is in no comparable writing, a visit to Italy by the author can be assumed. However, he mentions only briefly collections such as those of Settala in Milan or Imperato in Naples, by reference to Major's text. Perhaps this presumed journey to Italy explains his enhanced comprehension of museums compared to that of his predecessors. Italian art collections seem to have played a fundamental role, in comparison with others, because works like Pliny's *Historia naturalis* formed a kind of handbook for the collections. It was gradually realized that this work is not only an encyclopaedic enumeration of the works of nature, but that Pliny emphasizes the priority of man over nature. In Neikelius's eyes, by contrast, nature plays the role of master to the artist, who creates his works after the example of nature. Works of art become worthy of being explained, collected and evaluated according to measures of quality. The new museums had to do justice to new requirements and new ideas.

The four works which have been analysed here mirror only a small part of the abundance of such writings that appeared mainly in the eighteenth century. By modern standards of knowledge, Quiccheberg's treatise is singular in its kind and for its time. As mentioned repeatedly above, Quiccheberg's thoughts were obviously influential, although his contribution is never acknowledged; this is especially astonishing in the cases of Valentini and Neikelius, who otherwise set a high value on their extensive bibliographies. The three writings of the late seventeenth to the early eighteenth centuries, however, consciously refer to one another. The study of all four works provides new insights into what has been stated elsewhere about the early art of collecting,[37] and contributes to the evaluation of older theories. At no time were *Kunst- und Wunderkammern* indiscriminate medleys born of a purely encyclopaedic zeal for collecting, or out of mere pleasure in oddities or a passion for representation. They were formed according to values based upon the scientific knowledge of the time.

This has been elucidated by way of quotations from the authors discussed in this chapter. The pursuit of science was defined as the desire of man to accumulate encyclopaedic knowledge in order to define the natural phenomena that surrounded him. In order to justify this typically human trait, not only was reference made to classical authors such as Pliny, but the Bible too was used repeatedly. The Temple of Solomon was no longer synonymous merely with the habitation of God on earth, but was itself transformed into a collection. The climax was reached with the Book of Genesis being equated with an ideal but unachievable collection. This point having been reached at the beginning of the eighteenth century, Neikelius further developed consideration of the question at which Major had only hinted, namely the role of curious and studious man in this macrocosm ordered by God. Man, already favoured with a privileged position and with the power of reason, becomes himself the creator of an ordered microcosm. This resulted in the ordering of collections becoming increasingly detailed and in works of art gravitating to an isolated position within the collection. In Neikelius's estimation, for example, artistic endeavour of the highest merit is associated almost exclusively with works of Italian artists and with works from Antiquity. These he characterizes as the peak of human creation. Scientific activity is no longer confined to admiring the diversity of creation, but extends to evaluating works of human creation. Now, training the power of discrimination becomes the most important function of a collection. Thus scientific research within collections, up to then directed towards a passive glorification of creation, is superseded by a 'new science'. Catalogues, inventories and libraries for purposes of study, already demanded in the writings of Quiccheberg and Valentini, here take on a new weight.

It seems, however, that the time for manifesting the establishment of the concrete term 'museum' in the understanding of the public had not yet come. Neikelius certainly vigorously promoted the adoption of the term 'museum', but he acknowledged others such as 'Schatz-Raritäten-Naturalien-Kunst-Vernunft-Kammer' to be quite as valid. Neither should it be forgotten that the collections mentioned above were not initiated by the state, but were in the main developed through private initiative.

With the help of such early museological writings, we can justify the search for the beginnings of the movement towards fully-fledged museums in the late sixteenth century. Only the narrowness of our present-day understanding of the role of the sciences and of the character of the institutions currently called museums presents difficulties of access to understanding of the sciences and museums of earlier epochs.

This paper first appeared in Journal of History of Collections 2(2) (1990), pp. 205–18.

NOTES AND REFERENCES

1 O. Impey and A. MacGregor (eds) (1985) *The Origins of Museums. The Cabinet of Curiosities in Six-teenth- and Seventeenth-Century Europe*, Oxford; Oxford University Press.

2 W. Liebenwein (1977) *Studiolo die Entstehung eines Raumtyps und seine Entwicklung bis um 1600*, Berlin.

3 H. Beck (1985) 'Von der Kunstkammer zum bürgerlichen Wohnzimmer', in H. Beck and P. C. Bol (eds) *Natur und Antike in der Renaissance*, Frankfurt: Catalogue Leibighaus, 282–304.

4 Pliny, *Historia naturalis*, lib II, chap. 5.

5 G. Olmi (1985) 'Science–honour–metaphor. Italian cabinets of the sixteenth and seventeenth centuries', in Impey and MacGregor, op. cit., 5–16.

6 O. Hartig (1933) 'Der Arzt Samuel Quiccheberg, der ertse Museologe Deutschlands am Hofe Albrechts V in München', *Das Bayernland* 44: 630–3.

7 S. Quicche[l]berg (1565) *Inscriptiones vel tituli theatri amplissimi . . .*, Munich. 'Musea et officinae . . .' (chap. 2) and his explication for 'inscriptio tertia, classis prima'.

8 See Quiccheberg, op. cit., 'Digressiones et Declarationes secundum ordinem inscriptionum'.

9 See Quiccheberg, op. cit., 'Exempla ad Lectorem . . .', Chap. 'In Bavaria & Suevia'.

10 Quiccheberg, op. cit., heading of chap. 1.

11 Quiccheberg, op. cit., chap. 2.

12 Liebenwein, op. cit., 51, 161.

13 See for example, L. Seelig, 'The Munich Kunstkammer 1565–1807', in Impey and MacGregor, op. cit., 76–89; E. Scheicher, 'The collection of Archduke Ferdinand II at Schloss Ambras; its purpose, composition and evolution', in Impey and MacGregor, op. cit., 29–38; J. von Schlosser (190: 8) *Die Kunst- und Wunderkammern der Spätrenaissance. Ein Beitrag zur Geschichte des Sammelwesens*, Leipzig; new edn Braunschweig 1978.

14 See, for personal details of Major, *Allgemeine deutsche Biographie (AdB)* xx, Leipzig (1884), 112.

15 J. D. Major (1674) *Unvorgreiffiches Bedencken von Kunst- und Naturalien-Kammern insgemein*, Kiel, chap. 3 'Absonderlich von der ersten Gelegenheit Kunst- oder Naturalien-Kammern zu erfinden', see especially §3 und §4.

16 See Major, op. cit., chap. 1 'Von der natürlichen Zuneigung eines jedweden Menschen zur Betrachtung der Natur', see especially §1.

17 Major, op. cit., chap. 1 §4.

18 Major, op. cit., chap. 1 §7.

19 Major, op. cit., chap. 2 §2.

20 Major, op. cit., chap. 5 §19.

21 Major, op. cit., chap. 5 §20.

22 See Major, op. cit., Appendix chap. 6 'Ob König Salomon einige Kunst- oder Naturalien-Kammer zu Jerusalem gehabt'; chap. 8 'Von Königs Hiskia Schatz-Hause gleichfalls zu Jerusalem und denselben befindlichen Raritäten'.

23 See Major, op. cit., chap. 9 and chap. 10ff.

24 See J. Menzhausen, 'Elector Augustus's *Kunstkammer*: an analysis of the inventory of 1587', in Impey and MacGregor, op. cit., 69–75.

25 See, for example, A. Mayer-Meintschel (1986) 'Die Gemäldegalerie', in U. Arnold and W. Schmidt (eds) *Barock in Dresden, Kunst und Kunstammlungen unter der Regierung des Kurfürsten Friedrich August I von Sachsen und Königs August II von Polen 1694–1733 und des Kurfürsten Friedrich August II von Sachsen und Königs August II von Polen 1733–1763*, Leipzig, exhibition catalogue Villa Hügel, Essen, pp. 313ff.

26 See. H. von Brühl (ed.) (1755) *Kurzer Entwurf der königlichen Naturalienhammer zu Dresden*, Dresden and Leipzig.

27 For personal details of Neikelius, see Ch. G. Jöchers (ed.) (1816) *Allgemeines Gelehrten-Lexikon* suppl. 5 p. 467.

28 See C. F. Neikel[ius] [Jenckell] (1727) *Museographia . . .*, Leipzig and Breslau. Preface to part III concerning libraries, and p. 445.

29 See Neikelius, op. cit., part IV.

30 Neikelius, op. cit., part IV, chap. 1 p. 407.

31 Neikelius, op. cit., part I, p. 4.

32 Neikelius, op. cit., part III, chap. 3; and part I, p. 6.

33 Neikelius, op. cit., part IV, p. 409 and pp. 421–3, and for comparison Vitruvius lib. 4, chap. 4.

34 Neikelius, op. cit., part IV, p. 457.

35 Neikelius, op. cit., part IV, p. 454.

36 Pliny, op. cit., lib. XXXVI, 4 and lib. XXXV, 1. See also Neikelius, op. cit., p. 90.

37 See above all the collection of lectures from the symposium in Oxford 1983, in Impey and MacGregor, op. cit.

25

Another past, another context: exhibiting Indian art abroad

B. N. Goswamy

Cultural traditions outside that of Europe have their own approaches to the collection of material objects. This paper by Goswamy discusses the indigenous Indian aesthetic called rasa, *an aesthetic theory based on immediate emotional response to selected objects, which has its own elaborate intellectual history. Goswamy sets as his theme the nine* rasa *of Indian art, and describes how his two exhibitions were organized not according to chronology, type of objects, or artist, but by the aesthetic response of the viewer.*

> Pure aesthetic experience [*rasa*] is theirs in whom the knowledge of ideal beauty is innate; it is known intuitively, in intellectual ecstasy without accompaniment of ideation, at the highest level of conscious being; born of one mother with the vision of God, its life is as it were a flash of blinding light of transmundane origin, impossible to analyze, and yet in the image of our very being.
>
> (Viswanatha Kaviraja)

> A work of art elicits and accentuates this quality of being a whole and of belonging to the larger, all inclusive, whole which is the universe in which we live. This fact, I think, is the explanation of that feeling of exquisite intelligibility and clarity we have in the presence of an object that is experienced with aesthetic intensity. It explains also the religious feeling that accompanies intense aesthetic perception. We are, as it were, introduced into a world beyond this world which is nevertheless the deeper reality of the world in which we live in our ordinary experiences. We are carried out beyond ourselves to find ourselves.
>
> (John Dewey)

The two exhibitions upon the intimate experience of which I draw here ('Rasa: les neuf visages de l'art Indien', Grand Palais, Paris, 1986; 'Essence of Indian Art', Asian Art Museum, San Francisco, 1986)[1] began with the first visit of a group of French colleagues to India in 1983. The holding of the Festival of India in France had been negotiated and announced. Quite naturally, a major exhibition of Indian art was to figure prominently in it, but till then no real thought had been given to its theme or range. Things were wide open, and we were going to speak of various possibilities. In the course of discussions, when the subject of the exhibition of art at the Grand Palais came up, my French colleagues stated that they were interested in an exhibition that would not be just an expansion of the fine exhibition of Indian art that had been held at the Petit Palais a few years back,[2] nor a show that simply presented 'masterpieces' of Indian art. They were interested in an exhibition that *said* something. They had a highly sophisticated museum-going public that was not as easily appeased as audiences 'elsewhere', one of them stated with a Gallic twinkle.[3] I responded quickly by asking them if they would be interested in an exhibition that approached Indian art through *rasa*. The idea and even the word were unfamiliar to them, but there was a sudden spark of interest. I explained, in the broadest possible manner, how *rasa* (roughly, 'aesthetic delight') was related to art in the Indian tradition; conversely, how art was understood in the context of *rasa*. If one could take this approach to Indian art, it might become more accessible, I argued. An animated discussion ensued, at the end of which the mood was one of agreement and enthusiasm. Accessibility seemed to be the key word. We were vaguely aware that this was something of a dark plunge, for nothing along these lines had been essayed before in the area of the visual arts, even in India. Despite the hazard that such an approach involved, though, there was lurking excitement. We agreed to discuss and explore this idea further.

In the months that followed we all had our share of doubt and uncertainty. The French sent two bright young curators to work with me and to acquaint themselves with the collections that I was going to draw upon (and, I suspect, with the workings of my mind). They were legitimately unsure of how well the idea of *rasa* was going to come across to French audiences through objects. On my part, I was grappling with the concept and working out ways to present meaningfully what was, from the French viewpoint, an alien art and an alien conceptual framework. There was obvious appeal in the idea, but equally obvious pitfalls and difficulties. Not everything in Indian art could be approached from this angle; one might not be able to locate enough objects of high quality in each category of *rasa*; there was also the fear that, because of the unfamiliarity of the concept, the exhibition might become too wordy and the concept might eventually come to overshadow the art. I thought of falling back upon alternative, more conservative approaches: it was possible to present a selection of great paintings and sculptures as high points in Indian culture, but that had been done all too often before. It would also be possible to explore a given period in depth through objects, but to an audience generally unfamiliar with the history of Indian art, or even of India, that might mean very little; in any case there was a general wish that the exhibition should cover a wide range of Indian art, establishing its antiquity as much as its breadth. One could take a sharply defined category of great works, such as Chola bronzes, Mughal paintings or Gupta stone sculptures, but then that would leave out so much else. From the past of India it was not easy to take an individual artist and present his *œuvre*, for identifying the work of a single artist from a tradition that is for the most part emphatically anonymous presents almost insuperable difficulties.

Compared to all these possibilities, relating art to the experience of art appeared to be a far more attractive idea. Through the concept of *rasa*, it might be possible to provide the non-Indian general viewer with an entrée into Indian art, for the nine *rasas* were central to the context of Indian art. It might be unfashionable to speak of *rasa* now, but it was an experience that the Indian viewer traditionally always associated with art. In presenting art objects with reference to the emotions they aroused or heightened in the viewer's mind, one would be using categories that were appropriate to the art.

Rasa is a key to Indian art, and deserves to be better understood. It is easily the most important of terms in the Indian theory of art. The first reasoned treatment of it is found in Bharata Muni's *Natyasastra*,[4] which is datable to the early centuries of the Christian era and deals primarily with the arts of the theatre. The term has been used most often in the context of the arts of performance – theatre, dance and music – even though it is mentioned specifically in other texts[5] as extending to all the arts, and literary theorists have always adverted to it. Among the most refined discussions of the theory of *rasa* are those by rhetoricians of the medieval period.

In the most general of ways, the average listener, viewer or reader in India has often seen art as being intimately connected with *rasa*, indeed even as being valid only to the extent that it leads to a *rasa* experience (art being inherently 'a well-spring of delight, whatever may have been the occasion of its appearance'[6]). The idea of *rasa* is something that the average viewer or listener feels at home with, even if its subtleties, and the discussions that have centred on it for several centuries, are often beyond his or her ken.

At the physical level the word *rasa* means sap or juice, extract, fluid. It signifies, in its secondary sense, the non-material essence of a thing, the best or finest part of it – like perfume, which comes from matter but is not easy to describe or comprehend. In its subtlest sense, however, *rasa* denotes taste, flavour, relish; but also a state of heightened delight that can be experienced only by the spirit (*ananda*). When one experiences a work of art, the experience is likened to the tasting of a flavour, the taster being the *rasika* and the work of art the *rasa-vanta*. In the singular, *rasa* is used in the absolute sense, 'with reference to the interior act of tasting flavour unparticularised'.[7] In the plural, the word is used relatively with reference to the various, usually eight or nine,[8] emotional conditions that may constitute the burden of a given work and that the listener or viewer can experience. These conditions, or sentiments, are the erotic (*shringara*), the comic (*hasya*), the pathetic (*karuna*), the furious (*raudra*), the heroic (*vira*), the terrible (*bhayanaka*), the odious (*bibhatsa*), the marvellous (*adbhuta*) and the quiescent (*shanta*).

The notion is that *rasa*, or aesthetic delight, is a unity, but comes within the reach of the viewer through the medium of one of these sentiments. At the same time, *rasa* being essentially an experience, it does not inhere in the art object; it belongs exclusively to the viewer or listener, who alone can experience it. How *rasa* arises and is 'tasted' has been the subject of a sustained, refined debate among scholars and theoreticians for close to fifteen hundred years. But, broadly, the process is conceived thus: each *rasa* has its counterpart in what is called a *bhava*, a dominant feeling or mood. Thus, the erotic sentiment, the *rasa* called *shringara*, has *rati* (love) as its corresponding *bhava*; the comic sentiment has *hasa* (mirth or playfulness) as its *bhava*, and so on. *Bhava* belongs to the work, and can be consciously aimed at by its maker or performer. How this *bhava* (enduring psychological state) comes into being in its own turn has been described in fine, eloquent words by past theorists. For a specific *bhava* to rise to the surface in a work or performance, the mood is carefully built up with the use of appropriately chosen *vibhavas* (determinants), essentially 'the physical stimulants to aesthetic reproduction, particularly the theme and its parts, the indications of time and place and other apparatus of representation – the whole factibile'.[9] Another input is that of *anu-bhavas*, or appropriate consequents, consisting of gestures and movements in consonance with the mood of the work. There are then the complementary (transient) emotional states (*vyabhichari bhavas*), especially relevant to the arts of theatre and dance and comprising a wide range of emotions, from agitation to fright to envy and indecision. It is these determinants, consequents and complementary emotional states that work on the mind of the viewer or listener, 'churning his or her heart'. From this churning a dominant emotional state, a *bhava* that is durable, emerges.

But then suddenly something else happens: the *bhava* transmutes itself into *rasa*, which the viewer or listener experiences. This does not happen uniformly every time. There are many preconditions that the texts speak of: the viewer must be cultured or sensitive enough; the work or performance must be alive with *bhava*; the moment must be right; the heart must be capable of receiving; and so on. But if these and other conditions are present, wonderful things happen: a spark leaps from the performance to the viewer, suffusing his or her entire being. *Bhava* turns into *rasa*. The experience can be overpowering, for it comes often like a flash of lightning, catching the viewer unprepared for the moment, and leaving him or her deeply moved. This is the moment when, as later writers put it, 'magical flowers would blossom' in the viewer's awareness: *rasa* is tasted.[10] The experience cannot be consciously worked towards; the moment comes unpredictably; but when it comes, it does so with blinding swiftness, yielding the same inscrutable delight that the seeker experiences upon coming face to face with the unknowable.

It is clearly stated that the same viewer may have the *rasa* experience from viewing an object or performance at one time and not have it at another; the intensity one viewer experiences may be different from another's. There are many imponderables and many factors intervene, but the experience is real, and can be intense. It is stated again and again that the experience belongs to the viewer; the work of art is a vehicle. In the fine skein of this theory many strands of thought come together. Coomaraswamy puts it with his usual succinctness:

> The conception of the work of art as determined outwardly to use and inwardly to a delight of the reason; the view of its operation as not intelligibly causal, but by way of a destruction of the mental and effective barriers behind which the natural manifestation of the spirit is concealed; the necessity that the soul should be already prepared for this emancipation by an inborn or acquired sensibility; the require-ment of self-identification with the ultimate theme, on the part of both artist and spectator, as prerequisite to visualization in the first instance and reproduction in the second; finally, the conception of ideal beauty as unconditioned by natural affections, indivisible supersensual, and indistinguishable from the gnosis of God – all these characteristics of the theory demonstrate its logical connection with the predominant trends of Indian thought, and its natural place in the whole body of Indian philosophy.[11]

Much of this sounds esoteric and mysterious, and one cannot be sure how much the intel-lectual operations behind *rasa* and *bhava* were understood by the average Indian viewer of the past. But there seems to be little doubt that art and *rasa* were very closely con-nected in the Indian mind. It was not easy to think of one without the other. I have cited elsewhere my encounter with that great connoisseur of the arts of India, the late Rai Krishnadasa of Benares, to whom I once took a small enquiry of mine concern-ing the date and the style of a painting. Rai Krishnadasa heard my questions out with his usual grace and patience, but then he leaned back on the comfortable round bolster of his simple divan and said softly: 'These questions I will now leave to you eager historians of art. All that I want, at this stage of my life' – he was past seventy years of age then and in frail health – 'is to taste *rasa*.' Nobody knew better than Rai Krishnadasa the answers to the questions I had taken to him at that time, but somehow he had moved on to, or back towards, what in his eyes was the real meaning or purpose of art.

This paper first appeared in I. Karp and S Lavine (eds) (1991) Exhibiting Cultures: The Poetics and Politics of Museums Displays, *Washington, DC: Smithsonian Insitution Press, pp. 68–73, notes 76–7.*

NOTES

1 In 1983, the exhibition that was being discussed was meant only to figure in the Festival of India in Paris. It was decided at a much later stage that the Paris exhibition would travel to San Francisco in the fall of 1986. The catalogues of the two exhibitions, both written by me, vary somewhat from each other.

2 Apart from the 1960 exhibition 'Trésors de l'art de l'Inde', the Petit Palais saw another exhibition of Indian art in 1978 – 'Inde: cinq mille ans d'art'.

3 It is to be remembered that arrangements for the exhibitions connected with the Festival of India on the East Coast of the United States had already been made final by this time.

4 Bharata Muni's *Natyasastra*, perhaps the most comprehensive treatise of its kind on the arts of India, is variously dated by different authors. An English translation by Manmohan Ghosh is available under the title *Natyasastra* (Calcutta: Manisha Granthalaya, 1967).

5 Most early texts on painting, sculpture, or literature contain passages on *rasa* and its applicability to the various arts, although the treatment varies in length and detail. Thus, the celebrated *Vishnudharmottara* (part 3, trans. Stella Kramrisch, Calcutta: Calcutta University Press, 1928) has a whole chapter on *rasa*. Viswanatha Kaviraja's fourteenth-century *Sahitya-Darpana* (trans. J. R Ballantyne and Pramada-Dasa Mitra, Calcutta: C. R. Lewis, Baptist Mission Press, 1875) speaks of *rasa* at considerable length in relation to literature.

6 Ananda K. Coomaraswamy (1956) *The Transformation of Nature in Art*, New York: Dover.

7 Ibid., 48.

8 The *Natyasastra* mentions only eight *rasas*, but the ninth, *shanta*, was added by later theoreticians and is so widely accepted that one is wholly used to the phrase *nava-rasa* (nine *rasas*) in all the arts.

9 Coomaraswamy, op. cit. 52.

10 Among the first expositions of Bharata Muni's *rasa* theory is that by the great eleventh-century Kashmir scholar Abhinavagupta. It is he who speaks of these 'magical flowers'. See *Aesthetic Experience according to Abhinavagupta*, ed. Raniero Gnoli, Rome: Istituto Italiano per il Media ed Estremo Oriente, 1956.

11 Coomaraswamy, op. cit., 55.

26

Collecting reconsidered

Susan M. Pearce

All material now in museums has arrived there as the result of the collecting process, however elaborate or simple this may have been. In this paper Pearce examines some aspects of the collecting process, and distinguishes three characteristic modes of object accumulation. It is important to remember that any collection may embrace two or more of these modes, either at one time or in different phases of its existence.

Sweden. Lapp. Pouch made from a blackthroated diver (*Colymbus arcticus*). Male specimen, probably taken in the nuptial season.

Eastern Eskimo. Iglulik Tribe. Pouch made from the footskin of an albatross. Collected during Admiral Sir Leopold McClintock's expedition in H.M.S. Fox. 1859.

Faroe Islands. Strono Kvivig. House broom of four puffins' wings.
(Labels from the Pitt Rivers Museum, Oxford, quoted by James Fenton as Exempla 10, preceding his poem on the Pitt Rivers Museum (Fenton 1983: 79))

It is a truism, but still true, that museums hold the stored material culture of the past. They share this characteristic with a number of other institutions, like great houses, perhaps churches, perhaps libraries; but museums alone exist in order to hold material objects.[1] In a unique sense, our collections are what we are, and from this all our other functions flow. It is strange, then, that until very recently the study of these collections by museum people, and from a museological stance, has been comparatively neglected, certainly in comparison with the amount of effort which has been poured into this study from a field or discipline base. This, it seems to me, has been a major weakness, for it is only when practitioners turn their attention to the history and nature of their own field, and begin to develop a critical historiography proper to it, that the field can be said to have come of age. This has clearly been true of the history of science as a study, it is beginning to prove itself in archaeology (for example, Fahnstock 1984), and now a parallel development is gathering momentum among museum workers which, I think, can properly be called Collection Studies.

Collection Studies can be seen to embrace three broad areas. The one which has been most familiar to us is the large and complex area of collection policies, that range of issues, part philosophical and part practical, which include decisions about what any particular museum should and should not collect, why and how material may be disposed of, and the relationship between documentation systems and the kinds of research which can be generated. The second broad area covers the history of collections and of collecting from its beginnings in the ancient world up to the present day. The focus is upon the tracing of acquisitions and dispersals, the editing of relevant surviving documents and the biographies of collectors, together with themes like the relationship between collections and the idea of the museum. Study here is not new, but it has been put on a new footing by the work of Arthur Impey and Oliver Macgregor (Impey and Macgregor 1985; Macgregor 1983) and by the *Journal of the History of Collections* which they founded in 1989. The third area concerns the nature of the collections themselves and the reasons why people collect, both the explicit intellectual or 'presentable' reasons and the more obscure psychological or social reasons. Curators are now realizing that we must start to understand the history and nature of our collections and the reasons behind their formation, so that we can appreciate better the assumptions about knowledge and value which they embody (see Stewart 1984). This understanding lies at the heart of all interpretative activity. All three areas are intimately interwoven, and, in sum, Collection Studies present an exciting field for thought and work. I have chosen in this paper to concentrate on aspects of the nature of collections and of collecting, in an effort to explore some of the cultural implications.

Museums may hold the stored material culture of the past, but this stored archive has not arrived in bland, sanitized form in, as it were, uniform storage boxes coming in at so many on the first of every month. Quite the contrary: the material has come in fits and starts. It comes in all kinds of relationships to the progress of human lives, including bequests made after death. It comes incomplete, imperfect, and with associated documentation and information, itself immensely variable in quality and quantity. Above all, it comes in groups, in sets of material. Even the accession of a single object is perceived as part of a set, either in relation to others of its kind or in relation to the other elements in the life history of the original owner or collector. But, in fact, by far the greater proportion of the material in museums has arrived not in single objects but in groups. We are accustomed to call each of these groups 'a collection' and to refer to the whole assemblage as 'the collections'. The notion, then, of group identity is deeply embedded in the material itself and in museum language, the two combining to play a part in constructing the curator's world.

An attempt to understand the nature of these collections is one way of exploring our human relationship with the external physical world of which they are a part. The material comes as part of a context, part of the web of relationships, for which 'ideological' is a useful word, which involve persons and the material world. The forming of the collection is part of the relation between the subject, conceived as each individual human being, and the object, conceived as the whole world, material and otherwise, which lies outside him or her. The collections, in their acquisition, valuation and organization, are an important part of our effort to construct the world, and so it is with this large and fascinating area that this paper will be concerned. I shall try to distinguish three modes of collecting, to which it seems to me most of our collections belong, and these may be called 'collections as souvenirs', as 'fetish objects' and as 'systematics'. I shall try to draw out the characteristic features of each mode, using as framework some of the ideas usually described as phenomenological, and associated originally with Hegel, and especially the concept of 'objectification' abstracted by Miller (1987) from Hegel's ideas, which supposes a dual relationship of process between subject and object. 'Process' is an important word to which we shall return. These will be linked with concepts of the romantic, an important group of ideas which is now being applied to the history of collecting (Wainwright 1989), and which have been greatly developed over the last few decades. These two interlinked ideas are to the fore in contemporary cultural studies, in writers like Eagleton (1983) and Miller (1987) although naturally each author will make his or her own use of them, and to both I shall return in a moment.

Let us make a start with that material which I have characterized as souvenirs. These are the objects which take their collection unity only from their association with either a single person and his or her life history, or a group of people, like a married couple, a family or, say, a scout troop, who function in this regard as if they were a single person. They cover a huge range of possible objects. Examples chosen at random include children's toys in the York Castle Museum, a sampler in the Victoria and Albert Museum, a piece of patchwork in Exeter City Museum, a powder compact in Leicestershire Museums Service, and a small, modern blue-glazed pottery scarab made specifically to act as a souvenir of the Egyptian collection, which can be purchased in the British Museum shop for 5p. The range of such pieces formally accessioned into museums is, of course, only a tiny fraction of the number which actually exists out in the world, but they are, nevertheless, very characteristic types of museum accession.

They usually arrive as part of what curators call 'personalia' or 'memorabilia' and sometimes the personality to which they are attached was sufficiently interesting or notorious to throw a kind of glamour-by-association over the pieces, an interesting aspect of the way in which museum objects work, which is susceptible to analysis as signs and symbols but which must not delay us here (but see Pearce 1990). I am reminded of a playlet written by Laurence Binyon, formerly an Assistant Keeper at the British Museum. He imagines an altercation between two exhibits, the bust of a Roman emperor and the mummy of an Egyptian queen (quoted in Holmes 1953: 3). Each claims precedence on the grounds of past importance and present popularity. The lady makes good her claims in one devastating couplet:

> I lived in scandal and I died in sin;
> That's what the world is interested in!

Generally, however, the personalities are not particularly distinguished and unless the objects have acquired the kind of interest which accrues to survival through the passage of years and increasing rarity, like the Leicester powder compact made for Boots Ltd in the 1930s, they are experienced as boring and embarrassing. James Fenton, one of the few modern poets to have written a poem about a museum, says of the Pitt Rivers Museum:

> Outdated
> Though the cultural anthropological system be
> The lonely and unpopular
> Might find the landscapes of their childhood marked out
> Here, in the chaotic piles of souvenirs.
> The claw of a condor, the jaw-bones of a dolphin.
>
> (Fenton 1983: 82)

The Pitt Rivers aside, such objects will not be displayed unless they can be hooked on to a historical exhibition in which their personal connections will be mentioned.

And yet we know, in our hearts if not in our minds, that souvenirs are moving and significant to each of us as individuals; otherwise we would not keep them. What, then, is the nature of these pieces? Souvenirs are intrinsic parts of a past experience, but because they, like the human actors in the experience, possess the survival power of materiality not shared by words, actions, sights and the other elements of experience, they alone have the power to carry the past into the present. Souvenirs are samples of events which can be remembered, but not relived. Their tone is intimate and bittersweet, with roots in nostalgic longing for a past which is seen as better and fuller than the difficult present. The spiral is backwards and inwards as the original experience becomes increasingly distant and contact with it can only be satisfied by building up a myth of contact and presence. Souvenirs discredit the present by vaunting the past, but it is an intensely individual past – no one is interested in other people's souvenirs. Souvenirs speak of events that are not repeatable, but are reportable; they serve to authenticate the narrative in which the actor talks about the event. As a part of this they help to reduce a large and complex experience, like the Somme or the Western Desert, to a smaller and simpler scale of which people can make some sense. They make public events private, and move history into the personal sphere, giving each person a purchase on what would otherwise be impersonal and bewildering experiences (Stewart 1984: 132–50). Souvenirs, then, are lost youth, lost friends, lost past happiness; they are the tears of things.

They are also something else, and the phrase just used 'can make sense' was chosen deliberately. Souvenirs are intensely romantic in every way, and especially in the ways in which that idea is now often applied. The romantic view holds that everything and, especially, everybody has a place in the true organic wholeness which embraces human relationships, the traditional continuity of past into present, the landscape and the changing seasons. It asks us to believe that life is not fractured, confused and rootless, but, on the contrary, suffused with grace and significance. It is no coincidence that in Europe generally, and especially in England, the romantic movement came to birth at the moment in the late eighteenth century when religion had begun to lose its hold over the thinking classes and when the new factories were manifesting the shape of things to come. It was this dislocation between things as they are and things as they ought to be which aroused the characteristically romantic emotions of alienation and despair. In terms of a concept, and nowhere more than in its mystical and metaphysical side, romanticism is about as convincing as a leaking sieve, but, unquestionably, it has a powerful hold over our deepest hopes and feelings: it shows life as we would wish it to be.

It is in these hopes and feelings that the souvenirs belong. They are an important part of our attempt to make sense of our personal histories, happy or unhappy, to create an essential personal and social self centred in its own unique life story, and to impose this vision on an alien world. They relate to the construction of a romantically integrated personal self, in which the objects are subordinated into a secondary role, and it is this which makes them, all too frequently, so depressing to curate and to display.

This brings us to the second of our broad collecting modes, that which was described at the beginning as fetishistic collecting. This is in many ways an unfortunate, or even unpleasant, term, and perhaps a phrase like 'devoted', or even 'obsessive collecting' might be an improvement; but 'fetish' and 'fetishistic' are now enshrined in the literature to such an extent that to avoid the term would create more misunderstandings than it solves, so it will be used here on the understanding that nothing inherently pejorative is intended.

Our museum collections hold vast quantities of material which are almost never put on show; the reasons why this is so are part and parcel of the nature of these collections and we shall return to them later. These collections span the disciplines, and they are, significantly, usually known not by the location from which the material derived, nor by the subject upon which it concentrates, but by the name of its original owner and collector. In museums across the country, and in their equivalents across the world, the Pritchard Collection will turn out to be 15,000 foreign stamps, the Sandford Bequest 10,000 cigarette cards, and the John and Sarah Hart Loan over 2,000 crochet hooks.

Close spiritual kin to this kind of collecting are those accumulations which have been gathered by the so-called 'serious' collectors. These include very famous collections in the art and antiquities fields, like those of the Arundel or Townley classical marbles, which have always been valued for their perceived intrinsic, and therefore financial, quality and which have been taken correspondingly seriously by the museums which have come to hold them. Paralleling these are the major collections of curiosities, rarities and assorted *objets de vertu* accumulated by renowned collectors like the Tradescants, Sir Hans Sloane and Joseph Mayer which stand at the beginnings of some of our most important national collections, and the huge number of essentially very similar but much less famous collections, some in museums, but many now broken up. What links these collections with their humbler cousins of the matchbox tops and beer-mats is the lack of an intellectual rationale by which the material and its acquisition was informed, and this notwithstanding the fact that cigarette cards and the like are classified into sets which collectors try to complete: the sets have no rhyme or reason outside the covers of the album

A quantity of occasional verse has been perpetrated to make fun of this kind of collecting, from Sir Charles Hanbury Williams, a friend of Sir Hans Sloane, in the eighteenth century who wrote:

> The stone whereby Goliath died,
> Which cures the headache, well applied.
> A whetstone, worn exceeding small,
> Time used to whet his scythe withal.
> The pigeon stuff'd, which Noah sent
> To tell him when the water went.
> A ring I've got of Samson's hair,
> The same which Delilah did wear,
> St Dunstan's tongs, which story shows
> Did pinch the devil by the nose.
> The very shaft, as you may see,
> Which Cupid shot at Anthony.
> (Brooks 1954: 193)

to Ogden Nash in our own century who penned:

> I met a traveller from an antiques show,
> His pockets empty, but his eyes aglow.
> Upon his back, and now his very own,
> He bore two vast and trunkless legs of stone.
> Amid the torrent of collector's jargon
> I gathered he had found himself a bargain,
> A permanent conversation piece post-prandial,
> Certified genuine Ozymandial,
> And when I asked him how he could be sure
> He showed me P. B. Shelley's signature.
> (quoted in Bray 1981: 227)

The collecting practice lends itself to parody.

This kind of obsessive collecting, in which the intention is to acquire more and more of the same kind of pieces, and in which the accumulation stops only with death, bankruptcy or a sudden shift of interest, has been the butt of journals like *Punch* ever since the 1850s, and it has loomed large in the image which museums have been at great pains to dispel since the early 1960s. It would, however, be a major mistake to suppose that this kind of collecting belongs with our Victorian, or at least pre-Second World War, past, and is a part of our inherited museological baggage which can be decently buried in distant storage. A glance at the issue of *Exchange and Mart* dated 8 March 1990 (current when this paper was written) shows us 'Collecting' as a major heading. Here we find 'Muffin the Mule items wanted by collector, puppets, badges, annuals, etc.'; 'Wanted by collector pit checks, pay checks, time checks etc., . . . best prices paid for brass'; 'Must sell: dearly loved collection of 350 antique china half-dolls'. These have been picked at random from over 300 such advertisements, including those for large collectors' fairs. There are separate sections for bottles, cigarette cards, coins and medals, buttons and matchbox labels, and some hitherto unknown, at least to me, like smokiania, which turns out to include tobacco tins and cigarette packets. In a more up-market world, the sales catalogues of Sothebys and Christies tell exactly the same story. It is an important characteristic of these collections that they are bought, or sometimes exchanged, at an agreed valuation on the open market, in which the price reflects a perceived level of desirability. It is a fair guess that many of these collections, especially those which achieve substantial dimensions, will end up being offered to a museum, and probably accepted, with varying degrees of reluctance.

However, the reluctance on the part of our curatorial successors in the coming decades may be less than we think. There are signs that this kind of collecting, so widespread in the community that it clearly answers a fundamental need, is beginning to be given the serious attention which its social significance demands. In May–June 1990, Walsall Museum and Art Gallery, under the able guidance of Peter Jenkinson, mounted a new kind of exhibition called 'The People's Show'. Material for display was recruited by a flyer which says:

> We are looking for collections by Walsall people for a new exhibition at Walsall Museum and Art Gallery called The People's Show. If you collect anything as an interest or a hobby, or simply as a decoration in your home, we would like to hear from you. . . . If you have a collection which you think people in Walsall would enjoy seeing, please fill in this form.

The answers are being followed up by a questionnaire which is designed to discover the history of the collection, the process by which it was accumulated, the rationale behind the collection, how the owner is viewed by family and friends and what the future of the collection will be. At the time of writing, the museum has been offered collections of football shirts, eggcups, model frogs, Madonna posters and international travel sick bags taken from aircraft. When the data and the experience of this exhibition have been digested, the results should be extremely interesting.

I have said that the use of the word 'fetish' in relationship to objects and collections viewed in a particular way is now a normal part of discussion. A random dip into fairly recent writings in the related fields of literary and linguistic theory, material culture and museum studies begins to show us how the word is used. Terry Eagleton in his *Literary Theory: An Introduction*, published in 1983, discusses the nature of society in early industrial Britain. He says: 'In England, a crassly Philistine Utilitarianism was rapidly becoming the dominant ideology of the industrial middle class, fetishing fact, reducing human relations to market exchanges, and dismissing art as unprofitable ornamentation' (Eagleton 1983: 19). Two pages on, he continues: 'Art was extricated from the material practices, social relations and ideological meanings in which it is always caught up, and raised to the status of a solitary fetish' (1983: 21).

Daniel Miller in his 1987 discussion of material culture and modern mass consumption, speaks of how 'An approach to modern society which focusses on the material object always invites the risk of appearing fetishistic, that is of ignoring or masking actual social relations through its concern with the object *per se*' (Miller 1987: 3).

Three years ago, in the first of our Museum Studies International Conference series,

Peter Gathercole gave a paper entitled 'The fetishism of artefacts' where he explored the implications of the display of the Enigma Coding machine (Gathercole 1989). The idea of fetish objects has entered more generally into the world of writing. A poem by Fenton, entitled 'Nest of Vampires', which was published as a part of the collection already quoted and which strikes in some ways similar notes to those of the Pitt Rivers verses, says:

> In that chest there was a box
> Containing a piece of white coral,
> A silver cigar-cutter shaped like a pike,
> A chipping taken from the Great Pyramid
> And a tribal fetish stolen during the war.
> (Fenton 1983: 44)

'Fetish' and 'fetishistic' have come recently into museum and related studies from the broader field of cultural investigation. Psychologists use the word to describe a particular form of sexual orientation, unfortunately in many ways, because it is this that has given a useful idea an uncomfortable feel. The psychologists, however, had borrowed the concept from nineteenth-century anthropologists like E. B. Tylor, just as they have made use of kindred words like 'totem' and 'taboo'. The standard reference works trace the word back to the Portuguese *feiticos* meaning 'a charm', which was used in the fifteenth century to describe contemporary Christian relics, rosaries and holy medals. When they arrived on the African coast later in the same century, the Portuguese naturally applied the word to the local wooden figures, stones and so on, which were regarded as the residence of spirits and W. Bosman in his *Description of Guinea* of 1705 uses the word in this connection.

It is worth noting in passing that no racial or colour prejudice was involved: the devout Portuguese used the same word indiscriminately for religious objects regardless of origin, in the same way that contemporary descriptions of African settlements use an ordinary tone equally appropriate to the description of European towns. More to the purpose here, *feitico* also means 'made by man' and carries the idea of something 'artful' or 'magically active'. It was from this web of connections that the anthropologists appropriated the word, and used it to describe material objects which were worshipped for their magical powers, believed to be inherent rather than deriving from an indwelling god or spirit.

This begins to uncover the nature of fetishistic collections and collection-making. Such collections are often very private or rather, sometimes, the owner suffers a degree of tension between his urge for privacy and his desire to display his private universe to others. Joseph Mayer and his collection, which eventually went to the then Liverpool City Museum in 1867, makes the points very well. Between about 1830 and 1886 when he died, Mayer accumulated a very considerable, but very mixed, collection which included classical gemstones, Middle Eastern ivories, manuscripts, and Napoleonic memorabilia. Originally the collection was kept in a series of private homes where it seems to have been open only to close friends, but as it grew in size and fame, Mayer was moved to open his own museum originally called the 'Egyptian Museum' at 8 Colquitt Street, Liverpool (Gibson and Wright 1988).

The portrait of Mayer painted about 1840 by William Daniels gives us a vivid insight into the nature of this kind of collecting. Mayer sits in his study at 20 Clarence Terrace, Everton Road, Liverpool. He is seated in a throne-like chair in the Gothic taste, gazing reflectively at a Wedgwood urn, while light falls on Greek and Etruscan antiquities set out on the table and touches classical marbles and paintings further back in the room.

The collection is not organized, but merely arranged by its owner to what seemed to be its best advantage; indeed, it seems to have grown up around him as an extension of his person. This notion touches the heart of the matter: this kind of collection is formed by people whose imaginations identify with the objects which they desire to gather. Powerful emotions are aroused by the objects which the objects seem to return, stimulating a need to gather more and more of the same kind. The urge is towards samples, and as many of them as possible, rather than to examples, a point to which we shall return when we consider systematic collecting. The whole accumulation process is a deployment of the possessive self, a strategy of desire, in Stewart's memorable phrase. The fetishistic nature lies in the relationship between the objects and their collector, in which it is the collection which plays the crucial role in defining the personality of the collector, who maintains a possessive but worshipful attitude towards his objects. Such collections and their collector are at the opposite pole to souvenirs discussed earlier. Here, the subject is subordinated to the objects, and it is to the objects that the burden of creating a romantic wholeness is transferred.

We can take the story a stage further by reminding ourselves of the implications of that fact that the fetish concept was taken over not only by the anthropologists and psychologists, but also by the political scientists. In a passage of *Capital* famed for its obscurity, Marx says:

> It is a definite social relation between men, that assumes, in their eyes, the fantastic form of a relation between things. In order, therefore, to find an analogy, we must have recourse to the mist-enveloped regions of the religious world. In that world the productions of the human brain appear as independent beings endowed with life, and entering into relation both with one another and the human race. So it is the world of commodities with the products of men's hands. This I call the Fetishism which attaches itself to the products of labour, so soon as they are produced as commodities, and which is therefore inseparable from the production of commodities.

> (Marx 1906: 203)

This seems to mean that through the operation of the capitalist system, the commodities which people produce come to have a life of their own, irrespective of their makers, the circumstances of their manufacture, or personal relationships which all this involves. These commodities endowed-with-life then operate in an independent fashion, detached from direct social relationships, and capable themselves of being the partner in a relationship with humans, an operation which Marx saw as a distortion of the proper relation between men and goods, an abberant evil typical of mass-production society.

Leaving on one side the specific argument about the extent to which Marx was right in his analysis of modern capitalist society and of the artefacts which are part and parcel of it (but see Miller 1987), his extended notion of the nature of fetishes gives us an important clue to the nature of the collections which we are considering, and the kind of response which it is possible to make to them in a museum (or anywhere else). These collections are detached from any context, they are removed from the sphere of actual social relationships with all the tensions, efforts of understanding and acts of persuasion which these imply. This detachment is, indeed, a very substantial part of the attraction for their collectors who use them to create a private universe, but its sterility gives to the material that peculiarly lifeless quality which all curators recognize with a sinking heart. The detachment of fetish collections explains why they have so seldom been put on display: unless the collection contains objects deemed to be of intrinsic merit, usually in the art fields, or of historic interest, usually in relation to the early history of the museum, the collection languishes from decade to decade undisturbed. It will be interesting to see what impact on this the Walsall exhibition has.

Although souvenirs and fetishistic collections stand at opposite ends of the romantic pole in terms of the ways in which their human subject relates to them, as is so often true, there is a point where opposite ends meet. Both are part of an attempt to create a satisfactory private universe, and both do this by trying to lift objects away from the web of social relationships, to deny process and to freeze time. In museums, therefore, they are perceived as disassociated and static, floating in a kind of purposeless limbo. Very different is the way in which we appreciate what I shall call the systematic collections.

Historically, this kind of collecting can be traced back quite a long way, certainly into the Renaissance, and probably in some respects earlier still, but because this paper is concerned with intentions and implications rather than with historical analysis, I shall take Pitt Rivers and his collection as illustrating what I mean. Pitt Rivers believed two fundamental principles: first, that material culture reveals humankind's essential nature and development; and second, that the progress of artefactual development, and so of human nature, follows broadly Darwinian principles, so that types developed one from another according to a process of selection which modified their forms. The addition to this of diffusionist ideas about the spread of artefacts across the globe meant that the whole structure could be knit together into a kind of lattice-work in which there might be a place for everything..

Pitt Rivers presented his views in three lectures on 'Primitive Warfare' at the United Service Institute in 1867, 1868 and 1869, and offered a general statement of them in *The Evolution of Culture* published in 1875. As far as possible, the material in his own collections, and in the Pitt Rivers Museum, was arranged to demonstrate these principles, but this fell short of Pitt Rivers's ideal museum which would take the form of a rotunda building, arranged in concentric circles which would show the major human phases of artefactual evolution, with the innermost circle for the Palaeolithic, the next for the Neolithic, and so on. The rotunda would also be divided into wedges, so that 'separate angles of the circle might be appropriated to geographical areas' and allied civilizations would 'occupy adjacent angles within the same concentric ring' (Chapman 1985: 41, quoting Pitt Rivers; see also Chapman 1989). So would the conceptual lattice-work be made museum flesh.

The detail of Pitt Rivers's views about material culture has now been discredited, but this does not touch the fundamental idea which informed those views and which, of course, is shown by all the systematic collecting in the natural sciences (see Morgan 1986 and references there), and equally in the collections which result from planned anthropological expeditions, organized archaeological excavation, or the deliberate assemblage of historical material to create the period room, like those which the York Castle Museum has made famous. It is to the nature of this idea and of its implications that we must now turn.

Systematic collection depends upon principles of organization which are perceived to have external reality beyond the specific material under consideration, and which are held to derive from general principles deduced from the broad mass of kindred material through the operation of observation and reason; these general principles form part of our ideas about the nature of the physical world and the nature of ourselves. Systematic collecting, therefore, works not by the accumulation of samples, as fetishistic collecting does, but by the selection of examples, intended to stand for all the others of their kind and to complete a set, to 'fill in a gap in the collections' as the phrase so often upon curators' lips has it. The emphasis is upon classification, in which specimens (a revealing word) are extracted from their context and put into relationships created by seriality. This is achieved by defining set limits, which apparently arise from the material. Collecting is usually a positive intellectual act designed to demonstrate a point. The physical arrangement of the finds sets out in detail the creation of serial relationships, and the manipulation implicit in all this is intended to convince or to impose, to create a second and revealing context, and to encourage a cast of mind.

From this emerges a fundamental difference between the systematic collections and the other two modes discussed earlier. Systematics draw a viewer into their frame, they presuppose a two-way relationship between the collection, which has something public (not private) to say and the audience, who may have something to learn, or something to disagree with. This is one of the two reasons why curators generally give the lion's share of their blessings, and of their exhibition space, to this kind of collection. In our familiar phrase, 'you can do something with it', you can make a point, you can engage your public. The second reason is implicit in the nature of this kind of collecting. It is conceived as display, it requires organized space in which to demonstrate its serial relationships. If museum galleries and glass showcases had not existed, it would have been necessary to invent them; but, of course, museums as the public institutions which we know, and serial collecting, more or less grew up together, uniting to demonstrate the laying out of material knowledge.

But laying-out has another, and more sinister meaning. Collections and displays of this kind can be experienced as death-like, as mummification rather than interaction. Moreover, we who live in this godless postmodernist world know that there is no such thing as objective reality, at least as far as human beings are concerned, and that all knowledge is socially constructed and forever bound in the play of ideological relationships. Our systematic collections do not show us external reality; they only show us a picture of ourselves.

Hegel's concept of 'objectification' as developed by Miller may help us here. Hegel overcame the ancient dualism which separates subject and object, or humankind and the whole external world, and which must result in either the subordination of the object to a romantic vision of the essential self, as with souvenirs, or the subordination of the subject to romanticized objects, as with fetish collections: both are static, sterile, and take us nowhere. 'Objectification' is meant to describe the 'dual process by means of which a subject externalizes itself in a creative act of differentiation, and in return re-appropriates this externalization through an act [of] sublation' (Miller 1987: 28). Put rather crudely, this means that the human person as subject creates from within himself an entity of whatever kind – including material artefacts – which assumes an external existence as an object; but then takes back this creation to use it as part of the next burst of creative activity. In this way, the gulf between subject and object is healed and neither is elevated at the other's expense. The essence of the link is relationship, that relationship is always in process, and process is always bringing about change.

This, it seems to me, helps us to understand the nature of systematic collections. They are formed by the imposition of ideas of classification and seriality on the external world, but the world itself has, one way or another, given rise to these ideas. However, this is a process without beginning or end. No one starts to form or to display a collection without inheriting past process, and each collection or display in place contributes its mite to the dynamics of change. The whole continuous reconstruction is part of the concrete appreciation of the world, with all its awkwardness and dislocation, and each actor in the story can be involved in the struggle.

A principal actor is, of course, the curator, and this brings me to my last important point. The position of the curator, it seems to me, is a dilemma central to the profession at this time. On the one hand, there is our professional and discipline training through which we inherit a share in the received knowledge and wisdom of the western tradition, linked with a particular obligation to try to pass this on to others. On the other, we are aware that this knowledge, wisdom and tradition can have no intrinsic or absolute value, either moral or intellectual, that it is merely a product of specific social relationships, and therefore has no claim to any special position. In archaeological circles, to draw on my own discipline, this dislocation is seen as part of the reason for the growth of so-called 'alternative archaeology' which includes irrationalities like ley-line dowsing and abberations (from a classic position) like treasure-hunting (Gregory 1983; Williamson and Bellamy 1983).

The paradox may be eased by linking the idea of collection as process with the notion of consensus as it has been developed for the purpose of discussing the nature of theory in science by Thomas Kuhn (1970) and others. This supposes that there is a *research or professional community* made up of individuals who share a general interest and a network of communication, and a *speciality*, that is a segment of the general community which is interested in a particular problem, say the nature and implications of the nineteenth- and early twentieth-century collections of herbaria. The speciality segment will come to a broadly shared view of their subject which they will commend to the wider community, usually with some success. So is a consensus achieved, and the wider the ripples of this can spread, the better for all concerned. But the terms of the consensus are not written on tablets of stone; they are part of the same dynamic process of perpetual change which makes up the relationship between subject and object, between people and the material world of museum collections.

It is time to see, not where we have arrived, but perhaps how hopefully we have travelled. This paper has tried to open up discussion of the nature of collections as they actually are in our museums, as a particular area of social experience. It has suggested that philosophical ideas current in the broad field of cultural theory may help us here, and they have turned out to show us three common collecting modes, two at either pole, frozen and static, and the third engaging itself to bridge the gap. It must be stressed, of course, that many individual collectors and collections show elements of more than one mode, either at the same time or reflecting successive phases of activity. The analysis has thrown some light on why and how curators experience their collections, and so on why and how they are, or are not, put on exhibition.

All this, I am aware, is merely to scratch the surface of one part of collection studies. I have not attempted to discuss topics like the nature of relics, seen not merely as a specific medieval form but as a more general concept; or the idea of collection as deposition or dedication, a mode that links the centuries back to prehistoric times. The idea of collections as treasure is a fruitful one, linking them to the art and antiquities markets and so to the workings of the capitalist world: it is no accident that museums as we know them and modern capitalism came to birth at much the same time. These ideas beckon, and no doubt others lie yet in shadow beyond.

For the moment, we must leave the last word with the Pitt Rivers Collection, which has run through this paper. Fenton saw the Pitt Rivers Museum as full of souvenirs, and perhaps fetishes too. Pitt Rivers saw his collection as bringing systematic scientific classification to bear on the human material world, and curators have accorded him his historical place while disagreeing with his ideas. The Pitt Rivers labels quoted at the head of this paper can be read in all three modes, depending upon how one takes them at the time, which illustrates the notion of interaction and change. The labels remind us that, always, we are dealing with attitudes not facts, or, put another way, with human temperament. For the collectors of Walsall, for Joseph Mayer, for Pitt Rivers, as for us all, the glass of a showcase gives both a transparent vision and reflection of our own faces.

This paper first appeared in G. Kavanagh (ed.) (1991) Museum Languages, *Leicester: Leicester University Press, pp. 135–53.*

NOTE

1   This statement is not intended to exclude natural history specimens. Specimens from the natural world are, of course, to be studied and displayed according to the scientific principles which have been developed in zoology, botany, geology and related disciplines. Collections carry within them much which relates to the history of these disciplines, and are worthy of study on that count also. However, there is a further and very significant point. It is clear that the acquisition of a natural history specimen involves selection according to contemporary principles, detachment from the natural context, and organization into some kind of relationship (many are possible) with other, or different material. This classification process transforms a 'natural' piece into a humanly defined object, which is to say an artefact, and collections of natural history can probably be discussed in material culture terms just as can those in the other disciplines. This is an important part of the museological aspect of the history and philosophy of science, and requires correspondingly extensive treatment.

REFERENCES

Bray, W. (1981) 'Archaeological humour: the private joke and the public image', in J. Evans, B. Cunliffe and C. Renfrew (eds) *Antiquity and Man: Essays in Honour of Glyn Daniel*, London: Thames & Hudson, 14–27.

Brooks, E. (1954) *Sir Hans Sloane*, London: Batchworth Press.

Chapman, W. (1985) 'Arranging ethnology: A. H. L. F. Pitt Rivers and the typological tradition', in G. Stocking (ed.) *Objects and Others: Essays on Museums and Material Culture*, Milwaukee: University of Wisconsin Press, 15–48

—— (1989) 'The organizational context in the history of archaeology: Pitt Rivers and other British archaeologists in the 1860's', *Antiquaries Journal*, 69(1): 23–42.

Eagleton, T. (1983) *Literary Theory: An Introduction*, Oxford: Basil Blackwell.

Fahnstock, P. (1984) 'History and critical development: the importance of a critical historiography of archaeology', *Archaeological Review from Cambridge* 3(1): 7–18.

Fenton, J. (1983) *The Memory of War and Children in Exile: Poems 1968–1983*, London: Penguin Books.

Gathercolte, P. (1989) 'The fetishism of artefacts', in S. Pearce (ed.) *Museum Studies in Material Culture*, Leicester: Leicester University Press, 73–81.

Gibson, M. and Wright, S. (eds) (1988) *Joseph Mayer of Liverpool 1803–1886*, Liverpool: Society of Antiquaries, London and National Museums and Galleries on Merseyside.

Gregory, T. (1983) 'The impact of metal detecting on archaeology and the public', *Archaeological Review from Cambridge* 2(1): 5–8.

Holmes, M. (1953) *Personalia*, London: Handbook for Museum Curators, Part C, Section 8, Museums Association.

Impey, O. and Macgregor, A. (eds) (1985) *The Origins of Museums*, Oxford; Oxford University Press.

Kuhn, T. (1970) *The Structure of Scientific Revolutions* (2nd edn), Chicago: University of Chicago Press.

Macgregor, A. (1983) *Tradescant's Rarities*, Oxford: Oxford University Press.

Marx, K. (1906) *Capital: A Critique of Political Economy*, trans. S. Moore and E. Aveling, London: Cassell.

Miller, D. (1987) *Material Culture and Mass Consumption*, Oxford: Basil Blackwell.

Morgan, P. (1986) *A National Plan for Systematic Collections?* Cardiff: National Museum of Wales.

Pearce, S. (1990) 'Objects as meaning: or narrating the past', in S. Pearce (ed.) *Objects of Knowledge: New Research in Museum Studies* vol. 1, London: Athlone, 125–40.

Stewart, S. (1984) *On Longing: Narratives of the Miniature, the Gigantic, the Souvenir, the Collection*, Baltimore: Johns Hopkins University Press.

Wainwright, C. (1989) *The Romantic Interior*, New Haven: Yale University Press.

Williamson, T. and Bellamy, L. (1983) 'Ley-lines: sense and non-sense on the fringe', *Archaeological Review from Cambridge* 2(1): 51–8.

27

Psychological aspects of art collecting

Frederick Baekeland

Baekeland begins this paper with the question, what impels the art collector to acquire works of art? The paper takes a particular stance on the question of what distinguishes the collector from the accumulator ('active interest' as opposed to 'passive and critical') and then charts a way through the range of motives which may influence collecting practice.

> Nothing is enduring except change, nothing constant except death. Every beat of the heart strikes a wound in us, and life would be an eternal bleeding to death if there were not the art of poetry. It grants us what nature denies us: a golden age which does not rust, a spring which does not fade, cloudless happiness and eternal youth.
>
> (Ludwig Börne 1964: 741)

> It is doubtful, however, whether collectors have ever been unmindful of the investment value of art.
>
> (Richard H. Rush 1961: vii)

What impels the art collector to acquire works of art? Art historians have steadfastly turned their backs on this question, and psychiatrists and psychoanalysts have not had much to say on the matter either. Patients, after all, do not seek psychiatric services because they are collectors. Yet to anyone at all familiar with art collectors, it is clear that their reasons for collecting are both diverse and complex. They may range from relatively pure ones like those suggested in the passage from Börne, just as applicable to art as to poetry, all the way to the much crasser ones alluded to by Rush.

Here I shall have nothing to say about those who collect for profit pure and simple, who may even buy paintings in wholesale lots only to stash them away in a warehouse until they have risen in value. This breed, which has increased apace with the feverish growth of the art business in recent years, does not collect art for art's sake. It is rather to the collector whose motives for collecting are primarily non-monetary that I want to turn my attention.

First, we should be clear about what a collector is and is not. His or her similarity to the accumulator is not obvious although in some cases it may be a deep one. While the accumulator passively and uncritically amasses a motley assortment of things that pass his way, the collector actively seeks out only certain kinds of objects in which he is interested. The former maintains that the objects he accumulates may come in handy some day, hides them away, and finds them a source of displeasure and mild shame. The latter either cannot explain why he collects, says he buys art because it gives him pleasure, or else rationalizes his collecting as a form of investment. Instead of secreting his collection, he usually likes to exhibit it. The accumulator lacks self-definition, and he tends to defer decisions. The things he accumulates have no clear-cut symbolic significance (Phillips 1962). The collector, on the contrary, is often attached to certain kinds of objects rather than others because of their symbolic value, and he tends to use his collection and collecting activities to enhance his self-definition. However, some collectors buy so uncritically and in such large quantities that they resemble accumulators. This kind of collector is never a connoisseur.

Although the collector is not merely an accumulator, neither is he simply an art lover. Most ordinary art lovers, even if they could afford to do otherwise, are content to look and not to possess. Others occasionally buy art objects but in the long run spend little time at art dealers or auctions and certainly never own more pieces than they have room to exhibit at one time. Not so the collector. He may sacrifice everything else to his desire to enlarge and improve his collection, which often becomes so large that at any given moment part of it must be relegated to closets. The Frenchmen Victor Chocquet and Maurice Girardin were famous examples. Chocquet, a modest clerk in the customs department, died in 1891. In order to amass a great collection of Impressionist and Post-impressionist paintings, he went without an overcoat and on occasion was short of food. Similarly, the dentist Girardin, who died in 1954 and left the city of Paris an extremely important collection of modern French paintings, devoted most of his modest income to buying them. He was well known for his stinginess (Cabanne 1963: 45–6, 205, 221). Along the same lines, the famous financier J.P. Morgan, despite his great wealth, spent so much on his art-buying trips abroad that his accountants were sick with worry whenever he embarked on one (Allen 1949: 198).

What are the sources of this passion for collecting art – a passion that afflicts both the high and the low? In the case of the rich industrialist, especially if he is a self-made man with a limited background, vanity and a desire for social advancement seem to play major roles. In both the East and the West owning works of art has always been thought to imply education, cultivation and refinement. Indeed, in China and Japan an active interest in art was traditionally considered one of the hallmarks of the educated man. Nevertheless, the rich Japanese businessman who spends millions on currently fashionable western Impressionist, Postimpressionist and School of Paris paintings should be seen in no different a light than his western counterpart. As with Henry Clay Frick who used to sit reading the *Saturday Evening Post* amidst his Rembrandts and Holbeins (Behrman 1952: 89), owning paintings makes him feel more educated. Hence it should occasion no surprise that rich businessmen who themselves lack pedigrees are sometimes attracted to buying family portraits of dead aristocrats with whom they presumably would like to identify (Behrman 1952: 97–8). For the tycoon, collecting art also extends the range of competitive activities from the boardroom and market-place to the auction gallery and drawing-room. With rare exceptions he is apt to rely on experts or on dealers with access to famous experts not only to authenticate the expensive works of art he buys but also to suggest them. Thus, Mellon, Frick and Kress had their Duveen (who in turn could fall back on the prestigious art historian Bernhard Berenson), Charles Lang Freer and the Havemeyers had the painters Whistler and Mary Cassatt as advisors.[1] Girardin had this to say about such rich collectors, 'Big collectors are moneyed people who for personal or social reasons use their wealth under expert advice to bring together quickly a number of celebrated works of art and boast of their possession: they are usually financiers although some of them catch the 'fever' and become collectors' (Cabanne 1963: 206). Their motives have included vanity, the pleasure of buying a work from under the nose of a rival (Cabanne 1963: 26) and the need to compete with him. Other reasons that have been adduced are emotionally empty lives at home, acquisitiveness, and the need for immortality (Behrman 1952: 295–6). There is no reason to believe that the motives of the small, supposedly 'purer' collector, the kind I propose to examine, do not include some of the foregoing.

In what follows I rely on the scanty psychological literature, on my fairly extensive personal experience with collectors and on interviews with a number of collectors, dealers, museum curators and art historians of my acquaintance. The twelve collectors interviewed are a somewhat atypical group inasmuch as they are, with one exception, professional people; all but one of them collect Far Eastern or primitive art; and with one exception, they eschew the art of the present, preferring that of the past.

Do art collectors spring into being all at once as adults, or can we single them out in advance while they are children? At least 10 per cent of American children do collect something (Lehman and Witty 1927; Witty and Lehman 1930). Childhood collecting is favoured by the more intelligent child (Durost 1932) and seems to peak a few years before puberty (Whitley 1929). Unlike adults, children rarely collect art. Young J. P. Morgans who acquire medieval stained glass (Allen 1949: 140) must surely be great oddities even among scions of the rich. Adult collectors who focus on art are also in the minority, certainly in part because of its cost but also because their childhood experiences help determine the hobbies they choose (Nestrick 1939). Girls are more likely than boys to collect at all ages (Witty and Lehman 1930), but in contrast, most adult collectors in the formal, public sense of the word are men. Women art collectors are also relatively rare although it is not too hard to pick out famous examples such as Catherine the Great and Peggy Guggenheim.

Why do so few women collect art, especially in an era when they have more money to spend than ever before? While women who inherit from their husbands are apt to do so in the declining years, long after the age when new interests usually develop, women who are rich in their own right have always abounded. The key to the relative paucity of women art collectors must therefore be not merely economic but also psychological. First, we should not forget that many women privately amass personal possessions far in excess of any practical need, without any thought of public exhibition other than adornment: we rarely think of accumulations of dresses, shoes, perfumes china and the like as collections. They consist of relatively intimate and transient objects intended directly to enhance their owners' self-images, to be used until they are worn out or broken, and then to be discarded. Men's collections, however, be they of stamps, cars, guns or art, tend to have clear-cut thematic emphases and standard, external reference points in public or private collections. Thus women's collections tend to be personal and ahistorical, men's impersonal and historical, just as, traditionally, women have tended to have a relatively greater emotional investment in people than in ideas and men to some extent the reverse.

If we can assume that art collecting satisfies some kind of aesthetic need, then we can classify it with the few socially acceptable outlets that most American men have for such a need. According to traditional role definition, women can express their aesthetic side in clothing, in decorating their homes and in fashioning their gardens – in other words, in so-called feminine occupations. Traditional role definitions have also dictated that men be more aggressive and women more passive. In art collecting, men can simultaneously express strong, aggressive, competitive aspects of themselves and aesthetic ones. In addition to competing with other collectors, they may in effect compete with their wives as interior decorators as their art objects gradually dominate the house, fill collecting cases, and spread from room to room, sometimes directly outshining and displacing the more mundane objects with which their wives have chosen to decorate their homes.

Finally, women are creative in a sense in which men can only be creative symbolically: they bear children. It has been conjectured that this is one reason why women figure much less prominently than men in the creative arts and sciences, let alone collecting. However, family names are perpetuated through the man and not the woman, which may sensitize the man more than the woman to the issue of immortality and perpetuation of his name. One way he can do this is through his collection.

All these factors apply to the situation now. There is no reason it cannot change as the roles of men and women change, especially as wives have to defer less to their husbands in expression of interests and in accounting for expenditures.

THE COLLECTORS

It is probably no accident that all the collectors I know collected something when they were children. Most of them had adult collectors in the family who collected in different areas, not necessarily art. Typically, their collecting, like that of children studied in large-scale surveys, dropped off or disappeared entirely during adolescence. They subsequently started buying art in their twenties and thirties, usually when they could first afford to do so. All but one started collecting western art, mostly graphic work, which ranged from Impressionist to contemporary schools. Most of them soon found that western painting and sculpture were very expensive and that they could get more aesthetic value for their money in the more recondite areas of Far Eastern and primitive art. Their involvement in collecting deepened as they spent more and more time and money on it and developed personal relationships with other collectors, with dealers and with museum curators.

Inevitably, they started upgrading their collections. However, one collector I know dislikes either trading or selling any of his art works, a reluctance that seems connected with the striking and aggressive enthusiasm with which he acquires them. Similarly, the Swiss collector Emil-Georg Bührle never sold any of his pictures, with which he spent an hour a day alone. 'My pictures are part of me,' he said. 'If I were to sell one I should feel I was repenting a choice I had made, changing my own tastes, or betraying myself.' By contrast, another collector of my acquaintance keeps getting rid of works he has bought in an effort to upgrade his collection. The Dutchman D. B. van Beuningen was an extreme example of this kind of collector, keeping permanently only 10 per cent of the paintings he had bought (Cabanne 1963: 126, 135, 138, 141). In such persons it is not clear how much of the 'upgrading' may in fact be a rationalization of a restless need for change, or else a subtle displacement of hostility towards someone or something for which the art work stands – for example, an ex-wife in the case of one of my collector friends. In certain instances, financial considerations, sometimes abetted by a need to prove his foresight and validate his taste, may impel a collector to sell all of his collection in a given area. Thus, the American banker Thomas Benedict Arnold (1848–1931), who started collecting then unfashionable American paintings in 1872, sold his collection of 373 landscape and genre paintings at auction in 1899 for a probable 60–70 per cent profit in a sale which stimulated interest in American painting by setting record prices for a number of artists (Truettner 1971). He continued to collect in other areas, including American portraits (Constable 1964: 125, 142).

The collectors I know all read about art, one as much as several hours a day. They are assiduous museum and art gallery visitors, and most of them subscribe to domestic and foreign auction catalogues in their special fields of collecting. Their factual interest in the pieces they own ranges from an understandable concern with knowing something about the objects they buy to a deep scholarly preoccupation with many facets of art and its history. The desire for knowledge of the past or of other countries should not be minimized as a motive for collecting. It has sometimes led collectors to travel frequently and far afield, not merely to buy objects more easily and cheaply where they were made, but also better to understand the cultures that produced them. To this end they have on occasion even been driven to learn difficult Far Eastern languages.

All but one of the collectors I know still owns the first work of art he bought. Is this simply a sign of acquisitiveness, a derivative of the oral and anal trends with which some psychoanalysts have been content to explain collecting,[2] or is it something more? It is no secret that acquiring and owning material possessions makes most people feel more secure, provided they have the wherewithal to pay for them. It is not entirely clear why amassing art objects should enhance the collector's feelings of security, something they all describe. In some cases, as noted by Fenichel with respect to money in his paper 'The drive to amass wealth', it may satisfy his need for power. (Museum curators inevitably want to borrow his art objects for exhibition and hence are dependent on him.) In others it may stem from a childhood in which he was given material things rather than love so that objects came to stand for love and acquiring possessions became a way of assuring himself that he could be loved (Schwartz and Wolf 1958). In others it may be one way in which he can order and control his environment (the anal, compulsive aspect). The collector's need for order is secondarily satisfied by the task of arranging and cataloguing the objects he owns, a chore to which he is inevitably driven. Among these collectors, such activities vary according to the prominence of compulsive features in their personalities, to the time they have available, and to their background in scholarship.

Securing and buying an art object can also function as an oral analogue – as if it were another way of feeding or rewarding the collector. Several of those I interviewed reported having an urge to buy art objects when they feel frustrated or depressed because something has not worked out as they wished, and sometimes they succumb to this rather expensive form of impulse buying. William Randolph Hearst was a notorious self-feeder through art. His mother allegedly said, 'Every time Willie feels badly, he goes out and buys something' (Saarinen 1958: 76).

That simply owning art may comfort the collector is also suggested by those who rarely look at the items they own. Even if they actively examine many of their pieces, they usually have tucked away some that rarely, if ever, see the light of day. In some cases art objects may be what Laughlin defines as soterial objects – in other words, objects that are a source of feelings of comfort, security and well-being that seem out of proportion to the material value of the art. Owning them, he proposes, is a symbolic equivalent of possessing the earliest object of dependency, the nurturant mother – that is, soterial objects are libidinized objects.[3]

Nonetheless, something more than acquisitiveness, orality and anality seems involved when a collector keeps for ever the first art object he bought. A collection has a history just as much as the items of which it is composed. The owner's almost total recall of the circumstances of each purchase he has ever made suggests that the act of buying is an overdetermined one in which many motives have a hand. As I mentioned, competition, a derivative of aggression, must be one of them. Here both the collector and the psychoanalyst can be our guides.

One collector emphasizes the pleasure of being 'one up' when he buys art. His collecting career has successively involved two corners of western art that were at first inexpensive and unfashionable. He has usually bought from small dealers or at auction. 'In every auction,' he is fond of saying, 'there is at least one good buy provided you are the only one who knows it.' He has made many impressive finds. For him they validate his superior acumen. To others, who are duly informed, they proclaim it. Being one up is not as important to many other collectors.

When the collector makes a find and exults about it, the art work is almost a kind of trophy. Indeed, in 'Trophy and triumph' Fenichel has argued that the relationship between the owner and his art objects reflects the feeling, 'I have acquired something by force or fraud that originally belonged to someone more powerful, but which now is a talisman for me, or which connects me magically with the previous possessor.' It is as if merely by having them their current owner were imbued with the fame, riches, power or special abilities of a former owner. Examples of this kind of identification include collectors who acquire the portraits of noble or famous persons of the past, and the fact that objects that belonged to a famous collection are always more expensive and sought-after than those that did not. It is the rare collector who is totally indifferent to provenance.[4] That the need to identify with the past or with those who lived in it is an unconscious one is illustrated by one of the collectors I know. Both to get the most for his money and to prove his astuteness, he avoids buying any work whose provenance is known or which has been published (that is, a work that has been pictured or described in a catalogue, book or journal). Nevertheless, he paid a higher price for a painting than is his wont because it was accompanied by a letter in which the painter explained when and why he had painted it.

The collector's delight in detailing how he acquired an object reminds one of the Don Juan who must describe his triumphs. Like Don Juan, he is not satisfied with one conquest but must go on to more and more. Why does he keep on collecting even if his closets are bulging? A tag such as 'compulsive behaviour' only applies in some cases and then imperfectly. Although they have a compulsion to collect, not all collectors have compulsive personalities.

I draw attention to the fact that for the collector collecting can be just as much a way of life as his business or profession sometimes overshadowing his nominal vocation; certainly its rewards strongly reinforce his collecting. It involves regular personal and epistolary contacts with other collectors, with artists, with dealers and with museum staffs In many cases these contacts have broadened his social life by developing into friendships with people with very different personalities and backgrounds. Collecting also entails making regular rounds of the auction houses, antiques shops and art galleries. There is the ever-present possibility of making a find or of undergoing what can be, like falling in love, one of life's most compelling experiences: irresistible attraction to a beautiful work of art, suffusion with the desire to own it, and finally possession and enjoyment. The collector's life is thus one full of anticipation of potential pleasure and excitement. It may afford him more stimulation and gratification than his work or home life, a notion in line with Philippe Jullian's suggestion (1966) that the need to combat boredom is a major motive for collecting. Although most of the collectors I know are strenuously involved with their work and do not appear bored with it, the quality of their absorption with collecting seems more passionate than their concern about their work. A few of them frankly admit that it looms much larger in their lives than their professions, and one did start collecting art at the advice of a psychiatrist who felt that his bored and chronically depressed patient needed a hobby. In any event, whatever the origins of collecting, it encompasses a way of life which may be complete in itself. As such it has institutions that are analogous to more conventional ones. Thus, if museums are the churches of collectors, then the auction houses and art galleries are ecclesiastical merchants who purvey the objects necessary for domestic shrines.

A moment's reflection suggests that if the collector stopped buying works of art, the rationale for his network of personal art relationships and activities would begin to disintegrate. It would then lose much of its *raison d'être* and the future its aura of antici-pation. He would still have a collection, but he would no longer be a collector. Here, I think, lies one of the reasons for the mounting restlessness that most collectors report when considerable time has elapsed since they last bought a work of art.

The fallow period may be terminated by the purchase of an object of substantial merit or of one that is not up to the collector's usual standards. The latter often involves bargain-hunting. Some collectors buy only when they think they have a bargain. Bergler (1947) felt that bargain-hunters he treated as patients were all orally fixated people. He related bargain-hunting to a need to outsmart others. Be this as it may, only one collector of my acquaintance seems totally immune to the impulse to bargain-hunt. Not only does he have very little time for it, but he is also the one who is most likely to buy a published work of art, who is anxious to buy 'significant' objects and wants to have an 'important' collection. More than most, he is unwilling to risk buying a fake.

The collectors are remarkably uniform in their descriptions of how they feel when they choose an art object. To a man, they report that they usually know immediately whether or not a piece really appeals to them and whether they want to possess it. They often compare their feeling of longing for it to sexual desire. This suggests that art objects are confused in the unconscious with ordinary sexual objects, an idea that gets some confirmation from the fact that many collectors like to fondle or stroke the objects they own or to look at them over and over from every angle, both up close and at a distance, activities that are impossible in a museum. The only other context in which looking, fondling and caressing loom so large is sexual foreplay.

Once the collector knows that he wants an object, the decision to buy it is determined by mundane considerations such as price, value, available funds and the opinions of others. Depending on his relationship with his wife, she may make it easier or harder for him to buy a work of art that has seized his fancy. If the marriage is a poor one, his collecting may be but one of a number of disputed areas. If the wife feels unloved, she may resent any major interest he has, including art. Thus, one collector was reproached by his wife, who said, quite accurately, 'You are more interested in art than in me.' His collecting became such a source of conflict that finally he never brought his art friends home. He often left objects with the dealers from whom he had bought them for many months in order to forestall the resentment and arguments that disclosure of their purchase would inevitably engender when he took them home.

However, in a harmonious marriage the collector's wife usually enthusiastically approves of his collecting though she may at times be alarmed by the size or frequency of his purchases. If the collectors' wives I know are at all typical, the collector's spouse is more passively involved in art than he is and views his collecting with indulgence or pride. In any case, he is likely to discuss with her an object he has in mind and on occa-sion even to accept her objections to its purchase. If she has a better eye than he does, he may defer to her in deciding whether an object meets a high aesthetic standard. How-ever, he usually makes the final financial decision and almost always gets the credit, or blame, for the purchase. Such arrangements are more likely if the husband is a busi-nessman with a strong interest in the investment value of art and the area in which he collects is currently a very fashionable one. Since they are unflattering to the man, such marriages are rarely documented by art historians. A well-known example is that of the sugar millionaire H. O. Havemeyer. With his wife Louisine, he amassed an important collection of European old master and Impressionist paintings, most of which were ulti-mately left to the Metropolitan Museum of Art. In 1879, before he met Louisine, his collection, like that of most rich American collectors, consisted of currently fashionable

French and German salon painters with a sprinkling of Barbizon school artists (Strahan 1879). By 1889, six years after the marriage, under her tutelage his tastes had veered to Courbet and seventeenth-century Dutch paintings (Saarinen 1958: 158).

The concurrence of a fellow collector or of an expert can make it easier for the collector to divest himself of money for a purchase. The enthusiasm of the one may add competitive or acquisitive fuel to the fire of his desire. The authority of the other can make it easier for him to rationalize the money he is about to spend as a 'sound investment'. However, only rarely can a true connoisseur be led by someone else to buy an object towards which he has no natural leaning. Such arranged marriages are stoutly resisted.

The dealer may, however, be very influential in shaping the collector's tastes and decisions. He has at his disposal a number of more or less standard devices. He may intimate that someone else is interested in buying the object, that a certain museum curator has seen, approved and liked it, that it is published, that it came from a famous collection, that it is something very rare or even unique, that it fills an important gap in his collection, that it is an especially good buy, that objects like it will soon be unobtainable or prohibitively expensive, that it is a better piece than a similar example owned by another collector, and so forth. In using such manoeuvres, the dealer plays on the collector's belief in the good taste and judgement of experts (who may in fact err), on his desire to identify with famous people, on his need for uniqueness, on his compulsivity (the theme of having the complete collection), on his desire for bargains, on his need to possess the object, and on his competitiveness.

Why do collectors prefer certain works of art to others? Preferences range among sculpture, painting, prints and drawings or *objets d'art*; modern, classical, ancient or primitive art; large or small pieces; brightly coloured or subdued works; angular configurations or those with continuous curved lines; perfect items or slightly imperfect or repaired ones, and so forth *ad infinitum*. This area is not understood well, but it is likely that the preferences of a given collector can be explained by his temperament, his early childhood experiences, the nature of his past and present exposure to art, and his financial circumstances.

Several studies have linked extraversion and introversion to aesthetic preferences. Thus, Eysenck found that extraverts tend to prefer simple, vivid, strong art, introverts art that is complex, refined and subtle (1971: 211). Other researchers have reported that extraverts favour realistic or classical art, introverts art that is more abstract or romantic (Jamison 1972; Rosenbluh, Owens, and Pohler 1972). Along similar lines, conservatism has been connected with a preference for more representational art and a dislike of abstract and complex works (Wilson, Ausman and Mathews 1973).

Morris, however, related aesthetic preferences to the scheme of Sheldon and Stevens, who held that the three basic body types (mesomorph, endomorph and ectomorph) and temperament are correlated. He concluded that people tend to prefer paintings that symbolize their somatotypes (Morris 1957; Sheldon and Stevens 1942). Among the collectors of my acquaintance one is drawn to African art, which tends to be crude and vigorous, and he himself is a burly, roughhewn and forceful person. Another collector of primitive art, who is more slender and more ectomorphic, also is attracted to pre-Columbian art, which tends to be more highly finished. From sketchy data of this kind one could support almost any theory.

The influence of specific childhood and adolescent experiences on the kind of art collectors prefer can be seen in the life of George A. Hearn (1853–1913). A second-generation department store owner, Hearn who had a close relationship with his English immigrant father and was partly frustrated in realizing his social aspirations, collected eighteenth-

and nineteenth-century English painting (mostly portraits and landscapes) and contemporary American painting.[5] One collector I know, an elderly man born around the turn of the century, felt that his adolescence had been marred by the death of his father, with whom he had a good relationship and who was replaced by a stepfather whom he disliked intensely and who wronged him. (He still becomes emotional when he refers to his stepfather.) He has successively collected two different kinds of later nineteenth-century and early twentieth-century art, which may have helped him to recover the unsullied past of his father and grandfather's time. Another collector is deeply involved with Japanese art, an area associated with several close family members with whom he has identified both in his work and in his extracurricular interests. Yet another collector of Japanese art was also exposed to Japanese culture in his childhood by his father, who read him Lafcadio Hearn translations of Japanese legends and fairy tales.

Financial considerations, which always figure in collecting, are nowhere more cogent than for the collector with relatively modest means. On occasion he may find an unfashionable area he likes, where he can get excellent works at a relatively small cost. This is characteristic of all the collectors I know. Well-known past examples already cited include Victor Chocquet and Maurice Girardin, both of whom had modest incomes. George A. Hearn and Thomas B. Clarke, although rich, did not have great fortunes like those of Morgan, Kress and Mellon. Both businessmen, they certainly must have derived considerable satisfaction from getting the most for their money in buying American painting even though they could not successfully compete with richer businessmen in the area of European old masters.

It is only a few steps from the collector who likes to make a find and so to be one up to two other types. In one, active aggression and competition predominate. In the other, a special kind of snobbery, which is actually a more subtle and passive form of aggression, is the key. The first constantly compares his collection with those of others, whom he needs to surpass. Such comparisons may be made silently or aloud. He is likely to insist that any object he owns is the best example of its kind, or one of the best. Such a person is very anxious to have others see his collection but may show surprisingly little interest in carefully examining pieces owned by another collector if he feels sure that his own collection is more important. The snob collector is especially concerned that his area of interest be one that is followed by few, if any, others. His primary demand is for uniqueness. To a certain extent, western collectors of many kinds of Far Eastern art may be somewhat tainted with the snobbery that demands exclusivity. However, prestige rarely accrues through collecting oriental art as it is so little known and appreciated by the general public. The true connoisseur, in contrast to both of these types, is least likely to be driven by either fashion or the need to collect in an obscure area, which is a kind of ultrafashionability in reverse. The snob collector is somewhat different from the run-of-the-mill social snob, who, according to Bergler (1969), is an inner defeatist who settles for the proximity of the 'great', having unconsciously despaired of becoming 'great' himself. The portrait collector conforms more to the image of the social snob: he is a person who indulges in make-believe through identification.

Collecting may be an allowable pleasure for a person who finds it hard to indulge himself. For example, one collector is a very hard-working, highly organized and achievement-oriented person. For him the demands of work take precedence over almost everything else except collecting, which seems to serve him as a vicarious emotional outlet. Beyond this, he has in effect converted collecting into a second career. A famous example of this kind of collector was John D. Rockefeller, Jr, who gave the Cloisters to the Metropolitan Museum of Art. A reserved, self-disciplined, meticulous and methodical man, he was quite naturally drawn to craftsmanship and hence to *objets d'art* rather than to paintings. He

213

was especially fond of jewels. Collecting art was the closest he would allow himself to come to self-indulgence. He justified buying it on the grounds that the works of art would eventually go to a museum. When buying for himself as opposed to the Cloisters, he was often cautious and guilt-ridden (Saarinen 1958: 349–55).

Collectors are persons with a special emotional investment in art. As such, they partially overlap five other kinds of people in whose lives art is also important: people who frequently visit museums and galleries, art historians, art dealers, museum curators and artists. They share with all these groups a propensity to look at and evaluate works of art. Like museum curators, art historians and art dealers, when they go through museums they take note of much that escapes the average museum-goer. Almost as soon as they see a painting, they tend to examine the placard that tells who gave or lent it to the museum. However, unlike the other groups, they alone are likely mentally to divide the works they prefer into two groups: those they would like to own and those they wouldn't. Usually they want to know the dates, countries of origin, and authors of the objects in their collections but they may not necessarily be interested in understanding their historical context. This is the special domain of the art historian, on whom they tend to look down because of his apparent lack of emotional involvement with art objects; often the art historian seems less drawn to the art itself than to the photographs and slides with which he spends so much more time. Along with many other art appreciators who are not art historians, most collectors would agree with Paul Valéry, who wrote:

> In questions of art learning is a sort of defeat: it illuminates what is by no means the most subtle, and penetrates to what is by no means the most significant. It substitutes theories for feelings and replaces a sense of marvel with a prodigious memory. It amounts to an endless library annexed to a vast museum: Venus transformed into a document.
>
> (quoted in Rheims 1961: 3–4)

Collectors, like museum curators, identify, touch, care for, are nourished by and catalogue works of art. In buying and selling art they are both like curators, although they use their own money rather than that of others, and like artists and dealers, although they are more involved in buying than selling.

It is noteworthy that few art historians and museum curators are passionate collectors, in part because of their smaller incomes, in part because of the very high standards of artistic excellence set them by their professions. However, many dealers and artists collect.[6] A surprising number of art dealers started as collectors, only to turn into dealers as they began to do more and more trading and selling because collecting was beginning to strain their finances to breaking-point. Thus, collectors are least like simple art lovers and most like art dealers. However, unless they actually become dealers, they are often inefficient about selling objects they own, perhaps because they do not really want to. For example, one collector says that whenever he has decided to sell a piece, it suddenly seems much more desirable than it did before he made the decision.

All six groups share a deep involvement with some aspect of art, which presumably satisfies for them an array of psychological needs. Psychological literature has little to add to what I have already suggested about what distinguishes art lovers from those who are indifferent to it. However, Roubertoux (1970) found that high-school students whose exclusive cultural activity was visiting art exhibitions were much more self-restrained than those who favoured the theatre or had no cultural interests at all. This is consistent with the idea that for the collector art may have an indirect and vicarious expressive role. Indeed, the collectors I know are, with two exceptions, a self-contained and restrained lot. Although half of them deal with people in their professions, they do so only at a remove made safe by their roles as authority figures. The others are solitary workers who devote themselves to writing, composing and scholarly research.[7]

The expressive role of art is but one of the many functions which have been proposed for it at some time or other. These have included the idea that using any of our capacities is pleasurable, that learning to appreciate the ambiguities of art works prepares us to tolerate ambiguity in everyday life, that art helps to make the world seem orderly and intelligible, and that it is a form of play or exploratory behaviour. Any or all of these might be important in the case of a given collector. Thus, collectors presumably have a better eye for judging certain kinds of artefacts than those who are not interested in art. The exercise of a good eye is rewarding because it is a skill with both practical and emotional benefits. It helps the collector to build up a better collection for less money, since it betters his chances of making finds and good buys. It also sets him apart and above most others. It is not clear, however, whether the collector's ability to make effective comparative judgements of art works derives primarily from exposure to them before he started collecting, from his experience as a collector, or from an innate ability that is sharpened by experience. In any case, before he becomes a collector, someone may be totally unaware that he has a good eye. Thus, two of my acquaintances started collecting when they had to furnish bare walls. Both rapidly discovered that they had good eyes for art. All of the collectors I interviewed felt they had a better than average eye, which had sharpened with experience. On the basis of experimental work, it is clear that some people not involved with art are better than others in consistently agreeing with expert opinion (Berlyne 1971; Eysenck 1971: 206–7; Child 1968).

For some collectors, art seems to make their world more orderly and intelligible. One obvious way it can do so is by helping to structure their lives. The 'career' of collector is one that can enhance his self-definition by giving him a new role distinct from that afforded by his work, where he may be but one among many. It may also help him differentiate himself from a father who is or was an art collector. Thus, two collectors who had collector fathers bought art in fields that were very different from those in which their fathers were experts. Indeed, fathers and sons who have collected in exactly the same area are rare in the history of art.

Is collecting an outlet for skills and interests not expressed in the collector's vocation? Sometimes this seems to be the case. Two collectors, for example, painted before they submitted themselves to the rigours of their professions. In various ways all the collectors I interviewed who are involved with scientific work felt that collecting gave them an aesthetic and expressive dimension lacking in their work. One composed music and wrote fiction and poetry before he entered his very time-demanding profession. All but one of the collectors I know either fall into Strong's group 1 of occupations (artist, psychologist, physician, dentist, architect), which score high on his artist scale (Strong 1943: 108, 136–7, 314–22), or are creative or performing artists (composer, musician, writer). Although this may not be typical of collectors in general, according to Strong's results such professions do share a common factor that involves abstract-conceptual thinking. In any event, collecting art does seem to involve the expression of some kind of creative impulse. That there are creative artists who also collect – that is, who presumably satisfy their creative impulse in ways other than collecting – suggests that the collecting impulse has ingredients other than the aesthetic. One collector who is neither in the arts nor in a research profession feels that collecting helps him to satisfy his creative needs through identification with the creators of objects he owns – a point several collectors made.

What of the sublimatory and expressive function of art? Is it an important factor in art collecting? As one put it in psychoanalytic terms, 'In my work I am continually subjected to the constraint of logic and reason and am committed to secondary-process thinking and must be careful how I express myself. Through art and collecting I can express my libidinal and aggressive drives.' His statement mirrors the psychoanalytic notion of artistic satisfaction as an amalgam both of an indirect gratification of wishes and of a gratification derived from mastering the expression of such wishes. Thus, Menninger (1942) and Noy (1968–9), like most other analysts, believe that all hobbies are sublimations of libidinal and aggressive impulses and also that they are a refined form of play.

The psychoanalyst can also see other factors in collecting, such as exhibitionism, voyeurism and identification. Certainly, there must be elements of exhibitionism in the collector's desire to have others see his collection either *in situ* or in the context of public exhibitions. Here, as Fenichel pointed out in the case of acting, the collector may derive a kind of exhibitionistic and erogenous satisfaction – direct narcissistic satisfaction from applause, and narcissistic satisfaction from a sense of magical influence on the audience that is related to an unconscious aim of making it feel the same emotions he feels and displays (the collector indirectly displays his emotion through the works of art he owns).

While most collectors are only too eager to have everyone and anyone examine and praise their collections, others will only admit those who they feel are qualified. In rare instances, such as the case of the reclusive millionaire Caloustes Gulbenkian, they may let no one see them. The collector knows he has something others covet. Hence, if he is at all sophisticated, he may feel like the rich and beautiful woman who wonders whether she is loved for herself, her money or her looks. Accordingly, his friendships with museum curators and art dealers, who stand to profit from him, may be tempered with not a little scepticism about their motives. Collectors rarely lend anonymously, and I know only one who always does so. He cites four reasons for concealing his identity: (1) He did not produce the works of art so he can garner no real merit through owning them. (2) Anyone with a good eye or good advice, perseverance and money can form a good collection. (3) Anonymous lending discourages the unwelcome telephone calls of the curious and the even more unwelcome visits of burglars. (4) He is averse to publicity. Nevertheless, it is revealing that when he gives art works to museums, he does not do so anonymously but under his own name. One surmises that a passion for anonymity can be a defence against exhibitionism.

Voyeurism in art collecting seems blatant in the case of erotic art but can also be inferred from other kinds.[8] Freud (1915) first noted that exhibitionism and scoptophilia are different aspects – one passive, the other active – of the same partial instinct, to look. Fenichel has stressed the role of scoptophilia in identification. He proposed that looking at the object may have the unconscious meaning of growing to be like it.

The collector's identification with his collection is complex and may manifest itself in a number of ways. First, if someone questions the authenticity of a piece he owns, his usual reaction is either to brush off the suggestion without really considering its merits or else to become angry. Why should he become angry? Probably not only because his judgement – though very often it is the judgement of another, an expert – is being impugned but also because it is as if the critic had said, 'I don't value you. I don't like anything about you. You are false and worthless.' Another clue lies in the collector's preference for seeing his name attached to a work lent out for public display in a museum rather than for lending anonymously. A third lead is the difficulty with which collectors part with their art works. One I know carries some paintings along with him whenever he travels. He had a precedent in the nineteenth-century English collector Sir

George Beaumont, who always travelled with his favourite picture. Claude Lorrain's *Hagar and the Angel*, now in the National Gallery in London (Von Holst 1967: 17). The Sung poet, painter and calligrapher Mi Fu even used to travel with his whole collection (Beurdeley 1966: 17). To the collector, the prospect of ultimately permanently parting with his collection may be even more difficult. Thus, Cardinal Mazarin, a seventeenth-century Frenchman who amassed two great collections in the course of his life, lamented just before his death as he wandered through his galleries, 'All this I must leave behind me' (Taylor 1948: 30). His ancient Roman counterpart was the proconsul Verres, who had the finest sculpture collection in Italy. Prosecuted for his corruption by Cicero, he lived in exile for twenty-seven years until the orator died. Upon his return Marc Antony asked him for some of his Corinthian bronzes. His refusal to give them up led to his proscription and condemnation to death (Taylor 1948: 30).

Some collectors, unlike Egyptian pharaohs who could take their treasures to the tomb with them, have preferred to see them destroyed rather than have anyone else enjoy them. Thus, a few days before he died, Mi Fu called in his friends and asked them to burn all his paintings and calligraphy (Beurdeley 1966: 74). Some collectors, including one I know, question whether museums, which nowadays provide sterile, crowded and noisy settings for works of art, are appropriate places to which to leave their collections. Like the collector-writer Edmond De Goncourt, they may feel that works of art should 'not be consigned to the cold tomb of a museum and the uncultivated glance of the indifferent passerby' but the they should instead be dispersed at auctions, 'so that the joy the acquisition of each one of them has given me shall be again given in each case, to some inheritor of my taste'.[9]

Throughout history most collectors have preferred contemporary art. By collecting modern art they can feel that they are patronizing the artist. They may, also become personally involved with him and thus vicariously participate in and identify with the creative act. In some cases, they may even be able to dictate the content, and perhaps even the style, of the work of art. By contrast, the collectors I know have gravitated to the art of the past. The specific direction they have taken may have been determined in part by chance factors such as their financial circumstances and the dealers they first met, but other factors are obviously involved for not all modern art is more expensive than Far Eastern or primitive art, especially if the artist is unknown, and many dealers concentrate on such modern art. Preference for the already known and studied art of the dead rather than the relatively untested art of the living implies not only a wish to get the most for the least but also a certain conservatism. However, the collector's involvement with the past seems to go beyond conservatism. As one of them said, 'For me art unifies the past and present.' Several others find themselves dissatisfied with the current values of industrial society, which is in such a state of flux. For them the art of the past represents a vision of order and fixity. By identifying with it they are able to deny the primacy and transiency of the present, which then becomes part of the past, which is eternal. They can thus abrogate time and its passage.

A related need to obtain immortality through leaving their intact collections, bearing their names, to famous museums seems to have been a major motive of many collectors. By willing his treasures, the collector leaves behind a part of himself and perpetuates his name for all time, something often not possible through his children or his business and professional activities. If he has no children, his collection may literally become his offspring. One childless collector I know refers to his collection as his child and is concerned that it be properly recorded and published before he dies. A collection consequently may have the significance of an only child, a kind of self-portrait its owner wants kept intact after he dies.

The alert reader will object that I have overlooked a major reason for collecting, the owner's need to surround himself with beautiful objects. I would be the first to agree. Beyond exposure to the social training that teaches that what is beautiful is good, the collector does seem to have a strong awareness of beauty. Whether this awareness – this need – has a primary instinctual basis or is a derivative of other instincts is a moot point. At any rate, its gratification and the constant search for a more perfect and ideal beauty, the great object, keep him collecting and help to compensate for some of the drawbacks of his existence. At times his life may become particularly complicated and expensive. His wife or family may not appreciate the new directions his collecting interests have taken. He may worry about depriving his heirs of the money he puts into art. He may be so busy that he doesn't have enough time properly to contemplate and fully to enjoy all the works of art he has bought. His living quarters may no longer have enough room for both him and them. Both the work of cataloguing and the insurance premiums may have become onerous. The correspondence involved in collecting may have become overwhelming. At such times he should console himself with the thought that without him the artist might stop producing and that art historians, museum curators and art dealers might wither away.

This paper first appeared in Psychiatry 44 *(Feb. 1981), pp. 45–59.*

NOTES

1 Such examples are easily multiplied. See Aline B. Saarinen, *The Proud Possessors*, and Behrman for other examples.
2 See Freud 1908; Jones 1938; Menninger 1942; Fenichel 1945, p. 283.
3 Laughlin's concept of the soterial object for all practical purposes seems the same as Winnicott's notion of the transitional object (1953). See Laughlin (1967), pp. 609, 613, 620, 626.
4 Knowing an art object's provenance also has a very practical side. Like publication, it can help establish a work's authenticity, but also like publication it can rarely guarantee it. This is a point often overlooked by collectors, dealers, art historians and museum people in their need for certainty.
5 See Baekeland (1976); *The National Cyclopedia of American Biography* vol 16, New York: James T. White, 1937, 316–17; and unpublished correspondence and catalogues at the Metropolitan Museum of Art in New York regarding Hearn's collection and gifts.
6 There have always been artists who were collectors. Rembrandt and Rubens are notable examples from the past (Wittkower and Wittkower 1969: 275–6; Eagle 1971).
7 Donald Super found similar personality patterns among stamp-collectors (1941: 168).
8 For discussions of the erotic in art, see Lucie-Smith (1972), Peckham (1969), and Bowie and Christenson (1970).
9 De Goncourt's comment, published as an epigraph to the catalogue of his and his brother's collection of Far Eastern art, which was sold at auction in 1897, is worth quoting in full:

> My wish is that my drawings, prints, bibelots and books – the works of art which have been the joy of my life – should not be consigned to the cold tomb of a museum and the uncultivated glance of the indifferent passerby. I want them to be sold under the auctioneer's hammer, so that the joy the acquisition of each one of them has given me shall be given again, in each case, to some inheritor of my taste.
> [*The Connoisseur* 182 (1973): 77]

REFERENCES

Allen, F. L. (1949) *The Great Pierpont Morgan*, New York: Harper.
Baekeland, F. (1976) 'Collectors of American Painting, 1813–1913', *American Art Review* 3(6): 120–66.
Behrman, S. N. (1952) *Duveen*, New York: Random House.
Bergler, E. (1947) 'Psychopathology of "bargain hunters"', *Journal of Clinical Psychopathology* 1: 623–67.
—— (1969) 'A contribution to the psychology of the snob', *Selected Papers of Edmund Bergler, M.D. 1939–1961*, New York: Grune & Stratton.

Berlyne, D. E. (1971) *Aesthetics and Psychobiology*, New York: Appleton-Century-Crofts.
Beurdeley, M. (1966) *The Chinese Collector through the Centuries*, Rutland, Vt.: Charles Tuttle.
Börne, L. (1964) *Sämtliche Schriften* (1825) vol. 1, Düsseldorf: Josef Meyer.
Bowie, T. and Christenson, C. V. (eds) (1970) *Studies in Erotic Art*, New York: Basic Books.
Cabanne, P. (1963) *The Great Collectors*, New York: Farrar, Straus.
Child, I. L. (1968) 'Esthetics', in G. Lindzey and E. Aronson (eds) *Handbook of Social Psychology* (2nd edn) vol. 3, New York: Addison-Wesley.
Constable, W.G. (1964) *Art Collecting in the United States of America*, London: Thomas Nelson.
Durost, W. N. (1932) *Children's Collecting Activity Related to Social Factors*, New York: Columbia University, Teachers College, Contributions to Education no. 535.
Eagle, J. (1971) 'Artists as collectors', in J. Lipman (ed.) *The Collector in America*, New York: Viking Press.
Eysenck, H. J. (1971) *Dimensions of Personality*, New York: Kegan Paul, Trench, Trubner.
Fenichel, O. (1945) *The Psychoanalytic Theory of Neurosis*, New York: Norton.
—— (1953) 'The scoptophilic instinct and identification', in *The Collected Papers of Otto Fenichel. First Series*, New York: Norton.
—— (1954) 'The drive to amass wealth', 'On acting', 'Trophy and triumph', in *Collected Papers. Second Series*, New York: Norton.
Freud, S. (1953–74) *Standard Edition of the Complete Psychological Works*, New York: Hogarth. 'Character and anal erotism' (1908) vol. 9, 'Instincts and their vicissitudes' (1915) vol. 14.
Jamison, K. (1972) 'A note on the relationship between extraversion and aesthetic preference', *Journal of General Psychology* 87: 301–2.
Jones, E. (1938) 'Anal-erotic character traits', in E. Jones, *Papers on Psychoanalysis*, Baltimore: William Wood.
Jullian, P. (1966) *Les Collectionneurs*, Paris: Flammarion.
Laughlin, H. P. (1967) *The Neuroses*, Washington: Butterworths.
Lehman, H. C. and Witty, P. A. (1927) 'The present status of the tendency to collect and hoard', *Psychological Review* 34: 48–56.
Lucie-Smith, E. (1972) *Eroticism in Western Art*, New York: Praeger.
Menninger, W. C. (1942) 'Psychological aspects of hobbies', *American Journal of Psychiatry* 98: 122–9.
Morris, C. (1957) 'Significance, signification and painting', in R. Lepley (ed.) *The Language of Value*, New York: Columbia University Press.
Nestrick, W. V. (1939) *Constructional Activities of Adult Males*, New York: Columbia University, Teachers College, Contributions to Education, no. 780.
Noy, P. (1968–9) 'A theory of art and aesthetic experience', *Psychoanalytic Review* 55: 623–45.
Peckham, M. (1969) *Art and Pornography*, New York: Basic Books.
Phillips, R. M. (1962) 'The accumulator', *Archives of General Psychiatry* 6: 474–7.
Rheims, M. (1961) *The Strange Life of Objects*, New York: Atheneum.
Rosenbluh, E. S., Owens, G. B. and Pohler, M. J. (1972) 'Art preferences and personality', *British Journal of Psychology* 63: 44–3.
Roubertoux, P. (1970) 'Personality variables and interest in art', *Journal of Personality and Social Psychology* 16: 665–8.
Rush, R. H. (1961) *Art as an Investment*, New York: Prentice-Hall.
Saarinen, A. B. (1958) *The Proud Possessors*, New York: Random House.
Schwartz, E. K. and Wolf, A. (1958) 'The quest for certainty', *AMA Archives of Neurology and Psychiatry* 81: 69–84.
Sheldon, W. M. and Stevens, S. S. (1942) *The Varieties of Temperament*, New York: Harper.
Strahan, E. [Shinn E.] (1879) *The Art Treasures of America*, Philadelphia: George Barrie.
Strong, E. K., Jr (1943) *Vocational Interests of Men and Women*, Stanford: Stanford University Press.
Super, D. E. (1941) *Avocational Interest Patterns*, Stanford: Stanford University Press.
Taylor, F. H. (1948) *The Taste of Angels*, Boston: Little, Brown.
Truettner, W. H. (1971) 'William T. Evans, collector of American painting', *American Art Journal* 3: 59–79.
Von Holst, N. (1967) *Creators, Collectors and Connoisseurs*, New York: Putnam's.
Whitley, M. T. (1929) 'Children's interest in collecting', *Journal of Educational Psychology* 20: 249–61.
Wilson, G. D., Ausman, J. and Mathews, T. R. (1973) 'Conservatism and art preferences', *Journal of Personality and Social Psychology* 25: 286–8.
Winnicott, D. W. (1953) 'Transitional objects and transitional phenomena', *International Journal of Psycho-Analysis* 34: 89–97.
Wittkower, R. and Wittkower, M. (1969) *Born under Saturn*, New York: Norton.
Witty, P. A. and Lehman, H. C. (1930) 'Further studies of children's interest in collecting', *Journal of Educational Psychology* 21: 112–27.

28

No *two alike: play and aesthetics in collecting*

Brenda Danet and Tamar Katriel

This paper is a conceptual analysis of the elements of play and aesthetics in collecting. The main focus is on the process of collecting as a form of human experience among both children and adults. It draws on materials from popular literature on collecting as well as on interviews with about 165 adult and child collectors in Israel. The paper analyses the process by which objects become collectables and the basic aesthetic principle that guides the construction of a collection. The central hypothesis of the paper is that collecting is a means to strive for a sense of closure, completion or perfection.

One of the most famous collectors in our time was the writer Vladimir Nabokov. A life-long avid collector of butterflies, who published his findings in scientific journals, Nabokov began collecting as a young child growing up in a wealthy household in Russia. In his autobiography, *Speak, Memory,* he wrote

> From the age of seven, everything I felt in connection with a rectangle of framed sunlight was dominated by a single passion. If my first glance of the morning was for the sun, my first thought was for the butterflies it would engender. The original event had been banal enough. On the honeysuckle, overhanging the carved back of a bench . . . my guiding angel . . . pointed out to me a rare visitor, a splendid, pale-yellow creature with black blotches, blue crenels, and a cinnabar eyespot over each chrome-rimmed black tail. As it probed the inclined flower from which it hung, its powdery body slightly bent, it kept restlessly jerking its great wings and my desire for it was one of the most intense I have ever experienced
>
> (Nabokov 1969: 94)

Although few collectors are as eloquent as Nabokov about their passion, or as scholarly in their approach, collectors of all ages share his intense emotional involvement. In our work on collecting in Israel, we find that both children and adults are extremely eager to talk about their activities. Whatever people collect – and the range is truly remarkable, from stamps to key chains to empty soda cans, from pipes to old Dutch tiles to Chinese snuff bottles, from rare books to butterflies to Botticellis – collectors of all ages also share a distinctive pattern of experience.

ACADEMICS DISCOVER COLLECTING

Until very recently collecting was only rarely the subject of serious academic research. There is an abundance of novels,[1] biographies and autobiographies[2] about collectors and collecting, and several popular general treatments exist.[3] There is also a huge number of handbooks and guides for different kinds of collectors. In contrast to all this popular literature, until the mid-1980s there was remarkably little academic research on collecting. Suddenly, in the latter half of this decade, there has been a spurt of publications in a number of academic disciplines, for example Belk (1982) and Belk, Wallendorf, Sherry, Holbrook and Roberts (1988) in consumer research; Stewart (1984) in the interface between folklore and literature; Dannefer (1980, 1981), Olmsted (1987a, 1987b), Fine (1987a, 1987b) and Moulin (1984) in sociology; Robinson (1987) in human development; MacLeod (1987) and Saisselin (1985) in art history; Clifford (1985, 1988), Kirshenblatt-Gimblett (1982, 1987), Moody (1985), Spooner (1988) and Thompson (1979) in anthropology; and Stocking (1985), Lumley (1988), and Impey and MacGregor (1988) in museum studies.

This proliferation of research on collecting is one expression of a new interest among many academics in material culture in modern society. When sociologists traditionally think of the concept of culture, for example, it is usually norms, values, behaviour patterns – what people carry around in their heads – that come to mind, not material objects. The pioneering work of Csikszentmihalyi and Rochberg-Halton (1981) on the symbolic meanings of domestic objects in American middle-class homes has helped to put material culture on the agenda of contemporary social science. We concur with these authors that 'to understand what people are and what they might become, one must understand what goes on between people and things. What things are cherished, and why, should become part of our knowledge of human beings' (Csikszentmihalyi and Rochberg-Halton 1981: 1).

In contrast to all this new work on adult collecting, childhood collecting remains neglected. Of the above studies, only Mechling's pertains to childhood, focusing on collecting in the Boy Scouts. There was a passing flurry of interest in children's collecting in the United States in the early years of the twentieth century (Burk 1907; Whitley 1929; Witty and Lehman 1930). Three more recent studies – Furby's (1976) work on the psychology of possession and ownership, Sutton-Smith and Rosenberg's (1971) study of American children's game preferences, and an English study of 7-year-olds (Newson and Newson 1976) – treat collecting only secondarily at best.

PREVIEW OF THE PAPER

This paper aspires to add to the current intellectual ferment about collecting by elucidating two aspects not yet explored in the depth they deserve, the elements of play and of aesthetics in the activities of collectors. Unlike virtually all those now writing about collecting, we shall treat both children and adults. The work this paper draws upon is based in Israel. We are studying adult and child collectors, mainly among urban Jewish Israelis. To illustrate various points, we will provide examples from our materials from interviews with approximately 85 adult and 80 child collectors.

Our approach is primarily qualitative and phenomenological. The goal of the research is to illuminate the nature of individual collectors' experiences. The data are gathered mainly through semi-structured, tape-recorded interviews and are supplemented with observations of auctions and collectors' clubs. The approach is comparative in that, unlike Dannefer's (1980, 1981) or Fine's (1987a, 1987b) studies of the worlds of old-car and mushroom-collecting, respectively, we focus not on one specific type of collectable but on collecting as a general phenomenon. In addition, our research deals specifically with the collecting of material objects. We suspend the conventional distinction between high and low culture; thus the collecting of corkscrews, hatpins and old Coca-Cola machines is of as much interest to us as the collecting of fine paintings and sculpture. We are more interested in the experience and *process* of collecting than in the product – the collection.

The remainder of the paper will be divided into six sections. First, we analyse the elements of play in collecting. Next we discuss the processes by which objects become collectables. Third, we formulate a set of rules that constitute the collecting game. A fourth extensive section elaborates the basic aesthetic principle that guides the construction of a collection. The fifth section develops the hypothesis that collecting is a means to strive towards a sense of closure or completion. We present five strategies that collectors use to pursue closure. Finally, in the concluding section we offer some speculations on the significance of collecting as a cultural form.

COLLECTING AS PLAY

Like Stewart (1984), we view collecting as a form of play with classification. In its prototypic form it is voluntary activity, engaged in for its own sake (Huizinga 1955). It is a form of private leisure, outside the bounds of role obligations and the serious business of everyday life, in which the individual is free to develop an idiosyncratic symbolic world. In Csikszentmihalyi's (1977) terms, collecting provides a 'flow' experience: there is a merging of action and awareness. Nabokov's experience of butterfly-collecting is an extreme example: the ecstasy he experienced was nothing less than transcendental (Nabokov 1969: 109–10). Although dealers, museums and auction houses also collect, they will be excluded from this paper since for them these activities are work, not leisure. While there are potentially addictive aspects to collecting, and collectors are sometimes obsessive about the objects of their devotion, our approach stresses the social definition of the activity as voluntary.[4]

Contest is another feature of play frequently discussed in the literature (e.g., Caillois 1961; Huizinga 1955). It is present in the competition among collectors for the best items at flea markets. Collectors often arrive very early in order to have first pick of choice items. Similarly, there is tension in auctions when those interested in the same item attempt to outbid each other. An especially dramatic example of the tension surrounding an auction was Sotheby's 1988 sale of Andy Warhol's estate, which included both works of art and a good deal of 'junk'. The sale took place in an atmosphere that can only be characterized as hysterical.[5]

There is often competition among collectors as to who has the best collection of a given type. Collections are also a means to demonstrate or to claim high social status, *vis-à-vis* non-collectors as well as other collectors; the distinctiveness of the collection brings distinction to the collector (cf. Baudrillard 1981; Bourdieu 1984). The pinnacle of achievement is to have one's collection displayed by a museum.

Like many forms of play, collecting is fraught with paradox. One of these paradoxes is the tension between rationality and passion. Dannefer (1980) showed that the two exist side by side in old-car collectors. In fact they exist in *all* collectors. Rationality is present, for example, in the careful assessments collectors make about price in relation to quality and rarity, in the analyses they carry out to test authenticity, and in the budgets they set for new acquisitions. It is also present in the attempt to create a collection as a means to an end, for instance, as a means to gain status or make a good financial investment. At the same time there is much passion in collecting. Collectors 'fall in love with' objects, cannot resist buying them when they see them, go to great lengths to hunt for them, devotedly care for them, wax rhapsodic when talking about them, and so forth.

Still another feature of play is the presence of chance in the outcomes of certain kinds of activity (Caillois 1961). If contest is an expression of the skills and power of the actor, chance is the very opposite: outcomes are outside the control of the actor. It is a matter of chance what objects will be on view at a given flea market or auction, and who one's competitors will be.

'As-ifness', or the element of make-believe or fantasy, is present in many aspects of collecting. Among adults, collecting toys – teddy-bears, dolls, miniature trains – is sometimes a way of transporting oneself back to childhood. Thus, an Arab Israeli university lecturer who collects erasers especially treasures one in the form of a lantern, just like the lantern his family used when he was a child and before his village had electricity. Fantasy is also involved in adult collecting of objects from an exotic culture, such as primitive art or Japanese sword fittings, the objects being a way of imagining oneself in another time and place. Among adult collectors we interviewed in Israel, as-ifness was especially prominent in a 30-year-old collector of Chinese snuff bottles who wears a genuine eighteenth-century Chinese dragon robe and accessories to the annual banquet of the International Society of Snuff Bottle Collectors.

Some people collect 'real' objects while others collect imaginary representations of objects. Thus, while Nabokov hunted real butterflies in the fields, the Viscountess Lambton created a total environment for herself in which not only her clothes but nearly every item in her home had a butterfly emblem on it (Johnston and Beddow 1986). We found a similar phenomenon in the collection by an Israeli writer and retired diplomat of images of roosters. His roosters number 400 and fill not only the balcony but also the entrance hall and his study, creating a total environment of fantasy objects.

As-ifness is also present in the tendency for collectors to personify the objects of their devotion. A collector of Biblical archaeological objects we interviewed, a Franciscan priest, spoke of walking in the desert with a group of tourists he was guiding when suddenly his eye caught sight of an object half buried in the sand; he continued walking, but in the end he *had* to go back because the object 'kept calling' him. Old teddy-bears have recently become fashionable collectables. According to a staff member of a London auction house, buyers are attracted to them because 'they look lonely'.[6]

TYPES OF COLLECTABLES

Collecting always involves one or more of the five senses, and in our view is an effort to transcend the ephemerality of experience. At first glance it seems possible to make a sharp distinction between the ephemerality of sensuous experiences and the durability of material objects. In fact, however, the physical durability of objects is also relative, as so eloquently put in Shelley's famous poem 'Ozymandias', about the ruined monumental sculpture of an ancient ruler. Only the trunkless legs remained standing. 'Round the decay/Of that colossal wreck, boundless and bare/The lone and level sands stretch far away.' Viewed metaphorically then, concern with the durability of objects is also concern for the ephemerality of one's own existence.

Ephemeral experiences

Some people collect jokes, proverbs, tall tales. The recording of various genres of folklore necessarily involves one's sense of hearing and is meant to transcend the existential fact that sounds are inherently evanescent. By recording words, one keeps them from being forgotten.

223

Humphrey, an ethologist who has speculated about the possible biological roots of collecting (Humphrey 1984, chapters 9 and 11), recalled his own boyhood habit of standing on a railroad bridge to list numbers of trains as they went by (p. 143). Children sometimes do the same thing with licence numbers of automobiles. Birdwatchers collect sightings of birds. Stuffed specimens seen in natural history museums or even live ones seen in zoos don't count in this context.[7]

The classic Don Juan collects sexual experiences, each one with a different woman. Thus Tomas, the protagonist in Kundera's (1984) *The Unbearable Lightness of Being*, seeks to collect the millionth part of every woman that is unique. The senses of taste and smell are central to connoisseurship in wine-tasting, cigar-smoking and gourmet eating. Visual aspects may also be important: the connoisseur of wines pays attention to colour, and the gourmet to the composition of colours and shapes on the plate. Mushroom-collecting resembles bird-watching in that sighting specimens is important, but it is also a form of gastronomy since collectors eat their discoveries.

The sense of smell is central in the collecting and connoisseurship of incense and snuff. In medieval Japan the aristocracy cultivated the collecting and connoisseurship of incense (Earle 1986: 60).[8] Eighteenth-century French men and women collected snuffs, which were valued for their provenance, much as the provenance of a painting contributes to its value. A certain Madame de Verrue had more than sixty containers of different snuffs (Rigby and Rigby 1944: 216).

Material objects, animate and inanimate

More durable collectables may be animate or inanimate, and if inanimate they may be objects from the natural world such as shells or rocks or manufactured artefacts such as sculptures or antique hardware. A zoo is a collection of animals; usually, representation of types of species is important. A cactus garden may bring together many types of cactuses from around the world, juxtaposing shapes, colours and textures. While the conservation of material objects is a concern of all types of collectors (cf. Dannefer 1980), it is most paramount in the devotees of a type of collectable known as 'ephemera', defined by the author of a manual for collectors as 'the transient everyday items of paper – mostly printed – that are manufactured specifically to use and throw away' (Rickards 1978: 7).

Although the senses of sight and touch are probably the ones most often involved in the collecting of material objects, the other senses may be involved too. For example, Israeli children are interested in the smells of erasers, a popular collectable among them. Similarly, smell is important to collectors of soaps or perfume bottles, like 9½-year-old Eran, an Israeli boy who proudly displays his soap collection. One type of soap in Eran's collection smells like chocolate; he keeps it wrapped in aluminum foil to preserve the smell.[9]

THE RULES OF THE COLLECTING GAME

In everyday parlance, the terms 'saving', 'hoarding' and 'collecting' are sometimes used interchangeably, as when we say, 'I've collected a lot of clothes over the years; I really should give some away.' More precisely, the term for this activity is 'saving' – keeping that which one already possesses. In this paper the term 'collecting' is used more narrowly, to refer to a certain type or future-oriented activity; to collect is to set up an agenda for future action for oneself. Hoarding too is future-oriented, but while the hoarder is interested in quantity, the collector is interested in quality. Even though collectors are often interested in quantity too, the distinctive feature of their activities is their concern with making fine discriminations about items that may or may not enter the collection. Such discriminations are a product both of the general rules that define the collecting 'game' and of individuals' evolving personal tastes.

We have formulated four general rules that constitute prototypical collecting activity: the Reframing rule, the Classification rule, Procedural rules and the Discrimination rule.

For an object to become part of a collection it has to be *reframed* as a collectable, that is, as a potential member of a category of objects that can be treated as aesthetic objects. Different cultures and eras may have different definitions as to what can become a collectable.

For an assemblage of objects to become a collection, they must be defined as belonging to a superordinate *category*. Subcategories may be recognized within the superordinate one.

For collecting to be a socially appropriate activity, collectors must create and follow *procedures* for cultivating the collection. These procedures relate to the ways in which new objects are acquired, the care and display of objects, and the place of collecting in individuals' lives. The over-passionate collector is considered crazy, sick, etc, whereas some minimal level of activity is required for a person to be considered a collector. 'An excessive, sometimes even rapacious need to *have* is transformed into rule-governed, meaningful desire. Thus the self that must possess but cannot have it all learns to select, order, classify in hierarchies – to make "good" collections' (Clifford 1988: 218).

For an assemblage of objects to be considered a collection, each item must be *different* from all others in some way discernible to the collector. We call this the Principle of No-Two-Alike. This principle, which is critical to collecting as an aesthetic experience, will be elaborated on in the next section.

COLLECTING AS AESTHETIC EXPERIENCE

Reframing the object

Collectables as aesthetic objects

To relate to an object or an experience as a collectable is to experience it aesthetically. There is a long tradition of analysis of the features of the aesthetic attitude (e.g., Bullough 1957; Kant 1914; Maquet 1986; Osborne 1970; Stolnitz 1960). Hospers summarized three overlapping views of the nature of the aesthetic attitude as (a) non-practical, (b) non-cognitive, and (c) non-personal. The object is perceived for its own sake and not in order to pursue some goal by means of it; cognitive knowledge about the object is analytically distinct from immediate sensory experience of it; finally, the experience is disinterested – one experiences a portrait not as a picture resembling someone one knows but in terms of its formal characteristics (Hospers 1969: 4–5).

From rubbish to collectables

Its is a distinctive feature of contemporary collecting that many people collect recycled, formerly functional objects such as old telephones or Coca-Cola bottles. Following Malraux (1947, 1967) and Maquet (1986), we will speak of two types of aesthetic objects: those that are aesthetic objects by destination and those that become aesthetic objects by metamorphosis. Paintings and sculpture are aesthetic objects by destination – they were made to be objects of aesthetic contemplation; Coca-Cola bottles and old tools were not.

Thompson (1979) distinguishes between three categories of objects: transients, rubbish and durables (symbolic, not physical durables). Transients are objects of utility whose value declines over time as a result of wear and tear or obsolescence. When they are no longer considered to be of value, objects are relegated to the rubbish heap. The process by which objects are rescued from the rubbish heap and promoted to the status of durables, objects of lasting value, is a social and symbolic one – only in small part dictated by the physical qualities of the object, or even not at all.

There is yet another category of symbolic durables, of relatively recent vintage and deserving of research in its own right: the production of commercial, mass-produced 'instant collectables' like those made by the Franklin Mint in Pennsylvania such as figurines and miniature railroad cars. Mass advertising entices individuals to subscribe to receive entire sets of items over time and even to purchase the display stand specially made for the collection. Commercialization and manipulation of collectors exists in the world of stamps too. National postal services produce catalogues that specify which stamps have been issued and regularly issue special stamps and commemorative envelopes aimed primarily at collectors. Still another example is the recent craze among children to collect Garbage Pail Kid cards. So aggressive has the marketing strategy been in Israel in the past year that distributors passed out free albums in schoolyards in order to stimulate motivation to buy.

Ironic reframing: the pursuit of 'kitsch'

Collectors may play with the reframing process itself, as is true of the person who collects objects he or she regards as kitsch. Thus Henry (1979), who characterizes himself as a 'kitsch addict', pursues items such as a pillow with the word 'Mother' embroidered on it, or a pepper grinder in the form of the Eiffel tower. The uglier, the more grotesque, the more tawdry or sentimental – the more awful the item – the more he loves it. In contrast to most forms of collecting, this variety is ironic.

Aesthetic distance and objective distance from necessity

Theorists who stress the importance of disinterestedness in aesthetic experience often use the phrase '*aesthetic distance*' to characterize the orientation of the perceiver of the object (Kreitler and Kreitler 1972: 281–4). Bourdieu (1984) has taken this notion one step further by linking it to class relations and to freedom from economic necessity:

> The aesthetic disposition, a generalized capacity to neutralize ordinary urgencies and to bracket off practical ends, a durable inclination and aptitude for practice without a practical function, can only be constituted within an experience of the world freed from urgency and through the practice of activities which are an end in themselves.
>
> (1984: 54)

Recontextualization

To treat an object as a collectable is to take it out of its natural or original context and to create a new context for it, that of the collector's own life-space and the juxtaposition with other items in the collection. As Stewart (1984) has written,

> The collection is a form of art as play, a form involving the reframing of objects within a world of attention and manipulation of context. Like other forms of art,

its function is not the restoration of context of origin, but rather the creation of a new context, a context standing in a metaphorical, rather than a contiguous, relation to the world of everyday life.

(1984: 151–2)

The principle of no-two-alike

Reframing and recontextualizing individual objects do not in themselves make an individual into a collector. A person may hang an African mask on the living-room wall or place an antique copper cooking-pot on the shelf, to be admired as aesthetic objects, and yet not be a collector. In addition to orienting oneself to objects aesthetically, then, there must be a more or less conscious decision of the individual to acquire many items belonging to the same general category, and far more important, to acquire many different items belonging to this category.

Same-but-different: how objects rhyme

No matter what their ages or what they collect, collectors, at least of material objects, are usually not interested in having two of anything. Duplicates are usually viewed as spares to trade or sell, or to have just in case the best exemplar becomes damaged and needs replacing. This tendency to seek out items that are the-same-but-different is so basic to collecting that we highlight it by calling it the Principle of No-Two-Alike. The items are 'the same' because the collector perceives them as belonging to the same linguistic or cultural superordinate category (e.g., stamps from Finland, African masks, Coca-Cola paraphernalia). At the same time, each item is in some way discernible to the collector as different from all the others. If the Coca-Cola collector concentrates on bottles, for example, he or she will want exemplars of all the shapes produced by different factories, in different countries, in both green and white glass, etc.

The occurrence of repetition, of sameness-in-difference, within the flow of ever-changing experience creates the illusion of beauty. In Kundera's (1984) *The Unbearable Lightness of Being*, the chance recurrence of the number 6 in different situations becomes an integral part of the relationship between Tereza and Tomas, the protagonists; on the day they met, the church bells had chimed 6; on a later occasion bells chimed 6 just as he came to the door of their flat. So great was the impact of the coincidence on Tereza that 'a sense of beauty . . . cured her of her depression and imbued her with a new will to live' (Kundera 1984: 78).

Following the poet Gerard Manley Hopkins (1959), Humphrey has suggested that the paradigm for the experience of beauty in sameness-within-difference is rhyme. Just as a poem rhymes, so objects may rhyme:

> Consider the nature of a typical collection, say a stamp collection. Postage stamps are, in structuralist terms, like man-made flowers: they are divide into 'species,' of which the distinctive feature is the country of origin, while within each species there exists tantalizing variation. The stamp-collector sets to work to classify them. He arranges his stamp in an album, a page for the species of each country. The stamps on each page 'rhyme' with each other, and contrast with those on other pages.
>
> (Humphrey 1984: 132)

It should be evident that this preference for sameness-in-difference is a case of the more general aesthetic principle of unity-in-diversity (Gombrich 1984).[10]

Collecting and classifying objects and experiences is a source of joy to both children and adults. In children this sense of joy is fresh and spontaneous. Witness the poem written by 9-year-old Dana from Haifa who, like many Israeli girls of her age, collects erasers:

> I collect erasers
> All kinds of kinds
> All kinds of colors
> I have lots of erasers,
> Each one is different:
> One is round and one is square,
> One is purple and one is pink
> I have many erasers and each one is different.

Asked whether they sometimes think that collecting is silly or crazy, our child interviewees retort, 'Don't be ridiculous! Collecting is marvellous! It's beautiful! It's fun!' While in adults this simple pleasure in classification often becomes interwoven with many other satisfactions and preoccupations, and may appear buried under layers of sophistication, it is invariably present in them too. At the same time, for many adults there is often a good deal of ambivalence about collecting. Although the snuff-bottle-collector mentioned earlier thinks collecting is 'marvellous', quite a few other adults we interviewed spoke of it, metaphorically, as 'a disease', or a 'madness'.

Exceptions apparent of real?

There are some apparent exceptions to this general tendency to seek out items that are the-same-but-different. For example, a collector of salt and pepper shakers we interviewed buys them two at a time, virtually identical items of the same shape and style. In this case the pair, the *set*, is the collectable, not the individual salt or pepper shaker. Also among our interviewees, a pipe-collector was observed to own two identical enamel opium pipes from Iran. However, he displayed them with different groups of pipes in different rooms. If an item is particularly rare and fine, a collector might take special pride in owning and displaying two exemplars even if he or she doesn't particularly think of them as a set. As for the phenomenon of buying a sheet of stamps that are all alike, here, we would argue, one should think of the sheet as the collectable, and not the individual stamp. The more important trading is to collectors, the more likely they will keep a separate large stock of spares.

Dominance and aesthetics in collecting

In a fascinating analysis of the interrelations between dominance and affection, Tuan (1984) showed that the imposition of one's will is subtly, and sometimes not so subtly, present in a wide range of aesthetic and play phenomena, from the creation of gardens to the domestication of pets. Viewed through Tuan's lens, collecting is not an innocent activity. Collections are like pets: objects of affection: they are also objects of domination and control. It is not surprising that most collectables are inanimate objects. It is easier to dominate an inanimate object such as an antique typewriter than a living organism such as a plant; plants grow, change shape, die.

Collectors are in fact quite open about the centrality of control to their activities. Thus, when asked why owning objects was preferable to seeing them in a museum, a stamp-collector physicist stated, 'It's mine [the collection]. I can do with it what I want. I can arrange it in the album the way I want. I can display it in exhibits.' Ownership is also essential for another reason: the sensuous aspects of collecting – handling, touching, playing with, caring for the collection – are made possible by it. According to one woman collector of Judaica, 'the most important thing is that you are able to handle it, because once it's in the museum you can't – this way you can take it and feel it and look at it.'

Ownership of material objects is also a prerequisite for the sense of accomplishment that is one of the satisfactions of collecting. When asked 'What is the fun in collecting? Why do you like it?' quite a few children replied that they like to look at the collection and to think, 'Gee, I did all that! I collected all those coins [or erasers, or whatever].'

The theme of dominance is also reflected in the rules collectors have as to who may touch the collection. Nearly every child we interviewed specified some limitation, for example, 'Only my parents, not my brother, because he's little and might break things' or 'Anyone can look at them, but only I can take them out of the drawer'. An extreme illustration of the same point is the behaviour of an adult collector of Judaica – in his case spice-boxes used in the service to conclude the Sabbath. Not the collector himself, but a friend of the family whom we also happened to interview, revealed that he keeps his collection of about 400 spice-boxes locked in a special room in his home, and even his wife may not enter!

The preoccupation of many collectors with owning rare or unique items may also be an expression of a desire to dominate. Stewart recounts an often retold story of a book collector who paid another collector a huge sum of money for a book, only to throw it into the fire, just so he could be sure that his was the only copy in existence (Stewart 1984: 160). Since owning unique items is seldom feasible except for art objects, collectors often make do with rare ones. Even young children value rarity; young Avigail, a 10-year-old stamp-collector, was so proud of her rare stamp from Hitler's era in Germany that she mentioned it again and again. Feelings of dominance may be mixed with the sense of social distinction that comes from owning something unique.

STRIVING FOR CLOSURE

As for the aesthetic dimension of collecting, the central hypothesis of this paper is that the attractions of collecting have to do with the possibilities they offer for the pursuit of a sense of closure. Closure in turn has to do with tension and tension reduction.

Tension and tension release in collecting

In a synthesis of four main theories of the psychology of art, psychoanalysis, Gestalt psychology, information theory and behaviourism, Kreitler and Kreitler (1972) high-lighted the role of tension and tension release in the experience of art. Tension and tension release are important in collecting too: *collectors intentionally create an agenda for the production of, and reduction of, manageable tension.* Our materials strongly suggest that collectors toy with, pursue, aspire to, and sometimes actually manage to create a sense of closure, completion, perfection.[11] As Gombrich has written,

> we must ultimately be able to account for the most basic fact of aesthetic experi-
> ence, the fact that delight lies somewhere between boredom and confusion, if
> monotony makes it difficult to attend, a surfeit of novelty will overload the system
> and cause us to give up. . . . It is different with hierarchies which we can master
> and reconstruct. . . . The very ease of reconstruction allows us to go on and to enjoy
> that unity in complexity that has always appealed to paviors and other pattern-
> makers.
>
> (1984: 9)

If the relatively passive taking-in of pattern in decorative art is pleasing, then the active construction of pattern, of sameness-in-diversity, of a kind chosen by the collector, must be at least as pleasing.

Drawing on the gestalt theory of perception as well as writings on music and language, Herrnstein-Smith analysed the rhetorical devices that poets use to convey a sense of 'Ah-hah! that's the way it is', the click of things-coming-together or concluding that is the sense of closure:

> when a thematic connection or opposition is to some degree reinforced by syntactic correspondence and formal repetition, the linguistic structure so formed appears particularly stable and authoritative. . . . What distinguishes the snappy force of 'Look before you leap' from the flatness of 'Look before you jump' is simply the alliteration of the antithetical verbs.
>
> (Herrnstein-Smith 1968: 168)

Herrnstein-Smith goes beyond Hopkins (1959) and Humphrey (1984) by suggesting *why* rhyme and repetition are experienced as pleasing. We extrapolate still further by suggesting that just as poets may strive towards closure via language, collectors strive towards closure via manipulation of objects. A woman coin-collector was quite articulate about this. When asked about the satisfactions of collecting she replied, 'There is an aspiration to reach *shlemut* [completion, perfection], enrichment, interests, and very much the aesthetic aspect.'

Five ways to create a sense of closure

We have identified five types of strategies that collectors can use to work at producing a sense of closure. They are listed in Table 28.1. Note that the various strategies are divided into two groups: those that pertain to relations between objects and those that pertain to features of individual objects.

Completing a series or set

The first strategy is to strive towards completing a series or set. Even very young children can articulate their interest in completing series: virtually all the stamp- and coin-collectors we interviewed, both children and adults, told us this is something that interests them, usually very much. But why this fascination with series among collectors of all ages? In Stewart's words, 'To play with series is to play with the fire of infinity. In the collection the threat of infinity is always met with the articulation of boundary' (1984: 159).

The need for closure no doubt varies with the personality of the individual. It may be that those with a particularly strong need for closure will choose types of collectables that lend themselves to completing series or sets. When asked why he thought he had been attracted to stamps, one stamp-collector we interviewed replied, 'because you know exactly what you are missing'. A person less preoccupied with actually obtaining closure might choose instead to collect, say, scissors or thimbles – collectables that do not come in ready-made series.

A variation of this strategy is to aspire to acquire all of something. Thus a record-collector we interviewed sets as a goal the acquiring of all recorded performances of a given musical work. An adult stamp-collector told us, 'I try to reach *shlemut* in this area [sports stamps], and therefore I will acquire every sports stamp.' Acquiring exemplars of all editions ever published of, say, *Alice in Wonderland* would be another example.

Table 28.1 Strategies to pursue closure/completion/perfection

Strategy	Example
1 Completing a series or set	Completing a series of stamps
Acquiring all of something	Acquiring all editions ever published of a book
Assembling exemplars of subcategories	Collecting examples of pipes made by different manufacturers
Putting together items that 'go together'	Furnishing a room with country furniture
2 Filling a space	Filling a wall with a displayed collection of plates
3 Creating a visually pleasing, harmonious display	Attending to the composition created by a display of plates
4 Manipulating the scale of objects	
Collecting very small objects	Collecting miniatures, e.g., dollhouse furniture
Collecting very large objects	Collecting vintage cars
5 Aspiring to perfect objects	
Acquiring items in mint condition	Acquiring a mint condition vintage car
Restoring items to mint condition	Restoring a vintage car
Acquiring aesthetically perfect objects	Acquiring an exquisite painting
Improving the physical quality of items	Replacing a rusted stamp with one in better physical condition
Improving the aesthetic quality of items	Trading a painting for one of superior aesthetic quality

The Armand Hammer collection of Honoré Daumier's drawings, lithographs and bronzes shown in 1987 at the Israel Museum includes 'all Daumier's known lithographs and woodcuts, not counting the duplicates' (Ronnen 1987: 13) – some 4,000 works!

Sometimes collectors choose to pursue only selected subcategories out of a range of possible ones. Thus a woman collector of ceramic plates in our study collects only handmade pottery and not porcelain. A pipe-collector also chose this strategy, aspiring to have exemplars of the products of certain factories. Another variation is simply to assemble items that the collector perceives as going together in some fashion, for instance furnishing a room with pieces that all belong to the general category of country furniture, though they constitute neither a set nor exemplars of a fixed set of subcategories. Along the same lines, a collector of antique jewellery we interviewed creates what she calls suits. Say she has bought an antique coral necklace and earrings; she will then hunt for a ring, pin and bracelet to match the exact colour, texture, quality and style of work. In contrast to coin or stamp series, here the items were never intended by their makers as a series, it is the collector who has created the series.

Filling the space

A second, simple strategy is to identify a space as needing to be filled and trying to fill it, whether a page in a stamp album or the entire album, a shelf or a space on the wall.

Among the children we interviewed, Dorit, a young collector of stickers, was eager to fill the doors of her wardrobe with stickers. Similarly, an 8-year-old girl who collects stamps likes to paste many exemplars of the same stamp on a page. Better socialized stamp-collectors would smile at her behaviour; they would say she does not know how to collect stamps. Interest in filling the space is present in adults too. The collection of ceramic plates just mentioned fills an entire wall in the collector's dining-room. And the rooster collection described earlier fills a three-dimensional space. A biologist collector of antique travel books on the Holy Land spoke of how much he enjoys sitting opposite his now-filled shelves and 'taking in' how his collection fills them.

Creating a visually pleasing, harmonious display

Many collectors are interested in creating pleasing displays of their collections. Under what conditions does display become important to collectors? There is at least prelimi-nary evidence that it may be a more important concern in the West than in the Far East (Alsop 1982: 104–5; Clifford 1988).

Display is a prominent theme in many of our Israeli interviews. Our plate-collector put great stress on the importance of creating a harmonious pattern on the wall. In choosing what to put where, she seeks to mix smaller and larger ones, to contrast colours and designs, and to leave spaces in between them that are 'not too big and not too small'. And a collector of earrings took great pains to arrange her collection on three triangular shawls hung on her bedroom wall, with the various earrings arranged not in pairs but apart though symmetrically hung at opposite sides of the shawl.

Concern for creating visual pattern is particularly prominent in the collection of Islamic copperware belonging to a corporate executive in his 50s whom we interviewed. The collection is displayed on specially designed Perspex shelves.

Manipulating the scale of objects

One way to work towards closure is to manipulate the scale of objects (Strategy 4 in Table 28.1). This strategy is intermediate between those stressing relations between items and those focusing on the individual object, because some aspects of both are involved. There is probably the hint of an answer here to the intriguing question of why people are so often attracted to miniature objects. If one thinks about it, a good many collectables are in fact very small. In part of course, this is a matter of logistics, of hav-ing room in one's home to store them. Collectors also appreciate the virtuosity of the producers of tiny objects. Japanese *netsuke* for example, once used as toggles or counterweights to hold tobacco pouches and medicine cases to the belts of Japanese men, are now prized as fine miniature sculptures.[12]

But there is another reason for the fascination of dolls' houses and their accessories, of thimbles, *netsuke*, Chinese snuff bottles, tin soldiers, keys and other such small collec-tables: they facilitate the creation and perception of a small, coherent world. Smallness facilitates taking in the whole gestalt all at once. 'There are no miniatures in nature; the miniature is a cultural product, the product of an eye performing certain operations, manipulating, and attending in certain ways to the physical world' (Stewart 1984: 55). So popular is the idea of collecting and displaying miniatures today, among both chil-dren and adults, that commercially produced cabinets simulating printers' boxes are widely available for this purpose. It is also pertinent that a miniature world is a more perfect world; the blemishes visible to the naked eye in life-size objects are no longer visible. Kirshenblatt-Gimblett (1982, 1987) has noted the special interest of elderly people in miniatures: the easily grasped gestalt they have created helps to give them a sense of transcendent wholeness and unity, which is especially meaningful as death approaches.

Collecting objects that are very large can also, paradoxically, facilitate a sense of closure, this time by providing an entire frame within which the collector can transport himself or herself into a different world. Dannefer observed this in his vintage car-collectors: for financial and logistic reasons they may have only one car, but one is enough to slip into the 1920s or 1930s. To compensate for what they don't have in their 'stable', some of these car-collectors also collect miniature models (Dannefer 1980).

Striving for perfect objects

A fifth strategy towards closure is to include only perfect objects. One can strive either for physical or for formal/aesthetic perfection, or for both. Thus, child stamp-collectors are taught by their parents and older siblings that one should collect only stamps whose teeth are intact and which are free of rust. The correct number of teeth is also considered to be important. Similarly, 'To bring top dollar, [beer] cans usually have to be clean, dent free, and have no major scratches or rust' (Hughes 1984: 107). And the most desirable trade cards (commercial cards to advertise products and services, produced in the years 1870–1900 in the US) 'are crisp, clean, and free from any errant marks, tears, or creases' (Hughes 1984: 103–4).

One variation on the preoccupation with the physical condition of objects is the interest in restoring them to mint condition. In an adult education class on collecting observed by Katriel, the class was taught that if there is something physically wrong with an object, its value goes down. The teacher was not just informing prospective buyers about criteria of value, enabling them to avoid being cheated; they were also being socialized to the idea that whole or perfect objects are to be valued over blemished ones. In Dannefer's research on vintage car-collectors, he concluded that the process of restoration is the most valued aspect of the world of cars. 'There is ambivalence about finishing the job, not only because peers may find fault with the work, but also because the car will never be this good again' (Dannefer 1980: 403).

Quite a few of our Israeli collectors are involved in activities that maintain and preserve the objects, dusting, cleaning, and so on. Thus a collector of Haggadoth[13] airs out the collection once every few months, dusts it, repairs tears, and if necessary brings especially antiquarian ones in for professional conservation. Restoration and conservation are a way of seeking closure by turning back the hands of the clock so that the inexorable process of decay will be slowed down at least to some degree.

The pursuit of aesthetically perfect, formally beautiful objects is another course to take. Collectors of painting and sculpture typically come to mind here. They strive to become connoisseurs of their chosen objects, to be able to make very fine discriminations about the merits of individual objects and therefore are highly selective as to which items may enter the collection.

Systematicity, so prominent in stamp- and coin-collectors, can at the same time go with connoisseurship of individual objects. Consider a record-collector, a lawyer and recent immigrant to Israel from the United States, who aspires to own a recording of every performance ever recorded of a Mozart piano concerto. By listening to many different interpretations, he has taught himself to make very fine discriminations and to develop reasoned opinions as to what constitutes the best interpretation.

Another variation on the theme of striving for perfect objects is to improve the physical or aesthetic quality of what one has. Thus a stamp-collector might replace a slightly rusted stamp with an exemplar in better physical condition. And an art-collector may trade in a painting he or she no longer likes for one that is more pleasing. Collectors will even sell items at a loss so they do not have to look any more at those which, in their opinion, now betray poor taste.

An especially intriguing variation on the theme of the pursuit of perfection is, paradoxically, the hunt for *imperfection*. In the world of stamp-collectors, there is great interest in stamps with printing mistakes; they are extremely valuable. A certain 64-year-old political activist and trade-union official specializes in Israeli stamps with printing mistakes. When the post office first opened after Israel was declared a state in 1948, he bought six stamps and then discovered printing mistakes in them. This 'event', to use his charged term, changed his orientation to stamps thoroughly. He addressed three envelopes to himself, each with two of the faulty stamps on them, and mailed them. He took the envelopes with their cancelled stamps to a dealer, who paid him a high price for one of them. And thus began his romance with stamps with printing errors:

> Sometimes I would buy thousands of cancelled stamps . . . and I would sit at night with a magnifying glass and look for mistakes. Sometimes I would find a stamp without a price, or whose colour wasn't printed, or instead of three colours only two . . . the word 'Israel' deleted . . . I subscribed to the philately service, and thus I would follow all the new stamps. And by following continuously, I would discover a mistake. It really became an obsession with me, malaria in my bones. I would come home from work and sit for hour after hour into the wee hours of the night with the magnifying glass and check stamps.

His motivation for hunting stamps with mistakes is no doubt in part financial, since they are valuable. But the more important question is, why are they valuable? A case can be made that to identify imperfection is to control it. Or is there another explanation altogether? Perhaps touching stamps with mistakes is a way of being in touch with other human beings, fallible like ourselves. If this explanation is the more pertinent, then stamp-collectors who hunt for mistakes may have something in common with the Franciscan priest we interviewed who especially treasured a deformed Roman glass bottle because it had collapsed when blown.[14]

Playing with closure

It is evident that whatever objects are collected, collectors must live with a great deal of ambiguity about their prospects for producing closure. An empty stamp album stares one in the face. As Katriel's teenage stamp-collector daughter put it, 'the holes [in the album] hurt'. Seven figurines on the shelf beg for more. Committing oneself to hard-to-find categories, or to collecting items one can hardly afford, provide other constraints. Thus a host of factors may impede progress towards closure.

While all collectors thrive on the challenge of pursuing closure, few invite challenge and the accompanying tension to the extent revealed by a collector of Haggadoth interviewed by one of our students. A retired immigration official, a man of 70, once bought half of an antique Haggadah in New York many years ago. With much emotion he revealed that he had hunted for the other half for years and had finally found it in Mea Shearim, the orthodox Jewish quarter of Jerusalem! This extraordinary story demonstrates that collectors play with closure – this man more than most.

In a study of biology, behaviour and the arts, Peckham suggested that art is an expression of 'man's rage for chaos'.

Man desires above all a predictable and ordered world . . . and this is the motivation behind the role of the scientist. But because man desires such a world so passionately, he is very much inclined to ignore anything that intimates that he does not have it . . . Only in protected situations, characterized by high walls of psychic insulation, can he afford to let himself be aware of the disparity between his interests . . . and the data his interaction with the environment actually produces.

(Peckham 1967: 313)

Like art, we believe collecting is a sheltered way of confronting chaos and the ephemerality of human existence.

COLLECTING AS A CULTURAL FORM

Like any complex form of human activity, collecting has many meanings, both at the level of the individual and of the wider culture. An important question is, in what ways does contemporary collecting reflect themes specific to modern and postmodern society, and in what ways is its significance universal? Is it primarily an expression of late capitalism, bureaucracy and the consumer society? Of surplus income, fragmentation, isolation and powerlessness of the individual in an overly rationalized world (Berger, Berger and Kellner 1974; Dannefer 1980; Jameson 1983; Stewart 1984)? Or is it best understood as a continuation of the western drive that flowered in the Renaissance to explore, classify, make order in the physical world, to appropriate and domesticate the alien 'other' (Clifford 1985, 1988)?

At least some types of contemporary collecting reflect feelings of nostalgia for earlier times. Davis (1977) has suggested that such feelings flourish when there is discontent with the present, which is experienced as bleak, unsatisfying or even frightening. The nostalgia wave of the 1970s and 1980s in the United States and Britain has had its impact on collecting too. In a world in which an old teddy-bear can command the price of £5,000 and the going price for a 1950s jukebox is $3,850,[15] collectables cannot be viewed simply as pure aesthetic objects. We need to develop sophisticated ways of analysing the cultural meanings that such objects carry.

As the above suggests, a distinction should be made between the meanings of the activity of collecting and of the objects collected. In this paper we have not been able to consider in any detail the significance of the objects collected. One question is, to what extent has the legitimation for the collecting of recycled objects – twentieth-century collectables *par excellence* – come from developments in avant-garde art? Is there a relationship between the collecting of beer cans and comic books and Marcel Duchamp's 'ready-mades' – objects taken from everyday life and transformed into art objects – and Pop art images such as Andy Warhol's Campbell soup cans (cf. Crane 1987; Lippard 1985)? A proper understanding of collecting as a cultural activity must take into account its place and shape within the wider contemporary aesthetic scene, particularly the commodification and democratization of art.

Just as mechanical reproduction eroded the aura of the original work of art (Benjamin 1969b), so it has had an important impact on collecting. Collectors of paintings and sculpture continue to be interested in the authenticity of unique objects in the traditional sense. However, many of those who collect mass-produced, typically recycled objects are now preoccupied with the genuineness not of unique objects but of exemplars. For this reason vintage car-collectors prefer 'old old' parts, rather than 'new old' ones, that is, parts manufactured at the same time as the original car rather than virtually identical but recently manufactured replacement parts for antique cars (Dannefer 1980). The larger question for the cultural analyst is *why* collectors are preoccupied with authenticity.

The above discussion pertains primarily to the significance of collecting as a late twentieth-century activity. Alongside the time-bound aspects there remains the more fundamental question of its universal significance. In our opinion, in its contemporary form, and perhaps in all ages since it first blossomed about 3,000 years ago (Alsop 1982; Bazin 1967), collecting is an aesthetic activity that gives expression to the universal experience of the ephemerality of human existence. As Rochberg-Halton has written,

> We are mysterious creatures who mark our time on earth through tangible remembrances. We transform time itself, as it were, into tangible space through our makings and doings, personalizing our environment while objectifying ourselves. In our own time it might be said that things themselves have got the better of us, dominating our lives with their claim that buying and selling is the ultimate goal of existence. Yet in this economic age of possession, it remains possible, and indeed all the more essential, to reclaim significance from our surroundings. As Jorge Luis Borges has said, 'Time is the one essential mystery', and 'Our task is to turn memory into beauty.'
>
> (Rochberg-Halton 1986: 188)

This paper first appeared in Play and Culture 2(3) (1989), pp. 255–71.

NOTES

1 See Fowles, *The Collector* (1967); Balzac, *Cousin Pons* (1968, 1981); Connell, *The Connoisseur* (1974); Canetti, *Auto-da-Fé* (1974); Dreiser, *The Titan* (1925); Norris, *The Pit: A Story of Chicago* (1903, 1956); Radcliff, *Adventures of a Vintage Car Collector* (1972). See also the short story, 'The stamp collection', in Capek (1962), and the play *The Glass Menagerie* (Williams 1945, 1984).
2 In addition to Nabokov (1969), see Benjamin's essay, 'Unpacking my library' (Benjamin 1969a); Hazlitt (1897); Guggenheim (1980); Rheims (1980); Getty (Le Vane and Getty 1955); Templeton (1958); and Price (1959). Biographies of art collectors also abound: see Pollack (1962); Saarinen (1958); Cabanne (1963); Tharp (1965).
3 See Rigby and Rigby (1944); Taylor (1948); Alsop (1982); Jullian (1967); Rheims (1961, 1967); Eccles (1968); Carmichael (1971).
4 An orthodox Freudian approach would focus on the concepts of anal character, obsession and compulsion; for more on psychoanalytic approaches, see Freud (1962); Fodor and Gaynor (1950); Baudrillard (1968). For a thorough discussion of addictive aspects of collecting, see Wallendorf (1988).
5 See McGuigan (1988); Greenspan (1988); Kaylan (1988). Sotheby's contributed to this hysteria by issuing a pricey ($95) boxed set of six catalogues for the sale, obviously intended itself to be an instant collectable, by holding black-tie viewings of the objects before the sales and by making the sale into a media event. This extreme case illustrates how the element of contest in collecting can be manipulated in a symbiotic relationship between the media, dealers and auction houses.
6 Interview with Anna Marrett, Collectors' Department, Phillips Fine Arts and Antiques Auctioneers, London, March 1988. Dannefer adds that vintage car collectors often keep pictures of their cars in their wallets, along with photos of their families (Dannefer 1980).
7 Personal communication from Patricia C. Barry of the University of North Carolina, a veteran bird-watcher.
8 Perhaps no society has made such a cult of experiencing the ephemeral as has Japan. Keene (1981) identified four basic principles in Japanese aesthetics, one of which is perishability. 'Their favorite flower is . . . the cherry blossom, precisely because the period of blossoming is so poignantly brief. . . . Plum blossoms look much the same . . . but they are less highly prized because they linger so long on the boughs' (p. 24).
9 This is a very unusual collection for an Israeli boy. The most popular collections among boys are stamps, coins and keychains. Girls tend to collect table napkins, stationery and erasers, but also perfume bottles and soaps. Strong sex-typing is very much in evidence

10 With respect to more ephemeral experiences, the Principle of No-Two-Alike is apparently relaxed. Thus, connoisseurs of wine will buy a whole case of wine; cigar smokers will buy a whole box of fine cigars. While birdwatchers generally pursue the sighting of different birds on each occasion, Patricia C. Barry told us that a second sighting can occasionally be a satisfying test of one's skills of identification.
11 On the pursuit of completion in collecting, see also Belk *et al.* (1988).
12 See, for example, Barker and Smith (1976).
13 The *Haggadah* is the ceremonial service for the Passover Seder. Many editions of it have been produced over the centuries.
14 Stewart (1984) has suggested that collecting containers of various kinds (e.g., pots, vases, teapots, boxes, salt and pepper shakers) is yet another strategy towards closure. See Stewart (1984: 159).
15 Five thousand pounds sterling was the top price a teddy-bear commanded at auction in Phillips Fine Arts and Antiques auction house in London in recent years (interview with Anna Marrett, Collectors' Dept, Phillips, London, March 1988). The price of $3,850 for a 1950s jukebox was spotted in a collectables shop in the trendy Los Angeles area of Melrose Avenue in April 1988.

REFERENCES

Alsop, J. (1982) *The Rare Art Traditions: A History of Collecting and its Linked Phenomena*, New York: Harper & Row.
Balzac, H. (1968) *Cousin Pons*, trans, H. J. Hunt, Harmondsworth: Penguin. (Original work published 1848)
Barker, R. and Smith, L. (1976) *Netsuke: The Miniature Sculpture of Japan*, London: British Museum.
Baudrillard J. (1968) *Le Système des objets*, Paris: Gallimard.
—— (1981) *For a Critique of the Political Economy of the Sign*, trans. C. Levin, St Louis: Telos.
Bazin, G. (1967) *The Museum Age*, New York: Universe.
Belk, R. W. (1982) 'Acquiring, possessing, and collecting: fundamental processes in consumer behavior', in R. F. Bush and S. G. Hunt (eds) *Marketing Theory: Philosophy of Science Perspectives*, Chicago: American Marketing Association, 185–90.
Belk, R. W., Wallendorf, M. Sherry, J., Holbrook, M. and Roberts, S. (1988) 'Collectors and collecting', *Advances in Consumer Research* 15: 27–32.
Benjamin, W. (1969a) 'Unpacking my library', in W. Benjamin, *Illuminations*, ed. H. Arendt, trans. H. Zohn, New York: Schocken, 59–67.
—— (1969b) 'The work of art in the age of mechanical reproduction', in W. Benjamin, *Illuminations*, ed. H. Arendt, trans. H. Zohn, New York: Schocken, 219–53.
Berger, P. L., Berger, B. and Kellner, H. (1974) *The Homeless Mind*, Harmondsworth: Penguin.
Bourdieu, P. (1984) *Distinction: A Social Critique of the Judgment of Taste*, trans. R. Nice, Cambridge, Mass.: Harvard University Press.
Bullough, E. (1957) *Aesthetics: Lectures and Essays*, London: Bowes & Bowes.
Burk, C. F. (1907) 'The collecting instinct', in G. S. Hall (ed.) *Aspects of Child Life and Education* Boston: Ginn, 205–39.
Cabanne, P. (1963) *The Great Collectors*, London: Cassell.
Caillois, R. (1961) *Man, Play and Games*, Glencoe, Il.: Free Press.
Canetti, E. (1974) *Auto-da-Fé*, New York: Continuum.
Capek, K. (1962) 'The stamp collection', in K. Capek, *Tales from Two Pockets*, trans. P. Selver, London: Folio Society, 201–6.
Carmichael, B. (1971) *Incredible Collectors, Weird Antiques and Odd Hobbies*, Englewood Cliffs, N.J.: Prentice-Hall.
Clifford, J. (1985) 'Objects and selves: an afterword', in G. Stocking (ed.) *Objects and Others: Essays on Museums and Material Culture* Vol. 3, *History of Anthropology*, Madison: University of Wisconsin Press, 236–47.
—— (1988) *The Predicament of Culture: Twentieth-century Ethnography, Literature and Art*, Cambridge, Mass.: Harvard University Press.
Connell, E. S., Jr (1974) *The Connoisseur*, New York: Knopf.
Crane, D. (1987) *The Transformation of the Avant-garde: The New York Art World, 1940–1985*, Chicago: University of Chicago Press.
Csikszentmihalyi, M. (1977) *Beyond Boredom and Anxiety*, San Francisco: Jossey-Bass.
Csikszentmihalyi, M. and Rochberg-Halton, E. (1981) *The Meaning of Things: Domestic Symbols and the Self*, Cambridge: Cambridge University Press.
Dannefer, D. (1980) 'Rationality and passion in private experience: modern consciousness and the social world of old-car collectors', *Social Problems* 27: 392–412.

—— (1981) 'Neither socialization nor recruitment: the avocational careers of old-car enthusiasts', *Social Forces* 60: 395–413.

Davis, F. (1977) 'Nostalgia, identity, and the current nostalgia wave', *Journal of Popular Culture* 11: 414–24.

Dreiser, T. (1925) *The Titan*, Cleveland and New York: World.

Earle, J. (ed.) (1986) *Japanese Art and Design*, London: Victoria & Albert Museum.

Eccles, D. (1968) *On Collecting*, London: Longmans, Green.

Fine, G. (1987a) 'Trivial pursuits: mushroom collectors and the culture of nature', paper presented at the Conference on Qualitative Methodology, Hamilton, Ontario.

—— (1987b) 'Community and boundary: personal experience stories of mushroom collectors', *Journal of Folklore Research* 24: 223–40.

Fodor, N. and Gaynor, F. (eds) (1950) *Freud: Dictionary of Psychoanalysis*, New York: Philosophical Society.

Fowles, J. (1967) *The Collector*, New York: Dell.

Freud, S. (1962) *Standard Edition of the Complete Psychological Works of Sigmund Freud*, ed. J. Strachey, London: Hogarth Press & Institute of Psychoanalysis.

Furby, L. (1976) 'The socialization of possessions and ownership among children in three cultural groups: Israeli kibbutz, Israeli city and American', in S. Modgil and C. Modgil (eds) *Piagetian Research: Compilation and Commentary* vol. 8, Windsor: NFER Publishing, 541–64.

Gombrich, E. H. (1984) *The Sense of Order: A Study in the Psychology of Decorative Art*, London: Phaidon.

Greenspan, S. (April 1988) 'The rise and fall of Warhol Hall', *Art and Auction* 102–11.

Guggenheim, P. (1980) *Out of This Century: Confessions of an Art Addict*, Garden City, N.Y.: Anchor.

Hazlitt, W. C. (1897) *The Confessions of a Collector*, London: Ward & Downey.

Henry, L., Jr (1979) 'Fetched by beauty: confessions of a kitsch addict', *Journal of Popular Culture* 13: 197–208.

Herrnstein-Smith, B. (1968) *Poetic Closure: A Study of How Poems End*, Chicago: University of Chicago Press.

Hopkins, G. M. (1959) 'On the origin of beauty: a platonic dialogue', in H. House and G. Storey (eds) *G. M. Hopkins: Journals and Papers*, Oxford: Oxford University Press.

Hospers, J. (ed.) (1969) *Introductory Readings in Aesthetics*, New York: Macmillan.

Hughes, S. (1984) *Pop Culture Mania: Collecting 20th-century Americana for Fun and Profit*, New York: McGraw-Hill.

Huizinga, J. (1955) *Homo ludens*, Boston: Beacon.

Humphrey, N. (1984) 'The illusion of beauty', in N. Humphrey, *Consciousness Regained*, Oxford: Oxford University Press, 121–37.

Impey, O. and MacGregor, A. (1988) *The Origins of Museums: Cabinets of Curiosities in the Sixteenth and Seventeenth Centuries*, Oxford: Oxford University Press.

Jameson, F. (1983) 'Postmodernism and consumer society', in H. Foster (ed.) *The Anti-aesthetic: Essays on Postmodern Culture*, Port Townsend, Wash.: Bay Press, 111–25.

Johnston, S. and Beddow, T. (1986) *Collecting: The Passionate Pastime*, Harmondsworth: Penguin.

Jullian, P. (1967) *The Collectors*, trans. M. Callum, Rutland Vt. and Tokyo: C.E. Tuttle.

Kant, I. (1914) *Critique of Judgment* (2nd edn) trans. J. H. Bernard, London: Macmillan.

Kaylan, M. (April 1988) 'The Warhol collection: why selling it is a shame', *Connoisseur*, 118–28.

Keene, D. (1981) *Appreciations of Japanese Culture*, Tokyo and New York: Kodansha.

Kirshenblatt-Gimblett, B. (1982) 'In search of the paradigmatic: ethnic symbol building among elderly immigrants', paper presented at the International Symposium on Ethnic Symbol Building, Hungarian Academy of Sciences and American Council of Learned Societies, Budapest.

—— (1987) 'Authoring lives', paper presented at a conference on Life History as Cultural Construction/Performance, Budapest.

Kreitler, H. and Kreitler, S. (1972) *Psychology of the Arts*, Durham, N.C.: Duke University Press.

Kundera, M. (1984) *The Unbearable Lightness of Being*, London: Faber & Faber.

Le Vane, E. and Getty, J. P. (1955) *Collector's Choice: The Chronicle of an Artistic Odyssey through Europe*, London: W. H. Allen.

Lippard, L. R. (1985) *Pop Art*, London: Thames & Hudson.

Lumley. R. (ed.) (1988) *The Museum Time Machine: Putting Cultures on Display*, London: Routledge.

McGuigan, C. (April 1988) 'The selling of Andy Warhol', *Newsweek*, 61–4.

MacLeod, D. S. (1987) 'Art collecting and Victorian middle-class taste', *Art History* 10: 328–49.

Malraux, A. (1967) *Museum without Walls*, New York: Doubleday (French edition, 1947).

Maquet, J. (1986) *The Aesthetic Experience: An Anthropologist Looks at the Visual Arts*, New Haven: Yale University Press.

Moody, H. R. (1985) 'The collector', *Human Values and Aging Newsletter* 8: 1–2.

Moulin, R. (1984) *The French Art Market: A Sociological Analysis*, New Brunswick, N.J.: Rutgers University Press.

Nabokov, V. (1969) *Speak, Memory*, Harmondsworth: Penguin.

Newson, J. and Newson, E. (1976) *Seven Years Old in the Home Environment*, New York: Wiley.

Norris, F. (1956) *The Pit: A Story of Chicago*, New York. Grove (Original work published 1903)

Olmsted, A. D. (1987a) 'Stamp collectors and stamp collecting', paper presented at the Popular Culture Association Annual Meeting, Antiques and Collecting Section, Montreal.

—— (1987b) 'Collecting popular culture: identity and interaction in the mass society', unpublished manuscript.

Osborne, H. (1970) *The Art of Appreciation*, London: Oxford University Press.

Peckham, M. (1967) *Man's Rage for Chaos: Biology, Behavior and the Arts*, New York: Schocken.

Pollack, B. (1962) *The Collectors: Dr. Claribel and Miss Etta Cone*, Indianapolis: Bobbs-Merrill.

Price, V. (1959) *I Like What I Know: A Visual Autobiography*, Garden City, N.Y.: Doubleday.

Radcliff, A. (1972) *Adventures of a Vintage Car Collector*, New York: Bonanza.

Rheims, M. (1961) *The Strange Life of Objects*, New York: Atheneum.

—— (1967) *Art on the Market: Thirty-five Centuries of Collecting and Collectors, from Midas to J. Paul Getty*, trans. D. Pryce-Jones, London: Weidenfeld & Nicholson

—— (1980) *The Glorious Obsession*, trans. P. Evans, London: Souvenir.

Rickards, M. (1978) *This is Ephemera: Collecting Printed Throwaways*, London: David & Charles.

Rigby, D. and Rigby, E. (1944) *Lock, Stock and Barrel: The Story of Collecting*, Philadelphia: Lippincott.

Robinson, R. E. (1987) 'Why this piece? On the choices of collectors in the fine arts', paper presented at the 82nd Annual Meeting, American Sociological Association, Chicago.

Rochberg-Halton, E. (1986) *Meaning and Modernity: Social Theory in the Pragmatic Attitude*, Chicago: University of Chicago Press.

Ronnen, M. (3 April 1987) 'Merciless eye', *Jerusalem Post Magazine* 12–13.

Saarinen, A. B. (1958) *The Proud Possessors: The Lives, Times and Tastes of Some Adventurous American Art Collectors*, New York: Random House.

Saisselin, R. G. (1985) *Bricobracomania: The Bourgeois and the Bibelot*, London: Thames & Hudson.

Spooner, B. (1988) 'Weavers and dealers: the authenticity of an Oriental carpet', in A. Appadurai (ed.) *The Social Life of Things*, Cambridge: Cambridge University Press, 195–235.

Stewart, S. (1984) *On Longing: Narratives of the Miniature, the Gigantic, the Souvenir, the Collection*, Baltimore and London: Johns Hopkins University Press.

Stocking, G. (ed.) (1985) *Objects and Others: Essays on Museums and Material Culture* vol. 3, *History of Anthropology*, Madison: University of Wisconsin Press.

Stolnitz, J. (1960) *Aesthetics and the Philosophy of Art Criticism*, Boston: Houghton-Mifflin.

Sutton-Smith, B. and Rosenberg, B. G. (eds) (1971) 'Sixty years of historical change in the game preferences of American children', in R. E. Herron and B. Sutton-Smith (eds) *Child's Play*, New York: Wiley, 18–50.

Taylor, F. H. (1948) *The Taste of Angels: A History of Art Collecting from Ramses to Napoleon*, Boston: Little, Brown.

Templeton, A. (1958) *Alec Templeton's Music Boxes*, as told to Rachael Bail Baumel, New York: Funk.

Tharp, L. H. (1965) *Mrs. Jack: A Biography of Isabella Stewart Gardner*, Boston: Little, Brown.

Thompson, M. (1979) *Rubbish Theory*, Oxford: Oxford University Press.

Tuan, Y. (1984) *Dominance and Affection*, New Haven: Yale University Press.

Wallendorf, M. (1988) 'Addiction in collecting', paper presented at the Annual Meeting, Popular Culture Association, New Orleans.

Whitley, M. T. (1929) 'Children's interest in collecting', *Journal of Educational Psychology* 20: 249–61.

Williams, T. (1984) *The Glass Menagerie*, Harmondsworth: Penguin. (Original work published 1945)

Witty, P. A. and Lehman, H. C. (1930) 'Further studies of children's interest in collecting', *Journal of Educational Psychology* 21: 112–27.

29

Of mice and men: gender identity in collecting

Russell W. Belk and Melanie Wallendorf

This study examines the relationship between gender and collecting, based on approximately 200 interviews conducted with collectors over the past four years. It focuses on the objects they collect, the way these objects are collected, and the role these objects play in the collector's life and identity. Belk and Wallendorf present findings related to gender regarding each of these issues by using four detailed case-studies as well as brief descriptions of several others. Gender is one of the most important ways in which individuals construct their personal identities, and the collecting process has a significant relationship to this activity.

IS COLLECTING A GENDERED ACTIVITY?

The general thesis we wish to explore is that gender is expressed, shaped and marked through the process of collecting. We define collecting as the activity of selectively acquiring an interrelated set of objects, ideas or experiences.[1] Furthermore, in assembling these objects, ideas or experiences into a collection, the collector grants them non-utilitarian sacred status. Sacredness, in a Durkheimian or Eliadian sense, implies, in part, that the object is taken out of use.[2] Thus, stamps or coins in a collection are not regarded as appropriate for mailing a letter or making purchases. The objects in a collection are instead deemed sufficiently significant that they are removed from the ordinary and treated as extraordinary.

As with religious zealotry,[3] we also find that collecting often involves obsessive and compulsive behaviours on the part of collectors. Even if it is not the result of a compulsion, a collection is closely linked to the collector's identity; someone cannot excuse a collection by saying, 'Well, I just happened to pick that up somewhere', or 'someone gave that to me'. Because a collection results from purposeful acquisition and retention, it announces identity traits with far greater clarity and certainty than the many other objects owned. Collections are especially instrumental to identity among avid collectors.

Some of the identity work that goes on through collections involves striving for personal completion and perfection. Completing the collection, in a sense, completes the individual; the person who has a whole collection feels more like a whole person. Similarly, a representative collection confers on the collector a sense of being well-rounded. In striving for perfection in a collection, the collector also strives for an ideal self. Generally collectors try to upgrade their collections, based on a philosophy that only the best will do. If someone can bequeath a collection and if it remains intact and is identified with the collector, that collector is immortalized.

Collectors also seek acclaim through the achievement of building their collections. A collector of elephant replicas was interviewed after he opened an elephant museum to enshrine his collection. He offered the rather implausible hope that 'History will stand in awe of what I have done.' Assembling the elephants is his (hypothesized) means of achieving immortality and acclaim. Having ennobled the elephant replicas by gathering them in a collection, he has sought to legitimize the collection by establishing it as a museum. He hopes that society will appreciate his benevolence and foresight in collecting and assembling these objects.

Thus, collecting is a means of achieving and expressing identity. Gender is implicated in this process in several ways, three of which we discuss here. Gender is linked to collecting through the gendered meaning of essential collecting activities, the gender associations of the objects collected, and the gendered uses of collections.

The most basic question we address is whether the process of collecting is inherently a male or female activity. There is a small, but provocative, historic literature addressing this issue. In their important seminal book on collecting, Douglas and Elizabeth Rigby suggested in 1944 that:

> grand scale collecting almost always calls for aggressive and material ambition to a degree uncharacteristic of women, aside from women's historic economic position. Those who came within hailing distance of collecting giants were women who seemed to exhibit the masculine strain of a highly developed competitiveness, although this in no way detracts from the position of women as amateurs.[4]

In a somewhat related vein, Rémy Saisselin offers reasons why historically even a woman of means might not have been perceived as a 'serious' collector:

> By 1880 in France, women were perceived as mere buyers of bibelots, which they bought as they did clothing, in their daily bargain hunting. Men, of course, collected too, but their collecting was perceived as serious and creative. Women were consumers of objects; men were collectors. Women bought to decorate and for the sheer joy of buying, but men had a vision for their collections, and viewed their collections as an ensemble with a philosophy behind it.[5]

Since women are still seen in the primary role of consumers,[6] it is worth while considering what threat women collectors pose to society and to men in particular. In addition to offering the same competition that men now face from women in the workplace, collecting may pose an additional threat because it serves as a metaphor and metonym for capital accumulation. The fear of woman as collector rather than consumer may well be because she symbolizes a threat to male control of capital and power in society.

A related opinion is offered by Brenda Danet and Tamara Katriel. Before gathering data on collecting, they speculated that:

> traditionally sexist social structures force men to go out into the world and act upon it in order to make a living, while women take the more passive role of cultivating the home and family. Since collecting is a proactive form of behavior which develops a sense of mastery, it is very likely that males will, therefore, be more involved in it than females.[7]

Their subsequent research in Israel found that among adults this tends to be true, while among children, girls are somewhat *more* likely than boys to collect. Since historical data also suggest that girls are no less likely to be collectors than boys,[8] greater age-related female attrition among collectors may result from gender-role socialization.

Based on this small amount of literature, it appears that stereotypically masculine personality traits congenial to collecting include aggressiveness, competitiveness, mastery and seriousness. On the other hand, a set of collecting-congenial personality traits stereotypically regarded as feminine in western culture includes care, creativity, nurturance and preservation. So rather than being decidedly characteristic of one gender or the other, collecting activity benefits from both sets of traits in collectors. Traits defined as masculine seem especially useful in acquiring objects for a collection, while traits defined as feminine are important in curating and maintaining the resulting collection. Thus even within stereotypical gender-role definitions, it does not appear that the activity of collecting can be regarded as inherently masculine or feminine. Instead, collecting has certain aspects that have historically been regarded as masculine and others historically regarded as feminine in our culture.

ARE THE OBJECTS COLLECTED GENDERED?

We now consider whether objects collected tend to possess either masculine or feminine meanings. In this regard, it is interesting to note that Sigmund Freud's collection of 3,000–4,000 Roman, Egyptian, Greek and Chinese antiquities contains explicitly gendered objects that relate to Freud's work on sexual symbolism. A major category in his extensive collection is phallic amulets and other phallic objects. Although it may be true that 'Sometimes a statue is just a statue',[9] it is clear that the choice of these particular objects was not a mere coincidence. Similarly, regardless of whether guns and rifles are viewed as phallic symbols of power,[10] it is clear that gun collectors are almost uniformly male.[11]

Although not all objects are strongly gender-typed,[12] sometimes the gender of products is constructed in the design and manufacturing process, as when motor-scooters were crafted, created, advertised and sold in England as a feminine alternative to the masculine motorcycle.[13] In other cases, the engineered gender of objects is more subtly conveyed, as with brushes and pocket-knives that are distinctively designed for males or females and stereotypically convey certain gender role characteristics.[14] Thus, wristwatches intended for women or children are typically more delicate and ornamented, but less angular than those intended for men.

It should come as no surprise that such differences are also reflected in the objects that males and females choose to collect. Historical studies of the collections of American children reflect such biases. In 1931, Witty found that girls were more likely to collect decorative objects (e.g., flowers, pictures, monograms), jewellery, personal referent objects (e.g., souvenirs, autographs, valentines), dolls and doll items, household items, school objects and games. Boys were more likely to collect animal and insect parts, saleable junk, tobacco souvenirs, objects of war, hunting or fishing, game objects (e.g., marbles, tops, kites), and miscellaneous repair and maintenance objects (e.g., nails, oilcans, padlocks).[15] At approximately the same time, Durost found girls more likely to collect jewellery, beads, cloth and dance favours, while boys were more likely to collect auto licence tags, cigar tags, and birds' eggs and nests.[16] And in the same time period, Whitely found that boys were almost exclusively the collectors of tyres, radio parts, screws, tools, lumber and things having to do with hunting, fighting and war, while girls were almost exclusively the collectors of dolls and doll accessories.[17]

Among adults, a recent article in a collecting magazine suggests that:

> Traditionally male's [*sic*] have collected clocks, stamps, coins, guns, knives and
> other similar items associated with childhood, sports, or a profession. [Among

those who collected other items] Many kept their 'treasures' hidden in closets, under beds, or relegated to the basement or attic feeling uneasy that their adult friends might view them as foolish, extravagant, childish or even effeminate.[18]

In antiques collecting, one source recommends that appropriate objects for men to collect include guns, pocket-knives, artillery shells, snuffboxes, railroadiana, souvenirs of early flyers, lead soldiers, advertising trays, antique musical instruments, and chessmen.[19] Whereas antiques collecting was once almost exclusively a male avocation or vocation, during the Victorian era men turned to overstuffed Victorian furniture, leaving 'spindly' antiques to women.[20] While Hertz suggests a similar list of antiques that are sufficiently masculine for contemporary male collectors, he also suggests the rules that,

> decorative articles or those whose primary use is decorative are essentially feminine antiques; operating and functional articles are for the most part inherently masculine antiques . . . women are more inclined to the fragile rather than the substantial . . . while men lean toward more substantial materials such as iron and tin . . . women usually collect with decorative values or a definite decorative purpose in mind; men, for study from a technical or historical standpoint.[21]

Clearly such rules are not universally enacted. The Winterthur Museum houses the decorative arts collection of Henry Francis du Pont. However, the perspectives exemplified in both this museum and Hertz's guidelines echo Saisselin's observations about French attitudes a century ago: men's collections are taken seriously while women's purchases are regarded as frivolous consumption.[22]

While the sample of 192 collectors we have interviewed were not selected to be statistically representative of the population of collectors, some of the differences between the incidence of males and females in particular areas of collecting are strikingly clear. The categories in which there are more women than men collectors include animal replicas, housewares (dishes, silverware, utensils) and jewellery. In contrast, more men collect antiques, books, automobiles, sports-related objects, and tattoos. In order to account more deeply for these differences, it is useful to consider the contrasts evident in case studies of two collections: the Mouse Cottage and the Fire Museum.

The Mouse Cottage

Both the Mouse Cottage and the Fire Museum are collections institutionalized as museums by a wealthy retired businessman. The Fire Museum houses his own collection of fire trucks and fire-fighting equipment. He established the Mouse Cottage across town as a posthumous memorial to his former wife. It houses her collection of mouse replicas. The brochure from the Mouse Cottage invites the visitor to:

> Enter the Mouse Cottage and you'll squeak with delight! Once upon a time, in the early 1920's, there was a little girl so clever and charming in character and petite in stature that her mother quite naturally called her 'mouse.' The childhood name inspired the little girl's imagination with a life long passion for collecting mice of every description.

The mice replicas are displayed in and on pseudo-antique golden oak household furniture in a home-like setting inside a high-rent industrial warehouse near an upscale, suburban shopping district. The display is cluttered, casually arrayed, and almost chaotic. It includes mice ornaments hung on a Christmas tree with the packages beneath wrapped in mouse motif paper. A miniature Christmas tree is also displayed in the home-like family setting of a mouse dollhouse. This decor and holiday emphasis reflect the feminine character of the collection. Christmas is 'women's work', and is a family-focused activity in which men act primarily as recipients of food, gifts and affection.[23] This theme of subservience is echoed in the mice's diminutive and miniaturized nature – traits which reflect the powerlessness associated with women and children.[24] The museum also contains cribs and a number of motifs featuring Mickey Mouse, a character with an interesting gender history.

When Mickey Mouse was first introduced by Walt Disney, he had a deep voice and was rather rat-like in appearance – a strong male representation. However, in order to reach the popular imagination, Mickey Mouse was neutered.[25] His voice became higher pitched, he became clumsy around female mice, and his appearance was made puffier and more baby-like or androgynous. Mickey's sacrifice was thus to become a eunuch in order to achieve popular success. Consistent with the brochure for the Mouse Cottage, the childlike and powerless character of Mickey Mouse succeeds in his comic adventures with the wish-fulfilling guile and cleverness of a child contesting against menacing adults.

Thus in both its decor and contents, the Mouse Cottage represents that which is diminutive, homey and informal. It contrasts sharply with the Fire Museum.

The Fire Museum

The collection of Mouse's husband is housed in another museum in a larger industrial warehouse located in the same town. The Fire Museum brochure invites the visitor to:

> See the world's largest exhibit of fire-fighting equipment. Over 100 fully restored pieces dating from circa 1725 to 1950. . . . Learn about the history of the American firefighter – America's most dangerous profession – from Ben Franklin's Philadelphia volunteers to the modern era.

The exhibit is considerably more spacious than the Mouse Cottage. The fire trucks and other pieces of fire equipment are restored to perfection, and are individually presented in spacious roped-off areas that impart importance and honour to these objects. Carefully displayed exhibits of fire hats and other fire-fighting regalia line museum walls. Historic photos, along with dates and plaques, help to give the impression that this is a historical museum. Whereas the Mouse Cottage charges no admission and has no guidebook, both are found at the Fire Museum. The Mouse Cottage brochure positions that museum as a tribute to childhood, while the Fire Museum is organized as a place for an adult educational experience.

The seriousness of apparent purpose is not to deny that the Fire Museum caters to boyhood fantasies.[26] This theme of collecting representations of boyhood dreams featuring rugged adventure is borne out in two of this man's other collections. Displayed in separate rooms of the Mouse Cottage warehouse are his collections of western art, depicting cowboys and Native Americans, and animal trophies from an African hunting safari that the family took in the 1920s. As with the Fire Museum collection, it is difficult to imagine clearer contrasts to the Mouse Museum, even though both of these collectors seem to have been pursuing childhood fantasies of ideal self-images.

Mouse Cottage versus Fire Museum

In contrasting the Mouse Cottage to the Fire Museum, a number of distinctions emerge that we believe are prototypical of gender differences in materials collected. Mouse Cottage displays mice that, although small in nature, are often further miniaturized in

Table 29.1 Mouse Cottage is to Fire Museum as . . .

X is	*To Y*
Tiny	Gigantic
Weak	Strong
Chaos	Order
Home	World
Nature	Machine
Art	Science
Playful	Serious
Inconspicuous	Conspicuous

replicas; Fire Museum displays gigantic fire-engines. Mice are weak; men empowered by fire-engines are strong. Mice are chaotically displayed; fire-engines are in orderly rows. Mice are shown within the nurturing environment of home, whereas the fire-engines represent the ability to conquer the external world. Mice are a part of nature, whereas fire-engines are machines used to control nature. The mice replicas are a form of art, while fire-fighting is a mix of technology and science. The mice are playful and decorative, while fire-engines are serious and functional. Mice are inconspicuous, while fire-engines are intentionally conspicuous.

Although not entirely flattering to either gender, these traits parallel stereotypical gender role images. The woman is portrayed by her mouse collection to be small, weak, home-focused, natural, artistic, playful and inconspicuous. Her husband's collections suggest that he is large, strong, proactive, machine-like, scientific, serious and conspicuous. In Laing's terms, 'They are playing a game. They are playing at not playing a game.'[27] In this case, he is playing masculine; she is playing feminine.

ARE THE USES OF COLLECTIONS GENDERED?

In addition to looking at the collection, we can look more processually at the individual's use of the collection and ask how this use reflects or constructs gender identity. We examine two further case-studies to consider ways collectors use a plastic form to work through fantasies and construct a sense of self.

A collection allows the collector to play with multiple images of the self and multiple images of others. The first case-study is based on the Barbie Museum assembled by a woman named Flo. Flo began collecting Barbies eleven years ago, but had collected other dolls prior to that. Four years ago, she underwent a radical mastectomy that interrupted her collecting activity. She had reconstructive as well as extensive corrective surgeries due to complications from the mastectomy. Flo resumed her collecting activity two years later, after recovering from the last of these surgeries. She has two daughters: one collects dolls and the other collects art deco items and antiques. Flo buys dolls for her daughters and granddaughters, but is dismayed that they do not care for the dolls the way she thinks they should. She is appalled that her granddaughters actually play with them.

Flo uses her collecting activities to enact the feminine quality of generosity. Through the museum, she reportedly sells Barbie dolls and related items at reasonable prices to others seeking to complete their collections. If someone is missing a maroon shoe to go with a particular Barbie outfit, Flo says she will sell the collector that shoe at a very low price. When she attends Barbie conventions, Flo follows a convention custom of giving gifts to the other collectors seated at her dinner-table. She says that her gifts are very generous and widely sought. But she is alarmed to hear people say, 'Next year I want to sit at your table.' She is dismayed that her generosity breeds such greed and selfishness. She also reflected her generosity in saying that she views her collecting as a mothering activity, since mothers are supposed to keep things for their daughters.

The second way Flo uses her collection to reflect gender derives from her pride in its completeness. As a result of another collector's gift of a Pan Am stewardess outfit for Barbie, Flo now possesses a complete collection of the outfits manufactured by Mattel for Barbie, as well as at least one of each Barbie model ever produced. Her use of the collection to demonstrate completeness resonates deeply when contrasted with her difficulties following the removal of her breasts.[28] Through owning a full set of authentic Barbies, she is able to restore a sense of completeness. Not only does Barbie possess the kind of figure Flo no longer has, but collecting allows Flo to possess a complete set of these voluptuous dolls.

A second case-study illuminating the gendered use of collections is that of Brent and Barbie's house. This is a very vivid collection and we can learn a great deal about Brent through the Barbie dolls he collects. Although Brent collects the same objects as Flo, they serve a very different gendered purpose in his life. Because Brent's character is quite distinctive, it is easier to trace the process of identity expression through his collection than it sometimes is with more commonplace collections such as baseball cards. Although not all collecting activity is as vividly expressive as Brent's, we find other collections are put to gendered uses as well. While Brent's particular situation is idiosyncratic, it allows us to more clearly see how collections are used to construct meaningful understandings of the complexities of gender.

We can examine collections not just statically in terms of the objects contained in the collection, but also dynamically in terms of the collector's interaction with these objects. One day when one of the authors went to Brent's home to talk with him, she noticed a pile of Barbie clothes that he had just purchased lying on a table. This was the evening after his mother's funeral. Despite the author's concern about doing fieldwork at such a time, Brent said he would really like to talk to her. He said that he bought the Barbie clothes on his way home from the funeral because he felt depressed. Buying clothing for Barbie was his way of making himself feel better.

Collection use may not be limited to expressing the dichotomy of male and female biological sex or the socially prescribed masculine and feminine gender roles pertaining to a culture and time period. In a psychological sense enacted gender can be seen as more of a continuum than a dichotomy. By examining the uses of collections, we can explicate the multiple images that attach to femininity and masculinity. Brent's use of his collection is instrumental here. In his case the Barbies are used to mediate three types of gendered images: real-life images, worldly images, and otherworldly images. Real-life images are those that exist or previously existed in his everyday life. Brent's real-world images come from his life as a child, his former life as an exotic dancer and male prostitute, and his current life as a gay male employed as a hairdresser. Worldly images are expressed directly in the objects in the collection. Otherworldly images are the mythic characters evoked by the collection. In this tripartition, the worldly images of the collection are used to mediate images from everyday life with those that exist in a mythic realm. Thus, a collection can tangibilize the individuation process of constructing an identity through personal myth.[29] That is, a collection can be used at times to represent and reconstruct real life, as well as to fill in what is missing from real life with worldly images linked to mythic images.

We will first examine the feminine images represented in the collections of our case-studies, dividing these feminine images into good and evil, and then into a number of different types of image within each of these categories.

In Brent's collection of Barbie dolls as well as in Mouse's collection of mouse replicas, there are several kinds of feminine representations of good. One of these feminine images of good is the virgin bride. Mouse's collection contains a number of bride figures, including a celluloid of Minnie Mouse as Juliet. In addition, the room adjoining the Mouse Cottage displays family photos, including one of Mouse herself as a bride. Thus, parallels exist between the worldly images in the collection and real life of Mouse. The worldly image of the virgin bride also corresponds to an otherworldly image of woman as angel. This otherworldly image of a diminutive angel personifies goodness. The mice in Mouse's collection are often angelic little figures – like good little girls. This museum also contains a photograph of the woman, Mouse, as a little girl with a big bow in her hair. Again, worldly images in the collection seem to echo the real-life self-image of the collector.

In the house Brent built for Barbie, evidence that Barbie has put away the innocence of a little girl appears in the bedroom, where 'little girl' toys are relegated to the top of a wardrobe. Woman as good little girl is not the feminine image that Brent enacts through his collection of Barbie dolls.

The figure of loving mother is missing in Brent's collection. Not coincidentally, it is also missing in Brent's real-life experience. As a boy, Brent did not experience woman as the loving mother that would be represented in an otherworldly image of a Madonna. Flo's comments about Barbie suggest that the doll was not manufactured to represent the good mother image. She said that Barbie is not a 'baby-person', noting that Mattel had never produced maternity clothing or a baby for Barbie. Her euphemism was, 'Barbie is more a woman of leisure.'

In place of images of woman as loving mother, Brent's collection contains several surrogate mother images. One of these is a blonde doll dressed in blue, whom he named Carol. In real life, Carol was a babysitter Brent fondly recalls from his childhood. He refers to this doll as 'the wholesome one'. This adjective is particularly striking and distinguishes this doll from a number of his other dolls. In a poignant moment during

Table 29.2 Feminine images and characters

	Otherworldly	*Worldly*	*Real life*
Good	Angel	Virgin bride	
		Little girl	Self ('Mouse')
	Madonna	Mother	
	Fairy Godmother	Babysitter	Babysitter
Evil	Witch	Whore	Prostitute
		Temptress	Mother
		Maid	
		Voyeur	
		Ice Queen	Mother

the fieldwork, Brent displayed another doll representing a mythic replacement for the good mother. After arranging all of his male dolls for photographs, Brent perched another doll dressed as a fairy (male as godmother) reigning over the others. Expressing some of the gender identity issues Brent deals with both in real life and through his collection, Brent's fairy godmother image is his Gay Bob doll wearing a pink fairy costume. This display is meaningful to Brent; it also has meaning for our understanding of the uses of worldly images in a collection. Rather than always representing a direct correspondence between the collector's real life and the worldly images of the collection, rather than reflecting the real life of the collector in microcosm, collections also offer the collector an opportunity to construct a fully controllable world of objects in which mythic images and reconstructed reality can be manipulated. The controllable world of the collection is one in which fantastic gender images can be played with in a constructive and bounded way.

Feminine embodiments of evil are also often evident in collections. These images, together with the multiple images of good discussed, support the contention that masculine and feminine are categories of meaning that are more psychologically complex than a simple dichotomy. Masculine and feminine are complex categories of meaning, each represented by multiple images of both good and evil. Unlike sex, enacted gender is not readily dichotomized.

One feminine image of evil is that of woman as whore, linked to an otherworldly image of woman as witch. In his collection Brent has an oversize Barbie doll that he has painted with extremely heavy eye makeup. He described this doll disparagingly as 'a whore'. She had been placed next to a Miss Piggy doll – a deliberate connection between whore and swine.

The simultaneous anger and fascination with feminine images of evil expressed by Brent through this and other dolls is based in his real-life experience. He worked as a male prostitute and an exotic dancer for a short time to support himself while he attended beauty school. His verbal descriptions of these experiences are replete with scornful references to the women he served and entertained. During that time, the only help he received from his mother was a $25 cheque that he said she gave him so she could tell her friends she was helping put him through school. He very much resented this claim of assistance at a time when he needed so much more, and therefore he never cashed the cheque.

Brent expressed a similarly scornful attitude towards dolls representing the feminine evil image of the temptress. He dressed one Barbie in a silver lamé evening gown worn backwards to show more cleavage. Oddly, given his action in dressing her, he then verbally disparaged the doll's supposed desire to show off her breasts. This temptress image, too, is linked to Brent's recollection of his mother. After his parents divorced, Brent said his mother would bring other men to the house and he would hear her with them in the other room. Not only did he refer to some of his Barbie dolls as tramps, but just after his mother's funeral he also referred to her as a tramp.

Brent's anger at what he considered evil in other people was also periodically expressed through the subjugation of Barbie dolls in the collection. At one point during the fieldwork, particularly racist anger was directed towards his black Barbie dolls. He 'took-away their nice dresses', put them in maids' costumes and 'made them get down on the floor [of the Barbie house] and scrub it'. This punishment was prompted by his anger towards a black man in his real life.

Another feminine image of evil represented in Brent's collection is woman as voyeur. Like Brent's mother and those who hired him as an exotic dancer or male prostitute, the female voyeur is distanced and uses men for her own pleasure, without caring about them. There was a set of binoculars at the foot of one of Barbie's beds; Brent said that she used the binoculars to watch men and then pleasure herself. His description of this activity expressed simultaneous fascination and anger.

The most vivid feminine image of evil in Brent's collection is that of Ice Queen – a woman who is beautiful, coldly brittle and absolutely rejecting of males. The ice queen in the collection is Brent's 'number one Barbie', the first model Mattel sold. It is the most valuable doll in Brent's collection. When this one enters the room, Brent says that she makes the other dolls bow down. Thus, like Brent himself, the other dolls reportedly hate and fear the number one Barbie. Brent says he cannot keep the number one and the other dolls in the same room for fear of what would happen if they began fighting. Number one Barbie, says Brent, is vain and concerned only with her own appearance. Brent displays her in a red coffin-like box that he prepared for her. Much of Brent's description of this Barbie doll would also fit his real-life experience of his mother when he was a child. His simultaneous fascination with and contempt for women's vanity is perhaps especially understandable since he is a hairdresser.

Thus, a number of feminine images are included in collections and are used in the ongoing process of constructing personal gender identity and gender meanings. Similar identity work occurs through the use of masculine images. The Ken dolls in Brent's collection incorporate several masculine images of good. The worldly image of a businessman in a grey suit is similar to an otherworldly image of a king – a man who is wealthy, benevolent and powerful. The worldly image of a sailor or rugged outdoorsman corresponds to the otherworldly image of hero.[30] It is especially significant that all of these masculine images of good were absent in Brent's real life. Through his collection he finds a way to participate in their meaning.

Also in Brent's collection is a worldly image of a cowboy – an image also present in the western art collection of the man who founded the Fire Museum. The cowboy represents a hero who can round up other beings and corral them for his purposes. Brent's collection of masculine images of good also includes an athlete and a prep or college boy. These wholesome images are heroic masculine counterparts to the wholesome babysitter/surrogate-mother described earlier.

In other collections, different worldly, masculine representations of good are included. For example, man-as-rescuer in the worldly form of a fireman is celebrated at the Fire Museum. This worldly image can be linked to the otherworldly image of masculine saviour. In the Fire Museum, the tools and machines which transform man into a saviour

Table 29.3 Masculine images and characters

	Otherworldly	*Worldly*	*Real life*
Good	King	Businessman	
	Hero	Soldier, Sailor	
		Athlete	
		Cowboy	
	Saviour	Rescuer, Fireman	
		Boy	Self (Brent)
Evil	Devil	Nazi soldier	Father
	Snake	Wild beasts	
		Slave, Servant	

are enshrined. The same image of fireman is included by Mouse in the Mouse Museum, humorously diminished in size and reduced to the status of a mouse fireman holding an axe atop a doll house. This is a feminized version of the heroism enshrined in the Fire Museum. It is hardly believable that this little mouse could chop through the roof and save someone. In gender terms, the feminine qualities of the mouse make its attempts to undertake the masculine job of rescuing others and controlling nature laughable. In the comedy we find in this little mouse, we experience pleasurable release through the expression of an unconscious form of sexism.[31]

The final masculine image of good we will discuss is the little boy. Brent claimed that one boy doll in his collection represents him as a little boy. Brent displayed it in a box beside several other dolls. Brent got the adult male doll in the box when he was a little boy. It represents the good soldier father – not at all like Brent's real father. In Brent's display, this doll's arm had been pulled out of its rigid socket to permit the doll to put his arm proudly around the boy. In the same box is an image of a black evil mother and a sister, although in real life Brent's two siblings were brothers. In this one box, Brent includes good and evil images, masculine and feminine images, and worldly and otherworldly images with real-world referents.

Masculine images of evil are also included in collections. Brent's Nazi soldier doll represents an otherworldly image of the devil, as well as the real-world image of his father. Before his parents were divorced, Brent recalls that his father would destroy his toys by throwing them across the room, especially when he came home and found Brent playing with dolls. Brent's current interests in doll preservation and restoration are clearly linked to these experiences.

Another masculine image of evil is reflected in the collection of hunting trophies displayed by the man who started the Fire Museum. Here the collector is able to control the wild beasts that represent a masculine image of evil nature. Like the collection of fire-fighting tools displayed in the Fire Museum, this collection celebrates masculine domination over nature. The worldly images of these wild animal trophies correspond to an otherworldly image of the evil serpent. They are tamed through the collection – conquered, captured and hung on the wall. Similarly, after having an orangutan for a pet, this man symbolized his dominance over nature by having the orangutan stuffed and included in the collection when it died.

In Brent's collection, there are also masculine images of evil subjugated. At the time when Brent was dealing with the racially directed anger in his real life, besides making his black Barbies scrub the floor, he also subjugated a black male doll by casting him in the role of Barbie's servant/bartender. In this way, Brent took steps to control man's evil nature – his fear of the potential for evil within himself.

The feminine and masculine worldly images contained in a collection can be used to connect otherworldly meanings to real-world experiences. They do so by direct representation as well as by filling in what is otherwise missing in the person's life. Through these meanings, collections are used to mediate real world experience with otherworldly images in a way that attempts to reconstruct and resolve personal issues concerning gender.

ARE THE SOCIETAL FUNCTIONS OF COLLECTIONS GENDERED?

The final question we will address is the larger question of whether the societal functions served by collections are gendered. In answering this question, we will consider both the manifest and latent functions of collecting activity.[32]

From a societal perspective, collections represent and enact the achievement orientation of the collector. However, like other aspects of life, collections can represent two different kinds of achievement – two worlds of achievement in Carol Gilligan's terms.[33] That is, achievement may represent different ideas to men and women. Women's collections tend to represent achievement in the world of connection to other people – achievement of sentiment. A substantial number of the items in the Mouse Cottage were given to Mouse by other people who knew of her collection. The display of these gift items in the museum enshrines Mouse's connections to others. Also enshrined in that display is the belief that, through the museum, she brings happiness to others and makes it seem like Christmas all year long. The Christmas tree displayed year-round at the Mouse Cottage allows Mouse to fulfil the feminine achievement of delivering holiday happiness to a wider set of people than her own family.[34] The mouse collection also demonstrates her achievement in the world of interpersonal connection and senti-ment by illustrating her capacity to transform intruding pests into cute decorations, not unlike the way some mothers dress and otherwise treat their children.

The contrast of Mouse's collection to the collections of her husband shows how the masculine achievement world differs from the feminine. Here, the powerful achieve-ments of masculine control over nature are exemplified through killing wild beasts, conquering the west, and fighting fires. In such ways collections perform the societal function of gendering achievement worlds, while celebrating the societal importance of achievement.[35]

A second societal function served by collecting activity is pattern maintenance[36] within the economic sphere. Collecting activity serves to support economic activity through the purchase of objects that are not functionally necessary. Collected objects are regarded as desirable and valuable, even though they are removed from everyday use. Thus, collecting supports a consumer culture. It allows both genders to participate in the fem-inine world of consumption in a way that simultaneously supports the masculine world of production. Through the protectionism it engenders among collectors, collecting serves the societal function of pattern maintenance.

A third societal function of collecting is reification and integration of gender dialectics. Through collecting, culture is made visible.[37] Intrapersonally, collecting permits experi-mentation with androgyny as an individual participates in the masculine hunt for additions to the collection, as well as feminine nurturance in curating the collection. Interpersonally, collecting activity may bond couples, particularly those whose children have left home, in a gendered activity in which both can seek their specializations within the division of labour.[38]

CONCLUSIONS

Through the examination of these case-studies, we have explored several ways in which gendering is a component of collecting activity. In particular, gender is reflected in both the activities involved in collecting and the objects that are collected. Gender is con-structed through the uses to which collections are put, particularly in the mediation of real-life and otherworldly images. Even the societal functions of collecting solidify and maintain gender distinctions held by the culture. In these ways, collecting makes visible the gender distinctions governing social life.

This paper will appear in Kenneth L. Ames, Gender and Material Culture *(Winterthur, Delaware, forth-coming).*

NOTES

1 Russell W. Belk, Melanie Wallendorf, John Sherry, Morris Holbrook and Scott Roberts (1988) 'Collectors and collecting', in Michael Houston (ed.) *Advances in Consumer Research* vol. 15, Provo, Utah: Association for Consumer Research, 548–53; Russell W. Belk, Melanie Wallendorf, John Sherry and Morris Holbrook (forthcoming) 'Collecting in a consumer culture', in Russell W. Belk (ed.) *Highways and Buyways: Naturalistic Research from the Consumer Behavior Odyssey*, Provo Utah: Association for Consumer Research.

2 Russell W. Belk, Melanie Wallendorf, and John Sherry (1989) 'The sacred and the profane in consumer behavior: theodicy on the Odyssey', *Journal of Consumer Research* 16: 1–38.

3 Eric Hoffer (1951) *The True Believer*, New York: Harper & Row.

4 Douglas Rigby and Elizabeth Rigby (1944) *Lock, Stock, and Barrel: The Story of Collecting*, Philadelphia, Pa.: J. B. Lippincott, 326–27.

5 Rémy G. Saisselin (1984) *Bricobracomania: The Bourgeois and the Bibelot*, New Brunswick: Rutgers University Press, 68.

6 Diane Barthel (1988) *Putting on Appearances: Gender and Advertising*, Philadelphia, Pa.: Temple University Press; Mary Ann Doane (1987) *The Desire to Desire: The Woman's Film of the 1940s*, Bloomington, Ind.: Indiana University Press; Judith Goldstein (1987) 'Lifestyles of the rich and tyrannical', *American Scholar* 56: 235–47; Lynn Spigel and Denise Mann (1989) 'Women and consumer culture: a selective bibliography', *Quarterly Review of Film and Video* 11(1): 85–105.

7 Brenda Danet and Tamara Katriel (1986) 'Books, butterflies, Botticellis: a life-span perspective on collecting', paper presented at Sixth International Conference on Culture and Communication, Philadelphia, Pa., October 1986, p. 48.

8 Sara E. Wiltse (1891) 'Children's collections', *Pedagogical Seminary* 1: 2 34–7; Harvey C. Lehman and Paul A. Witty (1927) 'The present status of the tendency to collect and hoard', *Psychological Review* 34: 48–56; Paul A. Witty and Harvey C. Lehman (1933) 'The collecting interests of town children and country children', *Journal of Educational Psychology* 24: 170–84.

9 Peter Gay (1989) 'Introduction', in Lynn Gamwell and Richard Wells (eds) *Sigmund Freud and Art: His Personal Collection of Antiquities*, Binghamton, N.Y.: State University of New York, Binghamton, 15–19, at p. 19.

10 Don B. Kates, Jr and Nicole Varzos (1987) 'Aspects of a priapic theory of gun ownership', paper presented at 1987 Popular Culture Association Meeting, Montreal, Quebec, March 1987; Emanuel Tanay and Lucy Freeman (1976) *The Murderers*, Indianapolis, Ind.: Bobbs-Merrill, 25–43.

11 Al D. Olmsted (1990) 'Gun collecting in western Canada: the influence of popular culture and history', in William R. Tonso (ed.) *The Gun Culture and its Enemies*, Columbus, Ohio: Merrill; Barbara Stenross (1987) 'The meaning of guns: shooters, hunters, and collectors', paper presented at Popular Culture Association Meeting, Montreal, Quebec, March 1987.

12 Neil K. Allison, Linda L. Golden, Gary M. Mullett and Donna Coogan (1980) 'Sex-typed product images: the effects of sex, sex role self-concept and measurement implications', in Jerry C. Olson (ed.) *Advances in Consumer Research* vol. 7, Ann Arbor, Mich.: Association for Consumer Research, 604–9; Linda L. Golden, Neil Allison and Mona Clee (1979) 'The role of sex role and self-concept in masculine and feminine product perceptions', in William L. Wilkie (ed.) *Advances in Consumer Research* vol. 6, Ann Arbor, Mich.: Association for Consumer Research, 599–605.

13 Dick Hebdige (1988) *Hiding in the Light*, London: Routledge.

14 Adrian Forty (1986) *Objects of Desire: Design and Society from Wedgwood to IBM*, New York: Pantheon.

15 Paul A. Witty (1931) 'Sex differences: collecting interests', *Journal of Educational Psychology* 22: 221–8.

16 Walter N. Durost (1932) *Children's Collecting Activity Related to Social Factors*, New York: Teachers College, Columbia University Bureau of Publications.

17 M. T. Whitley (1929) 'Children's interest in collecting', *Journal of Educational Psychology* 20: 249–61.

18 Kenneth S. Hays (1989) 'The male collector', *Collectors' Showcase* 9: 62–5, at p. 62.

19 Albert C. Revi (1974) '*Spinning Wheel's Antiques for Men*, Hanover, Pa.: Spinning Wheel Books.

20 Louis H. Hertz (1969) *Antique Collecting for Men*, New York: Galahad Books.

21 Hertz, op. cit., 6, 8.

22 Saisselin, op. cit.

23 Theodore Caplow (1982) 'Christmas gifts and kin networks', *American Sociological Review* 47(3): 383–92; Theodore Caplow (1984) 'Rule enforcement without visible means: Christmas gift giving in Middletown', *American Journal of Sociology* 89(6): 1306–20; David Cheal (1987) '"Showing them you love them": gift giving and the dialectic of intimacy', *Sociological Review* 35(1): 150–69; David Cheal (1988) *The Gift Economy* London: Routledge.

24 Susan Stewart (1984) *On Longing: Narratives of the Miniature, the Gigantic, the Souvenir, the Collection*, Baltimore: Johns Hopkins University Press.
25 Fritz Mollenhoff (1939) 'Remarks on the popularity of Mickey Mouse', *American Imago* 1(3): 19–32; Stephen Jay Gould (1979) 'Mickey Mouse meets Konrad Lorenz', *Natural History* 88: 20–4.
26 Robert Lichty (1981) *Collecting and Restoring Antique Fire Engines*, Blue Ridge Summit, Pa.: Tab Books.
27 R. D. Laing (1970) *Knots*, New York: Vintage Books, 1.
28 Cf. Betty L. Feather, Susan B. Kaiser and Margaret Rucker 'Mastectomy and related treatments: impact of appearance satisfaction on self-esteem', *Home Economics Research Journal* 17: 127–39.
29 Carl Gustav Jung (1933) *Modern Man in Search of a Soul*, New York: Harcourt, Brace & World.
30 Joseph Campbell (1949) *The Hero with a Thousand Faces*, Princeton, N.J.: Princeton University Press.
31 Sigmund Freud (1960/1905) *Jokes and Their Relation to the Unconscious*, trans. James Strachey, New York: W. W. Norton.
32 Robert K. Merton (1957) *Social Theory and Social Structure* (revised and enlarged edn), Glencoe, Ill.: The Free Press.
33 Carol Gilligan (1982) *In a Different Voice: A Psychological Theory and Women's Development*, Cambridge. Mass: Harvard University Press.
34 Melanie Wallendorf and Eric Arnould (1990) '"We gather together": the consumption rituals of Thanksgiving Day', unpublished manuscript, Department of Marketing, University of Arizona; Caplow, 'Christmas gifts'; Caplow, 'Rule enforcement'; Cheal, 'Showing them'; Cheal, *Gift Economy*.
35 David McClelland (1961) *The Achieving Society*, Princeton: Van Nostrand.
36 Talcott Parsons (1951) *The Social System*, New York: The Free Press.
37 Grant McCracken (1988) *Culture and Consumption: New Approaches to the Symbolic Character of Goods and Activities*, Bloomington, Ind.: Indiana University Press.
38 Emile Durkheim (1933/1893) *The Division of Labor in Society*, trans. George Simpson, New York: The Free Press.

30

Objects of desire

Susan Stewart

Stewart's book offers a broad view of our relationship to objects, especially those which have been made deliberately gigantic or miniature, and those which are collected. Her book has been very influential and only a small sample of the style of Stewart's approach is given here. Her argument draws on the broad tradition of post-structuralist debate and relates to a discussion of the principles of organization which individuals use in the articulation of collections.

In contrast to the souvenir, the collection offers example rather than sample, metaphor rather than metonymy. The collection does not displace attention to the past; rather, the past is at the service of the collection, for whereas the souvenir lends authenticity to the past, the past lends authenticity to the collection. The collection seeks a form of self-enclosure which is possible because of its ahistoricism. The collection replaces history with *classification*, with order beyond the realm of temporality. In the collection, time is not something to be restored to an origin; rather, all time is made simultaneous or synchronous within the collection's world.

Like other forms of art, its function is not the restoration of context of origin but rather the creation of a new context, a context standing in a metaphorical, rather than a contiguous, relation to the world of everyday life. Yet unlike many forms of art, the collection is not representational. The collection presents a hermetic world: to have a representative collection is to have both the minimum and the complete number of elements necessary for an autonomous world – a world which is both full and singular, which has banished repetition and achieved authority.

Because the collection replaces origin with classification, thereby making temporality a spatial and material phenomenon, its existence is dependent upon principles of organization and categorization. Herein lies the difference between the collections of humans and the collections of pack rats. William James reported that a California wood rat arranges nails in a symmetrical, fortress-like pattern around his nest, but the objects 'collected' – silver, tobacco, watches, tools, knives, matches, pieces of glass – are without seriality, without relation to one another or to a context of acquisition. Such accumulation is obviously not connected to the culture and the economy in the same way that the collection proper is connected to such structures. Although the objects of a hobbyist's collection have significance only in relation to one another and to the seriality that such a relation implies, the objects collected by the wood rat are intrinsic objects, objects complete in themselves because of the sensory qualities that have made them attractive to the rat. James found the same propensity for collecting intrinsic objects among 'misers' in lunatic asylums:

'the miser' *par excellence* of the popular imagination and of melodrama, the monster of squalor and misanthropy, is simply one of these mentally deranged persons. His intellect may in many matters be clear, but his instincts, especially that of ownership, are insane, and their insanity has no more to do with the association of ideas than with the precession of the equinoxes.

(James 1950): 424)

Thus James concludes that hoarders have an uncontrollable impulse to take and keep. Here we might add that this form of insanity is, like anal retentiveness, an urge towards incorporation for its own sake, an attempt to erase the limits of the body that is at the same time an attempt, marked by desperation, to 'keep body and soul together'.

Although it is clear that there is a correspondence between the productions of art and the productions of insanity in these cases, it is equally clear that the miser's collection depends upon a refusal of differentiation while the hobbyist's collection depends upon an acceptance of differentiation as its very basis for existence. Thus the 'proper' collection will always take part in an anticipation of redemption: for example, the eventual coining-in of objects or the eventual acquisition of object status by coins themselves. But the insane collection is a collection for its own sake and for its own movement. It refuses the very *system* of objects and thus metonymically refuses the entire political economy that serves as the foundation for that system and the only domain within which the system acquires meaning. Baudrillard as well concludes that because of the collection's seriality, a 'formal' interest always replaces a 'real' interest in collected objects (Baudrillard 1968: 146). This replacement holds to the extent that aesthetic value replaces use value. But such an aesthetic value is so clearly tied to the cultural (i.e., deferment, redemption, exchange) that its value system is the value system of the cultural; the formalism of the collection is never an 'empty' formalism.

INSIDE AND OUTSIDE

To ask which principles of organization are used in articulating the collection is to begin to discern what the collection is about. It is not sufficient to say that the collection is organized according to time, space or internal qualities of the objects themselves, for each of these parameters is divided in a dialectic of inside and outside, public and private, meaning and exchange value. To arrange the objects according to time is to juxtapose personal time with social time, autobiography with history, and thus to create a fiction of the individual life, a time of the individual subject both transcendent to and parallel to historical time. Similarly, the spatial organization of the collection, left to right, front to back, behind and before, depends upon the creation of an individual perceiving and apprehending the collection with eye and hand. The collection's space must move between the public and the private, between display and hiding. Thus the miniature is suitable as an item of collection because it is sized for individual consumption at the same time that its surplus of detail connotes infinity and distance. While we can 'see' the entire collection, we cannot possibly 'see' each of its elements. We thereby also find at work here the play between identity and difference which characterizes the collection organized in accordance with qualities of the objects themselves. To group objects in a series because they are 'the same' is simultaneously to signify their difference. In the collection, the more the objects are similar, the more imperative it is that we make gestures to distinguish them.

Any intrinsic connection between the principle of organization and the elements themselves is minimized by the collection. We see little difference between collections of stones or butterflies and collections of coins or stamps. In acquiring objects, the collector replaces production with consumption: objects are naturalized into the landscape of the collection itself. Therefore, stones and butterflies are made cultural by classification, and coins and stamps are naturalized by the erasure of labour and the erasure of context of production. This impulse to remove objects from their contexts of origin and production and to replace those contexts with the context of the collection is quite evident in the practices of Floyd E. Nichols of New York City, a collector's collector. Rather than exhibit his many collected items according to type, Nichols would group objects together so that they told a story: 'For instance, with miniature cat, mice, whiskey glass, and whiskey bottle, he dramatizes the proverb, "One drink of moonshine whiskey would make a mouse spit in a cat's face",' and 'To miniature camels he attached a number 5 needle, the wire being shaped so that when it was pulled away from the needle, the camel mounted on the traverse section of the wire passed completely through the eye of the needle.' Nichols's practice exemplifies the replacement of the narrative of production by the narrative of the collection, the replacement of the narrative of history with the narrative of the individual subject – that is, the collector himself.

Whereas the space of the souvenir is the body (talisman), the periphery (memory), or the contradiction of private display (reverie), the space of the collection is a complex interplay of exposure and hiding, organization and the chaos of infinity. The collection relies upon the box, the cabinet, the cupboard, the seriality of shelves. It is determined by these boundaries, just as the self is invited to expand within the confines of bourgeois domestic space. For the environment to be an extension of the self, it is necessary not to act upon and transform it, but to declare its essential emptiness by filling it. Ornament, décor and ultimately decorum define the boundaries of private space by emptying that space of any relevance other than that of the subject.

The collector can gain control over repetition or series by defining a finite set (the Tiffany postal scales) or by possessing the unique object. The latter object has acquired a particular poignancy since the onset of mechanical reproduction; the aberrant or unique object signifies the flaw in the machine just as the machine once signified the flaws of handmade production. Veblen's critique of conspicuous consumption similarly concluded that the handmade object's crudity was, ironically, a symptom of conspicuous waste.

> Hand labor is a more wasteful method of production; hence the goods turned out by this method are more serviceable for the purpose of pecuniary reputability; hence the marks of hand labor come to be honorific, and the goods which exhibit these marks take rank as of higher grade than the corresponding machine product. ... The appreciation of those evidences of honorific crudeness to which hand-wrought goods owe their superior worth and charm in the eyes of well-bred people is a matter of nice discrimination.
>
> (Veblen 1953: 114)

Thus a measured crudity of material quality is presented in tension with an overrefinement of significance. This tension is further exaggerated by the juxtaposition of the unique and singular qualities of the individual object against the seriality of the collection as a whole.

Yet it is the museum, not the library, which must serve as the central metaphor of the collection; it is the museum, in its representativeness, which strives for authenticity and for closure of all space and temporality within the context at hand. In an essay on *Bouvard and Pécuchet*, Eugenio Donato has written:

> The set of objects the Museum displays is sustained only by the fiction that they somehow constitute a coherent representational universe. The fiction is that a

repeated metonymic displacement of fragment for totality, object to label, series of objects to series of labels, can still produce a representation which is somehow adequate to a nonlinguistic universe. Such a fiction is the result of an uncritical belief in the notion that ordering and classifying, that is to say, the spatial juxtaposition of fragments can produce a representational understanding of the world.

(Donato 1979: 223)

Thus there are two movements to the collection's gesture of standing for the world: first, the metonymic displacement of part for whole, item for context; and second, the invention of a classification scheme which will define space and time in such a way that the world is accounted for by the elements of the collection. We can see that what must be suppressed here is the privileging of context of origin, for the elements of the collection are, in fact, already accounted for by the world. And we can consequently see the logic behind the blithe gesture towards decontextualization in museum acquisitions, a gesture which results in the treasures of one culture being stored and displayed in the museums of another.

This paper first appeared in S. Stewart (1984) On Longing: Narratives of the Miniature, the Gigantic, the Souvenir, the Collection, *Baltimore: Johns Hopkins University Press, pp. 151–2; 153–5; 156–7; 160–1; 162.*

REFERENCES

Baudrillard, J. (1968) *Le Système des objects*, Paris: Gallimard.
Donato, E. (1979) 'The museum's furnace', in J. Harari (ed.) *Textual Strategies: Perspectives in Post-Structuralist Criticism*, Ithaca: Cornell University Press.
James, W. (1950) *The Principles of Psychiatry*, 2 vols, New York: Dover.
Veblen, T. (1953) *The Theory of the Leisure Class*, New York: New American Library.

31

Collecting ourselves

J. Clifford

Clifford's book has also been extremely influential. The Predicament of Culture *is a wide-ranging explanation of the context and implications of twentieth-century ethnography, literature and art. This extract is taken from the chapter which is concerned with collecting art and culture, particularly in the areas of tribal artefacts and cultural practice. It proposes a critical, historical approach to collecting which focuses on subjective, taxonomic and political processes. It offers an 'art-culture' system through which in the last century exotic objects have been contextualised and given value in the West, so contributing to western notions about 'Us' and 'the Other'.*

> Entering
> You will find yourself in a climate of nut castanets,
> A musical whip
> From the Torres Straits, from Mirzapur a sistrum
> Called Jumka, 'used by Aboriginal
> Tribes to attract small game
> On dark nights,' coolie cigarettes
> And mask of Saagga, the Devil Doctor,
> The eyelids worked by strings.

James Fenton's poem 'The Pitt Rivers Museum, Oxford' (1984: 81–4), from which this stanza is taken, rediscovers a place of fascination in the ethnographic collection. For this visitor even the museum's descriptive labels seem to increase the wonder ('. . . attract small game / on dark nights') and the fear. Fenton is an adult-child exploring territories of danger and desire, for to be a child in this collection ('Please sir, where's the withered / Hand?') is to ignore the serious admonitions about human evolution and cultural diversity posted in the entrance hall. It is to be interested instead by the claw of a condor, the jaw of a dolphin, the hair of a witch, or 'a jay's feather worn as a charm / in Buckinghamshire'. Fenton's ethnographic museum is a world of intimate encounters with inexplicably fascinating objects: personal fetishes. Here collecting is inescapably tied to obsession, to recollection. Visitors 'find the landscape of their childhood marked out / Here in the chaotic piles of souvenirs . . . boxroom of the forgotten or hardly possible'.

> Go
> As a historian of ideas or a sex-offender,
> For the primitive art,
> As a dusty semiologist, equipped to unravel
> The seven components of that witch's curse

> Or the syntax of the mutilated teeth. Go
> In groups to giggle at curious finds.
> But do not step into the kingdom of your promises
> To yourself, like a child entering the forbidden
> Woods of his lonely playtime.

Do not step in this tabooed zone 'laid with the snares of privacy and fiction / And the dangerous third wish'. Do not encounter these objects except as *curiosities* to giggle at, *art* to be admired or *evidence* to be understood scientifically. The tabooed way, followed by Fenton, is a path of too-intimate fantasy, recalling the dreams of the solitary child 'who wrestled with eagles for their feathers' or the fearful vision of a young girl, her turbulent lover seen as a hound with 'strange pretercanine eyes'. This path through the Pitt Rivers Museum ends with what seems to be a scrap of autobiography, the vision of a personal 'forbidden woods' – exotic, desired, savage and governed by the (paternal) law:

> He had known what tortures the savages had prepared
> For him there, as he calmly pushed open the gate
> And entered the wood near the placard: 'TAKE NOTICE
> MEN-TRAPS AND SPRING-GUNS ARE SET ON THESE
> PREMISES.'
> For his father had protected his good estate.

Fenton's journey into otherness leads to a forbidden area of the self. His intimate way of engaging the exotic collection finds an area of desire, marked off and policed. The law is preoccupied with *property*.

C. B. Macpherson's classic analysis of western 'possessive individualism' (1962) traces the seventeenth-century emergence of an ideal self as owner: the individual surrounded by accumulated property and goods. The same ideal can hold true for collectivities making and remaking their cultural 'selves'. For example Richard Handler (1985) analyses the making of a Québécois cultural *patrimoine*, drawing on Macpherson to unravel the assumptions and paradoxes involved in 'having a culture', selecting and cherishing an authentic collective 'properly'. His analysis suggests that this identity, whether cultural or personal, presupposes acts of collection, gathering up possessions in arbitrary systems of value and meaning. Such systems, always powerful and rule-governed, change histori- cally. One cannot escape them. At best, Fenton suggests, one can transgress ('poach' in their tabooed zones) or make their self-evident orders seem strange. In Handler's subtly perverse analysis a system of retrospection – revealed by a Historic Monuments Commis- sion's selection of ten sorts of 'cultural property' – appears as a taxonomy worthy of Borges's 'Chinese encyclopedia': '(1) commemorative monuments; (2) churches and chapels; (3) forts of the French Regime; (4) windmills; (5) roadside crosses; (6) commemo- rative inscriptions and plaques; (7) devotional monuments; (8) old houses and manors; (9) old furniture; (10) "les choses disparues"' (1985: 199). In Handler's discussion the collection and preservation of an authentic domain of identity cannot be natural or inno- cent. It is tied up with nationalist politics, with restrictive law, and with contested encod- ings of past and future.

Some sort of 'gathering' around the self and the group – the assemblage of a material 'world', the marking-off of a subjective domain that is not 'other' – is probably universal. All such collections embody hierarchies of value, exclusions, rule-governed territories of the self. But the notion that this gathering involves the accumulation of possessions, the idea that identity is a kind of wealth (of objects, knowledge, memories, experience), is surely not universal. The individualistic accumulation of Melanesian 'big men' is not possessive in Macpherson's sense, for in Melanesia one accumulates not to hold objects as private goods but to give them away, to redistribute. In the West, however, collecting has long been a strategy for the deployment of a possessive self, culture and authenticity.

Children's collections are revealing in this light: a boy's accumulation of miniature cars, a girl's dolls, a summer-vacation 'nature museum' (with labelled stones and shells, a hummingbird in a bottle), a treasured bowl filled with the bright shavings of crayons. In these small rituals we observe the channellings of obsession, an exercise in how to make the world one's own, to gather things around oneself tastefully, appropriately. The inclusions in all collections reflect wider cultural rules – of rational taxonomy, of gender, of aesthetics. An excessive, sometimes even rapacious need to *have* is transformed into rule-governed, meaningful desire. Thus the self that must possess but cannot have it all learns to select, order, classify in hierarchies – to make 'good' collections.[1]

Whether a child collects model dinosaurs or dolls, sooner or later she or he will be encouraged to keep the possessions on a shelf or in a special box or to set up a dollhouse. Personal treasures will be made public. If the passion is for Egyptian figurines, the collector will be expected to label them, to know their dynasty (it is not enough that they simply exude power or mystery), to tell 'interesting' things about them, to distinguish copies from originals. The good collector (as opposed to the obsessive, the miser) is tasteful and reflective.[2] Accumulation unfolds in a pedagogical, edifying manner. The collection itself – its taxonomic, aesthetic structure – is valued, and any private fixation on single objects is negatively marked as fetishism. Indeed a 'proper' relation with objects (rule-governed possession) presupposes a 'savage' or deviant relation (idolatry or erotic fixation).[3] In Susan Stewart's gloss, 'The boundary between collection and fetishism is mediated by classification and display in tension with accumulation and secrecy' (1984: 163).

Stewart's wide-ranging study *On Longing* traces a 'structure of desire' whose task is the repetitive and impossible one of closing the gap that separates language from the experience it encodes. She explores certain recurrent strategies pursued by westerners since the sixteenth century. In her analysis the miniature, whether a portrait or doll's house, enacts a bourgeois longing for 'inner' experience. She also explores the strategy of gigantism (from Rabelais and Gulliver to earthworks and the billboard), the souvenir and the collection. She shows how collections, most notably museums, create the illusion of adequate representation of a world by first cutting objects out of specific contexts (whether cultural, historical or intersubjective) and making them 'stand for' abstract wholes – a 'Bambara mask', for example, becoming an ethnographic metonym for Bambara culture. Next a scheme of classification is elaborated for storing or displaying the object so that the reality of the collection itself, its coherent order, overrides specific histories of the object's production and appropriation (pp. 162–5). Paralleling Marx's account of the fantastic objectification of commodities, Stewart argues that in the modern western museum 'an illusion of a relation between things takes the place of a social relation' (p. 165). The collector discovers, acquires, salvages objects. The objective world is given, not produced, and thus historical relations of power in the work of acquisition are occulted. The *making* of meaning in museum classification and display is mystified as adequate *representation*. The time and order of the collection erase the concrete social labour of its making.

Stewart's work, along with that of Phillip Fisher (1975), Krzysztof Pomian (1978), James Bunn (1980), Daniel Defert (1982), Johannes Fabian (1983), and Rémy Saisselin (1984), among others, brings collecting and display sharply into view as crucial processes of western identity formation. Gathered artefacts – whether they find their way into curio cabinets, private living-rooms, museums of ethnography, folklore or fine art – function within a developing capitalist 'system of objects' (Baudrillard 1968). By virtue of this system a world of *value* is created and a meaningful deployment and circulation of arte-facts maintained. For Baudrillard collected objects create a structured environment that substitutes its own temporality for the 'real time' of historical and productive processes: 'The environment of private objects and their possession – of which collections are an extreme manifestation – is a dimension of our life that is both essential and imaginary. As essential as dreams' (1968: 135).

A history of anthropology and modern art needs to see in collecting both a form of western subjectivity and a changing set of powerful institutional practices. The history of collections (not limited to museums) is central to an understanding of how those social groups that invented anthropology and modern art have *appropriated* exotic things, facts and meanings. (*Appropriate*: 'to make one's own', from the Latin *proprius*, 'proper', 'property'). It is important to analyse how powerful discriminations made at particular moments constitute the general system of objects within which valued arte-facts circulate and make sense. Far-reaching questions are thereby raised.

What criteria validate an authentic cultural or artistic product? What are the differential values placed on old and new creations? What moral and political criteria justify 'good', responsible, systematic collecting practices? Why, for example, do Leo Frobenius's wholesale acquisitions of African objects around the turn of the century now seem exces-sive? (See also Cole 1985 and Pye 1987.) How is a 'complete' collection defined? What is the proper balance between scientific analysis and public display? (In Santa Fe a superb collection of Native American art is housed at the School of American Research in a building constructed, literally, as a vault, with access carefully restricted. The Musée de l'Homme exhibits less than a tenth of its collections; the rest is stored in steel cabinets or heaped in corners of the vast basement.) Why has it seemed obvious until recently that non-western objects should be preserved in European museums, even when this means that no fine specimens are visible in their country of origin? How are 'antiquities', 'curiosities', 'art', 'souvenirs', 'monuments' and 'ethnographic artefacts' distinguished – at different historical moments and in specific market conditions? Why have many anthropological museums in recent years begun to display certain of their objects as 'masterpieces'? Why has tourist art only recently come to the serious attention of anthro-pologists? (See Graburn 1976; Jules-Rosette 1984.) What has been the changing inter-play between natural-history collecting and the selection of anthropological artefacts for display and analysis? The list could be extended.

The critical history of collecting is concerned with what from the material world specific groups and individuals choose to preserve, value and exchange. Although this complex history, from at least the Age of Discovery, remains to be written, Baudrillard provides an initial framework for the deployment of objects in the recent capitalist West. In his account it is axiomatic that all categories of meaningful objects – including those marked off as scientific evidence and as great art – function within a ramified system of symbols and values.

To take just one example: the *New York Times* of 8 December 1984 reported the wide-spread illegal looting of Anasazi archaeological sites in the American Southwest. Painted pots and urns thus excavated in good condition could bring as much as $30,000 on the market. Another article in the same issue contained a photograph of bronze age pots and jugs salvaged by archaeologists from a Phoenician shipwreck off the Coast of Turkey. One account featured clandestine collecting for profit, the other scientific collecting for knowledge. The moral evaluations of the two acts of salvage were sharply opposed, but the pots recovered were all meaningful, beautiful and old. Commercial, aesthetic and scientific worth in both cases presupposed a given system of value. This system finds intrinsic interest and beauty in objects from a past time, and it assumes that collecting everyday objects from ancient (preferably vanished) civilizations will be more *rewarding* than collecting, for example, decorated thermoses from modern China or customized T-shirts from Oceania. Old objects are endowed with a sense of 'depth' by their historically minded collectors. Temporality is reified and salvaged as origin, beauty and knowledge.

This archaizing system has not always dominated western collecting. The curiosities of the New World gathered and appreciated in the sixteenth century were not necessarily valued as antiquities, the products of primitive or 'past' civilizations. They frequently occupied a category of the marvellous, of a present 'Golden Age' (Honour 1975; Mullaney 1983; Rabasa 1985). More recently the retrospective bias of western appropriations of the world's cultures has come under scrutiny (Fabian 1983; Clifford 1986). Cultural or artistic 'authenticity' has as much to do with an inventive present as with a past, its objectification, preservation or revival.

Since the turn of the century objects collected from non-western sources have been classified in two major categories: as (scientific) cultural artefacts or as (aesthetic) works of art.[4] Other collectables – mass-produced commodities, 'tourist art', curios, and so on – have been less systematically valued; at best they find a place in exhibits of 'technology' or 'folklore'. These and other locations within what may be called the 'modern art–culture system' can be visualized with the help of a (somewhat procrustean) diagram.

A. J. Greimas's 'semiotic square' (Greimas and Rastier 1968) shows us 'that any initial binary opposition can, by the operation of negations and the appropriate syntheses, generate a much larger field of terms which, however, all necessarily remain locked in the closure of the initial system' (Jameson 1981: 62). Adapting Greimas for the purposes of cultural criticism, Fredric Jameson uses the semiotic square to reveal 'the limits of a specific ideological consciousness, [marking] the conceptual points beyond which that consciousness cannot go, and between which it is condemned to oscillate' (1981: 47). Following his example, I offer the following map (see Fig 31.1) of a historically specific, contestable field of meanings and institutions.

Beginning with an initial opposition, by a process of negation four terms are generated. This establishes horizontal and vertical axes and between them four semantic zones: (1) the zone of authentic masterpieces, (2) the zone of authentic artefacts, (3) the zone of inauthentic masterpieces, (4) the zone of inauthentic artefacts. Most objects – old and new, rare and common, familiar and exotic – can be located in one of these zones or ambiguously, in traffic, between two zones.

The system classifies objects and assigns them relative value. It establishes the 'contexts' in which they properly belong and between which they circulate. Regular movements towards positive value proceed from bottom to top and from right to left. These movements select artefacts of enduring worth or rarity, their value normally guaranteed by a 'vanishing' cultural status or by the selection and pricing mechanisms of the art market. The value of Shaker crafts reflects the fact that Shaker society no longer exists: the stock is limited. In the art world work is recognized as 'important' by connoisseurs and collectors according to criteria that are more than simply aesthetic (see Becker 1982). Indeed, prevailing definitions of what is 'beautiful' or 'interesting' sometimes change quite rapidly.

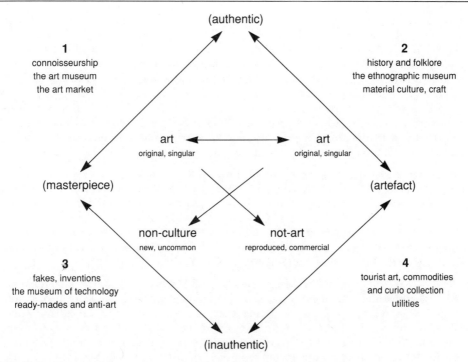

(authentic)

1
connoisseurship
the art museum
the art market

2
history and folklore
the ethnographic museum
material culture, craft

art ⟷ art
original, singular   original, singular

(masterpiece)

(artefact)

non-culture   not-art
new, uncommon   reproduced, commercial

3
fakes, inventions
the museum of technology
ready-mades and anti-art

4
tourist art, commodities
and curio collection
utilities

(inauthentic)

Fig. 31.1 The art–culture system: a machine for making authenticity

An area of frequent traffic in the system is that linking zones 1 and 2. Objects move in two directions along this path. Things of cultural or historical value may be promoted to the status of fine art. Examples of movement in this direction, from ethnographic 'culture' to fine 'art', are plentiful. Tribal objects located in art galleries (the Rockefeller Wing at the Metropolitan Museum in New York) or displayed anywhere according to 'formalist' rather than 'contextualist' protocols (Ames 1986: 39–42) move in this way. Crafts (Shaker work collected at the Whitney Museum in 1986), 'folk art', certain antiques, 'naive' art all are subject to periodic promotions. Movement in the inverse direction occurs whenever art masterworks are culturally and historically 'contextualized', something that has been occurring more and more explicitly. Perhaps the most dramatic case has been the relocation of France's great Impressionist collection, formerly at the Jeu de Paume, to the new Museum of the Nineteenth Century at the Gare d'Orsay. Here art masterpieces take their place in the panorama of a historical-cultural 'period'. The panorama includes an emerging industrial urbanism and its triumphant technology, 'bad' as well as 'good' art. A less dramatic movement from zone 1 to zone 2 can be seen in the routine process within art galleries whereby objects become 'dated', of interest less as immediately powerful works of genius than as fine examples of a period style.

Movement also occurs between the lower and upper halves of the system, usually in an upward direction. Commodities in zone 4 regularly enter zone 2, becoming rare period pieces and thus collectables (old green glass Coke bottles). Much current non-western work migrates between the status of 'tourist art' and creative cultural-artistic strategy. Some current productions of Third World peoples have entirely shed the stigma of modern commercial inauthenticity. For example Haitian 'primitive' painting – commercial and of relatively recent, impure origin – has moved fully into the art–culture circuit. Significantly this work entered the art market by association with zone 2, becoming valued as the work not simply of individual artists but of *Haitians*. Haitian painting is surrounded by special associations with the land of voodoo, magic and negritude. Though specific artists have come to be known and prized, the aura of 'cultural' production attaches to them much more than, say, to Picasso, who is not in any essential way valued as a 'Spanish artist'. The same is true, as we shall see, of many recent works of tribal art, whether from the Sepik or the American Northwest Coast. Such works have largely freed themselves from the tourist or commodity category to which, because of their modernity, purists had often relegated them; but they cannot move directly into zone 1, the art market, without trailing clouds of authentic (traditional) culture. There can be no direct movement from zone 4 to zone 1.

Occasional travel occurs between zones 4 and 3, for example when a commodity or technological artefact is perceived to be a case of special inventive creation. The object is selected out of commercial or mass culture, perhaps to be featured in a museum of technology. Sometimes such objects fully enter the realm of art: 'technological' innovations or commodities may be contextualized as modern 'design', thus passing through zone 3 into zone 1 (for example the furniture, household machines, cars, and so on displayed at the Museum of Modern Art in New York).

There is also regular traffic between zones 1 and 3. Exposed art forgeries are demoted (while nonetheless preserving something of their original aura). Conversely various forms of 'anti-art' and art parading its unoriginality or 'inauthenticity' are collected and valued (Warhol's soup can, Sherrie Levine's photo of a photo by Walker Evans, Duchamp's urinal, bottle rack or shovel). Objects in zone 3 are all potentially collectable within the general domain of art: they are uncommon, sharply, distinct from or blatantly cut out of culture. Once appropriated by the art world, like Duchamp's ready-mades, they circulate within zone 1.

The art–culture system I have diagrammed excludes and marginalizes various residual and emergent contexts. To mention only one: the categories of art and culture, technology and commodity are strongly secular. 'Religious' objects can be valued as great art (an altarpiece by Giotto), as folk art (the decorations on a Latin American popular saint's shrine), or as cultural artefact (an Indian rattle). Such objects have no individual 'power' or mystery – qualities once possessed by 'fetishes' before they were reclassified in the modern system as primitive art or cultural artefact. What 'value', however, is stripped from an altarpiece when it is moved out of a functioning church (or when its church begins to function as a museum)? Its specific power or sacredness is relocated to a general aesthetic realm.

It is important to stress the historicity of this art–culture system. It has not reached its final form: the positions and values assigned to collectable artefacts have changed and will continue to do so. Moreover a synchronic diagram cannot represent zones of contest and transgression except as movements or ambiguities among fixed poles. As we shall see at the end of this chapter, much current 'tribal art' participates in the regular art–culture traffic *and* in traditional spiritual contexts not accounted for by the system (Coe 1986). Whatever its contested domains, though, generally speaking the system still confronts any collected exotic object with a stark alternative between a second home in an ethnographic or an aesthetic milieu. The modern ethnographic museum and the art museum or private art collection have developed separate, complementary modes of classification. In the former a work of 'sculpture' is displayed along with other objects of similar function or in proximity to objects from the same cultural group, including utilitarian artefacts such as spoons, bowls or spears. A mask or statue may be grouped with formally dissimilar objects and explained as part of a ritual or institutional complex. The names of individual sculptors are unknown or suppressed. In art museums a sculpture is identified as the creation of an individual: Rodin, Giacometti, Barbara Hepworth. Its place in everyday cultural practices (including the market) is irrelevant to its essential meaning. Whereas in the ethnographic museum the object is culturally or humanly 'interesting', in the art museum it is primarily 'beautiful' or 'original'. It was not always thus.

Elizabeth Williams (1985) has traced a revealing chapter in the shifting history of these discriminations. In nineteenth-century Paris it was difficult to conceive of pre-Columbian artefacts as fully 'beautiful'. A prevailing naturalist aesthetic saw *ars Americana* as grotesque or crude. At best pre-Columbian work could be assimilated into the category of the antiquity and appreciated through the filter of Viollet-le-duc's medievalism. Williams shows how Mayan and Incan artefacts, their status uncertain, migrated between the Louvre, the Bibliothèque Nationale, the Musée Guimet and (after 1878) the Trocadéro, where they seemed at last to find an ethnographic home in an institution that treated them as scientific evidence. The Trocadéro's first directors, Ernest-Théodore Hamy and Rémy Verneau, showed scant interest in their aesthetic qualities.

The 'beauty' of much non-western 'art' is a recent discovery. Before the twentieth century many of the same objects were collected and valued, but for different reasons. In the early modern period their rarity and strangeness were prized. The 'cabinet of curiosities' jumbled everything together, with each individual object standing metonymically for a whole region or population. The collection was a microcosm, a 'summary of the universe' (Pomian 1978). The eighteenth century introduced a more serious concern for taxonomy and for the elaboration of complete series. Collecting was increasingly the concern of scientific naturalists (Feest 1984: 90), and objects were valued because they exemplified an array of systematic categories: food, clothing, building materials, agricultural tools, weapons (of war, of the hunt), and so forth. E. F. Jomard's ethnographic classifications and A. H. L. F. Pitt Rivers's typological displays were mid-nineteenth-century culminations of this taxonomic vision (Chapman 1985: 24–5). Pitt Rivers's typologies featured developmental sequences. By the end of the century evolutionism had come to dominate arrangements of exotic artefacts. Whether objects were presented as antiquities, arranged geographically or by society, spread in panoplies, or arranged in realistic 'life groups' and dioramas, a story of human development was told. The object had ceased to be primarily an exotic 'curiosity' and was now a source of information entirely integrated in the universe of Western Man (Dias 1985: 378–9). The value of exotic objects was their ability to testify to the concrete reality of an earlier stage of human Culture, a common past confirming Europe's triumphant present.

With Franz Boas and the emergence of relativist anthropology an emphasis on placing objects in specific lived contexts was consolidated. The 'cultures' thus represented could either be arranged in a modified evolutionary series or dispersed in synchronous 'ethnographic presents'. The latter were times neither of antiquity nor of the twentieth century but rather representing the 'authentic' context of the collected objects, often just prior to their collection or display. Both collector and salvage ethnographer could claim to be the last to rescue 'the real thing'. Authenticity, as we shall see, is produced by removing objects and customs from their current historical situation – a present-becoming-future.

With the consolidation of twentieth-century anthropology, artefacts contextualized ethnographically were valued because they served as objective 'witnesses' to the total multidimensional life of a culture (Jamin 1982: 89–95; 1985). Simultaneously with new developments in art and literature, as Picasso and others began to visit the 'Troca' and to accord its tribal objects a non-ethnographic admiration, the proper place of non-western objects was again thrown in question. In the eyes of a triumphant modernism some of these artefacts at least could be seen as universal masterpieces. The category of 'primitive art' emerged.

This development introduced new ambiguities and possibilities in a changing taxonomic system. In the mid-nineteenth century pre-Columbian or tribal objects were grotesques or antiquities. By 1920 they were cultural witnesses and aesthetic masterpieces. Since then a controlled migration has occurred between these two institutionalized domains. The boundaries of art and science, the aesthetic and the anthropological, are not permanently fixed. Indeed anthropology and fine arts museums have recently shown signs of interpenetration. For example the Hall of Asian Peoples at the New York Museum of Natural History reflects the 'boutique' style of display, whose objects could never seem out of place as 'art' on the walls or coffee-tables of middle-class living-rooms. In a complementary development downtown the Museum of Modern Art has expanded its permanent exhibit of cultural artefacts: furniture, automobiles, home appliances and utensils – even hanging from the ceiling, like a Northwest Coast war canoe, a much-admired bright green helicopter.

While the object systems of art and anthropology are institutionalized and powerful, they are not immutable. The categories of the beautiful, the cultural and the authentic have changed and are changing. Thus it is important to resist the tendency of collections to be self-sufficient, to suppress their own historical, economic and political processes of production (see Haacke 1975; Hiller 1979). Ideally the history of its own collection and display should be a visible aspect of any exhibition. It had been rumoured that the Boas Room of Northwest Coast artefacts in the American Museum of Natural History was to be refurbished, its style of display modernized. Apparently (or so one hopes) the plan has been abandoned, for this atmospheric, dated hall exhibits not merely a superb collection but a moment in the history of collecting. The widely publicized Museum of Modern Art show of 1984, '"Primitivism" in Twentieth Century Art', made apparent (as it celebrated) the precise circumstance in which certain ethnographic objects suddenly became works of universal art. More historical self-consciousness in the display and viewing of non-western objects can at least jostle and set in motion the ways in which anthropologists, artists and their publics collect themselves and the world.

At a more intimate level, rather than grasping objects only as cultural signs and artistic icons (Guidieri and Pellizzi 1981), we can return to them, as James Fenton does, their lost status as fetishes – not specimens of a deviant or exotic 'fetishism' but *our own* fetishes.[5] This tactic, necessarily personal, would accord to things in collections the power to fixate rather than simply the capacity to edify or inform. African and Oceanian artefacts could once again be *objets sauvages*, sources of fascination with the power to disconcert. Seen in their resistance to classification they could remind us of our *lack* of self-possession, of the artifices we employ to gather a world around us.

This paper first appeared in J. Clifford (1988) The Predicament of Culture, *Cambridge, MA: Harvard University Press, pp. 216–29.*

NOTES

1 On collecting as a strategy of desire see the highly suggestive catalogue (Hainard and Kaehr 1982) of an exhibition entitled 'Collections Passion' at the Musée d'Ethnographie, Neuchâtel, June to

December 1981. This analytic collection of collections was a *tour de force* of reflexive museology. On collecting and desire see also Donna Haraway's brilliant analysis (1985) of the American Museum of Natural History, American manhood, and the threat of decadence between 1908 and 1936. Her work suggests that the passion to collect, preserve and display is articulated in gendered ways that are historically specific. Beaucage, Gomilia and Vallée (1976) offer critical meditations on the ethnographer's complex experience of objects.

2 Walter Benjamin's essay 'Unpacking my library' (1969: 59–68) provides the view of a reflective devotee. Collecting appears as an art of living intimately allied with memory, with obsession, with the salvaging of order from disorder. Benjamin sees (and takes a certain pleasure in) the precariousness of the subjective space attained by the collection.

> Every passion borders on the chaotic, but the collector's passion borders on the chaos of memories. More than that: the chance, the fate that suffuse the past before my eyes are conspicuously present in the accustomed confusion of these books. For what else is this collection but a disorder to which habit has accommodated itself to such an extent that it can appear as order? You have all heard of people whom the loss of their books has turned into invalids, of those who in order to acquire them became criminals. These are the very areas in which any order is a balancing act of extreme precariousness.
>
> (1969: 60)

3 My understanding of the role of the fetish as a mark of otherness in western intellectual history – from DeBrosses to Marx, Freud and Deleuze – owes a great deal to the largely unpublished work of William Pietz; see 'The problem of the fetish, 1' (1985).

4 For 'hard' articulations of ethnographic culturalism and aesthetic formalism see Sieber 1971; Price and Price 1980; Vogel 1985; and Rubin 1984. The first two works argue that art can be understood (as opposed to merely appreciated) only in its original context. Vogel and Rubin assert that aesthetic qualities transcend their original local articulation, that 'masterpieces' appeal to universal or at least transcultural human sensibilities. For a glimpse of how the often incompatible categories of 'aesthetic excellence', 'use', 'rarity', 'age', and so on are debated in the exercise of assigning authentic value to tribal works, see the richly inconclusive symposium on 'Authenticity in African Art' organized by the journal *African Arts* (Willett *et al.* 1976).

5 For a post-Freudian positive sense of the fetish see Leiris 1929, 1946; for fetish theory's radical possibilities see Pietz 1985, which draws on Deleuze; and for a repentant semiologist's perverse sense of the fetish (the 'punctum') as a place of strictly personal meaning unformed by cultural codes (the 'studium') see Barthes 1980. Gomila (1976) rethinks ethnographic material culture from some of these surrealist-psychoanalytic perspectives.

REFERENCES

Ames, Michael (1986) *Museums, the Public and Anthropology: A Study in the Anthropology of Anthropology*, Vancouver: University of British Columbia Press.

Barthes, Roland (1980) *La chambre claire*, trans. Richard Howard as *Camera Lucida*, New York: Hill & Wang, 1981.

Baudrillard, Jean (1968) *Le Système des objets*, Paris: Gallimard.

Beaucage, Pierre, Gomila, Jacques and Vallée, Lionel (1976) *L'Expérience anthropologique*, Montreal: Presses de l'Université de Montréal, 71–133.

Becker, Howard (1982) *Art Worlds*, Berkeley: University of California Press.

Benjamin, Walter (1969) *Illuminations* (ed.) Hannah Arendt, New York: Schocken Books.

Bunn, James (1980) 'The aesthetics of British mercantilism', *New Literary History* 11: 303–21.

Chapman, William (1985) 'Arranging ethnology: A. H. L. F. Pitt Rivers and the typological tradition', in George Stocking (ed.) *History of Anthropology* vol. 3, *Objects and Others*, Madison: University of Wisconsin Press, 15–48.

Clifford, James (1986) 'On ethnographic allegory', in James Clifford and George Marcus (eds) *Writing Culture*, Berkeley: University of California Press, 98–121.

Coe, Ralph (1986) *Lost and Found Traditions: Native American Art: 1965–1985*, Seattle: University of Washington Press.

Cole, Douglas (1985) *Captured Heritage: The Scramble for Northwest Coast Artifacts*, Seattle: University of Washington Press.

Defert, Daniel (1982) 'The collection of the world: accounts of voyages from the sixteenth to the early eighteenth centuries', *Dialectical Anthropology* 7: 11–20.

Dias, Nelia (1985) 'La fondation du Musée d'Ethnographie du Trocadéro (1879–1900): un aspect de l'histoire institutionelle de l'anthropologie française', thesis, troisième cycle, Ecole des Hautes Etudes en Sciences Sociales, Paris.

Fabian, Johannes (1983) *Time and the Other: How Anthropology Makes its Object*, New York: Columbia University Press.

Feest, Christian (1984) 'From North America', in William Rubin (ed.) *'Primitivisim' in Twentieth Century Art*, New York: Museum of Modern Art, 85–95.

Fenton, James (1984) *Children in Exile: Poems 1968–1984*, New York: Random House.

Fisher, Philip (1975) 'The future's past', *New Literary History* 6(3): 587–606.

Gomila, Jacques (1976) 'Objectif, objectal, objecteur, objecte', in Pierre Beaucage, Jacques Gomila and Lionel Vallée (eds) *L'Expérience anthropologique*, Montreal: Presses de l'Université de Montréal, 7–133.

Graburn, Nelson (ed.) (1976) *Ethnic and Tourist Arts*, Berkeley: University of California Press.

Greimas, A. J. and Rastier, François (1968) 'The interaction of semiotic constraints', *Yale French Studies* 41: 86–105.

Guidieri, Rémo and Pellizzi, Francesco (1981), Editorial, *Res* 1: 3–6.

Haacke, Hans (1975) *Framing and Being Framed*, Halifax: The Press of the Nova Scotia College of Art and Design.

Hainard, Jacques and Kaehr, Rolland (eds) (1982) *Collections passion*, Neuchâtel: Musée d'Ethnographie.

Handler, Richard (1985) 'On having a culture: nationalism and the preservation of Quebec's *patrimoine*', in George Stocking (ed.) *History of Anthropology* vol. 3, *Objects and Others*, Madison: University of Wisconsin Press.

Haraway, Donna (1985) 'Teddy bear patriarchy: taxidermy in the Garden of Eden, New York City, 1908–1936', *Social Text* Winter: 20–63.

Hiller, Susan (1979) Review of *Sacred Circles: 2,000 Years of North American Art*, *Studio International* Dec.: 8–15.

Honour, Hugh (1975) *The New Golden Land*, New York: Pantheon.

Jameson, Fredric (1981) *The Political Unconscious: Narrative as a Socially Symbolic Act*, Ithaca: Cornell University Press.

Jamin, Jean (1982) 'Objets trouvés des paradis perdus: à propos de la Mission Dakar-Djibouti', in J. Hainard and R. Kaehr (eds) *Collections passion*, Neuchâtel: Musée d'Ethnographie, 69–100.

—— (1985) 'Les objets ethnographiques sont-ils des choses perdues?' in J. Hainard and R. Kaehr (eds) *Temps perdu, temps retrouvé: voir les choses du passé au présent*, Neuchâtel: Musée d'Ethnographie, 51–74.

Jules-Rosette, Benetta (1984) *The Messages of Tourist Art*, New York: Plenum.

Leiris, Michel (1929) 'Alberto Giacometti', *Documents* 1(4): 209–11; trans. J. Clifford (1986) in *Sulfur* 15: 38–41.

—— (1946) *L'Age d'homme*, Paris; Gallimard; trans. Richard Howard (1985) as *Manhood*, Berkeley: North Point Press.

Macpherson, C. B. (1962) *The Political Theory of Possessive Individualism*, Oxford: Oxford University Press.

Mullaney, Steven (1983) 'Strange things, gross terms, curious customs: the rehearsal of cultures in the late Renaissance', *Representations* 3: 40–67.

Pietz, William (1985) 'The problem of the fetish, 1', *Res* 9 (Spring): 5–17.

Pomian, Krzysztof (1978) 'Entre l'invisible et le visible: la collection', *Libre* 78(3): 3–56.

Price, Sally and Price, Richard (1980) *Afro-American Arts of the Suriname Rain Forest*, Berkeley: University of California Press.

Pye, Michael (1987) 'Whose art is it anyway?', *Connoisseur* (March): 78–85.

Rabasa, José (1985) 'Fantasy, errancy, and symbolism in New World motifs: an essay on sixteenth-century Spanish historiography', PhD diss, University of California, Santa Cruz.

Rubin, William (ed.) (1984) *'Primitivism' in Modern Art: Affinity of the Tribal and the Modern*, 2 vols, New York: Museum of Modern Art.

Saisselin, Rémy (1984) *The Bourgeois and the Bibelot*, New Brunswick, N.J.: Rutgers University Press.

Sieber, Roy (1971) 'The aesthetics of traditional African art', in Carol F. Jopling (ed.) *Art and Aesthetics in Primitive Societies*, New York: Dutton, 127–45.

Stewart, Susan (1984) *On Longing: Narratives of the Miniature, the Gigantic, the Souvenir, the Collection*, Baltimore: Johns Hopkins University Press.

Vogel, Susan (1985) 'Introduction', in *African Masterpieces from the Musée de l'Homme*, New York: Harry Abrams, 10–11.

Willett, Frank *et al.* (1976) 'Authenticity in African art', *African Arts* 9(3): 6–74 (special section).

Williams, Elizabeth (1985) 'Art and artifact at the Trocadéro', in George Stocking (ed.) *History of Anthropology* vol. 3, *Objects and Others*, Madison: University of Wisconsin Press, 145–66.

32

The filth in the way

M. Thompson

How the value of objects is constructed, and the implications of this within economic and political action, have proved to be questions of great complexity and subtlety. Thompson looks at these interrelated problems by proposing three object categories, which he calls 'transient', 'durable' and 'rubbish'. Objects move between these categories in complicated ways. Does the category membership of an object determine the way we act towards it, or does the way we act towards it determine its category membership? Particularly important here is the impact which the collecting process has upon object values and the ways in which they change.

There is a status difference between the condition of being rich and the condition of being poor, the former being higher than the latter. The condition of richness or poorness is determined by the quantity of objects one possesses: a poor person possesses few objects, a rich person many objects. But how can one tell whether a person is rich or poor? Apart from tramps, most people choose not to carry all their possessions around with them and really rich people would be physically incapable of doing so even if they wanted to and even assuming they could overcome the problems of security and insurance that such ostentatious behaviour would entail. Well, the answer is that one cannot always be sure of recognizing a rich or poor person, but one sure indication of status which one may sometimes be fortunate enough to witness is how many objects people are able to discard. A poor man, since he has few possessions, can afford to discard very little; a rich man will be able to discard much more.

Obviously a poor man who discards more valueless objects than a rich man in no way threatens the social order. For the social order to be maintained there has to be some measure of agreement as to what is of value. People in different cultures may value different things, and they may value the same things differently, but all cultures insist upon some distinction between the valued and the valueless.

An advertisement in *The Times* promoting *The Times*'s classified advertisement columns, and the service provided by *The Times* staff who advise on the best wordings for the classified ads, shows a pair of identical vases of oriental style. One is labelled, in crude block capitals, 'Secondhand'; the other, in elegant copperplate within a black border, 'Antique'. The inscription above the vases reads: 'It's not what you say, it's the way that you say it.'

Our appreciation of the advertisement is adequate proof that objects may be seen in two very different ways, one aesthetically and economically superior to the other, and moreover that in certain circumstances we may be able, to our considerable advantage, to control the way in which we ourselves and others see an object. The pair of vases has been chosen to illustrate this flexibility. The label 'Secondhand' leads us to see the vase on the left as a worthless piece of tat, a grotesque present from a grotesque relative. The label 'Antique' leads us to see its mate as the real thing; a beautiful, delicate, valuable, old, Chinese ceramic *objet d'art*.

This flexibility does not extend to all objects. Most objects are only visible in one or other of these two ways, and their identities are so certain that the labels 'Secondhand' and 'Antique' are superfluous. The used car in the back-street car mart and the Queen Anne walnut tallboy advertised in *Country Life* are perhaps more typical, in their unequivocal natures, of objects in general, than *The Times*'s borderline vases.

Let us start by identifying two very different ways in which objects can be seen. They form an element in our perception of the physical and social environment, our world-view. The element can be described like this. In our culture objects are assigned to one or other of two overt categories which I label 'transient' and 'durable'. Objects in the transient category decrease in value over time and have finite life-spans. Objects in the durable category increase in value over time and have (ideally) infinite life-spans. The Queen Anne tallboy, for example, falls into the durable category, the used car into the transient category.

The way we act towards an object relates directly to its category membership. For instance, we treasure, display, insure and perhaps even mortgage the antique vase, but we detest and probably destroy its secondhand mate. Obviously, when it comes to objects, there is a relationship between our view of the world and our action in that world, but what is the nature of this relationship? Does the category membership of an object determine the way we act towards it, or does the way we act towards an object determine its category membership? So far as the unequivocal Queen Anne tallboy and the used car are concerned, simple observation of the market in these objects reveals that their category membership determines the way we act towards them: that is, world-view is prior to action. They are located within a region of fixed assumptions. But when we look at the two vases we find that the way we act towards them, that is whether we treat them as antique or secondhand, determines their category membership: that is, action is prior to world-view. They lie in a region of flexibility somewhere between the inflexible regions inhabited by Queen Anne tallboys and used cars (see Fig. 32.1).

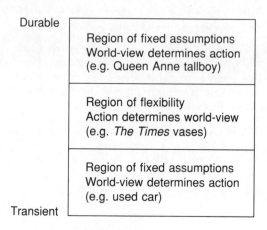

Fig. 32.1 'Transient' and 'durable' objects

This is an obvious example of what I feel is a general phenomenon and as an anthropologist I should be able to provide a formal description – an adequate theory – to account for what is going on here. For categories are not free just to float about. They are closely tied to the social situation that they render meaningful. A common response for the theorist is to treat the data *as if* the category framework determined the social action, and then to treat it again *as if* the social action determined the category framework – rather like physicists who can treat light as made up of waves or of particles and who choose whichever approach is best suited to their particular problem. The trouble is that neither approach is much help in understanding the conceptual equivalent of 'muddling through' that must go on when, despite the clear separation between them, equivocal objects become unequivocal and vice versa. I have to come at it from a different direction altogether.

Innovation and creativity arise within the region of flexibility, but access to innovation and creativity is not freely available to all members of our society. Differential access is imposed through the social order. For those near the bottom there really is no region of flexibility; for those near the top there may be a wide range of manipulative freedom (and, of course, *The Times* is a paper for top people!).

By relating these differences in the breadth of the region of flexibility to the various social levels, we can uncover the control mechanism within the system: the manner in which durability and transience are imposed upon the world of objects. This is perhaps the first stumbling-block in presenting rubbish theory, for we all tend to think that objects are the way they are as a result of their intrinsic physical properties. The belief that nature is what is there when you check in is reassuring but false: the belief that it is made anew each afternoon is alarming but true. We have to recognize that the qualities objects have are conferred upon them by society itself and that nature (as opposed to our idea of nature) plays only the supporting and negative role of rejecting those qualities that happen to be physically impossible.

The operation of this control mechanism would seem inevitably to give rise to a self-perpetuating system. Briefly: it is decidedly advantageous to own durable objects (since they increase in value over time whilst transient objects decrease in value). Those people near the top have the power to make things durable and to make things transient, so they can ensure that their own objects are always durable and that those of others are always transient. They are like a football team whose centre-forward also happens to be the referee; they cannot lose.

A paradoxical question now arises. How can such a self-perpetuating system ever change itself? How, as it were, can the other side ever score a goal? In this case the equivalent of such a goal is the transfer of an object from the transient to the durable category: a transfer which defies the powerful control mechanism that results from combining the roles of centre-forward and referee yet nevertheless does happen. We are all familiar with the way despised Victorian objects have become sought-after antiques; with bakelite ashtrays that have become collectors' items; with old bangers transformed into vintage motor cars. So we know the changes take place, but how? The answer lies in the fact that the two overt categories which I have isolated, the durable and the transient, do not exhaust the universe of objects. There are some objects (those of zero and unchanging value) which do not fall into either of these two categories and these constitute a third *covert* category: *rubbish*.

My hypothesis is that this covert rubbish category is not subject to the control mechanism (which is concerned primarily with the overt part of the system, the valuable and socially significant objects) and so is able to provide the path for the seemingly impossible transfer of an object from transience to durability. What I believe happens is that a transient object gradually declining in value and in expected life-span may slide across into rubbish. In an ideal world, free of nature's negative attitude, an object would reach zero value and zero expected life-span at the same instant, and then, like Mark Twain's 'one hoss shay', disappear into dust. But, in reality, it usually does not do this; it just continues to exist in a timeless and valueless limbo where at some later date (if it has not by that time turned, or been made, into dust) it has the chance of being discovered. It may be discovered by a creative *Times* reader and successfully transferred to durability (Fig. 32.2).

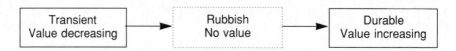

Fig. 32.2   The covert 'rubbish' category

Only if one remains within severe cultural and temporal confines can one sustain the commonsense belief that rubbish is defined by intrinsic physical properties. Step outside these limits and one sees that the boundary between rubbish and non-rubbish moves in response to social pressures.

The interesting feature of this category system is that membership is not fixed for all time but is to some greater or lesser extent flexible. A member of the transient category can, and usually does, gradually transfer to the rubbish category and a member of the rubbish category can, under certain conditions, transfer to the durable category. The other transfers that would complete the diagram do not happen. So dynamically:

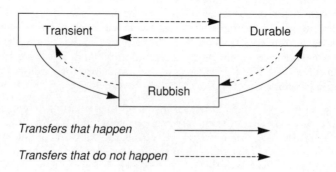

Fig. 32.3   Dynamic system of cognitive categories

This then is the dynamic system of cognitive categories, and the problem now is to enquire how this cultural system can be related to the social order in such a way as to recognize that they are closely tied to one another yet, at the same time, are not in general mutually reinforcing and self-perpetuating. The arrows on the diagram, indicating those transfers that happen and those that do not, provide an obvious clue to the identity of the third and missing element between cultural and social order: control.

The explanatory framework in terms of the three categories, transient, rubbish and durable, and of the permitted transfers between these categories, is all very pretty but it does leave some unanswered questions. What happens to the durable item in the long run, when, still increasing in value, it disappears off the top right-hand corner of the graph? What happens when a supposedly impossible transfer occurs? For example, when something durable becomes transient or rubbish; when moth or rust corrupt or when thieves break through and steal; when an old master painting is slashed to ribbons, a Venetian glass goblet dropped and smashed into a thousand pieces, or a Georgian silver teapot overwarmed on the hot-plate and melted into a glistening lump? What about the situations where a new item suddenly appears out of the blue, or where an existing one suddenly disappears in an equally mystifying fashion? That is, how does this dynamic category system relate to the processes of production and consumption?

Ideally, durables last for ever and increase in value over time. In such a system items continually enter the durable category yet never leave it, and the fact that they all must increase in value simply exacerbates an already expansive or even explosive trend. We must ask whether this is what actually happens or whether in the long run other factors intervene to provide an upper ceiling or at least some retardation of what must otherwise be a runaway situation. Does the system carry within it the seeds of its own destruction?

One limit which durables undoubtedly approach, and which some classes of durable items actually attain, is total removal from circulation. This represents a perfect solution to this runaway problem, since the removal from circulation retards the expansion without in any way imposing on the durable items properties that would be incompatible with their membership of the durable category. The complete transfer of a class of items to museums and public collections is consonant with a general belief that, if only those items were in circulation, they would be increasing in value. In other words, they are so durable they are priceless.

The almost inevitable occasional destruction of durable items also helps to bring about this total removal from circulation, but it is in this case that the category system is in fact threatened. Of course, we all know that no physical object can last for ever and in consequence the durable category must logically be a class with no members. In practice, this seemingly insurmountable obstacle is easily overcome. Objects in the durable category do not have to last for ever, just long enough. As long as the majority of the items in the durable category survive the lifetime of the individual culture-bearers, and, more important, as long as during this time people act towards those objects *as if* they were going to last for ever, then the category boundary is unthreatened.

The rubbish to transient transfer is, theoretically, impossible for the following reason. Both the value and expected life-span of an item in the rubbish category are zero. In the transient category they are positive and decreasing. The transfer of rubbish to transience would involve a change from zero to a positive quantity which inevitably entails an increase (the criterion for membership of the durable category), and in consequence would exclude the item from the transient category. But do such theoretically impossible transfers occur in practice? They do occur to a limited degree, which does not seriously threaten the boundary maintenance, in the business affairs of the dealer. The successful dealer operates by manipulating the value and expected life-span of an item: by depressing them in one transaction and elevating them in the subsequent transaction. The secondhand car dealer is successful to the extent that he is able to delay the transfer of an item from the transient to the rubbish category; the antiques dealer is successful to the extent that he is able to emphasize the durability of an item. The transfer of rubbish to transience occurs in the limiting case which exists in the context of the totter, the rag-and-bone man, the Gypsy and the scrap-dealer.

The theoretically impossible transfers of transient to durable and durable to transient can be considered together. They correspond to the seemingly impossible market situation where some people are expecting to pay less and less for a particular item whilst others are expecting to pay more and more. Such a situation, should it exist, would be inherently unstable and would alter until the market wholly excluded those who were expecting to pay less and less. Similarly, in a crisis such as the Wall Street crash we could envisage a hypothetical situation where the sudden loss of confidence meant that those people who expected to pay more and more for, say, antique silver rapidly became fewer and fewer, with the result that those people who expected to pay less and less, and who presumably wanted the silver for brewing tea in and eating with, could enter and take over the entire market. It is evident that the long-term survival of the category system and the existence of transient to durable and durable to transient transfers are incompatible. Such transfers are an automatic threat to boundary maintenance and their appearance would seem to signal the imminent collapse of the durable category – as happened, for instance, with the destruction of the middle classes in Weimar Germany or the wartime privations that caused the (regretted) exchange of old masters for tins of corned beef. People become aware that they live in troubled times, not just because of the real physical dangers, but because of the real conceptual dangers as well. It is very alarming when objects cease to conform to the properties expected of them. Of course, these properties expected of objects and of ideas constitute our values, our civilization, and it is because of perceived threats to these properties that wars are fought.

But there is another possibility. We can imagine the establishing of a permanent cultural boundary between those who expect to pay more and more and those who expect to pay less and less whereby those who expect to pay more and more take over the market entirely, and those who expect to pay less and less accept their exclusion from the market by denying the relevance, for them, of durable items. Such a boundary effectively eradicates competition in terms of the items defining it: it would be the sort of boundary which exists between castes rather than classes. Only the existence of this cultural boundary can account for the observed facts that a considerable proportion of British society consistently behave as though there were no such things as durables and that some, if not all, of them continue to behave like this, even though they are fully aware that durables do exist, for the very good reason that they are 'not for them'. This is not said in any detrimental or patronizing sense. Such a person may be very well aware that, within his social context, five pounds spent on drinks for old or potential friends and acquaintances is a much better investment than five pounds' worth of unit trusts.

Generalizing, we can say that this cultural boundary, when competition is eliminated, separates castes and, when competitions persists, separates classes. And competition is made possible by the existence of the transfers from transient to rubbish to durable. It follows then that under conditions where the possibilities of these transfers are progressively reduced the social stratification will tend to change from class-based to caste-based. The explanation is quite simple: the transient rubbish/durable category system permits the uneven distribution of power and status within our society and is the basis for the cultural differences between the classes that are ranged along that distribution. The permissible, but carefully controlled, transfers between these categories allow the degree of social mobility sufficient to modify these classes so that they accurately reflect the inevitably changing distribution of power within our society. That is, they permit the continuous realignment of power and status.

Now, you might say, 'But power and status always go together, so how can they need realigning?' Well, in the West this indeed has tended to be the case, thanks to the transfers between categories, but in India, for instance, there were virtually no transfers through rubbish and power and status varied quite independently. The meat-eating Prince, for example, sat firmly at the head of the power structure but he deferred to the vegetarian Brahmin within the hierachy of caste. This is the difference between class and caste, and there is no reason why power and status should not begin to vary independently here in the West as well.

The degree of control needed to ensure this constant realignment of power and status without, at the same time, threatening to destroy the cultural boundaries between the classes is not easily achieved. If control is too tight, then the distribution of power and the distribution of status will tend to drift apart, since the transfers that would keep them aligned are not allowed to happen. In this way, power and status will increasingly vary independently of one another: those near the top of the prestige league concerning themselves less and less with objects as sources of power and more and more with the embracing of some objects, and with the rejection of others, as indicators of purity and of separation. Social stratification will change from class-based to caste-based. If control is too loose, power and status will remain aligned but the status differential will be eroded as too much is transferred too rapidly between the categories, and it will no longer be possible to maintain the emphatic differences between them. That is, stratification will decrease, the durable category will disappear, and the society will move towards the egalitarian pole, becoming increasingly organized around differences only of a universal kind such as age, sex and physical characteristics.

We can now see that by pushing the argument for a dynamic sociology to its logical extreme and considering not only the possibilities of transfers between cultural categories but also the possibilities of the various permutations that result from the total elimination of some of these categories as a consequence of these transfers, we obtain a simple triangular range of transformations within which those supposedly fundamental social dimensions, stratification and competition, emerge as secondary abstractions (see Fig. 32.4).

The generalization does not have to stop at this stage. This 'rubbish triangle' provides, in outline, a description of all the ways in which the goods in circulation in any society may be conceptualized and of the manner in which these conceptualizations relate to the entire possible range of variations of the fundamental properties of social systems. In other words, it depicts the social laws that govern distribution and exchange. We can now ask how this model of all the socially realizable variations of the modes of distribution and exchange relates to the other two departments of economic activity, production and consumption, but first we should clarify the relationship between the 'rubbish triangle' and the model that has been used in the analysis of Stevengraphs and North London houses. This latter model is represented in Fig. 32.5.

This model represents just one specific possibility within the total range of socially realizable possibilities given by the 'rubbish triangle'. It is, in fact, that possibility corresponding to the top right-hand corner of the triangle, the clearly defined class-based society characterized by high levels of stratification and competition. It is a description of one of the historic conditions of distribution and exchange. In contrast, the 'rubbish triangle' provides, in outline, a description of all such historic conditions, both those that have actually occurred and those that, although possible, may not have occurred yet. It is a description therefore of the universal qualities of distribution and exchange.

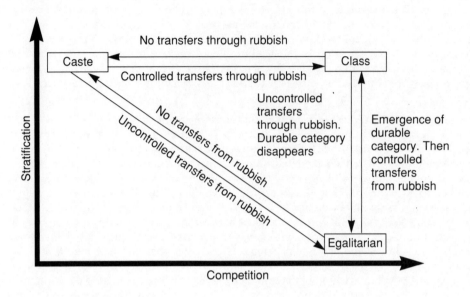

Fig. 32.4 The rubbish triangle

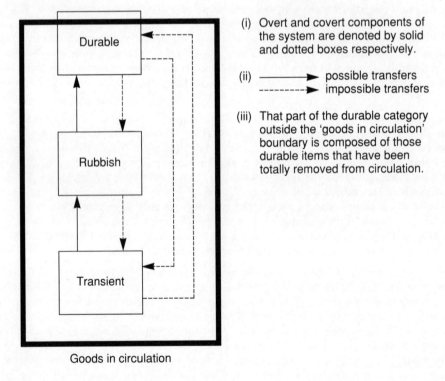

Fig. 32.5 Model representing one of the historic conditions of distribution and exchange

The universal (or natural) condition of these departments is, according to Marx, the identity of production and consumption but this identity is obscured by the interposition of the historic (or cultural) conditions of distribution and exchange which prevent us from perceiving it. This historic separation of production and consumption is contradicted by the existence of processes that can only occur if they are not separate, productive consumption (the use of a product in a new process of production) and consumptive production (the reproduction of human life). This state of affairs can be visualized as two contradictory forces, the historic condition separating production and consumption so that one becomes the beginning and the other becomes the end, the universal condition linking them together again to form a closed circle that makes nonsense of the idea of beginnings and ends. The manner in which the historic condition intervenes to obscure the universal unity can, with the help of a chicken-and-egg image, be represented as in Fig. 32.6.

Concerning the various possible and impossible transfers on the diagram, those within the 'goods in circulation' section have already been accounted for (as too have Marx's self-evident yet troublesome productive consumption and consumptive production) but we should now look more closely at those transfers crossing from 'production' to 'goods in circulation' and from 'goods in circulation' to 'consumption'.

Taking the impossible one first, that from durable to consumption, we can see that this is ideally impossible since durable objects ideally last for ever. They may be removed from circulation (as is represented by that area of the durable category which extends beyond the goods in circulation boundary) but they may not cease to exist, that is, be

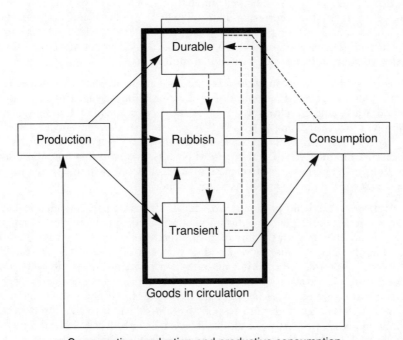

Fig. 32.6   Chicken-and-egg image representing various possible and impossible transfers

consumed. This transfer is simply a variation of the ideally impossible transfer from durable to rubbish which has already been dealt with. It corresponds to the destruction of a durable which leaves no residue to be disposed of, as happens for instance when a diamond is dropped into a furnace. If this transfer did become possible and began to occur quite frequently it would herald the collapse of the durable category (by its absorption into the transient). That is, this particular historic condition would shift towards the egalitarian apex of the 'rubbish triangle'.

Theoretically, the other five transfers (from 'production' to 'goods in circulation' and from there to 'consumption') are feasible and we should look to see whether they occur in practice and, if so, to what sort of common-sense everyday transactions they correspond. The production to transient transfer presents no problems. It is, as it were, the norm. It corresponds to what we usually consider the whole point of production to be: the creation of useful things. Some of these useful things, like foodstuffs, may be used up very quickly; others, like cars and washing-machines, less quickly; and still others, like books and houses, very slowly indeed, but the essential feature is that as they get used they get used up and as they get used up they make the transfer from transient to consumption. So this transfer from transient to consumption also corresponds to the norm, and indeed the normal route from production to consumption is via the transient category. All other routes are generally considered quite abnormal, and the very existence of such abnormal routes is frequently ignored and sometimes even denied.

The production to rubbish transfer, at first sight, appears rather unlikely. After all, who would go to all that expense and trouble to produce rubbish. Of course, nobody would do this deliberately but inevitably the production of useful things often involves the production of rubbish as well, as an unwelcome but unavoidable by-product. So the transfer 'production to rubbish' corresponds to all that is produced that is persistent and useless. This is an aspect of production that is often disregarded and may even be denied. Currently, in certain quarters, however, it is the subject of much attention. The production to rubbish transfer corresponds to pollution.

The transfer 'rubbish to consumption' is quite common. It occurs whenever rubbish is got rid of, for example, refuse collection and incineration, sewage treatment, the reinstatement of waste land, the clearance of slums, the deportation of undesirable aliens and, at its most extreme, the gassing of Jews and Gypsies in Nazi Germany. Such consumption is generally seen as a social service: a necessary transfer, but one which nevertheless is a burden on the community. The real horror of Nazi Germany resides not in its collective madness but in the perfect reasonableness of the behaviour in terms of the particular category framework that constituted its historic condition.

The last transfer, that from production to durable, is extremely uncommon but does sometimes occur. It corresponds to the starving artist's dream come true. Certain categories of person operate with the intention that their products shall be assigned directly to the durable category, but this very seldom happens. A particularly well-established painter may achieve this, especially if his rate of production is low. Recent examples would be Bacon, Coldstream or Hundertwasser. The same may sometimes happen with other hand-crafted objects such as Fabergé Easter eggs, Tiffany lamps, and Lutyens mansions, but those objects that go straight from production to the durable category represent a minuscule proportion of all the objects being produced. Objects which make this transfer are clearly distinct from those involved in the other transfers that have just been described; they are art. (All objects which make the direct transfer 'production to durable' are art but not all art objects make this particular transfer.)

This paper first appeared in M. Thompson (1979) Rubbish Theory, *Oxford: OUP.*

33

Art museums and the ritual of citizenship

Carol Duncan

Viewed from the perspective of Thompson's scheme most material in public museums, and probably also in the major private collections which have received public recognition of their importance, would belong within the 'durable' category: this material, we might say, has achieved the status of 'heritage'. Duncan suggests that this material historically has been deployed as a secular ritual of the modern state in which 'the spiritual heritage of the nation' is offered as a public reinforcement of political values. The recognized great individuals and periods of western history – Greece and Rome, the Renaissance, nineteenth-century Europe – become the inheritance which legitimizes the present. Museums, therefore, make an important statement when they admit a new body of work.

The French Revolution created the first truly modern art museum when it designated the Louvre Palace a national museum. The transformation of the old royal palace into the Museum of the French Republic was high on the agenda of the French Revolutionary government. Already, public art museums were regarded as evidence of political virtue, indicative of a government that provided the right things for its people. Outside France, too, educated opinion understood that art museums could demonstrate the goodness of a state or municipality or show the civic-mindedness of its leading citizens. By the middle of the nineteenth century, almost every western nation would boast a national museum or art gallery. Even Washington, D.C., was, for a time, slated to have a national gallery of art in what is now the Renwick Building, which was designed in 1859 with the Louvre's architecture very much in mind.

The West, then, has long known that public art museums are important, even necessary, fixtures of a well-furnished state. This knowledge has recently spread to other parts of the world. Lately, both traditional monarchs in so-called underdeveloped nations and Third World military despots have become enthralled with them. Western-style art museums are now deployed as a means of signalling to the West that one is a reliable political ally, imbued with proper respect for and adherence to western symbols and values. By providing a veneer of western liberalism that entails few political risks and relatively small expense, art museums in the Third World can reassure the West that one is a safe bet for economic or military aid.

So in 1975 Imelda Marcos put together a museum of modern art in a matter of weeks.[1] The rush was occasioned by the meeting in Manila of the International Monetary Fund. The new Metropolitan Museum of Manila – it specialized in American and European art – was clearly meant to impress the conference's many illustrious visitors, who included some of the world's most powerful bankers.[2] Not surprisingly, the new museum re-enacted on a cultural level exactly the same relations that bound the Philippines to the United States economically and militarily. It opened with dozens of loans from the Brooklyn Museum, the Los Angeles County Museum of Art, and the private collections of Armand Hammer and Nathan Cummings.[3] Given Washington's massive contribution to the Philippine military budget, it is fair to assume that the museum building itself, an unused army building, was virtually an American donation.

The Shah of Iran also needed western-style museums to complete the facade of modernity he constructed for western eyes. The Museum of Contemporary Art in Teheran opened in 1977 shortly before the regime's fall.[4] Costing over $7 million, the multilevel modern-style structure was filled mostly with American art from the post-World War II period – reputedly $30 million worth – and staffed by mostly American or American-trained museum personnel. According to Robert Hobbs, who was the museum's chief curator, the royal family viewed the museum and its collection as simply one of many instruments of political propaganda.[5]

Meanwhile in the West, museum fever continues unabated. Almost weekly, newspapers publicize plans for yet another new museum or an expansion or renovation of an old one in London, Paris, New York, Los Angeles, or some other national or regional capital. As much as ever, having a bigger and better art museum is a sign of political virtue and national identity — of being recognizably a member of the civilized community of modern, liberal nations.

Recently, there has been much concern with how western museums represent other cultures — how museum displays of 'primitive', Third World, or non-western art often misrepresent or even invent foreign cultures for what are ultimately political purposes. The question of what museums do to other cultures often leaves unexamined what I believe is a prior question: what fundamental purposes do museums serve in our own culture and how do they use art objects to achieve those purposes? My essay, then, will be concerned not with the representation of foreign or non-western cultures but with what art museums say to and about our own culture – what political meanings they produce and how they produce them. I should immediately say that I am concerned with the most familiar kind of public art museum, the typical capital or big-city museum dedicated to a broad sweep of art history. The Louvre is the prototype of this kind of museum.

THE MUSEUM AS RITUAL

I will be treating art museums as ceremonial monuments. My general approach grows out of work I have done in the past, much of it in collaboration with Alan Wallach.[6] In referring to museums as ceremonial monuments, my intention is to emphasize the museum experience as a monumental creation in its own right, a cultural artefact that is much more than what we used to understand as 'museum architecture'. Above all, a museum is not the neutral and transparent sheltering space that it is often claimed to be. More like the traditional ceremonial monuments that museum buildings frequently emulate – classical temples, medieval cathedrals, Renaissance palaces – the museum is a complex experience involving architecture, programmed displays of art objects, and highly rationalized installation practices. And like ceremonial structures of the past, by fulfilling its declared purposes as a museum (preserving and displaying art objects) it also carries out broad, sometimes less obvious political and ideological tasks.

Since the Enlightenment, our society has distinguished between the religious and the secular. We normally think of churches and temples as religious sites, different in kind from secular sites such as museums, courthouses or state capitols. We associate different kinds of truths with each kind of site. The distinction, rooted in Enlightenment struggles against authoritative religious doctrines, makes religious truth a matter of subjective belief, while the truths belonging to museums, universities or courts of law claim to be self-evident to reason, rooted in experience and empirically verifiable. According to this tradition, we think of religious truth as addressed to particular groups of voluntary believers, while secular truth has the status of objective or universal knowledge and functions in our society as higher, authoritative truth. As such, it helps bind the community as a whole into a civic body, identifying its highest values, its proudest memories and its truest truths. Art museums belong decisively to this realm of secular knowledge, not only because of the branches of scientific and humanistic knowledge practised in them – conservation, art history, archaeology – but also because of their status as preservers of the community's cultural heritage.

In contrast, our concept of ritual is normally associated with religious practices, with real or symbolic sacrifices or spiritual transformations. Clearly, such events can have little to do with so secular a place as a museum. But, as anthropologists now argue, our supposedly secular culture is full of ritual situations and events.[7] Once we recognize the ideological character of our Enlightenment vocabulary and question the claims made for the secular – that its truths are lucid, rationally demonstrable and objective – we may begin to conceptualize the hidden (or perhaps the better word is *disguised*) ritual content of secular ceremonies. We can also consider the advantages of a ritual that passes as a secular, and therefore objective and neutral, occurrence.

The very architecture of museums suggests their character as secular rituals. It was fitting that the temple facade was for two hundred years the most popular signifier for the public art museum.[8] The temple facade had the advantage of calling up both secular and ritual associations. The beginnings of museum architecture date from the epoch in which Greek and Roman architectural forms were becoming the normal language for distinctly civic and secular buildings. Referring to a pre-Christian world of highly evolved civic institutions, classical-looking buildings could well suggest secular, Enlightenment principles and purposes. But monumental classical forms also brought with them the space of rituals – corridors scaled for processionals and interior sanctuaries designed for awesome and potent effigies.

Museums do not simply resemble temples architecturally; they *work* like temples, shrines and other such monuments. Museumgoers today, like visitors to these other sites, bring with them the willingness and ability to shift into a certain state of receptivity. And like traditional ritual sites, museum space is carefully marked off and culturally designated as special, reserved for a particular kind of contemplation and learning experience and demanding a special quality of attention – what Victor Turner called 'liminality'.[9]

In all ritual sites, some kind of performance takes place. Visitors may witness a drama – often a real or symbolic sacrifice – or hear a recital of texts or special music; they may enact a performance themselves, often individually and alone, by following a prescribed route, repeating a prayer or certain texts, reliving a narrative relevant to the site, or engaging in some other structured experience that relates to the history or meaning of the site. Some individuals may use ritual sites more knowledgeably than others; they may be more educationally prepared to respond to their symbolic cues. Ritual is often regarded as transformative: it confers identity or purifies or restores order to the world through sacrifice, ordeal or enlightenment.

So visitors to a museum follow a route through a programmed narrative – in this case, one or another version of the history of art. In the museum, art history displaces history, purges it of social and political conflict, and distills it down to a series of triumphs, mostly of individual genius. Of course, what the museum presents as the community's history, beliefs and identity may represent only the interests and self-image of certain powers within the community. Such deceit, however, does not necessarily lessen the effectiveness of the monument's ritual structure as such.

THE POLITICS OF PUBLIC ART MUSEUMS

I want to return now to the question with which I began, namely the political usefulness of public art museums. Some museum history will help bring this political use into focus.

Ceremonial sites dedicated to the accumulation and display of treasures go back to the most ancient of times. It is tempting to extend our notion of the museum back in time and discover museum-like functions in the treasuries of ancient temples or medieval cathedrals or in the family chapels of Italian baroque churches. But however much the public art museum may resemble these other kinds of places as a structured experience, historically the modern institution of the museum grew most directly out of sixteenth- and seventeenth-century princely collections. These collections, often displayed in lavishly decorated galleries built especially for them, anticipated some of the functions of later museums. Beginning in the eighteenth century, public art museums would appropriate, develop and transform the central function of the princely gallery.[10]

Typically, princely galleries were used as reception halls, providing sumptuous settings for official ceremonies and magnificent frames for the figure of the prince. Princes everywhere installed their treasures in such galleries in order to impress both foreign visitors and local dignitaries with their splendour and, often through special iconographies, the rightness or legitimacy of their rule. This function of the princely gallery as a ceremonial reception hall wherein the state presented and idealized itself would remain central to the public art museum.

The Louvre was not the first royal collection to be turned into a public art museum, but its transformation was the most politically significant and influential. In 1793 the French Revolutionary government, looking for a way to dramatize the creation of the new republican state, nationalized the king's art collection and declared the Louvre a public museum. The Louvre, once the palace of kings, was reorganized as a museum for the people, to be open to everyone free of charge. It thus became a powerful symbol of the fall of the *ancien régime* and the creation of a new order.

The new meaning that the French Revolution gave to the old palace was literally inscribed inside, in the heart of the seventeenth-century palace, the Apollo Gallery, built by Louis XIV as a princely gallery and reception hall. Inscribed over its entrance is the French Revolutionary decree that called into existence the Museum of the French Republic and ordered its opening on 10 August 1793 specifically to commemorate 'the anniversary of the fall of the tyranny'. Inside the Apollo Gallery, a case holds three crowns from the royal and imperial past, now ceremonially displayed as public property.

Other art museums could hardly boast such politically dramatic origins or so historically rich a setting. But every major state, monarchical or republican, understood the usefulness of having a public art museum. Such public institutions made (and still make) the state look good: progressive, concerned about the spiritual life of its citizens, a preserver of past achievements and a provider for the common good. The same virtues accrue to the individual citizens who, in the Anglo-American tradition, bring about public art museums. Certainly vanity and the desire for social status and prestige among nations and cities as well as among individuals are motives for founding or contributing to art museums, as they were in the creation of princely galleries. But such motives easily blend with sentiments of civic concern or national pride. And since public museums are, by definition, accessible to everyone, they can function as especially clear demonstrations of the state's commitment to the principle of equality. The public museum also makes visible the public it claims to serve. It produces the public as a visible entity by literally providing it with a defining frame and giving it something to do. Meanwhile, the political passivity of citizenship is idealized as active art appreciation and spiritual enrichment. Thus the art museum gives citizenship and civic virtue a content without having to redistribute real power.

In all this, the work of art, now displayed as public property, becomes the means through which the relationship between the individual as citizen and the state as benefactor is enacted. In order for art to become useful in this way, however, older concepts of art and art collecting had to be reconceived. In the princely gallery, paintings, statues and other rare and precious objects were understood as luxurious decorations and enviable displays of wealth or as trophies of military exploits.[11] In one way or another, displays of objects demonstrated something about the prince – his splendour, glory, or wisdom. To fulfil their task in public art museums, the same objects had to acquire yet another layer of meaning, a layer that could obliterate, contradict or radically distort previous meanings and uses. In the museum, the prince's treasures, along with other things – altarpieces, for example, taken from yet another ritual context – now had to become art-historical objects, repositories of spiritual wealth, products of individual and national genius. Indeed, the museum environment was structured precisely to bring out these meanings and to suppress or downplay others. The museum context is, in this sense, a powerful transformer: it converts what were once displays of material wealth and social status into displays of spiritual wealth.

The form that this new kind of wealth takes in the museum is the work of art as the product of genius, an object whose true significance lies in its capacity to testify to the creative vitality of its maker. This reinvestment of meaning was made possible by the new discipline of art history, whose system of classification was immediately employed by the state as an ideological instrument. Thus recontextualized as art history, the luxury of princes could now be seen as the spiritual heritage of the nation, distilled into an array of national and individual genius. Displayed chronologically and in national categories along the museum's corridors, the new arrangement illuminated the universal spirit as it manifested itself in the various moments of high civilization. Significantly, the new value discovered in the prince's old treasures could be distributed to the many merely by displaying it in a public space. To be sure, equality of access to the museum in no way gave everyone the relevant education to understand the new art-historical values of these old treasures, let alone equal political rights and privileges; in fact, only propertied males were full citizens. But in the museum, everyone was in principle equal, and if the uneducated were unable to use the cultural goods the museum proffered, they could – and still can – be awed by the sheer magnitude of the treasure.

In a relatively short time, the Louvre's directors (drawing on some German precedents) worked out a whole set of practices that came to characterize art museums everywhere. Very early on, the Louvre's galleries were organized by national school. By its 1810 reopening as the Musée Napoléon, the museum, now under the direction of Vivant Denon, was completely organized by school, and within the schools works of important masters were grouped together. The new art history thus provided the authoritative text upon which the public art museum was to structure its ritual. The vestibule of the

Musée Napoléon (the Rotunda of Mars), dedicated in 1810 and still intact today, already states the new art-historical programme. Four medallions in the ceiling celebrate what art history early designated as the most important moments in the history of art. Each contains a female personification of a national school along with a famous example of its sculpture. Egypt holds a cult statue, Greece the *Apollo Belvedere*, Italy Michelangelo's *Moses*, and France Puget's *Milo of Crotona*.[12] The message reads clearly: France is the fourth and final term in a narrative sequence that comprises the greatest moments of art history. Simultaneously, the history of art has become no less than the history of the highest achievements of western civilization itself: its origins in Egypt and Greece, its reawakening in the Renaissance, and its flowering in nineteenth-century France. As promised by the vestibule's decorations, the sculpture collection was organized as a tour through the great schools.

Even though almost two centuries have passed since the Louvre opened as a museum, and even though there have been and still are expansions, alterations, reorganizations and reinstallations, the museum is still remarkably coherent both as a series of ceremonial spaces and as a programmed sequence of collections that maintains the nineteenth-century bias for the great epochs of Civilization. Strong doses of classical art are still administered early in the tour and visitors soon see Italian Renaissance art, the importance of which is stressed, no matter what route one takes, by the monumentality and centrality of the halls devoted to it.

In the nineteenth century, when these museum meanings were still novel, the ruling authorities spelled them out on the Louvre's ceilings. At first, the ceilings hammered home the image of the state or monarch as protector of the arts. Using traditional princely iconography, images and insignia repeatedly identified this or that government or monarch in that role. But increasingly the iconography centred on artists. In the Musée Charles X, dating from the 1820s, ceiling after ceiling celebrates great patron-princes of the past – popes, kings and cardinals; but famous artists are also abundantly present, their names or portraits, arranged into schools, decorating the entablatures. Ever greater expanses of overhead space would be devoted to them as the century wore on. Indeed, the nineteenth century was a great age of genius iconography, and nowhere are genius ceilings more ostentatious than in the Louvre. Predictably, after every coup or revolution, new governments would vote funds for at least one such ceiling, prominently inscribing their own insignia on it. Thus in 1848, the newly constituted Second Republic renovated and decorated the Salon Carré and the nearby Hall of the Seven Chimneys, devoting the first to great artists from foreign schools and the second to French geniuses, profiles of whom were alphabetically arranged in the frieze.

It should be obvious that the demand for Great Artists, once the type was developed as a historical category, was enormous – they were, after all, the means by which, on the one hand, the state could demonstrate the highest kind of civic virtue, and on the other, citizens could know themselves to be civilized. Not surprisingly, quantities of Great Artists were duly discovered and furnished with properly archetypal biographies by the burgeoning discipline of art history. We should also recall that artists such as Ingres and Delacroix were very aware of themselves as candidates for the category of Great Artist so lavishly celebrated on the museum's ceilings, and plotted their careers accordingly. The situation continues today in the institution of the giant retrospective. A voracious demand for Great Artists, living or dead, is obligingly supplied by legions of art historians and curators trained for just this purpose. Inevitably some of the Great Artists recruited for this purpose – especially premodern masters – fill out the role of museum art star with less success than others. Even so, a fair or just good Great Artist is still a serviceable item in today's museum business.

CIVILIZATION ON THE WANE

The United States followed the English tradition of relying mainly upon private citizens to found museums. Nevertheless, museums in the United States have played the same ideological role as their state-founded equivalents in Europe, just as they adopted the essentials of the ceremonial programme first perfected by the Louvre.

New York's Metropolitan Museum of Art, for example, was directly inspired by the Louvre. Until a few years ago, the museum's commitment to the great-epochs approach was unmistakable. From the museum's vast, monumental entry hall, all the main axes led either to antiquity or to the Renaissance: Greece and Egypt to the right and left, Italy up the stairs. Other collections were fitted in behind these. Thus, as in the Louvre, the three great moments of western civilization were programmatically emphasized as *the* heritage of the present. These arrangements were echoed by every major American museum and scores of minor ones. When no Greek or Roman originals were on hand, as they were not in many museums, the idea was conveyed by plaster casts of classical sculpture or Greek-looking architecture, the latter often embellished with the names of Great Artists; such facades are familiar sights everywhere.

The general museum ideal I have been describing went through a variety of particular developments in the various nations of the West, where it was subject to different sets of tensions and pressures. Nevertheless, it remained remarkably viable and coherent as an ideal until around the 1950s, when its hold on the museum community began to wane – at first in the United States and then internationally. The frenzy of museum building that began in the 1950s and continues to this day has left us with many new museums dedicated to modern art. Modern art museums (or modern wings in older museums) differ from traditional museums not only because their collections consist of more recent art, but also, and more important, because they introduce a different museum ritual. The concept of the public and the reverence for the classical western past that informed the older museum do not operate in the modern one, just as the new, more alienated kind of individualism celebrated there is very different from the idealized citizen–state relationship implicit in the older museum.

These shifts are dramatically visible in many traditional museums that, like the Museum of Fine Arts, Boston, have been expanded or altered in recent years. In the old Museum of Fine Arts, everything was organized around the central theme of Civilization. Behind the monumental classical entry facade, the entire sequence of world civilizations followed one upon the other: Greece, Rome and Egypt on one side, balanced by their eastern counterparts on the other. The rest of art history came after, all in its proper order, with the Renaissance centrally placed. This arrangement is still intact today, but the recent addition of the new East Wing has seriously disrupted the order in which it unfolds. Because the new wing has in practice become the museum's main entrance, the classical galleries, the old museum's opening statement, now occupy the most remote reaches of the building – remote, that is, in relation to the new entrance. The museum's opening statement now consists of a large gallery of modern art, three new restaurants, a space for special exhibitions, and a large gift-and-book store. It is now possible to visit the museum, see a show, go shopping and eat and never once be reminded of the heritage of Civilization.

In the same way the new primitive-art wing at the Metropolitan Museum of Art decidedly upstages the Greek collection, which had to be moved to create an access first to the new primitive-art galleries and then later to the new twentieth-century wing, an arrangement that decidedly blunts the museum's earlier claims about Greece as an antecedent to modern civilization. As constructed by the museum, the modern soul yearns not for the light of classical antiquity but for the presumably dark and incomprehensible creations of supposedly precivilized, ahistorical cultures. In other museums, so-called primitive art is frequently mixed up with twentieth-century avant-garde art, where it validates every possible modern style from early cubism to surrealism to current neo-expressionism and neo-primitivism.

Museums can be powerful identity-defining machines. To control a museum means precisely to control the representation of a community and some of its highest most authoritative truths. It also means the power to define and rank people, to declare some as having a greater share than others in the community's common heritage – in its very identity. Those who are in the greatest accord with the museum's version of what is beautiful and good may partake of this greater identity. It is they who are best prepared to recognize the history presented by the programme and who have most cultivated the skills to produce the particular kind of associations or, as the case may be, the aesthetic attention, implicitly demanded by the museum's isolated objects. In short, those who best understand how to use art in the museum environment are also those on whom the museum ritual confers this greater and better identity. It is precisely for this reason that museums and museum practices can become objects of fierce struggle and impassioned debate. What we see and do not see in our most prestigious art museums – and on what terms and whose authority we do or don't see it – involves the much larger questions of who constitutes the community and who shall exercise the power to define its identity.

This paper first appeared in I. Karp and S. Lavine (eds) (1991) Exhibiting Cultures: The Poetics and Politics of Museum Display, *Washington, DC: Smithsonian Institution, pp. 88–103.*

NOTES

1 'How to put together a museum in 29 days', *ARTnews* (Dec. 1976).
2 *New York Times*, 5 Oct. 1976, 65, 77.
3 'How to put together a museum.'
4 Sarah McFadden (1981) 'Teheran Report', *Art in America* 69(10).
5 Robert Hobbs (1981) 'Museum under siege', *Art in America* 69(10).
6 See especially Carol Duncan and Alan Wallach 'The universal survey museum', *Art History* 3.
7 See, for example, Victor Turner (1977) 'Frame, flow and reflection: ritual and drama as public liminality', in Michel Benamou and Charles Caramello (eds) *Performance in Postmodern Culture*, Milwaukee: Center for Twentieth Century Studies, University of Wisconsin, 33–5.
8 See Nikolaus Pevsner (1976) *A History of Building Types*, Princeton: Princeton University Press, 118ff.; Neils von Holst (1967) *Creators, Collectors and Connoisseurs*, trans. Brian Battershaw, London: Thames & Hudson, 228f.; and Germain Bazin (1967) *The Museum Age*, trans. Jane van Nuis Cahill, New York: Universe, 197–202.
9 Turner, op. cit.
10 For princely galleries see Bazin, op. cit., 129–39; von Holst, 95–139 and *passim*; Thomas da Costa Kaufmann (1978) 'Remarks on the collections of Rudolf II: the Kunstkammer as a form of representations', *Art Journal* 38; Pevsner, op. cit. 112ff.; and Hugh Trevor-Roper (1976) *Princes and Artists: Patronage and Ideology at Four Habsburg Courts 1517–1633*, London: Thames & Hudson. For the beginnings of public art museums, see Bazin, op. cit., 141–91 and *passim*.
11 The princely gallery I am discussing is not the cabinet of curiosities, which mixed together found objects, such as shells and minerals, with man-made things, but the large, ceremonial reception hall, such as the Louvre's Apollo Gallery. For a discussion of the differences, see Bazin, op. cit. 129ff.
12 Christiane Aulanier (n.d.) *Histoire du Palais et du Musée du Louvre*, Paris: Editions du Musées Nationaux, 5: 76.

34

'The People's Show'

Cathy Mullen

In 1991 Peter Jenkinson organized a new kind of exhibition at Walsall Museum in the English West Midlands. For what was called 'The People's Show' people in the town of Walsall were invited to offer their own collections for display in the museum. The response was very large, and the resulting exhibition so successful that it had obviously chimed in with people's needs and aspirations; as a result Walsall Museum has followed up with further People's Shows, and other museums in the area and elsewhere in Britain have adopted the same strategy. Clearly, the exhibition has much to say both about the collectors themselves, and about the relationship between museums and culture, both 'high' and 'popular', themes which link up with the previous paper.

As cultural pluralism becomes more and more of a guiding force in shaping the responsibilities of cultural institutions, a pluralist concept of knowledge and its social construction has never been more important. Schools are not the only institutions that have an important educational mission in a heterogeneous society. Museums and art galleries play an increasingly important role in the construction of cultural knowledge. That role need not be confined to preserving and disseminating established, legitimated cultural knowledge; it can also be one of facilitating the social construction of a broad range of cultural knowledge, and so contribute to the cultural empowerment of a broad range of people. What can museum and gallery professionals do to aid, or even lead a person's or a group's construction of knowledge of and about their own cultural practices? What projects or practices are there that have succeeded in putting the ethos of cultural pluralism to work, by encouraging public recognition of cultural practices that don't fall within traditional boundaries of 'legitimate' culture or 'high art'. A community art gallery in Walsall, England, on the outskirts of Birmingham, provides an excellent example.

A COLLECTION OF COLLECTORS

The simple idea behind 'The People's Show'[1] was to present what local residents collect. It was an exhibit rich in exuberance, diversity and sentiment. I entered a gallery filled from floor to ceiling. Plexiglass-covered cases held arrangements of eggcups, valentines, thimbles, hotel soaps, toy cars. The walls were covered with groupings of Hindu religious pictures, neckties, T-shirts. There were shelves laden with tea mugs, plaster portrait busts, vegetable motif salt-shakers, souvenir plates and plastic ware. Suspended from the gallery's ceiling were rows of souvenir scarves, tea-towels, model aeroplanes and clip-on furry toys. Partitions enclosed a few spaces for 'installations': in one, ceramic frogs, rabbits and otters mingled on a carpet of moss; in another, a teenager had re-created his bedroom, decorated entirely with Madonna memorabilia.

The exhibition design established the human contexts for these diverse objects, and also gave a structural and interpretive coherence to what otherwise would have been just an assembly of mass-produced miscellanea, with no sense of personal significance.

Through accompanying photographs and quotations from each collector, I was able to associate the objects with the faces of the collectors and their comments about collecting. Each collector was presented in this way (except a few who chose to remain anonymous; in those cases, names and photographs were omitted). There were Tom Holmes's neckties, Maureen King's blue glass vases, James and Andrew Lovell's toy cars and planes, Bob Cordon-Champ's Velosolex mopeds.

The photographs and the quotations played a key role, both by communicating cultural information and by maintaining a connection between that information and particular people who were the source of that information. The inherently social process that constructed both the exhibition itself and the cultural knowledge that it presented were neither concealed nor disregarded.

A series of quotations displayed on a central panel in the main gallery offered further insight into dispositions and motivations for collecting:

- 'I get enjoyment from searching out the most horrendous ties.'
- 'I prefer the furry ones to the plastic ones.'
- 'Many of the items are incredibly rare and very old and represent my entire life from childhood to adulthood.'
- 'Most of them were bequeathed to me . . . a hat can transform your mood.'
- 'There are some people who know, others who sort of think how peculiar it is.'
- 'Some of them were bought by people who have since died.'
- 'I get a little thrill from the thought that I recycle them from the ragman.'
- 'I just buy them, I just want them, it's a passion.'
- 'It's part of my childhood . . . it means a lot to me. They used to think it was a phase I'd grow out of.'

These comments communicate knowledge experienced as meaning grounded in the concrete particulars of these people's lives.

NOT A TYPICAL ART EXHIBITION

'The People's Show' prompts me to consider it according to the distinctions between 'popular culture' and 'high culture'. One of the reasons the exhibition stands out is because it is not what usually happens in an art gallery. Beyond the doors of these rooms, one found the museum's permanent collection of 'fine art' objects, the bequest of avid collectors Kathleen Garman, Lady Epstein (widow of the sculptor Sir Jacob Epstein) and Sally Ryan, an American sculptor and student of Epstein. Those displays communicated the legitimacy and status we have come to expect of objects found in art museums and galleries; we learn to respond with regard and reverence, and to respect a process of mystification that has bestowed upon them a sacred aura.

The gallery environment created by 'The People's Show' evoked quite different responses. It was not a sparse arrangement of objects whose significance required the viewer to adopt an exclusively aesthetic disposition or to utilize specialized academic knowledge.[2] Rather, this abundant array of cultural artefacts invited viewers to refer to their feelings and understandings of family, friends, special events, vacation trips, gift-giving, eating, dressing and decorating their homes. Rather than eschewing associations with that which entertains, these objects revel in being curious, silly, ironic, adorable, sentimental. On the other hand, I noted an important similarity between these collectors and those who collect 'fine art'. Like their counterparts in the ranks of the 'high culture' public, these collectors exercise a good measure of passion, obsession, selectivity, discipline and eccentricity. Their responses to their objects are complex, including aesthetic pleasure in materials, colours and textures, as well as engagement with symbols as diverse as mythologized celebrities, consumer products and self-images derived from mass media.

PLURALIST PRECEDENTS

The pluralist ethos inherent in the gallery staff's initiative in this project emanates from the strong regard for cultural pluralism that exists among many British cultural professionals, especially those involved in regional and grass-roots programmes. The exhibit was focused specifically on members of the general public. I associate this focus with well-known exhibitions celebrating British working-class culture, at the York Castle Museum and the People's Palace in Glasgow. These museums' exhibits are powerful contributors to the construction of legitimated knowledge of the working-class people in their respective communities. 'The People's Show' was intentionally created to move on from these exhibitions of a homogenized representation of 'working-class culture' to acts that celebrate diverse cultural practices existing now.

A PROCESS OF ENQUIRY

Perhaps this exhibition can best be seen as the concrete product of a social process of enquiry. According to Peter Jenkinson, manager of the gallery's small group of staff and student interns, that process was quite a challenge. To begin, participants were solicited by leaflets in local newspapers and announcements on local radio stations. Staff then answered a flood of responses, and a committee chose from those a total of 63 collectors to exhibit. (While the final selection included collectors of different age, gender, race, ethnic and socioeconomic designations, it could best be described as being indicative rather than 'representative' of the local population.) Student interns did fieldwork-style interviews with each collector, and a hired photographer documented each collector and collection *in situ*. Finally, the exhibition designers figured out a way of displaying the gathered material in two modestly sized rooms. The entire process of soliciting, selecting, inventorying, then displaying some 16,000 objects was accomplished in a mere two months.

THE PROCESS CONTINUES

The gallery staff's efforts have been rewarded with overwhelming success. One measure of the show's popular success came in visitorship: about 10,000 people viewed the exhibition, the single biggest attendance in the gallery's recent history. It also drew extensive national media coverage and a proposal currently being developed, for a television series. Further afield, the exhibition has received widespread attention and recognition in the community of museum and gallery professionals.[3]

Encouraged by such positive response, Jenkinson and his staff are already planning a second exhibition for 1992. Besides repeating such adjunct events as a young collectors' fair and swap meeting plans include events for museum professionals, scholars and students in related academic disciplines (including a conference on collecting and ancillary publications). These additions will enable people with professional and academic expertise to join in the social process put in motion by 'The People's Show', enabling them to share their collecting proclivities and passions, and to contribute their own meanings to the cultural knowledge being constructed.

The knowledge that has been constructed – through the preparatory process of enquiry and the exhibition itself – is powerful because it maintains an intimate connection to the people by whom and for whom it exists. That knowledge has not been distanced from people's lived experiences; nor has it been depersonalized by generalization or abstraction. In planning for future events, I hope that the gallery staff can preserve that close connection, which is the source of cultural empowerment.

This paper first appeared in Visual Sociology Review *6(1) (Summer 1991), pp. 47–9.*

NOTES

1 'The People's Show', May–June 1990, the Walsall Museum and Art Gallery, Lichfield Street, Walsall, England.
2 I am drawing here from Pierre Bourdieu's (1984) distinction of elite and popular tastes. See *Distinction: A Social Critique of the Judgement of Taste*, trans. Richard Nice, Cambridge, Mass.: Harvard University Press.
3 See, for example, Mark Suggitt's (1990) 'Emissaries from the toy cupboard', *Museums Journal* 90(12): 30–3.

35

Leicester Contemporary Collecting Project's questionnaire
Susan M. Pearce

This questionnaire was sent out by post in 1993 to 1,500 randomly chosen residents of Britain whose names appear on the current electoral register, using the methodology described by D. A. Dillman in his Mail and Telephone Surveys: The Total Design Method *(1978, John Wiley, New York). It formed part of a research project carried out in 1993–4 aimed at investigating collecting practices in contemporary Britain, mounted by the Department of Museum Studies, University of Leicester. The questionnaire was designed to draw out information about what, why and how people see themselves as collecting, and how this relates to personal factors like gender and social background. The response rate to the questionnaire was good (roughly 61 per cent). The completed questionnaires, and related information, are now undergoing analysis.*

Department of Museum Studies
University of Leicester
Contemporary Collecting
Project

Please tick the box that applies to you. Tick more than one box if you like. Please also write what you like for the other questions. If you have more than one collection, please choose one and answer for it.

<u>Do you collect anything?</u>

Yes ☐   No ☐

If No, then please turn to the back page, fill in the 'background' section and return the form.

<u>We would like to know the history of your collection.</u>

What do you collect? _____

_____

How many items are there in your collection?

1–10 ☐   11–20 ☐   21–50 ☐   51–100 ☐   over 100 ☐

Have you   collected constantly ☐   collected off and on ☐

If you have ticked the last box, why did you stop and then start again? _____

_____

Do you belong to a collectors' club?   Yes ☐   No ☐

<u>We would be interested to know how you got your collection.</u>

Did you get some of you collection

by purchases ☐   as birthday/Christmas/other presents ☐   swapping with others ☐

belonging to a collectors' club ☐   informal contacts ☐   other ☐

If purchase, was it from

shop ☐   auction ☐   car boot/jumble sale/market ☐

other private collectors ☐   mail order from magazine ☐   other ☐

What do you reckon to spend on a piece?

5p–£1 ☐   £1.05–£5 ☐   £5.05–£10 ☐   over £10 ☐

Do you

seek out pieces actively ☐   wait for pieces to appear ☐   are you offered pieces you don't want? ☐

How do you look after your collection?

Are you interested in remembering

where you acquired each piece ☐   what you paid for it ☐   how you found out about it ☐

Are you interested in finding out

how the objects were made ☐   when ☐   where ☐

by whom ☐   how they were used in the past ☐

Do you make a record of any of this? .... yes ☐ no ☐

in a notebook ☐   on a card ☐   on a computer ☐   on a sheet of paper ☐

Do you think about it much between times? .... yes ☐ no ☐

Do you put a personal mark of any kind on each piece? .... yes ☐ no ☐

If yes, what do you put? _____

Do you collect material relevant to your collection, e.g. newspaper articles? .... yes ☐ no ☐

Do you spend time collecting and looking after your collection?

every day ☐   2 or 3 times a week ☐   once a week ☐

once a month ☐   other ☐

If 'other', how often? _____

Where do you keep your collection?

in your bedroom ☐   living room ☐   kitchen ☐

garage ☐   shed ☐   spare room/attic/loft ☐

Is your collection

in a chest of drawers ☐   boxes ☐   on display e.g. on shelves ☐

Anywhere else? _____

How is your collection arranged?

no special order ☐   put on show so that it looks good ☐   divided up in a particular way ☐

What way? _____

Who knows you collect?

family ☐   friends ☐   wide range of people ☐   nobody ☐

Who do you show your collection to especially? _____

Why? _____ When? _____

What do people seem to think of you? _____

<u>We would like to hear why you collect.</u>

Do you collect

just because you like them ☐   to get complete sets ☐   because they bring back memories ☐

If memories, then what memories? _____

Any other reasons? _____

Is it easy to say why you like them? _ yes ☐ no ☐

Can you put down some reasons, e.g. they look decorative/may be an investment? _____

_____

Were you encouraged to collect because you found one thing and carried on from there? yes ☐ no ☐

What thing? _____

Where did you get it? _____

because it linked up with your home? _ yes ☐ no ☐

how? _____

because you were encouraged by somebody? _ yes ☐ no ☐

who? _____

Does you collection link up with another hobby or activity? _ _ _ _ _ _ _ _ _ _ _ _ _ _ _ yes ☐ no ☐

What hobby/activity? _____

Does your collection have anything to do with your work? _ _ _ _ _ _ _ _ _ _ _ _ _ _ _ _ yes ☐ no ☐

What? _____

<u>How do you feel about your collection?</u>

How important is it to you?

very important ☐   fairly important ☐   quite important ☐   take it or leave it ☐

Does it seem a part of you? _ yes ☐ no ☐

Do you use your collection at all? _ yes ☐ no ☐

how? _____

If a piece turned out to be very valuable, would you sell? .... yes ☐ no ☐

Will your collection ever be complete? .... yes ☐ no ☐

Why, or why not? _____

Do you have a favourite piece? What is it? Why? _____

_____

Do you sometimes see something you __must__ have? .... yes ☐ no ☐

Does it ever make you feel guilty? .... yes ☐ no ☐

Why? _____

Do you wish you had never started? .... yes ☐ no ☐

Would you do it again? .... yes ☐ no ☐

What will you do with it in the end?

sell it ☐   pass it on to somebody ☐   bequeath it to somebody ☐

give it to a museum ☐   not given the matter any thought ☐   other ☐

If 'other', what _____

We would like to have a little background about you

sex   male ☐   female ☐

age   18–25 ☐   26–35 ☐   36–45 ☐   46–55 ☐   56–65 ☐   over 65 ☐

Do you think of yourself as   white ☐   Afro-Caribbean ☐   Asian ☐   other ☐

Do you live in   big city centre ☐   big city suburb ☐   large town ☐   small town/village ☐

Where were you born (please given town and county)? _____

What is/was (if retired) the occupation of the main wage-earner in your family? _____

Do you have access to a car? .... yes ☐ no ☐

Are you living with a partner? .... yes ☐ no ☐

Do you have children? .... yes ☐ no ☐

Does anybody else in your family collect? _____

THANK YOU VERY MUCH FOR YOUR HELP

If you would not mind a follow-up contact, please put your name and address below.

_____

_____

If you object to your name and address being held on computer, please tick box ☐

36

Beyond the Odyssey: interpretations of ethnographic writing in consumer behaviour

Annamma Joy

The literature on the use of naturalistic enquiry in consumer behaviour focuses primarily on the researcher and the research process, although the ethnographic account and the reader are often implied. The focus of this paper is on the crafting of such interpretative accounts – realist, confessional, impressionist and jointly constructed. It is argued that ethnographic accounts are not only interpretations of a culture but texts that raise theoretical, philosophical and epistemological issues. By using alternative frameworks and methodologies, ethnographics create the 'other' in order to understand the 'self'. Joy examines these issues through discussion of a swap meet, the Odyssey Project (see also the following paper by Belk) and two gift stores.

The last few years have witnessed both ideological and intellectual ferment in consumer behaviour over what constitutes knowledge and how it is generated, interpreted and generalized across situations (Anderson 1983; Belk, Sherry and Wallendorf 1988; Belk, Wallendorf and Sherry 1989; Hirschman 1986; Holbrook 1987a; Holbrook, Bell and Grayson 1989; Hudson and Ozanne 1988; McCracken 1988; Mick 1986; Sherry 1987a, 1988: Stern 1990). To date, there are very few publications in the *Journal of Consumer Research* that use naturalistic enquiry[1] (although Sherry and Camargo (1987) predates the Odyssey Project), and doubts remain in some scholars' minds as to the usefulness of such alternative paradigms and research techniques in the field of consumer behaviour. There is some unease about such deconstruction processes[2] where knowledge creation and dissemination become the focus of analysis (Anderson 1986; Holbrook 1989).

Since the consumer behaviour Odyssey Project (Kassarjian 1987), there has been a concerted effort to use alternative methodologies to understand consumption patterns, processes and meanings (Arnould 1989; Belk, Sherry and Wallendorf 1988; Belk, Wallendorf and Sherry 1989; Hirschman 1989; Sherry and McGrath 1989). Without exception, all these accounts have questioned some of the underlying premises of what is known in the field of consumer behaviour and our ways of knowing. They have used the ethnographic mode to rethink some key concepts and revise many of our long-held assumptions. This process of questioning our established ways of thinking is referred to in anthropology as 'defamiliarization' (Marcus and Fischer 1986: 138).[3] In consumer behaviour, for instance, Belk, Wallendorf and Sherry (1989) do use this technique in their study of the sacred aspects of consumption. They state that revelatory incidents directly experienced by the researchers caused them to re-evaluate some of the field's fundamental constructs for understanding marketplace and consumer behaviour. They provide three examples of such revelatory vignettes (1989: 2).

> Each of these vignettes reflects a dimension of a buyer and seller world previously undescribed in consumer research. Each is an example of the ritual substratum of consumer behaviour. These observations make it apparent that consumption involves more than the means by which people meet their everyday needs. Consumption can become a vehicle for transcendent experience: that is, consumer behavior exhibits certain aspects of the sacred.

The focus of this paper is on the crafting of such interpretive accounts, whether they are narratives of one's own culture or of cultures other than one's own. Further, this paper incorporates some of the insights provided by feminist discourse that poses new challenges to the writing of ethnographies at home and abroad. Since the consumer behaviour Odyssey Project was confined geographically to the US, the ethnographic narratives linked to this project primarily consider issues relating to the 'self' and 'other' in the context of one's own culture. Consequently, gender concerns or cross-cultural issues are only peripherally raised. To fill this gap, I examine at some length Sherry and McGrath's (1989) comparative ethnography of two gift stores (feminist discourse). In addition, I also make references to a few other ethnographies that help in elucidating key issues raised in this account.

While ethnographic writing is still in its infancy in consumer research, researchers, some of whom have training in fields with long histories of ethnography and case-studies, have veered rapidly towards such rich documentation processes (Wallendorf and Belk 1989). It is my contention that the creation and production of the text is the logical outcome of the hermeneutic process[4] and should be given importance not only because it plays a major role in the dissemination of knowledge but because it raises ethical, political and epistemological issues. One of the central concerns of this paper is to argue that by not reflecting on the text-writing process or on the reading of the text, we objectify the text. This self-reflexivity is central to the claims made by the naturalistic mode of enquiry (Belk *et al.* 1988, 1989). Thus the four components – the researcher, the research process, the reader and the text – are inextricably entwined, and no one factor can be considered without the others. However, this form of demystification need not be confined to accounts using a naturalistic mode of enquiry but must be applied to texts written in a positivist mode as well.

There is a danger, however, in focusing on the textualization process.[5] Post modernist[6] accounts suggest that writing is autonomous and that we can talk about the 'other' without situating the discourse in a political context (Polier and Roseberry 1989). This approach contains an interesting blindspot – it refuses to be self-reflexive, even though it elevates the process of self-reflexivity (Rabinow 1986: 250).[7] The very same argument is applicable to this paper as well. While I have had the opportunity to receive feedback from some of the consumer researchers whose works I have selected, I as the author, have the final say. The attempt at using a dialogic mode[8] remains partial because of the authorial voice I use.

To write a piece such as this at a critical time in the history of consumer behaviour is also to highlight the political processes – at both a macro and a micro level. The macro level has already been alluded to in terms of discussing paradigm diversity arising out of dissatisfaction with existing theories and explanations (Anderson 1986; Firat, Dholakia and Bagozzi 1987; Holbrook 1989). At the micro level, power relations involve the university community and the publication process that includes readings by informants prior to publication, editorial control and the review process (Sherry 1988).

Any discussion of interpretive textualization cannot be understood out of the social contexts of knowledge production (Crick 1982; Flacks and Turkel 1978).

In what is to follow, I explore, through a close reading of the ways in which each author has constructed the text, the ways that selected authors using the ethnographic mode arrive at their conclusions. It is subjective in that it is one reader's interpretation of the texts. Yet any interpretation is also a socially located activity and involves selecting the elements to be included, translating these elements into standard parts, and then arranging them into a text (Becker 1986). Such a process does not occur in a vacuum but follows from the conventions of a collective tradition – in this case, an anthropological/ feminist approach. While the ethnographic mode is alive and well in sociology, and eminently applicable to consumer behaviour, this paper focuses primarily on anthropological texts.

WHAT IS AN ETHNOGRAPHY

An ethnography is a written account that arises out of fieldwork rather than from the description of the fieldwork experience itself (Marcus and Fischer 1986).[9] It is the systematic description of a culture, based on first-hand observation. There are two facets to this – the actual observation and collection of data, and the transformation of such knowledge into the text. The written account of fieldwork in some form in the text is what distinguishes an ethnographic account from all others.

The writing of the ethnographic text has moral and ethical implications, since writing about other cultures involves participation in the culture, and first-hand knowledge of a culture denies any form of neutrality. Ethnographic accounts point to the numerous ways of defining what it is to be human. More recently, ethnography has been a way of talking about theory, philosophy and epistemology while maintaining the traditional task of interpreting different ways of life (Marcus and Fischer 1986). One of the ways in which this is accomplished is by the conscious examination of 'self' *vis-à-vis* the 'other'.[10] This 'other' could be either one's own culture or a different one. In trying to explain differences, however great or small, ethnographers have to deal with complex relations between their cultural constructions of reality and those of others.

How can these concepts of 'self' and 'other' be applied to consumer behaviour? At a very general level, the 'other' can be applied to the study of consumption in our own society as well as to those that are different from our own. In the first instance, we make the familiar strange; and in the second, we make the strange familiar. At another level, the 'self' refers to constructs and methods that are dominant in the field (for instance, the construct of consumer involvement understood through a positivist mode of enquiry). This familiar construct can be made strange by subjecting it to scrutiny and reanalysis using a naturalistic mode of enquiry. Such an exposure to deconstruction and reconstruction of the meaning of this construct through an alternative framework brings forth new recognition and newer understanding.

Belk, Wallendorf and Sherry (1989: 3) provide some insights into this process. They state, with reference to the use of naturalistic enquiry,

> This approach differs from surveys or experiments which assume that the researcher understands the phenomenon prior to doing the research, so that hypothesis and fully specified data collection and analysis plans are possible. In naturalistic inquiry, no such assumption is made. Instead, researchers build an understanding of the phenomenon as it occurs *in situ*, later testing the veracity of that understanding also *in situ*.

Later (p. 31), regarding the construct of involvement, they observe,

> Involvement has been glossed as focused activation (Cohen 1983), whether its duration is situational or enduring (Bloch and Richins 1983). Even when it has been considered as more than merely repeat purchase, loyalty is reduced to a function of decision-making, utilitarian, evaluative processes (Jacoby and Kyner 1973). . . . We have described the sacred and the profane as conceptual categories that animate consumer behaviors. We have incorporated the spirit of these constructs into a more inclusive and culturally grounded process in which consumers routinely harness the forces of material and mental culture to achieve transcendent experience.

In reading a text, a person understands it not only in terms of his/her own individual concerns but also as a collective effort. Reading is a learned and socially organized activity (Becker 1986; Peterson 1976). As an anthropologist I am familiar with the set of conventions that has been used in interpreting a text. These conventions were developed over time and have changed over the years through debate over the problems of representation and interpretation (Becker 1986). When changes are made in conventions, it suggests that the authoritative voices of the past have been replaced by those of a new interpretive community. The political dimension in the interpretive process is thus crucial.

That being said, I must identify the conventions that I used to read and interpret the ethnographic texts presented below. For these purposes I rely heavily on articles by Marcus and Cushman (1982), by Flax (1987) and Strathern (1987), although I have developed my own style of reading and interpretation. On my first reading. I form a general impression of the text. In my subsequent readings. I flesh out the salient features identified in my first reading.

Salient characteristics of ethnographic accounts

1 Its particular genre – realist, confessional, impressionist or jointly constructed.
2 The location of fieldwork, duration, number of researchers, reasons and choice of locale(s), references to establishing rapport, conditions of fieldwork, linguistic competence (if applicable), choice of key informants, methods used to gather data, as well as references to field notes and journals on which the account is based.
3 Organization of the text. How does the author establish a narrative presence? How does s/he present the problem (event, ritual, concept) and how is it analysed? What stance does the author take on the subject?
4 Documentation on any prolonged contact with informants through revisits.
5 Field experience. While the writer may choose to exclude what happens in the field, the reader must be convinced that the writer presents a world that is known to him or her through first-hand experience. This includes not only written statements but maps, drawings, films, videos and photographs as well
6 Generalizations from particular sets of data. For instance, are the cases presented treated as 'typical' or are they acknowledged for their individuality when the author tries to interpret them?
7 Linguistic competence in studying cultures other than one's own. I examine the ways the author uses contextual explications of native concepts in organizing the text.
8 The ways by which the author establishes his/her authority. In any interpretation, this means examining the individual's biases and judgements and the ways they are present. How does the author locate his/her study with interpretations that have

gone before? What is the problem and how does it unfold? The concern here is with the story line and the fleshing out of the details. What point of view does the author take in narrating the story? Do the data presented stay close to the contexts from which the cultural materials are drawn or are they abstracted from the contexts in which they are elicited?

9 The form of cultural critique the text offers. Is it through cross-cultural comparison or through a critique of theory?

10 Gender implications – that is, the author's gender, the gender of the informants, and the types of questions that are asked that reflect gender concerns. This is very closely linked to the stance taken by the author(s). While this may not be critical to all texts, the sensitivity to such issues I consider crucial.

11 Closure, consistency and formality of presentation.

12 Authenticity or plausibility of the explanation. I consider the sensitivity the author displays in presenting the informant's perspective. Does s/he use an 'us-them' difference or a 'me-they' form of contrast, and how is it presented in the text?

13 Audience. Is the author writing for a readership, some of whom are unfamiliar with this framework?

Having outlined the criteria I use for evaluating and interpreting an ethnographic account, I will now discuss the different genres available. They are expertly discussed by Van Maanen (1988), upon whose text I rely heavily for what is to follow.

Types of ethnographic texts

A historical description of ethnographic genres sets the stage for the examination of ethnographies in consumer behaviour. Through these accounts, we have the benefit of knowledge that has gone before, thus providing a potentially greater variety of textual modes. Consumer ethnographies, however, combine elements of each of these genres while emphasizing one or the other.

Realist tales are documentary, are written in the third person, and make reference to typical individuals in the society under study. Ultimately what distinguishes this genre of ethnographic writing from others is the authoritativeness with which the fieldworker presents the culture. The formal rendition of the 'I was there' narration appears only in the introduction or the footnotes or the appendix. The informants and accounts are presented as abstract or ideal types, and the narrator fades into insignificance after the initial introduction (Marcus and Cushman 1982; Van Maanen 1988).

A modified attempt at realism is provided by Arnould (1989: 241) in his study of consumption practices in Zinder, a province in the Niger Republic. He notes,

> Data for this study comes from the author's fieldwork in Zinder province of the Niger Republic. . . . Ethnographic data collection began in 1977 in several villages (Lepdo, Don Doukou, and Riga) and one urban neighborhood. . . . Multiple data sources (both quantitative and qualitative), constant working back and forth between hypotheses and reality tests of them, and intimate knowledge of a group's daily life earned through long-term participant observation provide internal validity checks on the data (Kirk and Miller 1986: 24–5). As in any discipline, peer review provides external validity checks for published material. . . . For this study, formal interviews provided data about consumer behavior (Wallendorf and Arnould 1988).

Realist portrayals gave way to more conscious accounts of the encounter with other cultures and gave rise to *confessional* tales, written in the first person. They exist today, in a modified form. Confessional tales question the assumptions of objectivity in studying other cultures and, more importantly, attempt to deal with this issue in the writing of ethnography.

An example of a confessional is provided by Van Maanen (1988: 83) in his study of the police. He writes,

> Three rather personal and perhaps pivotal factors seem best to explain my particular choice to study the police. First, when I began thinking seriously of the police as a topic for research in the late Sixties, the police were prominently fixed in the imagery of the day. . . . Second, however, not much seemed to be known about the police. Third, the available literature did not seem to square with my own random observations and run-ins with the police.

The 1970s witnessed a radical change in the role of ethnography and the importance of writing ethnographic accounts. In particular, *impressionist* tales made their appearance, exemplified by Geertz (1973). These writings were more reflexive, although episodic and complex, and reflected the tenuous nature of the link between researcher and informants (Van Maanen 1988).

The reader is aware of the nuances and subtleties of the culture as expressed in the vignettes of the ethnographer, establishing a rapport with the informants (Geertz, 1973). The reader peeks over the narrator's shoulder in much the same way as the narrator reads over the shoulders of informants in deciphering cultural principles. However, in this view, the independence of the text and its stable and structural properties are challenged. Detail and intimacy provide proximity between the ethnographer, the informant and the cultures they each come from.

An excellent example of impressionist writing is evident in 'the Balinese cockfight'. Geertz (1973: 4) writes,

> In Bali, to be teased is to be accepted. It was the turning point so far as our relationship to the community was concerned and we were quite literally 'In.' . . . Getting caught, or almost caught in a vice raid is perhaps not a very generalizable recipe for achieving that mysterious necessity of anthropological fieldwork, rapport, but for me it worked very well.

The process of editing informant voices out of the text has the effect of distancing the reader. Distancing lends authenticity to the text. Changes in the account are made in relation to prior knowledge and less from encounters in the field even in the skilled hands of Geertz (1973).

> What the cockfight says it says in a vocabulary of sentiment – the thrill of risk, the despair of loss, the pleasure of triumph. . . . Attending cockfights and participating in them is, for the Balinese, a kind of sentimental education. . . . If, to quote Northrop Frye again, we go to see Macbeth to learn what a man feels like after he has gained a kingdom and lost his soul, the Balinese go to find out what a man, usually composed and aloof, almost obsessively self-absorbed, a kind of moral autocosm, feels like when, attacked, tormented, challenged, insulted, and driven in result to the extremes of fury, he has totally triumphed or been brought totally low. The whole passage takes us back to Aristotle.

There are no exemplary impressionist narratives in consumer behaviour although the article by Sherry and Camargo (1987: 183) on English language labelling in Japan provides some insights.

Marcus and Fischer (1986) refer to the newer modes of impressionist tales as experimental ethnographies, or *jointly constructed tales*, which reflect on writing itself and the contrived nature of the cultural accounts. These accounts use the dialogical mode, wherein the focus is on the actual discourse of fieldwork. They seriously question the substantiality and independence of the text and highlight the tenuous and collaborative nature of the ethnographic account (Crapanzano 1980: Clifford 1983, 1986a). They recognize the role of rhetoric in the persuasion process (Sangren 1988). Dwyer (1982: 221) provides an interesting attempt to produce jointly a tale based on his fieldwork in Morocco. He writes,

> D: Now, I'd like you to think about this question. When I came here for the first time, when Bukhensha brought me here, what did you think then?
> A: I wasn't thinking anything. Just ... 'welcome', that's all. What would be on my mind?
> D: You must have thought something.
> A: No.

(Dwyer observes that this question leads to an immediate dead end. But since it is an important issue, he pursues it further.)

> D: Let's see – what did Bukhensha say to you then?
> A: Well, he said it in front of you: all things considered, this Rumi wants to come here and wants to rent your little room in the village. I have gotten to know him and I am making his concerns mine . . .

In consumer behaviour, there are no exemplary accounts that use the dialogic mode, although Sherry (1990: 33) provides some insights. The author introduces parts of the dialogue (not between himself and an informant as Dwyer does) that a consumer had with a vendor. He quotes,

> P: Will you take $10 for it?
> V: I'd feel like I was giving it away. I'd hate myself.
> P: I wouldn't hate you.
> V: I'd hate myself.
> P: I'll split the difference with you – $12.50
> V: What's it marked?
> P: $18
> V: Can't do it. I'll go $14[00].
> P: Sorry, thanks.
> V: No, thank you.

The focus in such accounts is on using rhetorical devices rather than on rendering quoted speech. Inspired by the new literary criticism, these accounts show how rhetoric can be used to communicate the meaning of a text (Burke 1969). They also enhance the reader's understanding of the ethnographer's aim of communicating a point of view. Just as self-reflexivity regarding the role of the informant and researcher sharpened earlier renderings into meaningful accounts, the new rhetorical devices lend credence to the subversive possibility that the account is unstable and indeterminate. But this must always be seen within a particular context.

Documenting culture is embedded in a specific way of creating knowledge. No text stands by itself: it is constructed within fields of power and privilege and must be seen as such (Mascia-Lees, Sharpe and Cohen 1989; Polier and Roseberry 1989: 251). One way is to introduce elements of critical enquiry into the narrative, which becomes particularly important in cross-cultural contexts. A political economy framework, especially a feminist framework, provides insight into this process. *Critical tales* try to high-light the structural and historical connections among specific customs, institutions or nations without adopting a normative commitment to social solidarity or stressing functional integration (Polier and Roseberry 1989: 257).

To write about writing ethnographic accounts is itself a political process. In consumer behaviour, the politicization of pluralism has been referred to as an unfolding drama – a clash of interests between paradigm bearers, the positivist and post-positivist researchers (Thompson, Loccander and Pollio 1989; Sherry 1988; Belk 1990). The people have been identified, and critical incidents vary from the ACR presidential address to the Odyssey Project of 1986. While tensions mount, an impasse is avoided by reparation made to the situation, evidenced in major changes made to the *Journal of Consumer Research*. Sherry (1988) views this politicization process as a revitalization movement in the history of the discipline. The choice of the performative metaphor opens up the process of dialogue about social complexity rather than reducing it to the single argument of the writer (Marcus and Fischer 1986).

Standard conventions in the crafting of an ethnographic text

In the construction of a tale, there are some common conventions regarding data collection and interpretation observed by ethnographers, regardless of the genre. Field data in any form (audio and visual) and the keeping of a field journal are central to the interpretive process (Wallendorf and Belk 1989).

The preliminary process of recording data is the earliest act of interpretation. Field data are constructed from talk and observation. These field notes provide the opportunity for self-reflection, since the researcher has to make conscious choices as to what is to be recorded, how, when and why it is to be recorded. Values and attitudes determine what are to be recorded as events. A good example of this process is provided by Belk, Wallendorf and Sherry (1989) in their discussion of revelatory incidents that helped them focus on the sacred aspects of consumption. These events or observations, in turn, do not speak for themselves. An interpretation is necessary because what we see or choose to see imposes constraints on us (Polier and Roseberry 1989). In combination with the journal kept by the researcher, it forms a powerful basis for the textualization process. This is why any interpretation is unstable and precarious.

Second, transforming oral and visual into written text can take many forms. Particularly in realist writings, the authors are conscious of the effort to represent the 'other's' point of view. The authenticity of the text (realist tales) was expected by the interpretive community to be enhanced by the actual words, translated and edited by the author. Yet this form of polyphony was used not so much as a consideration of the uses of rhetoric as a desire to lend objectivity to the text.

Third, textualization also raises the epistemological issue of visualism (Clifford 1986a, 1986b; Fabian 1983). Hence the emphasis on quantification, diagrammatic representation, maps and charts. By examining cross-cultural contexts which emphasize the importance of other human senses (Howes 1989), the arbitrariness associated with vision and cognition in our culture is revealed (e.g. 'I see' suggests 'I understand'). In consumer behaviour, Sherry and McGrath (1989), as well as Sherry (1990), pay attention to extrasensory modalities in different retail contexts. Sherry and McGrath (1989: 162) note,

> The reduction of atmospherics to just four sensory features – visual, aural, olfactory, and tactile notions are noted by Kotler (1974) – blunts the exploration of

simultaneous perception and synaesthesia which more accurately characterize ambience.

A particular twist to visualization involves the recording of fieldwork in the form of photographs and videos. While this fits well with the visual metaphor and is used precisely for these reasons, it opens the possibility of evoking polyphony and the multidimensionality of the account. As Wallendorf and Belk (1989: 72) note,

> In our experience, there is generally much more to gain in obstrusively, openly and honestly videorecording and talking to consumers than completely foregoing this opportunity and relying only on unobtrusive observation.

Audio and visual data challenge the givenness of the tale and speak with a different voice (McDougall 1978).

Jointly constructed ethnographies deal with the idea of polyphony in a different manner. They identify the philosophical issues of mediation and problems of meaning involved in presenting the informant's point of view. These authors know that the story can be told in a way which the author wants to tell it. Expertise is not so much at issue as is the knowledge that he or she is both voice and vehicle of meaning transfer. The emphasis is on fragmentation and discourse, not on the text. Narrative form is not a prior issue but one that evolves from the dialogical process. In consumer behaviour, there are no exemplary accounts, although Sherry (1990: 37) provides some insights. He notes,

> The flea market is essentially a multilogue, as Emerson construes such discourse (Fernandez 1986: 239), with many voices communicating. Or, rather, in keeping with the 'alternative' status of the periodic market. . . . As a polylogue, the flea market is a booming, buzzing confusion negotiated at the emic level by transactors, and at the etic levels by the analyst. . . . The flea market is a polylogue whose semiotic intensity is apparent to all participants but whose multiple meanings may be apparent to only a few. The subject of this polylogue (and ultimately its object) is the nature or essence of the marketplace in contemporary U.S. society.

Recognizing multiple voices in the text further necessitates the use of an intersubjective temporal structure which reduces the distance between the informant and the ethnographer. The assumption in such a situation is that the researcher and the informants are equal and share the same concept of time (Fabian 1983). The difficulties of doing so have been identified earlier. At the present time it seems that the experience of the consumer researcher is given temporal anchoring in the past in order to lend logical credence to the description. Realism is preferred, as in the article by Arnould (1989: 242). He notes,

> The first case describes the historical context for contemporary consumer behavior in Zinder. . . . In the nineteenth-century state of Zinder (or Damagaram), mass access to luxury goods was limited by macromarketing factors: the narrow span of the market system, long channels, cumbersome media of exchange (cowrie shells, foreign coins, and slaves), and the absence of written accounting systems (Baler 1974, 1977).

Later, in the discussion of contemporary contexts of consumption, the author states (p. 247),

> A critical periodic consumption event that provides scope for expression and innovation of preferences is the marriage ceremony. . . . A typical marriage today often involves expenses well in excess of annual per capita income.

Likewise, in the presentation of the account, the format used (expository substructures) varies, depending on the nature of the account. Thus Belk, Wallendorf and Sherry (1989: 2) observe,

> Explicit recognition of the sacred status accorded to many consumption objects illuminates aspects of contemporary North American consumer behavior that, while basic and pervasive, have not been explained by prior theory and research. The substantial body of social science theory on the role of the sacred in religion is used here in developing an understanding of sacred aspects of consumption. . . . However, the processes of meaning investment and divestment – the sacralization rituals we treat at length in this article – are resistant to such distanced exposition.

ETHNOGRAPHIC NARRATIVES

THE CONSTRUCTION OF 'SELF' IN ONE'S OWN CULTURE

Ethnographies, among other objectives described above, construct the 'self' in the process of constructing 'otherness' (Marcus and Fischer 1986). This 'other' can refer to a society very different from that of the ethnographer or can be the same one from which he/she comes. Instead of a cross-culturally based probing, 'otherness' is constructed from within the researcher's own culture. This form of cultural criticism is not new and is predominant in such fields as anthropology, sociology, literature and fine arts (Barthes 1973; Csikszentmihalyi and Rochberg-Halton 1981). There are two general directions in which this style of cultural criticism has evolved. The first involves the deconstruction of pure reason and the idea of social progress that results (Rabinow and Sullivan 1987). The second form of criticism arises from the study of social institutions and cultural forms. More recent studies, especially in sociology, deal with the production of cultural forms such as music, the text and art (Becker 1986; Griswold 1987; Petersen 1976). The latest form of cultural criticism, a combination of the two styles is self-reflexive, conscious about the positioning of the critique *vis-à-vis* one's own society, and provides alternatives to what is being critiqued (Marcus and Fischer 1986).

Thus a study of the researcher's own culture allows for the construction of 'otherness' from a new vantage point. Being an insider and yet providing a cultural critique privileges one: on the other hand, it makes the researcher more vulnerable to cultural criticism. But the benefit of such a process is that it minimizes cultural chauvinism that has often accompanied the interpretation of an exotic 'other'. 'Otherness' is comprehended as being both participant and interpreter. Second, by virtue of this dual position, the ethnographer is able to identify the various possibilities and alternatives as they exist in reality. However, such a perspective is not without problems: there are a number of blindspots for the ethnographer studying her/his culture (Wallendorf and Belk 1989). Two examples are examined below.

A naturalistic enquiry into buyer and seller behaviour at a swap meet (Belk, Sherry and Wallendorf 1988)

The importance of this article can be appreciated when one considers the background information and critical political underpinnings of the consumer behaviour Odyssey project. Dissatisfaction with the existing logical positivist philosophy expressed by a number of consumer researchers since the early 1980s eventually led to the coalescing of efforts by 'a substantial and sociometrically-central minority' to question the appropriateness of this position (Belk 1990). This group then decided to embark on the Odyssey project, which was to employ a variety of naturalistic methods to explore American consumption. In order to receive funding from the Marketing Science Institute (MSI), it was decided that a subset of the larger group would do a pilot project. The article on the Red Mesa Swap Meet was the outcome.

The purpose of the article on the Red Mesa Swap Meet is to document both the process and the outcome of interpretive research. It is essentially a tutorial and takes the reader through the various research stages encountered by the authors at a swap meet. Consequently, the first half of the paper is an explanation of data collection methods, data recording techniques, the creation of field notes and the keeping of the field journal. Together they form the basis for the written account. Since the purpose is not to focus on the crafting of the text itself, the latter half of the paper deals briefly with their findings.

It is the first account of its kind in the consumer behaviour literature to deal explicitly and systematically with alternative methodologies and paradigms for doing research, although Hirschman's article (1986) attempts to do the same. The framework used is described as 'naturalistic', although the authors are sensitive to current issues in the field of anthropology and sociology (Wallendorf and Belk 1989).

This account of the swap meet is a prelude to the Odyssey Project. It is based on traditional fieldwork at a single venue and explores a variety of significant actors, events and processes. As in other ethnographic accounts, etic and emic differences are well documented.

The reader is introduced to the site and is provided with a map of the meet. This is followed by some general information about the organization of the vendor area. Next, a brief description of the line-up and ambience is provided. The authors provide a brief description of the sellers and buyers, followed by a discussion of the emergent themes and possible hypotheses that could be tested further.

The authors' concern with the scientific nature of the study is particularly important, given the newness of the framework in consumer research and the considerable hostility of some researchers in the field towards such a paradigm (Sherry 1988). The pilot was critical to the launching of the Odyssey Project. Too much was at stake and, as Belk (1990: 13) notes,

> I doubt that MSI ever got more effort, energy, or material out of $1000 than they did out of the seed grant that got us started. It was partly a labor of love, partly that this effort promised larger rewards in potential funding for the summer project, and partly that it was now time to 'put up or shut up' about the project.

'Otherness' is represented by the alternative methodology and the paradigms that are used by the researchers. By juxtaposing the richer findings garnered from such alternative methods in specific consumption contexts to established concepts in the field, they raise havoc with our thinking and conventional modes of studying consumer behaviour. In their words (p. 467),

> The field has attained some elegance and precision but lacks soul, feeling and sensitivity to natural consumption contexts. . . . But because naturalistic inquiry studies consumers *in situ* and provides thick qualitative insights, it can potentially inject the richness that Tucker saw as missing in our research.

The dialogic mode that is used is not so much the process of joint construction by informant and researcher as the dynamic chorus of styles identified by Bakhtin (1981), which includes both the team's voice and individual voices (e.g., p. 462 they state 'yet for each of these rules we saw several violations'); narrative action: the reported speech of informants (e.g., p. 461: 'if we come out here and spend $10, $15 or $20, it is money well spent'); the teller's commentaries (e.g., p. 461: 'Bill is one of a group of people who sell miscellaneous furniture and used household items. When we first talked to them, they were sitting in upholstered reclining chairs drinking beer and appeared to have been all day'); evaluate remarks (p. 461: 'Bill had never heard of Wroe Alderson, but he nonetheless explained Alderson's sorting concept perfectly'); and interpretive remarks (p. 462: 'Freedom is an important motivation for both buyers and sellers at the swap meet and often transcends economic motivations').

The use of old field notes and journal excerpts in the text, especially by researcher's name, suggests self-reflexivity in the research and writing process. One introspective field note excerpt on p. 465 (some researchers separated field notes from the journal) is particularly poignant. It reflects a sensitivity to the informant as well as gender concerns that explicitly drew me into the text.

> I talked to one young woman who was selling household items in the regular area. She moved to New York about a year ago and had flown back into town for the weekend to sort through the things she had left there. She was trying to sell some of them at the swap meet. . . . A woman friend was helping her sell her things. She said the things that were sentimental she was shipping to New York. These things that she was selling were just things that could be used. I asked about an old waffle maker. She said that if she didn't sell that, she would take it with her because her grandmother gave it to her. But she said that she felt okay about selling it. It appeared to be a U.S.-made waffle maker rather than one that had come from Norway. It was, however, fairly old (1950's) and was probably given to her used [MW].

The instability and precariousness of the interpretation, the simultaneity and intimacy of the moment are all evoked in the reader. Wallendorf's interaction with the woman informant centres around the topic of personal and family ties and how sacred commodities are converted into profane commercial wares in impersonal market (public) contexts. The author is also sensitive to the ambiguity the woman informant felt about selling the waffle-maker because it straddled both categories. It was sacred, Wallendorf argues, in that it was a gift from the woman's grandmother, yet it was not as sacred as those objects given to her that were made in Norway.

From such a poignant moment, we are drawn back into the team's effort to provide substantiality to the text and legitimize the process of naturalistic enquiry. We are told of the value of triangulation methods, of researchers, as well as of the usefulness of auditors. The ethnographic account as a record of facts also becomes apparent in the author's discussions of choice of site, the ambience at site, the profiles of buyers and sellers, and the themes that emerged over the course of doing fieldwork.

The map, the profiles, the categories and themes are all intended to convince the reader of the factuality of the text. The blow-by-blow description of events and the process of temporal anchoring in the past lend validity to the description. The politics of writing culture is revealed only by examination of field entries by the researchers. The use of photographs and the video is an ingenious mechanism to suggest the presence of researchers and help in the interpretive process. However, while there is a commitment to the hermeneutic process, there is a preoccupation with establishing the credibility and legitimacy of naturalistic enquiry in consumer behaviour. The field journals kept by some of these researchers suggest this dilemma. Sherry (1986: 15) makes the following observations regarding the use of video equipment:

> I find that I am relying too much on video as aid to memory, and trying too hard to sustain the interview rather than absorbing all that is being said. . . . The naturalistic context we are after is distorted by this intercept procedure and is being sacrificed to some extent in favor of producing a particular kind of product to the proposal package. Once again, I found myself quite conscious of the camera, in the sense that I attended more to directing the interview than I did to absorbing the sense of his discussion. This time-constrained research – blitzkrieg ethnography is how I am coming to think of it – with a video product objective is disrupting my own natural rhythm, and I'll have to monitor that closely.

In the final analysis, the pilot project accomplished what it set out to do, despite its explicitly exploratory goals. What's more, it helped to establish procedures that were to be used in the main project and became a tangible marker for what was to come for the larger number of researchers who were keenly awaiting the results.

The sacred and the profane in consumer behaviour: Theodicy on the Odyssey (Belk, Wallendorf and Sherry 1989)

The editorial (although an extra-authorial intrusion over which the authors have little control) that accompanies the publication of this article signals the importance of the piece (Lutz 1989).

The use of vignettes as a rhetorical device at the very outset prepares the reader for what the authors try to do – that is, to question our taken-for-granted assumptions of the process of consumption as well as our day-to-day understanding of what is sacred and profane. The authors argue that consumption is more than the means by which individuals satisfy their material needs. It is a vehicle, they say, for a transcendent experience. Further, despite the recognition of sacrality associated with objects in North America, such concepts have not been explained by prior research and theory in consumer behaviour.

The authors demonstrate that the use of naturalistic modes of enquiry is more suitable for revealing such fundamental aspects of consumer behaviour. The iterative and discursive fashion in which they read the literature and interpret their field experiences is an effort to explain, deconstruct and reconstruct theories for us. In this, it is multidisciplinary and is intended as a conceptual contribution to parallel disciplines and as an empirical contribution to consumer research.

That being said, this is how they do it. While the pilot project used a conventional mode of data collection – participant observation at one site – the Odyssey Project involved several researchers and multiple sites. The intent was to pursue a phenomenon that transcended specific sites.

Having established personal authority through the identification of sampled sites, they launch into a discussion of the properties of the sacred as drawn from theories of religion. This section is tutorial in intent, since this material is presumed to be unfamiliar to researchers in consumer behaviour.

Following this is a discussion of the shifting boundaries of the sacred and the profane. What constitutes the sacred is outlined at some length to tutor the reader and make him/her aware of the paucity of such data in the field. This knowledge, they claim, is new and powerful – not amenable to quantitative analysis but best understood through qualitative research. The closest analogues in consumer research are the concept of consumer involvement and extended self, which barely touches upon the nature and experience of sacrality.

'How do certain possessions attain sacred status?' they ask. Through several processes, they answer, such as ritual, pilgrimage, quintessence, gift-giving, collecting and inheritance. They flesh out these ideas through field notes and observations informed by cultural theory and provide a thick text of the processes of sacralization. Each of these topics requires much in-depth plumbing through field data and recursive reading of theories and material and is done, for instance, by Belk, Wallendorf, Sherry and Holbrook (1990) in their paper on collecting.

This section is followed by a discussion of how sacrality is perpetuated. This includes spatial and temporal separation, sustaining rituals, specialized uses of objects, gift-giving, bequests and tangibilized contamination. Again, field notes are used to substantiate each of these methods of maintaining sacredness.

The Odyssey data included 800 pages of field notes, journals, 4,000 still photographs and slides, 137 videotapes, a dozen audio tapes, and few dozen artefacts – a very impressive amount of information that supports both the significance and the generalizability of their observations. The insights drawn from religious theories seem to provide ample insights into the phenomena they observed, allowing the authors to make 'thick descriptions'.

The use of field notes rather than reported speech is an important means by which they establish scientific authority and objectivity. For instance, on page 16, the authors state,

> He exhibited typical Japanese unwillingness to offend by claiming to have difficulty picking a favorite place he has been in America. . . . He doesn't like the crowded areas and said that the West is like the real America for him.

The distancing of the account from the simultaneity of the moment is what gives it scientific authority. There is no question in the reader's mind that the authors were there. Of the twenty-four instances of fieldwork material woven into the tale, more than half were taken from the field notes themselves. These detailed observations sometimes include short statements by informants. On occasion, the name of the informant is provided (e.g. p. 18: 'John's favorite toy is . . .'). The rest were extracted largely from the interviews and presented within quotation marks.

A very interesting attempt to construct the interpretation jointly is done on pages 19 and 22, where the authors provide extracts from the interviews that use both voices – the questions they asked and the responses they received. A touching moment is presented in the text when they describe a woman selling handcrafted dolls (p. 22). They state, 'She kissed the baby as she sold the doll (one object with two communicative voices).' Self-reflexivity is also evident on another occasion when they describe a situation in which they were corrected by their informants (p. 26). One other rhetorical device they use effectively is to bring the same information into the text from time to time. By spreading the field notes and quotations from a single informant over the entire text, the reader begins to develop a sense of the person and not just the faceless 'informant'.

The discussion of triangulation of researchers and methods raises an element of reflexivity, although this is not pursued: the reader is told that they get a bi-gender team with multidisciplinary specialists. In part, this can be explained by the fact that not all researchers were involved in the complete duration of the Odyssey Project (Belk 1990). Self-reflexivity is at its lowest when methodology and the theoretical discourse on the sacred and the profane are provided. The blow-by-blow description of the various stages of research and the interpretation process not only provides clinical description but helps to substantiate the text.

THE 'OTHER' AS IRRECONCILABLE WITH 'SELF'

If in realist, impressionist and jointly told tales the self and other are seen as important elements to be dealt with one way or another, feminist discourse offers yet another dimension to ethnographic writing in its irreconcilable stance between 'self' and 'other'.

Why should feminist discourse be a consideration in writing ethnographic texts in consumer behaviour? The answer to that is as follows: if self-reflection is a cornerstone of ethnographic accounts, the uncritical examination of gender issues that invariably arise in fieldwork is not tenable (Strathern 1987). More eloquently stated,

> Feminist theory is an intellectual system that knows its politics, a politics directed toward securing recognition that the feminine is as crucial an element of the human as the masculine and thus a politics skeptical and critical of tradition 'universal truths' concerning human behavior.
>
> (Mascia-Lees, Sharpe and Cohen 1989: 8)

The above authors state that constructing the 'other' entails relations of domination. While postmodern anthropologists speak for the 'other' (women in our culture, and both men and women in other cultures), the feminist speaks from the position of the 'other' (p. 11). This insight is brought home to us with greater force when we consider the paucity of such analyses in consumer behaviour (Schmitt, Leclerc and Dubé-Rioux 1988; Stern 1990).

Gender discourse refers not only to the ethnographer and the construction of gender in her/his own culture but also to the informants and their constructions of gender. In cross-cultural contexts, this becomes particularly significant, since universal theories of asymmetry are questionable. In consumer behaviour, the construction of gender is not so much an issue as is its manifestation (e.g. Jackson, McDaniel and Rao 1985). The key construct in feminist discourse is domination embodied in the general principle of patriarchy and, more concretely, in men. Men are the 'other' in this discourse (Strathern 1987), and the feminist task is to expose and destroy the authority of the 'other' in order to determine the female experience. Yet within feminist discourse itself, the dialogic process is pursued. The 'self' and 'other' are reconcilable, despite the varying interpretations and divergent cultural experiences of women. With men, however, there is no collaboration, no parity, only asymmetry. Dominance and patriarchy must constantly be recognized in order to maintain self and identity (Strathern 1987). The danger in such a perspective is the reification of the differences that are the sources of oppression that feminism is keen on destroying. One positive outcome of this binary thinking, however, is the emphasis on the worth of some of these 'feminine' qualities (Holbrook 1989). It has countered the negative valuation of women, as well as provided a critique of general cultural values that foster aggression and narrow individualism (Hare-Mustin and Marecek 1989) and allowed women to speak for themselves.

In the consumer behaviour literature, there are a few accounts that deal tangentially with some of the issues raised above (Fischer 1989; Sherry and McGrath 1989). It is to a discussion of this theme in the Sherry and McGrath article that we now turn.

Unpacking the holiday presence: a comparative ethnography of two gift stores (Sherry and McGrath 1989)

While this article is not informed by feminist discourse that sees asymmetry and conflict, there is an attempt to recognize the role of the female voice and the female experience in the construction of the text. Thus of all the texts discussed hitherto, this the most self-reflexive regarding gender considerations.

The authors begin the narrative with the stated objective of studying the institutional focus of discovery and the production of meaning. The two researchers chose sites that are comparable, especially in relation to the backgrounds of the owners and clientele who shopped at the stores. Each week, for a period of two months, 12–24 hours were spent doing fieldwork. The researchers' concern with short-term ethnography made them reluctant to give anything other than tentative generalizations and suggest explanatory frameworks. This sense of incompleteness and missing data set the mood for the reader, who could now join in the interpretive process. Multiple voices were also presented. For instance, the authors note (informant's voice),

> – I'd love to receive a gift from here but would never buy anything here for myself. Buying here is a time investment. It shows that people really care if they take the time to shop here.

and

> – This [expensive piece of jewellery] is a present from me to me.

The introduction to the two gift stores (Baubles and the Mouse House) is richly descriptive. There is detail and there is attention to preparing the reader for what is to follow. Expectations of the reader are met in the discussion of appropriate subtopics such as ambience, merchandise, history, choice heuristic, personnel, seasonal cycle, range of shopping activity, backstage activity and giving to oneself. The differences in text, albeit very few, are apparent in the slight deviations in topics by the ethnographer of Baubles, who introduces subtle nuances in her discussion of the importance of place and the marketing mix involved.

The propositions they offer are illuminating. They also challenge some taken-for-granted assumptions in marketing. The importance of sense of place in understanding buyer behaviour is evident in the authors' discussion of synaesthesia, which accompanies perception. Kotler's concept of 'atmospherics', which refers to the use of the sense of touch, smell, vision and taste, they argue, barely touches this issue.

Object–person relationships through gift-giving processes is a mechanism by which individuals make and re-make themselves *vis-à-vis* others, they note (Sherry 1983). The ludic and hedonistic qualities embedded in gift-giving activity is more important than its utilitarian function, they argue. Through rich descriptions, metaphor and point of view, the authors allow the reader to share in the construction and narration of the text. Most importantly, the authors state that gift-giving is the work of women (Fischer 1989). Since gift-giving behaviour is part of kin work that women do, the authors amplify our existing knowledge of kin work and, by extension, its importance to consumer behaviour. Further, by raising this issue, they signal the importance of kin work and thus defamiliarize the concept of work itself and what constitutes men's work and women's work. They even suggest that a gendered mediation between gift exchange and market might provide a model for a more personalized political economy and more humane workplace cultures.

CONCLUSIONS

The purpose of this paper is to provide a sequel to the discussions on naturalistic enquiry that have appeared in the consumer behaviour literature. It suggests that the openness associated with such an endeavour, once begun, must go on. The paper raises the issue of the links between the researcher, the research process, the reader and the narrative.

In the above discussion, I explored some of the many ways in which ethnographic accounts are being crafted – be they realist, critical, impressionist or jointly constructed tales. This paper is my interpretation of the selected accounts. Yet any interpretation is also socially constructed and is guided by conventions used by an interpretive community (anthropologists/feminists in this instance).

Ethnographic accounts reflect and construct cultural variation in an otherwise homogenizing world. They point to the multiplicity of being human. In the process, they question and challenge existing knowledge and the aims of such knowledge in consumer behaviour. More recently, these have been mechanisms by which theoretical and ethical issues are discussed.

Writing an ethnographic tale does not occur in a vacuum. It is embedded in a specific way of creating knowledge. In particular, ethnographies in consumer behaviour, reflect political turmoils within the field. While they provide alternative frameworks for an epistemological critique of the discipline, there are differences of opinion among the researchers themselves that reflect these larger concerns. The politicization of pluralism and the mission of legitimizing naturalistic enquiry have led some authors to restrict the textualization process. This gate-keeping function can limit the creativity of these accounts.

Based on the studies that have been discussed earlier, the following observations can provide some guidelines for interpreting a text:

1 The crafting of the text is central to the hermeneutic process because it raises theoretical, philosophical and ethical issues.
2 Field notes are the first type of interpretation that occurs. It is close to what the informants say and do and reinforces the constructed nature of interpretation.
3 Field journals allow for self-reflection that informs not only the keeping of field notes but also the interpretive process. In conjunction with field notes, they are necessary manifestations of in-depth observation and interviews and form the basis from which the ethnography is written.
4 The visual metaphor that guides the creation of an ethnographic account contributes to the emphasis on diagrams, charts and maps. However, they have the potential for using multiple voices and presenting the 'other's' point of view and must be explored by researchers.
5 While photos and videos add to the substantiality of the text, they also evoke multiple readings of the text and must be plumbed for its uses. In addition, these videos/photographs may themselves be presentational media (as exemplified by the video 'Deep meanings in possessions: naturalistic research from the consumer behavior Odyssey' (Wallendorf and Belk 1987).
6 The temporal structure that is essential to the structure of the text raises issues of intersubjectivity in the crafting process. While informant and ethnographer share the same time during fieldwork, distancing occurs through the use of narrative structure.
7 Likewise, writing an account cannot be divorced from its political and social context. Concerns over legitimizing naturalistic enquiry, editorial control and the review

process may lead to the use of expository substructures that provide for more realist accounts.

8 The use of multiple voices depends on the stance taken by the researcher(s) and varies with the account. Realist accounts, such as Arnould's (1989), provide data on typical individuals in the field, yet offer a critical perspective. Polyphony is maximally evoked by Sherry (1989) and presented differently in the dynamic chorus of styles in Belk, Sherry and Wallendorf (1988).

9 Finally, the mutuality of the 'self' and the 'other' is challenged in instances that are written in a feminist mode. The constructed nature of gender rather than the acceptance of gender manifestations is dealt with, at least tangentially, in Sherry and McGrath (1989) and offers us insights into how gender can inform writing in consumer behaviour.

The writing of ethnographic accounts is recent in consumer behaviour, hence there is not a large section of documents. Importantly, research monographs that do justice to the multiple dimensions of the text are only beginning to be considered. Journal articles, however comprehensive, are constrained by the requirements made by reviewers in their ability to flesh out the multiple voices of informants, professional standards in doing fieldwork, the self-reflection of the authors, and the nature of field experience itself.

This paper, it is hoped will encourage researchers working within this tradition to consider the interpretive process reflexively. While Belk, Sherry and Wallendorf (1988) provide guidelines for doing research, this paper poses questions about how such accounts are written and read.

This paper first appeared in R. Belk (1991) Highways and Buyways, *Association for Consumer Research, pp. 216–33.*

NOTES

1 Belk, Sherry and Wallendorf (1988) define *naturalistic enquiry* as a set of methods that are used in a natural occurring context, which are typically qualitative and represent a systematic set of procedures for assessing the credibility of the findings.

2 *Deconstruction* is an approach to literary interpretation which suggests that texts can generate a variety of meanings over and above what is intended. Further, the meaning of a text is generated by what it says as well as what it does (Stern 1990).

3 Defamiliarization is a term used by anthropologists to critique our own culture, by examining the form and content of ethnographies written about cultures other than our own (Marcus and Fischer 1986: 138). The authors describe two ways of doing so – through cross-cultural juxtaposition and through epistemological critique. The former makes use of data from other cultural contexts to probe and describe cultural reality at home. Defamiliarization by epistmological critique is more abstract and refers to the process by which knowledge generated on the periphery of a Eurocentric world can be brought back to examine the assumptions at the centre. This helps us to realize the culturally constructed and arbitrary nature of other societies as well as our own.

4 *Hermeneutics* refers to the theory of interpretation that is based on a subjective understanding of the significance of human actions, utterances, products and institutions. It is associated with philosophical attempts to investigate the human condition and the nature of human existence.

5 *Textualization* is a term used by Ricoeur (1973) to refer to the process by which unwritten behaviour, beliefs and practices become coded and classified as data, which then form the basis for interpretation. It is embodied in field notes kept by researchers. It is thus at least once removed from the immediate situation in which the ethnographer participates.

6 *Postmodernism* is a feature associated with advanced capitalist societies and is a controversial term referring to experimental tendencies in the arts, social sciences and architecture since the 1940s. It is confusing as a term, since it suggests that modernism is over, yet what are characterized as

successor movements are dependent on what has gone before (Mascia-Lees *et al.* 1989). The post-modern condition is devoid of authority, unity, continuity, purpose and commitment. In its place, there is rupture, fragmentation and crisis (Marcus and Fischer 1986).

7 *Self-reflexivity* is a term commonly used by anthropologists to refer to the consideration of the 'self' in the interpretive process. It arises out of the concerns with ways of knowing as presented in positivist philosophy and language. The 'self' in such discourse, although recognized, is minimal and unintrusive. Hermeneutics challenges this notion of the neutral or objective self and consciously draws it into the research process such that knowing is contingent on the knower. The self thus becomes a vehicle of meaning transfer.

8 The *dialogical mode* is used in ethnographic accounts that are jointly constructed. It provides cultural materials that are elicited in the interaction between informant and researcher and depends on the representation of the actual discourse of fieldwork (Marcus and Cushman 1982: 43).

9 *Fieldwork* refers to the systematic, first-hand participant observation and in-depth interviews that are conducted by researchers in the field. Prolonged contact and linguistic competence are generally considered necessary to the creation of an ethnographic account. Field notes and a field journal are systematically kept as tools for self-reflection, observation and interpretation. They are the preliminary steps to the interpretive process.

10 The terms '*other*' and '*otherness*' have been used extensively in the sociological and anthropological literature (Marcus and Fischer 1986). 'Self' and 'other' are seen as inhabiting the same world, although the 'other' lives a separate life, with its own centre distinct from the 'self'. The attempt in phenomenological understanding is to focus on the similarities of the self and other that make mutual understanding possible. Putting oneself in the shoes of another allows one to see the similarities between one's own behaviour and that of the other. A particular twist to this process of understanding involves making the other strange. In other words, knowledge of the other is possible only through further defamiliarization of the strange or unfamiliar as part of the other.

REFERENCES

Anderson, Paul F. (1983) 'Marketing, scientific progress and scientific method', *Journal of Marketing* 47 (Fall): 18–31.

—— (1986) 'On method in consumer research: a critical relativist perspective', *Journal of Consumer Research* 15(1): 133–73.

Arnould, Eric, J. (1989) 'Toward a broadened theory of preference formation and the diffusion of innovations: cases from Zinder Province, Niger Republic', *Journal of Consumer Research* 16(2): 239–67.

Bakhtin, Mikhail (1981) *The Dialogic Imagination: Four Essays* (ed.) M. Holquist, Austin: University of Texas Press.

Barthes, Roland (1973) *Mythologies*, London: Paladin Press.

Becker, Howard (1986) 'Telling about society', in H. Becker (ed.) *Doing Things Together*, Evanston: Northwestern University Press.

Belk, Russell (1986) 'Journal, Odyssey Project', unpublished text.

—— (1987) 'A modest proposal for creating verisimilitude in consumer-information-processing models, and some suggestions for establishing a discipline to study consumer behavior', in A. Fuat Firat, Nikhilesh Dholakia and Richard Bagozzi (eds) *Philosophical and Radical Thought in Marketing*, Lexington, Mass.: Lexington Books, 361–72.

—— (1990) 'The history and development of the Consumer Behavior Odyssey', in Russell Belk (ed.) *Highways and Buyways: Naturalistic Research from the Consumer Behavior Odyssey*, Provo, Utah: Association for Consumer Research.

Belk, Russell, Sherry, John and Wallendorf, Melanie (1988) 'A naturalistic inquiry into buyer and seller behavior at a swap meet', *Journal of Consumer Research* 14(4): 449–70.

Belk, Russell, Wallendorf, Melanie and Sherry, John (1989) 'The sacred and profane in consumer behavior: theodicy on the Odyssey', *Journal of Consumer Research* 16(1): 1–38.

Belk, Russell, Wallendorf, Melanie, Sherry, John and Holbrook, Morris (1990) 'Collecting in a consumer culture', in Russell Belk (ed.) *Highways and Buyways: Naturalistic Research from the Consumer Behaviour Odyssey*, Provo, Utah: Association of Consumer Research.

Burke, Kenneth (1969) *A Rhetoric of Motives*, Berkeley and Los Angeles: University of California Press.

Clifford, James (1983) 'On ethnographic authority', *Representations* 1 (Spring): 118–46.

—— (1986a) 'Introduction: partial truths', in James Clifford and George E. Marcus (eds) *Writing Culture: The Poetics and Politics of Ethnography*, Berkeley, Calif.: University of California Press, 1–26.

—— (1986b) 'On ethnographic allegory', in James Clifford and George E. Marcus (eds) *Writing*

Culture: The Poetics and Politics of Ethnography, Berkeley, Calif.: University of California Press, 98–121.

Crapanzano, Vincent (1980) *Tuhaml: Portrait of a Moroccan*, Chicago: University of Chicago Press.

Crick, Malcolm (1982) 'Anthropology of knowledge', *Annual Review of Anthropology* 11: 287–313.

Csikszentmihalyi, Mihaly and Rochberg-Halton, Eugene (1981) *The Meaning of Things: Domestic Symbols and the Self*, New York: Cambridge University Press.

Dwyer, Kevin (1982) *Moroccan Dialogues: Anthropology in Question*, Baltimore, Johns Hopkins University Press.

Fabian, Johannes (1983) *Time and the Other: How Anthropology Makes its Object*, New York: Columbia University Press.

Flacks, Richard and Turkel, Gerald (1978) 'Radical sociology', *Annual Review of Sociology* 4: 193–238.

Flax, Jane (1987) 'Post-modernism and gender relations in feminist theory', *Signs* 12(4): 621–43.

Firat, A. Fuat, Dholakia, Nikhilesh and Bagozzi, Richard (eds) (1987) *Philosophical and Radical Thought in Marketing*, Lexington, Mass.: Lexington Books.

Fischer, Eileen (1989) 'This the season to be jolly? Tensions and trends in Christmas shopping', paper presented at *ACR*, October 1989.

Geertz, Clifford (1973) *The Interpretation of Cultures*, New York: Basic Books.

Griswold, Wendy (1987) 'The fabrication of meaning: literary interpretation in the United States, Great Britain and the West Indies', *American Journal of Sociology* 92: 1077–1117.

Hare-Mustin, Rachel and Maracek, Jeanne (1989) 'The meaning of difference', *American Psychologist* 43(6): 455–64.

Hirschman, Elizabeth (1986) 'Humanistic inquiry in marketing research: philosophy, method and criteria', *Journal of Marketing Research* 23: 237–49.

—— (1989) *Interpretive Consumer Research*, Provo, Utah: Association for Consumer Research.

Holbrook, Morris (1987a) 'What is consumer research?' *Journal of Consumer Research* 14(1): 128–32.

—— (1987b) 'From the log of a consumer researcher: reflections on the Odyssey', unpublished journal and fieldnotes from the Odyssey Project.

—— (1989) 'President's column', *ACR Newsletter* 1–9.

Holbrook, Morris, Bell, Stephen and Grayson, Mark W. (1989) 'The role of humanities in consumer research: close encounters and coastal disturbances', in E. C. Hirschman (ed.) *Interpretive Consumer Research*, Provo, Utah: Association for Consumer Research.

Howes, David (1989) 'Sensorial anthropology', unpublished manuscript, Department of Anthropology, Concordia University.

Hudson, Laurel and Ozanne, Julie (1988) 'Alternative ways of seeking knowledge in consumer research', *Journal of Consumer Research* 14(4): 508–21.

Jackson, Ralph W., McDaniel, Stephen W. and Rao, C. P. (1985) 'Food shopping and preparation: psychographic differences of working wives and housewives', *Journal of Consumer Research* 12: 110–13.

Kassarjian, Harold H. (1987) 'How we spent our summer vacation: a preliminary report on the 1986 Consumer Behaviour Odyssey', in Melanie Wallendorf and Paul Anderson (eds) *Advances in Consumer Research* 14, Provo, Utah: Association for Consumer Research, 376–7.

Lutz, Richard (1989) 'Editorial', *Journal of Consumer Research* 16: 1.

McCracken, Grant (1988) *Culture and Consumption: New Approaches to the Symbolic Character of Consumer Goods and Activities*, Bloomington, Ind.: Indiana University Press.

McDougall, David (1978) 'Ethnographic film: failure and promise', *Annual Review of Anthropology* 7: 305–426.

Marcus, George E. (1986a) 'Contemporary problems of ethnography in the modern world system', in James Clifford and George E. Marcus (eds) *Writing Culture*, Berkeley, Calif.: University of California Press, 165–93.

Marcus, George E. and Cushman, Dick (1982) 'Ethnographies as texts', *Annual Review of Anthropology* 11: 25–69.

Marcus, George E. and Fischer, Michael (1986) *Anthropology as Cultural Critique: An Experiemental Moment in the Human Sciences*, Chicago: University of Chicago Press.

Mascia-Lees, Frances, Sharpe, Patricia and Cohen, Colleen B. (1989) 'The postmodernist turn in anthropology: cautions from a feminist perspective', *Signs* 15(1): 7–33.

Mick, David (1986) 'Consumer research and semiotics: exploring the morphology of signs, symbols and significance', *Journal of Consumer Research* 13(2): 196–213.

Peterson, R. A. (1976) *The Production of Culture*, Beverley Hills: Sage Publications.

Polier, Nicole and Roseberry, William (1989) 'Tristes-tropes: post-modern anthropologists encounter the other and discover themselves', *Economy and Society* 18(2): 245–64.

Rabinow, Paul (1986) 'Representations are social facts: modernity and postmodernity in anthropology', in James Clifford and George E. Marcus (eds) *Writing Culture*, Berkeley, Calif.: University of California Press, 234–61.

Rabinow, Paul and Sullivan, William (1987) 'The interpretive turn: a second look', in Paul Rabinow and William Sullivan (eds) *Interpretive Social Science: A Second Look*, Berkeley, Calif.: University of California Press, 1–30.

Ricoeur, Paul (1973) 'The model of the text', *New Literary History* 5: 91–120.

Sangren, Steven (1988) 'Rhetoric and the authority of ethnography', *Current Anthropology* 29(3): 405–35.

Schmitt, Bernd H., Leclerc, France and Dubé-Rioux, Laurette (1988) 'Sex typing and consumer behavior: a test of gender schema theory', *Journal of Consumer Research* 15: 122–8.

Sherry, John F., Jr (1983) 'Gift-giving in anthropological perspective', *Journal of Consumer Research* 10: 157–68.

—— (1986) 'Odyssey pilot: fieldnotes and Journal', unpublished text.

—— (1987a) 'Journal and fieldnotes on the odyssey Project', unpublished text.

—— (1987b) 'Keeping the monkeys away from the typewriters: an anthropologist's view of the consumer behavior odyssey', in Melanie Wallendorf and Paul Anderson (eds) *Advances in Consumer Research*, 14, Provo, Utah: Association for Consumer Research, 370–3

—— (1988) 'Post-modern alternatives: the interpretive turn in consumer research', in Harold Kassarjian and Thomas Robertson (eds) *Handbook of Consumer Theory and Research*, Englewood Cliffs, N.J.: Prentice-Hall.

—— (1990) 'A socio-cultural analysis of a Midwestern American flea market', *Journal of Consumer Research* 17(1): 13–30.

Sherry, John F. Jr and Camargo, J. (1987) 'May your life be marvellous: English language labelling and the semiotics of Japanese promotion', *Journal of Consumer Research* 14: 174–88.

Sherry, John F. Jr and McGrath, Mary Ann (1989) 'Unpacking the holiday presence: a comparative ethnography of two gift stores', in Elizabeth Hirschmann (ed.) *Interpretive Consumer Research*, Provo, Utah: Association for Consumer Research.

Stern, Barbara (1990) 'Literary criticism and consumer research: overview and illustrative analysis', *Journal of Consumer Research* 16(3): 322–35.

Strathern, Marilyn (1987) 'An awkward relationship: the case of feminism and anthropology', *Signs* 12(2): 276–96.

Thompson, Craig J., Loccander, William B. and Pollio, Howard R. (1989) 'Putting consumer experience back into consumer research: the philosophy and method of existential-phenomenology', *Journal of Consumer Research* 16(2): 133–46.

Van Maanen, John (1988) *Tales of the Field*, Chicago: University of Chicago Press.

Wallendorf, Melanie (1986) Journal observations on the Odyssey Project, unpublished text.

Wallendorf, Melanie and Belk, Russell (1989) 'Assessing trustworthiness in naturalistic consumer research', in Elizabeth Hirschman (ed.) *Interpretive Consumer Research*, Provo, Utah: Association for Consumer Research.

37

Collectors and collecting
Russell W. Belk

By one estimate, one out of every three Americans collects something (O'Brien 1981). Collecting is a common, intensely involving form of consumption. Yet it has been the subject of almost no prior work in the field of consumer research. This paper defines collecting and presents some initial findings from qualitative research on collectors. Propositions are derived for further investigation concerning the appearance and nature of collecting in contemporary American society.

ACQUIRING, POSSESSING, HOARDING AND COLLECTING

Distinctions are necessary between collecting and several related, but distinct consumption processes, including accumulation, possession and hoarding. We reject, for example, the suggestion that collections are necessarily intentional (Duroust 1932) or must involve series-completion (Rigby and Rigby 1949), but accept these as characteristics of some important types of collections. Kron (1983) suggests that collectors are more *selective* (and classificatory) than indiscriminate accumulators. Belk (1982), Kron (1983) and Danet and Katriel (1986) all specify that collecting involves acquiring an *interrelated set* of possessions. Duroust (1932) specifies that objects (or ideas) in a collection must be valued for more than their utilitarian or even their aesthetic qualities. While items collected may have utilitarian or aesthetic appeals, they must have additional significance to the collector due to their *importance in contributing to the 'set'* of items that comprise the collection. Although both coin collectors and misers accumulate money, the criterion of selectivity suggests that the miser is not a collector because he/she views money as a commodity (Simmel 1971/orig. 1907). We would further suggest that collected items take on a *non-utilitarian 'sacred' status*, as discussed below.

Items in a collection, as we construe it, may be *material objects, ideas or experiences* (e.g., travel, restaurant or concert experiences, either with or without tangible manifestations of these experiences). For the sake of brevity we will not focus on the possession-related activities of caring for, cataloguing or displaying a collection. These we label curatorial aspects of collecting and they differ from the acquisitive aspects of collecting *per se*. This distinguishes the collector from the possessor of a collection assembled by someone else (although the acquirer of several such previously assembled collections would be a collector of these collections). A similar distinction might be drawn between two types of non-collectors: the accumulator (who is acquisitive, but lacks selectivity) and the hoarder (who is possessive, but views the items possessed – e.g., food, toilet-paper; McKinnon, Smith and Hunt 1985 – primarily as utilitarian commodities rather than extra-utilitarian sacred items). The acquisitive activities of both collectors and hoarders can become *obsessive and compulsive* (Jensen 1963). Indeed at least some degree of obsession is required to distinguish the hoarder and the collector from the mere possessor of items.

METHODS

Our insights about collecting derive from data collected by the Consumer Behavior Odyssey. Since the data collection and analysis methods from this project have been described elsewhere (Wallendorf and Belk 1987), they will not be described here other than to say that the Odyssey was a transcontinental interdisciplinary research project undertaken in the summer of 1986 by a team of researchers from fifteen universities in the United States and Canada (Belk 1987a: Holbrook 1987b: Kassarjian 1987; Sherry 1987; Wallendorf 1987). The project employed a naturalistic paradigm (Lincoln and Guba 1985) to explore consumption phenomena in accord with Tucker's (1967) seminal call for open-ended investigation of fundamental consumer behaviours.

It should be noted however, that the focus on collecting behaviour in this project was not sustained enough to allow a complete development and testing of a theory of collecting based solely on these data. Therefore, the following discussion describes tentative propositions that are warranted based on these data. This preliminary work both contradicts and elaborates upon the existing literature on collecting.

PROPOSITIONS ABOUT COLLECTING

Collections seldom begin purposefully

Contrary to traditional wisdom, our findings and those of Johnston and Beddow (1986) indicate that collections of a particular type of item often begin with an incidental or accidental start. Rigby and Rigby suggest that 'Perhaps the average collector chooses his given subject in much the same way that people find friends and mates among those individuals whom chance has included into their small orbit' (Rigby and Rigby 1949: 341). They further recognize that collections can and often do begin without conscious intent (p. 398). For many, a gift (Lee 1984; Leerburger 1986) or a seemingly serendipitous discovery of some item (Schwarz 1984) starts a collection. A survey of 215 collectors also round that, for many, fascination with a single item that had been acquired led to a quest to acquire similar items (Treas and Brannen 1976). This desire to find replicable material pleasures is consistent with our interpretation of collecting as a materialistic activity.

In a sense, many collections are 'discovered' by their creators long after the materials have been gathered. Among our informants, one had amassed a number of paintings, wall hangings and other artefacts representing animals (see Holbrook forthcoming). This 'collection' did not register as such in his consciousness, but was rendered apparent upon reflection.

In some instances a collector began with inherited 'seed' objects or an intact 'starter' collection that primed the adoption of a collector role. For instance one informant had received such a 'starter' set of Christmas plates.

Gifts may act as a seed around which collections accrete. One informant, nicknamed 'Bunny', received rabbit replicas as gifts from her friends, and purchased others for herself. Another informant traced his collecting behaviour, which developed into a museum and gift shop, to a wedding gift given to him by a relative. Other informants reported receiving 'collectables' as gifts and subsequently embarking on quests to complete the collection.

The origins of hoards, as distinct from collections, were quite different. They existed less as discretely bounded, thematically unified wholes than as caches or eclectic assortments, and typically arose from accumulation by consumers who experienced traumatic deprivations, such as the loss of family networks or the weathering of the Great Depression. In some cases, these hoards were shared with others under the rubric of 'good neighbourliness'. One elderly informant had assembled several garages full of assorted utilitarian objects such as hardware, furniture and the like, which he dispensed to neighbours. Collectors are also unlikely to be as altruistic.

Addiction and compulsive aspects pervade collecting

Collecting is often likened by the collector, and perhaps more frequently by his or her family and friends, to an addiction, while search behaviour is frequently described as both an obsession and a compulsion. Both our interviews and others' examinations of collecting have suggested that collecting is addictive (e.g., Kron 1983; Johnston and Beddow 1986; Danet and Katriel 1986; Rigby and Rigby 1949; Olmsted 1987; Meyer 1973; Brady 1975; Holbrook 1987a; Brough 1963). Despite their incidental start, many collections are seen as becoming an addictive activity in which adding items to the collection constitutes a 'fix'. As with other addictions, the object of the addiction is relatively unimportant; it could be almost anything and acts only as the focus of release from other fears or feelings of inadequacy (Delattre 1986). While it might be debated whether avid collectors can be considered to be clinically addicted, the fact that collectors themselves admit to being addicted is telling, for, as described by Peele (1985), addiction is by no means a positive condition. He suggests that insecurity prompts the addicted individual to seek reassurance through a repeated ritualized activity. While feelings of well-being may increase as a result, the addict's other interests narrow until they focus solely on the external object of the addiction. The fact that many collectors readily admit to being addicted indicates the power of the attraction or of the social sanction bestowed upon compulsive activity when it is legitimized with the label 'collecting'. Association with other compulsive collectors further supports this feeling of positive addiction (Glasser 1976).

The altered states of consciousness produced through the collector's search and acquisition are commonly described as mood swings resembling the euphoria and depression induced by chemicals. Collectors frequently experience a holistic, autotelic sensation described as 'flow' (Csikszentmihalyi 1975). The search process is clearly a thrill-seeking experience for many collectors, which may engender distress as well as eustress. Collectors often report feeling both a craving and a loss of control with respect to their acquisition habits, and occasionally experience negative consequences in other spheres of their personal and social activity as a result of their chronic collecting. The coincidence of collecting and chemical dependency, or the incidence of symptom substitution or displacement (from chemicals to collectables) is sufficiently high as to warrant extended investigation. While many collectors belong to voluntary associations connected with their particular pattern (e.g., the Midwest Association of License Plate Collectors), many also lament the lack of self-help groups designed to arrest compulsive collecting. Some collectors forestall completing collections for fear of the withdrawal symptoms. As might be expected, 'dual or poly dependencies' commonly occur, with a collector diversifying into a number of collectables. So also is intergenerational transfer of collecting (although perhaps not of the same collectable) a commonplace occurrence.

One informant in particular embodied the interplay of stresses of compulsive collecting. A recovering polydrug abuser, he described his current collecting behaviour as an addiction. He has accumulated a large collection of Mickey Mouse memorabilia, and often obtained his 'Mickey fix' (an emic term) in lieu of paying rent or meeting other financial obligations. The thrill of collecting and displaying these objects eventually threatened his well-being, so he stopped collecting 'cold turkey' (again an emic term).

Collection legitimizes acquisitiveness as art or science

For the collector (and perhaps the hoarder to a lesser degree), the recognition of the collection by others as being 'worthwhile' legitimizes what is otherwise seen as abnormal acquisitiveness. This can give the collector not only a sense of purpose (e.g., Goldberg and Lewis 1978), but a sense of *noble* purpose in supposedly generating knowledge, preserving fragile art, or providing those who see it with a richer sense of history. Having one's collection accepted into a museum collection or in some instances even having it *become* a museum is the ultimate in legitimization of the activity (e.g., Hughes 1987; Pollay 1987). Having items *like* those that one collects appear in a museum is a less direct means of legitimizing one's collecting activities (Meyer 1979).

The distinction between art and science in collecting seems to appear in the two (pure) types of collectors detected by Danet and Katriel (1986). Their 'Type A' collector employs affective criteria to choose items for the collection. Such collectors try to improve their collections, but have no sense of a series needing completion. The 'Type B' collector uses cognitive criteria to choose items that add to a series and help improve their knowledge rather than the beauty of the collection. We agree that these two types, while sometimes mixed, represent the two distinct approaches of art and science as ways of legitimizing a collection (Belk 1986). In either case, a halo effect of sorts occurs, such that search and acquisition are ennobled through association with the collection itself. In turn, the effort invested in search and acquisition further legitimizes the collection. This effort raises these activities in the eyes of the collector to the level of art, if not science. Collecting is not mere stockpiling or warehousing, mean acquisition or sheer accumulation. Collectors exhibit a variant of the 'commercial libido' that Malinowski attributed to Zapotec merchants (Malinowski and Fuente 1982). The ardour and passion driving search behaviour is nurtured by a sense of purpose and worth.

Profane to sacred conversions occur when an item enters a collection

This legitimization and sanctioning of acquisitiveness is related to another phenomenon that occurs in collecting – the transformation of ordinary profane commodities into sacred icons. The terms 'sacred' and 'profane' are not used here in a vernacular religious sense. Instead profane is taken to mean mundane, ordinary and common, while sacred is taken to be extraordinary, special and capable of generating reverence (see Belk, Wallendorf and Sherry 1987). Collectors 'singularize' (Kopytoff 1986) items enshrined in collections when they remove an item from the secular, profane, undifferentiated realm of the commodity, and ritually transform it into a personally and socially significant object. The sacralized item becomes a vehicle of transcendent experience which exceeds its utilitarian and aesthetic endowment.

Sacred conversions are accomplished in a number of ways. The sheer bringing together of items under the rubric of 'collection' is the most basic transformation. By metonymic association, the sacrality of each item is enhanced. The container (whether it be envelope, box or room) chosen to house the collection defines a sacred space. Conventions for handling the collection and schedules for interacting with it provide the ritual grounding for maintaining its sacredness. As Kopytoff (1986) notes, the function of the collection in sacralizing formerly ordinary objects is aided by these objects being removed from the sphere of commodity exchange and also from their ordinary utilitarian roles. Thus collected automobiles or furniture must be sufficiently old that they are not merely seen as 'used' rather than rare antiques. Informants who were collectors of automobiles, if they drove these cars at all, drove them sparingly and for special occasions because they were regarded as primarily non-utilitarian icons. Coins that are no longer circulated gain some rarity by this status, but also make it clear that they lack utilitarian properties. Hoarding items merely for their investment value is not collecting because it invokes a utilitarian reason for the accumulation.

Another means of sacralizing a collectable object is by its having been 'contaminated' (in a positive sense) by contact with prominent persons. One antique collecting informant treasured a musical box that had once belonged to Winston Churchill. Other objects were seen by their collectors as contaminated with sacredness by connection to actors or to the collector's ancestors. An item can also gain sacred significance by having been a part of a famous collector's collection. Thus collectors may refer to a Walferdin Boucher, a Weil-Picard Fragonard, or a Gangnat Renoir (Rheims 1961). For this reason, an auction house such as Sotheby Parke Bernet or Christie's carefully explains the price-inflating provenance of an item for sale when it has a famous history. This contamination of property is also why collections are devalued and desacralized by the discovery of a forged work (Belk 1987c). If the utilitarian or aesthetic qualities of the item were paramount, the forgery would not matter. But because a collection depends instead upon other qualities for its sacredness, the forgery loses its value for the collection upon discovery (unless it enters a new type of collection where it is esteemed for its curiosity value).

Informants provided the strongest evidence of the sacredness of their collectables when asked about the saleability of the items. Except to upgrade, there was no consideration of this possibility. The Mickey Mouse collector, an elephant figure collector and an antique bronze collector all had businesses in their areas of specialization. Nevertheless, once an item entered their private collections, it would never be considered saleable. They said this would be unthinkable and would clearly be 'wrong'.

Collections serve as extensions of self

Our self-definition is often highly dependent upon our possessions (Belk 1987b). The collection is especially implicated in the extended self because it is often visible and undeniably represents the collector's judgements and taste (Stewart 1984). In addition, the time and effort spent in assembling a collection means that the collector has literally put a part of self into the collection. Sometimes collections involve a particular theme that is symbolic of one's occupation, family heritage or appearance (e.g., Fusco 1984; Lee 1984). Data from which this proposition is drawn include a grocery store owner's collection of antique consumer product packages, an advertising historian's collection of advertising artefacts, an amateur musician's collection of the recordings of musicians he admires, an engineer's collection of pocketwatches, and even the efforts of our research team in spending the summer travelling across country to amass our collection of data.

Because collections are seen as extensions of self, to lose one's collection is to experience a diminished sense of self. Because of this connection to self-definition, collections have been seen as aiding in children's development (e.g., Witty 1931; Tooley 1978). In the sense that nations are also collectors of art and artefacts, concern with loss of national pride results in efforts to repatriate such objects when they are in the hands of other nations and to prevent further loss of national heritage in this way (Venables 1984). The deep sense of loss experienced when a collection is accidentally destroyed was highlighted by the destruction of one informant's lifelong record album collection in a flood. He, too, felt destroyed by the flood, as if it had taken a part of him.

The notion that collections represent one's extended self accounts for many of the self-enhancing motives given for collecting, such as seeking power, knowledge, reminders of one's childhood, prestige, mastery and control. Data on a wealthy female informant's collection of monogrammed silver spoons inherited from her husband's mother indicates that it served as a mnemonic device conveying the importance of family name (through the monogram), wealth and social position. Several informants who saw themselves as cosmopolitan collected intangible travel experiences which some tangibilized with collections of T-shirts or glassware from each place visited.

Collections are used not only to express aspects of one's direct experiences; they are also used to express fantasies about the self. This proposition is based on data illustrated by a baseball-card collector (himself a middle-aged man) who thinks middle-aged men collect baseball cards 'to keep alive their fantasies of being ball players'. Since these fantasy aspects of the self aren't lived on an everyday basis, they are experienced through the collection, as was true for a fire buff (he enjoys watching fires and firefighting) who collects fire department items. The collector of Mickey Mouse items collects them because he is 'an overgrown kid'. The housewife nicknamed Bunny collects bunny replicas partly because she thinks her teeth make her look like a bunny and partly because, as she half-jokingly mused, people think she looks like a 'Playboy' bunny.

Other collectors expressed even grander fantasies, which are poignant in their underlying expression of self-doubt. The collector of elephant replicas, a man fond of showmanship, fantasized about adding a live elephant to the collection to attract the publicity he craves. Similarly, an overweight 8-year-old boy with a prominent scar indicated that he collects swords in order to 'make me equal to the other kids' when they play duel with each other. A 6-year-old girl entered in a beauty pageant wanted to collect pins from pageants to put on her sash because they would make her feel pretty.

Organized groups of collectors, such as the networks of elephant replica and Mickey Mouse collectors, support their mutual identity not only by trading with each other, but also delighting in showing their new acquisitions to each other. Only in such groups does a collector find knowledgeable others with sufficient understanding to feel appreciative and envious of the collector's acquisitions.

Just as a personal collection serves to shape the self-definition of a collector, so do museum collections serve to define the identity of a region or historical period. As with personal collections, a part of this identity is grounded in reality, and a part in fantasy and myth. This extension of the proposition was derived from instances like a museum of pioneer farm life in the Midwest which attempted to create a regional identity by displaying such household items as Limoges china, ornate parlour tables, pianos and sideboards, china cupboards with leaded glass fronts, and lace dresses. Such items may have been found in the town banker's house, but are certainly not representative of the area lifestyle at the turn of the century. Yet, through the collection, a nostalgic image of life is constructed as the identity of the region's past.

Collections tend towards specialization

While collections may begin broadly, there has been a trend towards specialization in the West since the eighteenth century (Defert 1982; von Holst 1967; Wittlin 1970; Impey and Macgregor 1985; Praz 1964; Hodgen 1964). This has helped the collector define a more manageable collecting task and narrow the competition so one's chances of being unique are improved (Rochberg-Halton 1986).

One informant was proud that she had all of the 'retired' (no longer in production) Precious Moments figurines, but would not consider purchasing any of the current figurines. Such increasing specialization was commonly mentioned, as with the elephant replica collector. He indicated that at that time he was seeking only the rare advertising pieces, he had recently purchased an entire collection of 500 elephant replicas in order to obtain the 20 in which he was interested. A jazz collector said he likes the music of only about 20 musicians, and has mainly their albums. The collector of Mickey Mouse items focused only on replicas produced during a certain time period. He indicated that he knows some collectors who specialize only in either authorized or non-authorized Disney toys. Such specialization produces expert consumers with greater knowledge than sellers, an unusual market phenomenon. It is perhaps appropriate to note that the researchers, as data collectors, evinced a similar tendency. As emergent design unfolds, the specification of appropriate sampling units becomes more focused in order to challenge developing ideas.

Post-mortem distribution problems are significant to collectors and their families

If collections are extensions of self, keeping one's collection intact may be a way to gain a sort of immortality (Rigby and Rigby 1949). Having lived to such a degree through the collection (e.g. definition of self, fulfilment of fantasy, development of a sense of mastery, construction of meaning and purpose in life), the collector's desire for immortality through the collection is not surprising. Another reason that collectors are concerned with the fate of their collection involves its perceived sacred status. They fear that it might fall into the hands of someone who would profane it by failing to appreciate it and care for it properly (Rheims 1961; Johnston and Beddow 1986; von Holst 1967). Some collectors have disinherited their children, finding them to be unworthy of their collections (Cabanne 1961).

In the data there is a tendency with age for both the collector and his or her family to begin to be concerned with post-mortem disposition. However, as with death, it is difficult for them to talk with each other about these concerns. Cultivating an heir is one solution, but quite often other family members are not interested (Olmsted 1987). Where a family member has some interest, there may be a substantial 'education' that must be imparted so the inheritor can fully appreciate the meaning of items in the collection (McCracken 1987). Again, the analysis turns to the collector of elephant replicas, who said he plans to leave the entire collection to his granddaughter, although she was only a year old. He has already given her several elephant toys (he says he is making a point of it) as well as an elephant print dress. He will not leave the collection to his daughter or to his wife because he doesn't think they would continue it. He wants to believe that the collection is historically important and that people will some day appreciate what he has accomplished. This type of inheritance pattern requires further research to determine its structure and consequences.

In contrast, a 79-year-old man who had accumulated three garages of functional materials to share with neighbours (properly a hoard rather than a collection) indicated that his children wanted him to get rid of all of it. He resisted until he was put in the position of serving as the executor of an even older neighbour's estate. When we visited him in follow-up interviews, he had in fact begun clearing things out of the garages. Although the strategies differ, both informants are making some efforts to resolve the dilemma posed by their life-long pattern of acquisitiveness.

There is a simultaneous desire for and fear of completing a collection

The desire to complete a collection has been cited as a feature that distinguishes human collecting from more innate hoarding tendencies in certain animal species (Rowed 1920). Desire for completing a collection has also been taken as evidence of compulsiveness among collectors (Wiseman 1974). Given notions of extended self, what is being completed, is really the collector (see Wicklund and Gollwitzer 1982), at least to the 'Type B' collectors (Danet and Katriel 1986). At the same time there seems to be a paradoxical fear of completing a collection (e.g., Dannefer 1980; Olsmsted 1987). For if one is a collector and there is nothing left to collect, who is one then? This fear also emphasizes the commonly heard justification that the fun is in the hunt and acquisition rather than in the possession of a collection. Only continual acquisition reinforces the sense of mastery and prowess. A common strategy to avoid completion is to redefine or add new collecting interests as completion nears. A different sort of problem occurs when financial means, time or space prohibit enlarging one's collection, as with car collecting for those with moderate means. Two strategies are possible. One is to improve one's collection continually, either by modifying the items owned or by trading-up. The other strategy is to develop a 'serial collection' in which the items in the collection are owned sequentially rather than simultaneously.

The desire for closure is seen in a baseball-card collector who wanted to have one card for each major league player in a particular year, and a man who had travelled to all but one continent and would like to go to Antarctica just to complete the set. At the same time, the fear of completion is shown in such strategies as developing higher standards as a way of ensuring that the collection is never complete. A collector of baseball cards can try to trade up to have a collection that is in 'mint' condition. Commercial sources often aid in expanding even highly specialized categories. Just as new Precious Moments figurines are constantly introduced into the marketplace, previous models are constantly removed from production, thereby increasing the set of 'retired' figurines that a collector can seek. Similarly, there are now several companies that issue series of baseball cards, so a collector can start a second company's series if one nears completion. And collectors also expand to prevent completion by beginning to collect peripheral items. A jazz-record collector also collects magazines about jazz. An antiques collector with a house filled with furniture said she was now looking for accessories.

CONCLUSION

Because no comprehensive integrated model of collecting exists in the social science literature, we have advanced a number of propositions towards such an end. Our data suggest that collections may be fruitfully classified on at least three dimensions or distinctions: conscious/unconscious, vertical/horizontal and structured/unstructured. We shall discuss each of these distinctions briefly, as an illustration of the utility of thick description to effective model-building. A deep understanding of collecting, based on additional field data and etic constructs, is forged in a subsequent treatment.

The *conscious/unconscious* dimension refers to the extent to which a recurrent theme is intentional, purposive, recognized and/or formally instituted as opposed to unintended, haphazard, below the level of awareness and/or informally organized. Collections high or low on all four of these attributes lie at the extremes of this dimension; mixed cases fall towards the middle range. A prototypical example is the collection of advertising artefacts which was found to be a goal-oriented, organized activity that intentionally provides a clearly recognized focus for the collector's life's work and hobbies to the point where he has officially instituted an archive and designated himself as its curator. By contrast, careful observation and photographic documentation uncovered an unconscious theme in another informant's collection of art objects in which a recurring animal motif lay below the level of conscious awareness (see Holbrook forthcoming).

The *vertical/horizontal* dimension reflects the degree to which a collection is housed in one centrally located array (often literally 'vertical' in its position on the wall or on shelves) as opposed to being spread or scattered throughout a space (so that visiting the entire collection requires 'horizontal' movement). An illustrative example from the data is a collection of figurines, statuettes and small porcelain objects that occupied two glass-enclosed display cases on both sides of the fireplace of one informant's living-room; in a sense, if an object were removed from these vertical arrays, it would no longer belong to the collection. In vivid contrast, another informant's vast collection of hearts, ducks, geese, apples and strawberries has expanded horizontally throughout her house; these objects pervade her space and appear in the most unsuspected places, which turned our photographic exploration of her home into a hunting expedition for hearts and geese.

Finally, the *structured/unstructured* dimension relates to how strongly the collection evinces aspects of order, balance and symmetry as opposed to entropy, collative properties and disarray. A structured collection is illustrated by a collection of silver spoons that hangs in a well-ordered, carefully balanced, highly symmetric display in an informant's dining-room. Indeed, its structured regularity may reflect a tendency on her part towards the pursuit of symmetry whose visual manifestations reach their apotheosis in the meticulously matching patterns of the bedspreads, wallpapers and curtains in her newly constructed master bedroom and recently redecorated guestroom. At the other extreme, another family's collection of stuffed animals lies around the house with no particular indication of organization or planning. Similar evidence of the ability to tolerate or even to prefer asymmetric arrangements appears in the flawed pattern of knobs on this family's kitchen cabinets, in the violated gestalt or negative synergy that characterizes one corner of the master bedroom, and in the comparatively lopsided positioning of the objects in and around the master bed. This latter arrangement contrasts vividly with the exaggerated symmetry of the master bedrooms in the other houses we visited in the same town.

Combining the conscious/unconscious, vertical/horizontal and structured/unstructured dimensions into one three-dimensional space and treating each as a simple dichotomy or trichotomy produces an eight- or twenty-seven-celled typology of collections that sets forth the conceptual possibilities in this particular classification scheme. Empirically, some combinations appear more likely than others; in other words, in actual fact, the dimensions or distinctions are related. Conscious-vertical-structured and unconscious-horizontal-unstructured collections appear more probable than others, as in the spoon and Hummel figure collections as contrasted with the animal artwork and stuffed animal collections. These two types were most evident in the household collections documented by Ruesch and Kees (1956). We also expect that the former is more related to Danet and Katriel's (1986) Type B collector, while the later should be more typical of Type A collectors. However, other combinations also occur and, conceptually, still others are possible. The hearts and geese were conscious-horizontal-unstructured; a pesticide collection was unconscious-vertical-semistructured (Holbrook forthcoming).

These dimensions, as well as a number of other structural and processual features, are essential to capturing the complexity of collecting behaviour. As our naturalistic enquiry into collecting proceeds, these eight propositions will be further refined or recast, and the phenomenon more thoroughly interpreted through the prism of consumer research.

This paper first appeared in Association for Consumer Research, Advances in Consumer Research, Vol. 15 (1988), pp. 548–53.

NOTE

Full references were omitted from the original article.

38

Why they collect: collectors reveal their motivations

Ruth Formanek

This paper reviews traditional psychoanalytic ideas on the motivations of collectors as well as newer 'relational-model' psychoanalytic approaches focusing on the develop-ment and stability of the self. Descriptive data on motivations are presented, based on 112 collectors' responses to a questionnaire and 55 letters from collectors. Categoriza-tion of motivations was based on the meanings of collecting (1) to the self; (2) to others; (3) as preservation, restoration, history, and a sense of continuity; (4) as financial invest-ment and (5) as addiction. Suggestions for future research include the use of in-depth interviews with collectors over a period of years in efforts to further explore motiva-tions as well as changes in collecting patterns over time.

Collecting is an important part of some people's lives as attested by the many magazines on collecting and by fairs inviting collectors' participation. Despite its importance, most examinations of collecting have appeared in the popular press and relatively few scholarly papers have been published. The first part of this paper surveys a portion of this scholarly work, focusing on psychoanalytic theories of the motivations of collectors. The second part offers preliminary data from an empirical study of collectors who were asked to speculate on the motivation to collect.

We shall first refer to Freud and his followers, who derived the individual's relation-ship to possessions and to collecting from the sexual drive. We shall then discuss notions about possessions and collecting from one of the newer 'relational-model' theories.

EARLY PSYCHOANALYTIC THOUGHT

Early contributions to the motivation to collect derive from Freud's biological drive model (1963), and were elaborated on by Jones (1950), Abraham (1927) and Fenichel (1945). These writers asserted a continuity between infant experience and adult per-sonality traits. During one of the 'psychosexual stages', the 'anal' stage, when infants' libidinal pleasures are related to sphincter control, a connection was asserted to exist between these anal-erotic impulses and certain traits of adults. This connection was twofold: (1) between faeces, the first product 'created' and overvalued by the infant, and the overestimation of things symbolic of faeces in adult life, and (2) certain traits orig-inating during toilet training and its attendant struggle with parental authority and the adult personality traits of obstinacy, orderliness and parsimony.

Jones (1912) described

> the refusal to give and the desire to gather . . . collect, and hoard. All collectors are anal-erotics, and the objects collected are nearly always typical copro-symbols: thus, money, coins (apart from current ones), stamps, eggs, butterflies, . . . books, and even worthless things like pins, old newspapers, etc. . . . A more edifying manifestation of the same complex is the great affection that may be displayed for various symbolic objects. Not to speak of the fond care that may be lavished on a given collection – a trait of obvious value in the custodians of museums and libraries.
>
> (1912: 430)

Abraham (1927) further suggested a similarity between collecting, or the love of possessions, and the love of a human being: the

> excessive value he (the collector) places on the object he collects corresponds completely to the lover's overestimate of his sexual object. A passion for collecting is frequently a direct surrogate for a sexual desire . . . a bachelor's keenness for collecting often diminishes after he has married.
>
> (1927: 67)

According to Fenichel (1945), childhood attitudes towards success or failure during toilet training are often continuous with later attitudes towards personal achievements. Such attitudes vary between self satisfaction and discontent, or vacillate between the two. Anal conflicts include two components – fear of loss and enjoyment of an erogenous pleasure. These conflicts may be displaced onto collecting. For example:

> A patient with the hobby of excerpting everything he read and arranging the excerpts in different files enjoyed in so doing (a) an anal-erotic pleasure: what he read represented food; his files represented the feces, into which the food had been turned by him; he liked to look at his feces and to admire his 'productivity'; (b) reassurance: the filing system was supposed to prove that he had things 'under control',
>
> (1945: 383)

again an allusion to toilet training.

Lerner (1961) appears to have been the only investigator who searched for an empirical basis for the presence of anal conflicts and their sublimation in collecting. He contrasted an experimental group of 15 stamp-collectors with a control group of 15 non-collectors. A list of 22 'anally-connotative' words was constructed and matched with neutral words. He determined auditory and visual thresholds of perception for each word. Data were analysed for differences within each subject and between groups of subjects, with regard to perceptual thresholds for anal and for neutral words. Lerner hypothesized that some subjects would show 'defence' effects, i.e., would respond more slowly, while others would show 'vigilance' effects, and would respond more rapidly when shown 'anally-connotative' words. Evidence in support of the hypothesis that collectors would differ in their perception of anal and neutral words was found, and Lerner believed that his study offered experimental evidence for the validity of the anal-character concept, as well as for the concept of sublimation.

Another motivation underlying collecting derives from psychoanalytic drive theory (Loewenstein, personal communication, 1988). Freud had hypothesized the existence of two drives, libido and aggression. Collecting might be viewed as deriving not from libido, i.e., the anal-erotic impulse, but from the aggressive drive. In many respects collecting resembles hunting: one locates the prey, plans for the attack, acquires the prey in the presence of real or imagined competition for it, and feels elated. The prey becomes a trophy – a symbol of one's aggression and prowess.

NEWER PSYCHOANALYTIC THOUGHT

During the last twenty post-Freudian years, 'relational-model' theories have begun to dominate psychoanalytic thinking. While the theories differ from one another, according to Mitchell's (1988) account, they draw on a vision of human development different from Freud's. Human beings are portrayed in them not as driven by sexual and/or aggressive impulses, but as shaped and embedded, and understood only within a matrix of relationships with other people. The mind is viewed as dyadic and interactive, seeking contact and engagement with other minds. Psychic organization and structures are based on patterns which have accompanied early interactions with caretakers.

Self Psychology, one of the relational-model theories, contributes to our understanding of the motivations of collectors. This theory concerns itself with the development of a healthy, cohesive, stable sense of self. According to Kohut (1984), the self develops dyadically out of close early relationships called 'selfobject relationships'. Self Psychology does not reduce all human experience and motivation to two inborn drives, as Freud had proposed. Thus sexuality is no longer the central motivator of behaviour. In fact, Self Psychologists view an overconcern with sexuality as an indication that the individual has perceived a threat to his/her stability and now attempts to fortify it. Thus, heightened sexual concerns and behaviour are viewed negatively, as desperate attempts at shoring up a fragile sense of self. This dethroning of sexuality also means that collecting is no longer viewed as a sublimation of anal sexuality, or as evidence of the trait of parsimony. Rather, collecting represents a need of the individual to explore, be in contact with others, and search for personal stability.

Wolf (1980) has attempted to chart the development of the self over the lifespan. In infancy, a close relationship to a primary caretaker permits the development of self structures, the creation of 'selfobjects'. With increasing maturation, other family members, friends or peers may substitute for the earlier relationship. Eventually, in adulthood, the need for a close relationship to another human being may also be transferred onto abstractions – to one's country, one's language, religion, profession. And to one's collecting. The motivation to collect may thus be viewed as partly arising out of the impulse to explore and seek contact with others, as well as representing a later development of early needs for close relationships with others.

William James (1892) and others (Beaglehole 1974; Furby 1978; Csikszentmihalyi and Rochberg-Halton 1981) have also asserted a close connection between personality and relationship to property. James, in particular, discussed the concept of the self, and applied it to collecting. Possessions, to him, are extensions of the self:

> A man's Self is the sum-total of all that he can call his, not only his body, and his psychic powers, but his clothes and his house, his wife and children, his ancestors and friends, his reputation and works, his land and horse and yacht and bank account.
>
> (James 1892: 177)

Moreover, if acquiring things aids our maintaining the continuity and cohesiveness of the self, their loss is bound to have adverse effects. According to James, people feel 'personally annihilated if a life-long construction of their hands or brains – say an entomological collection or an extensive work in manuscript – were suddenly swept away'.

A loss of possessions leads to 'shrinkage of our personality, a partial conversion of ourselves to nothingness' (p. 178).

James seems to allude to a connection between a loss of possessions and depressed feelings. He is echoed by Freud's observations of his own collecting: 'on the next rainy day I shall walk down to my beloved Salzburg; the last time I was there I picked up a few old Egyptian things. Those things cheer me and remind me of distant times and countries' (1954: 291). And William Randolph Hearst's mother allegedly remarked that 'every time Willie feels badly, he goes out and buys something' (Saarinen 1958: 76).

EMPIRICAL WORK

Empirical research on collecting has been summarized by Belk, Wallendorf, Sherry, Holbrook and Roberts (1988) and Olmsted (1991). While both summaries refer to motivations, no researchers have addressed motivations. And with good reason! Representative samples are probably unobtainable. Questionnaires are inadequate in view of the complexity of the issue. And, as many collectors are familiar with popular writings on collecting, their own ideas of collecting are no doubt influenced by what they've read. In view of this familiarity, the collectors' own speculations about their collecting cannot be used to validate hypotheses. Despite these difficulties, we decided to construct a questionnaire and search for collectors to respond to it. What follows is a preliminary and descriptive report of the responses to this questionnaire, as well as excerpts from collectors' letters.

METHOD

Subjects

Our sample includes responses from 167 subjects: out of 300 questionnaires sent to professors at Hofstra University (Long Island, New York) for class distribution, 32 responses were received from students, 12 from professors, and 7 from members of students' or professors' families; 32 collectors and 7 dealers who responded to our 'author's query' in the *New York Times,* or to notices in *The Antique Trader, Clocks Magazine* and other specialized collectors' publications, and who subsequently filled out questionnaires, and 5 collectors taking a course on collecting at another university. Seventeen respondents were recruited through personal contacts. Fifty-five letters were received from collectors and/or dealers who responded to the notices in the above-mentioned publications but who did not fill out questionnaires. This procedure of finding subjects is of course highly selective and permits no more than a glimpse into the personalities and the behaviour of some highly verbal collectors. It underrepresents those who do not attend private universities or read the *New York Times* and magazines for collectors. It also excludes those whose concern for their valuable collections led some to contact the author but who refused to fill out questionnaires, even when anonymity was promised.

Some demographic information is presently available on the first 97 questionnaires. Fifty-five respondents were female, 40 were male, and no information is available on two. Three respondents were between the ages of 9 and 16; 7 between 17 and 24; 25 between 25 and 39; 30 between 40 and 54, and 32 were over 55.

Nine people had been collecting between 1 and 4 years; 26 between 5 and 10 years; 12 between 11 and 15 years, and 46 longer than 16 years. No information is available on

4. Sixty-two collectors stated that they researched their collected items in books and/or magazines, and one researched in a museum. Information is missing on the other respondents.

Instrument

The questionnaire further asked about how collectors added items to their collections (e.g., find, trade, auctions, gifts, buy); how their collections are displayed; whether items are researched (e.g., in books, magazines, journals, museums); how much money is spent annually on the collection; what got collectors started on collecting, and how many different collections they had.

In addition to these factual questions, the questionnaire also addressed more intimate aspects of collecting, such as: When you acquire a new item, what do you feel? When you show your collection to others, does it matter to you that they react as you do, or admire your collection and your work as the collector? When do you work on your collection? When do you feel you want to add items to it? (e.g., when your life feels busy and full? when you're feeling a bit down? when you have lots of time?) Do you worry that your impulse to collect may get out of control and that you will spend too much money? Do you give any thought to the disposition of your collection?

We were most interested in the questions on motivation: Why do you think people collect? What motivates them? Why do you collect? Do you think collectors as a group differ from non-collectors? How important is your collection to you? Are there similarities in the personalities of collectors of similar items?

RESULTS

Out of the total of 112 questionnaires, 90 responded to the question on motivation. Some of the letter-writers also commented on motivation and are identified below by 'L' before their number. Of the 90, 3 (who identified themselves as psychologists!) did not respond, and 19 wrote that people collected for 'fun', 'interest', 'because it's a hobby', thus not really answering in any detail.

Multiple motivations

Twelve respondents listed multiple motivations. For example, No. 32, who collects prints, photographs, drawings, oils, wine, netsukes, books and other things: 'The challenge of the hunt; increasing and refining one's knowledge; patronage of an artist; having beautiful objects that retain or increase their value.' She adds, 'I think I enjoy objects more than people.' No. 48, a collector of military flags and flag items: 'Some collectors are in it for the hunt, others are hoarders, and some are preservationists or artefact conservators.' He collects for the 'experience of the past through historical objects that were used in struggles, and to appreciate lost values and workmanship.' No. 66, a pottery collector: 'Esthetic or historical satisfaction; excitement of the hunt and actual acquisition. Having something no one else has. Potential for financial appreciation.' No. 19, a collector of antique drinking-vessels: 'To have something that will "live" after them; to build ego: I have something you don't; to complete sets; to accumulate wealth; to satisfy yearnings for the good old days.' He adds that he has found good friends via his hobby, and that some of these friends have become more important to him than the hobby itself.

Collecting has meanings in relation to the self

Thirty responses were classified as pertaining in one way or another to the self – a motivation described by William James (1892) and Csikszentmihalyi and Rochberg-Halton (1981), referred to by Belk *et al.* (1988), and extrapolated from the work of the relational-model theorists. We have tried to divide this group into (a) those who collect as a defence against feeling low, (b) those for whom collecting appears to be a challenge, a wish for expertise, knowledge or mastery, and (c) those for whom collecting has a narcissistic function, that is, is essential for the maintenance of their self esteem.

(a) One would expect some collectors to refer to their being motivated by a need to counteract a sense of loss, low spirits or depressed states, and by a need for elation. Yet only one collector (No. 27) expressed such a motivation: 'I can focus my entire attention on searching out blue glass and can release my mind from other concerns. My collecting intensified after my mother died.'

(b) No. 90, an antiques collector: 'Collecting serves as an extension of the collector and his creativity; and brings a sense of excitement and purpose to one's life.' No. 87 collects seashells: 'People have a primal urge to collect, probably a connection to an early childhood pleasurable experience or a sense of order and control about possessing something.'

(c) The term 'narcissism' refers to the search for the maintenance of self-esteem. Mental activity is narcissistic to the degree that it functions to maintain the self as cohesive, stable and with positive affect (Stolorow and Lachmann 1980). This activity is frequently directed towards others – human beings and things – that become the source of supply for self-esteem. It is characteristic of some narcissists that the supplies only temporarily aid in maintaining their self-esteem, and that new sources of supplies must be found. 'I'm thrilled when I buy a new item', wrote antiques collector, No. 101. 'It gets special attention from me for a while. I show it to my friends before it goes in with the others. Then I slowly lose interest and look for new items.' And No. 56: 'I enjoy having something that others don't have.'

No. 69, a doll-collector: 'Some people want to have something special of their own and have a compulsion for perfection.'

Collecting has meanings in relation to other people

Eight respondents referred to the relationship between collecting and love of people – a motivation also consistent with relational-model theories. The items collected may represent close relationships to others, and the sharing and communicating with a group of like-minded people contributes to the individual's sense of well-being. For example, No. 42, who collects antique automobiles, spoke of the 'world of friendship that is opened to other collectors around the world'. No. 72, a collector of dolls, coins and musical boxes: 'People are motivated by sharing with others a segment of their personality.' No. 75, who collects books, records and shrubs: 'Some collect because their collections are their friends, and for some sharing with others has great value.' The relationship to people may also further status ambitions, as suggested by No. 112, who collects figurines: 'The desire to belong and become a part of an acceptable group of people.' Or, from L54: 'A new item becomes part of my collection and part of my family, or a close friend.'

Collecting as preservation, restoration, history and a sense of continuity

The need to restore and preserve was mentioned by four collectors. No. 27, who collects antique phonographs: 'The passion to preserve items for other people to enjoy. Getting an item back to pristine condition and working.' No. 40, a rock-collector: 'God created the world either by some unfolding principle or by a Big Bang. Rocks are part of this. It should make us realize that there is a great wondrous God. I am only a laborer and not very intelligent. . . . People collect to protect and preserve.' No. 57 collects old linens and lace: 'I collect for the love of old things. I like to see them saved for the future and when there will be none around.'

One of the six collectors who mentioned history as a motivation, No. 59, collects clocks and watches. He is motivated by the 'intrigue and history of time pieces'. No. 89, who collects fibre-related antiques, mercury glass, standard poodle miniatures, and snow eagles: 'For history buffs, it's a way of touching the past.' No. L23, who collects political buttons: 'I see collecting presidential memorabilia as a real service to our country.' No. L60, who collects postcards, pictures of royal families, letters from celebrities, all cut from newspapers, said that her scrapbooks 'make the past live again. These treasures hold everything there for you at a moment's notice . . . and it's special because you chose to cut it out and save it. . . . They all offer solace – a quiet world – you own what you've cut out, planned and ordered. I have pictures of movie stars that I cut out at age six – these pictures represent me.'

Collecting as financial investment

Eight collectors mentioned primarily financial motivations, but those who listed multiple motivations included them as well.

Collecting as an addiction

An important motivation is the feeling of excitement and elation. Referred to but as yet unexplored in the literature, is the collector's 'addiction' to collecting (Belk *et al.* 1988). The terms 'obsession' or 'compulsion' are mentioned chiefly in the popular literature (Olmsted 1991) and are not distinguished from addiction. Nine respondents mentioned addiction, obsession and compulsion, but definitions and introspective data are missing. Only one collector reported on his state of mind:

I looked forward for weeks to the day of this annual book sale and felt like a child waiting for Christmas. That date seems to organize my life; not only did I have to arrange to be on time, but I had to be there at least one hour before the opening in order to secure one of the first places in line. Once on line, I could feel a sense of arousal and excitement (release of endorphins?), heightened by overhearing conversations expressing similar excitement. Some of the talk is of treasures found at other book sales. Strategies are considered – which section to attend to first. The doors finally open. The crowd surges in. Chaos reigns until the collectors disperse to their areas of interest where they begin to place books into bags or boxes from which they will make their final selections. Elation continues during the hard work of scanning books as either fit for my collection, unfit or doubtful and to be decided on later. The next anticipated pleasure is to examine my purchases at home. Yet, with a few exceptions, after some time has elapsed, I can't exactly tell which book was bought where. Moreover, I sometimes wonder what made me buy a particular book. But I look forward to my next fix: another book sale, auction, or visit to a book dealer.

Miscellaneous motivations

There is a considerable popular and anecdotal literature on unusual and/or pathological collecting (see Carmichael 1971). In our sample an unusual motivation was expressed by No. L13. He felt 'a real compulsion to collect, but just for the sake of doing so, without any real interest'. He collected newspapers, stored them in his garage, and soon accumulated high stacks. He was unemployed. When his mother urged him to get a job, he felt compelled first to read all the accumulated newspapers since he thought he might miss something going on in the world. A slow reader, he remained unemployed for years.

No. L73 collects music: 'I try to learn more about a particular piece of music because I am intimidated by the intellectual jargon of the Arts Establishment. So I contrived my own approach to an understanding of the works without having to cope with scholarly disciplines beyond my reach.' He collected live performances, on tape, of over 1,000 pieces predetermined by his idiosyncratic taste. One might interpret his collecting as motivated by anti-establishment attitudes which lend him a sense of adequacy.

Our questionnaire further asked collectors about their views of the differences among collectors: Are there similarities in the personalities of collectors of similar items? Would you expect coin-collectors as a group to differ from book- or car-collectors? In what ways? Neither this question nor a question pertaining to differences between collectors and non-collectors yielded much information. Baekeland (1981) has suggested differences among collectors as based on a possible linkage of introversion and extraversion to aesthetic preferences, or of conservatism as leading to a dislike of abstract and complex art works, or the possibility that the three basic body types (mesomorph, endomorph and ectomorph) determine a preference for paintings. People tend to prefer those paintings that symbolize their somatotypes. This is another issue in need of research.

DISCUSSION

We have categorized our collectors' statements under five rubrics in addition to a category of collectors offering multiple motivations: collecting has meanings (1) in relation to the self, (2) in relation to other people, (3) as preservation, restoration, history and a sense of continuity, (4) as financial investment and (5) as addiction. While the categories are empirically derived, some reflect the emphasis of 'relational-model' psychoanalytic theories.

As expected, evidence for the existence of sublimated anal-erotic impulses in collecting was not found. Such evidence has traditionally derived from the couch rather than from the laboratory, from interpretation rather than from direct observation. Lerner's perceptual study is the only exception. And even his carefully designed research rests on the interpretation of the speed of responses in line with psychoanalytic drive theory.

Our research was designed to explore rather than to test hypotheses. We believe that our collectors' insightful responses have added to our understanding of the myriad of motivations to collect and will stimulate further research.

In view of the diversity of motivations found, one may speculate on the function of collecting to the individual personality. What seemed to be characteristic of our collectors, but less so of the literature surveyed, and what further complicated any efforts to reconcile our data with existing speculations on the collector's motivation, were references to changes in collecting interests and behaviour over time. While the literature suggests a linearity in regard to factors determining collecting and influencing the collector, our data suggest that collectors have experienced and observed changes within themselves. Collecting may be in the service of whatever motivations or needs dominate the individual at any given time, and may satisfy different personality needs at different times. This view also leads away from the search for one or more 'basic' motivations, and permits one to understand changes in an individual's collecting behaviour over time. It further suggests that questionnaire approaches are inadequate to the study of motivations and should be followed up by introspective reports, longitudinally, and by in-depth interviews to determine changes in collecting as reflective of changes in the collector's life and personality.

What is common to all motivations to collect, and what appears to be the collector's defining characteristic, is a passion for the particular things collected. This passion which, in some, resembles sexual excitement, may have led Jones, Abraham and Fenichel to consider collecting as the sublimation of anal-erotic impulses. In our sample, collectors alluded to their passion but could not fully describe it nor give evidence of understanding it. The adolescent Gustave Flaubert (1954) could describe it in a story about a book collector: 'he took the cherished book, devoured it with his eyes, . . . and loved it as a miser does his treasure, a father his daughter, a king his crown' (p. 10).

This paper first appeared in Journal of Social Behaviour and Personality 6(6), pp. 275–86.

REFERENCES

Abraham, K. (1927) *Selected Papers on Psychoanalysis*, London: Hogarth
Baekeland, F. (1981) ' Psychological aspects of art collecting', *Psychiatry* 44: 45–59.
Beaglehole, E. (1974) *Property*, New York: Arno Press. (Original work published 1932)
Belk, R. W., Wallendorf, M., Sherry, J. F., Holbrook, M. and Roberts, S. (1988) 'Collectors and collecting', *Advances in Consumer Research* 15: 548–53.
Carmichael, M. F. (1971) *Incredible Collectors, Weird Antiques and Odd Hobbies*, Englewood Cliffs, N.J.: Prentice Hall.
Csikszentmihalyi, M. and Rochberg-Halton, E. (1981) *The Meaning of Things*, Cambridge: Cambridge University Press.
Fenichel, O. (1945) *The Psychoanalytic Theory of Neurosis*, New York: Norton.
Flaubert, G. (1954) *Bibliomania: A Tale*, London: Rodale Press. (Original work published 1836)
Freud, S. (1954) *Sigmund Freud Letters: The Origins of Psychoanalysis*, New York: Basic Books.
—— (1963) 'Character and anal erotism', in P. Rieff (ed.) *Character and Culture*, New York: Collier.
Furby, L. (1978) 'Possessions: toward a theory of their meaning and function throughout the life cycle', in P. B. Baltes (ed.) *Lifespan Development and Behavior* vol. 1, New York: Academic Press.
James, W. (1892) *Psychology, Briefer Course*, New York: Holt.
Jones, E. (1950) 'Anal-erotic character traits', in *Papers on Psycho-analysis* (5th edn), London: Bailliere Tindall & Cox. (Original work published 1912)
Kohut, H. (1984) *How Does Analysis Cure?* Chicago: University of Chicago Press.
Lerner, B. (1961) 'Auditory and visual thresholds for the perception of words of anal connotation: an evaluation of the "sublimation hypothesis" on philatelists', doctoral dissertation, Ferkauf Graduate School of Education, Yeshiva University, New York.
Mitchell, S. A. (1988) *Relational Concepts in Psychoanalysis: An Integration*, Cambridge, Mass.: Harvard University Press.
Olmsted, A. D. (1991) 'Collecting: leisure, investment or obsession?' in F. W. Rudmin (ed.) 'To have possessions: a handbook on ownership and property' [special issue], *Journal of Social Behavior and Personality* 6(6): 287–306.
Saarinen, A. B. (1958) *The Proud Possessors*, New York: Random House.
Stolorow, R. and Lachmann, F. (1980) *Psychoanalysis of Developmental Arrest* New York: International University Press.
Wolf, E. S. (1980) 'On the developmental line of selfobject relations', in A. Goldberg (ed.) *Advances in Self Psychology*, New York: International University Press.

Further reading

The books listed here add some key texts to those already presented, and should be regarded as follow-up reading.

Barthes, R. (1977) *Image, Music, Text*, New York: Hill & Wang.
Baudrillard, J. (1968) *Le Système des objets* Paris; Gallimard.
Bourdieu, P. (1977) *Outline of a Theory of Practice*, Cambridge: Cambridge University Press.
—— (1984) *Distinction: A Social Critique of the Judgement of Taste*, trans. R. Nice, Cambridge, Mass.: Harvard University Press.
Briggs, A. (1990) *Victorian Things*, London: Penguin Books.
Bronner, S. (ed.) (1985) *American Material Culture and Folklore: A Prologue and Dialogue*, American Material Culture and Folklore Series, Ann Arbor: University of Michigan Press.
Bryant, C. and Jary, D. (eds) (1990) *Giddens' Theory of Structuration*, London: Routledge.
Collingwood, R. (1946) *The Idea of History*, Oxford: Oxford University Press.
Crook, J. M. (1973) *The British Museum: A Case-Study in Architectural Politics*, London: Penguin Books.
Douglas, M. and Isherwood, B. (1979) *The World of Goods: Towards an Anthropology of Consumption*, London: Allen Lane.
Eagleton, T. (1983) *Literary Theory: An Introduction*, Oxford: Blackwell.
Eysenck, H. (1991) *Decline and Fall of the Freudian Empire*, London: Penguin Books.
Fekete, J. (ed.) (1984) *The Structural Allegory: Reconstructive Encounters with the New French Thought*, Manchester: Manchester University Press.
Foucault, M. (1972) *The Archaeology of Knowledge*, London: Tavistock Press.
Fyfe, G. and Law, J. (eds) (1988) *Picturing Power*, Sociological Review Monograph 35, London: Routledge.
Giddens, A. (1979) *Central Problems in Social Theory: Action, Structure and Contradiction in Social Analysis*, London: Macmillan.
—— (1984) *The Constitution of Society*, Cambridge: Polity Press.
—— (1991) *Modernity and Self-Identity*, Cambridge, Polity Press.
Gombrich, E. (1962) *Art and Illusion: A Study in the Psychology of Pictorial Representation*, London: Phaidon Press.
—— (1984) *The Sense of Order: A Study in the Psychology of Decorative Art*, London: Phaidon Press.
Habermas, J. (1987) *The Philosophical Discourse of Modernity*, trans. F. G. Lawrence, Cambridge: Polity Press.
Haggett, P. (1965) *Locational Analyses in Human Geography*, London: Arnold.
Harvey, D. (1989) *The Condition of Postmodernity* Oxford: Blackwell.

Hawkes, T. (1977) *Structuralism and Semiotics*, London: Methuen.

Herrmann, F. (1972) *The English as Collectors*, London: Chatto & Windus.

Hodder, I. (1986) *Reading in Past*, Cambridge: Cambridge University Press.

Jackson, L. (1991) *The Poverty of Structuralism: Literature and Structuralist Theory*, London: Longman.

Jameson, F. (1991) *Postmodernism: or The Cultural Logic of Late Capitalism*, London: Verso Books.

Leach, E. (1976) *Culture and Communication*, Cambridge: Cambridge University Press.

Merriman, N. (1991) *Beyond the Glass Case: the Past, the Heritage and the Public in Britain*, Leicester: Leicester University Press.

Miller, D. (1985) *Artefacts as Categories*, Cambridge: Cambridge University Press.

—— (1987) *Material Culture and Mass Consumption*, Oxford: Blackwell.

Moulin, R. (1987) *The French Art Market: A Sociological View*, trans. A. Goldhammer, New Brunswick: Rutgers University Press.

Pocius, G. (ed.) (1991) *Living in a Material World: Canadian and American Approaches to Material Culture*, St John's, Newfoundland: Institute of Social and Economic Research, Memorial University.

Popper, K. (1979) *Objective Knowledge: An Evolutionary Approach* (revised edn), Oxford: Oxford University Press.

Rees, A. and Borzello, F. (eds) (1986) *The New Art History*, London: Camden Press.

Schlereth, T. (ed.) (1982) *Material Culture Studies in America*, Nashville, Tenn.: American Association for State and Local History.

Shanks, M. and Tilley, C. (1987a) *Re-Constructing Archaeology*, Cambridge: Cambridge University Press.

—— (1987b) *Social Theory and Archaeology*, Cambridge: Polity Press.

Simmel, G. (1978) *The Philosophy of Money*, London: Routledge & Kegan Paul.

Stocking, G. (ed.) (1986) *Objects and Others: Essays on Museums and Material Culture* vol. 3, *History of Anthropology*, University of Wisconsin Press.

Suleiman, S. and Crossman, I. (eds) (1980) *The Reader in the Text*, Princeton, N.J.: Princeton University Press.

Wainwright, C. (1989) *The Romantic Interior: the British Collector at Home 1750–1850*, New Haven: Paul Mellon Centre for Studies in British Art, Yale University Press.

Wierzbicla, A. (1985) *Lexicography and Conceptual Analysis*, Ann Arbor, Mich.: Karoma.

Index

Abraham, K. 327, 328
academics 220–1
acquisition 153–4, 317–18, 320
action objects 148
actual objects 25
addiction 319–20, 333, 334
addition 327
Aegina marbles 95
aesthetic experience of collecting
220–37; closure, striving for
229–35; dominance and
aesthetics 228–9; no-two-alike
principal 227–8; reframing object
225–7
aesthetic theory see rasa
aesthetics see play and aesthetics in
collecting
Albrecht, V. 176, 177, 179
Aldrovandi 183, 184
Alexandria Museum 164
Allen, F.L. 206, 207
Ames, M. on politics of interpretation 98–105, 263
analysis 3, 67, 116, 134, 135
'Anatomie Theater' (Leyden) 183
Anatomy School of Oxford
University collection 183
Anderson, Lieutenant H. 19, 20,
23, 25, 26
Anderson, P.F. 296, 297
Apollo Gallery (Louvre, Paris) 282
Appadurai, A. 101, 102, 104; on
commodities and politics of value
76–90
archaeology: analysis 71–2;
perspective 125–32; theoretical
48–52; see also New Archaeology
Ariana Museum (Geneva) 161
Arnould, E.J. 253, 296, 300, 304,
313
art museums and ritual of
citizenship 279–86; civilization
on the wane 285–6; museum as
ritual 280–2; politics 282–4
art and objects 142
art-culture system 258, 263, 270
artefacts 9, 11, 61, 78, 260–1, 264,
266; Columbian 265; studies
125–32; tribal 258
Arundel classical marbles 197
Asian Art Museum (San Francisco)
188
Assembly of First Nations 103, 105
Attalids of Pergamum 168

Baekeland, F. on psychological
aspects of art 205–18, 334
Bagozzi, R. 297
Bakhtin, M. 306
Balfe, J.H. 102
Balicki, A. 63
Barbarossa, F. 167
Barbie Museum 245–50
Barker, N. 93
Barley, N. 131
barter 80, 81
Barthes, R. 17, 267, 305; material
culture interpretation 67, 69, 74;
objects as meaning 21, 23, 28
Batchelor, R. on multifaceted
interpretation of objects 4,
139–43
'battleship-shaped' curve 30, 32, 33
Baudrillard, J. 17, 158, 159, 255,
261; commodities and politics of
value 79, 82, 87–8
Beaglehole, E. 329
Beaumont, Sir G. 216–17
Becker, H. 262, 298, 299, 305
Bedard, J. 100
Beddow 318, 319, 323
behavioural action 39
behavioural interaction 38–40
Behrens, P. 142
Behrman, S.N. 206, 207, 218
Belk, R.W. 5, 158, 252, 330, 333;
on collectors and collecting
317–26; ethnographic writing in
consumer behaviour 296, 297,
298–9, 303, 304, 305–10, 312,
313; on gender identity in
collecting 240–53
Bell, S. 296
Bellamy, L. 203

Belli, V. 93
Berenson, B. 206
Bergler, E. 211, 213
Berlyne, D.E. 215
Beuningen, D.B. van 208
Beurdeley, M. 217
Beutel, T. 183
bhava 190, 191
Bibliothèque Nationale (Paris) 265
Binford, L.R. 48, 50, 67
Binyon, L. 195
Birket-Smith, K. 63
Boas, F. 49, 62, 65, 99, 265
Bohannan, P. 83, 86
booty 165–7
Börne, L. 205
Bosman, W. 199
Botticelli forgery 96
Boucher, W. 321
Bourdieu, P. 16, 17, 81–2, 290
Brady 319
Brannen 318
Bray, W. 197
Bredius, A. 96
British Museum 92, 195
Brooklyn Museum 280
Brooks, E. 197
Brough 319
Bührle, E.-G. 208
buildings 56–7
Bunn, J. 260
Burke, K. 302
buyer and seller behaviour 305–8

Cabanne, P. 206, 208, 323
Cabinet des Médailles (Paris) 93
Camargo, J. 296, 301
Cambridge Material Culture study
school 44
Campbell, S.F. 86
Canadian Artists of Native
Ancestry Society 104
capital 79
Carmichael, M.F. 334
Casaubon, I. 94
Cassady, R. Jr 86
categories see coding

Catherine the Great 207
Chamberlain, J. 141, 142
Chapman, A. 79, 80
Chapman, W. 201, 265
Charles V, King 168, 169, 172
Charles VI, King 168
Charles VII, King 169
cherubs 30, 32, 33, 34, 36
Child, I.L. 215
Chocquet, V. 206, 213
Christie's 321
Churchill, W. 321
Cicero 181
cities 56
Clark, K. 96
Clarke, D. 4, 15, 51; on culture
   (Metropolitan Museum of Art)
   as a system with subsystems
   44–7
Clarke, T.B. 213
classes 148
classification rule 225
Clement VI, Pope 169
Clifford, J. 5, 302, 303; on
   collecting ourselves 258–67
Cloisters (Metropolitan Museum of
   Art) 213
closure, striving for 229–35;
   display 232; filling a space
   231–2; objects, manipulating
   scale of 232–3; objects,perfect
   233–4; set or series completion
   230–1; tension and tension
   release 229–30
coding categories and definitions
   27, 146–54; acquisition 153–4;
   home 154; meaning classes 148;
   non-persons 149–52; object
   146–8; person 152–3
Coe, R. 264
Cognacq-Jay Museum (Paris) 161
Cohen, C.B. 299, 302, 310
collectables 223–4, 225
collecting 149, 160–74, 317–18; as
   aesthetic experience 225–9;
   collection of collections 163–9;
   and collectors 317–26; as
   cultural form 235–6; invisible
   and visible 170–4; ourselves
   258–67; process 193–204
collection of collections 163–9;
   funeral objects 163–4; gifts and
   booty 165–7; offerings 164–5;
   relics and sacred objects 167–8;
   royal treasures 168–9
collectors and collecting 208–18,
   317–26
collectors and their motivations
   327–35; empirical work 330;
   method 330–1; psychoanalytic
   thought 327–30; results 331–4
commodities and politics of value
   76–90; by destination 84; by

diversion 84; by metamorphosis
   84; candidacy 83; circulation 76;
   context 84; coupons 88
comparative data 114, 116, 117,
   121–2; *see also* data
completion of collection 324
completion of series or set 230–1
compulsion 319–20; *see also*
   fetishistic collecting
Comte, A. 49
Concord, temple of (Rome) 167
Constable, W.G. 208
Constantine medals 93
construction of object 116, 117,
   118; class process 110, 111, 112,
   114; comparative data 121–2;
   observable data 120
consumer behaviour 296–313, 318
consumptive production 277
contemplation objects 148
Contemporary Art Museum
   (Teheran) 280
content 134–5
continuity 327, 333, 334
conversions 320–1
Coomaraswamy, A.K. 191, 192
craft 107–8, 150
Crapanzano, V. 302
Crick, M. 298
Csikszentmihalyi, M. 5, 305, 329;
   on home interview questionnaire
   144–54
culture 17, 44–7, 83, 110, 258
Cumberland Sound collections 60,
   61
Cushman, D. 299–300, 314

Damon, F.H. 86, 87
Danet, B.: collectors and collecting
   317, 319, 320, 324, 326; gender
   identity in collecting 241, 252;
   on play and aesthetics in
   collecting 220–36
Daniels, W. 199
Dannefer 324
data: comparative 114, 116, 117,
   121–2; observable
   114, 116, 117, 120–1; supplementary 114, 116, 117, 122–3
dead objects 26
death's head 30, 32, 33, 34, 35
deconstruction 313
deduction 133, 134, 135
Deetz, J. 9, 48, 50; on gravestones
   and motifs 30–7
defamiliarization 313
Defert, D. 260, 323
Delacroix, F.V.E. 284
Denon, V. 283
Derrida, J. 67, 72, 74
description 133, 134, 138, 150–1
design of object 110
Dethlefsen, E.S. 4, 48; on grave-

stones and motifs 30–7
Dholakia, N. 297
diacritical sign 67–8
dialogical mode 314
Dias, N. 265
Dillman, D.A. 291
dimensions 325–6
discrimination rule 225
display 231, 232
distribution problems 323–4
dominance and aesthetics 228–9
Dominguez, V.R. 98, 99, 100, 101,
   102, 103, 105
Donati, L. 95
Donato, E. 256–7
Douglas, M. 11, 16, 17, 53, 82, 88
Doxator, D. 100–1, 104
Dresden collection 183, 184
Dubé-Rioux, L. 310
Dummot, I. 77, 81, 88
Duncan, C., on art museums and
   ritual of citizenship 5, 279–86
durable objects 269, 270, 271, 272,
   273, 274, 276, 277, 278, 279
Durkheim, E. 42, 48, 49, 50, 240,
   253
Durost, W.N. 157, 158, 207, 242,
   252, 317
Dwyer, K. 302

Eagleton, T. 194, 198
'Egyptian Museum' (Liverpool) 199
Elgin Marbles 95
Elliot, R.S., on material history
   methodology 4, 5, 109–24
emotional response 136
empires 56
Engels, F. 79, 80
enjoyment 150
ephemeral experiences 223–4
Epstein, Sir J. and Lady 288
Erasmus, G. 103, 105
Errington, S.E. 99, 102
ethnic associations 149
ethnography 298–305; comparative
   310–11; narratives 305–10;
   salient characteristics 299–300;
   texts 300–5; writing in consumer
   behaviour 296–313
evaluation of objects 110
ex-commodities 84
Exeter City Museum 195
'Exotic Illusions' 101, 102, 105
experience 150
Eysenck, H.J. 212, 215

Fabian, J. 260, 262, 303, 304
factual description *see* identification
   of object
Fahnstock, P. 193
fakes 92–7
Federico Marés Museum
   (Barcelona) 161

feminine images and characters 247
Fenichel, O. 209, 210, 216, 218, 327, 328
Fenton, J. 193, 195, 199, 203, 258–9, 266
Ferdinand II 179
fetishistic collecting 194, 196–201, 264
filling a space 231–2
Fine Arts Museum (Boston) 285
Firat, A.F. 297
Fire Museum 243, 244, 245, 249, 250
First Peoples–Canadian Museums Association Task Force 104
Firth, R. 77, 86
Fischer, E. 310, 311
Fischer, M. 296, 298, 302, 303, 305, 313, 314
Fisher, P. 260
Flacks, R. 298
Flannery, K.V. 49, 52
Flaubert, G. 335
Fletcher, R. 51
'Fluffs and Feathers' 101, 104
Forde, C.D. 15
forgeries see fakes
Formanek, R. on collectors and their motivations 5, 327–35
Forster, E.M. 139
Foucault, D. 101
Foucault, M. 67, 70, 74
Fragonard, W.-P. 321
French Republic Museum (Louvre) 279, 282
Freud, S.: gender identity in collecting 242, 253; motivations of collectors 327, 328, 329, 330; psychological aspects of collecting 216, 218
Frick Collection (New York) 161
Frick, H.C. 206
Friedman, J. 15
Frobenius, L. 261
Fuente 320
function of object 116, 117, 118; class process 110, 111, 112, 113, 114; comparative data 122; observable data 121; supplementary data 122–3
functions, societal 250–1
funeral objects 163–4
Furby, L. 329

Gardner House (Boston) 161
Garman, K. 288
Gathercole, P. 199
Geertz, C. 105, 301
gender identity in collecting 240–53; Fire Museum 244, 245; Mouse Cottage 243–5; societal functions 250–1; uses of collections 245–50

Gibson, M. 199
gifts 81, 82, 149, 154, 165–7, 311
Gilligan, C. 251, 253
Girardin, M. 206, 213
Glassie, H. 134, 138
Glenbow Museum 103
Goering, H. 96
Goldberg 320
Gollwitzer 324
Goncourt, E. De 217, 218
'goods' 9, 11, 78
Goswamy, B.N., on Indian art abroad 5, 188–92
Graburn, N. 261
Grand Palais (Paris) 161, 188
gravestones 30–7
Grayson, M.W. 296
Gregory, C.A. 81
Gregory, T. 203
Greimas, A.J. 262
Griswold, W. 305
Guba 318
Guggenheim, P. 161, 207
Guidieri, R. 266
Gulbenkian, C. 216

Haccke, H. 266
Haddon, A. 13
Haggett, R. 130
Hamy, E.-T. 265
Handler, R. 259
Hanka, V. 94
Hare-Mustin, R. 310
Hart, K. 81, 84
Hartig, O. 175–6, 178, 181
Havemeyer, H.O. and L. 206, 211–12
Heans family 123, 124
Heard Museum 100, 101
Hearn, G.A. 213
Hearst, W.R. 209, 330
Hegel, G.W.F. 194, 202
heirloom 149
Heraclius medal 93
heritage 279
hermeneutics 313
Hermitage Museum (Leningrad) 161
Herodotus 170, 171
Hezeki'ah, King 179, 181, 183
Hill, J.N. 49
Hill, Sir G. 92
Hill, T. 104
Hirschmann, E. 296, 306
Historic Monuments Commission 259 history 327, 334; of collecting and museums 175–87, 333; see also provenance
hoarding 317–18
Hobbs, R. 280, 286
Hodder, I. 4, 13, 16, 41, 67, 71, 72; on symbolic meanings 12; on

theoretical archaeology 48–52
Hodgen 323
Holbrook, M. 252, 296, 297, 310, 330; collectors and collecting 318, 319, 326
Holmes, M. 195
home interview questionnaire 144–54
Honour, H. 262
Howarth, D. 20
Howes, D. 303
Hudson, L. 296
Hughes 320
Hunt 317
Hyde, L. 81

ideal, embodiment of 151
identification of object 110
Imperato, F. 181, 184, 185
Impey, O. 187, 194, 323
Impressionist collection 263
Indian art abroad 188–92
Ingres, J.A.D. 284
interpretation of collections 157–335
interpretation of material culture 67–74; from language to culture 68–9; metacritical sign and polysemy 72; Saussure and diacritical sign 67–8; and structure 69–72
interpretation of objects 9–154; multifaceted 139–43
intrinsic qualities 150–1
invention 140
investment 327, 333, 334
Iser, W. 19, 26, 27, 38
Isherwood, B. 11, 16, 17, 82

Jacknis 99, 100
Jackson, R.W. 310
Jacquemart-André Museum (Paris) 161
James, W. 254–5, 329–30
Jamin, J. 265
Jamison, K. 212
Jannasch, N. 122
Jenkinson, P. 5, 198, 287, 289, 290
Jenness, D. 64
Jensen 318
John and Sarah Hart Loan 196
Johnston 318, 319, 323
Jomard E.F. 265
Jones, E. 327, 328
Jones, M., on fakes 4, 92–7
Joy, A., on ethnographic writing in consumer behaviour 5, 296–313
judgements see evaluation of objects
Jules-Rosette, B. 261

Kaiser, S.B. 253
Kanold, Dr J. 183

Kassarjian, H.H. 296, 318
Katriel, T. 241, 252, 317, 319, 320, 324, 326; on play and aesthetics in collecting 220–36
Kaviraja, V. 188, 192
Kees 326
kitoums 86, 87
'kitsch', pursuit of 226
Kleivan, I. 64
Kluckhohn, C. 100
Knight, R.P. 95
Kohut, H. 329
Kopytoff, I. 83, 85, 320–1
Kress (art collector) 206, 213
Kron 317, 319
Kuhn, T. 59, 203
kula system 86, 87

Laclau, E. 10
Lady Franklin Point collections 60, 61, 62
langue 2, 21, 25, 67, 68
Laughlin, H.P. 209, 218
Làzaro Galdiano Museum (Madrid) 161
Le Berry, H. 169
Le Grand Camée 169
Leach, E. 4, 23, 25, 59, 65, 86, 87; on structuralism 41–3; on structuralist theory 53–8
Leach, J.W. 86
Leclerc, F. 310
Lee 318, 321
Lee, Lord 96
Leerburger 318
Lehman, H.C. 207, 252
Leicester Contemporary Collecting Project 5, 291–5
Leicestershire Museums Service 195
Leiris, M. 267
Lerner, B. 328, 334
Lévi-Strauss, C. 53, 68–9, 70, 131, 138
Levine, S. 264
Lewis, C.R. 192, 320
Ligota, C. 94
Lincoln 318
Liverpool City Museum 199
Lorrain, C. 217
Los Angeles County Museum of Art 280
Louis XIV 282
Louvre 265, 279, 280, 282, 283, 284, 285; *see also* Musée Napoléon
Lowie, R. 14
Lubbock (writer) 13, 14
Ludwig, A. 32
Lutz, R. 308

McClung Fleming, E. 110, 124, 125, 126, 127, 132
McCormick, C. 103, 104

McCracken, G. 253, 296, 323
McDaniel, S.W. 310
McDougall, D. 304
McFeat, T.F.S. 99
McGhee, R. 4, 131; on prehistoric technology 59–65
McGrath, M.A. 296, 297, 303, 310–11, 313
Macgregor, A. 187, 194, 323
McKinnon 317
McManus, G. 104
Macpherson, C.B. 259, 260
Major, J.D. 175, 179–80, 181, 182, 183, 184, 185, 186
Malinowsk, B. (anthropologist) 41–2, 43, 49, 173, 320
manufacture of objects 140–1
Maquet, J. 84
Maracek, J. 310
marbles, classical 197
Marcos, I. 279
Marcus, G.E. 296, 298, 299–300, 302, 303, 305, 313, 314
Maritime Museum of the Atlantic (Halifax) 122
Mark, K. 44
marketing of objects 141
Martin, W. 125
Marx, K. 5, 16, 70, 200, 260, 277; commodities and politics of value 76, 77, 78, 79, 80, 81, 82, 84, 85, 90
Mascia-Lees, F. 302, 310, 313
masculine images and characters 249
material culture 9, 13–17; analysis of meaning 22; hypotheses 137; interpretation *see* interpretation of material culture; and structure 69–71; subsystem 45, 47; theory and method 133–8
material history methodology 109–24; class process 109–15; and construction of objects 118; function 118; method application 119–24; model description 115–19
material of object 116, 117–18, 140; class process 110, 111, 112, 114; comparative data 121; observable data 120; supplementary data 122
material objects, animate and inanimate 224
Mathews, T.R. 212
Mathiassen, T. 59
Mauss, M. 63, 77, 81
Maximilian II, Emperor 176
Mayer, J. 197, 199, 204
Mazarin, Cardinal 217
meanings, symbolic 12, 53
Medici, collection of 181
'Medusa' style 35, 36

Mellon (art collector) 206, 213
mementoes 149
memories 149
Menninger, W.C. 216, 218
metacritical sign 72
Metropolitan Museum of Art (New York) 211, 213, 218, 263, 285
Metropolitan Museum (Manila) 279
Meyer 319, 320
Mi Fu 217
Michelangelo 185, 284
Mick, D. 296
Miller, D. 4, 78, 194, 198, 200, 202, 300; on material culture 13–17
Mitchell, S.A. 329
Modern Art Museum (New York) 161, 264, 266
Moko Mead, S. 104
Montesquieu, C.-L. 49
Montezuma, King 181
Montgomery, C. 126
Morgan, J.P. 206, 207, 213
Morgan, P. 201
Morris, C. 212
Morris, W. 108
motifs 30–7
motivations 331, 334
Mouffe, C. 10
Mouse Cottage 243–4, 247, 250, 251, 311
Mullaney, S. 262
multiple-halo designs 35
Muni, B. 189, 191, 192
Munich Glypothek 95
Munn, N.D. 86, 87
Murdoch, J. 63, 64
Musée Charles X 284
Musée de l'Homme 261
Musée Guimet 265
Musée Napoléon 283–4
Museum of the Nineteenth Century (Paris) 263
Museum Studies Department 291
Museum Studies International Conference 199

National Air and Space Museum (Washington, D.C.) 10
National Army Museum (London) 19
National Gallery (London) 217
National Museum of Canada 99
Native American art collection (Santa Fe) 261
Naylor, J. 20
Nehru, J. 99, 100, 101
Neikelius, C.F., and history of collecting and of museums 175, 183, 184, 185, 186, 187
Nestrick, W.V. 207
New Archaeology 48, 49, 50, 51

New Brunswick University 109
New York Museum of Natural
History 266
Newby Hall (Yorkshire) 95
Nichols, F.E. 256
Nicks, T. 104
Nissim de Comondo Museum
(Paris) 161
no-two-alike principle 225, 227–8
Nogent, G. de 171

objects 9, 10, 12, 78; categories
146–8, 269–78; of desire 254–7;
historical meaning 30–7;
manipulating scale 231, 232–3;
as meaning 19–28; multifaceted
interpretation 139–43; perfect
233–4; values 269
Objects of Culture symposium 99,
105
O'Brien 317
observable data 114, 116, 117,
120–1; *see also* data
obsessive collecting *see* fetishistic
collecting
Odyssey Project 5, 296–313
offerings 164–5
Olmi, G. 175–6, 178, 181
Olmsted, A.D. 252, 319, 323, 324,
330, 333
O'Rourke, D. 98
'other' 310–11, 314, 327, 332, 334
'otherness' 314
Owlijoot, T. 102, 103
Ozanne, J. 296

Palais Galliera (Paris) 161
Parezo, N.J. 98–9, 103
parole 2, 3, 21, 25, 67, 68
patterning, social 53
Pausanias 165, 167, 171
Pearce, S.M. 4, 5, 48, 67; on
artefact studies 125–32; on
behavioural interaction with
objects 38–40; on the collecting
process 193–204; on collection
definitions 157–9; on Leicester
contemporary collecting project's
questionnaire 291–5; on museum
objects 9–11; on objects as
meaning 19–28
Peggy Guggenheim Foundation
(Venice) 161
Pellizzi, F. 266
People's Palace (Glasgow) 289
People's Show Project 5, 198, 201
perfection 231
Perlin, F. 78
person codes 152–3
personal values 151–2
personification 152
Peterson, R.A. 299, 305
Petit Palais 188, 191

Phillips, R.M. 105, 206
Picasso, P. 265
Piero Sraffa 78
Piltdown Man 92
Pistrucci, B. 95
Pitt Rivers, A.H.L.F. 13, 14, 199,
201, 204, 265
Pitt Rivers Museum (Oxford) 193,
195, 203, 258–9
play and aesthetics in collecting
220–36; academics 220–1;
aesthetic experience 225–9;
collectables 223–4; rules 224–5
Pliny the Elder 165, 166–7, 171;
history of collecting and of
musuems 175–6, 178, 181, 183,
185, 186
Pohler, M.J. 212
Polier, N. 297, 302–3
politics and public art museums
282–4
politics of value and commodities
26–90; paths and diversions
85–9; spirit of the commodity
78–85
Pollay 320
polysemy 72
Pomian, K. 5, 260, 265; on
collecting 160–74
Pont, H.F. du 243
Porter, J. 125
possession 317–18
post-structuralism 74
postmodernism 313
Praz 323
prehistoric technology 59–65
preservation and collecting 327,
333, 334
'Preserving our Heritage' conference (1988) 102, 103, 105
Price, J.A. 84
Pritchard Collection 196
production 80, 277, 278
products 78, 79, 80
propositions of collectors and
collecting 317–26; acquisitiveness
legitimation 320; addiction and
compulsive aspects 319–20;
completion 324; conversions
320–1; distribution problems
323–4; self, extensions of 321–2;
specialization 323; unconscious
intent 318–19
provenance 116, 117, 118–19;
class process 110, 111,
112, 113, 114; comparative data
122; observable data 121;
supplementary data 123
Prown, J. 4, 5, 110–12, 124, 139;
on material culture theory and
method 133–4
psychoanalytic thought 327–30
psychological aspects of art 205–18

psychological subsystem 45,
47

Quiccheberg, S. and history
of collecting and museums 175,
176, 177, 178, 179, 180, 181,
183, 184, 186

Rabasa, J. 262
Rabinow, P. 297, 305
Radcliffe-Brown, A.R. 41, 42, 43,
48, 49
Rao, C.P. 310
rasa 188, 189, 190, 191, 192
Rasmussen, K. 63, 64, 65
Rastier, F. 262
recollection 149
recontextualization 226–7
reframing 225–7
release 150
relics 167–8
religion 45, 47, 149
Renfrew, C. 51
Renwick Building (Washington,
D.C.) 279
research 137
restoration 327, 333, 334
Rheims, M. 214, 321, 323
Ricoeur, P. 313
Riegl, A. 136, 138
Rigby, D. and E. 241, 252, 317,
318, 319, 323
rivers 57–8
Roberts, S. 252, 330
Rochberg-Halton, E. 5, 153,
305,323, 329; on home interview
questionnaire 144–54
Rockefeller, J.D. Jr 213
Roseberry, W. 297, 302–3
Rosenbluh, E.S. 212
Roubertoux, P. 214
Rowlands, M. 15
Royal Anthropological Institute 13
royal treasures 168–9
'rubbish': objects 173, 269, 271–2,
274, 276, 277, 278; to collec-
tables 225–6; to consumption
278; triangle 275, 276, 278
Rucker, M. 253
Ruesch 326
rules of collecting 224–5
Rush, R.H. 205
Ruskin, J. 108
Ryan, S. 288

Saarinen, A.B. 209, 212, 214, 218,
330
sacred objects 167–8
Sahlins, M. 50, 51, 81, 82
Saisselin, R.G. 241, 243, 252, 260
Salmon, M.H. 49
Salon Carré 284
same-but-different objects 227–8

Sandford Bequest 196
Saussure, F. de 19, 21, 22, 67–8
Savard, R. 64, 65
Schledermann, P. 60, 61
Schmitt, B.H. 310
Schulz, E. on history of collecting and museums 5, 175–87
Schwartz, E.K. 209, 318
Schwimmer, E.G. 65
Science Museum (London) 139, 143
Seddon, D. 78
'self' 152, 305–8, 321–2, 327, 332, 334; *see also* 'other'
self-reflexivity 312–13
seller *see* buyer and seller behaviour
sensory engagement 135–6
Settala collection (Milan) 183, 185
Shabaka Stone 93
Shanks, M. on craft 74, 107–8
Sharpe, P. 302, 310
Sheldon, W.M. 212
Sherry, J.F. Jr 252, 296, 297, 318, 320, 330; ethnographic writing 298–9, 301, 303, 304, 305–8, 308–9, 310–11, 313
sign 23, 25
signes 21, 25
signified/signifiers 21, 68
Silumiut collection 60, 61
Simmel, G. 17, 317; commodities and politics of value 76, 77, 78, 80, 82, 83
Singer, M. 99, 100
Sloane, Sir H. 197
Smith 317
Smith, Dr. S. 109
Soby, R.M. 64
sociocultural system 45, 46, 47
Solomon, King and Temple of Solomon 179, 181, 182, 183, 186
Sothebys 222, 321
Soule, E. 36
souvenirs 149, 194, 195, 196, 201
specialization 323
specimens 9
speculation 133, 134, 136–7
Stanford, D. 60, 61
Steadman, P. 14
Stefansson, V. 64
Stern, B. 296, 310, 313
Stevens, S.S. 212
Stewart, S. 20, 252, 260, 321; and the collecting process 194, 196, 200; on objects of desire 254–7
Strahan, E. 212
Strathern, A.J. 86
Strathern, M. 299, 310
Strong, E.K. Jr 215
structuralism 41–3
structuralist theory 53–8
style 151

subsystem 45, 47
supplementary data 114, 116, 117, 122–3; *see also* data
swap meet 305–8
symbol 23, 25
systematic collection 201–2
systematics 194

T-shaped element 35, 36
Talley, M.K. Jr 96
Tambiah, S.J. 81, 82
Taussig, M.T. 81
Taylor, F.H. 217
Taylor, J. 93
Taylor, L. 38, 39
Taylor, W.E. 62
tension and tension release 229–30
text 27
textualization 313
Thackeray, W.M. 23, 25
'Theatrum' 176, 177, 178
'things' 9, 10
Thompson, C. 303
Thompson, E.P. 24
Thompson, M. 5, 89, 279; on object categories 269–78
Thorwaldsen, B. 95
Thule culture 59–65
Tilley, C. on material culture interpreting 4, 67–74, 76
Titus Petronius 166
Tooley 322
Townley classical marbles 197
Tradescant Collection (London) 184, 197
transient objects 269, 270, 271, 272, 273, 274, 276, 277, 278
Treas 318
Tribuna of the Uffizi collection 185
Trocadéro 265
Truettner, W.H. 208
Tucker 318
Turkel, G. 298
Turner, V. 53, 281, 286
Type A collector 320, 326
Type B collector 320, 324, 326

unconscious intent to collect 318–19
uniqueness 150
urn-and-willow stones 33, 34
uses of collections 245–50
uses of objects 142–3
Utah, University of 5

Valentini, M.B. 175, 180, 182–3, 184, 186
Valéry, P. 214
Valois, P. de 169
value 116, 117, 119, 157; class process 110, 111, 112, 114; comparative data 122; observable data 121; supple-mentary

data 123; tournaments of 87
values, personal 151–2
Van Maanen, J. 300, 301
Van Meegeren (forgerer) 96
vaygu'a 173
Veblen, T. 17, 256
Vegetable Lambs of Tartary 93
Venables 322
Venus 95
'Vermeer' forgery 96
Verneau, R. 265
Verres (Roman collector) 166, 217
Victoria and Albert Museum (London) 107, 195
Virgil 183
Vitruvius 166, 181, 183, 185
Von Holst, N. 217, 323

Wainwright, C. 194
Walakpa assemblage 60, 61
Wallach, A. 280, 286
Wallendorf, M. 5, 318, 320, 330; ethnographic writing in consumer behaviour 296, 297, 298–9, 300, 303, 304, 305–10, 312, 313; on gender identity in collecting 240–53
Walsall Museum and Art Gallery 5, 198, 201, 204, 287
Warhol, A. 264
Watts, D. 103
Weiner, A.B. 86
Welsh, P.H. 99, 100, 102, 104, 105
Whistler, J.A.M. 206
Whitehorne, A.C. 19
Whitley, M.T. 207, 252
Whitney Museum 263
Williams, E. 265
Williams, Sir C.H. 197
Williamson, T. 203
willow tree 30
Wilson, E.O. 38, 39, 42
Wilson, G.D. 212
Wiltse, S.E. 241, 252
Winterthur Museum (University of Delaware) 126, 243
Wiseman 324
Wittlin 323
Witty, P.A. 207, 252, 322
Wolf, A. 209
Wolf, E.S. 329
Wolff, J. 16
Woodland Indian Cultural Education Centre (USA) 100, 101
Wright, E. and F. 93
Wright, S. 199

York Castle Museum 195, 201, 289

'Zinoviev letter' 93